To My New British Friend,
From Your New American Friend.

Wishing you + your Family all the Best that Life Has to Offer!

Yours in Jaycees,

Nick Hrbovich Jr
United States Junior Chamber of Commerce
National Vice President

11/19/98

NIAGARA

ATTRACTING THE WORLD

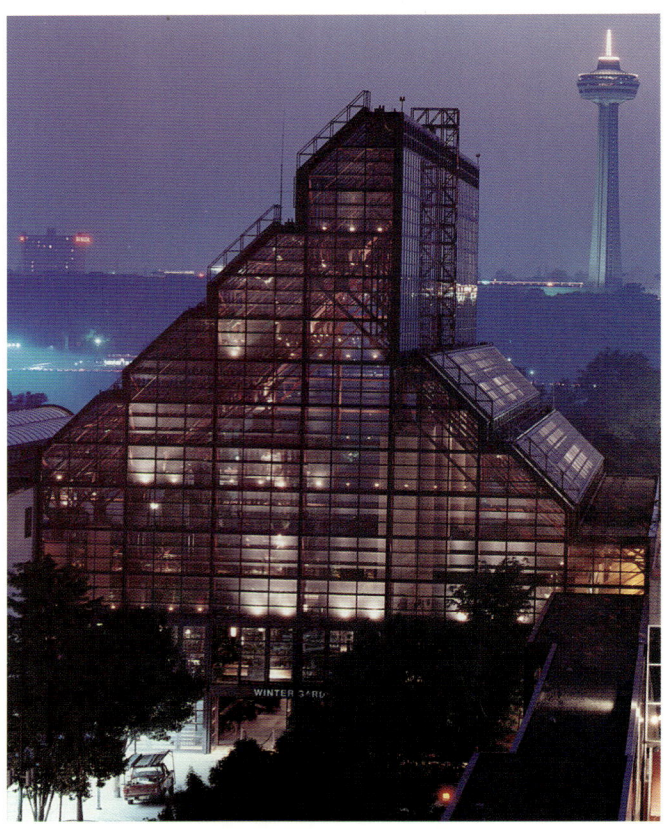

Niagara Falls Winter Garden photo by Marc Murphy.

by

Philip Nyhuis

Corporate Profiles by

Blair Boone and Maria Scrivani

Featuring the Photography of

James P. McCoy

Contributing Photographer

Marc Murphy

Produced in cooperation with

Greater Buffalo Partnership

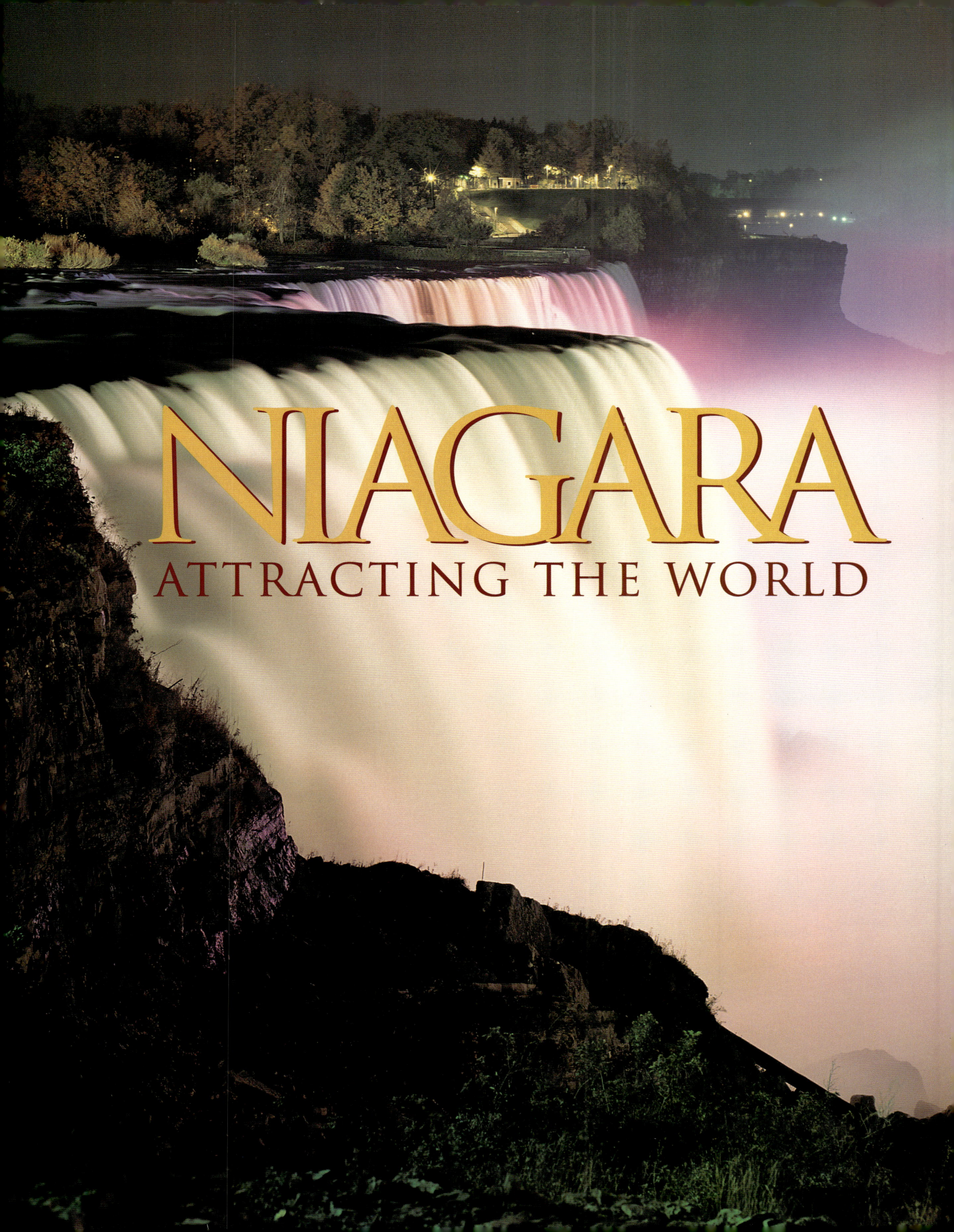

NIAGARA
ATTRACTING THE WORLD

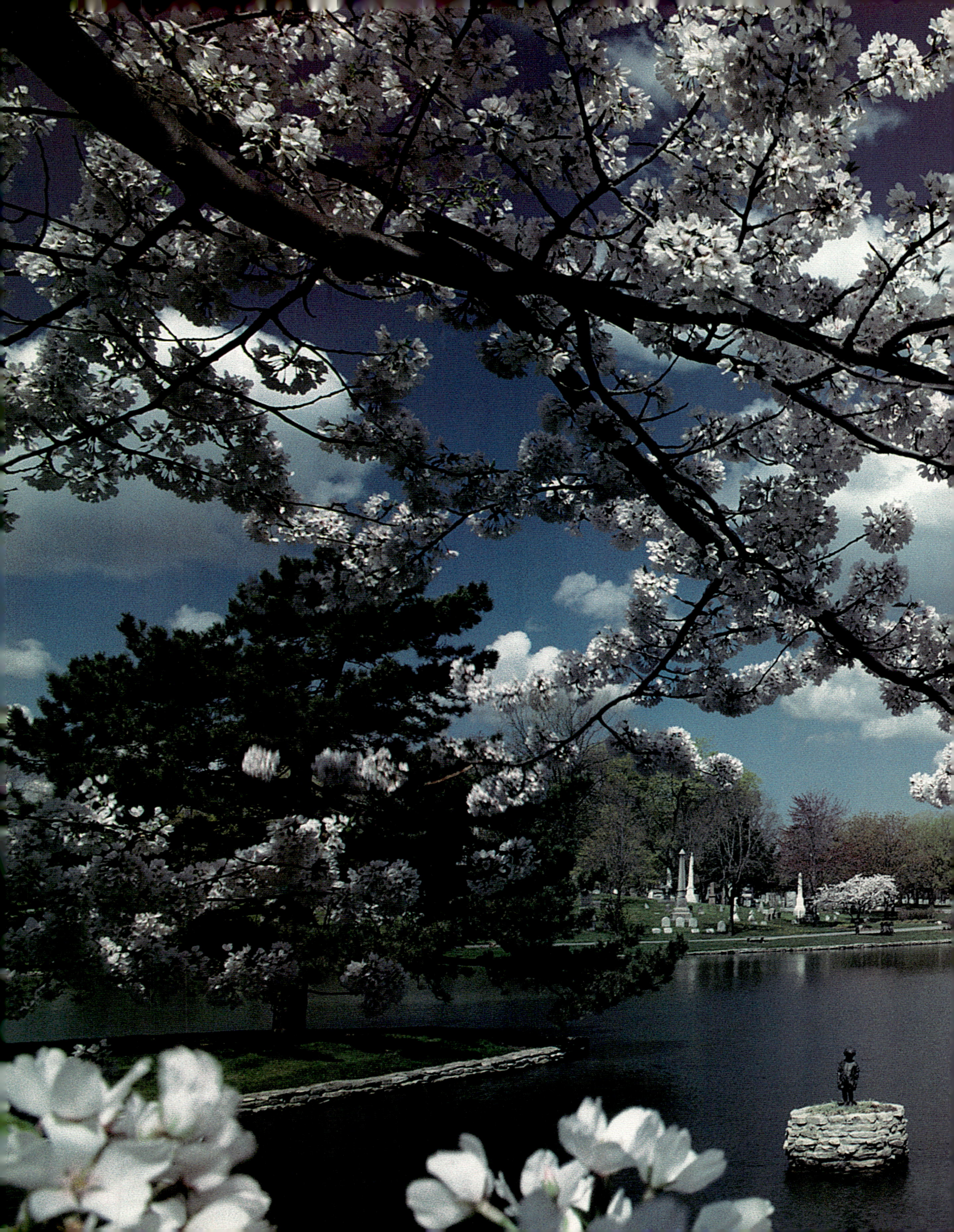

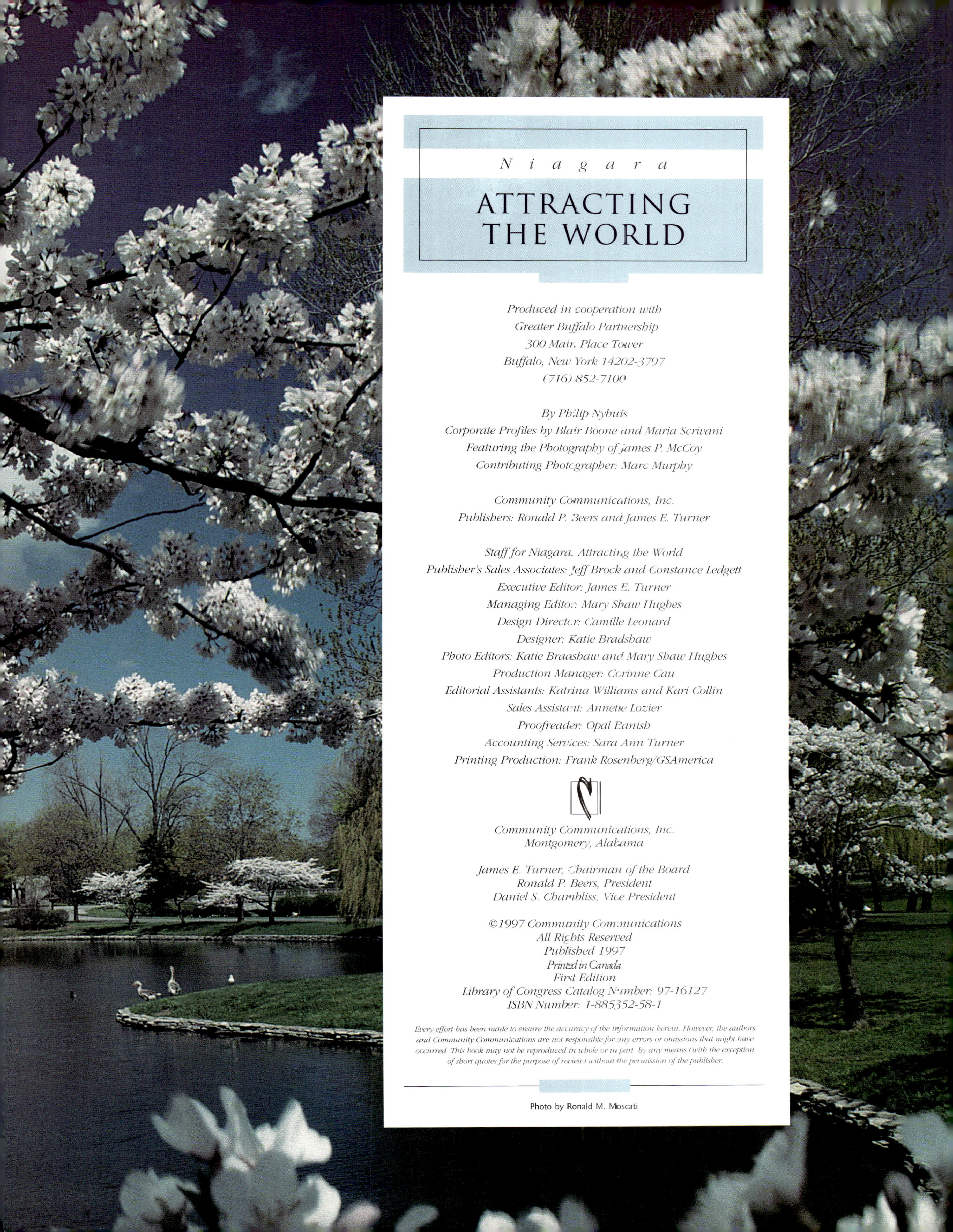

N i a g a r a

ATTRACTING
THE WORLD

Produced in cooperation with
Greater Buffalo Partnership
300 Main Place Tower
Buffalo, New York 14202-3797
(716) 852-7100

By Philip Nyhuis
Corporate Profiles by Blair Boone and Maria Scrivani
Featuring the Photography of James P. McCoy
Contributing Photographer: Marc Murphy

Community Communications, Inc.
Publishers: Ronald P. Beers and James E. Turner

Staff for Niagara: Attracting the World
Publisher's Sales Associates: Jeff Brock and Constance Ledgett
Executive Editor: James E. Turner
Managing Editor: Mary Shaw Hughes
Design Director: Camille Leonard
Designer: Katie Bradshaw
Photo Editors: Katie Bradshaw and Mary Shaw Hughes
Production Manager: Corinne Cau
Editorial Assistants: Katrina Williams and Kari Collin
Sales Assistant: Annette Lozier
Proofreader: Opal Eanish
Accounting Services: Sara Ann Turner
Printing Production: Frank Rosenberg/GSAmerica

Community Communications, Inc.
Montgomery, Alabama

James E. Turner, Chairman of the Board
Ronald P. Beers, President
Daniel S. Chambliss, Vice President

Photo by Ronald M. Moscati

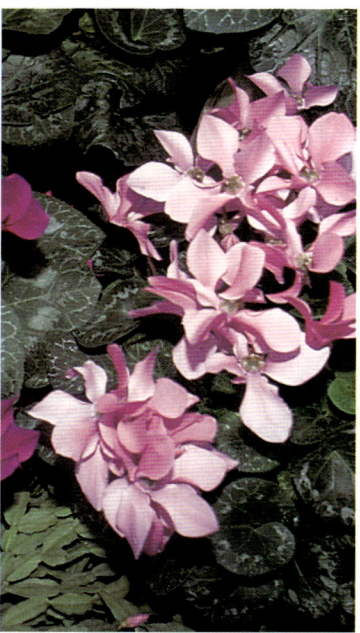

Photos on pages 171 & 199
by James P. McCoy.

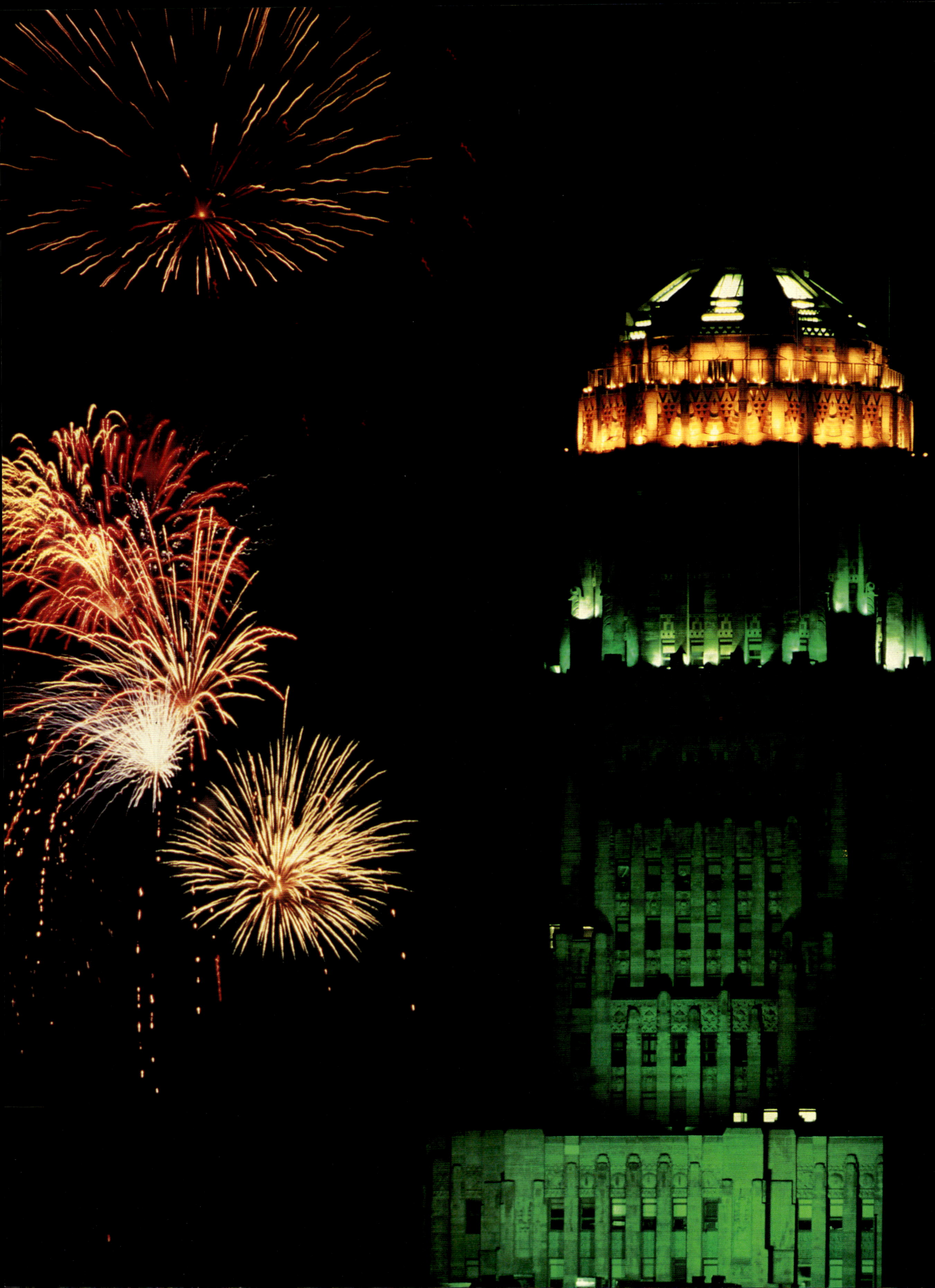

FOREWORD

As we move into a new millennium, this region is going forward with a renewed sense of itself, not as a set of separate communities, nor as the "Queen City of the Great Lakes," Greater Buffalo, or even as the Niagara Frontier, but simply as Niagara— a binational region encompassing the eight counties of Western New York State and the Niagara Peninsula of Ontario, Canada.

In geographic terms, Niagara is an area located on the eastern and northern portion of the North American continent. Its landmass runs along the shorelines of two Great Lakes, a mighty river, and a spectacular waterfall that provides aesthetic pleasure as well as hydroelectric power to millions of people.

In political terms, it is a place where two countries, friends and trading partners for many years, use this mighty river as their international border and its surrounding land as a "hub" for their many common interests and pursuits.

In terms of its inhabitants, so many have come to settle here— Native North American, English, Irish, German, Italian, Polish, African-American, and Hispanic all have a distinct presence and influence in Niagara. But no matter which side of the river residents call home, frequent crossing of this international border is a way of life.

In terms of its creativity, it's a place that has spawned art and artists, a place where ideas are regularly exchanged, and cultures partake and celebrate each other.

The Greater Buffalo Partnership is pleased and proud to present a book that has attempted to capture the essence of the wonderful region we call home. As you look throughout these pages, it will become abundantly clear why Niagara attracts the world.

Photo by James P. McCoy.

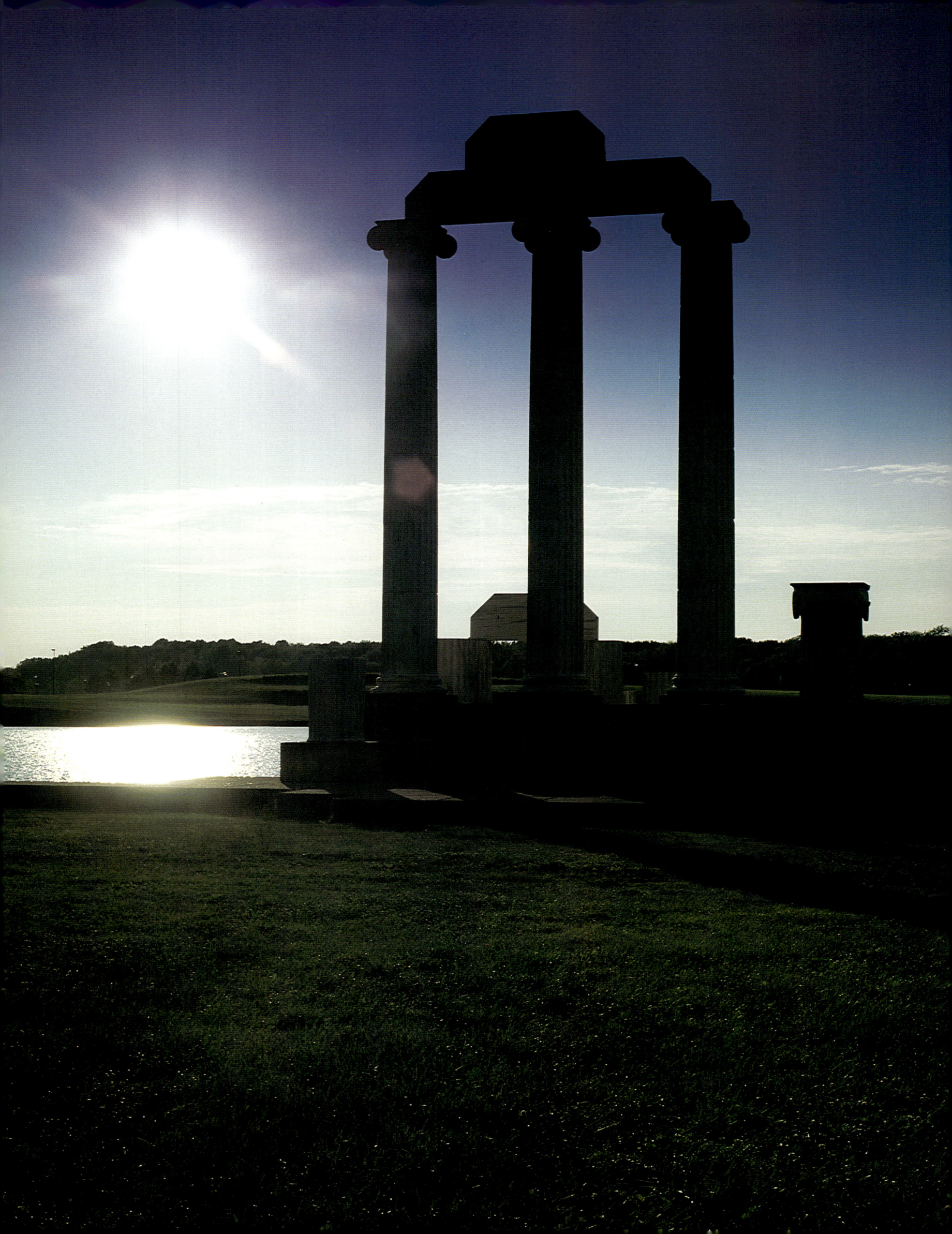

PREFACE

Since the mid-19th century, the Niagara area has earned a reputation as a tough, hard-working industrial region. But more than muscle, it is also heart: a place of great spirituality, beauty and romance. From its forests, farmlands, deep gorges, and magnificent waters to the architecture, art, and enterprise of its vital urban centers, Niagara draws you close to reveal its secrets and enfold you in its history.

I would like to thank Mary Hughes for asking me to write this book and for her patience and valuable suggestions throughout. It could not have been written without the help of dozens of people throughout Niagara who cheerfully provided information on the region's abundant resources: its schools, institutions, companies, and diverse organizations. My thanks to them and to the wonderful staff of the Buffalo and Erie County Public Library. Special thanks to Jim McCoy and Marc Murphy for their beautiful photography; to Linda Soltis, Julie Hazzan and the Greater Buffalo Partnership for conceiving the project and providing the opportunity for me to work on it; to Tracey Eastman for suggesting me for the project; to Mary Beth Spina at the University at Buffalo News Services for her good cheer and invaluable help; and to my wife Sharon for her encouragement and support. This book is dedicated to my parents, Edson and Lillian, and to my daughters, Colby, Theya, and Alexis.

—Philip Nyhuis

Photo by James P. McCoy.

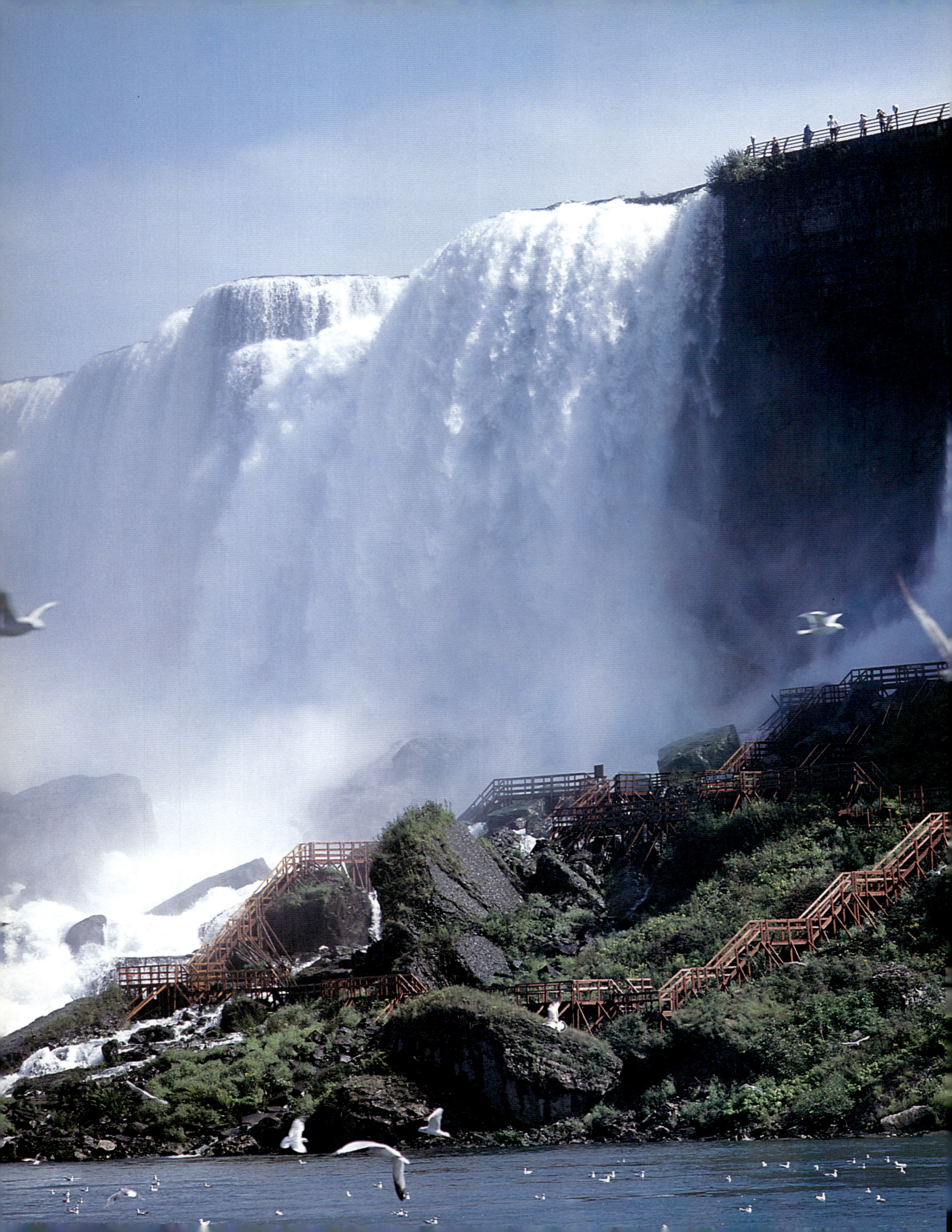

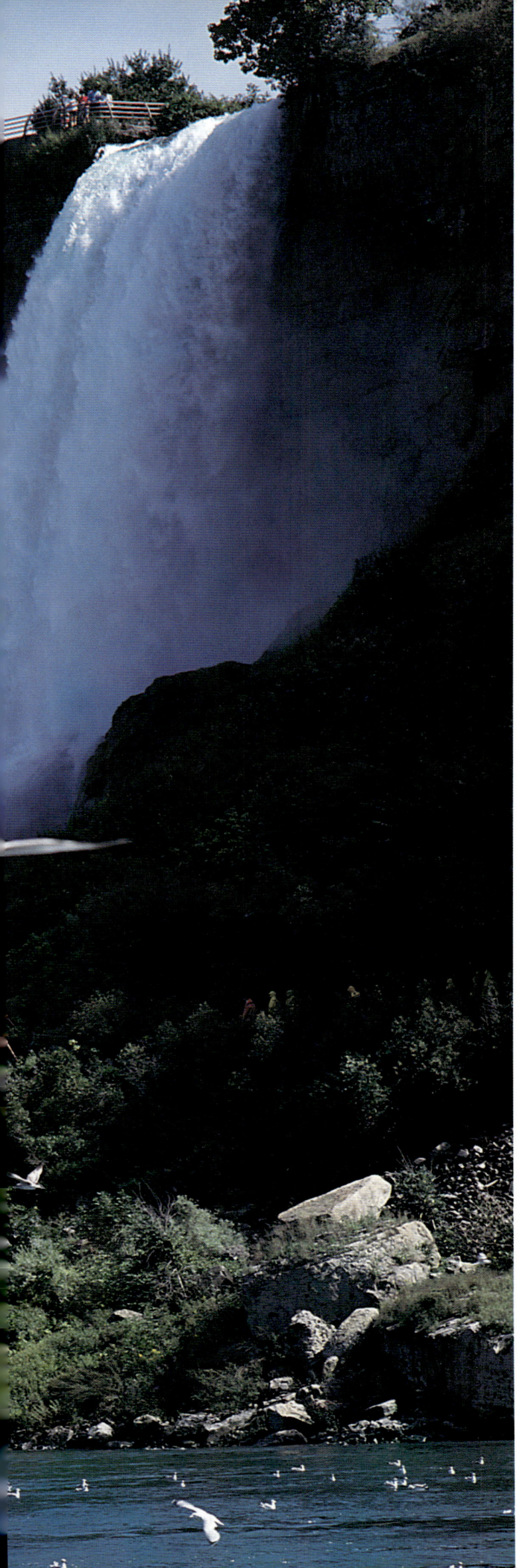

OVER THE RAINBOW

Niagara is an important center of commercial, cultural, and social relations between the United States and Canada. Its binational geography includes the eight counties of Western New York State and the Niagara Peninsula of Ontario, Canada. While the mighty Niagara River is the official dividing line between the United States and Canada, the seamlessness of the border is apparent to any resident or visitor.

Photo by James P. McCoy.

Within the region of Niagara, the two countries

share some beautiful and fascinating geography.

Two of the five Great Lakes, Erie and Ontario, are

connected by the Niagara River that leads to Niagara

Falls, a wonder that can be seen and visited on

either side of the border. Fourteen million tourists

annually visit this natural phenomenon.

While trends come and go, Niagara's principal strength has remained. It is, and always has been, an important center for international trade. Its unique location, both from a political and geographic standpoint, has given Niagara this enduring economic niche. Niagara's six international bridges handle 28 percent or $92 billion in the annual trade of goods and services between the United States and Canada, the world's two largest trading partners.

The Can-Am aspect of Niagara is only the beginning of its diversity. The region's remarkable panorama includes the urban hub of Buffalo, the beautiful rural areas, pleasant suburban communities, spectacular waterfront vistas, and geological wonders. You can visit a Van Gogh at the Albright-Knox Art Gallery or take in a rowing regatta at the Royal Canadian Henley course in St. Catharines. For theater lovers, downtown Buffalo has the drama of six live theaters while Niagara-on-the-Lake is home to the second-largest company in North America, the Shaw Festival. Just above the American village of Lewiston lies Artpark, a public park devoted to the visual and performing arts. Fun lovers flock to Darien Lake theme park in Genesee County, and one million skiers visit the popular ski resorts of Cattaraugus, Chautauqua, Erie, Genesee, and Allegany counties each year. You'll find the famous Falls and quaint surrounding towns in Niagara County, and rich, rolling farmland in Orleans and Wyoming counties. If you'd like to see well-tended vineyards and discover the places where wine is made, Niagara has 40 wineries from which to choose. For sports fans, Niagara has both amateur and professional venues, including the Bills, Sabres, Bisons, Bandits, and Blizzard. Throughout the region, there is almost always a game, race, or match going on. It could be softball, soccer, rugby, rowing, volleyball, or the sport from one of many organized leagues. Or you can simply lie on a beautiful Lake Erie beach or take a hike through a forest in Allegany County. In Niagara, the choices seem endless.

Dominating the geography of the region, the Niagara River flows north from Lake Erie to Lake Ontario, a 326-foot descent. Responsible for most of that drop is the Niagara

Escarpment, also known as the Giant's Rib, which originally met the Niagara River seven miles from Lake Ontario where Queenston, Ontario, now looks down on Lewiston, New York. At this point, a gash in the scarp winds upriver to Niagara Falls. This spectacular canyon constitutes the Niagara Gorge. Twelve thousand years ago, Niagara Falls tumbled over the escarpment at Queenston/Lewiston. Over the years, the force of the Falls and the annual freezing and thawing of the river fractured the brittle dolostone caprock and seeped into the shale below, eroding it and causing the dolostone to break off in huge chunks and slabs. As a result, the Falls inched upriver to its present location, creating a succession of gorges now united in the Lower Niagara.

In Niagara's southern geography, another scarp snakes across Chautauqua, Cattaraugus, and Wyoming counties, overlooking Lake Erie, hillside vineyards, checkerboard farms, and rural villages with names like Mayville, Summerdale, Maple Springs, Forestville, Cherry Creek, Springville, Little Valley, and Ashford Hollow. This is the Portage Escarpment, so called because Native North American travelers and early European explorers had to walk their canoes and bateaux over it to get from Lake Erie to Chautauqua Lake and south to the Allegheny, Ohio, and Mississippi rivers: the great inland waterway.

North of the Portage Escarpment lies the fertile farmland of the Erie Plain. Concord grapes flourish here, nurtured by sunshine, rainfall, favorable soils, and the temperate winds of Lake Erie. On this land where the Erie, Wenro, and Neutral Indians once planted squash, corn, and beans, today's farmers grow wheat, hay, soybeans, potatoes, melons, berries, pumpkins, cauliflower, and broccoli, as well as sweet corn, zucchini, snap beans, and other cash crops. Up north on the Ontario Plain, apple and peach orchards march across much of the countryside. On a clear fall day, you can bite into a scarlet Macintosh and gaze across the lake at the towers of Toronto.

The first explorers to the region found wild fruit trees growing in the congenial climate of the Niagara Peninsula around Lake Ontario. Peach orchards were planted in the mid-19th century, and the area soon became noted for the sweetness and abundance of its fruit. Throughout the spring and summer, the tilled land from Grimsby to Jordan Station to Niagara-on-the-Lake is filled with the color and fragrance of blossoming and ripening cherries, apples, peaches, raspberries, strawberries, grapes, currants, gooseberries, pears, and plums. This area, once completely under water, has created a microclimate where acres of vineyards cover the land.

The Niagara Peninsula is home to the largest flower-growing and exporting business in Canada. The region also exports a formidable list of ready-made goods like computer equipment, auto parts, chemicals, plastics, machine tools, medical supplies, and wood products to a global market. Buffalo, the urban hub of Niagara, is the flour-milling capital of the world. It is also the center of a burgeoning medical-dental-pharmaceutical manufacturing corridor and the site of several renowned medical research facilities. Buffalo is home to New York's largest public university as well as an abundance of architectural treasures, a thriving theater and arts community, and a fascinating array of attractions and entertainment venues.

With its solid copper-capped towers, white marble angels, art work in oils and stained glass, and great 80-foot dome, **Our Lady of Victory Basilica** in Lackawanna is a triumph of Baroque Revival architecture and an enduring monument to the leadership and charitable work of Fr. Nelson H. Baker, who also established an orphanage and a hospital nearby. Photo by James P. McCoy.

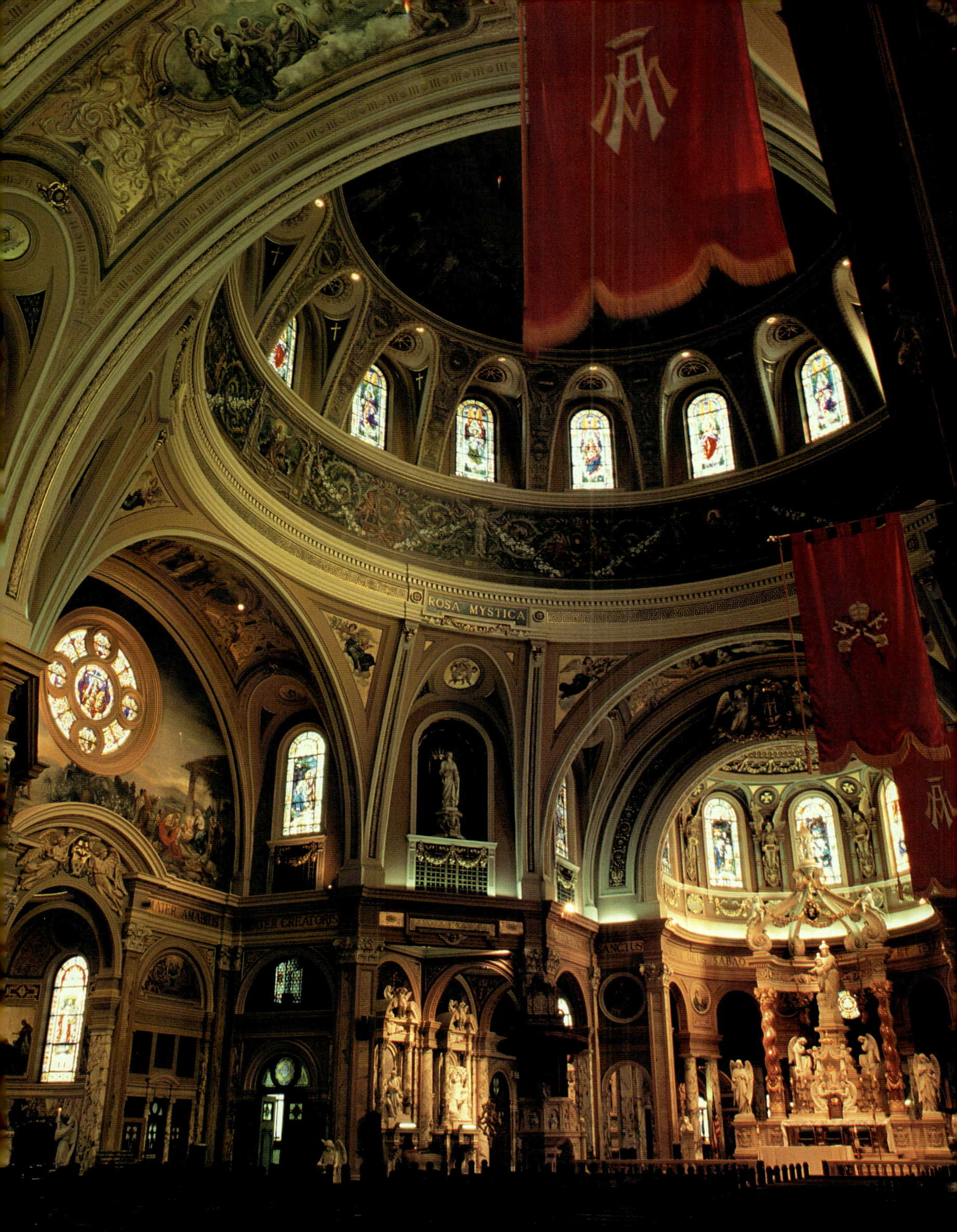

Founded by Yankee transplants from New England and other eastern regions, Buffalo was built by the muscle and grit of immigrant Irish, Germans, Poles, Italians, Hispanics, and African-Americans whose descendants continue to adhere to the strong work ethic, family ties, and community involvement of their forbears. These civic commitments and strengths of character were cited by national observers when Buffalo was designated an All-America City by the National Civic League in 1996. Criteria for the award included the city's ability to devise successful ways of solving contemporary urban problems by creating citizen-driven programs for improving the quality of life. These programs included Kids Escaping Drugs, the Skating Association for the Blind and Handicapped, and Forever Elmwood, a dynamic neighborhood revitalization and preservation effort.

Niagara is a wonderful place for people who enjoy the out-doors. With hundreds of miles of lakeshore, rivers, gorges, waterfalls, streams, and ponds, the area is a recreational haven for hikers, boaters, sailors, rafters, kayakers, anglers, cyclists, and skaters. In downtown Buffalo, plans are under way to create an inner harbor designed for all-weather, year-round water-front access. The area will feature residential neighborhoods, parks, bike paths, boat slips, a nature sanctuary, museums, and eventually an entertainment and nightlife district.

In Niagara, life on the border means the best of both worlds. It means easy access to some of the prettiest beaches on the Great Lakes, more than 20 ski resorts that annually attract a million skiers to the slopes, and a legacy of historic events, landmarks, and geological wonders. It means a short journey to the vitality of Toronto for a Blue Jays game, a business conference, or a dim sum lunch. It means 30 colleges and professional programs—from large public universities to small private colleges—with several cooperative programs between Canadian and American schools.

Although there are differences in outlook and style between the two nations of Niagara, those differences enrich the cross-cultural exchange and create a keener understanding and a greater appreciation for Niagara's common interests and goals. ❖

Four vehicular bridges and two railroad bridges span the Niagara River between Lake Erie and Lake Ontario. Together, the traffic bridges account for $92 billion in trade and 28 percent of all border crossings between the United States and Canada: over eight million vehicles a year. Designed by Edward Payson Lupfer, the **Peace Bridge** opened in 1927 with ceremonies attended by the Prince of Wales (later Edward VIII). Its graceful procession of arches across the river ends in a through truss over the ship canal, where a vertical clearance of 100 feet was built to accommodate high-masted lake vessels. Photo by James P. McCoy.

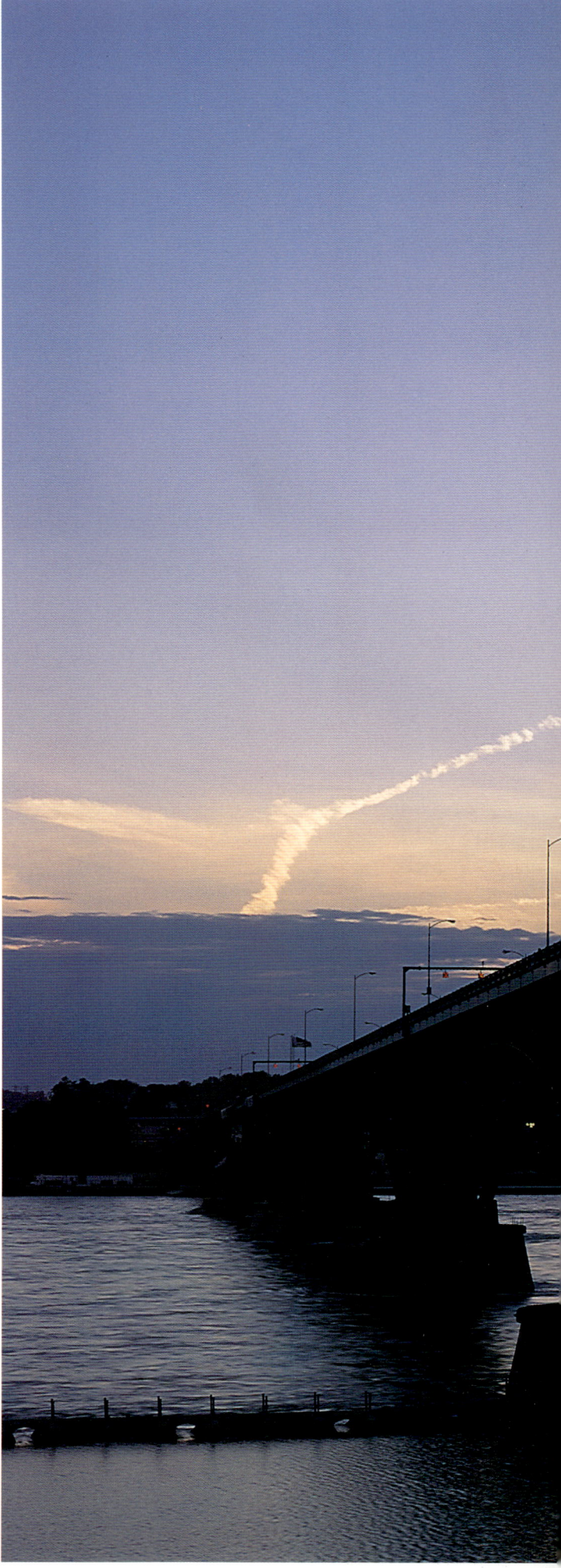

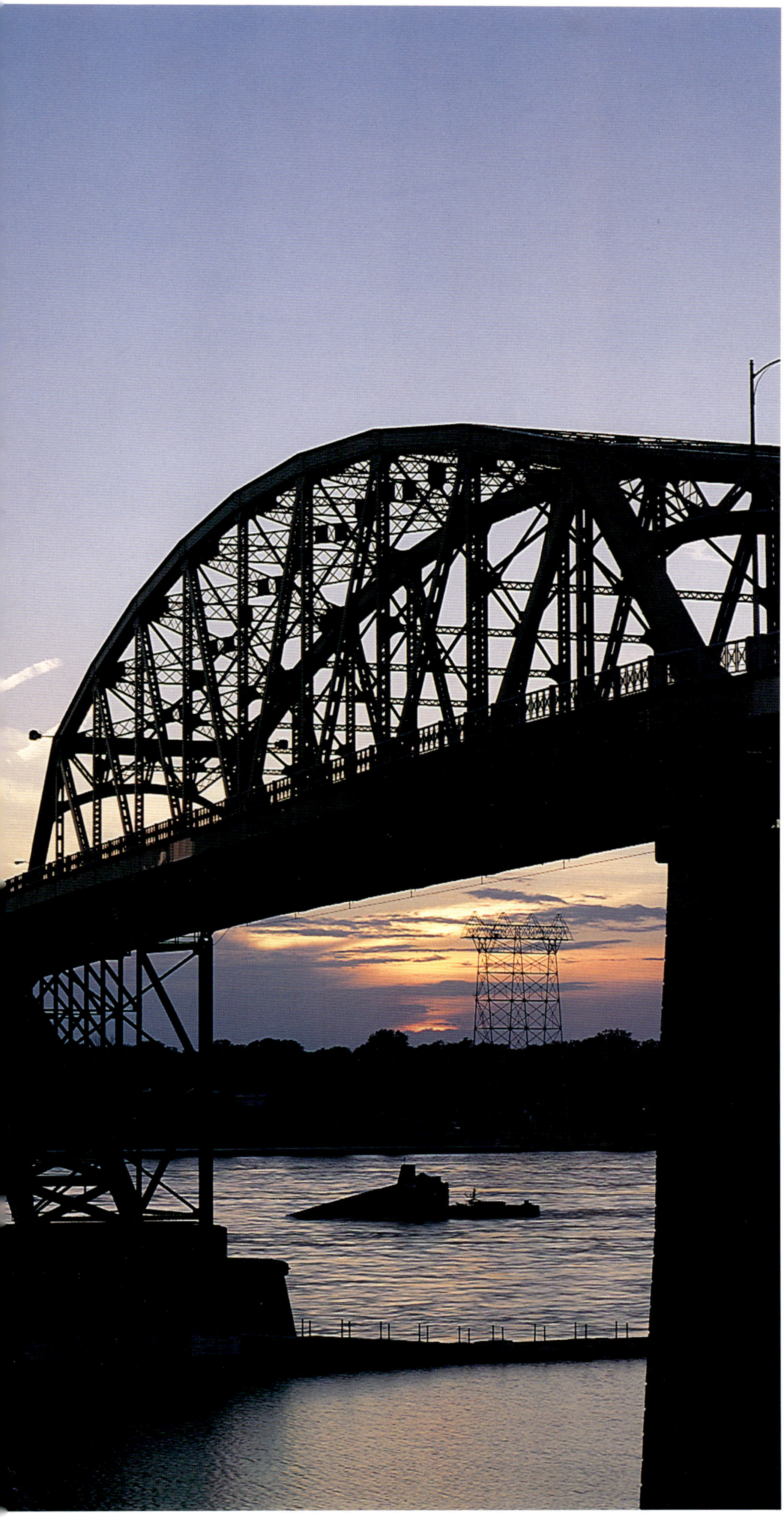

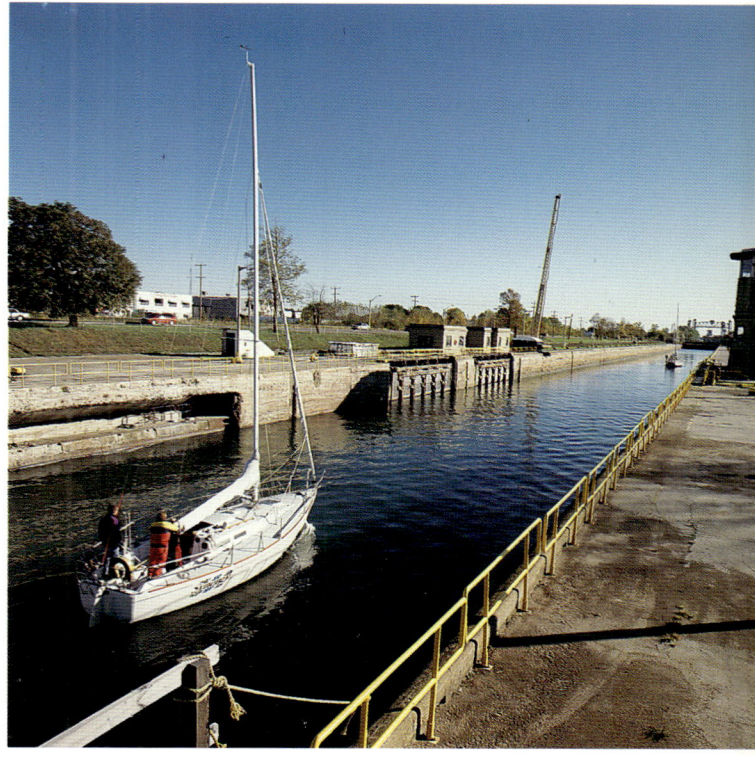

Allowing ships to bypass Niagara Falls, the **Welland Ship Canal** cuts a 27.6-mile waterway through the Niagara Peninsula between Port Colborne on Lake Erie and Port Weller, near St. Catharines, on Lake Ontario. A series of eight locks lifts sailboats, lake steamers, and oceangoing freighters over the Niagara Escarpment. The original Welland Canal opened in 1829 for local and regional trade and connected Port Dalhousie to Port Robinson on the Welland River, which in turn connected to the Niagara River. The present Welland Canal is an international commercial waterway and integral part of the St. Lawrence Seaway, which directly links nearly 100 Canadian and U.S. ports with Western Europe. Each day, great vessels laden with wheat, coal, iron ore, and other cargo make the 12-hour passage through the 27-foot-deep canal.
Photo by James P. McCoy.

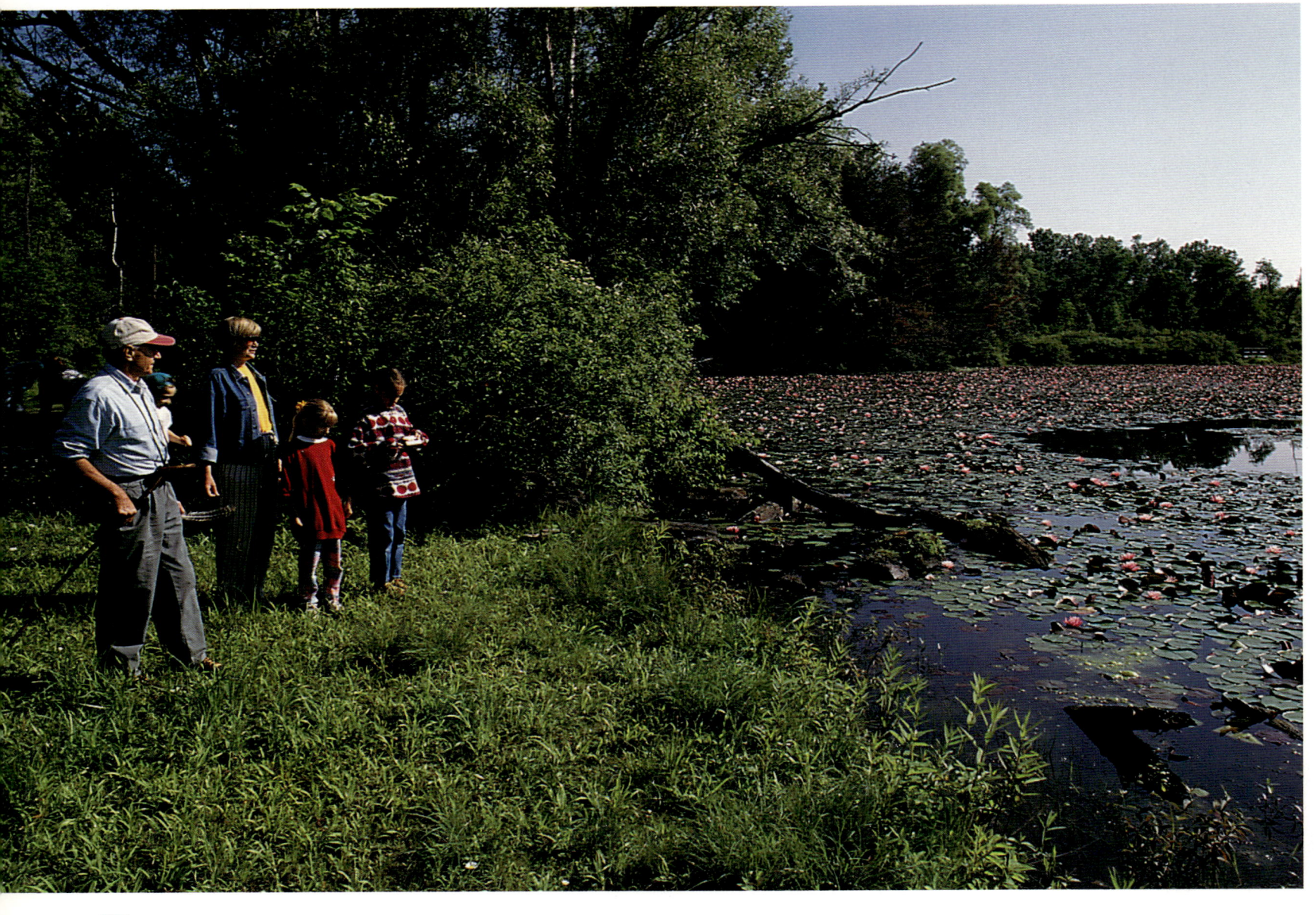

In the Buffalo suburb of Cheektowaga, surrounded by perfectly manicured neighborhoods, shopping malls, and busy thoroughfares, there's a place of prehistoric natural beauty. The **Reinstein Woods State Nature Preserve** is an 80-acre ancient forest abounding with venerable trees, diverse wildlife, serene lakes, secluded ponds, rare wildflowers, and reedy marshes. One of the largest virgin forests in New York State, it is also one of the few old growth forests still flourishing in the midst of a metropolitan environment. The preserve was the gift of Dr. and Mrs. Victor Reinstein to be protected in perpetuity as forever wild.
Photo by James P. McCoy.

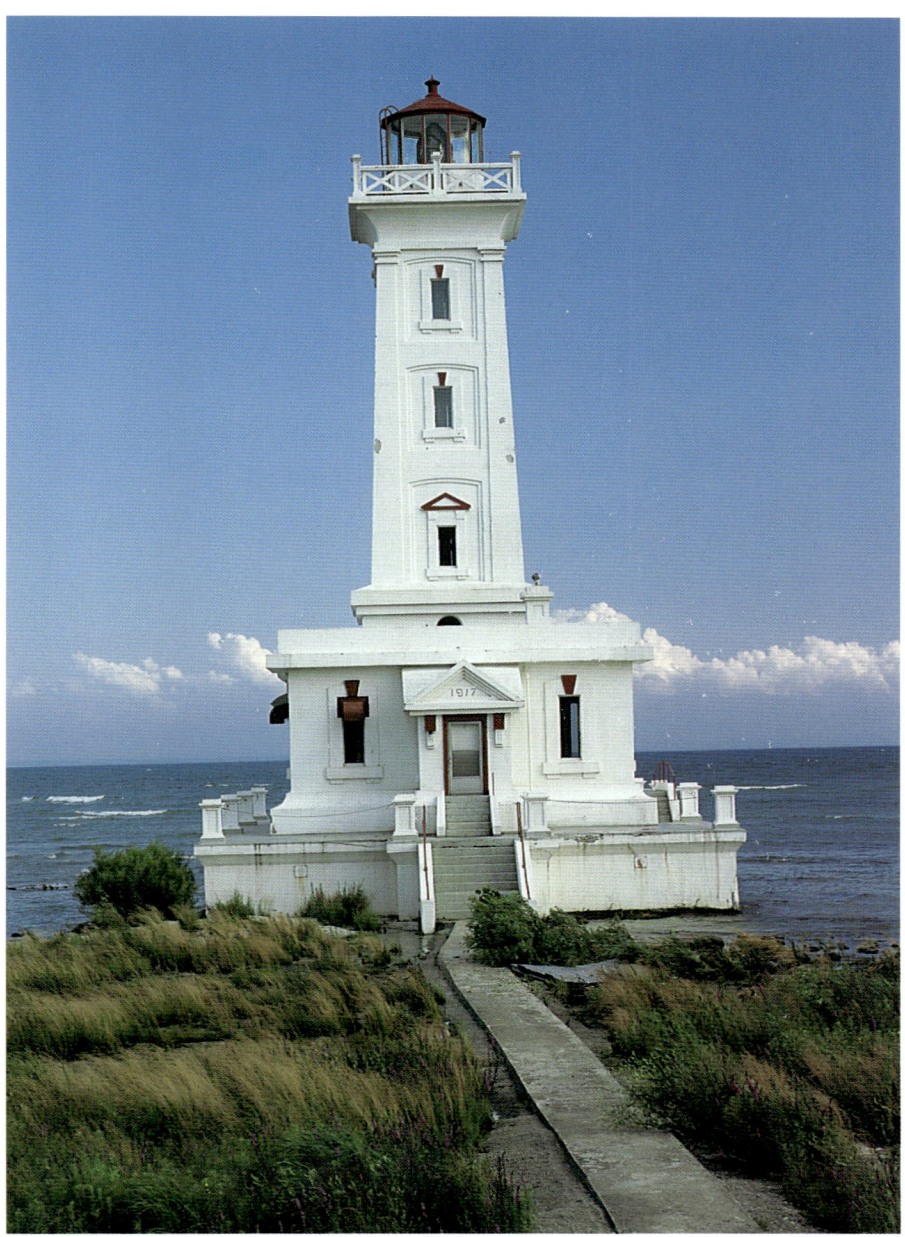

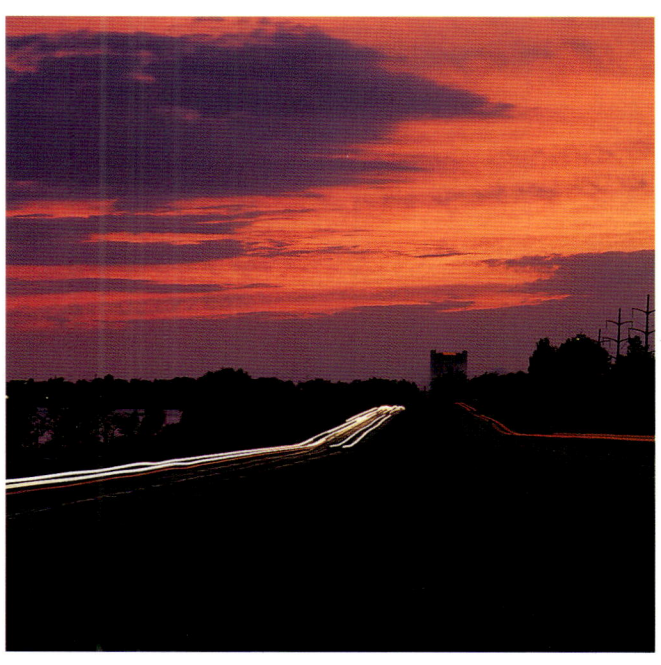

About halfway between the Niagara River and the Welland Canal, a small peninsula points straight into Lake Erie. Local legend has it that a French Jesuit priest, the Rev. Claude Aveneau, built a small cabin and lived here for a few months sometime around 1690. Adopting a less Gallic form of the pére's name as its own, Point Abino gradually developed into a small 19th-century industrial park with a sawmill, a lime kiln, a sand-mining operation, and boardinghouses for workmen. In 1892, a group of 21 American investors bought the land from the Halloway family and began developing it as a private summer resort community, which it remains to this day. Point Abino was always notorious among lake seamen for its treacherous shoal that snared many ships and barges blown in by squalls or faulty navigation. The **Point Abino Lighthouse** was built in 1917 and equipped with a foghorn that could be heard 16 miles out into the lake. With the opening of the St. Lawrence Seaway and the shifting of the shipping lanes, the lighthouse became less important as a navigational aid to lake vessels. In 1992, the Canadian Coast Guard switched the lighthouse over to an automatic system without the foghorn familiar to generations of Point Abino residents. In 1996, the lighthouse was decommissioned and a lightbouy was placed at the end of the shoal.
Photo by James P. McCoy.

Winston Churchill called it "the prettiest Sunday afternoon drive in the world." **The Niagara Parkway** is a magnificent stretch of scenic greenbelt that meanders along the Canadian side of the Niagara River from Lake Erie, through Chippawa, right past Niagara Falls and over the Niagara Escarpment all the way to Lake Ontario. The parkway between Queenston and Niagara-on-the-Lake is one of the oldest roads in Ontario. During the War of 1812, the road was a strategic link between Fort George near Newark and Fort Erie. In 1931, with the approved crossing of the Military Reserve near Fort George, the final link of the parkway opened and the continuous boulevard from lake to lake was completed. The Niagara River Recreation Trail, a 35-mile-wide paved path, accompanies the parkway for its entire run from Old Fort Erie to Niagara-on-the-Lake.
Photo by James P. McCoy.

In 1874, a manufacturer and a Methodist bishop began a training program for Sunday school teachers in a tent village illuminated by burning pine knots. Word of this interdenominational assembly quickly spread, and within a few years, thousands of people were attending the **Chautauqua Institution** each summer. In 1974, Chautauqua celebrated its centennial year as a world-famous religious convocation, fine arts colony, recreational playground, and learning center. But Chautauqua is more than an institution. It's also a leafy little Victorian village with gingerbread houses, porches with bright geraniums, sprawling old hotels, a post office, a bookstore, and a population of year-round residents. Its eight-week cultural program includes concerts by a professional resident symphony orchestra, a resident opera company, a resident theater company, and recitals and concerts by nationally renowned jazz, pop, and classical artists. Chautauqua's summer school offers courses in music, dance, and art, as well as a wide variety of special interest courses that range from mushrooming to surfing the Net. Photo by James P. McCoy.

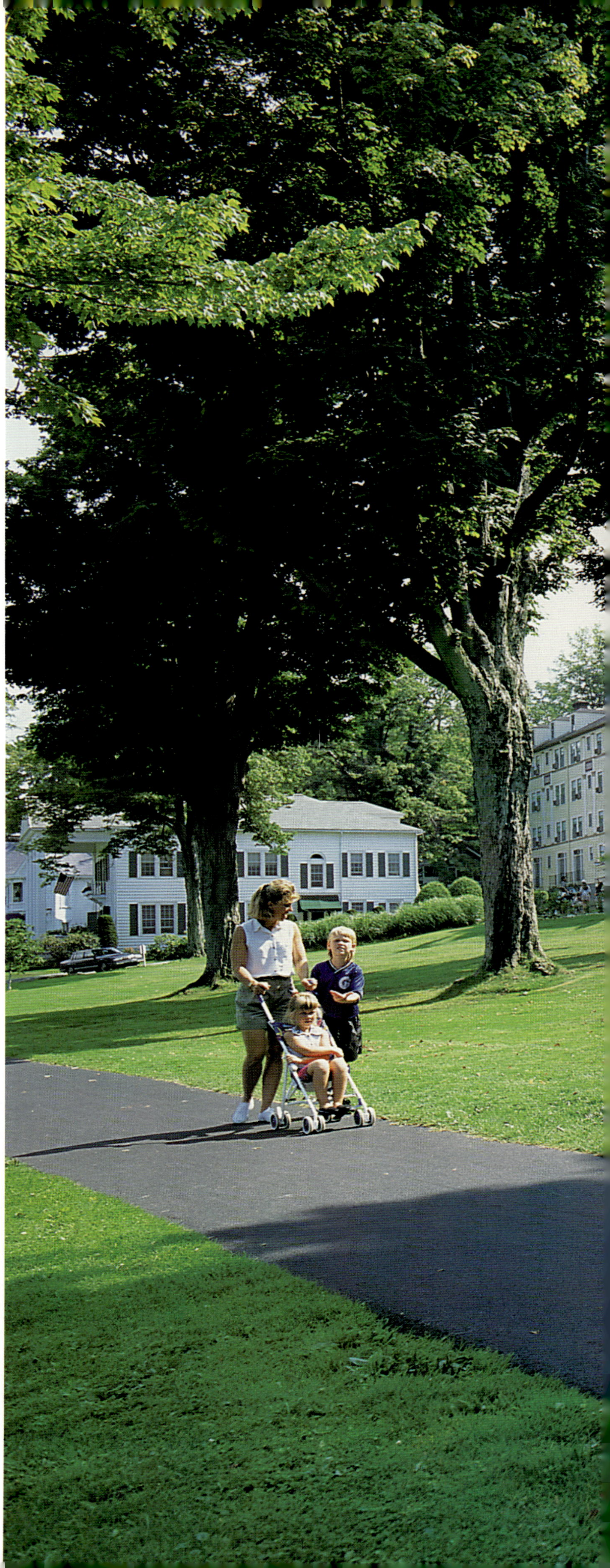

Every summer, Niagara celebrates its unique heritage and its legacy of importance to U.S./Canadian international relations and trade with a week of music, fireworks, spectacle, and fun. Drawing some of the largest crowds of any event in North America, the **Freedom Festival** presents symphony and rock concerts, an air show, equestrian events, arts and crafts, Highland games, and a great opportunity to strengthen the ties of friendship on both sides of the border. Photo by James P. McCoy.

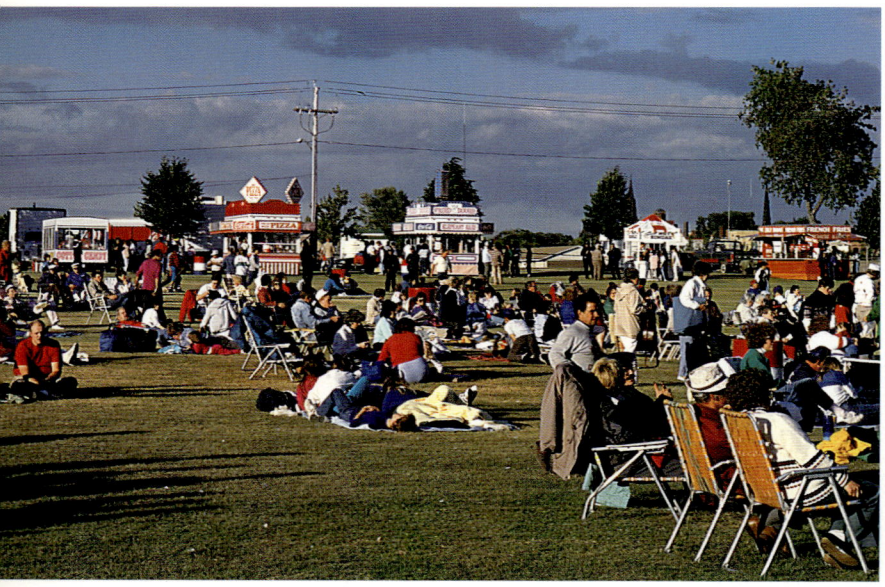

ATTRACTING THE WORLD

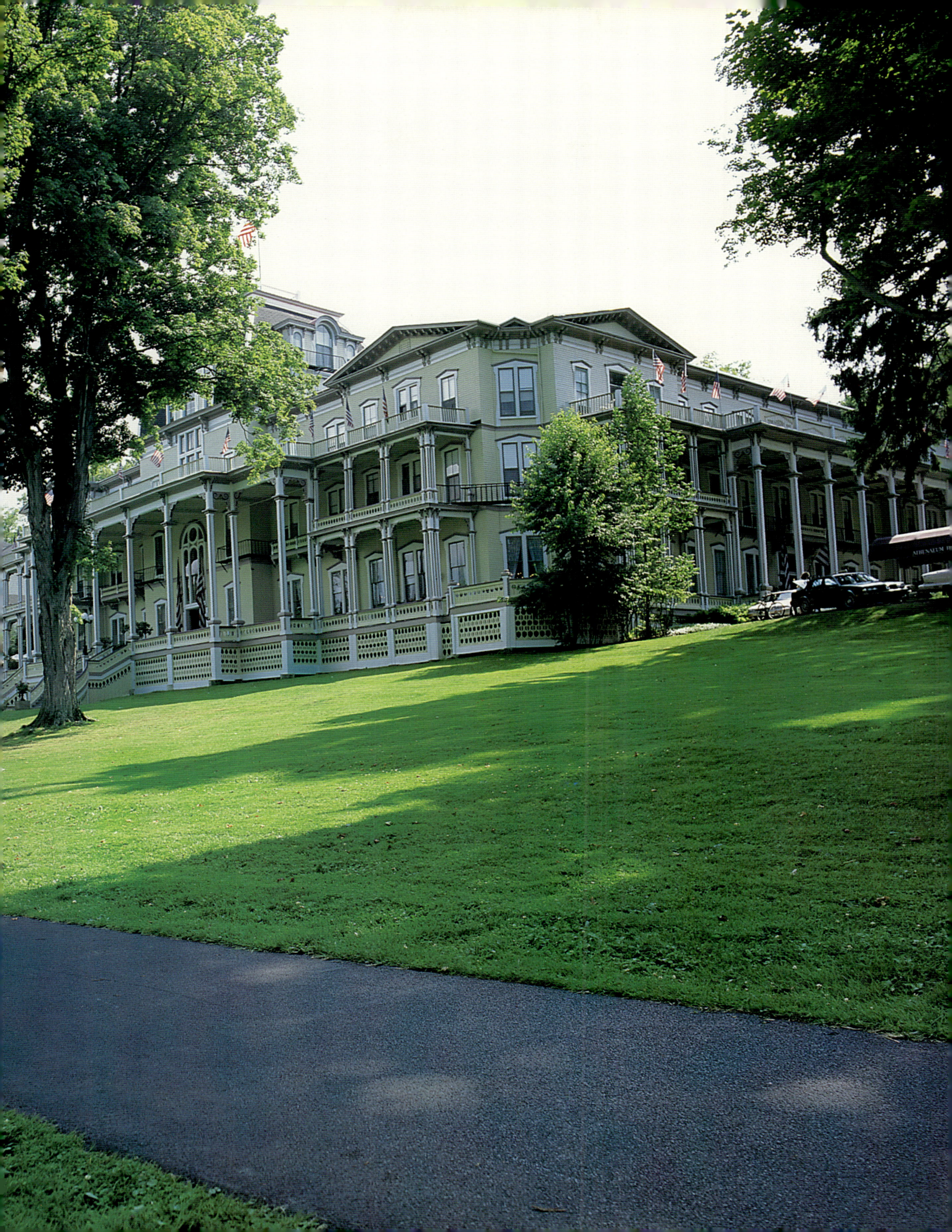

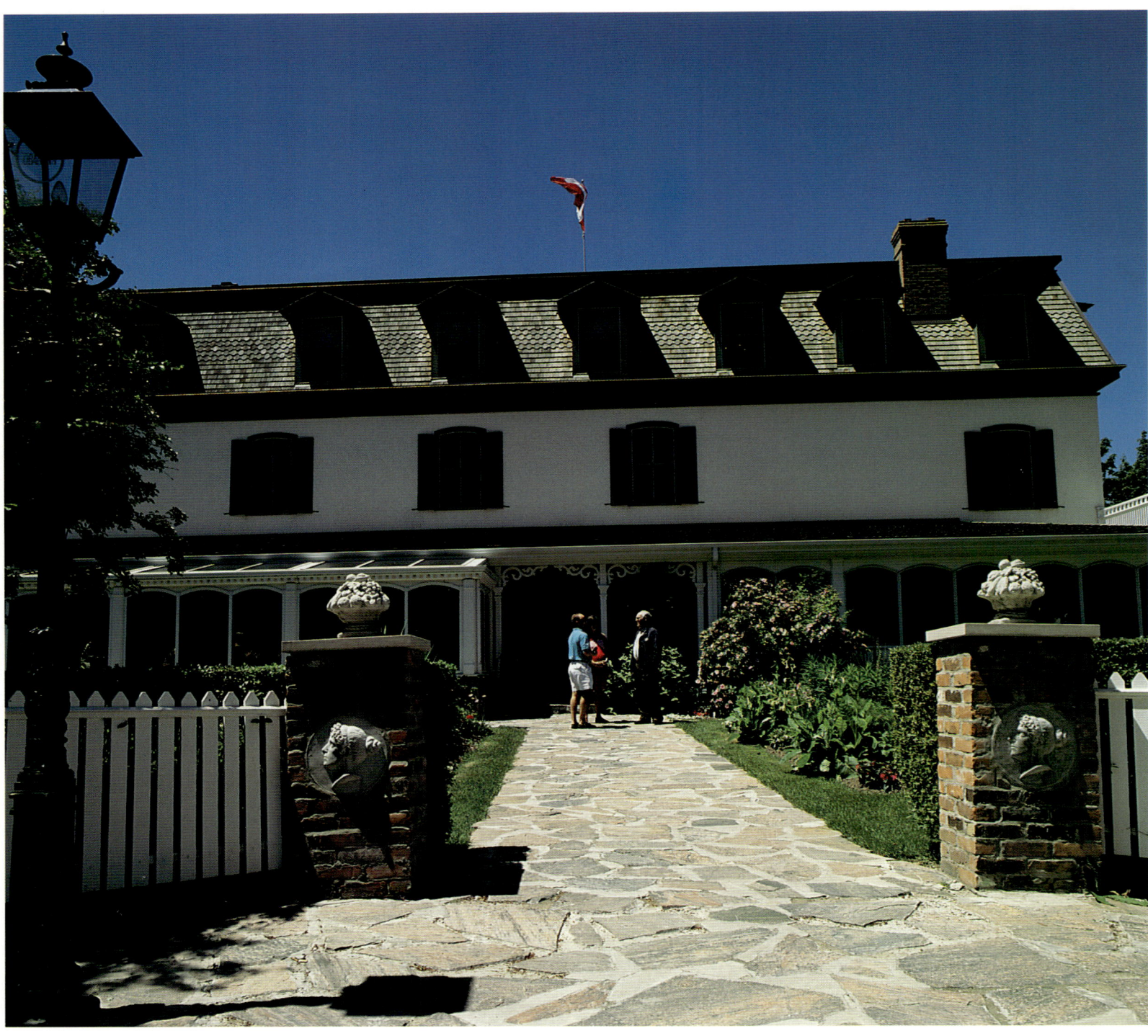

Originally called Newark, this charming 19th-century village was rebuilt after it was burned by American forces during the War of 1812. Once the capital of Upper Canada, it is now home to the Shaw Festival, the second-largest theater company in North America and the only one specializing in the works of George Bernard Shaw and his contemporaries. With Canada's largest collection of 19th-century Georgian architecture, **Niagara-on-the-Lake** commands a splendid view of Lake Ontario and the mouth of the Niagara River. Guests at the **Oban Inn** keep tradition alive by taking afternoon tea on the terrace.
Photo by James P. McCoy.

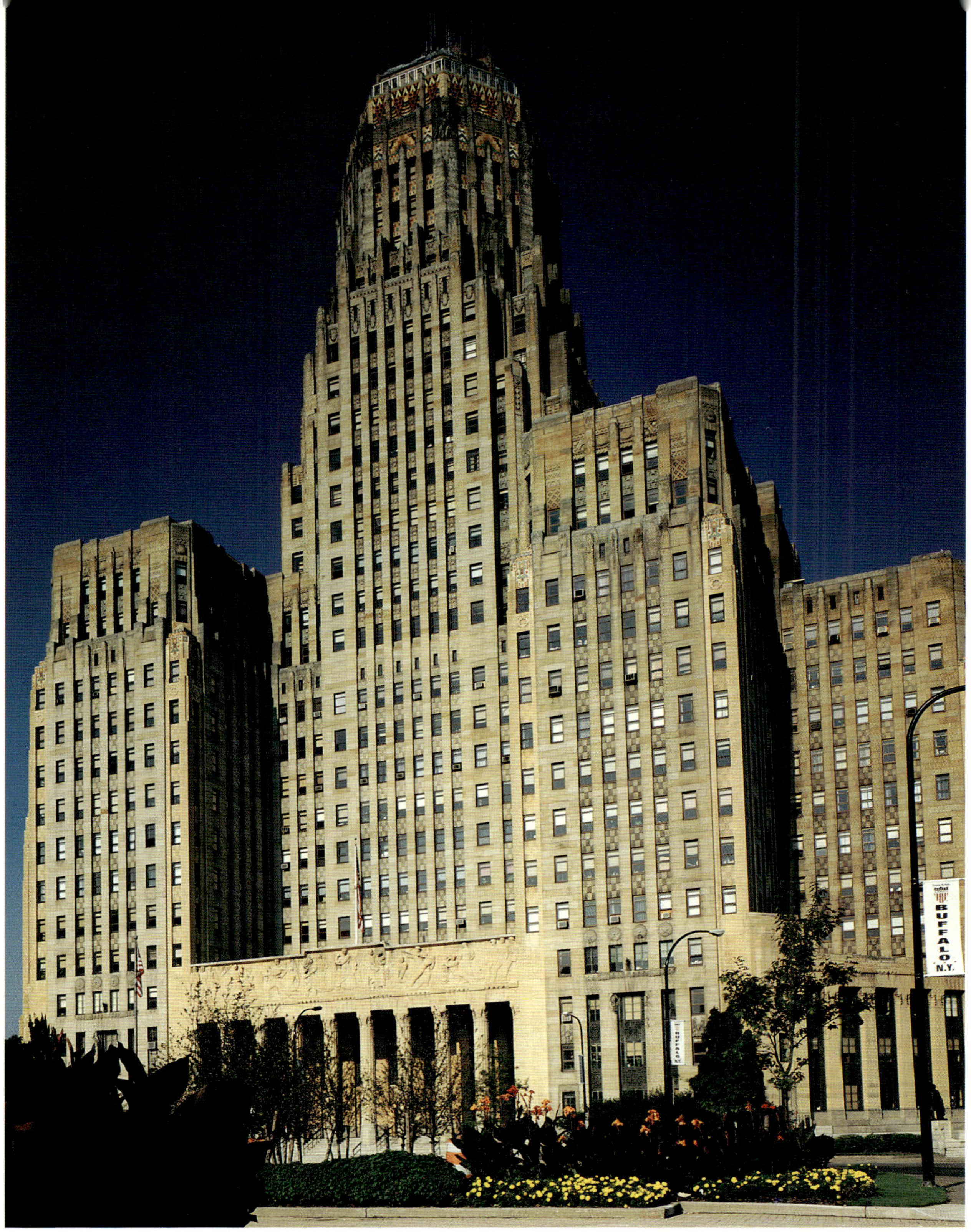

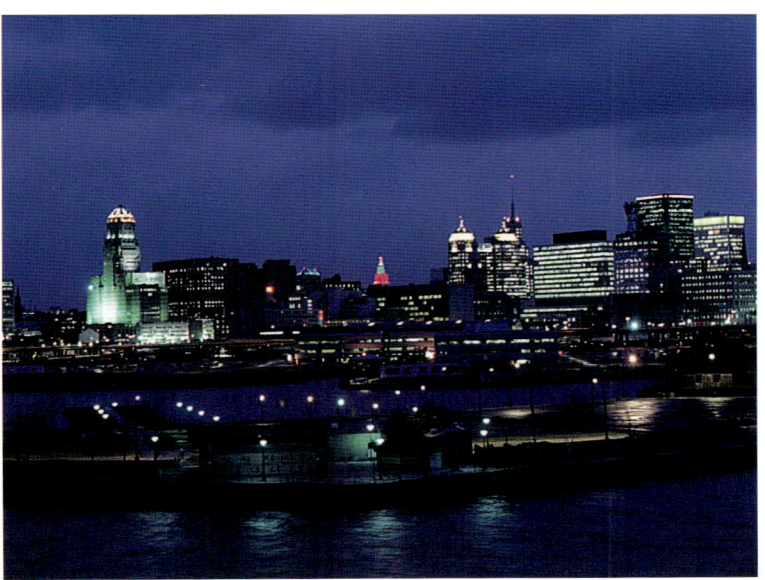

Like many North American cities, Buffalo was settled first at its waterfront and then pushed gradually inland. **Buffalo's waterfront** became one of the world's busiest after the opening of the Erie Canal, which ended here at the "Queen City of the Great Lakes" and provided transportation to eastern ports for lumber, grain, livestock, and iron. Although grain ships can still be seen unloading their cargo at the massive elevators that tower above the Buffalo River and the City Ship Canal, today's waterfront is primarily a mecca for sailboats, power yachts, sunset gazers, ice cream lovers, strollers, and real estate developers. Photo by James P. McCoy.

The **Buffalo City Hall** is a monument to the Art Deco decorative art and architecture movement of the 1920s and 1930s. From the 28th floor observation deck on a clear day, you can see the mist rising from Niagara Falls. Photo by Marc Murphy.

The **Maid of the Mist** tour boats bring visitors through the roar and the crashing spray to behold up close the panoramic power of the Horseshoe Falls. The Maid of the Mist is one of the oldest businesses in Niagara and has been making voyages from both sides of the river to the base of the cataract for 150 years.
Photo by James P. McCoy.

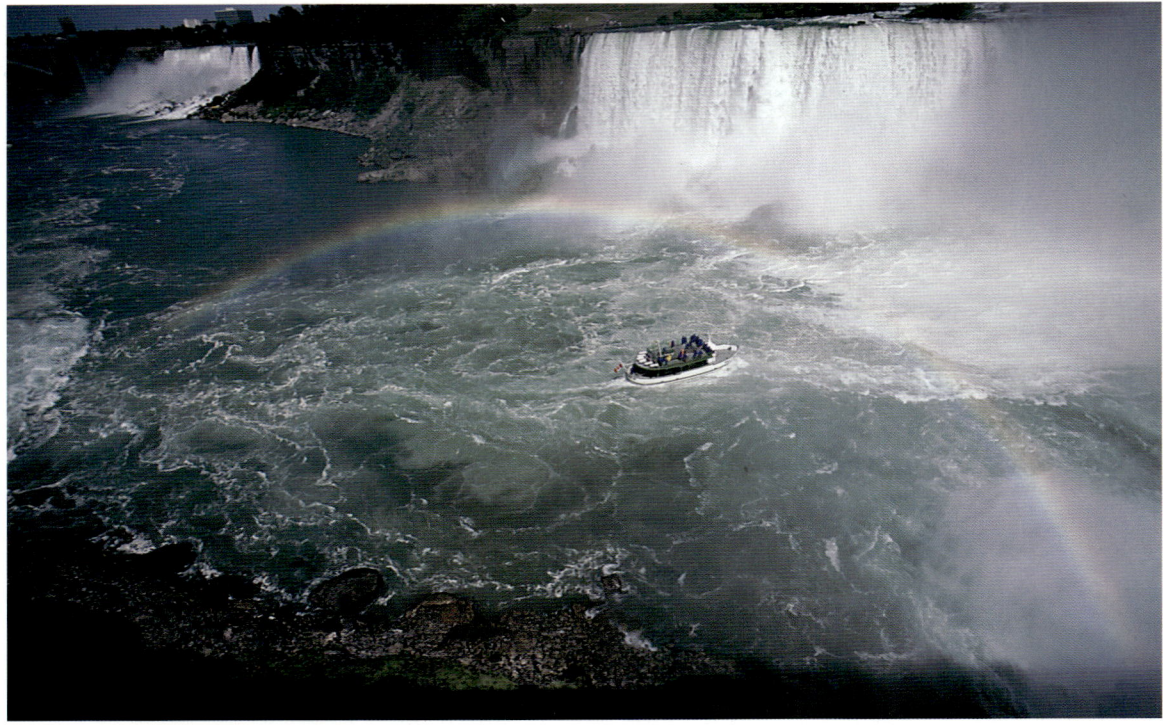

Sponsored by the Buffalo Audubon Society, the **Beaver Meadow Nature Center** is a 324-acre sanctuary with hiking trails, an astronomical observatory, and a visitor center with meeting rooms, wildlife exhibits, a library, and a gift shop. Beaver Meadow is equipped with a walkway for blind and handicapped visitors and offers guided tours, family programs, a summer day camp, and a year-round calendar of nature events.
Photo by James P. McCoy.

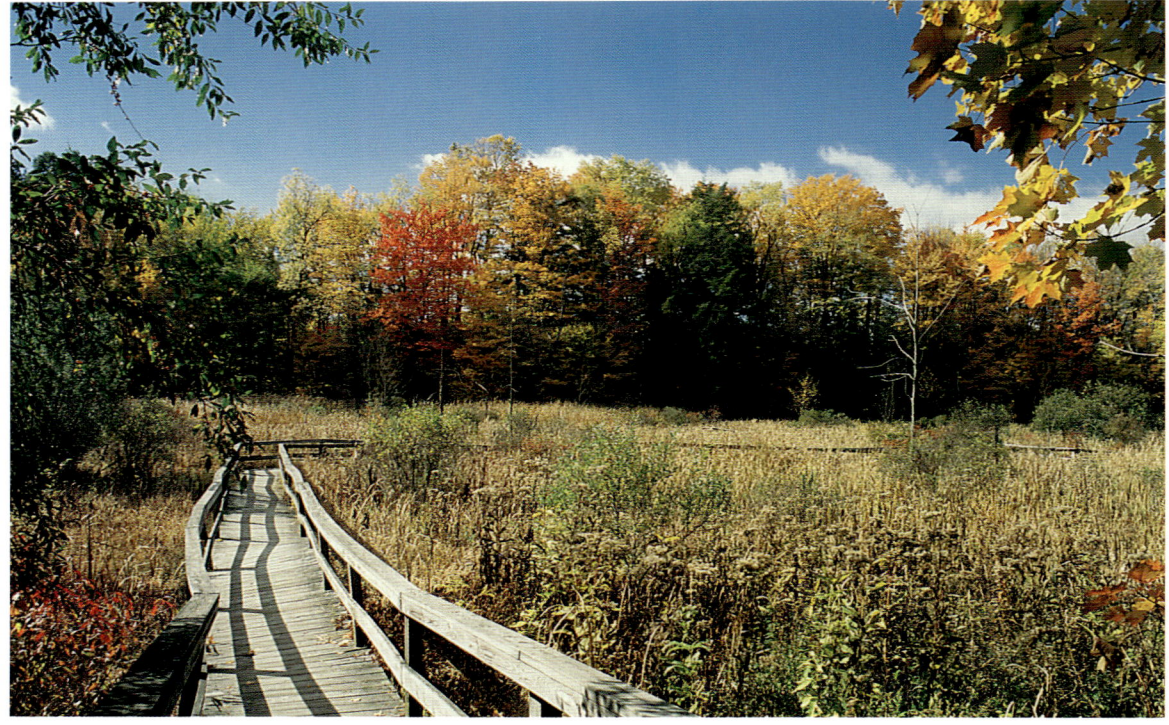

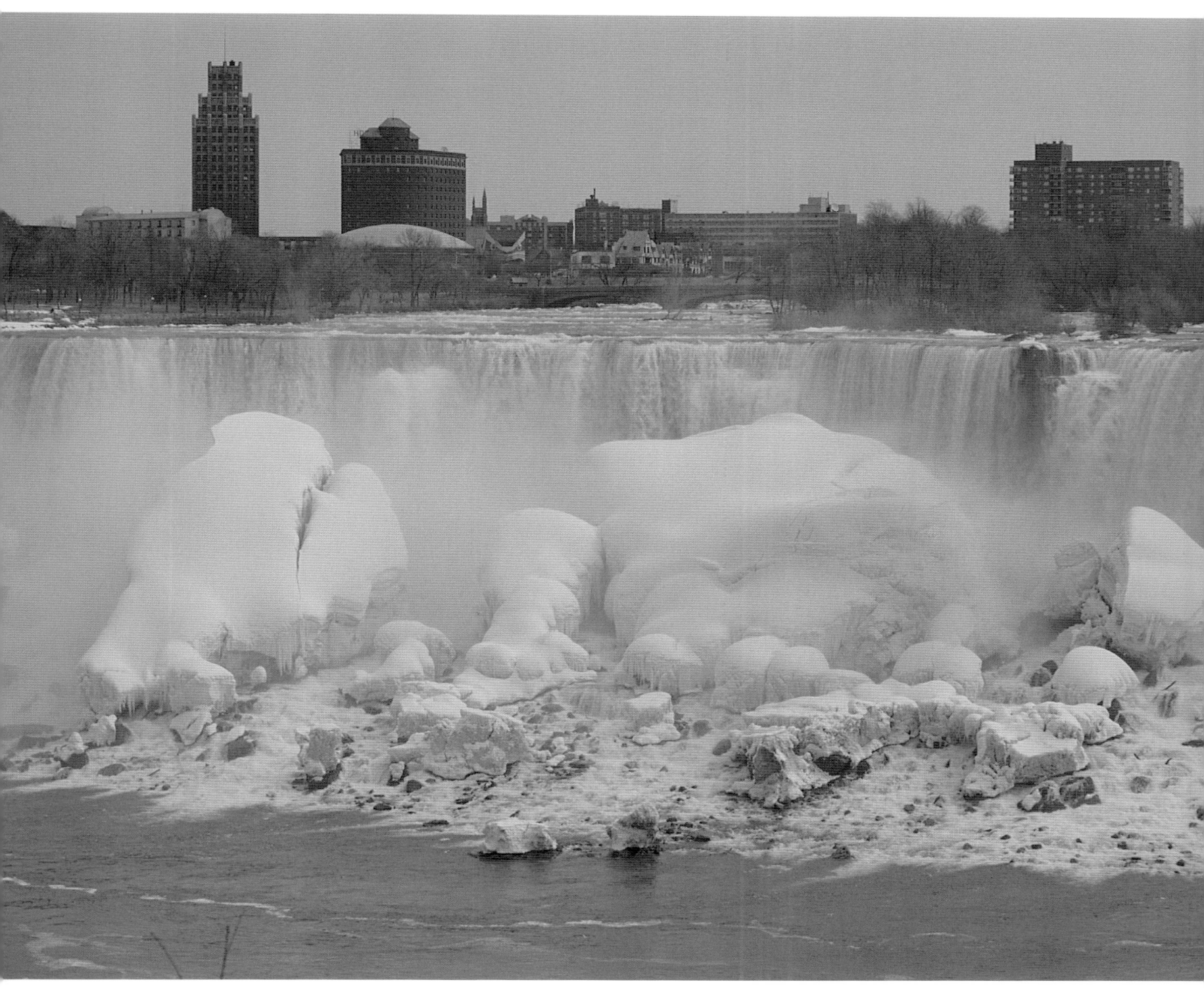

Great winter ice bridges occasionally form below **Niagara Falls**. The ice bridges are sometimes created in January when relatively mild weather followed by a strong southwest wind breaks up Lake Erie ice and hurls it down the Niagara River over the Falls. Forced up out of the water below the Falls, the wet ice freezes into a huge glacial mass. In 1964, a floating timber ice boom was placed in Lake Erie at the headwaters of the Niagara to help control the flow of ice down the river. Photo by James P. McCoy.

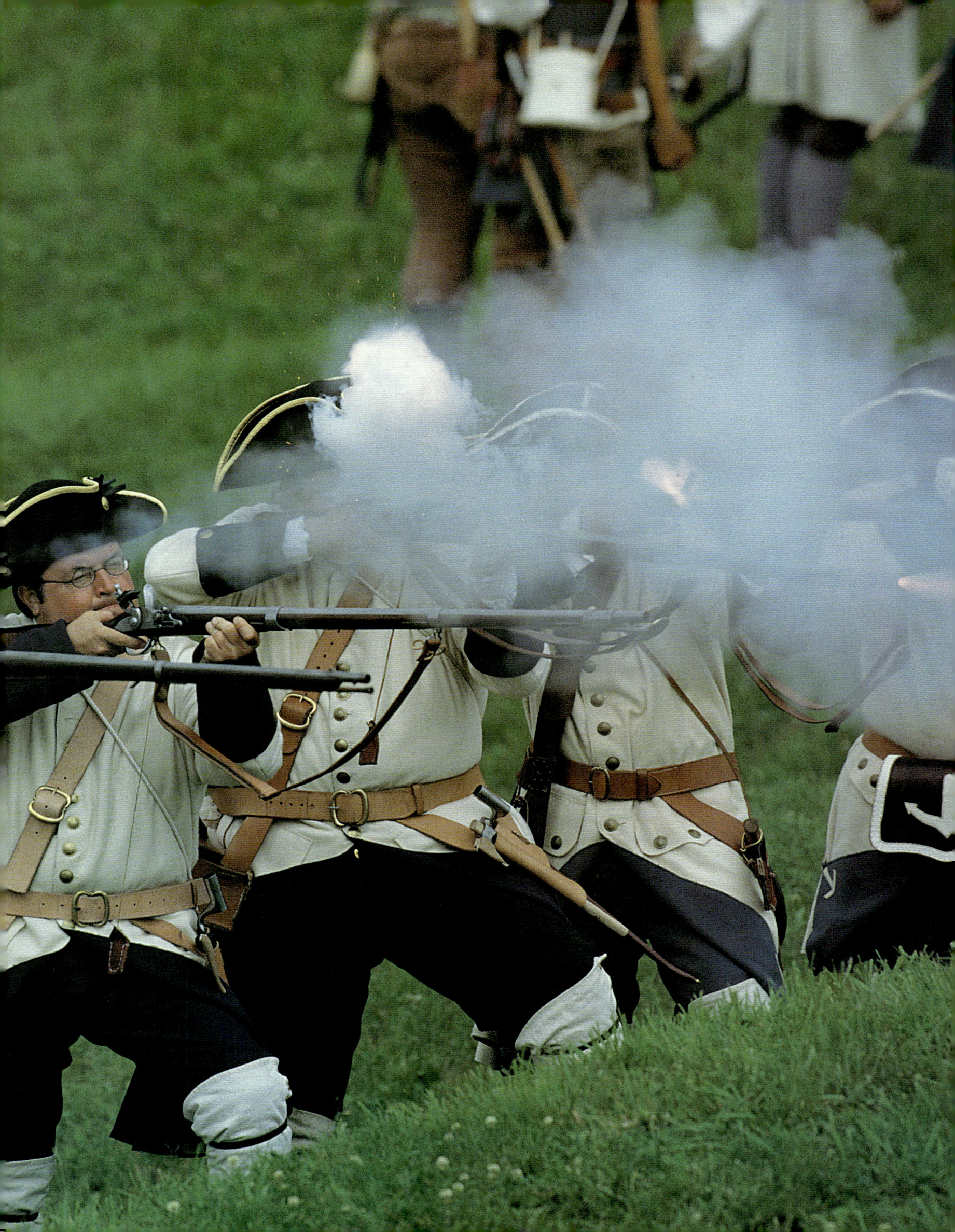

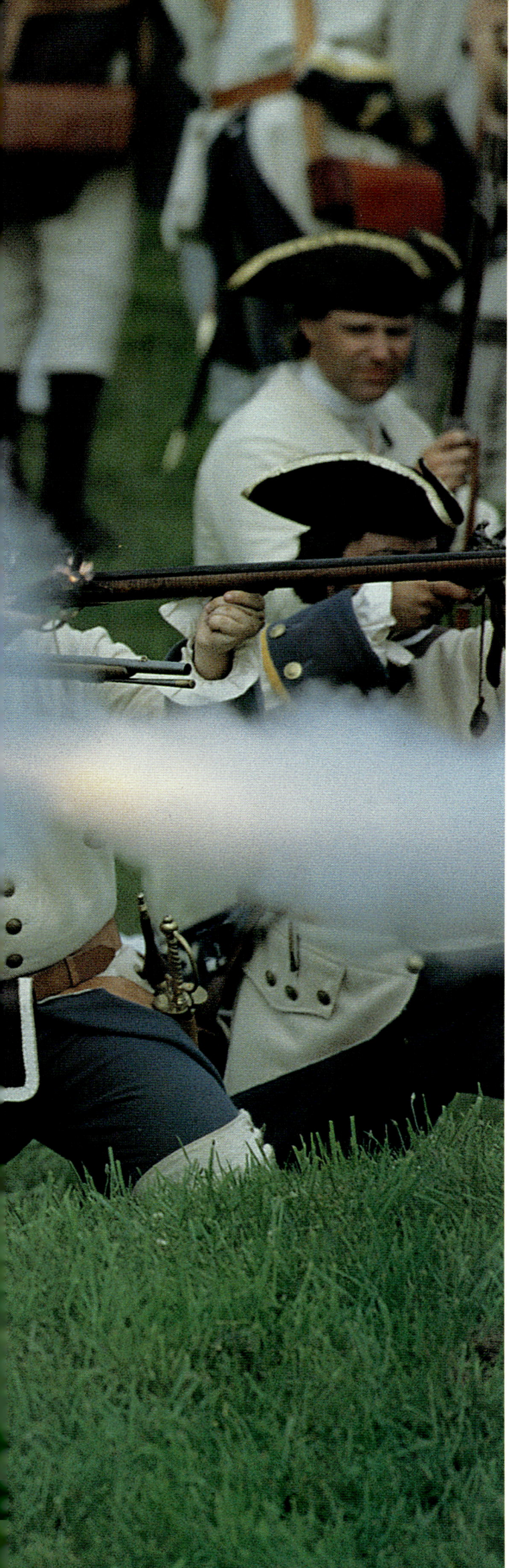

THE ATTRACTION BEGINS

Around 12,000 years ago, the glaciers of the last Ice Age retreated, Niagara Falls was created, and the first humans arrived in Niagara. The land was primarily tundra and spruce forest and inhabited by nomadic hunters, the Clovis people, who camped along the old shoreline of Lake Erie and probably hunted mastodons, caribou, elk, and moose with stone spears. Some 9,000 years ago, a deciduous forest covered most of the Niagara Peninsula. The hunter-gatherers of the Archaic Period subsisted here by hunting in small groups and fishing throughout the year.

Fort Niagara photo by James P. McCoy.

Long after the building of the Pyramids at Giza, a strong agricultural society took root in Niagara. The people of the Iroquois culture planted beans, corn, and squash and built villages of domed-roofed longhouses covered with sheets of elm bark and enclosed by palisades. They called the river Onguiaahra, meaning "the straight." In their leisure, they invented the game of baggataway, a rough and tumble game they regarded as excellent training for combat. The French later named the game lacrosse because the racquet reminded them of a bishop's crosier.

In Ontario, the peaceful Huron, the Petun, and Neutral confederacies were dispersed by intertribal warfare with the Iroquois. In 1651, the Neutrals were destroyed by the Iroquois over a fur trade rivalry. Today, the descendants of two Iroquois tribes still live in Niagara: the Seneca and the Tuscarora.

The Tuscarora were the last group of native people to join the League of the Iroquois, a confederacy of native tribes formed in the late 15th or 16th century. Forced out of the North Carolina area, the Tuscarora were attracted to the fertile lands and teeming rivers of Niagara and joined the League in 1722, creating the Six Nation Iroquois. The other five Iroquois nations, collectively known as "the people of the longhouse," were the Mohawk, Oneida, Onondaga, Cayuga, and the Seneca.

The Iroquois, whose names are reflected across the modern map of New York State, essentially controlled the lands between the Hudson River and the Great Lakes. With a total population of less than 12,000 and some 2,200 warriors, the Iroquois were able to dominate neighboring tribes and contain the French, Dutch, and English for two centuries.

The first serious threat to Iroquois dominance of Niagara came in 1678 with the arrival of the expedition of René-Robert Cavelier, Sieur de La Salle, which attempted to establish French sovereignty over the region. La Salle built a timber fort at the mouth of the Niagara River at Lake Ontario, which he called Fort Conti, but it was soon consumed by fire. Nearly 50 years later, the French built Fort Niagara at the same site, where it still stands today.

Traveling with the La Salle expedition was the Franciscan missionary, Father Louis Hennepin, who wrote and published detailed accounts of the new land, including the first description of "a vast and prodigious cadence of water that falls down after a surprising and astonishing manner, insomuch that the Universe does not afford its parallel."

Although the British colonies on the Atlantic seaboard were flourishing in the late 17th century, France was still the dominant European power in Niagara. Vastly outnumbered by the English colonists, the French had a larger military, better trained troops, and stronger alliances with the Indians than had the British. But the tide was turning, and by the outbreak of the French and Indian War in 1754, France was clearly on the defensive. The turning point in Niagara came with the surrender of Fort Niagara to British forces on July 25, 1759.

After the American victory in the Revolutionary War, Fort Niagara was ceded to the United States of America at the Treaty of Paris in 1783. The British, in turn, got all of Canada. Thirteen years later, the British finally withdrew from Fort Niagara and built a new post, Fort George, directly across the river at Newark (now Niagara-on-the-Lake).

Meanwhile, the Dutch, who in 1624 had established Fort Orange at Albany and then founded New Amsterdam on Manhattan Island (later captured by the English and named for James, Duke of York, brother of Charles II), now looked to profit in Western New York. (The area didn't acquire its capital W until the mid-20th century.) The Holland Land Company, a consortium of Dutch firms created in Amsterdam in 1792, speculated in over five million acres in Western New York and northern Pennsylvania. To plot out and sell its newly acquired real estate in Western New York, they hired a young Pennsylvania surveyor named Joseph Ellicott.

Ellicott was a fourth-generation American whose great grandfather Andrew, a Quaker, had emigrated from Devonshire, England, and settled in Bucks County, Pennsylvania, where he manufactured woolen goods. Hired as a surveyor, Ellicott quickly rose to the powerful position of Resident Agent for the Holland Land Company in Western New York. He arrived in 1800 and laid out plans for a village he planned to call New Amsterdam.

Fortunately for posterity, Ellicott had the advantage of his brother Andrew's influence in the design of the city that would become Buffalo. Andrew Ellicott was a surveyor with Pierre-Charles L'Enfant, the French-born architect and engineer and the principal designer of Washington, D.C. It is no accident that both cities are characterized by broad, radiating avenues converging into circular intersections and public squares.

During and after the American Revolution, the Niagara Peninsula of Ontario, at the time in British hands, became increasingly populated by English Loyalists who emigrated from the United States. During the War of 1812, Niagara became a bloody battleground. Niagara was pulled into the war because of its location, not because its animosity or emotions ran high on war issues. To the American war hawks, led by Secretary of War William Eustis, the Niagara peninsula of Canada seemed both desirable (good soil and climate) and vulnerable (the British forces at Quebec were hundreds of miles away). Important battles took place at Fort Erie, Queenston Heights, Fort George, Stoney Creek, and Fort Niagara. On December 10, 1813, after evacuating previously captured Fort George, American troops burned the village of Newark, leaving several hundred families homeless in midwinter.

In retaliation, the British stormed and recaptured Fort Niagara, then laid waste to the American side of the river, burning the villages of Lewiston, Youngstown, Manchester (later Niagara Falls), and Buffalo. The next July, Brigadier General Winfield Scott's American brigade, in its gray uniforms, won an important victory at Chippawa. (General Scott later told historians that to commemorate this battle, gray was subsequently adopted as the color of cadet uniforms at the U.S. Military Academy at West Point.) Less than three weeks after Chippawa, the Battle of Lundy's Lane was fought near Niagara Falls. This battle, often described as the fiercest of the entire war, ended with the withdrawal of the Americans back to Fort Erie. The War of 1812 is credited with creating Canadian nationalism and fostering a new sense of Canadian culture separate and distinct from its U.S. neighbors.

Hostilities officially ended with the signing of the Treaty of Ghent, and Canada and the United States have enjoyed continuous peace ever since, with one small exception. On May 31, 1866, a self-appointed general named John O'Neill and some 1,200 Fenians invaded Canada from the village of Black Rock, just north of Buffalo. The Fenians, who planned to win Irish independence by conquering Canada, attacked at Ridgeway and met the Canadian militia in a short-lived battle that ended with the arrest of O'Neill and several followers by the commander of a U.S. gunboat.

After the War of 1812, Queenston became a thriving community and Chippawa rebuilt itself into a prosperous center of factories and distilleries. At Niagara Falls during the 1820s, a stairway was constructed into the gorge at Table Rock and a ferry service began operating across the lower Niagara to the United States. By 1827, there was a paved road leading from the ferry landing up to the top of the Canadian bank. This area became known as Clifton Hill after the Clifton House Hotel was built there in the 1830s.

With the opening of the Erie Canal in 1825 and the arrival of thousands of settlers, immigrants, and fortune seekers, Niagara became more than a natural wonder; it became a place writers and orators continually declared destined for development, trade, prosperity, and success. The Erie Canal was 363 miles long, required 83 locks and had cost $9,000,000 to build, but it lowered the cost of shipping freight from $100 a ton to less than $10 a ton. At once, Buffalo became both a destination and a port of embarkation for travelers and pioneers coming west on the canal, then boarding the lakeboats for Detroit, Cleveland, and the Western Reserve. In 1842, Joseph Dart built the world's first mechanical grain elevator in Buffalo, and by midcentury, these great vertical structures, filled with western grain by steam-powered buckets

and the shovels and sweat of Irish scoopers, dominated the city's waterfront. In 1860, over 31 million bushels of grain arrived in Buffalo for storage, milling, and transshipment.

Firmly established as a shipping center, Buffalo next became a railway hub with 14 major trunk lines and a railway bridge over the Niagara River between Black Rock and Bridgeburg (a town that grew up around the bridge and was later annexed to Fort Erie).

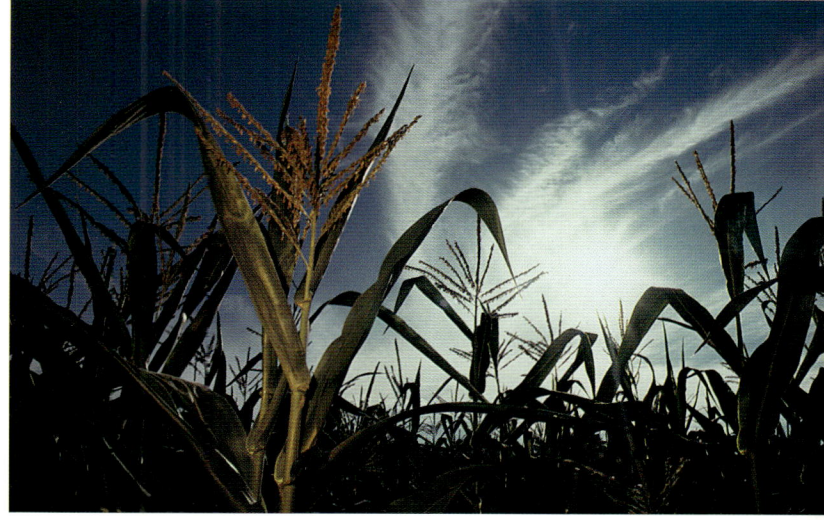

During the 19th century, Niagara Falls flourished first as a playground for the rich and later, given the rise of the railroad industry, as a popular recreation spot. As railroads made travel for the lower classes possible, Niagara Falls became a popular place for the new phenomenon, "the honeymoon." By the turn of the century, Niagara was attracting the world in droves. Buffalo, a great commercial and industrial center, had the fourth-busiest harbor in the country, the largest coal distribution facility, a booming flour milling industry, 19 breweries producing a million barrels of beer annually, and a huge stockyard and meat-packing industry. Over 250 passenger trains arrived at Buffalo's 5 terminals each day. Two of the city's adopted sons—Millard Fillmore and Grover Cleveland—had already risen to be president of the United States.

In 1896, electricity had been shot through wires to Buffalo from the great power generators in Niagara Falls. Streetcars, electric lights, and industrial engines were humming with the energy harnessed by Nikola Tesla, George Westinghouse, Thomas Edison, Jacob Schoellkopf, and other pioneers of electric power. The entire scientific world was preoccupied with the Falls and its technological implications. The chemical industry, previously limited by its huge need for power, set up shop in Niagara to produce a huge variety of chemical substances. Some were natural such as aluminum, which soon became a household product. Others were invented like Carborundum, the revolutionary inexpensive substitute for industrial diamonds. The time was right for a great celebration worthy of Niagara and reflective of an age of unbounded optimism and faith in the wonders of technology to transform the world.

On May 1, 1901, the Pan-American Exposition opened in Buffalo, drawing visitors from around the world. Predating Disney by decades, the Exposition was a fairy tale of opulent temples, classical and rococo structures, magnificent fountains, and wide promenades dominated by a 409-foot electric tower complete with a 70-foot waterfall and topped with a winged Goddess of Light.

At night, every window, cornice, and roofline of the Exposition sparkled with dazzling electric lights. Streetlights

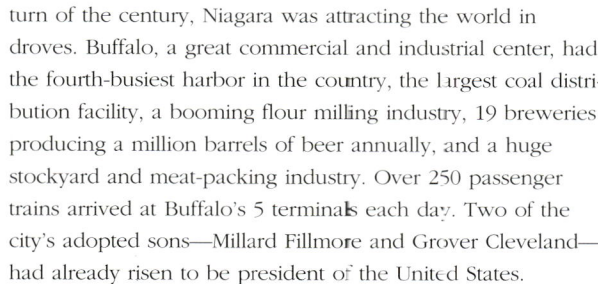

Rich farmland and a favorable growing climate make **agriculture** a top industry in Niagara. Photo by James P. McCoy.

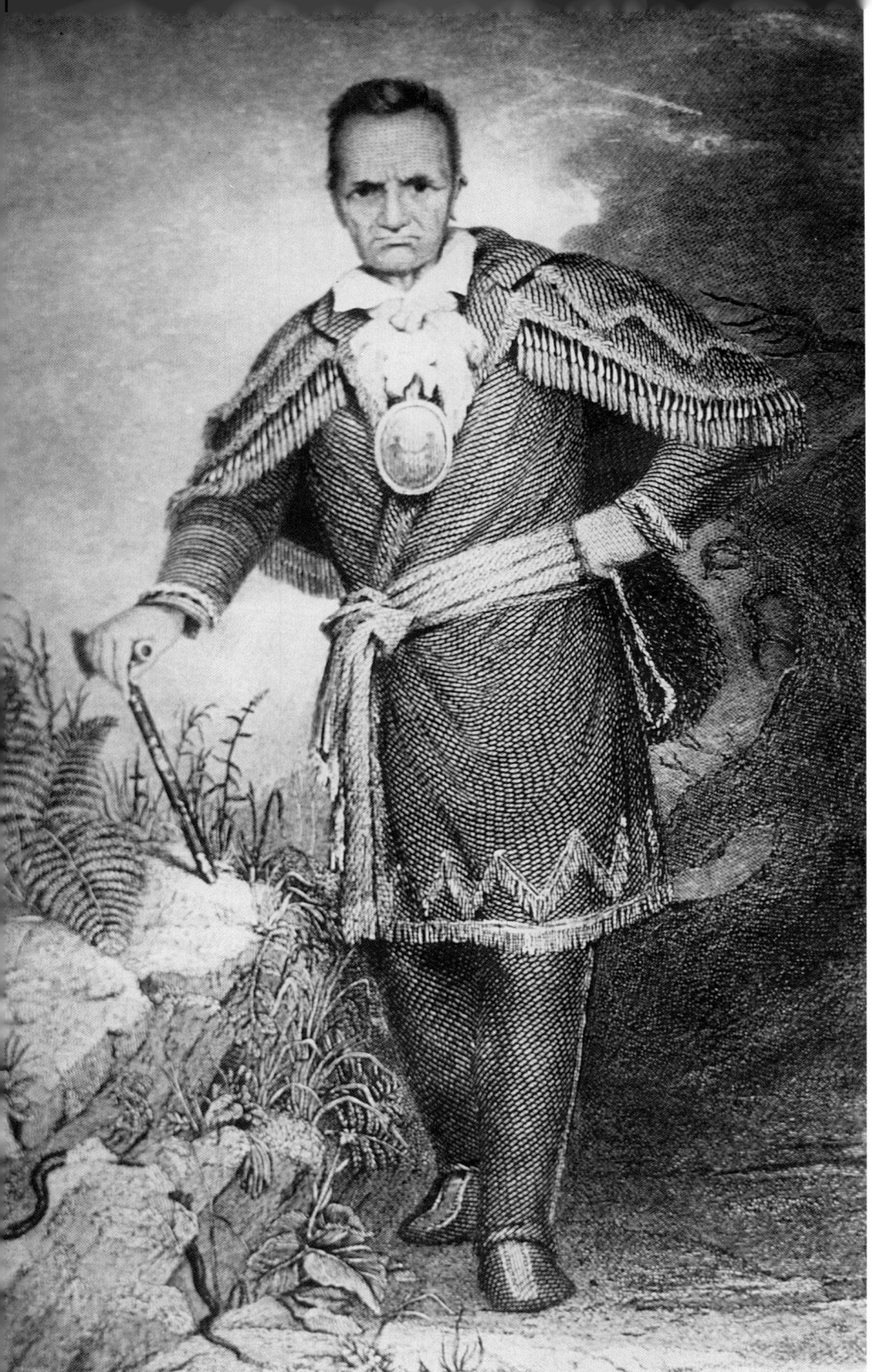

cast a soft glow over the grand boulevards and shimmered in the reflecting pools. By day, thousands of people visited elaborate exhibitions and viewed shows, parades, and midway entertainments. There was a simulated trip to the moon, a Venetian Grand Canal, and an African village built and inhabited by 150 authentic Africans.

Funded by a $2.5 million bond issue, the Exposition was 5 years in the planning, ran for 6 months, and produced at a total cost of $7 million. Between May 1st and November 2nd, 8 million visitors came and marveled. Among them was President William McKinley, who was shot by an anarchist while greeting the public in a reception line at the Temple of Music. Eight days later he died at the home of John Milburn, the president of the Exposition. Vice President Teddy Roosevelt, vacationing in the Adirondacks, rushed to Buffalo to take the oath of office at the Ansley Wilcox home on Delaware Avenue, just a few blocks south of the Milburns. It was an unsettling beginning to a revolutionary century.

By 1930, Buffalo's daily grain-milling capacity was greater than that of Minneapolis. With the construction of one of the largest and most modern steel plants in the world in Lackawanna, a huge automobile tire factory and a chemical plant in Tonawanda, automobile factories and windshield wiper plants in Buffalo, and the opening of new railroad stations across the area, Niagara was a major player in the modern industrial world. Prosperity continued unabated through World War II when the Buffalo region became an important center of war-related contracts at Bell Aircraft, Trico Products, Dunlop Tire, and many other area companies.

The interplay of social, political, and economic forces since the postwar period has fashioned a whole new role for Niagara in the late 20th century. With the decline of traditional heavy industry, the region is redefining itself as a center of tourism, trade and distribution, and specialized technical manufacturing, such as medical products. ◈

The Seneca, the westernmost Iroquois Nation, had prosperous settlements in the Genesee Valley until they were attacked and defeated in 1779 by Major General John Sullivan, U.S. Army, and 4,000 American troops. This was the price the Seneca paid for assisting the British cause with Chief Joseph Brant's Mohawk loyalists. After their defeat, the British helped the Seneca reestablish themselves in villages and farms in Western New York. By the late 1700s, some 1,600 Seneca were living along Buffalo Creek at the area of present-day South Buffalo. Here the Six Nations held councils with the British and later the Americans to negotiate the boundaries of their land. The celebrated and skilled Seneca orator **Red Jacket** was a leading participant in these councils. Red Jacket, whose Seneca name was Sagoyewatha, was a sachem, or civilian leader, of the Six Nations. His succession of red coats were gifts from his British allies, and his large silver medallion was given to him by President Washington.

Red Jacket was a brilliant and articulate spokesman who stirred his people with passionate invective against the encroaching white civilization. He was fiercely opposed to the undermining of Seneca customs, language, and religion by the missionaries, teachers, and land developers of the dominant white culture. Red Jacket died in 1830, but his remains were removed from his tribal burial ground and re-interred in a place of honor in Buffalo's Forest Lawn Cemetery on October 9, 1884. Today, the Seneca Nation occupies three reservations in Niagara.
Photo courtesy of *Buffalo News*.

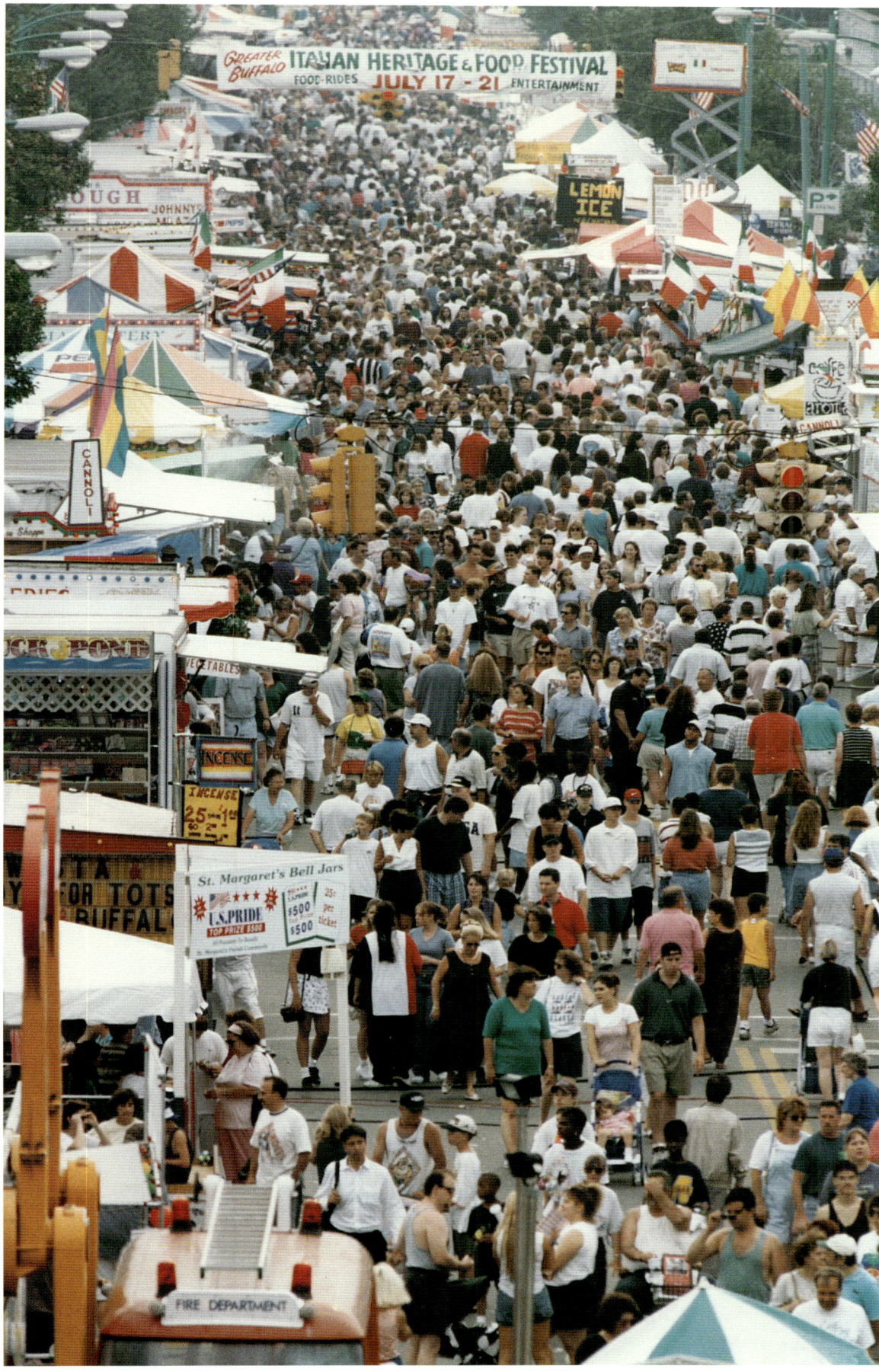

The first wave of **European immigrants** to Niagara came when the **Irish** arrived in the 1820s to provide much of the manpower for the building of the Erie Canal. At about the same time, **German** immigrants were also being drawn to the area with the hope of more freedom and greater financial opportunity. The first **Polish** immigrants to the area were Yiddish-speaking **Jews** fleeing religious persecution and conscription into the regiments of the Russian czar. For the Catholic Poles who came to Niagara in the late 19th century, the transition from the farms of rural Poland to life in the industrial heartland of Niagara was also a struggle. The largest Italian community flourished on Buffalo's West Side until the exodus to the suburbs began in earnest in the mid-20th century. Each summer, Hertel Avenue in Buffalo swings to the sounds of tarantellas and big band jazz as the descendants of Italian immigrants and those from other areas celebrate old traditions and new friendships. Basking in the aromas of red sauce, hot pizza, and spicy sausage with green peppers and onions, the **Italian Festival** is one of the area's many summer ethnic festivals.
Photo by James P. McCoy.

(following Page) Fort George photo by James P. McCoy.

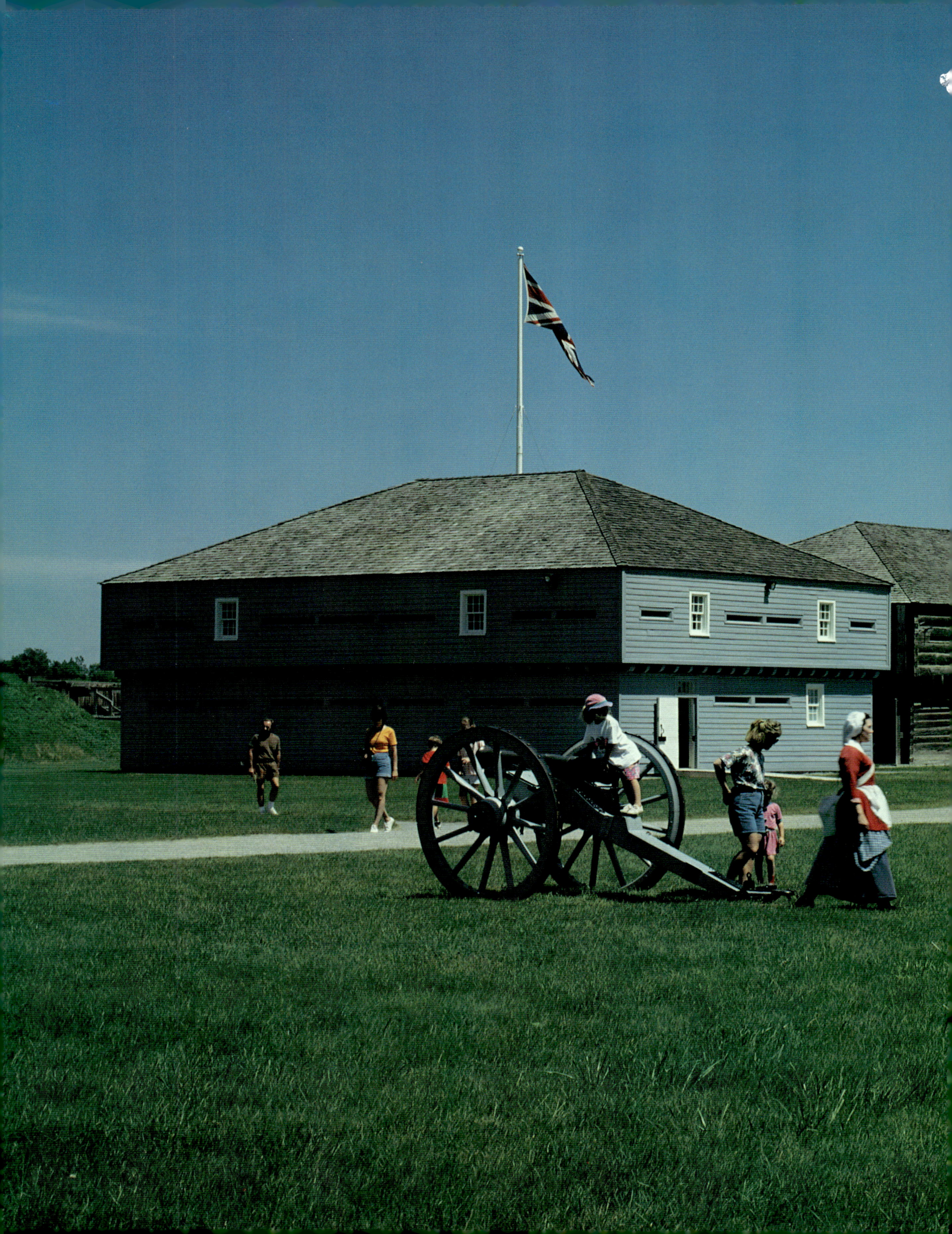

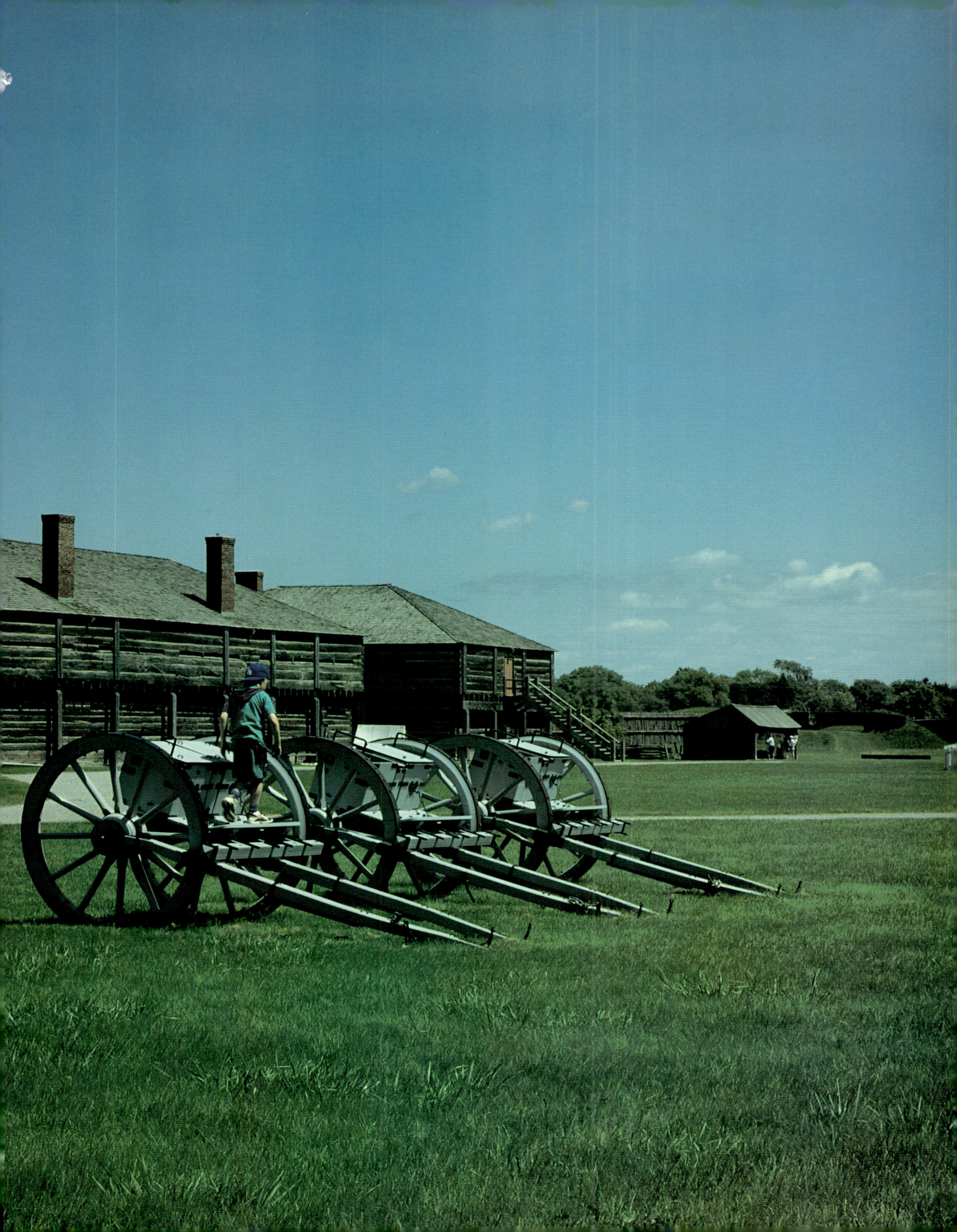

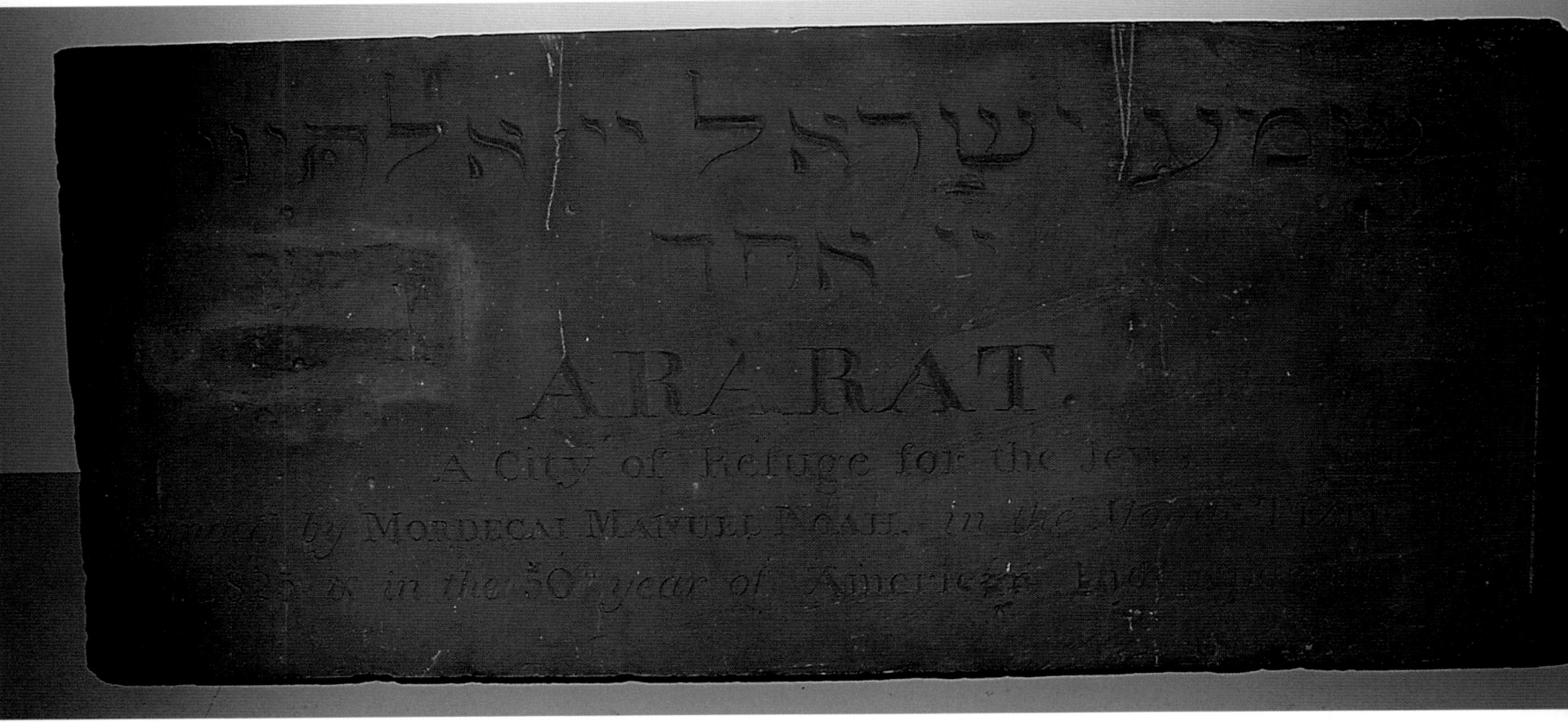

In 1825, the year the Erie Canal opened, Mordecai Manuel Noah acquired over 2,000 acres on Grand Island, a heavily wooded haven in the middle of the Niagara River, for the purpose of building a "city of refuge for the Jews." As Noah envisioned it, the city would have been located directly across the river from the Erie Canal. He planned to call his city Ararat, after the mountain in Turkey where his namesake, the Biblical Noah, and his Ark came to rest after the Deluge. Alas, crossing the Niagara River for dedication ceremonies on Grand Island proved too perilous, and Noah soon left the area without ever having set foot on the briefly promised land. The inscribed **Ararat Stone**, the intended cornerstone of the city, can be seen at the Buffalo Historical Society. Photo by James P. McCoy.

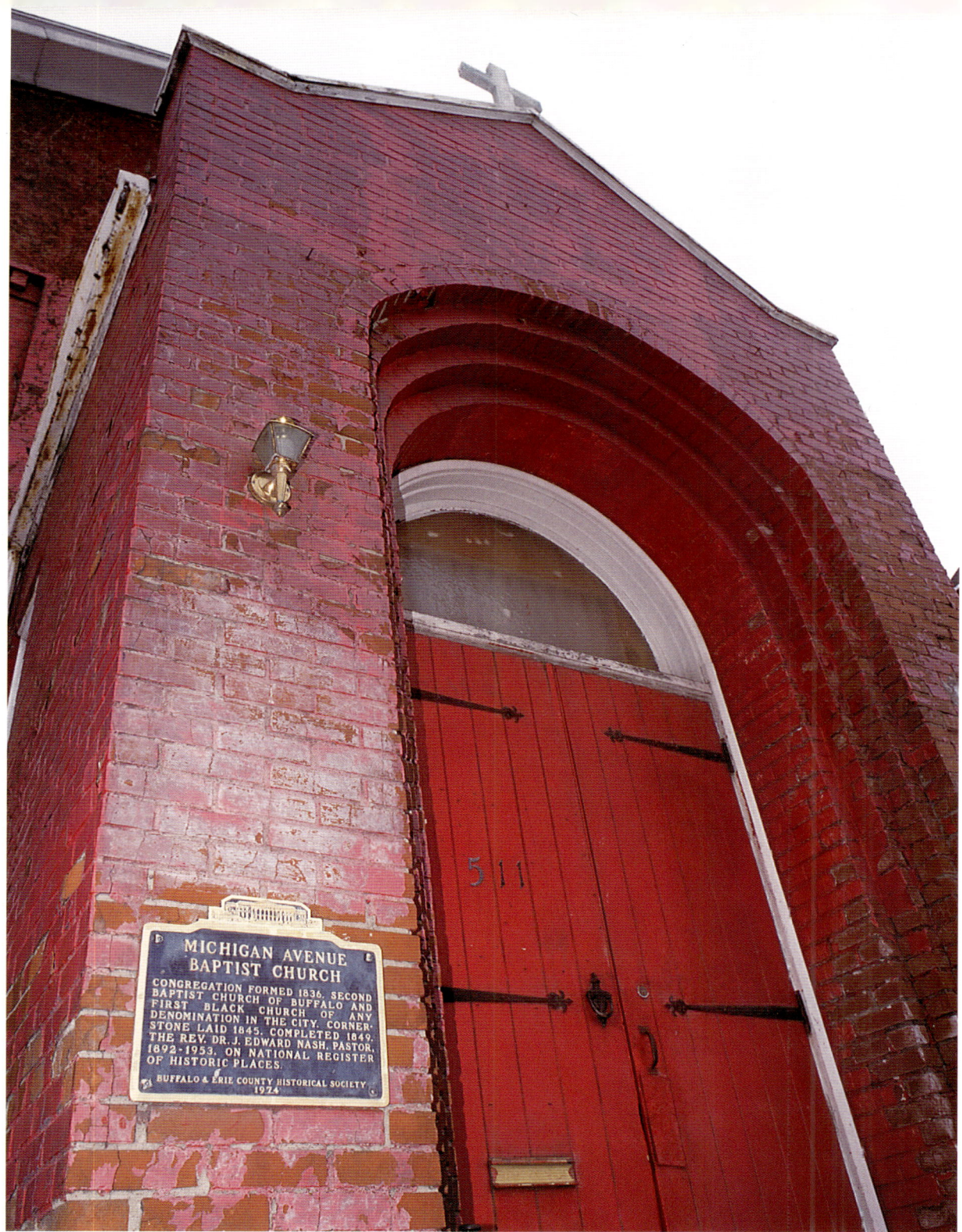

MICHIGAN AVENUE
BAPTIST CHURCH

CONGREGATION FORMED 1836. SECOND
BAPTIST CHURCH OF BUFFALO AND
FIRST BLACK CHURCH OF ANY
DENOMINATION IN THE CITY. CORNER-
STONE LAID 1845. COMPLETED 1849.
THE REV. DR. J. EDWARD NASH, PASTOR,
1892-1953. ON NATIONAL REGISTER
OF HISTORIC PLACES.
BUFFALO & ERIE COUNTY HISTORICAL SOCIETY
1974

A final station on the Underground Railroad, the **Michigan Avenue Baptist Church** in Buffalo was a haven for fugitive slaves from the South. Because of the safety of Canada, which was beyond the reach of slave hunters, Niagara was an important destination in the smuggling of human contraband from the oppression of slavery. One of the reasons for the Underground Railroad was the existence of the Fugitive Slave Law, which mandated the return of escaped slaves to their owners. That legislation was signed in 1850 by Millard Fillmore. The church was built in 1845 and was visited over the years by many important black leaders such as Frederick Douglass, Booker T. Washington, and W.E.B. DuBois. Mary Burnett Talbert, an active parishoner, was a key participant in the Niagara Movement, the forerunner of the National Association for the Advancement of Colored People(NAACP).
Photo by James P. McCoy.

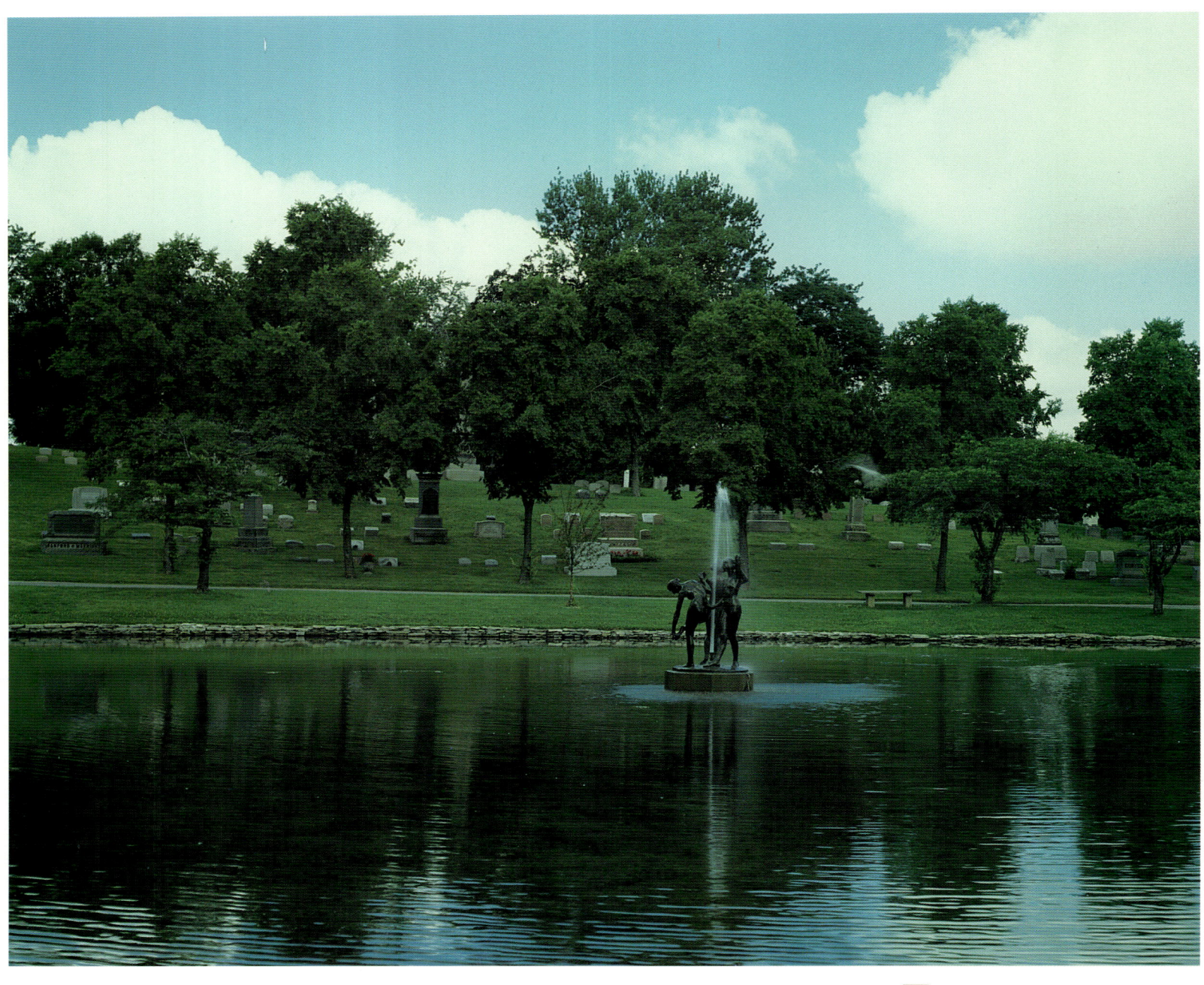

Established in 1849 as part of an American movement to rural, park inspired cemeteries, **Forest Lawn Cemetery** comprises 269 acres of hills, hollows, lakes, streams, graceful bridges, diverse species of trees, Victorian monuments and obelisks, and the graves of over 144,000 people, including many of the area's most prominent former citizens.
Photo by James P. McCoy.

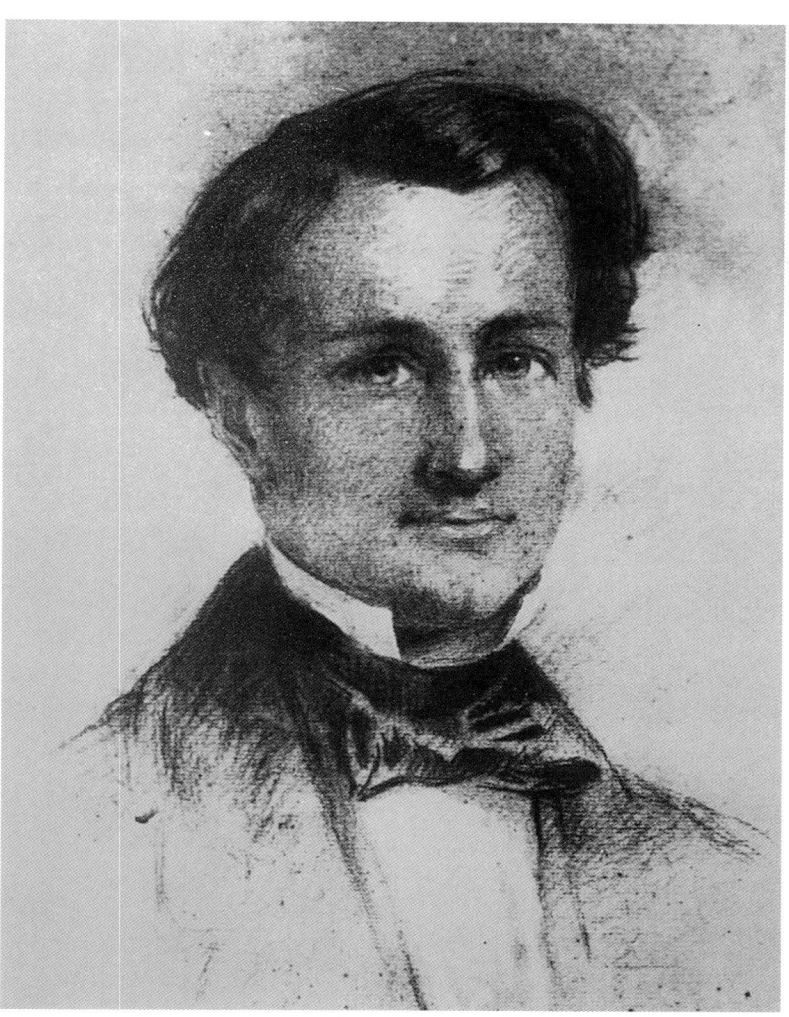

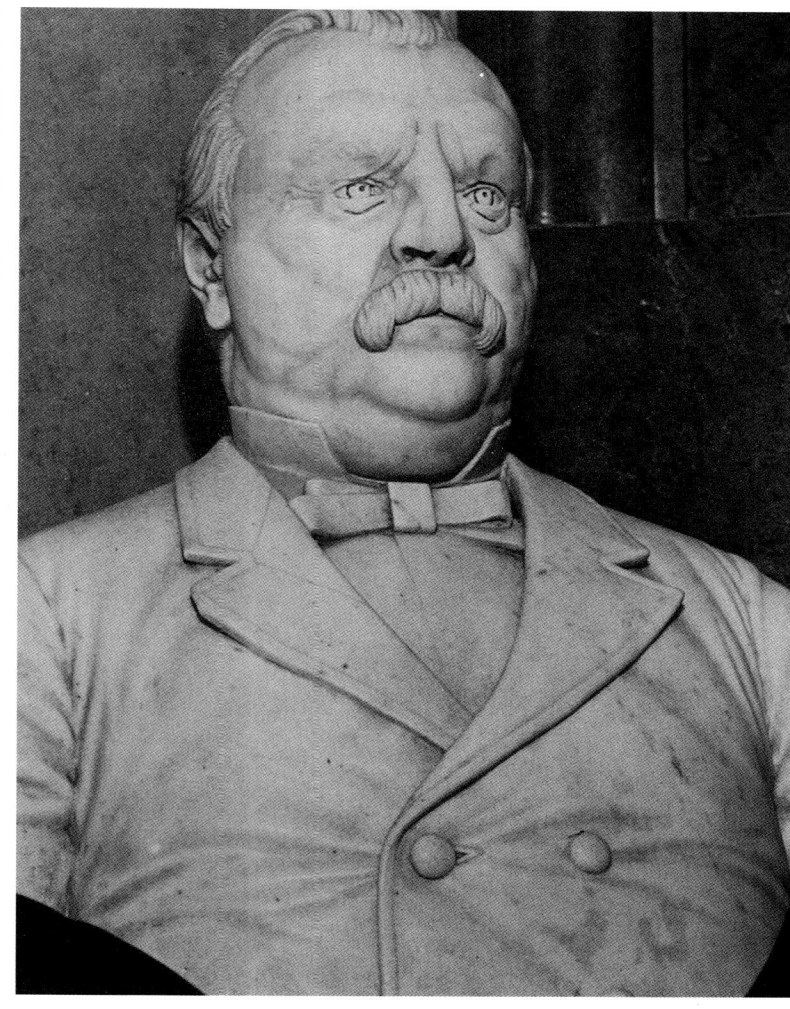

In 1820, a young **Millard Fillmore** arrived from Cayuga County to take a job as a schoolteacher in East Aurora. Ten years later, after being admitted to the bar and opening a law office in East Aurora, he joined a prestigious Buffalo law firm and was soon elected to the U.S. House of Representatives. Fillmore claimed he personally abhorred slavery but signed the Fugitive Slave Law because he believed the white South had to be assuaged to prevent war and preserve the Union. In his early law practice, he was a progressive reformer who supported the building of the Erie Canal and sided with the Agrarian Movement in its protest against the policies of the Holland Land Company. Fillmore's greatest legacy to national policy is undoubtedly his initiative in breaking the ice with Japan by dispatching Commodore Matthew C. Perry with a fleet of warships to coax the Japanese out of centuries of isolationism and into a trade and diplomatic relationship with the West.
Photo courtesy of *Buffalo News*.

Stephen Grover Cleveland was the nephew of Lewis F. Allen, a leading Buffalo businessman who arrived from New England and New York City in 1827 and made a fortune here in insurance, real estate, and lumbering. When young Grover visited Buffalo on his way to Ohio, Uncle Lewis talked him into staying and pursuing a legal career in Niagara. Cleveland soon began another career as a reformist, corruption-fighting politician that led to a classic rise as sheriff of Erie County, mayor of Buffalo, governor of New York, and president of the United States. He was the first president to marry in the White House and the only president ever to serve two nonconsecutive terms.
Photo courtesy of *Buffalo News*.

If there was one person who under-stood the inherent beauty of Niagara and wished to enhance it for the public pleasure, that person was **Frederick Law Olmsted**. While traveling in Europe, Olmsted was struck with the beauty of English landscaping. In 1857, Olmsted and Calvert Vaux, a young British architect, entered and won a competition to design Central Park in New York City. For Olmsted, it was the beginning of a long and distinguished career as a landscape architect, park designer, and urban planner. In 1868, Olmsted designed a park system for Buffalo consisting of several large parks connected by wide tree-lined avenues or parkways interspersed with monumental circles at the intersection of other major avenues. Meanwhile, at Niagara Falls, public sentiment was growing on both sides of the river against increasing commercial and industrial encroachment of the natural wonder. A grand design incorporating parkland, river, and water-falls by Olmsted and Vaux did a great deal to convince the state of New York to buy out the private landowners. On July 15, 1885, to the accompaniment of brass bands, a 400-voice choir, and a 100-gun salute, Niagara Falls was offi-cially declared free of spectator tolls and presented to the people. Two years later, inspired by Olmsted and led by the powerful Canadian entrepreneur, Colonel Casimir Stanislaus Gzowski, Canada passed the Queen Victoria Niagara Falls Park Act. The province of Ontario also had its first public park. Painting of Olmsted by John Singer Sargent. Photo courtesy of *Buffalo News.*

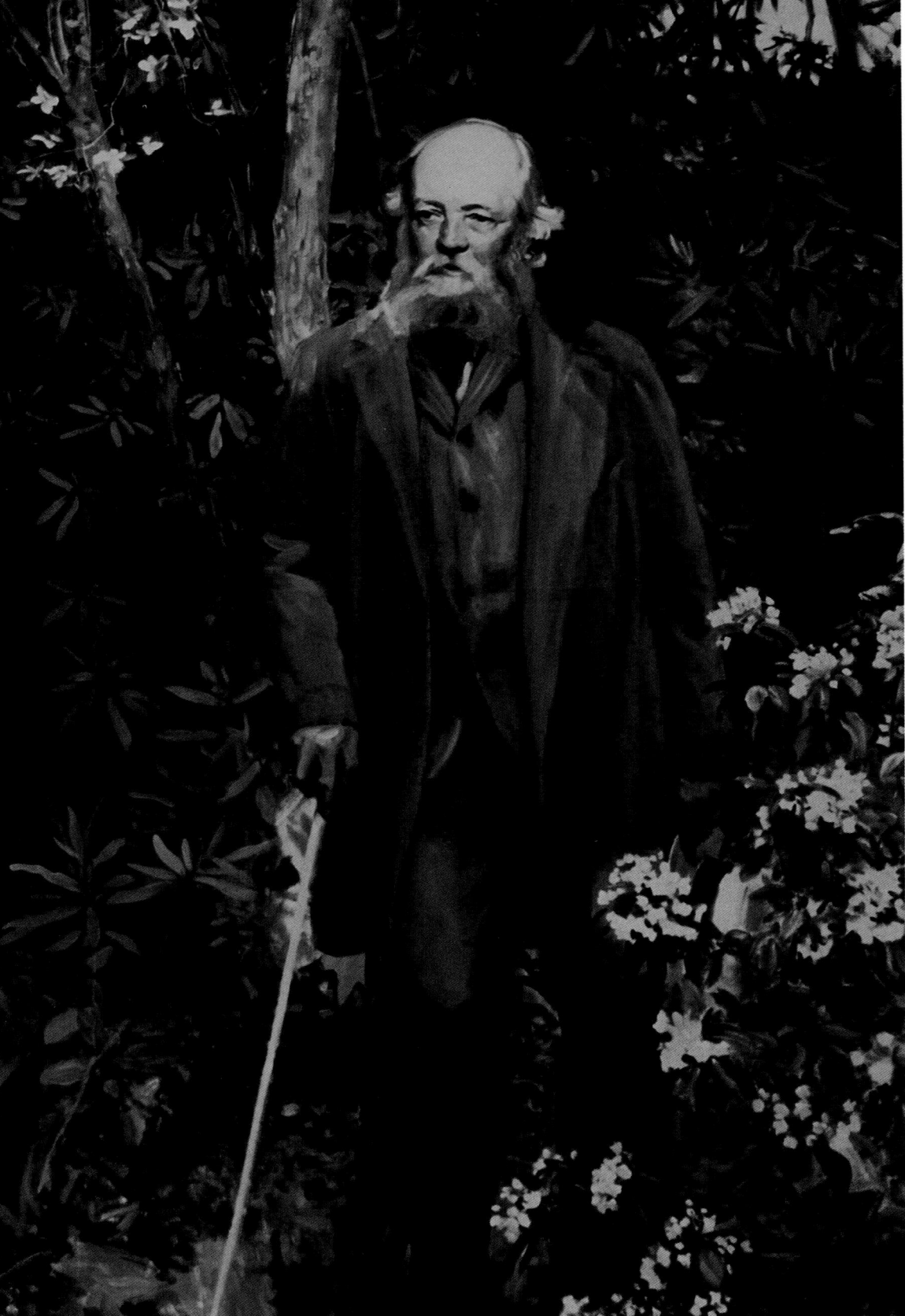

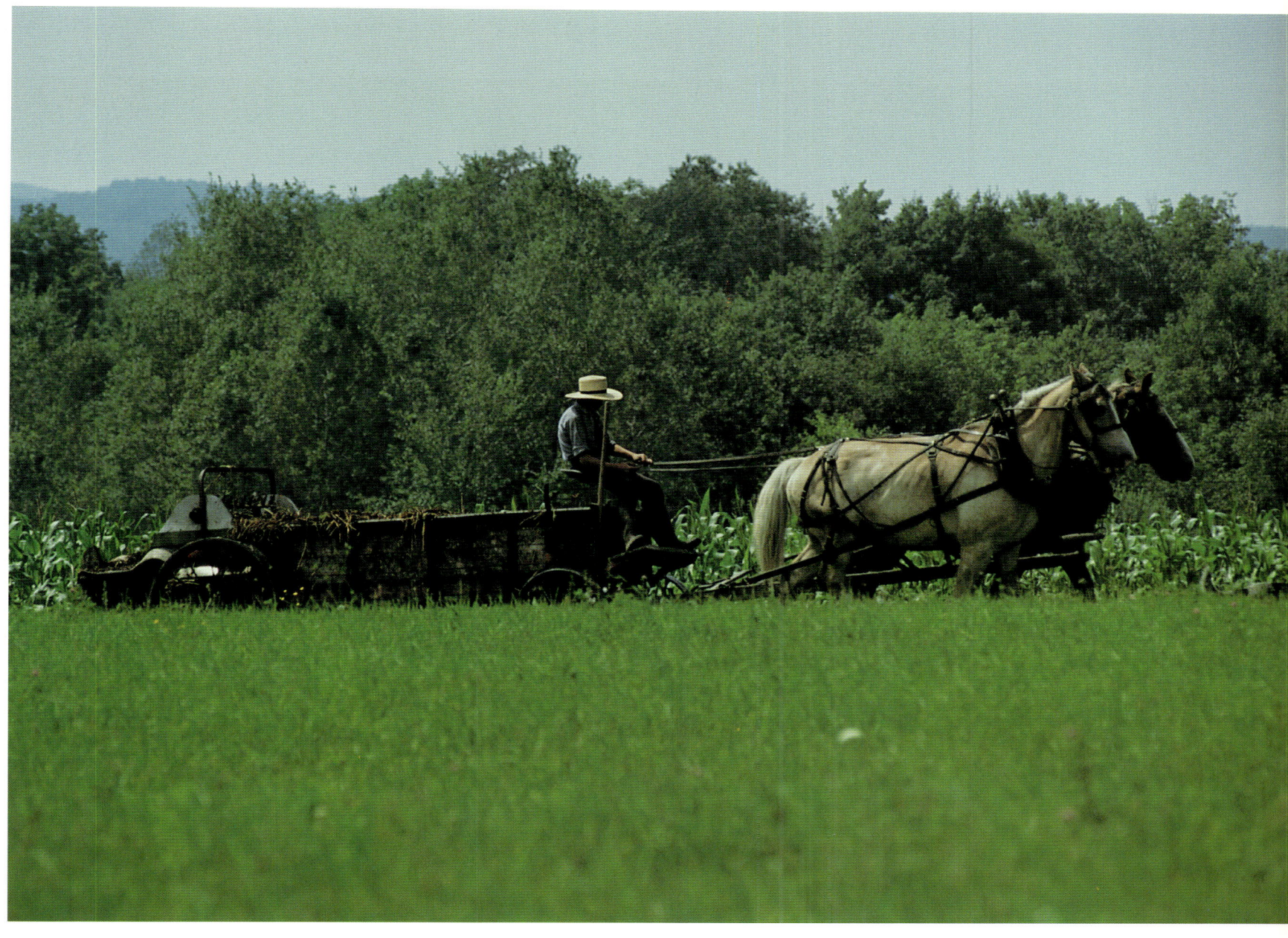

The Amish came from Lancaster County, Pennsylvania, and settled in the southern tier counties of Chautauqua, Cattaraugus, and Allegany, just north of the Pennsylvania border, where the rolling hills and fertile farmland seemed the perfect setting for their life of spiritual strength and honest toil. In the Conewango Valley of Cattaraugus and around the towns of Ellington, Randolph, Rushford, Cuba, and Franklinville, scenes of **Amish life** often appear plucked from the mid-19th century.
Photo by James P. McCoy.

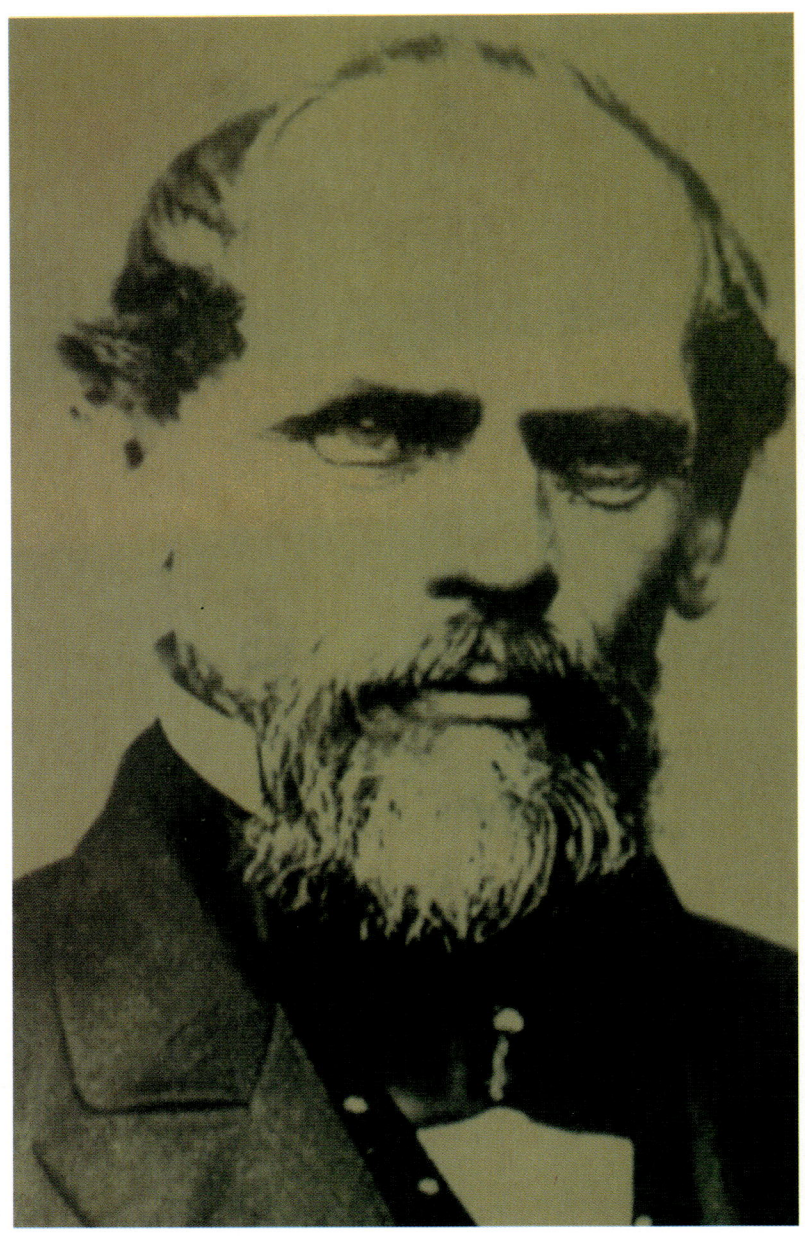

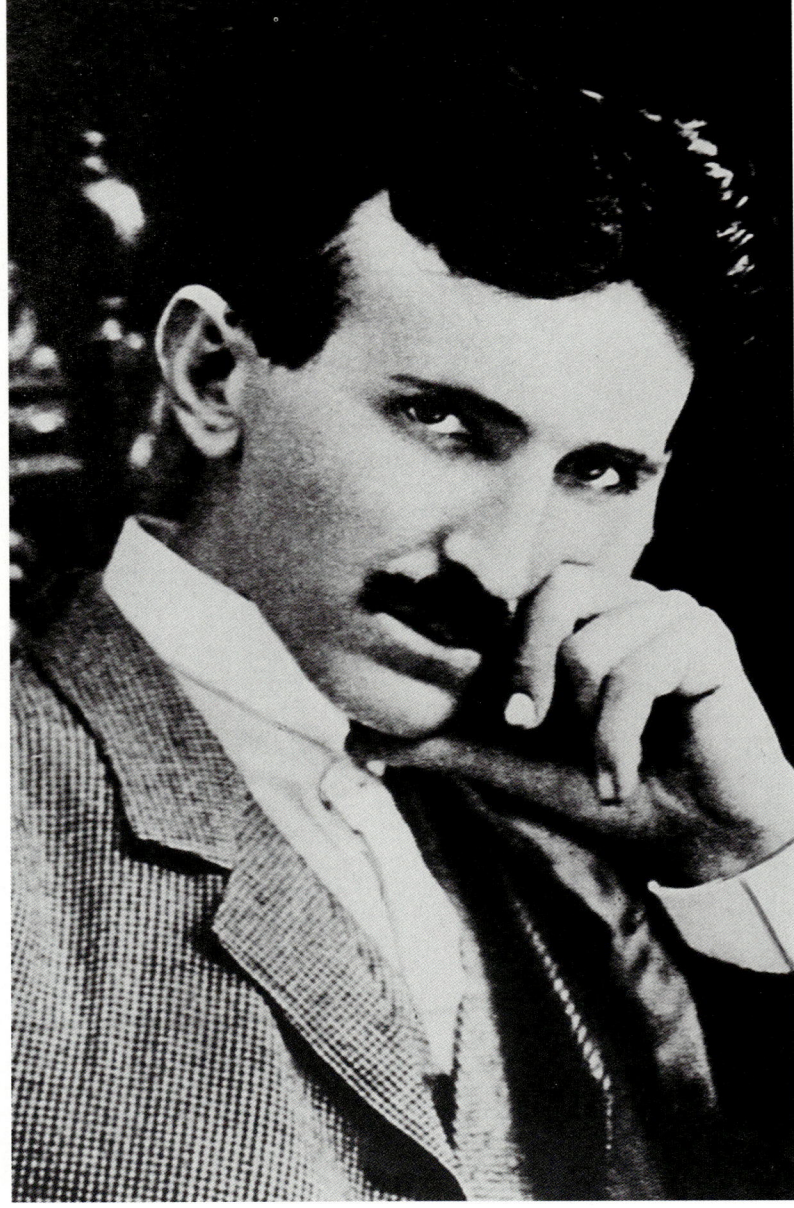

Although it wasn't the first bridge across the Niagara Gorge, John Roebling's Niagara Railroad Suspension Bridge was the first serious bridge across the chasm and the one that brought the world to Niagara by the trainload. **John Augustus Roebling**, a tough-minded, strong-willed German engineer who immigrated to the United States from Thuringia, had built a wire rope factory in Trenton, New Jersey where he manufactured cable to haul canal barges over the Allegheny Mountains. As railroads replaced canal boats, Roebling turned his attention to suspension bridges to incorporate his proven wire rope design. Niagara would provide the world with tangible proof of Roebling's ability to incorporate wire rope and stiffening trusses to create a firm, stable suspension bridge. Begun in 1851, Roebling's creation was a two-tiered bridge, 820 feet long, 24 feet wide, and 20 feet deep with railroad tracks and a pedestrian walk on the upper level and a plank roadway for carriage traffic on the bottom.
Photo courtesy of *Buffalo News*.

Mystical genius and inventor of alternating current, **Nikola Tesla** created the enormous polyphase motors that produced the first electrical current able to transfer electricity over some distance at Niagara Falls. Tesla tore up a contract that would have paid him a fortune in royalties so that George Westinghouse could continue his campaign to put the country on a system of alternating current.
Photo courtesy of *Buffalo News*.

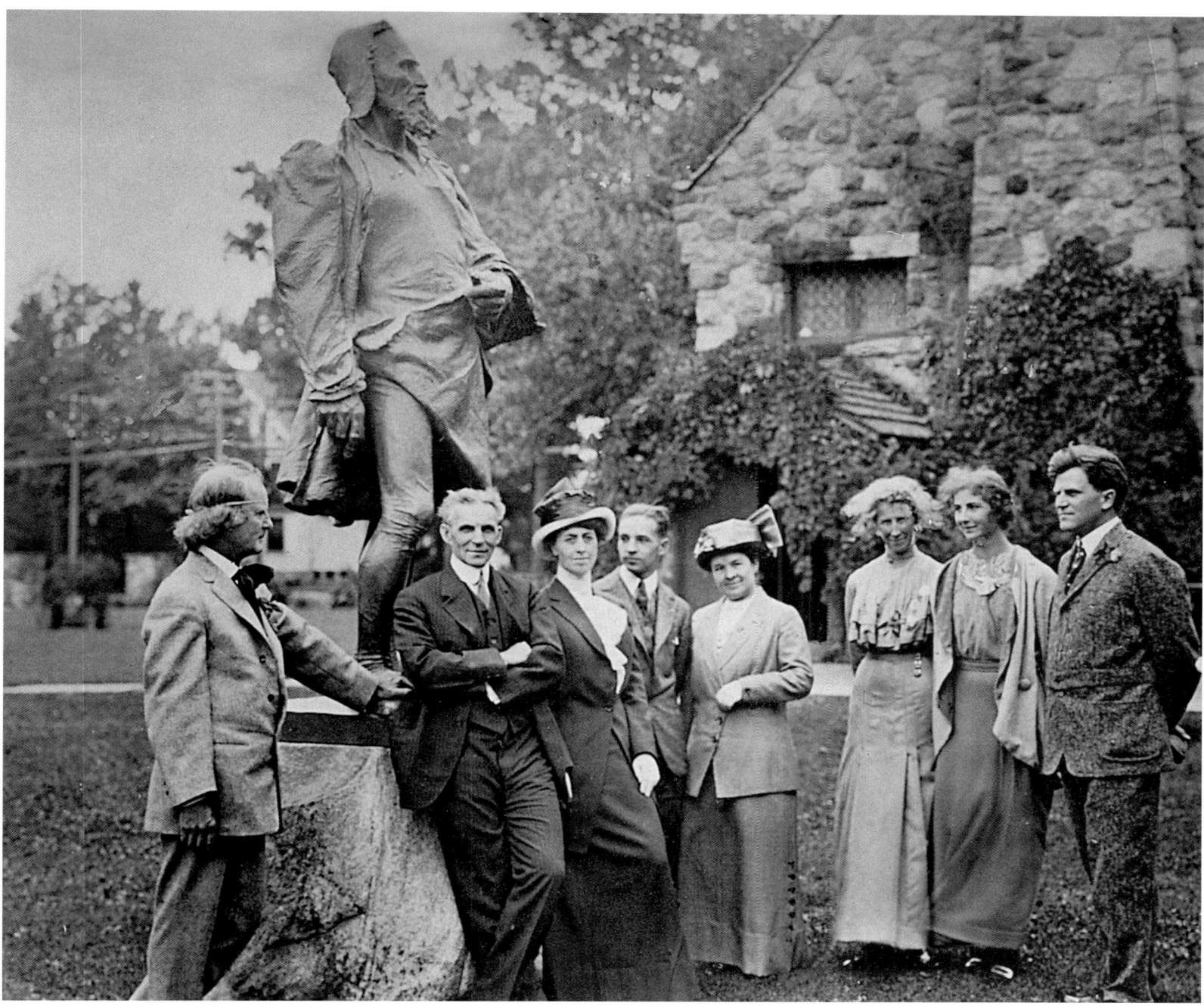

Elbert Hubbard was a marketing wizard and partner at the Larkin Company, an early mail-order firm whose Buffalo headquarters was designed by Frank Lloyd Wright. Hubbard made his fortune with Larkin and retired to East Aurora where he founded the **Roycroft**; a magazine, *The Philistine: A Periodical of Protest*; and a community of craftsmen and artisans. A passenger on the *Lusitania*, he perished when the British liner was sunk by a German submarine in 1915. The Roycroft Inn was reopened in 1995 after a major restoration that included the work of 57 companies and 500 workers.
Photo courtesy of *Buffalo News.*

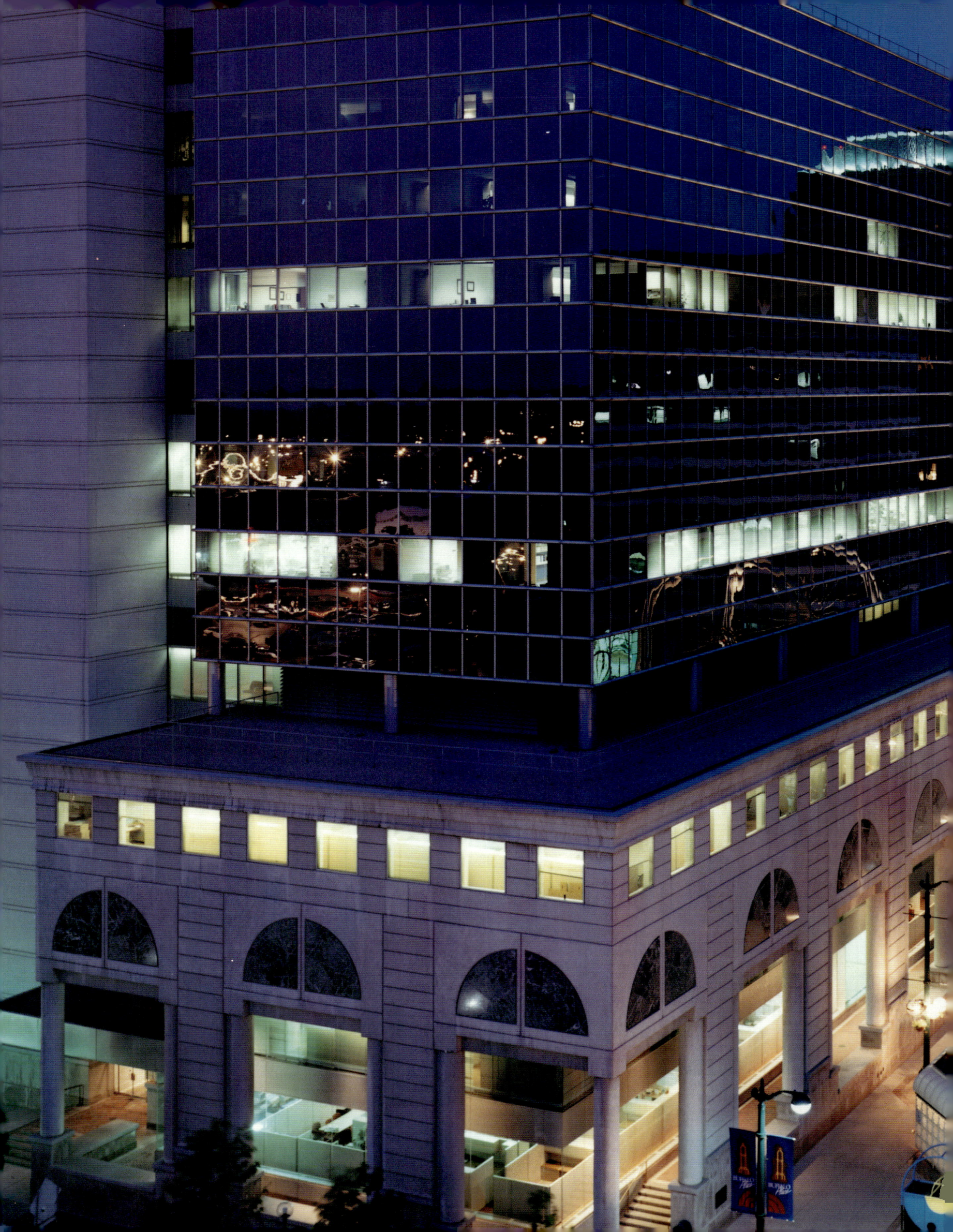

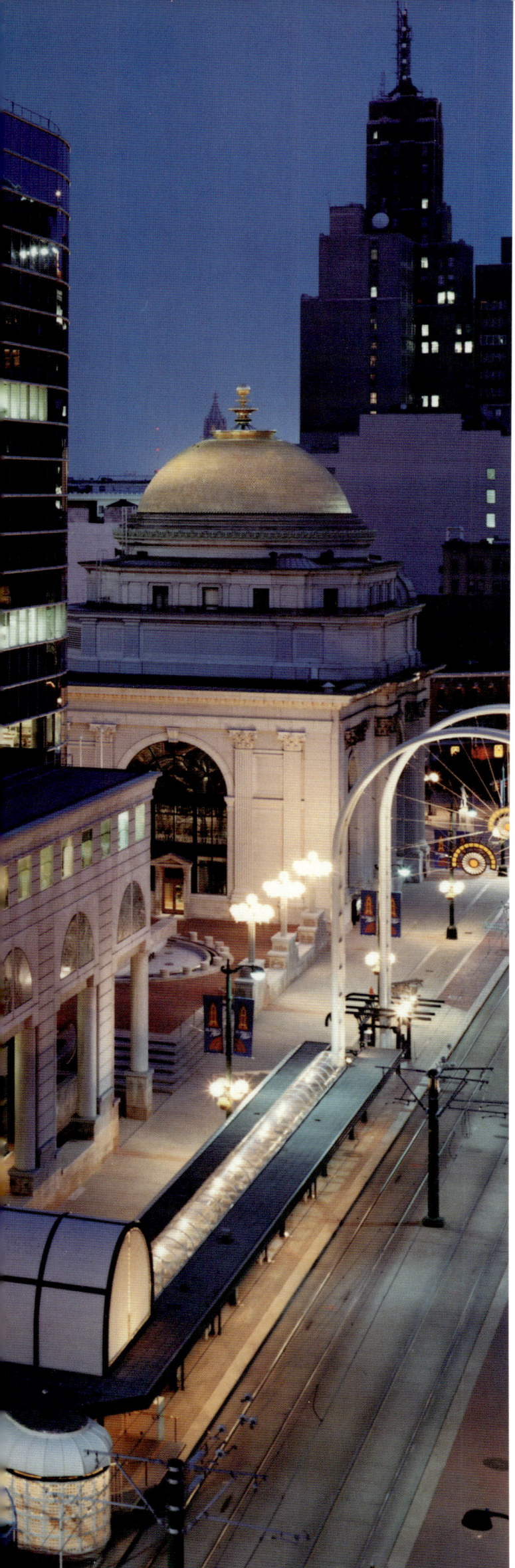

A STRATEGIC CENTER OF
INTERNATIONAL BUSINESS, TRADE, & TOURISM

In 1678, the French explorer La Salle envisioned a fort at the mouth of the Niagara River commanding passage from Lake Ontario to the region's great waterway and the lakes, streams, and forests beyond. The Five Nations Iroquois vetoed the notion, protective of their ancestral hunting grounds and opposed to an encroachment on their sovereign territory. So La Salle countered by building another structure. Aware of the Iroquois interest in European consumer goods, he ordered a storehouse and trading cabin constructed at the foot of the ancient portage where Lewiston stands today.

M&T Bank photo by Marc Murphy.

Although it took almost another 50 years for the French to build a permanent post at Fort Niagara, trade would flourish and continue to dominate the economy and the politics of the region for more than three centuries. From Chabert de Joncaire's fur trade to the Erie Canal to the Welland Canal to NAFTA, Niagara's geography and resources have thrust the region into its role as a vital center of trade in North America.

In 1817, Irish immigrants and other laborers were paid 80 cents a day to dig a canal through the fields, forests, and swamps of central and western New York. Triumphantly completed in 1825, the Erie Canal created the first direct, reliable link between Great Lakes shipping and the Atlantic seaports of New York, Boston, and Philadelphia. It brought unlimited trade potential and undreamed of prosperity to the Niagara region.

At about the same time, Canadian entrepreneur William Hamilton Merritt was constructing another canal, one that would create a navigable waterway between Lake Erie and Lake Ontario, bypassing Niagara Falls, its rapids, and whirlpool. In 1829, the first Welland Canal opened, carrying ships from Lake Ontario through a system of locks over the Niagara Escarpment to Lake Erie via Twelve Mile Creek, the Welland River, and the Upper Niagara. Four years later, the canal was extended directly south to Port Colborne on Lake Erie. With the construction of the modern Welland Ship Canal in 1932 and the opening of the St. Lawrence Seaway in 1959, Niagara became the gateway for oceangoing vessels from the Midwest to the Maritimes.

Niagara remains a locus for international trade routes linking the United States and Canada, the world's largest trading partners. Its six international bridges (4 vehicular and 2 rail) form essential infrastructure for this trade. Niagara and the Buffalo customs district account for nearly $92 billion in annual import-export traffic. Buffalo has been ranked by *World Trade* magazine as the nation's fifth-busiest port in the mid-1990s, with Canada, Japan, and the United Kingdom as the area's most active trading partners. Automotive products are among the region's leading exports while nickel, aluminum plates, and gold are among the district's fastest-growing imports.

Plant the point of your compass in the middle of the Peace Bridge and describe a circle with a 125-mile diameter on a map of the region. Within that circle is a market of nine million consumers. For companies like Molson Breweries, U.S.A., Christian Salvesen, Inc., and Norfolk Southern Corp., Niagara offers a prime location for warehousing and distribution centers because of its proximity to some of the largest consumer markets on the continent.

Within one day's drive of 55 percent of all U.S. population and 62 percent of Canadian, Niagara means easy access to nearly half of the U.S. population. In fact, 28 percent of all border crossings from Canada to the United States are through Niagara.

In Fort Erie, the new $12 million Peace Bridge Commercial Centre opened in 1995, providing more space for warehouse, office, and inspection facilities. The complex also includes areas for small freight shippers and customs brokers and is designed to speed the movement of freight into Canada and help eliminate inspection backups. A $26 million truck processing center exists on the Canadian side. With a dramatic new second span scheduled for completion in 2002, the Peace Bridge is preparing for its growing role in Niagara's expanding trade opportunities. The Peace Bridge handles $80 million a day in trade. The annualized figure is equal to all trade transacted along the entire U.S.-Mexican border.

Niagara's economic development, production, and ingenuity have often been at the forefront of historic enterprises. Beginning with its prominence as a Great Lakes port and Erie Canal terminus, Buffalo next became an important railroad hub, livestock, and grain-milling center. In the early 20th century, aviation pioneers Glenn Curtiss and Lawrence Bell created historic aircraft here. Curtiss built fighters for World Wars I and II, while Bell Aircraft Corporation built the nation's first jet aircraft and the world's first supersonic jet.

The automobile industry was attracted by Niagara's location, transport advantages, labor, and materials. The heyday of American steel production was exemplified by the roaring blast furnaces of Bethlehem and Republic Steel. Today, although still a vital part of the industrial heartland, Niagara has also become a center of medical research and a leader in the development and manufacture of medical products.

Wilson Greatbatch, Ltd., the world's leading maker of lithium batteries for pacemakers, has built a $6 million office and manufacturing complex next to its headquarters in Clarence in 1997. The company, which employs over 500 high-tech workers and also makes batteries for implantable defibrillators, passed up offers to relocate to warmer states.

The area's nationally renowned industrial muscle and strong work ethic keep productivity high at top manufacturers like General Motors, Delphi Harrison Thermal Systems, Ford Motor Company, Dresser-Rand, Moog, Bush Industries, Dunlop Tire, TRW Canada, Rich Products, DuPont, Cummins Engine, and Atlas Specialty Steels, while attracting new companies like American Axle and Manufacturing, Ingram Micro, Fujisawa, TeleTech, and Softbank Services.

One of North America's most productive automotive manufacturing areas, Niagara is home to assembly plants, original equipment manufacturers, and aftermarket firms. The industry provides the area's largest base of import/export trade, with cars, trucks, tractors, and engines constituting the fastest-growing exports in the region.

Exemplifying the generally high level of relations between management and labor in the region, United Auto Workers Local 774 at GM's Town of Tonawanda Powertrain Engine Plant and General Motors received the coveted Leadership Award from the Work in America Institute in 1996. The award recognized the commitment of the company and the union to mutual cooperation, increased productivity, and the continuous improvement of both products and manufacturing techniques. The plant was also selected by General Motors to produce its "world engine," a four-cylinder dual overhead cam engine designed for the 1998 Saturn Innovate. Tonawanda Powertrain is GM's most productive engine plant in North America and the world's largest operation of its kind.

White-collar companies also find Niagara's location and work ethic attractive. Ingram Micro, the world's largest distributor of computer software and hardware, announced plans to double its work force of 1,200 in Amherst by the year 2000. The Japanese pharmaceutical company Fujisawa is expanding its Grand Island operation with a $18.2 million plant, while in Niagara Falls, New York, Denver's TeleTech, Inc. built a customer service center for 750 workers. Computer Task Group, a company specializing in information technology services, continues to expand its business with industry giants like IBM. CTG employs over 5,000 people in its offices worldwide.

Elsewhere in the service sector, Niagara boasts an important financial community with some 25 banks and savings & loan institutions doing business across the area.

For the region's companies, good business means more than great location. It also means the support and services of many business-friendly agencies and organizations designed to assist new companies and help build a stronger economic environment for established firms. The State University of New York at Buffalo provides an outstanding resource for business with its work force education and training programs, advanced laboratory facilities, industrial effectiveness programs to retain workers and create new jobs, technology transfer services, and the UB Foundation Incubator for fledgling technology-based companies.

Working with the UB Greater Regional Industrial Technology program, the Empire State Development Corporation helps companies by providing access to state and local programs for financing, training, and market development. The Greater Buffalo Partnership nurtures business, community, and economic growth through its many programs and collaborative resources, including seminars, workshops, forums, networking events, publications, and advocacy efforts.

The Buffalo Enterprise Development Corporation works with private sector leaders and city, state, and federal officials to create project grants for renovation, downtown and inner-city business initiatives, private investment in Buffalo's Economic Development Zones, Theatre District revitalization, retail development, and retention and expansion of the city's core industries.

As a stimulant to increased trade between the United States and Canada, the New Exporters to Border States program helps thousands of Canadian firms do business in

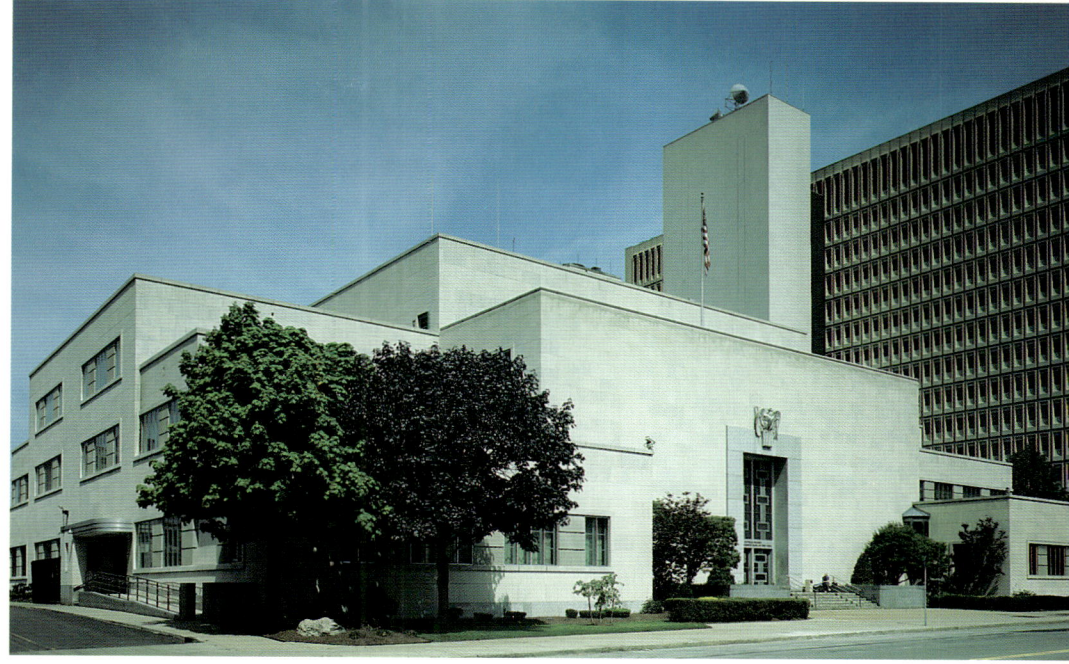

Western New York. In fact, 9 out of every 10 new Canadian exporters began by establishing relationships in Western New York.

Quick, effective communication and on-time deliveries are also warm rays of sunshine. Business mail moves with extraordinary efficiency in Niagara thanks to the award-winning work of the United States Postal Service. During the mid-1990s, the Western New York Postal Service team was the only such group in the nation to consistently score over 90 percent in both the Customer Satisfaction Index and the External First-Class Measurement System.

Soon after its discovery by Europeans, the Falls at Niagara became more than a spectacular natural wonder. For the Falls were imbued with what many perceived as a far higher calling: a perpetual source of electrical energy. A corollary to this belief was the conviction that great wealth would reward those who could devise a way to tap all that energy and create marketable power.

The first attempts to harness the Falls began with mill races and canals to drive gristmills, sawmills, paper mills, and other mechanical industries by using the rushing water from the upper rapids. In 1881, electricity was first produced at Niagara Falls as a by-product of Jacob Schoellkopf's milling operations.

With the throwing of two switches—in Niagara Falls and Buffalo—in 1896, electricity was transmitted for the first time over a long distance to provide power for a major city. Suddenly the energy of Niagara had traveled 20 miles to illuminate Buffalo's streetlights and run its streetcars. Through the alternating current technology developed by Nikola Tesla and promoted by George Westinghouse, the hydroelectric power developed at Niagara would completely transform modern civilization.

By 1925, electrical power output had expanded to 360,000 kilowatts. Beginning with the Pittsburgh Reduction Company (later ALCOA), electrochemical companies and other firms built a corridor of industry in Niagara Falls to take advantage of its hydroelectric power. Carborundum Company, Union Carbide, Hooker Electro Chemical Company, DuPont, the Shredded Wheat Company, Kimberly-Clark, Olin, and many

Each month, the Buffalo Branch of the **Federal Reserve Bank of New York** supplies more than $500 million in cash, much of it in crisp new currency and freshly minted coins, to 109 financial institutions in the 34 westernmost counties of New York State. In 1992, the branch became one of only five sites in the nation that handles U.S. Savings Bond transactions, processing an average of 20,000 applications a day. The Buffalo Branch also plays an important role in monitoring the key economic indicators that shape monetary policy. The Federal Reserve Bank is an independent entity that is not a part of the U.S. government. Its Federal Open Market Committee sets interest rates based on prevailing economic conditions. Photo by Marc Murphy.

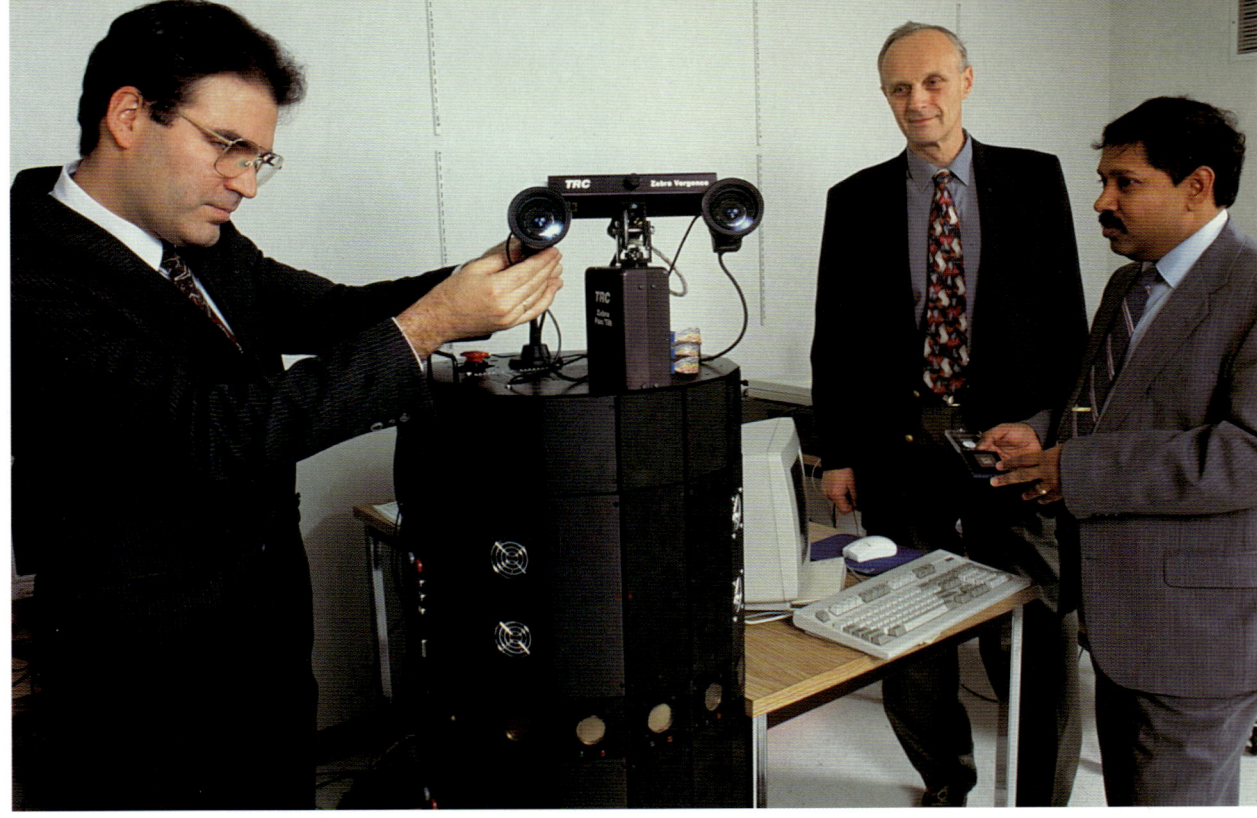

other companies set up manufacturing operations in the "Power City" during the first half of the 20th century.

Today, although Triscuit® crackers are now baked in place of shredded wheat at the Nabisco plant, Niagara Falls, New York, is still an industrial center and home to many manufacturing companies such as Goodyear Tire & Rubber, Carbide/Graphite Group, TAM Ceramics, Pyron Corporation, and Washington Mills. At the Robert Moses Power Station in New York and the Sir Adam Beck Power Stations across the gorge in Ontario, hydroelectric power production is now measured in millions of kilowatts.

Each year, 14 million people visit Niagara Falls, marvel at its awesome spectacle, and bring business to hotels, restaurants, parking lots, amusement parks, historic attractions, performing arts venues, tours, and shopping malls. That number is increasing dramatically as casino gambling lures more visitors to the gaming tables on the Canadian side of the Falls. Casino Niagara, a glitzy gambling palace overlooking the famous waterfall, opened for business in 1996. The Niagara Parks Commission, a self-sustaining government agency that administers Ontario's park system along the Niagara River from Lake Erie to Lake Ontario, takes in $57 million a year from gift and souvenir shops, food sales, site admissions, hydropower revenues, and other sources.

Certain to attract more visitors to Buffalo, an ambitious waterfront project to develop the city's inner harbor between Marine Midland Arena and the Erie Basin Marina is slated to include a new hotel, public spaces, and development of a vibrant new retail and restaurant district. The $27 million attraction will also feature inlets and docks for museum ships and tour boats, a new transit station, and a scenic harborwalk beside the water.

Conventioneers, tourists, and business travelers can expect a more efficient and pleasant arrival to the region at the dramatically redesigned Buffalo Niagara International Airport. The $187 million reconstruction project opened in the fall of 1997 showcasing a new terminal, three-level parking structure, and new access roadways. A wide connecting corridor between the ticketing lobby and the concourse areas is a welcoming harmony of original art and consumer-friendly

retail. The corridor's terrazzo floor beautifully depicts the area's geography and history, while its concession complex features retail shops offering name brands at regular retail prices.

Driving over the area's country roads admiring the fields, farms, and woodlands, a visitor is easily captivated by the picturesque beauty of the landscape and may momentarily lose sight of the economic importance of rural Niagara. From the vineyards of Chautauqua County to the orchards of Niagara and Orleans counties along Lake Ontario, Western New York accounts for $520 million in farm sales annually. With 6,570 farms and 1,017,500 acres in cropland, the eight-county region is a leading producer of milk and dairy products, grapes, wine, plums, prunes, sweet cherries, apples, peaches, maple syrup, vegetables, nursery plants, and flowers.

In the lake-tempered climate of the Niagara Peninsula's fruitlands in Ontario, there are 2,706 farms and an annual farm products sales total of $319 million. Here average individual farm products sales of $118,000 are 22 percent above the Canadian national average. Although grapes, peaches, and apples are the major crops in the region, Niagara's greenhouses are the predominant flower producers in the province. The peninsula is also an increasingly important wine center with award-winning Chardonnay, Pinot Noir, Reisling vintages, and icewine. Representing over 80 percent of Ontario's $215 million wine industry, Niagara vintners have cultivated a thriving tourist attraction as visitors tour the wine route that skirts the towns of Beamsville, Jordan, Vineland, and Niagara-on-the-Lake for estate tastings. ◆

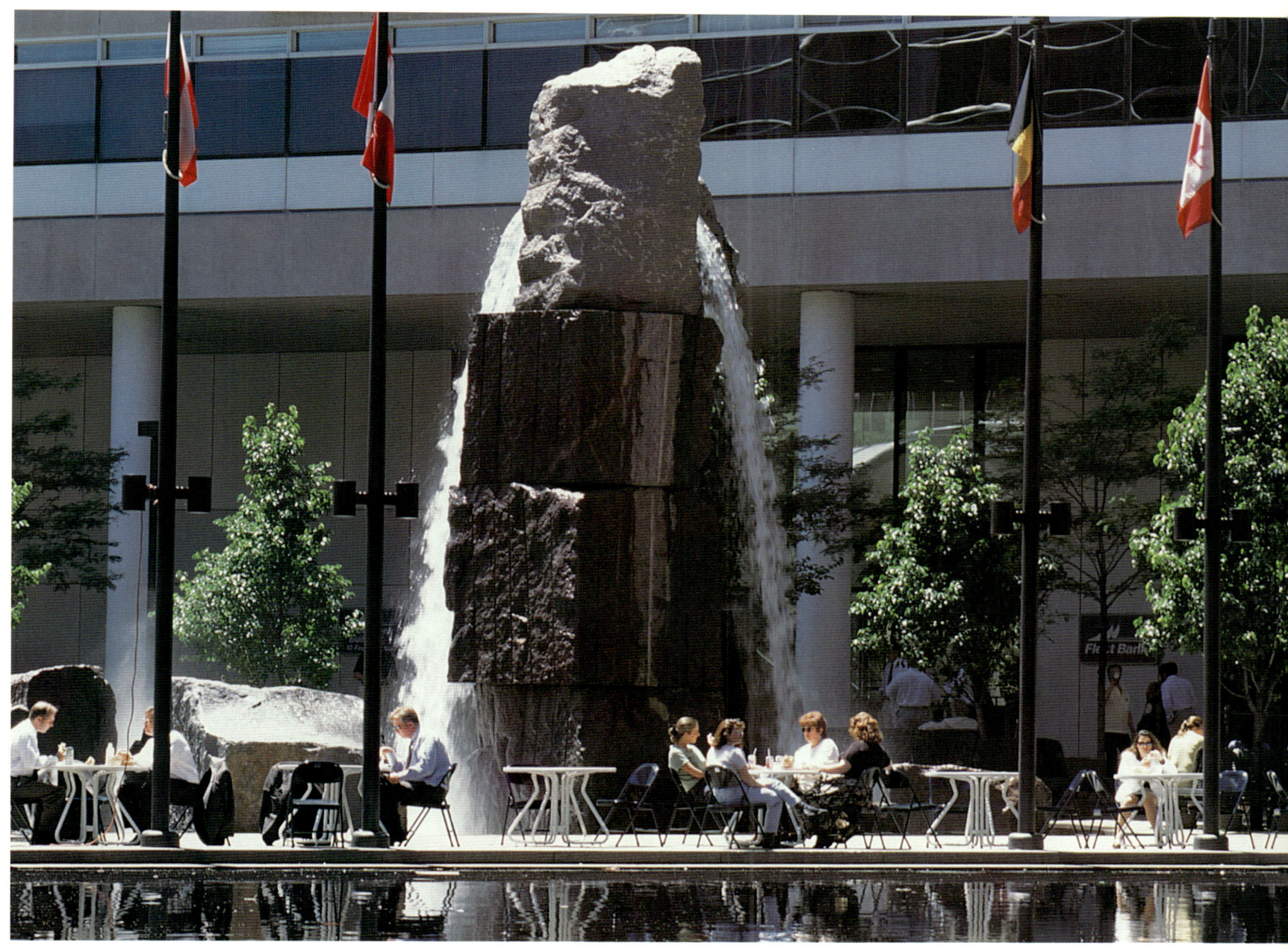

The splashing fountains and serene reflecting pool at **Fountain Plaza** provide a pleasant spot for an alfresco business lunch. The convergence of the two towers of **Key Center** and the regional headquarters of **Fleet Bank** creates a dramatic urban canyon where shoppers, businesspeople, and passers-by pause to chat, rest, daydream, plan an agenda, or grab a quick bite.
Photo by James P. McCoy.

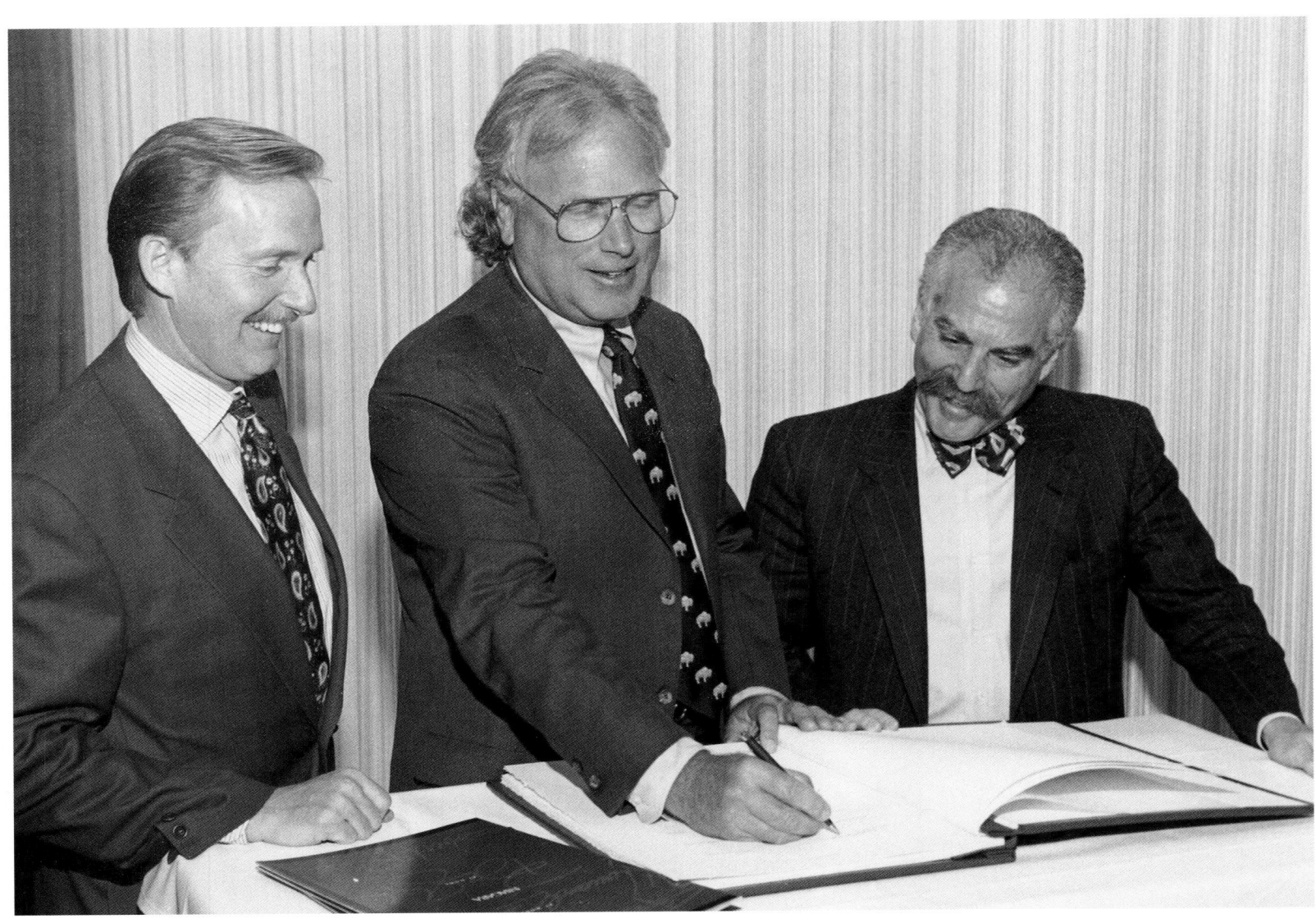

Pledging their support and commitment to the region, the signers of the **Niagara Compact** include the area's most prominent corporate leaders. The Niagara Compact, drafted in 1995, articulates a declaration of support for the eight counties of Western New York and the Niagara Peninsula as a unique bi-national region and vital area for international trade, industry, tourism, medical research, and cultural diversity. Compact signers agree to retain their operations in the region, seek to strengthen the area's economy through business investment, serve as ambassadors for the region, and encourage new businesses to locate to Niagara. Pictured here are three of the founding signers, (left to right) Brian Lipke, chairman & CEO, Gibraltar Steel; Bob Rich, president, Rich Products; and Dr. Andrew Rudnick, president of the Greater Buffalo Partnership. Photo by D. Zintech, Photographics 2.

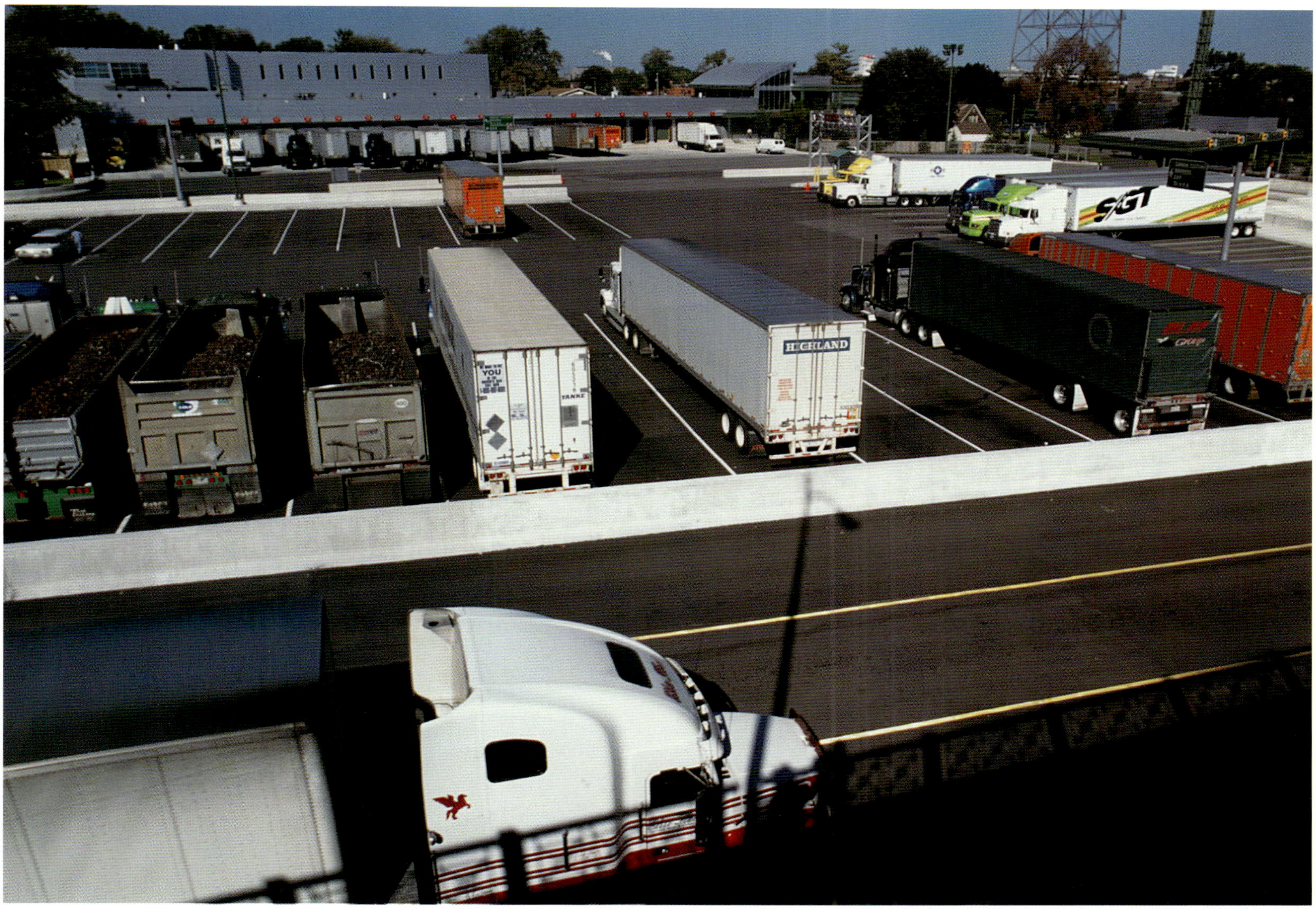

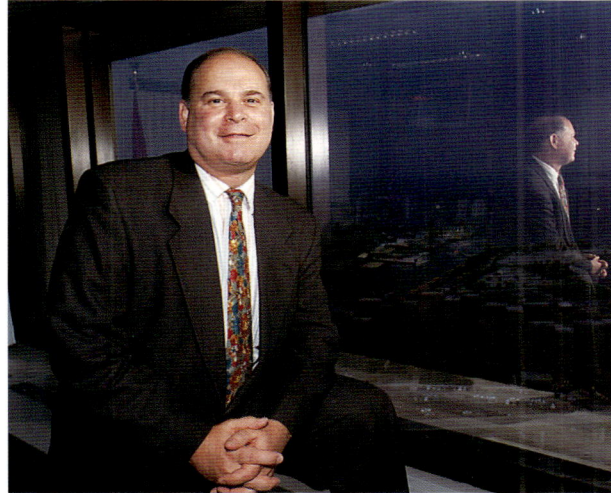

The **Canadian Consulate General** in Buffalo promotes trade, fosters tourism, oversees immigration, and provides information about Canada to the region of upstate New York, Western Pennsylvania, and the state of West Virginia. The consulate's Trade and Investment Division assists investors on both sides of the border in the creation of joint ventures, partnerships, licensing arrangements, and other business opportunities while helping manufacturers navigate the shoals of customs regulations and procedures. **Consul General Mark Romoff**, a Canadian diplomat formerly based in Tokyo, was appointed to head the Buffalo consulate in 1996.
Photo by James P. McCoy.

As the volume of trade heats up at the U.S.-Canadian border, so does the **customs brokerage business**. Nearly 20 brokerage firms in Western New York and 62 in Ontario handle the logistics to keep the freight moving across Niagara's bridges. Brokers act as agents for importers and exporters on both sides of the border. Brokers must be up to speed on the nontariff U.S. laws administered by more than 40 U.S. government agencies such as the USDA, the EPA, the FDA, and the FCC, as well as customs requirements related to the North American Free Trade Agreement. The Buffalo customs district includes the area's international bridge crossings plus all foreign traffic at the ports of Buffalo, Rochester, and Syracuse.
Photo by James P. McCoy.

(following page) Five hundred and sixty-six dairy farmers in the Western New York milk marketing area make milk the number one farm product in the region's agricultural production. Although the number of **dairy farms** has decreased during the past decade, milk production has increased by 20 percent. Monthly milk output in the area generally runs between 85 and 100 million pounds (8.6 pounds to the gallon). Less than half of the area's milk production is sold as drinking milk. The rest is used for dairy products like ice cream, cottage cheese, hard cheese, butter, and powdered and evaporated milk. Photo by James P. McCoy.

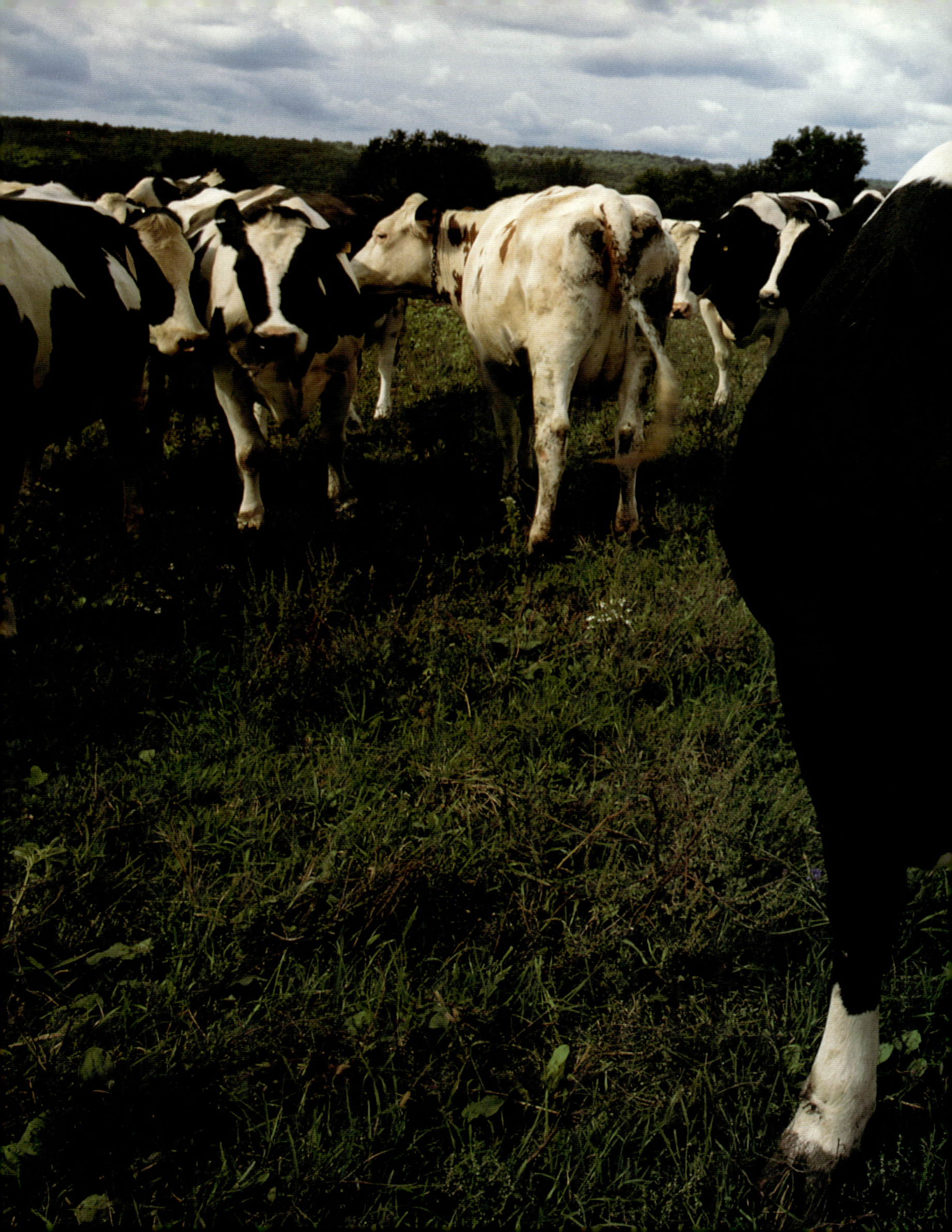

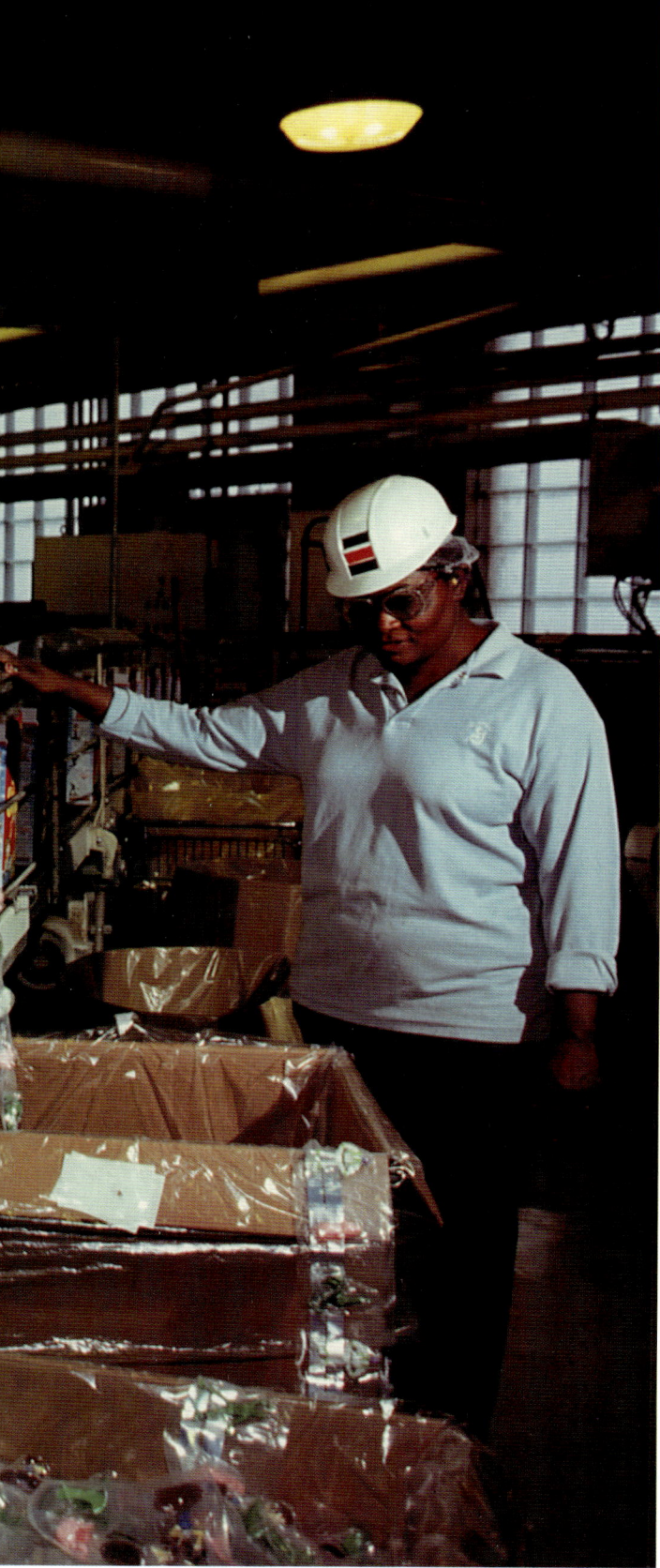

At the **General Mills** complex on Kelly Island, grain is ground into flour and the flour is used to create Kix®, Cheerios®, Wheaties®, and Total®. Here at General Mills' oldest cereal plant, 470 employees produce 20 percent of all General Mills breakfast cereals. Says Michigan native and Plant Manager Wayne Clive, "I like the people here. I like their work ethic, their friendliness, and their pride in themselves and what they do."
Photo by James P. McCoy.

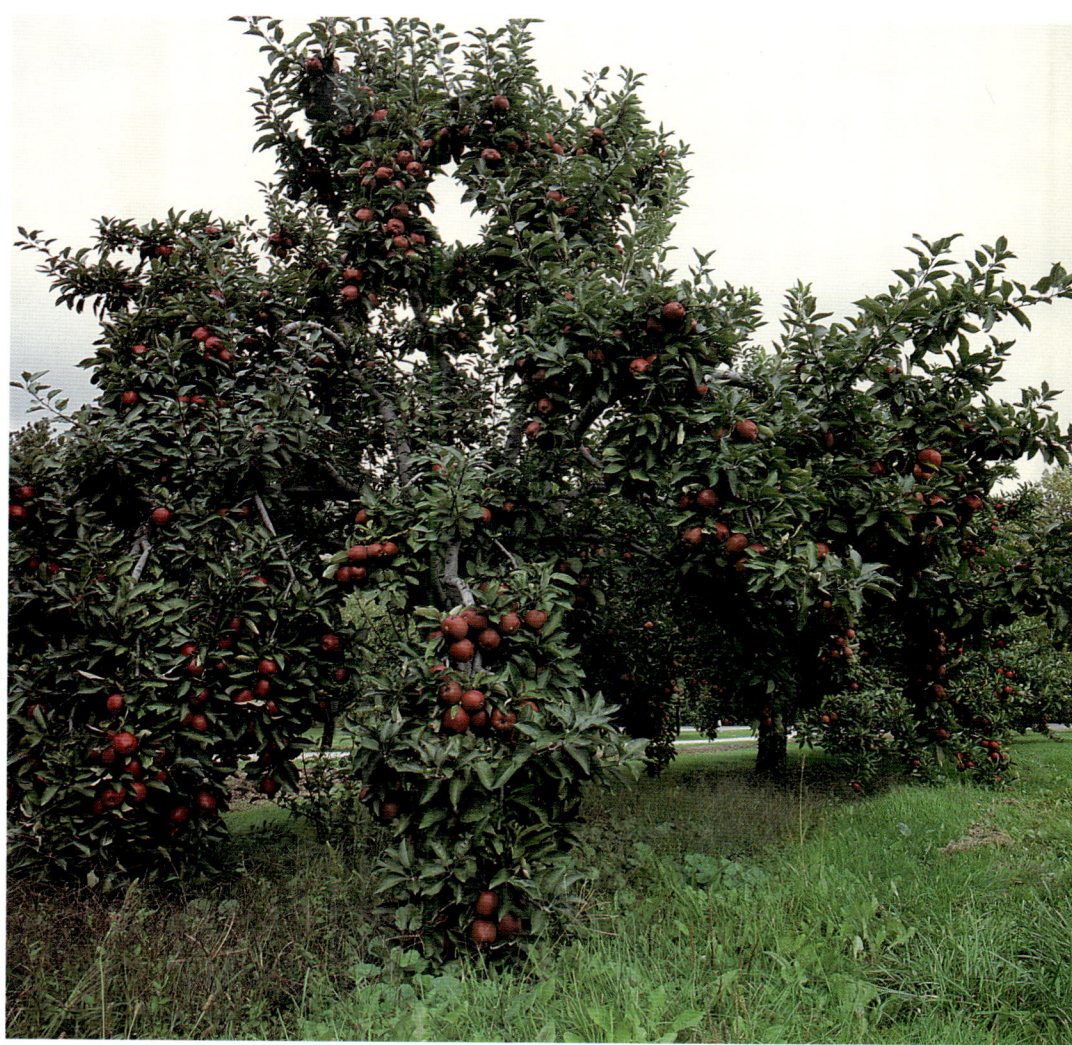

As one of the **top apple-growing regions** in New York State, Western New York orchards annually produce some 18 million bushels of old favorites like Empire, Cortland, Macintosh, Idared, Jonathan, Romes, and Red and Golden Delicious, as well as other tasty varieties like Crispin, Jonagold, Spartan, Jonamac, Macoun, Ginger Gold, Honey Crisp, Gala, and Fuji. There are approximately 185 growers in the eight-county area with the vast majority of orchards along the shores of Lake Ontario in the counties of Orleans and Niagara.
Photo by James P. McCoy.

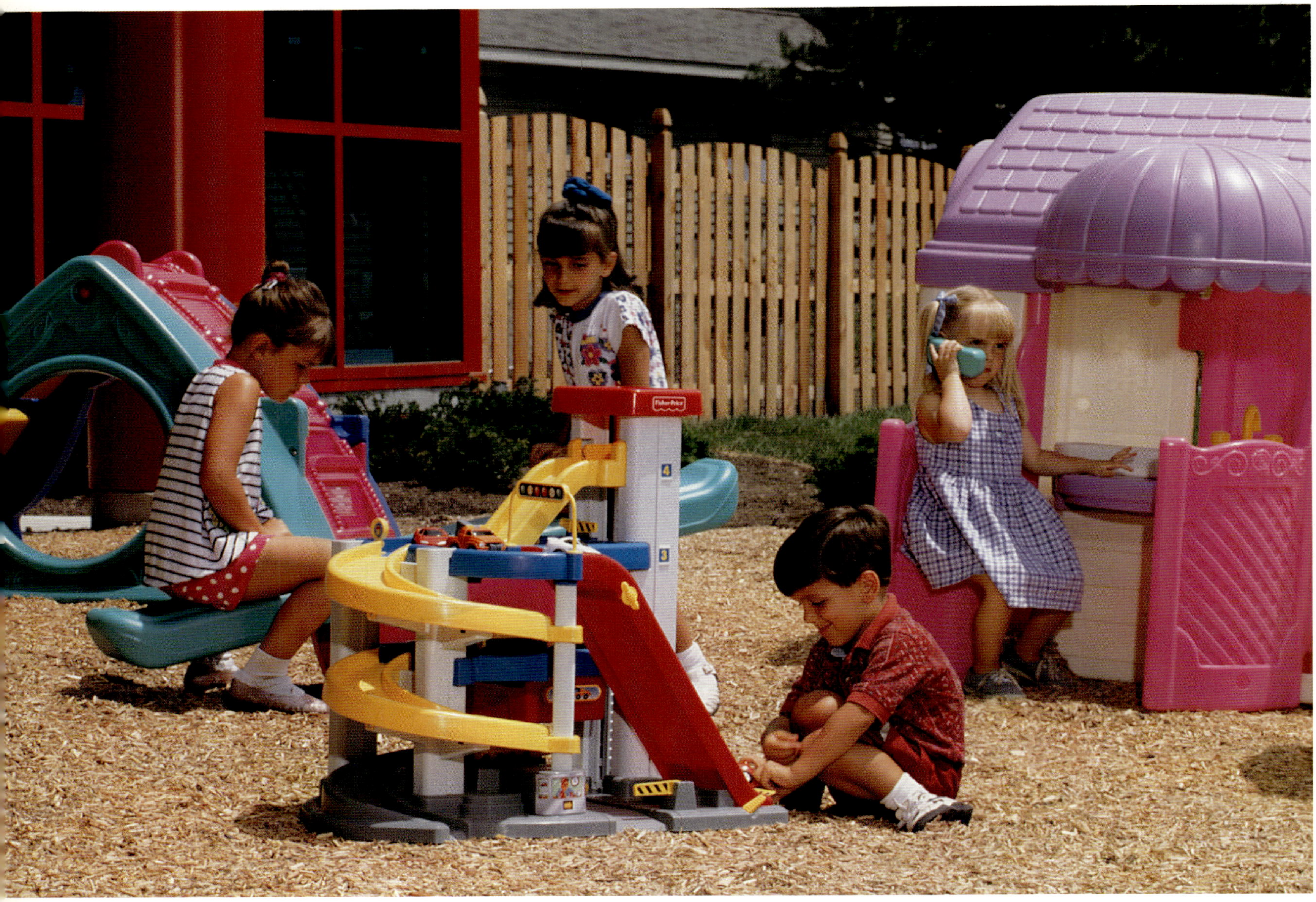

Fisher-Price, headquartered in Niagara, began making toys in East Aurora in 1930 and quickly became one of the nation's most popular creators of toys for preschool children. Many of the company's early successes were with colorful animal pull toys that delighted children with their realistic movements and funny sounds. Today, Fisher-Price's business is focused on infant toys, preschool toys, and children's products such as nursery monitors, strollers, carriers, high chairs, outdoor play equipment, as well as children's furniture and car seats.
Photo by James P. McCoy.

Leica, the Swiss optical company, manufactures microscopes at its Buffalo facility, the only Leica plant in the United States, and the largest manufacturer of microscopes in the nation. Leica's wide range of precision microscopy products includes stereomicroscopes for inspection and assembly in industrial applications, compound microscopes for educational uses, and refractometers for measurement and analysis in the pharmaceutical, industrial fluids, chemical, and plastics industries. Leica is the leading U.S. supplier of forensic microscopes, often used by police specialists to compare bullet grains.
Photo by James P. McCoy.

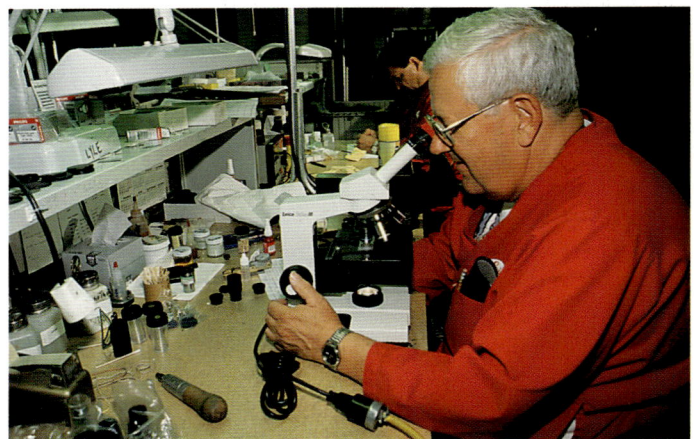

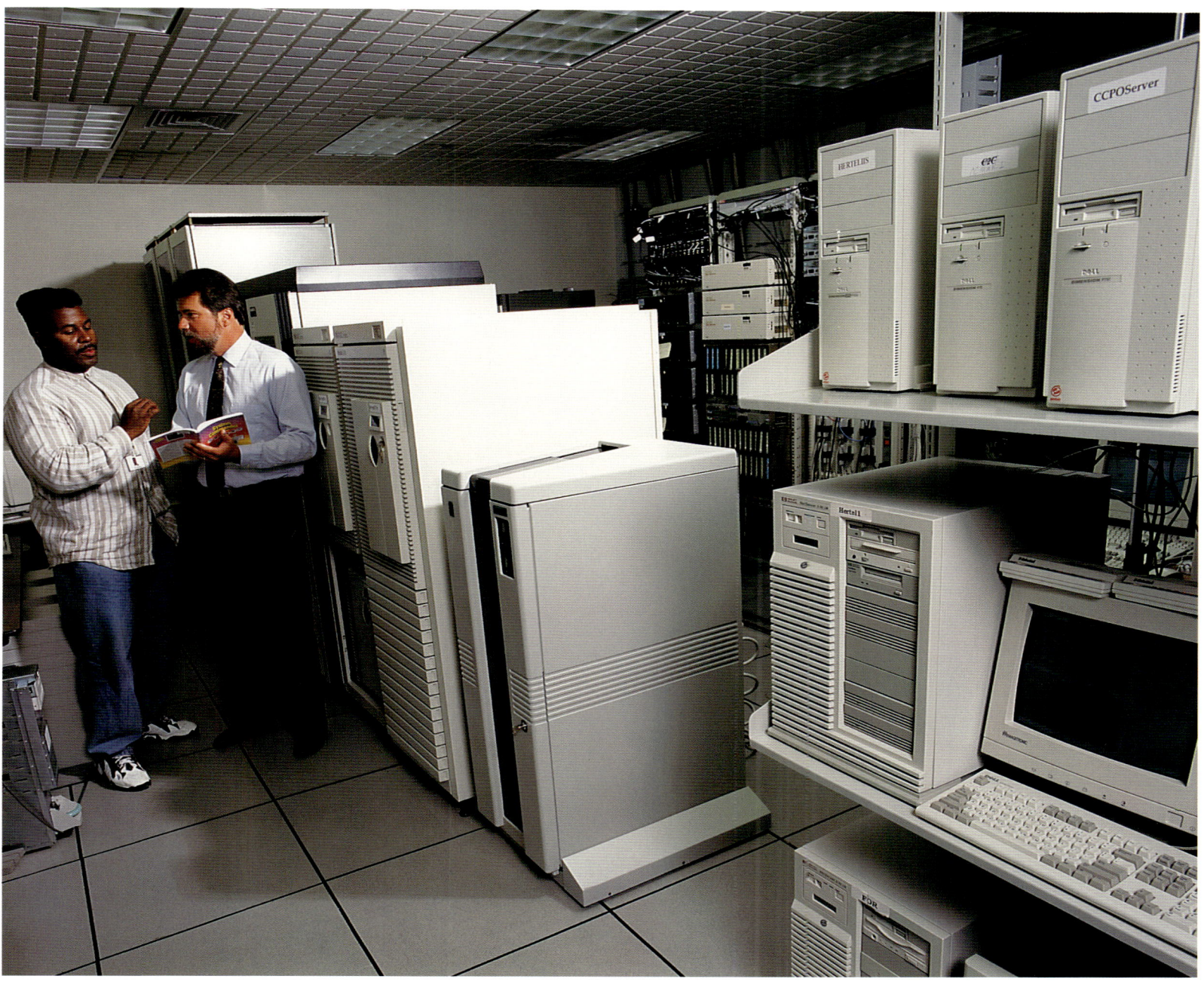

With a staff of 2,000 telephone sales and service agents, call centers in North America and Europe, and a growing distribution business, **Softbank Services Group** provides direct marketing, fulfillment, and tech support to Microsoft and other computer and software companies. The company's associates field nine million telephone calls annually for its roster of some 70 major clients worldwide. Softbank Services Group, which was formed in 1995 by the merger of the industry's two leading direct-marketing outsource companies, is headquartered in Buffalo. Photo by James P. McCoy.

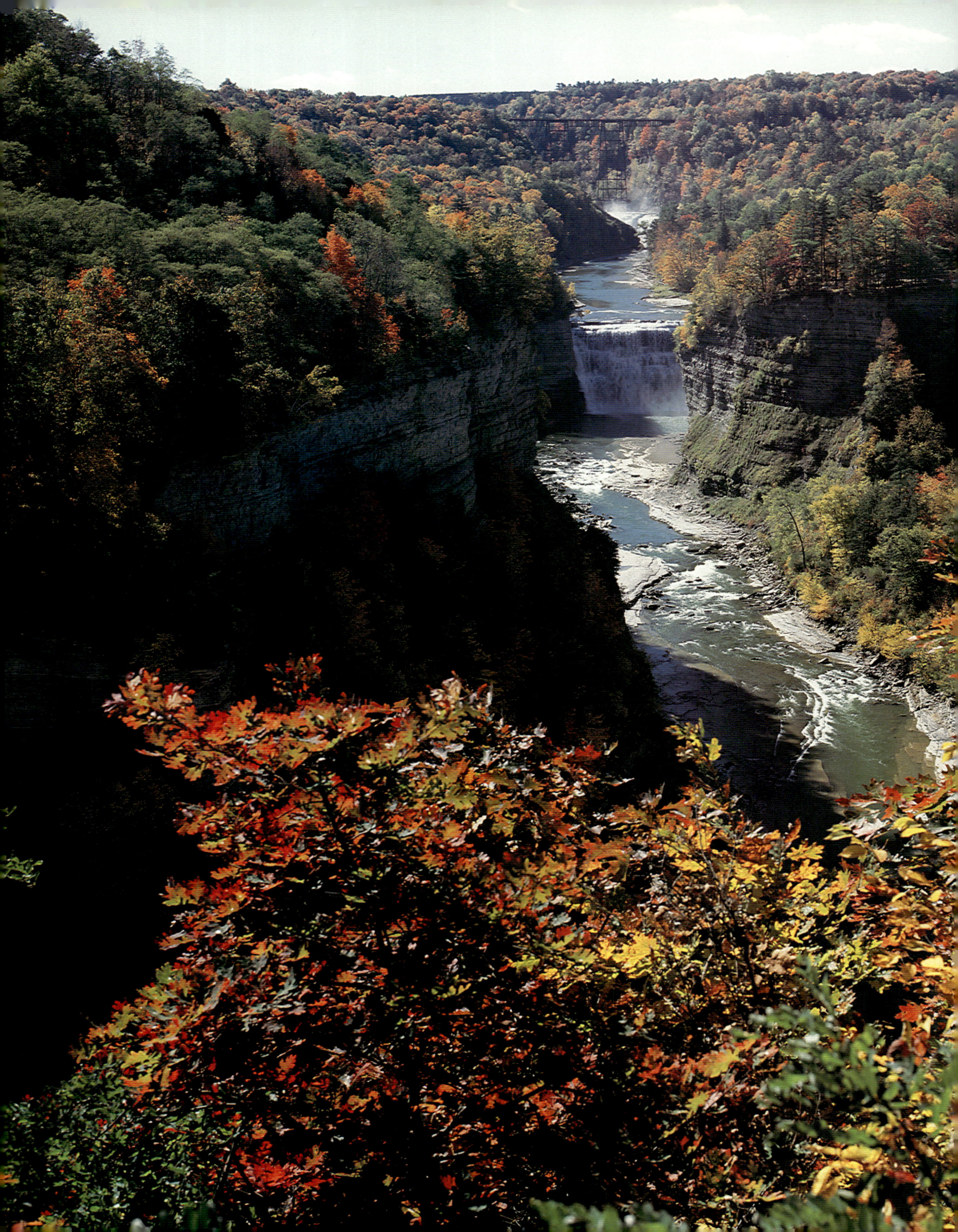

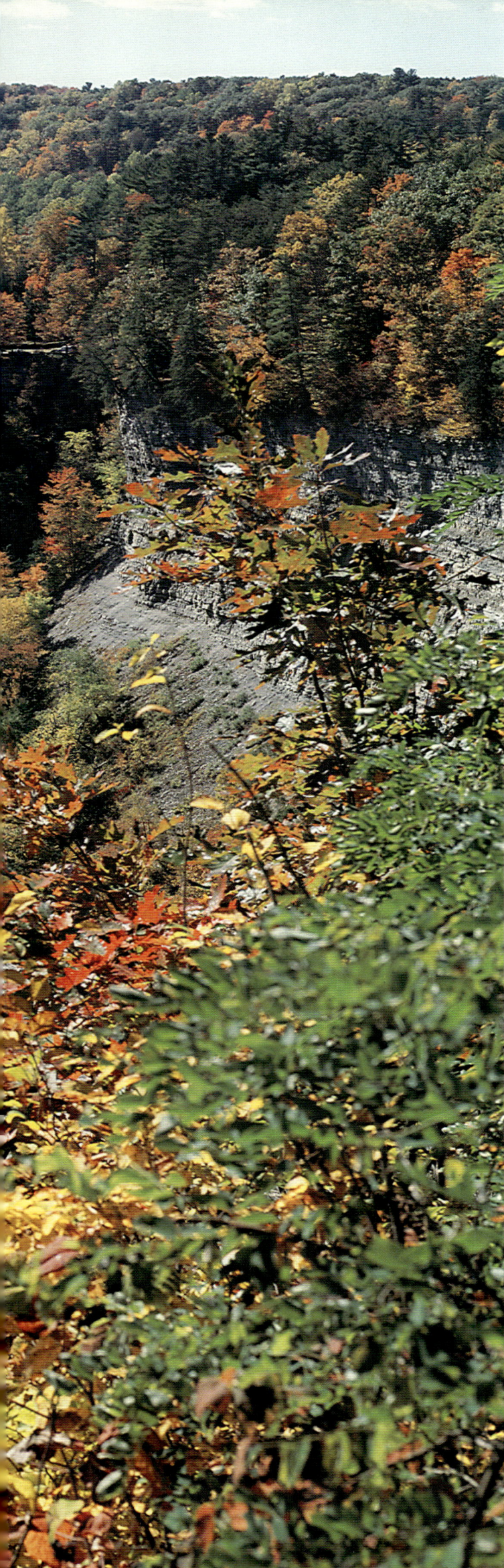

THE SPLENDOUR OF THE FOUR SEASONS

In March, the maple sap drips into buckets in the sugar bushes of the Southern Tier. Springtime in Cattaraugus, the soil sends up green shoots that bring a lush carpet of grasses, hay, and winter wheat across rolling fields. In the forests of Allegany State Park, the skunk cabbage and wild leeks push up through the mud and broadloom of last season's leaves. As summer nears, the small towns of Niagara are ablaze with forsythia, and one can smell the fragrance of lilacs.

In the fertile farms of Eden, people emerge from the long winter and haul out tractors, rototillers, shovels, spades, fertilizer, rakes, hoes, and hammers to bang in tomato stakes and row markers. Students at Brock University in St. Catharines open windows and are greeted by leaves on schoolyard oaks and maples. At the historic glass conservatory of the Buffalo and Erie County Botanical Gardens, the lilies, hyacinths, tulips, and daffodils are the stars of the annual Easter show. Along the lakeshore and the Niagara Parkway, Canada geese, Arctic ducks, and trumpeter swans fly in for their annual spring layover. Gliding with four-foot wing spans, the harriers return to nesting sites in the Buckhorn Island Marsh. The Tulip Festival in Holland commences. Soon, the strawberries will ripen and be offered for sale by the farmers at the Clinton-Bailey Market. The Lake Erie ice boom has opened and the river, now a white stampede of melting floes, carries the last remains of winter on a final journey through the heart of Niagara and over the Falls.

As evenings lengthen and the sun sets later over the round red brick Victorian water intake house at the entrance to the Buffalo harbor, families gather to eat ice cream and watch the sailboats drift past the old 1833 harbor lighthouse and into the Buffalo River. A Miss Buffalo cruise boat rounds the breakwater with deck lights blazing and a Dixieland band playing at full tilt. Along the path through the woods that leads to the hidden beach at Thunder Bay, wild raspberries and blackberries grow among the rotting logs and trillium. The orchard fruit ripens, the sweet fragrance of fresh cut alfalfa rises from the hayfields, and wild turkeys roost in the hemlocks of the Brokenstraw State Forest.

In the summer, Niagara is filled with celebrations. There are festivals to art, antiques, food, folklore, friendship, heritage, jazz, kids, kites, llamas, catfish, movies, cheese, cherries, sausage, wine, and roses. Ethnic fests honor Greeks, Italians, African-Americans, Irish, Germans, and Polish-Americans. Old canal towns, like Lockport, Medina, and Tonawanda, host historic festivals that feature parades with brass bands, old red fire trucks, fancy fiddlers, folks in period costumes, kazoo players, colorful clowns, and cotton candy. There are golf tournaments, regattas, rodeos, tractor pulls, custom car shows, air shows, craft shows, barbecues, clam bakes, corn roasts, doubleheaders, picnics, sidewalk sales, and flea markets. There are peach parties, walleye tournaments, bass derbys, canoeing championships, county fairs, and a skydiving boogie.

In late August, the goldenrod suddenly blossoms in the fields and roadsides and swarms of purple asters peek out from the hedgerows. Then, with the passing of Labor Day and the beginning of a new school year, summer quickly fades into what many regard as Niagara's finest moment. Autumn is aglow in oranges, scarlets, russets, mahoganies, heliotropes, and magentas. A drive or a hike in any direction on a sunny Sunday afternoon reveals a constantly changing diorama of deciduous color. Fall is filled with football games, pumpkin contests, apple cider, wine tastings, and woodchopping.

When the first snowflakes arrive in November, skiers, snowboarders, chair lift operators, alpinists, snowmobilers, and ice fishermen rejoice. Others mourn the passing of the glorious autumn and curse the arrival of the cold. As winter comes in earnest to Niagara Falls, the spray will coat sidewalks, handrails, cliffsides, trees, and bushes in a glistening patina of ice, a frozen tableau of nature's delicate tracery. At Beaver Meadow, visitors snowshoe over drifted trails or gaze at the splendor of the winter sky through the 12-and-a-half-inch reflecting telescope at the nature center's observatory. Festivals of lights and trees, winter carnivals and snow sculpting contests, holiday pageants and parties, and snug saloons offer solace and cheer, and remind us of the springtime pleasures waiting to burst forth in another season of renewal and growth. ◆

(previous page) William Pryor Letchworth was another prominent Niagara citizen who had the determination and the means to leave an area of natural beauty for eternal public enjoyment. Letchworth, a steel magnate who was also active in overseeing the distribution of charity to the poor and the placement of children for adoption, bought 1,000 acres along the Genesee River beginning in 1859. Today, **Letchworth State Park** is a 14,000-acre tract of land surrounding the Genesee River between Portageville and Mt. Morris. The river runs through a series of deep gorges with depths of up to 600 feet, then plunges over three spectacular waterfalls in its 15-mile northern journey through the park. There are also several smaller scenic waterfalls from other streams cascading over the gorge walls down to the river. Photo by James P. McCoy.

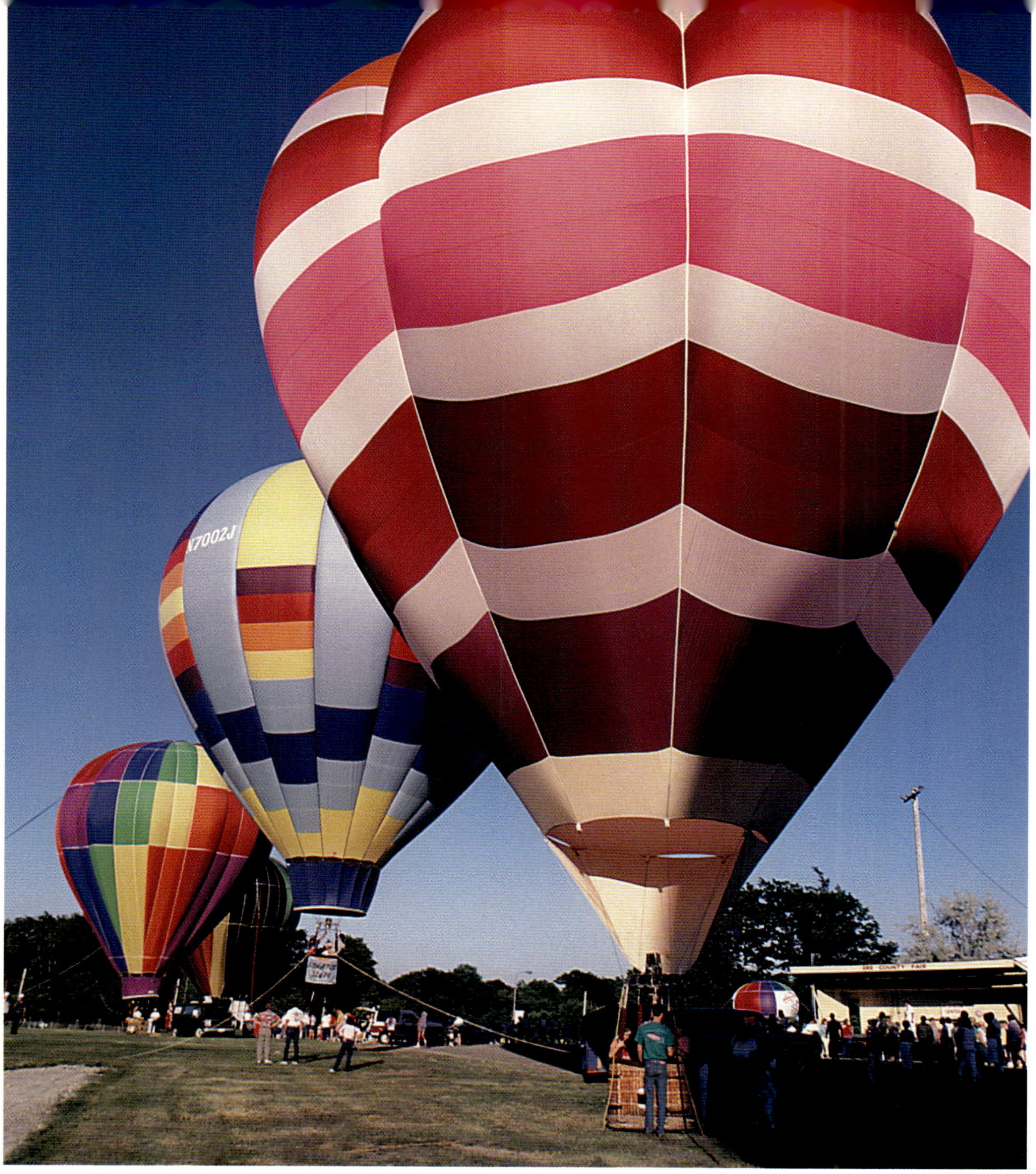

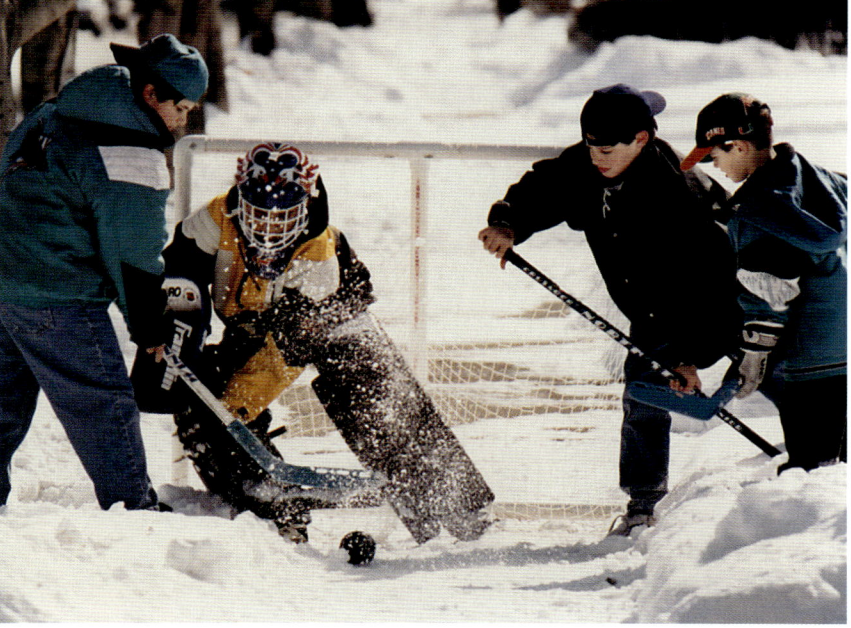

In mid-July, the skies over Wellsville are a pageant of color as dozens of hot-air balloons lift off at the annual **Great Wellsville Balloon Rally**.
Photo by James P. McCoy.

With strong influence from Canadian legends, **hockey** is a year-round sport in Niagara, with pick-up games played on rollerblades® in the summer, and on the ice whenever possible. But the best arena is often an empty street, a net, and a strong roster of friends.
Photo by James P. McCoy.

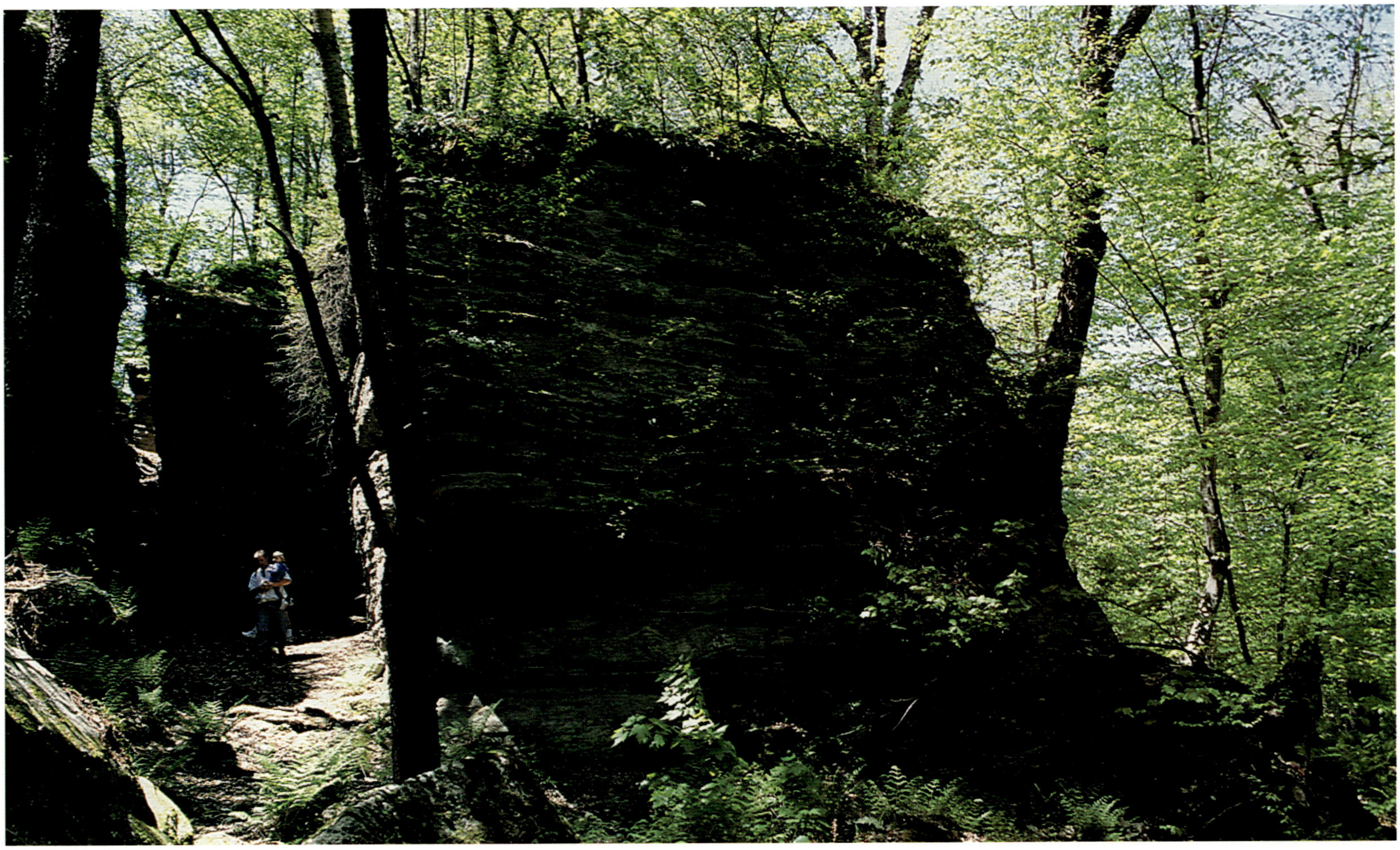

Over 300 million years ago, the **rocks at Panama** were the sand and pebbles of the beach on an ancient inland ocean. The rock is a conglomerate sometimes called puddingstone with imbedded stones of quartz, spar, flint, and bloodstone. Glacial freezing and thawing fractured the great monoliths and created a labyrinth of passageways and crevices that was eventually overgrown with trees and forest floor cover. Other "cities of rock" can be found at Little Valley and south of Olean near the Pennsylvania border.
Photo by James P. McCoy.

On a crisp winter day, you stand on top of the highest hill in **Chestnut Ridge Park** with the Erie Plain, Lackawanna, Buffalo, and Lake Erie spread out before you. Then it's pile onto the toboggan and a mad rush down the hill screaming and hanging on to anything you can grab. When it's time to warm up, you head for the big stone and timbered casino, where there's always a roaring fire and hot cocoa waiting.
Photo by James P. McCoy.

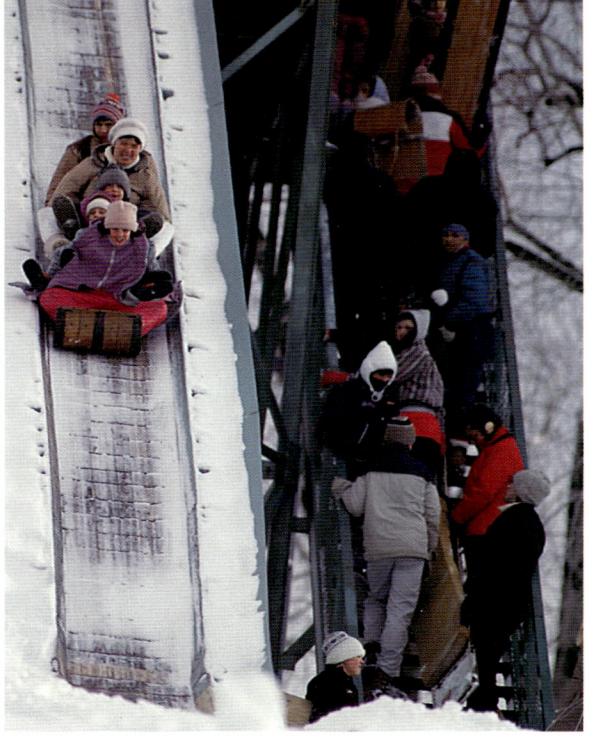

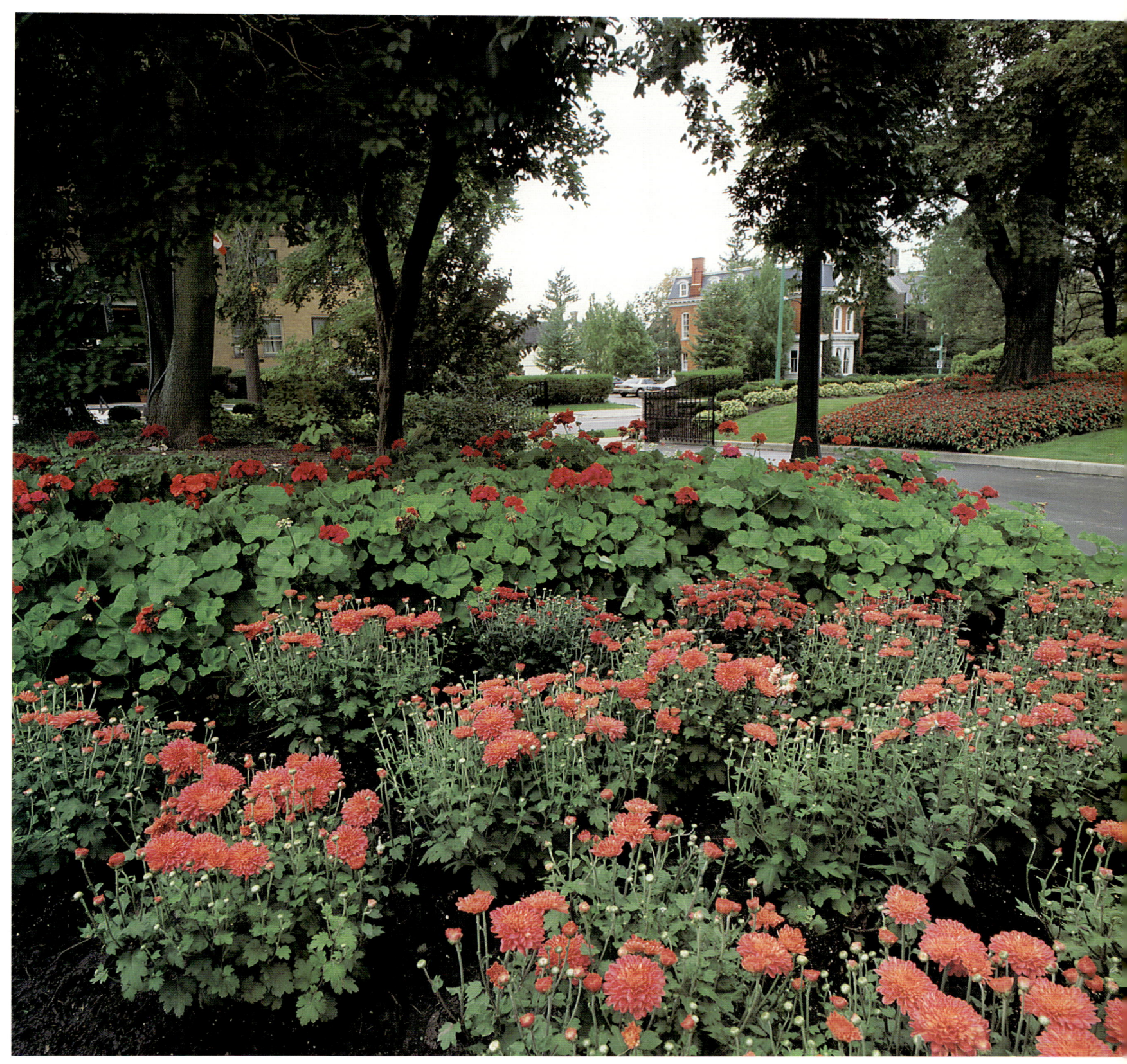

Gardening pride blossoms in Buffalo each year when corporate sponsors provide the resources for **Buffalo in Bloom**, a neighborhood flower gardening competition offering cash prizes for the most attractive residential gardens in each of the city's nine council districts. Businesses, institutions, municipal agencies, and community gardens also compete in separate categories for the honor of recognition and the pleasures of urban beautification.
Photo by James P. McCoy.

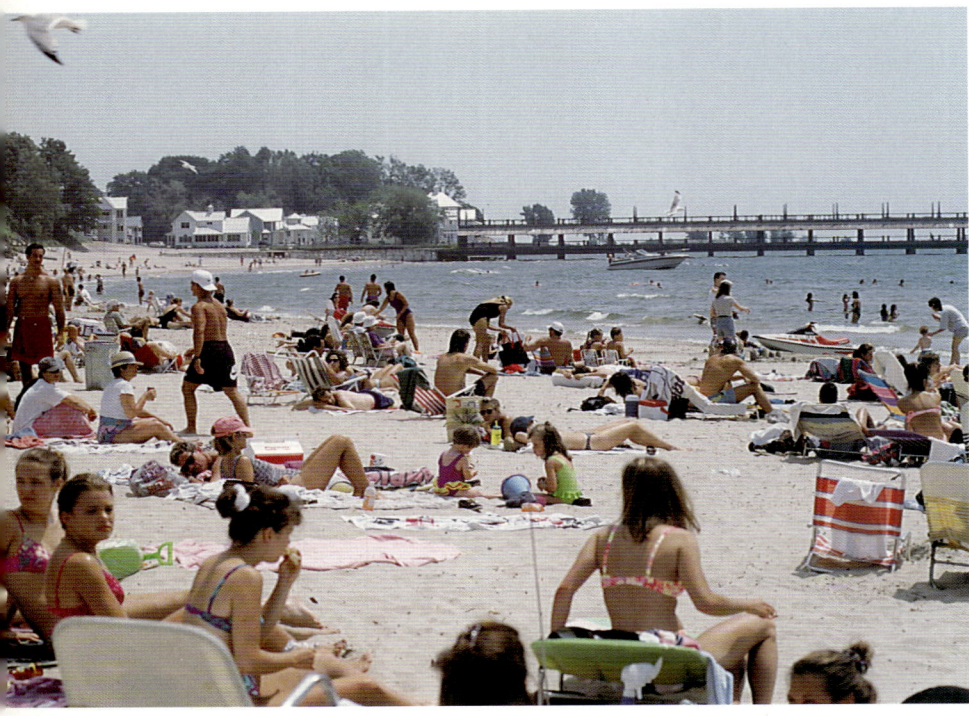

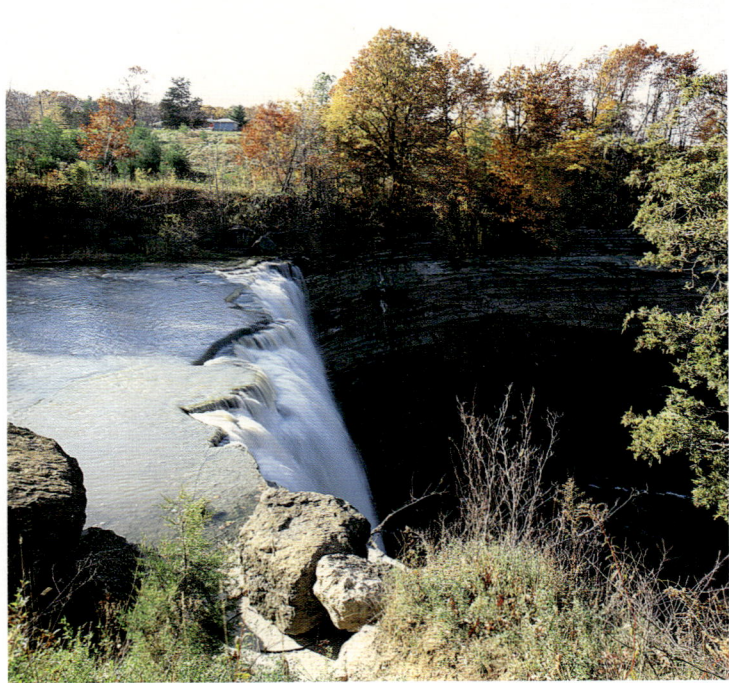

Just a 10-minute drive from downtown Buffalo are the sandy beaches of the **Canadian shore of Lake Erie**. On a summer's day in Niagara, few pleasures equal those available from a wicker settee on a shaded lawn or a beach chair or towel on the sand at Waverly Beach, Crescent Beach, Thunder Bay, Point Abino, or the Sherkston Beaches. Photo by James P. McCoy.

In the early 19th century, George Ball built a gristmill, a sawmill, and a woolen mill at the spot where Twenty Mile Creek falls 90 feet over the Niagara Escarpment. Today, the remains of the industrial community Ball founded are part of a 210-acre conservation area that includes scenic hiking trails, **Balls Falls**, and an arboretum. Photo by James P. McCoy.

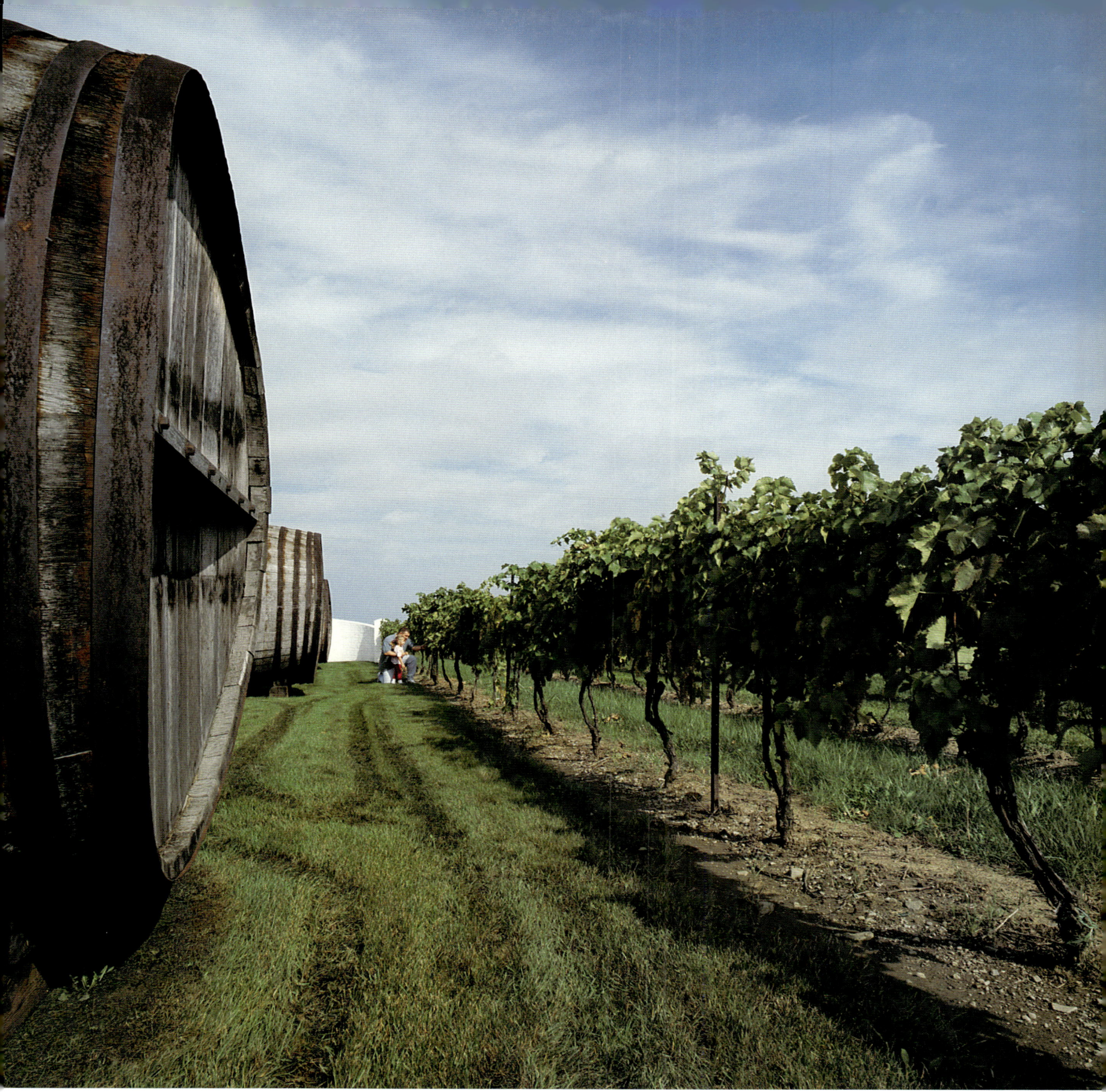

Like two great heat exchangers, Lakes Erie and Ontario provide the moderating temperatures to support a thriving viticulture along their southern shores. Niagara is home to 40 wineries growing Chardonnay, Pinot Noir, Pinot Gris, Cabernet Sauvignon, and **Niagara grapes**.
Photo by James P. McCoy.

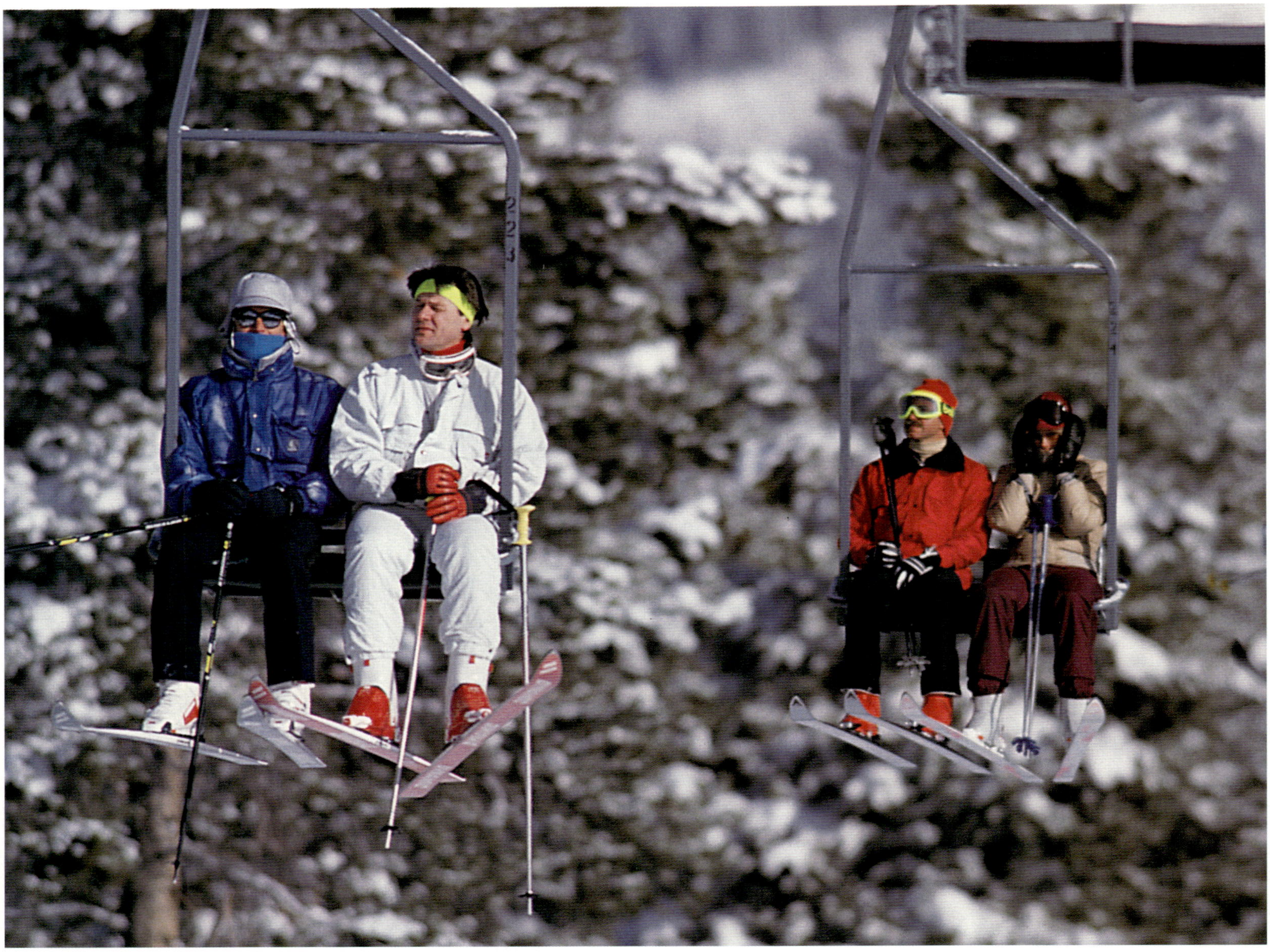

With one of the country's leading ski resorts and all the charms of a carefully preserved and restored Victorian village, **Ellicottville** attracts over one million skiers, snowboarders, golfers, and other year-round visitors from across Ontario, Pennsylvania, Ohio, and New York State. Once the seat of Cattaraugus County, the village was named for Joseph Ellicott, the general agent of the Holland Land Company, who laid out its streets, lots, and the village square. Photos by James P. McCoy.

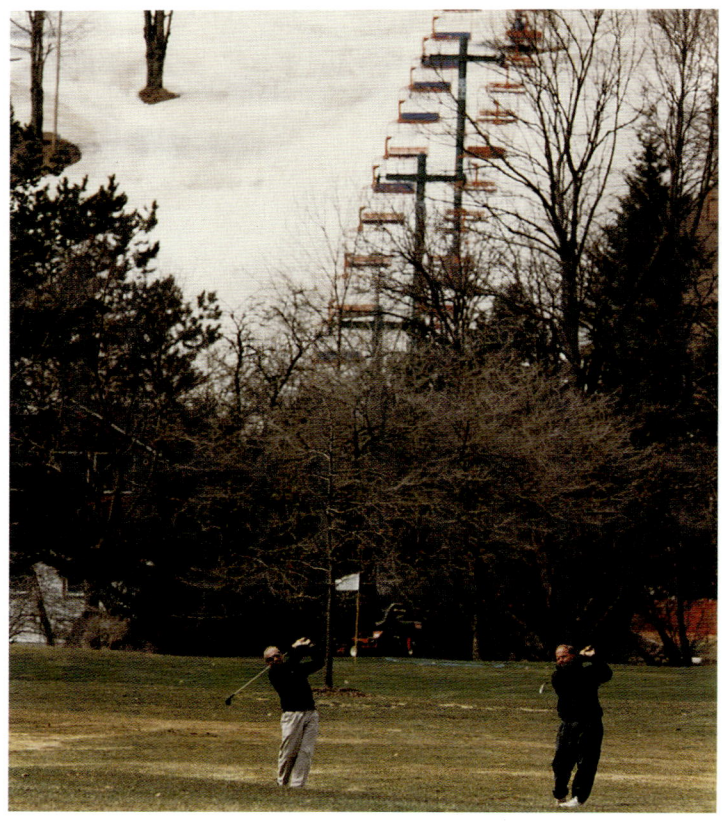

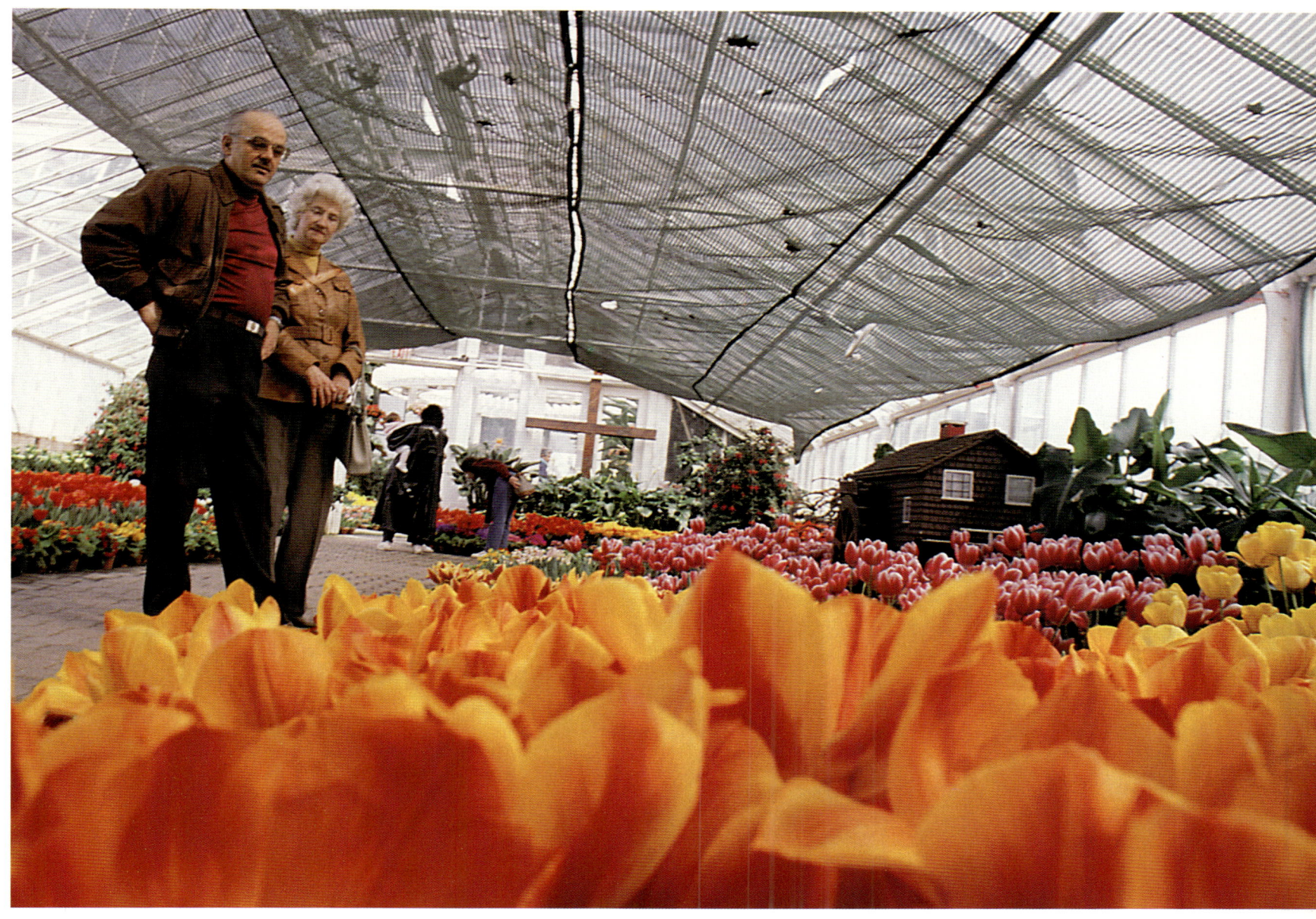

Every spring, autumn, and winter, the Show House at the **Botanical Gardens** presents a seasonal floral display under the great end dome. Other special events are also held at the gardens throughout the year. The conservatory is the crown jewel of South Park, originally designed by Frederick Law Olmsted as part of an interconnected system of Buffalo parks.
Photo by James P. McCoy.

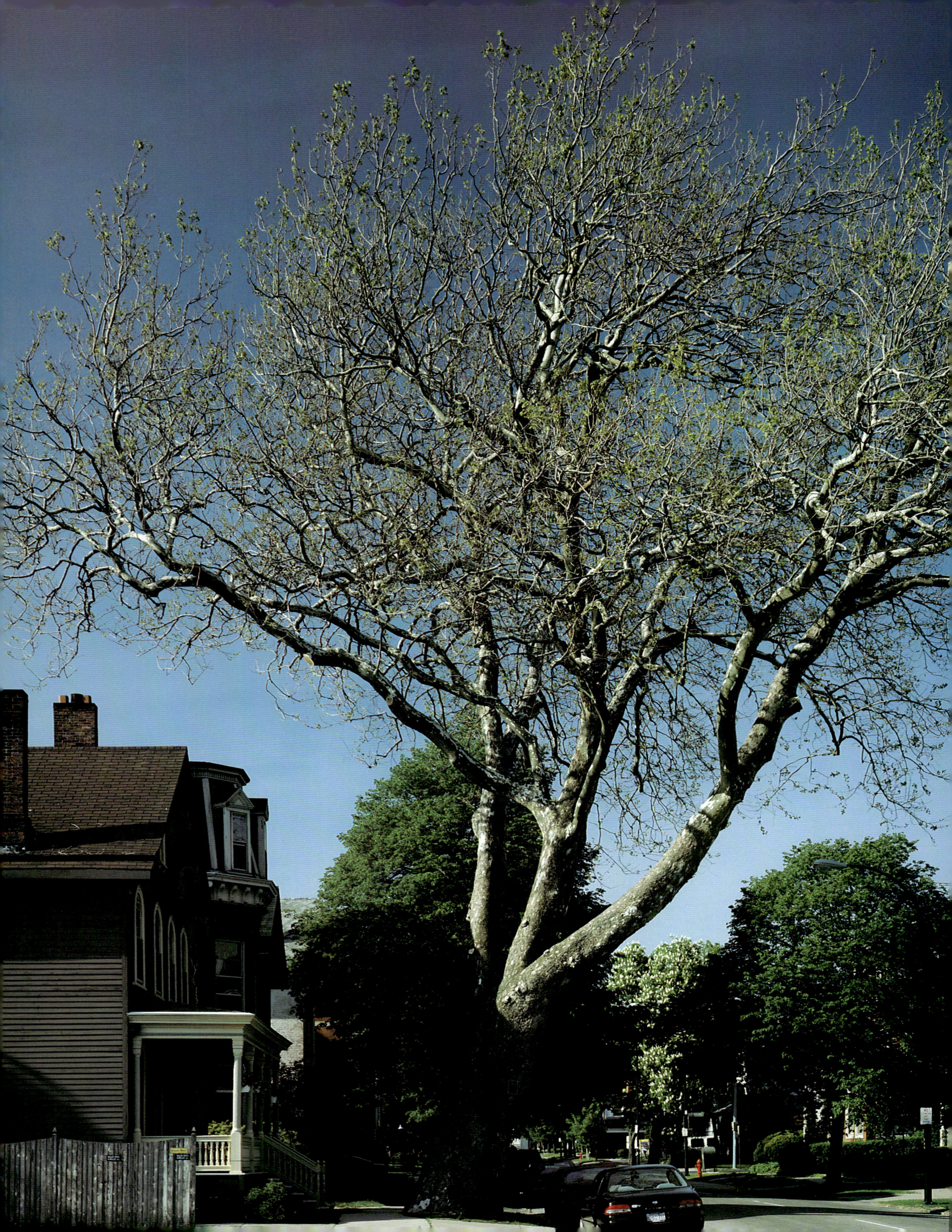

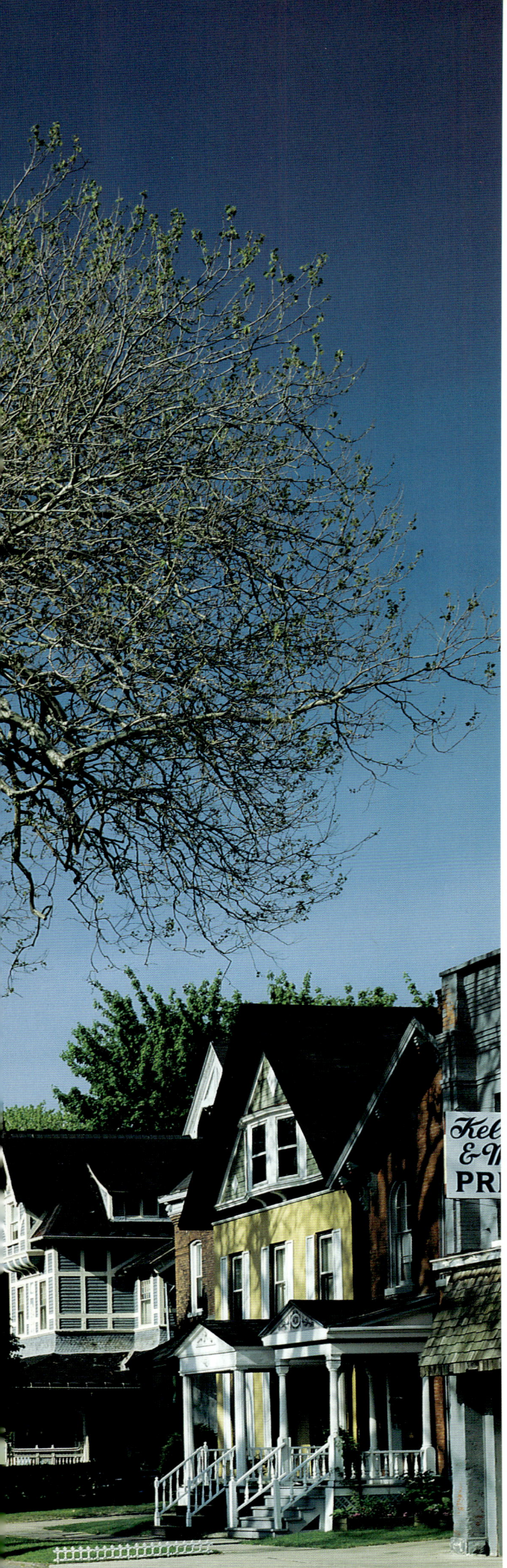

A LEGACY OF LIVING ALTERNATIVES

One of the delights of living in

Niagara is the possibility of discovering

another interesting neighborhood, village,

or town just around the next corner. It

could be an urban cul de sac, a row of

historic townhouses, an English tea

room, a tree-lined boulevard, a rural

village, a woodsy suburban hideaway,

or a splendid old farmhouse restored

to its former glory.

This sycamore tree is believed to be the oldest tree in Buffalo.
Photo by Marc Murphy.

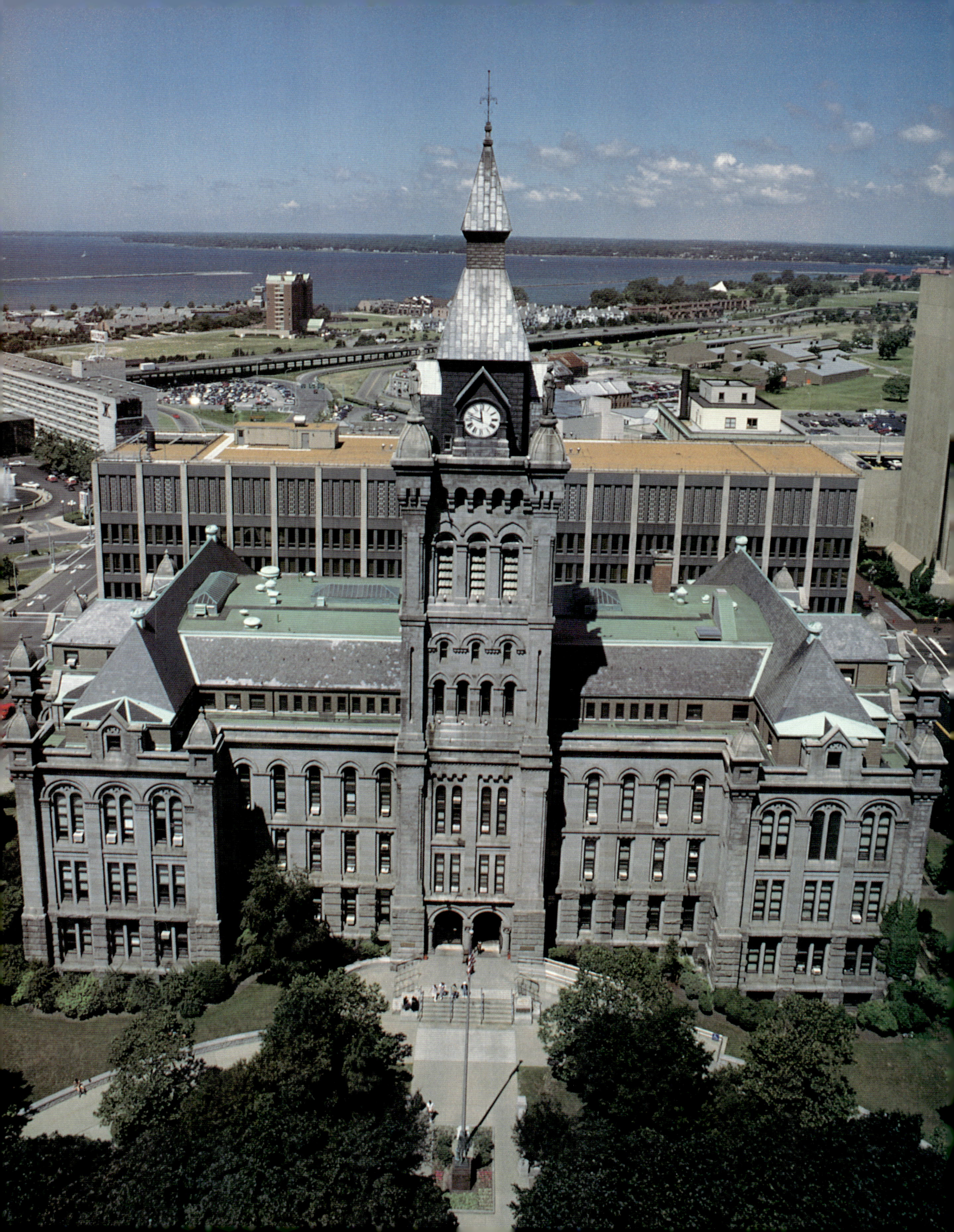

The area's first communities sprang up around the rivers and the lakes, from the early native encampments and longhouse villages to the forts, garrisons, mill towns, and farming hamlets of the European colonists and their descendants. From Niagara-on-the-Lake to North Tonawanda, from St. Catharines to Cattaraugus, the past is palpable in the brick, beams, stone, and timbers of Niagara's 19th-century architectural heritage.

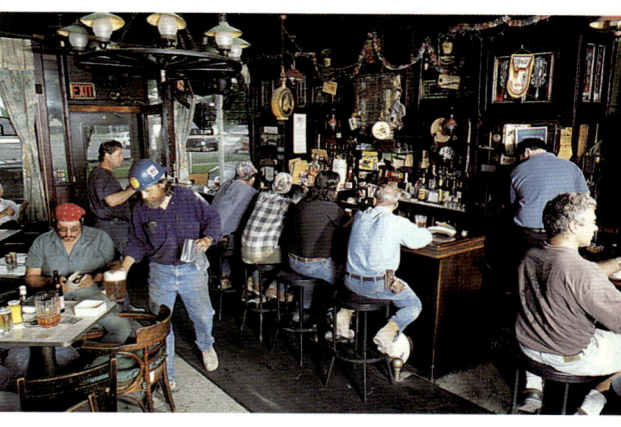

When this landmark Buffalo watering hole opened as a grocery-saloon in 1868, its East Side neighborhood was a solid German enclave and the center of Buffalo's brewing industry. Named for Mike Ulrich, "the last of the old-time German saloon-keepers" and the man who once served potato pancakes to Grover Cleveland, **Ulrich's Tavern** is a fascinating repository of Buffalo and American history. The upstairs, known then as the Hassenpfeffer Club, operated as a speakeasy during Prohibition. Owners Jim and Erica Daley bought the tavern in 1954, and keeping things exactly the way Mike Ulrich left them, turned Ulrich's into an amiable Irish bar with a celebrated German kitchen and dining room.
Photo by James P. McCoy.

Although some of Buffalo's earliest neighborhoods are now the focus of archeological digs, the city's oldest extant residence, the Coit House, is still inhabited (moved from its original downtown location) in Allentown. Allentown, site of a summer art festival, may be Buffalo's best-known neighborhood, a lively quarter where Victoriana meets pita, souvlaki, and caffe latte. Where Lewis Allen's cows once grazed, today you'll gaze on pretty little streets of well-kept houses, thriving antique emporiums, artists' ateliers, bookstores, coffee houses, eclectic shops, celebrated restaurants, and nightspots.

Traveling up Richmond Avenue from Symphony Circle to the parkways and circles that lead into Delaware Park, the broad boulevards, the statuary and fountains recall Olmsted's grand design for this historic city. The park, now bisected by a busy expressway, is still surrounded by grand houses with columns, pillars, porticos, gardens, circular drives, and arcadian vistas.

Buffalo's neighborhoods are replete with spacious two-family flats and large homes often rehabbed into handsome apartments with hardwood floors, fireplaces, and crafted woodwork. This is particularly true in the Parkside and North Buffalo neighborhoods, where solid, well-built homes dating from the 1920s include those built by the founders of the Pierce-Arrow Motor Car Company. Here, the canopied green streets spill onto Hertel Avenue, a cosmopolitan thoroughfare that rivals Elmwood for its interesting mix of shops, stores, bakeries, ethnic restaurants, bars, banks, mom & pop cafes, and the venerable North Park, the city's last single screen movie theater.

What's particularly interesting about Buffalo's neighborhoods is their great diversity within a relatively small area. Ethnic enclaves continue to flourish throughout the city with Polish- and African-Americans on the East Side, Italian and Hispanic communities on the West Side, and Irish in South Buffalo.

South Buffalo is also home to Cazenovia Park, the Erie County Botanical Gardens, the drama of the Buffalo River industrial landscape, and the ancestral fiefdom of countless distinguished Irish-American politicians and community leaders. Here the South Park and South Abbott neighborhoods are among the most stable and well-maintained in the city. Ethnic pride enriches the soul while ethnic food feeds everybody during celebrations like the St. Patrick's Day Parade, Dyngus Day, Juneteenth, and the Hispanic, Italian, and Hellenic Festivals.

Easy access is a hallmark of life in Niagara. For those whose pulses quicken in traffic jams and who enjoy conducting business by cell phone from the throes of gridlock, Niagara's rush hours may seem uncommonly tame. But newcomers from more frazzled cities report an easy transition to the extra time available at work or at home as a result of Buffalo's low-stress commute.

Niagara's growing suburbs and surrounding towns and countryside offer a great deal of variety in lifestyles and personalities. Beyond the near suburbs of Kenmore, Tonawanda, Cheektowaga, and West Seneca lie other attractive communities. Amherst, fourth-largest municipality in upstate New York, is home to the neighborhoods of Williamsville, Getzville,

Erie County Hall, Gothic Revival masterpiece, was built during the 1870s at Franklin Square, site of the original village of Buffalo that was burned by the British during the War of 1812. The sculptures by Giovanni Sala flanking the double-roofed clock tower represent Justice, Mechanical Arts, Agriculture, and Commerce.
Photo by James P. McCoy.

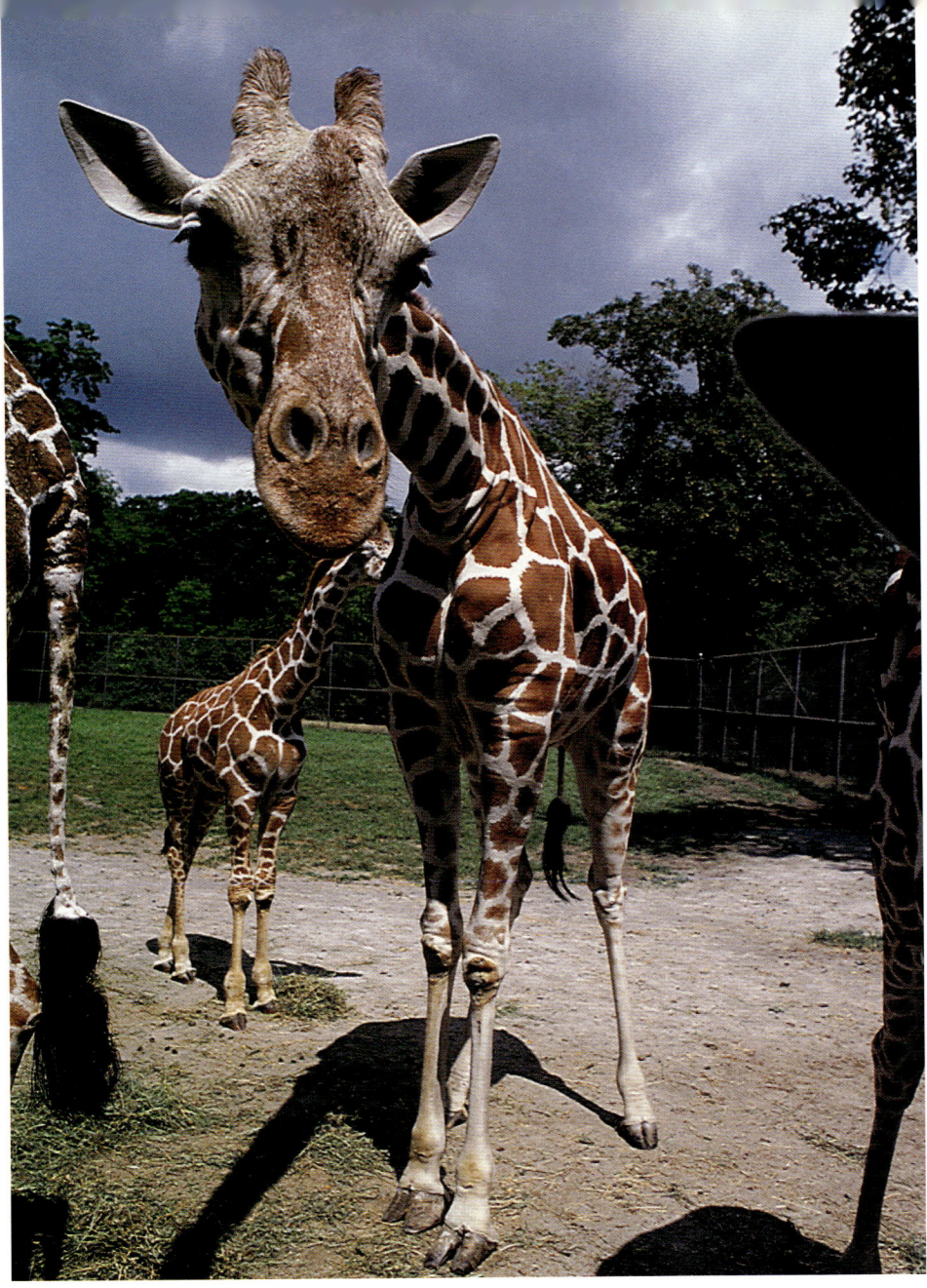

Delaware Park was designed by Olmsted and Vaux as the crown jewel of their ambitious Buffalo park system. In keeping with Olmsted's philosophy that the setting should provide solace and spiritual renewal in the urban environment, the centerpiece of the 350-acre park is a vast meadow hidden by trees at the original roadway intersections to keep the city at bay. The meadow, now a public golf course, is bordered by a circular roadway used by runners, walkers, in-line skaters, and bicyclists. The **Buffalo Zoo** occupies the northeast corner of the park. The Albright Knox Art Gallery and the Erie County Historical Museum are at the opposite end of the Delaware Park perimeter. Photo by James P. McCoy.

Snyder, Eggertsville, and East Amherst. In addition to its shopping malls, hotels, high-tech industries, retail businesses, and the North Campus of the State University of New York at Buffalo, Amherst also boasts the lowest crime rate of any U.S. city over 100,000 people.

Woods, water, and wide-open spaces distinguish Grand Island, which comprises 33 square miles and is home to beautiful Beaver Island State Park. On the West River State Parkway, sprawling ranch houses stare serenely across the water from their commanding heights opposite the Canadian shore. At Niagara Falls, many lovely neighborhoods are situated just downstream from the great cataract. Further north, the historic Niagara County village of Lewiston nestles in the original plunge basin where Niagara Falls once fell over the escarpment. On the southern shores of Lake Ontario, the towns of Wilson and Olcott are well known for their beautiful beaches and well-equipped marinas.

Lockport is a scenic old Niagara County town that grew around the locks of the Erie Barge Canal. Here, when the original canal was built, a twin set of five-flight locks was blasted out of the rock to allow canal boats to cross the Niagara Escarpment. Today, the magnificent houses built by the men who made their fortunes from the canal and other 19th-century enterprises still stand in the southeast quarter of the city, just a 20-mile commute from Buffalo and 18 miles east of Niagara Falls.

On the outer ring of Buffalo's suburbs, Clarence is the oldest township in Erie County and home to many commuters seeking a more rural lifestyle within the metropolitan environs. Antiquarians sometimes disappear for days in the flea markets and antique shops of Clarence Hollow.

Home of the Buffalo Bills, Orchard Park was founded as a Quaker community in 1805. Nowadays, Orchard Park still has the distinctive look and feel of a neighborly village, while the town's southern subdivisions expand into rolling wooded areas not far from the Colden ski resorts, Eighteenmile Creek, Sprague Brook, and other recreation areas.

Hamburg, putative birthplace of the world-famous ground beef sandwich, is another Southtowns suburb of pleasant neighborhoods. Site of the Erie County Fair, Hamburg is both a charming village and a township whose western border extends to the Lake Erie shore. Its attractions include well-maintained parks and beaches, golf courses, and shoreline homes with spectacular views of the lake and the Buffalo skyline.

In the summer, the Lake Erie shore between Fort Erie and Port Colborne becomes the playground of some 10,000 American cottagers, many of whom commute to work across the Peace Bridge. Fort Erie is named for the historic fort first built by the British in 1764, which later became a key battleground between British and American forces during the War of 1812. The fort was in ruins from 1814 until 1937 when it was restored by the provincial and federal governments of Canada.

Another interesting, off-the-beaten-track neighborhood can be found in the town of Port Dalhousie, where vessels traversing the original Welland Canal once entered the open waters of Lake Ontario. Just half an hour from the Peace Bridge, Port Dalhousie's location on the peninsula between Martindale Pond and the big lake provides the perfect setting for its inviting section of shops, restaurants, bookstores, and galleries.

Niagara also has its special interest neighborhoods. At Lily Dale near Cassadaga, spiritualists gather each summer as they have for more than a century to consult with mediums and attend lectures at the Lily Dale Spiritualist Assembly. In Niagara-on-the-Lake, summer activities revolve around the theater productions on the three stages of the Shaw Festival. Come winter, the village of Ellicottville is a welcoming haven for thousands of skiers arriving from the eastern United States and Canada.

No matter which neighborhood you choose in Niagara, you're never far from something of historical, geographic, recreational, or cultural interest. Or, to put it another way, there's a lot of fun for little or no admission charge. If quality of life is determined by the character of a place and the spirit and energy of its people, Niagara falls over the top.

And did we mention the gastronomic attractions? Ah, but that's another book. 𝗡

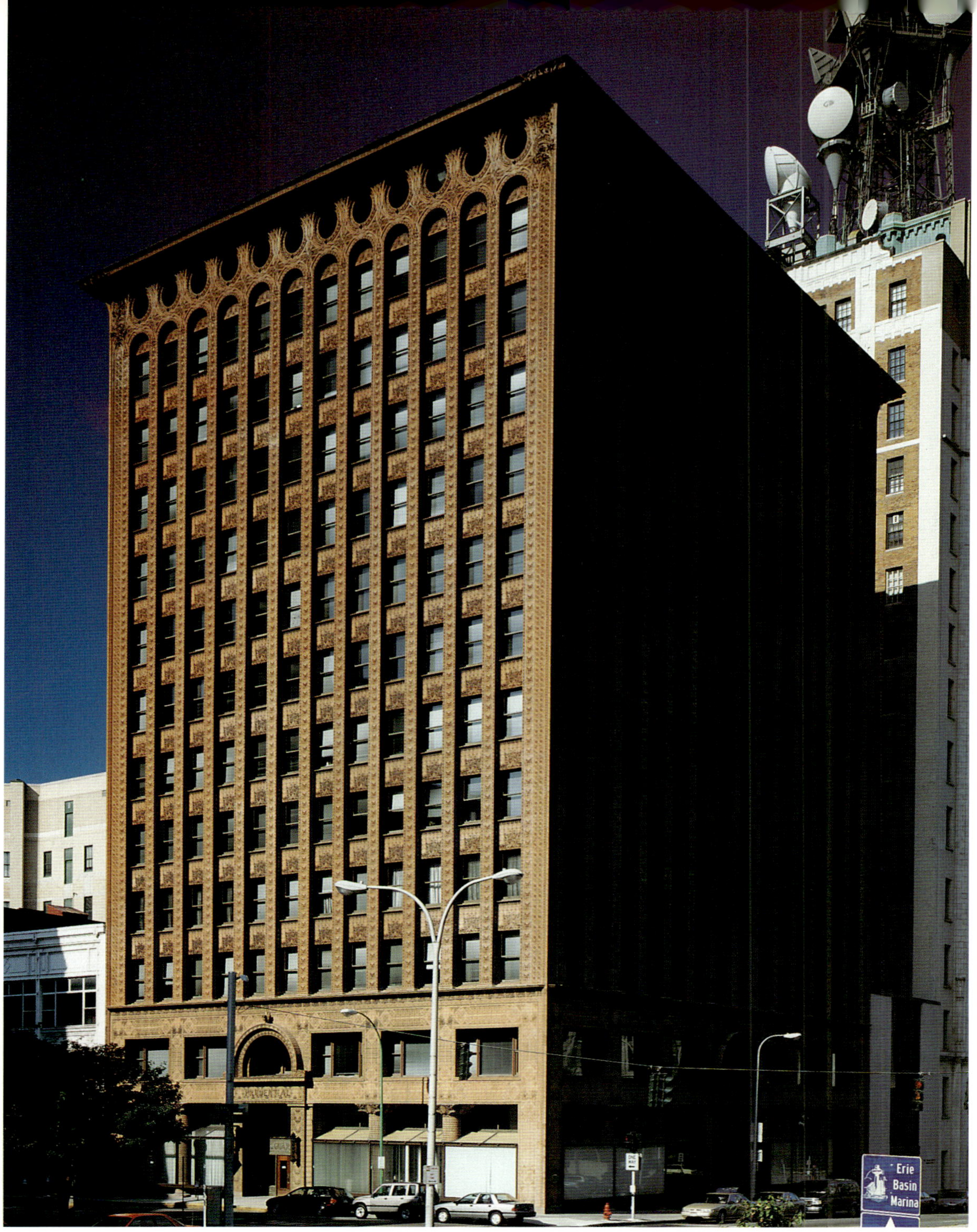

Regarded as one of famed architect Lewis Sullivan's most impressive works, this early steel-frame skyscraper was completed at the corner of Church and Pearl Streets in 1896. **The Guaranty Building's** lavish red terra cotta ornamentation is an Art Nouveau rendering of a nature theme based on sprouting seeds and growing plants. Photo by Marc Murphy.

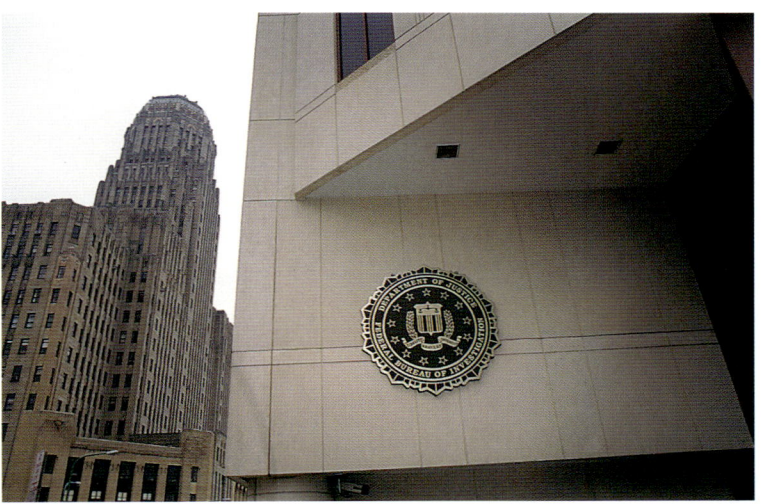

The federal government continued to demonstrate its confidence in the future of downtown Buffalo with the commission of this new three-story office building for the 17-county Western New York region of the **Federal Bureau of Investigation** in 1995. The privately owned building, called One FBI Plaza, joined three other federal office buildings within a few blocks of Niagara Square. Photo by James P. McCoy.

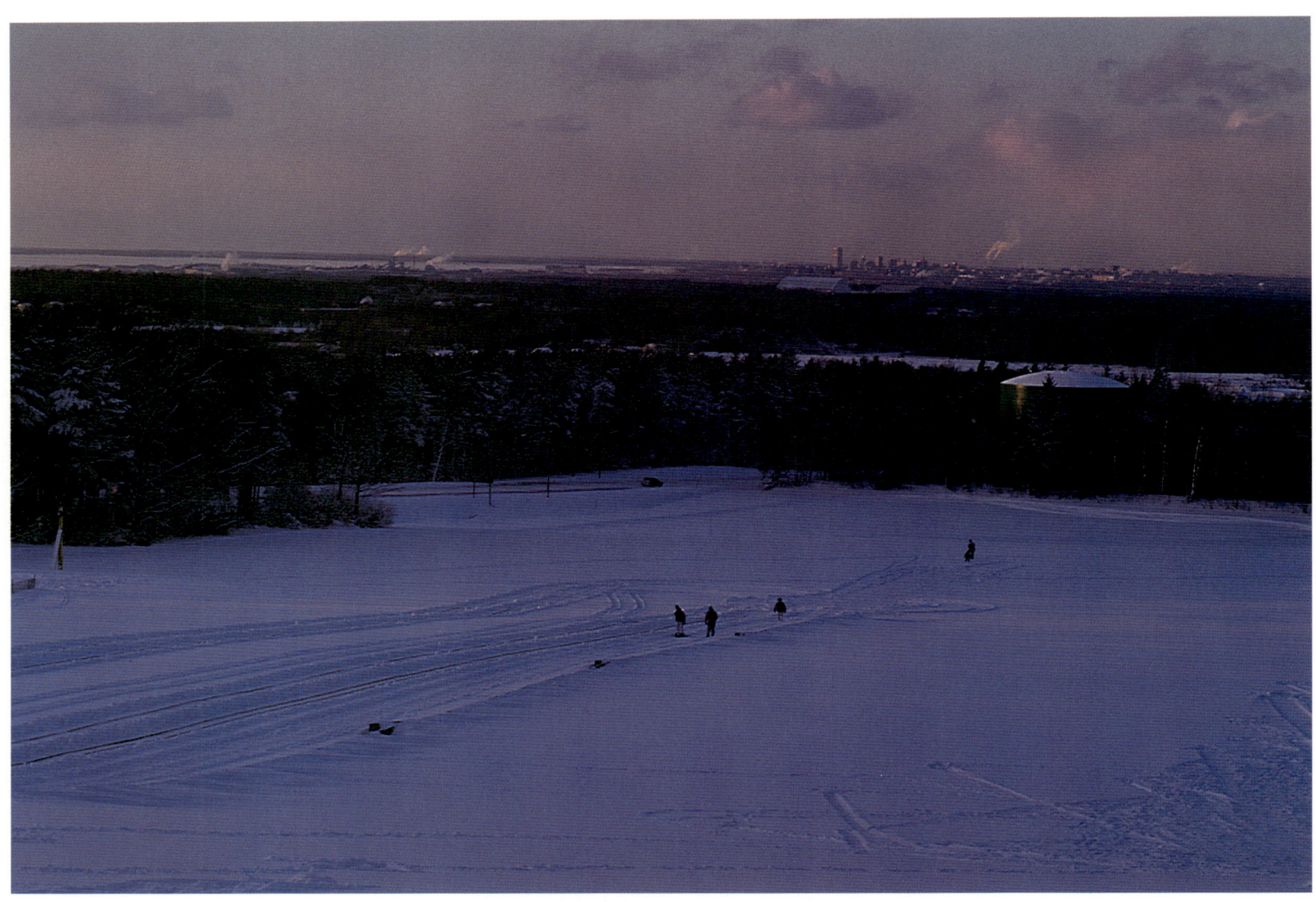

Atop Chestnut Ridge Park's toboggan
hill in **Orchard Park**, New York, a clear
day offers a panoramic view of Niagara
including the Buffalo Bills stadium and
Ralph Wilson Fieldhouse nearby,
with the Buffalo city skyline
glimmering in the distance.
Photo by James P. McCoy.

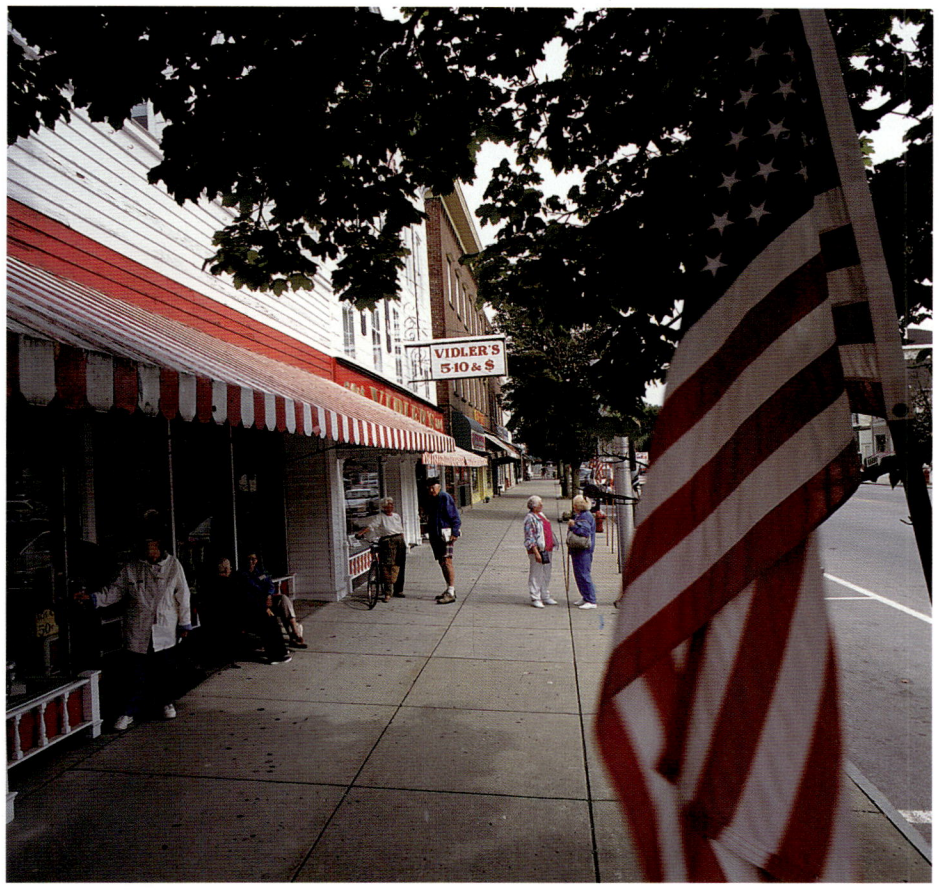

The euphoniously named village of **East Aurora** is famous both as the former residence of Millard Fillmore and the home of Elbert Hubbard's Roycroft craftsmen's guild. Beloved by residents for its graceful, quiet streets and neighborly Main Street business district, the town is also well known as the birthplace and headquarters of the Fisher-Price toy company.
Photo by James P. McCoy.

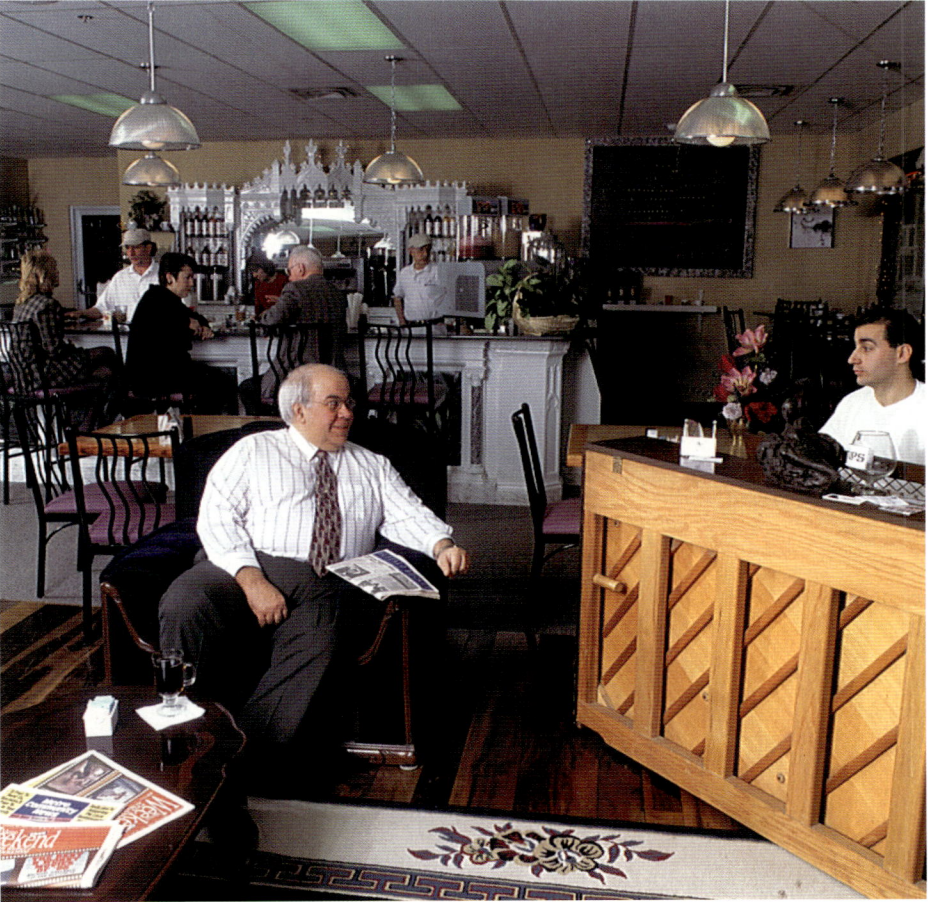

Less self-consciously chic than Elmwood, **Hertel Avenue** is more reflective of its surrounding neighborhood of Italian, Sicilian, Jewish, and Greek ethnic groups. In the bars of Hertel Avenue, they're more likely to be talking defense than deconstructivism.
Photo by James P. McCoy.

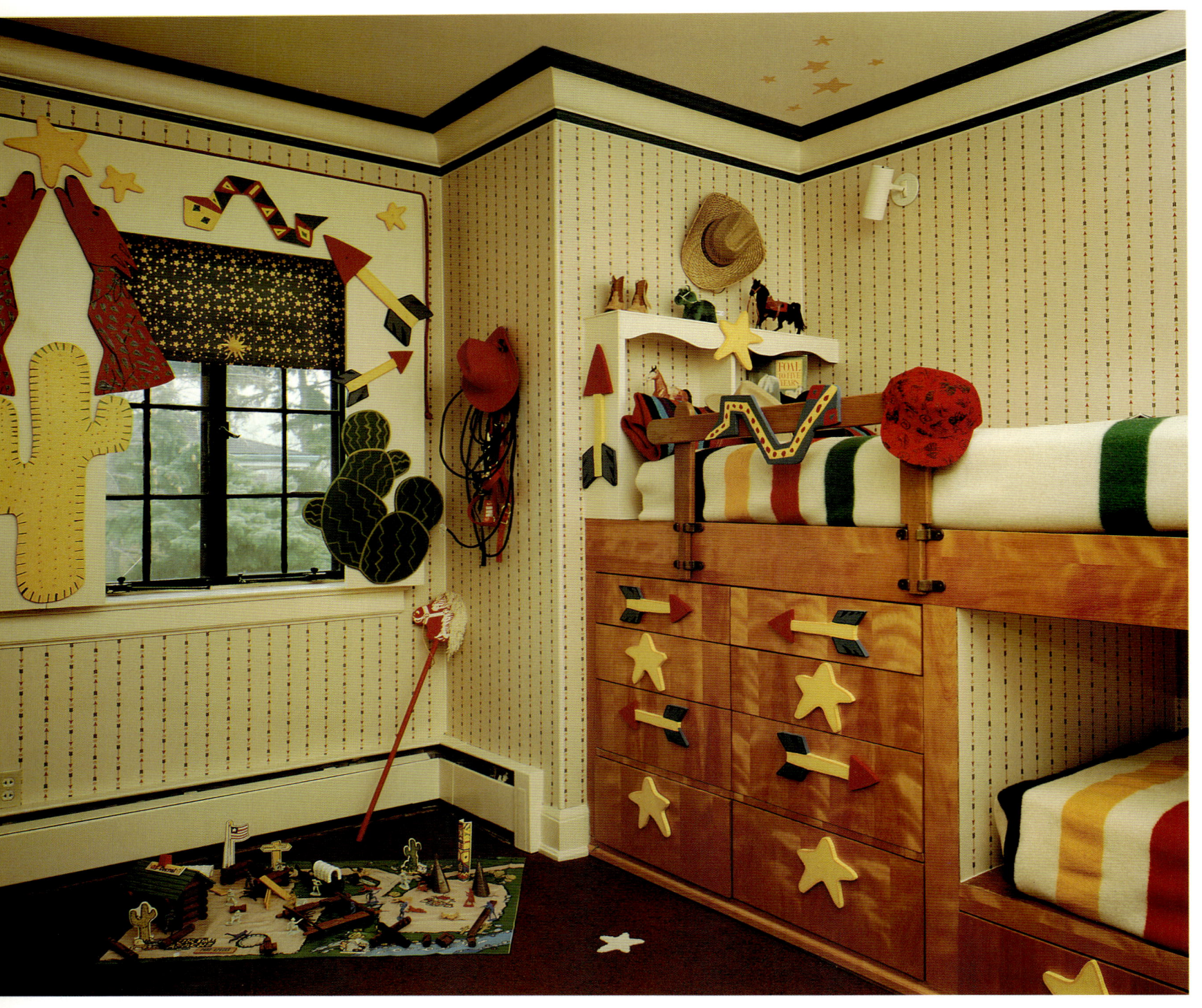

This interesting biennial event combines architectural tourism with charitable fund-raising. Sponsored by the Junior League and the *Buffalo News*, the **Decorators' Show House** displays the talents and creativity of local interior designers and decorators in a house of historical or architectural significance. The event also includes lectures, group tours, and special viewings of the house. Interior decorators get three months to transform the house, the public gets a grand tour of the mansion (for a nominal admission), and the selected charity receives the proceeds. Photo by Marc Murphy.

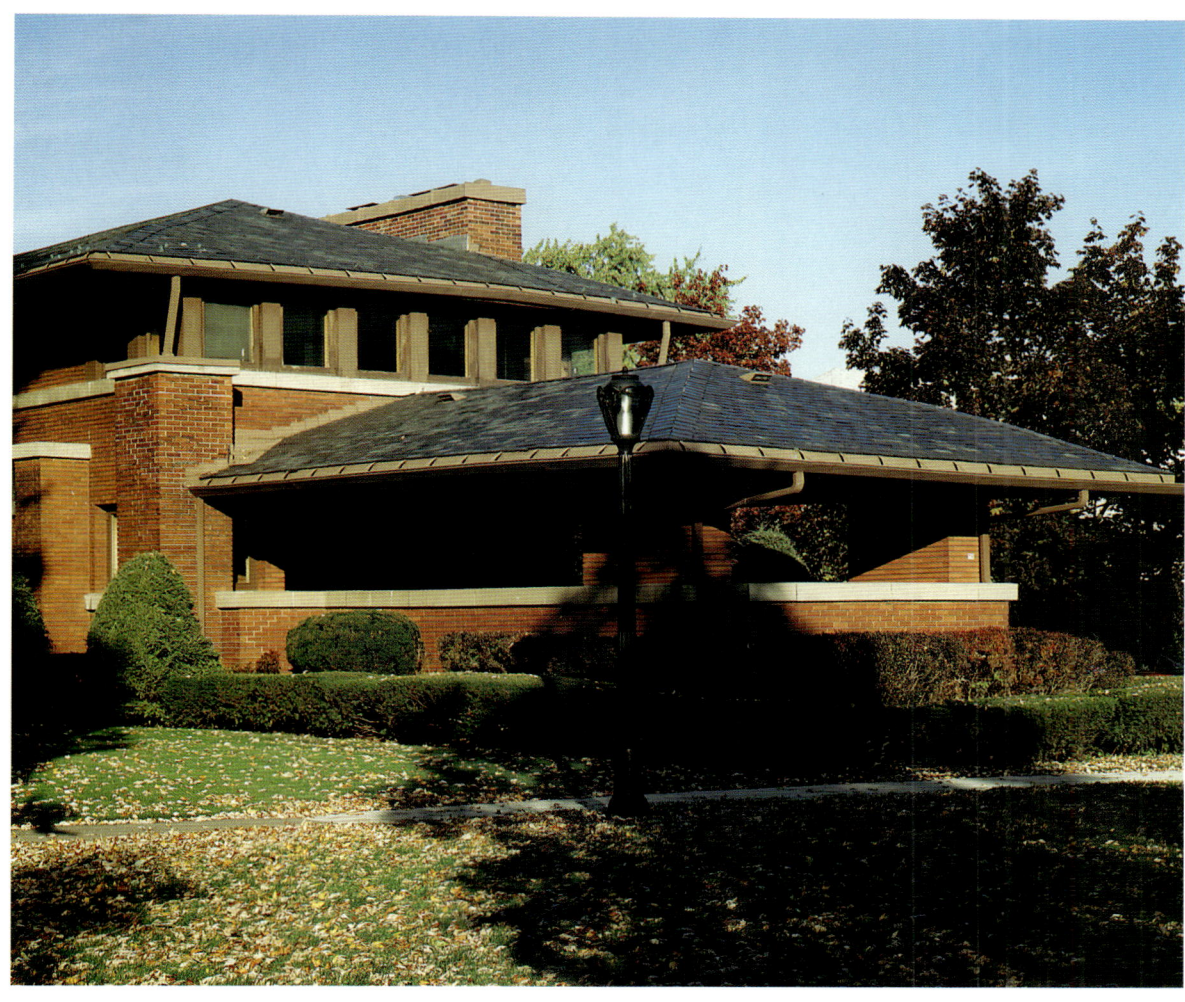

The **Heath House** at Soldier's Place and Bird Avenue was designed by **Frank Lloyd Wright** for William R. Heath and his family in 1904-05. The house, which has many similarities to Wright's Robie House in Chicago, is a fine example of the prairie style built on a long narrow lot. William Heath worked as office manager and vice president of the Larkin Company. Mrs. Heath was the sister of Elbert Hubbard, another Larkin executive, who later founded the Roycroft community in East Aurora.
Photo by Marc Murphy.

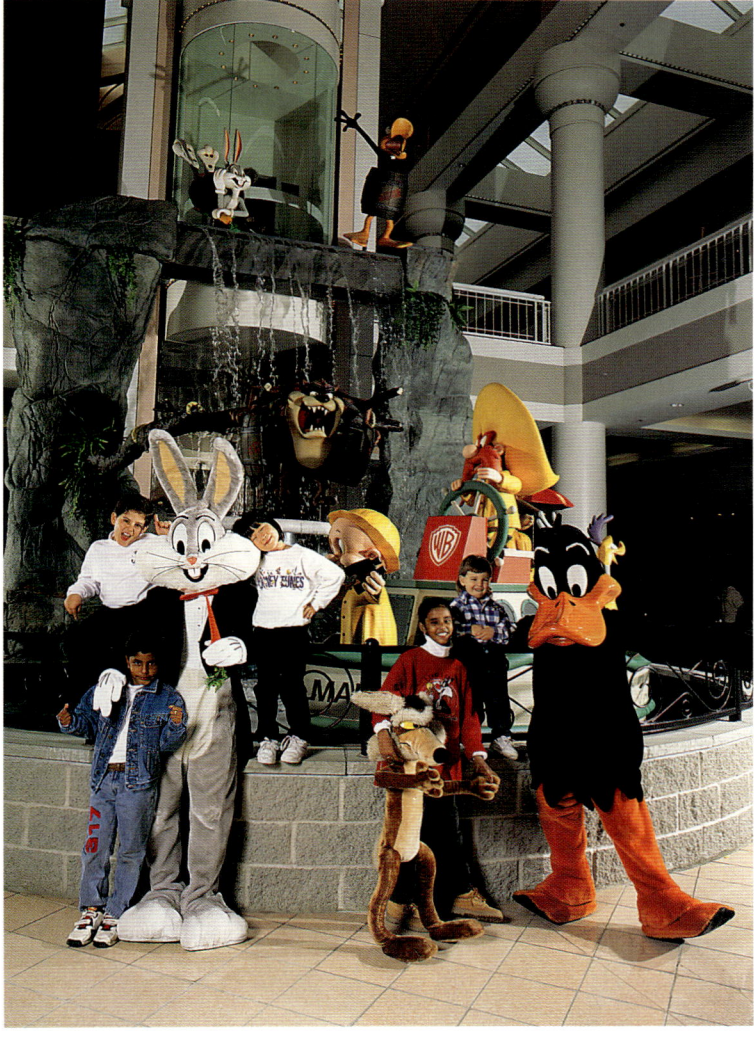

The Walden Galleria Mall, 1.6 million square feet of upscale retailing, has brought a boom of construction and a diverse array of new stores, restaurants, and supercenters to this sprawling eastern Buffalo suburb of Cheektowaga. With over 220 Galleria stores doing in excess of $350 million in business annually, Walden Galleria is the anchor for many successful new commercial enterprises in the area. Each year, the Galleria attracts 16 million shoppers, each of who travel an average of 30 miles to shop at the two-story mall.
Photo by James P. McCoy.

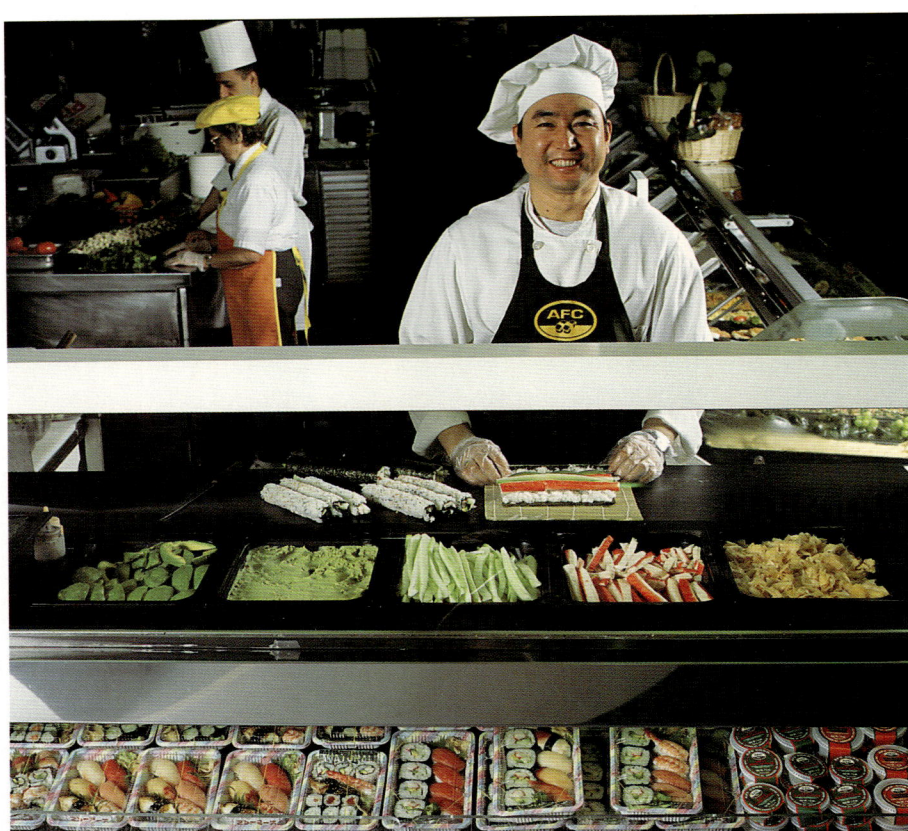

Got a craving for sushi but not in a restaurant mood? At many **Tops Friendly Markets**, you can pick up some freshly prepared California rolls or sashimi and slip them in your shopping cart next to the breakfast cereal. Tops, the area's leading supermarket with over 35 stores, also offers its superstore customers a dazzling array of imported beers and aisle after gleaming aisle of groceries and other products.
Photo by James P. McCoy.

Three days a week during the growing season, the pickups, vans, and delivery-size trucks arrive in the predawn hours and back into their familiar stalls at the **Clinton-Bailey Market** on Buffalo's East Side. In these early hours, some 25 to 50 farmers and growers do a brisk wholesale business selling produce to buyers for area restaurants, hotels, small stores, and supermarkets. After daybreak, the retail crowd arrives to inspect the fresh fruits and vegetables, homemade baked goods, honey, cider, plants, flowers, shrubs, and trees. In operation since 1931, the market is open for retail business six days a week.
Photo by James P. McCoy.

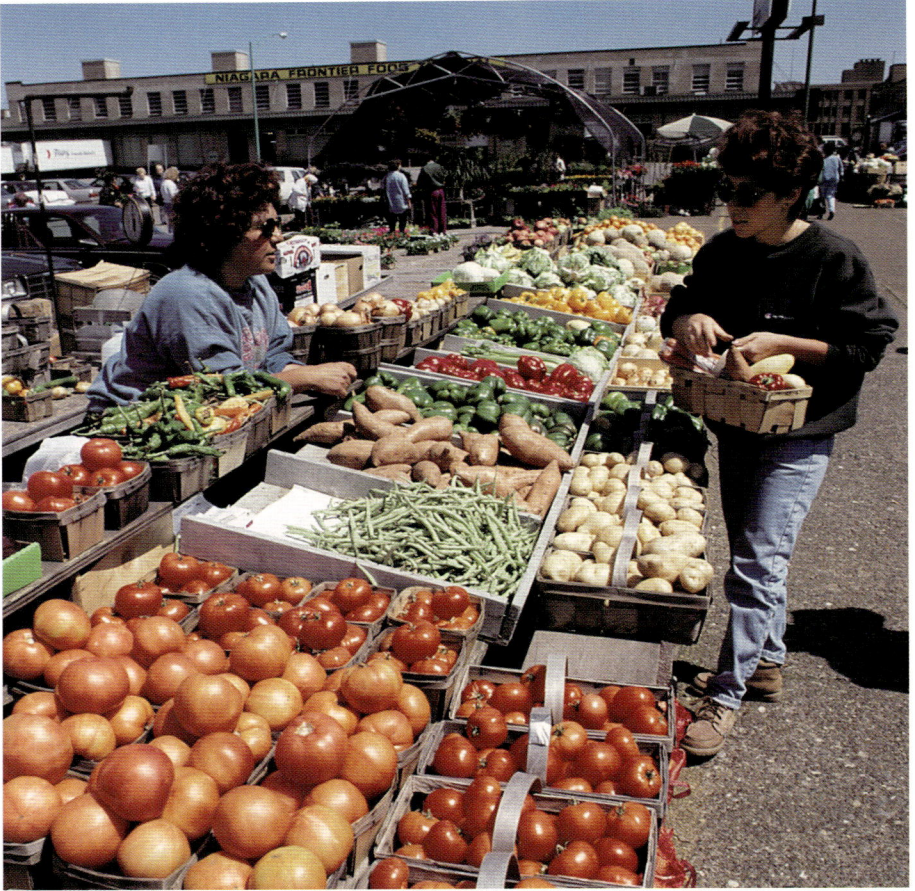

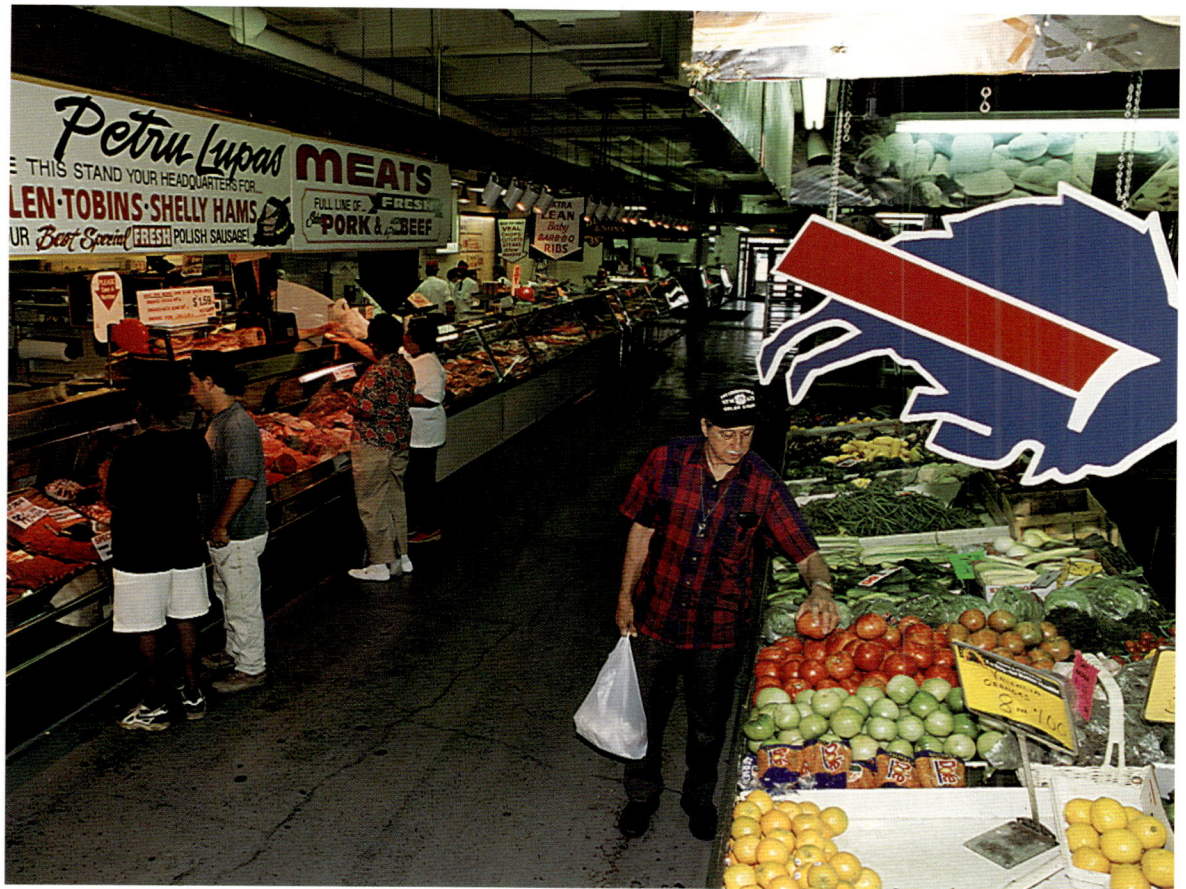

In the early years of the 20th century, the Broadway-Fillmore area was the heart of Buffalo's Polish community and the second-busiest commercial district in the city, after downtown. Today, although most of the heirs of Polonia have moved to Cheektowaga and other suburbs, the **Broadway Market**, a large enclosed public marketplace of ethnic specialty shops and stalls, still serves the remaining Poles as well as the growing African-American community. On weekends and holidays the market is packed with suburbanites shopping for Polish sausage, homemade pierogi, fresh horseradish, baked placek and chruschki, fancy candy, and butter lambs. And who can resist a quick lunch of beef on weck or a fried bologna sandwich?
Photo by James P. McCoy.

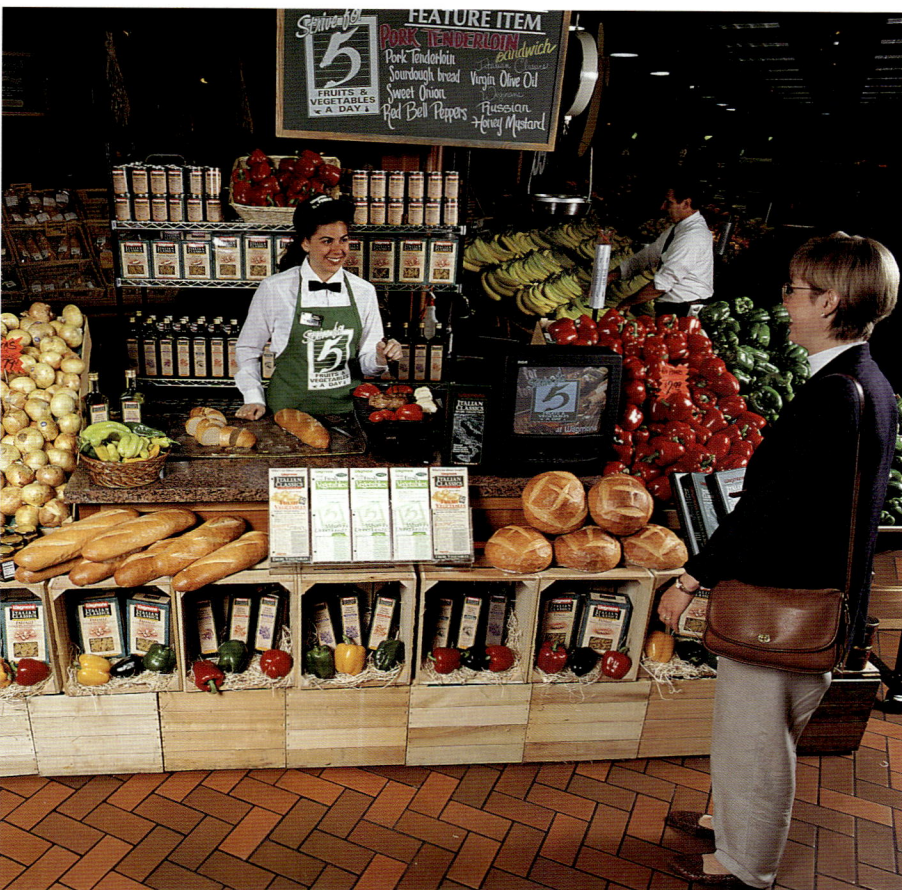

Wegmans, which began as a Rochester fruit market, is now the number two supermarket in Buffalo and its suburbs and renowned throughout Niagara for its exceptional open market-style produce departments and gourmet takeout foods.
Photo by James P. McCoy.

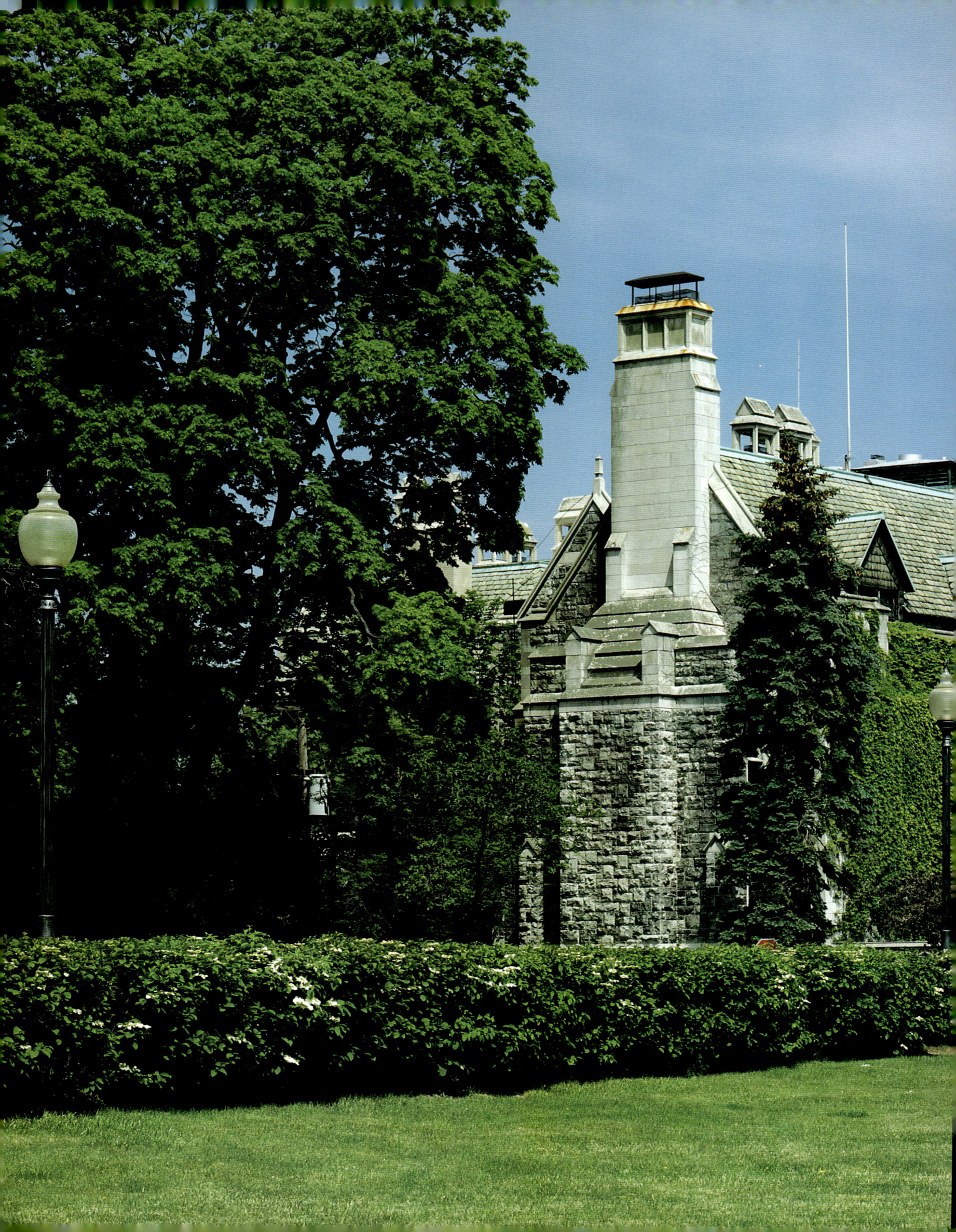

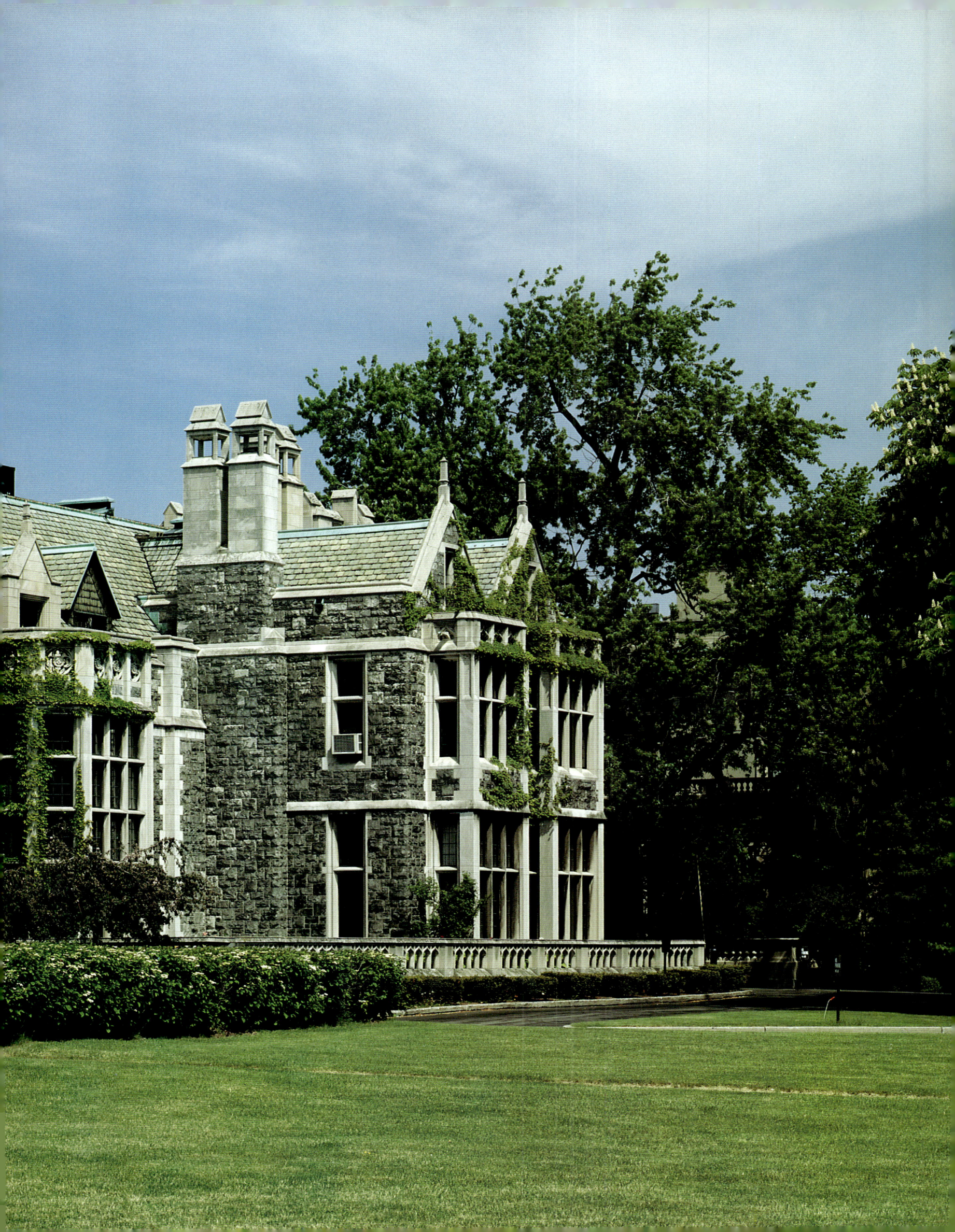

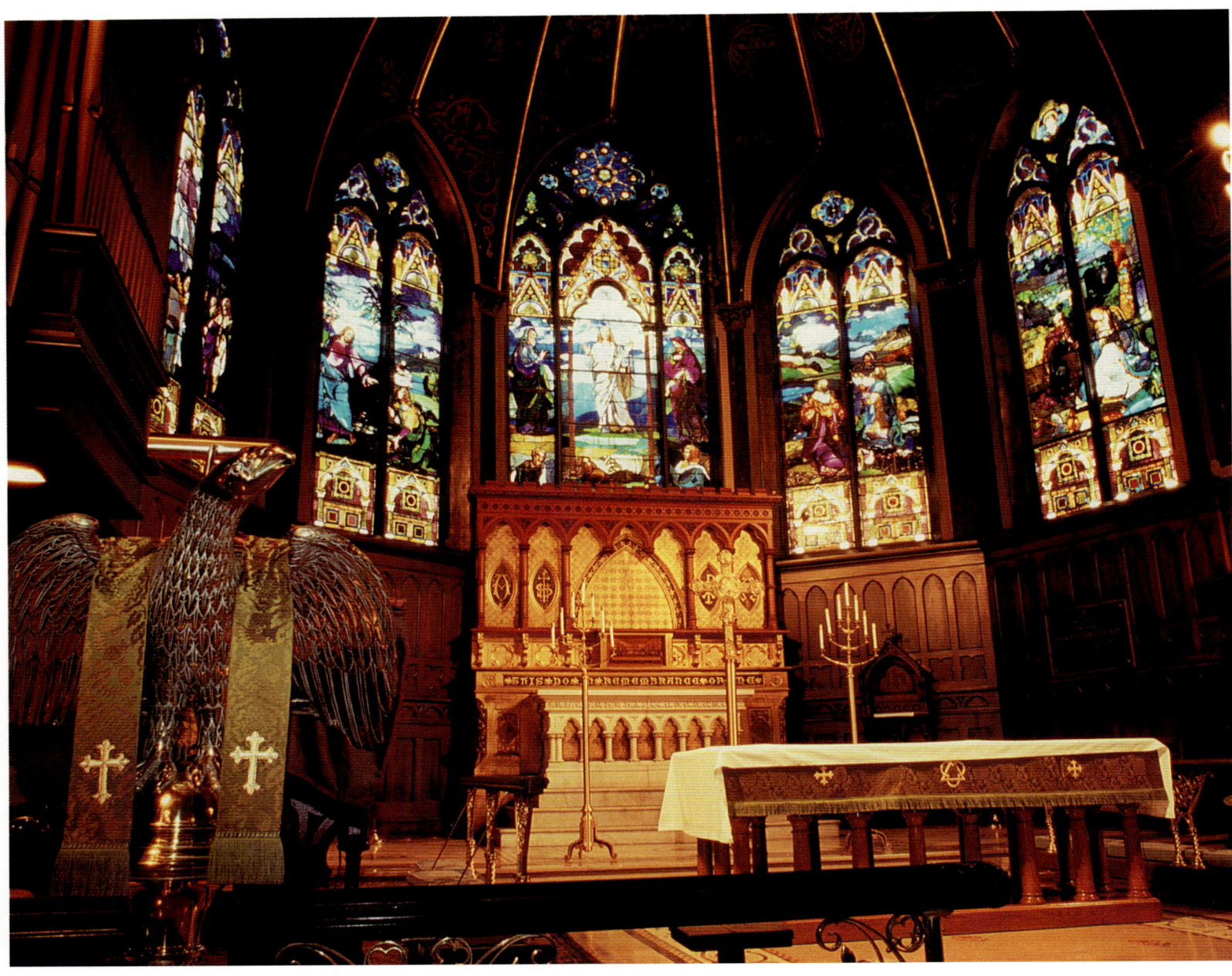

(previous page) At the close of the 19th century, **Delaware Avenue** was regarded as one of the most impressive residential streets in the nation. Beginning with Dr. Ebenezer Johnson's domed Palladian villa on 25 acres between Chippewa and Tupper in 1833, a procession of increasingly elaborate and expensive mansions went up on Delaware as Buffalo expanded northward from Niagara Square to Forest Lawn Cemetery. This mansion is now home to the American Red Cross.
Photo by Marc Murphy.

In the 1880s, **Trinity Episcopal** was built on the foundations of an earlier church designed by Arthur Gilman of Boston in 1869 but never completed. Trinity, with its great beamed ceiling and magnificent stain-glass windows by John La Farge and the Tiffany studios, is an exceptionally beautiful sanctuary. In *The Grand American Avenue*, Francis R. Kowsky describes the effect from the pews: "On a bright day, the procession of colored windows that ring the dark and spacious interior glow like gems."
Photo by James P. McCoy.

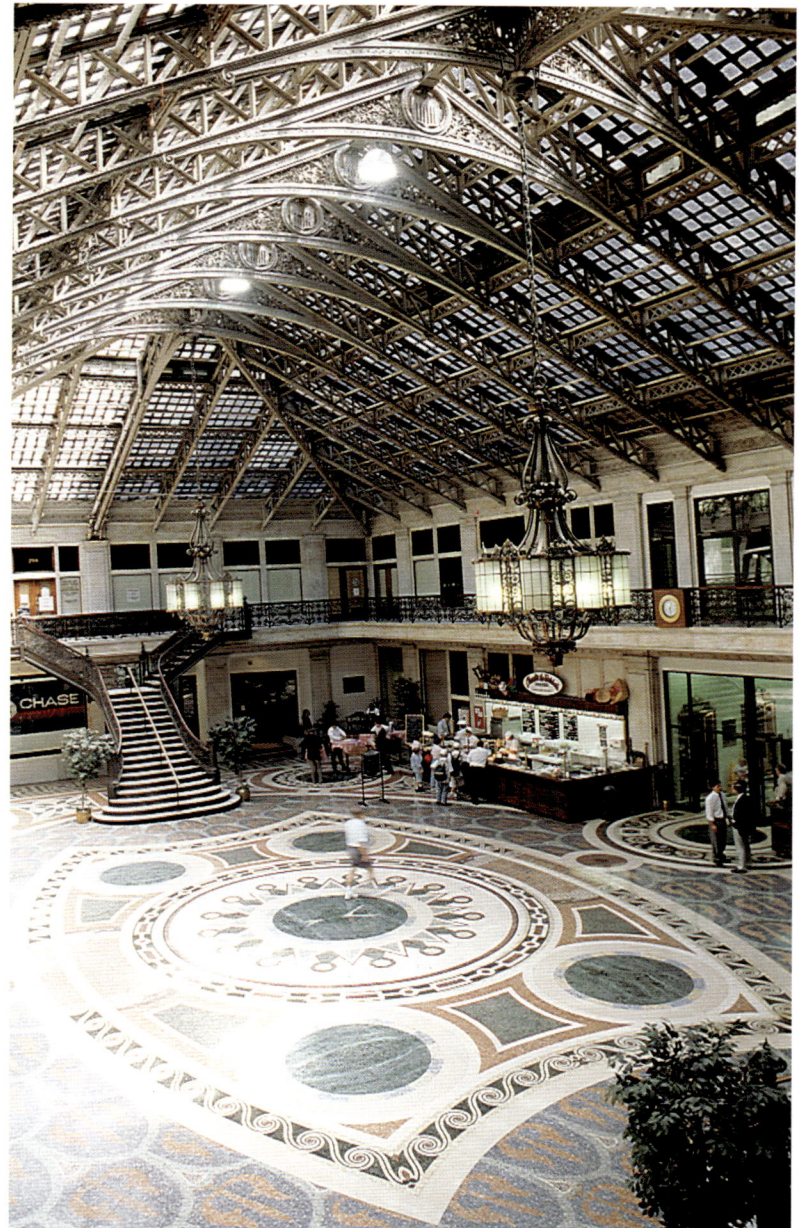

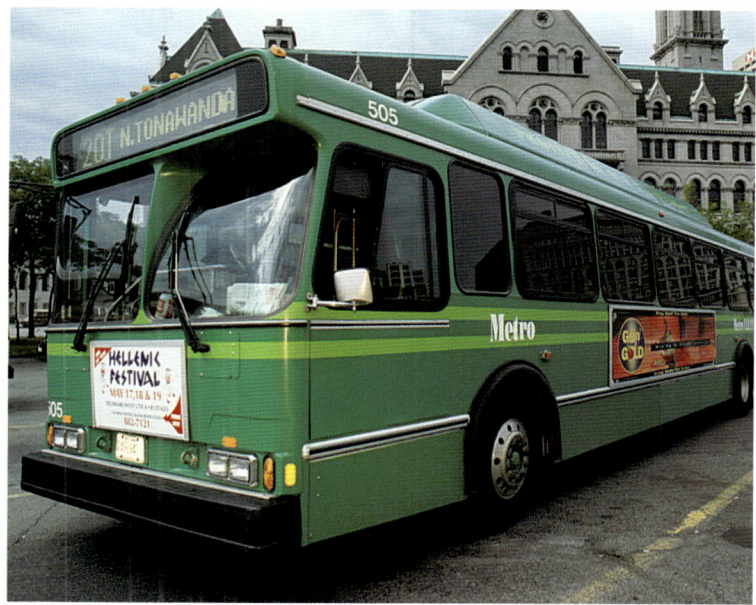

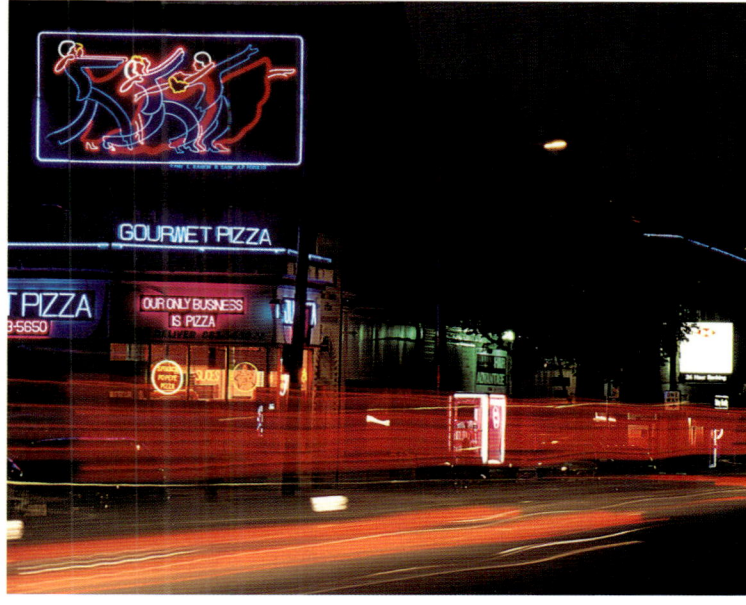

Once the world's largest office building, **Ellicott Square** comprises an entire city block and encloses a huge atrium covered by a great steel and glass skylight. From the grand central court, twin curving wrought-iron stairways sweep up to a second story balustrade. An Italian mosaic floor is inlaid with colorful sun symbols. Bronze elevator doors at both entrances feature panels engraved with symbols of the city's history.
Photo by James P. McCoy.

A ride on the bus is also part of a drive for cleaner air when you board a **Green Machine**, a bus powered by compressed natural gas. The Niagara Frontier Transportation Authority currently operates five natural gas buses as part of a federally assisted program to study alternative fuels. Natural gas reduces exhaust emissions and burns more efficiently than gasoline.
Photo by James P. McCoy.

Once Buffalo's great avenues were canopied with tall elm trees that the French writer André Maurois, gazing out from his room at the Hotel Lenox in 1941, described as "seas of verdure." The elms long ago fell to the fungus *Ceratocystis uimi* spread by elm bark beetles, and today Elmwood Avenue is best known as a successful commercial street centering on a diverse district of restaurants, bars, bookstores, coffeehouses, record stores, and gift shops. Close to downtown, the waterfront, the border, the Buffalo State campus, and surrounded by a strong, stable neighborhood, the vitality of the **Elmwood Strip** attracts visitors from all over Niagara.
Photo by James P. McCoy.

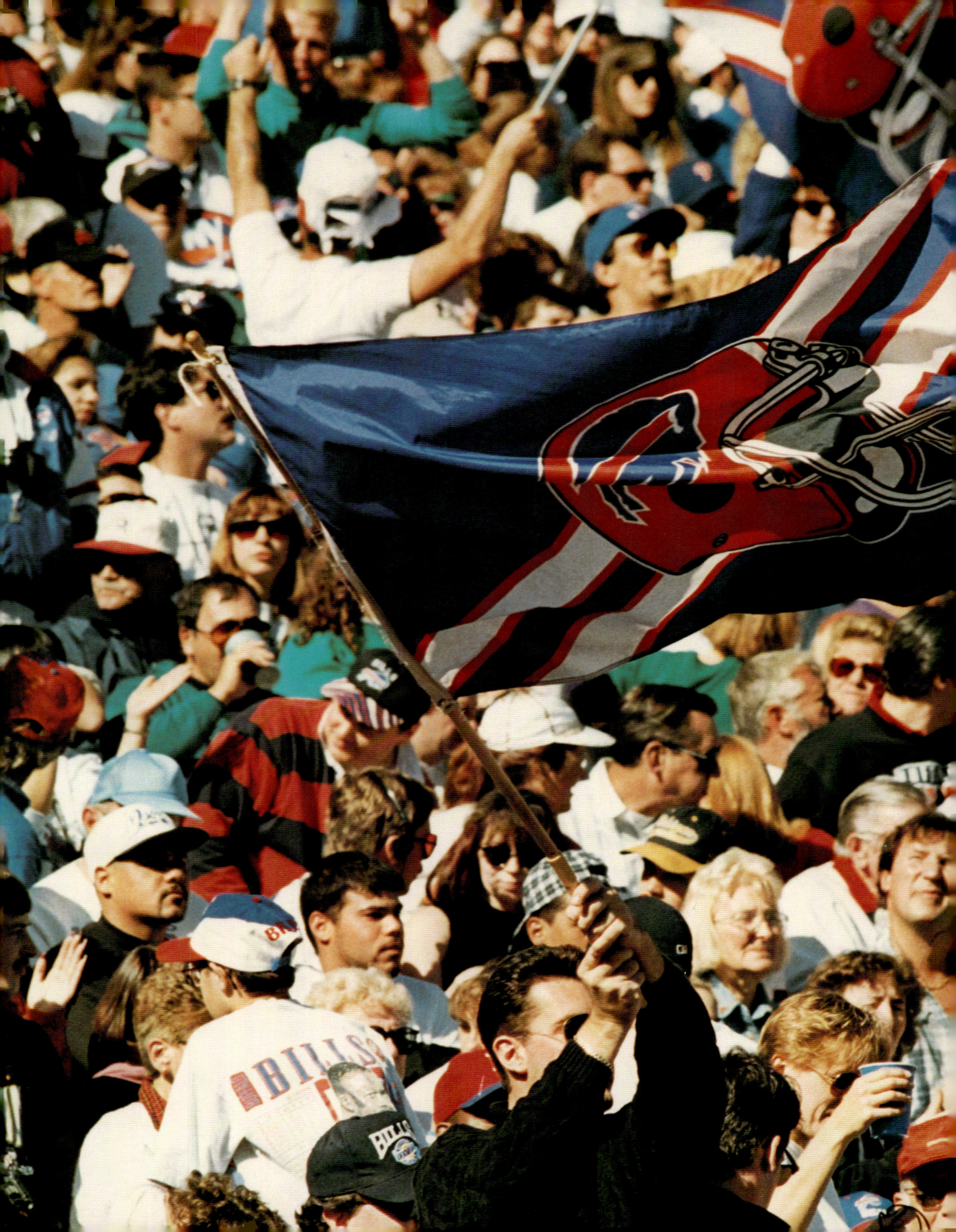

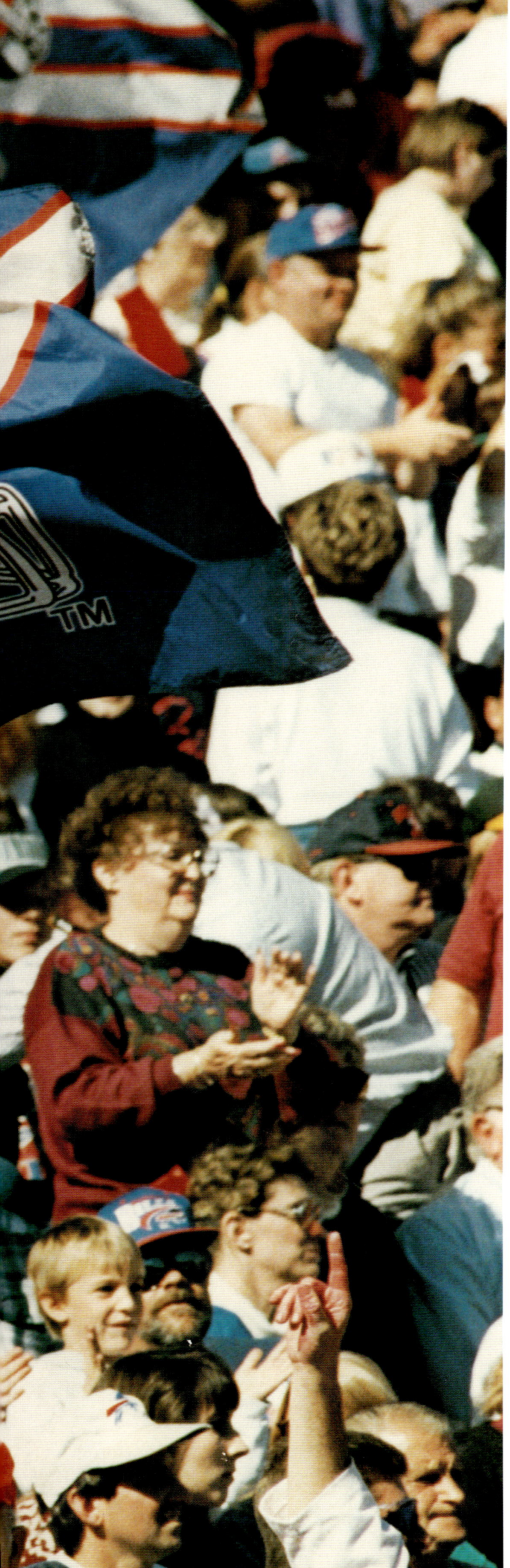

THE SPORTING LIFE

It's a gorgeous Sunday afternoon and the streets are practically deserted. People don't answer their phones. A car door slams and the aroma of fresh pizza drifts across the street. Another door opens and a stream of sound pours out—shouting, cheering, laughing, whoops, and hollers—that nearly drowns out the excited professional tones of a television announcer in the background. The door closes and the street is quiet again. World Series? Super Bowl? Stanley Cup? The Summer Olympics? No, it's just another Bills game day in Niagara.

Photo by James P. McCoy.

In the world of professional team sports, few teams have managed to inspire the kind of fan loyalty and passion that seems to affect the mental health of an entire region. Buffalo Bills fans have taken fandom to near fanaticism, maybe even to the edge of madness. In Bills Country, it's not just guys in the stands festooned with red, white, and blue warpaint and naked to the waist singing "Shout!" in the depths of December. It's not just transplanted fans routinely driving hundreds of miles one way through the snow for a regular season game. It's not just thousands of people packed into Niagara Square for a Bills celebration the day after they lost a Super Bowl. When the Bills come charging out of the tunnel and onto the field, it's pure, unconditional, to-die-for love.

Other professional teams also draw enormous financial and emotional support from area fans. Buffalo Sabres NHL hockey, Bison International League baseball, Bandits championship indoor lacrosse, and Blizzard soccer provide year-round thrills and excitement.

The Sabres, who began life as an NHL expansion team in 1970, were the creation of Seymour Knox III and his brother Northrup Knox, longtime Buffalo-area sportsmen. Within just five seasons, the Sabres, led by the brilliant "French Connection" of Gilbert Perreault, Rick Martin, and Rene Robert, reached the Stanley Cup playoffs where they defeated the Montreal Canadiens in an exciting semifinal series, then lost to the Philadelphia Flyers in the finals.

Today, a glittering new sports facility on downtown Buffalo's waterfront is home for the Sabres, the Bandits, the Blizzard, and host to college basketball and major concerts and events. Marine Midland Arena, a $127.5 million public and private joint venture, is the anchor for the restoration and development of the Cobblestone district, a 19th-century commercial and industrial area distinguished by its historic buildings and streets of stone and brick.

Next door, along the Buffalo River, an Inner Harbor project is taking shape that will include a harborwalk around the river linking the Cobblestone area with the Naval and Servicemen's Park, the Erie Basin Marina, La Salle Park and the Riverwalk trail extending to North Tonawanda. Plans are also afoot for a swing bridge to provide hiking and biking access from the Inner Harbor to the Outer Harbor and its gallant old 1831 lighthouse.

Just a few blocks north of the Marine Midland Arena, another premier sports venue, North AmeriCare Park, is home to the International League's Buffalo Bisons, one of the nation's most successful minor league baseball clubs. The Bisons average annual attendance is over 1,000,000, a figure higher than that of some major league parks. In six of its first eight years at the park, the Buffalo Bisons set all-time minor league single-season attendance records.

The World University Games came to Niagara in the summer of 1993 and left a legacy of sports facilities. The pool at the Burt Flickinger Athletic Center, the Lewiston-Porter soccer stadium, and the track and field stadium at the University of Buffalo all host major national and regional amateur sports events. In 1996, the Empire State Games returned to Buffalo, and in the late 1990s, UB is the site of the NCAA Men's and Women's Division I Track and Field Championships. Meanwhile, in Batavia, the Clippers, a community-owned professional baseball team that has played continuously since 1939, opened their 1996 season in another new Western New York sports venue, the 2,500-seat Dwyer Stadium.

While the opening of the spacious Marine Midland Arena in 1996 was cause for celebration, fans that year also said a bittersweet goodbye to its predecessor, Memorial Auditorium. The Aud opened in 1940 with a ceremony dedicated to the memory of those who died in World War I. Over the next 56 years, the Aud played host to hockey, college basketball, soccer, lacrosse, circuses, Sinatra, Elvis, the Stones, ice shows, rodeos, tennis, boxing, and many other sports and entertainment events. For several seasons in the 1970s, the Buffalo Braves brought NBA basketball fever to the Aud behind their high-scoring star center, Bob McAdoo.

At the Sabres last game in the Aud, the team's patriarch, Seymour Knox III, represented the community's affection for the aging auditorium as he concluded his remarks with a brief adieu. "Farewell, old friend," said Knox with his brother at his side.

Alongside the thrills and memorable moments of professional team sports, Niagara is a hotbed of competitive and recreational sports. High school and college teams, summer softball leagues, golf, skiing, bowling, cycling, racing, running, sailing, synchronized swimming, tennis, squash, handball, and other sports activities lure hundreds of thousands of participants and spectators throughout the year.

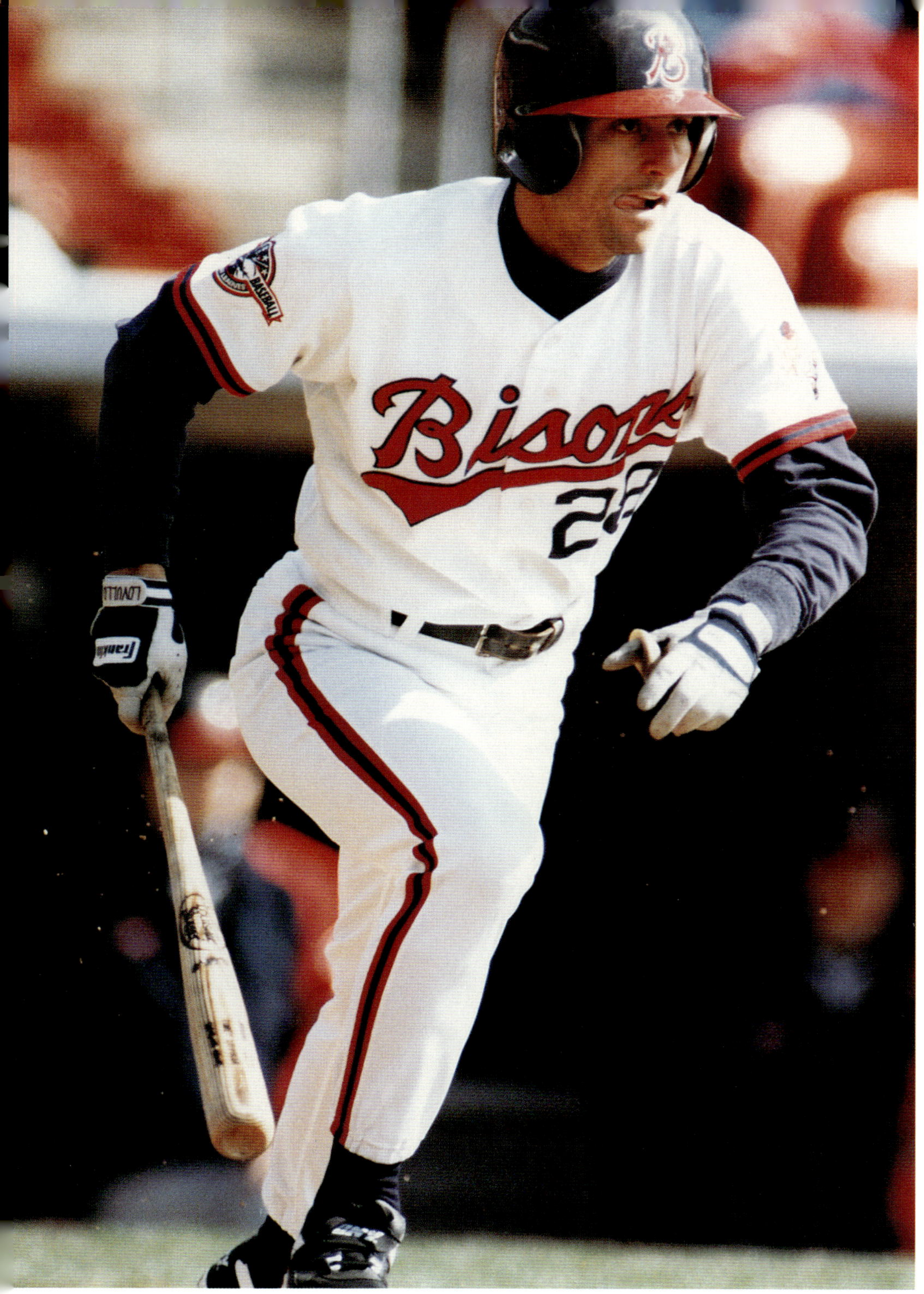

Since Robert E. Rich, Jr. brought Triple-A baseball to Buffalo in 1984, the city has renewed its love affair with the grand old game and the Bisons now are part of the International League. **Professional baseball** began in Buffalo in 1877, and many of the great former **Bison** players and managers are now enshrined in the Baseball Hall of Fame in Cooperstown. Among them are Connie Mack, Joe Tinker, Bill Dickey, Gabby Hartnett, Joe McCarthy, Lou Boudreau, Bucky Harris, Johnny Bench, and Ferguson Jenkins.
Photo by James P. McCoy.

Built for the World University Games, the Olympic-size swimming **pool at Erie Community College's Burt Flickinger Athletic Center** has been called one of the 10 best pools in the United States by athletic officials. The pool, which can accommodate eight 50-meter lanes lengthwise or sixteen 25-yard lanes across its width, is the site of the 1997 Senior Nationals. The athletic center also houses a basketball field house, classrooms, and a community athletic club with memberships available to all residents of Erie County.
Photo by James P. McCoy.

The Royal Canadian Henley Regatta is a renowned international rowing competition on one of the oldest rowing courses in North America. Every summer since 1903, this five-day event has been rowed on historic Martindale Pond near Port Dalhousie, Ontario. Twenty-three hundred rowers from Peru, Cuba, Europe, and North America competed in the 1996 Royal Canadian Henley Regatta. The 2000-meter Canadian Henley course has been selected as the site of the 1999 World Rowing Championships.

Itching to hit the fairways? There are 100 public and private golf courses across Niagara. Fishing for excitement? Lake Erie is great for bass and walleyes, Lake Ontario offers lake trout and king salmon, and the inland lakes are a haven for walleyes, northern pike, crappies, bluegills, sunfish, and perch. Fly fishermen net brook, brown, and steelhead trout in dozens of scenic creeks and streams. Niagara's southern tier counties are home to abundant wildlife. Hunters bag pheasant, wild turkey, deer, grouse, raccoon, fox, squirrel, rabbit, woodcock, and waterfowl in area fields, forests, and ponds. ⸙

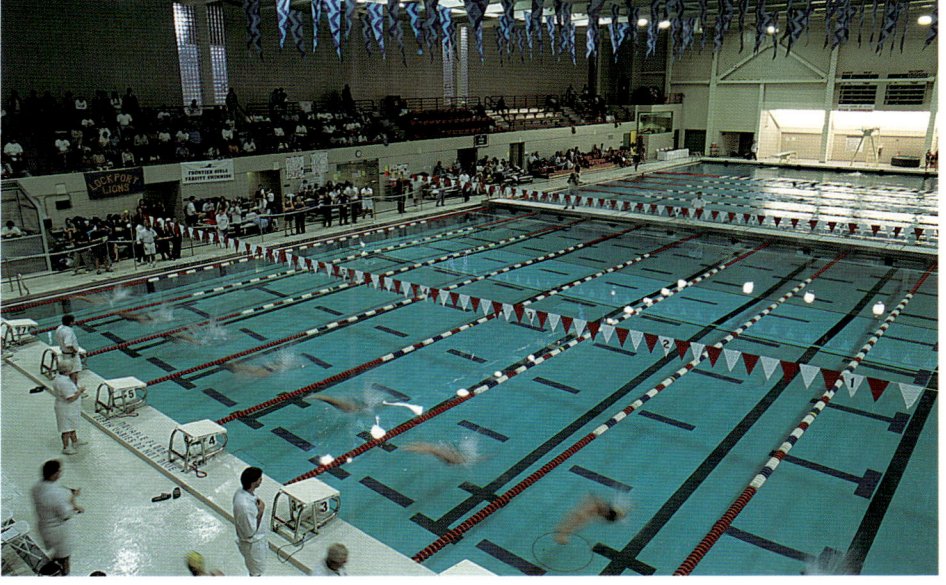

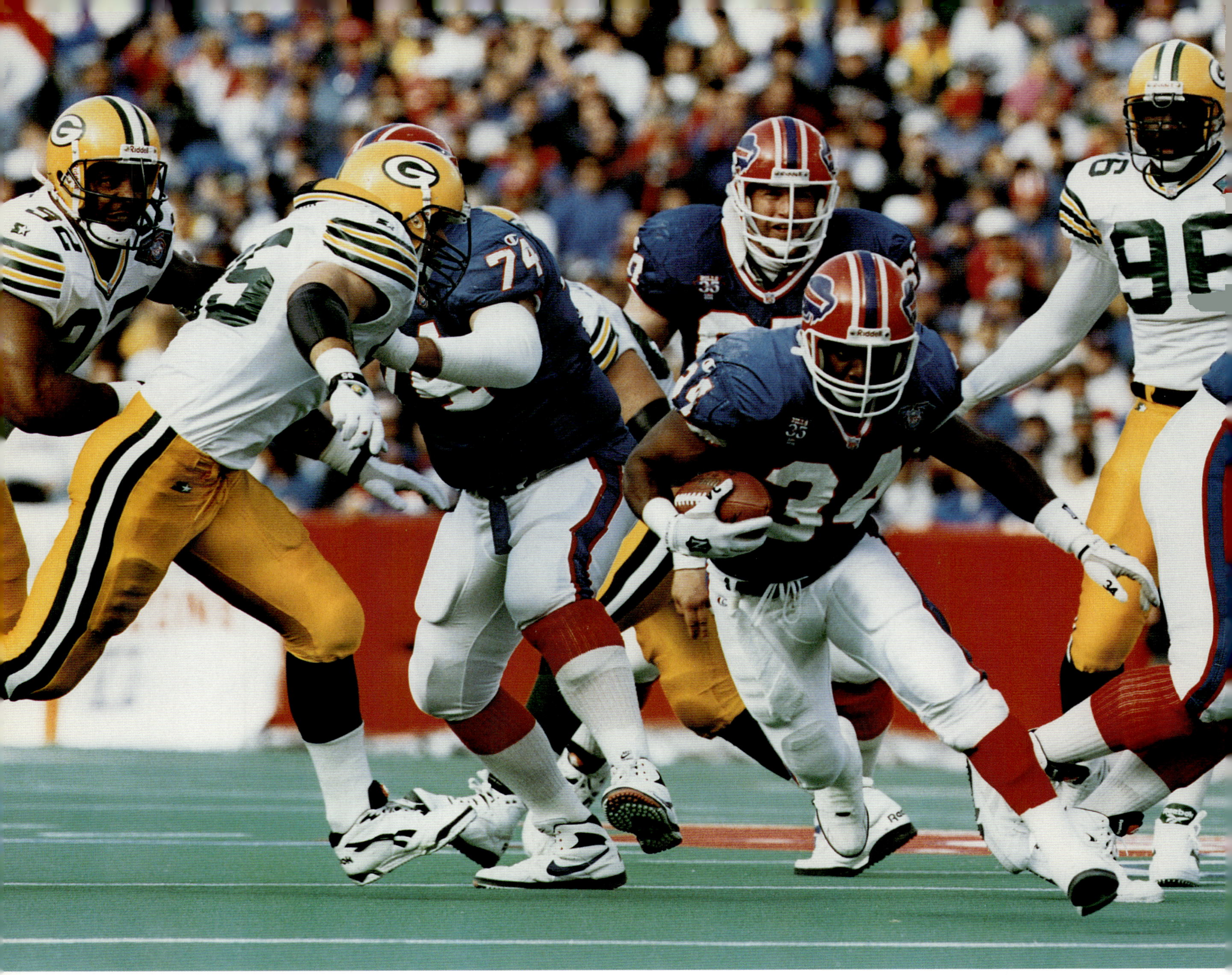

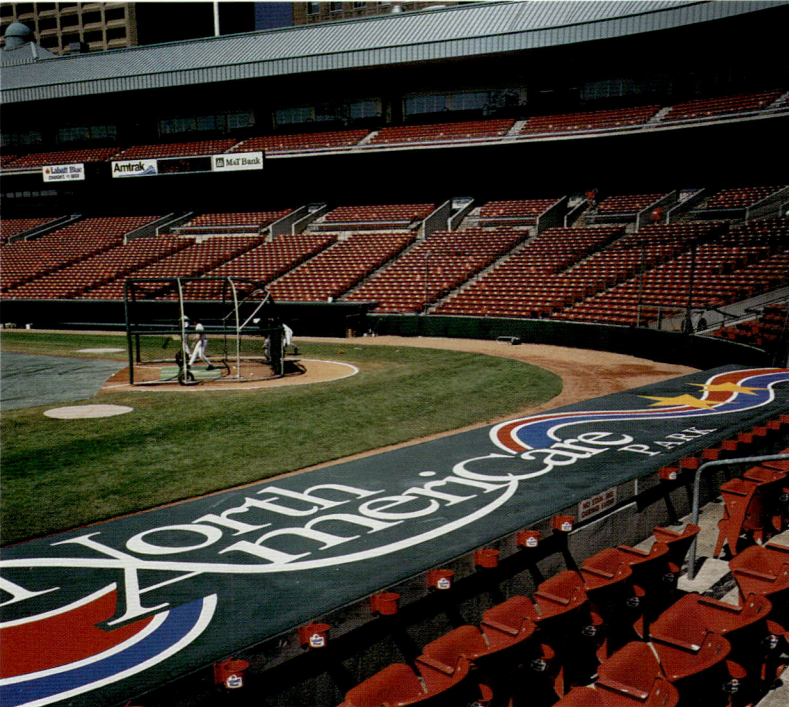

An autumn afternoon in Orchard Park with the beloved **Buffalo Bills** on the move—for 80,000 fans, there's no better place to be. The only team ever to play in four consecutive Super Bowls, the Bills are also one of a select group of NFL teams to have had just one owner— Ralph C. Wilson, Jr.—for the team's entire existence, almost 40 years. Photo by James P. McCoy.

North AmeriCare Park is home of the International League Buffalo Bisons baseball team. The ballpark is known as one of the finest baseball facilities in the nation, designed by H.O.K., whose many major league parks include Jacob's Field and Oriole Park at Camden Yards. Although primarily a baseball park, it has been host to a number of events and has drawn over 10 million fans since it first opened on April 14, 1988. Photo by Marc Murphy.

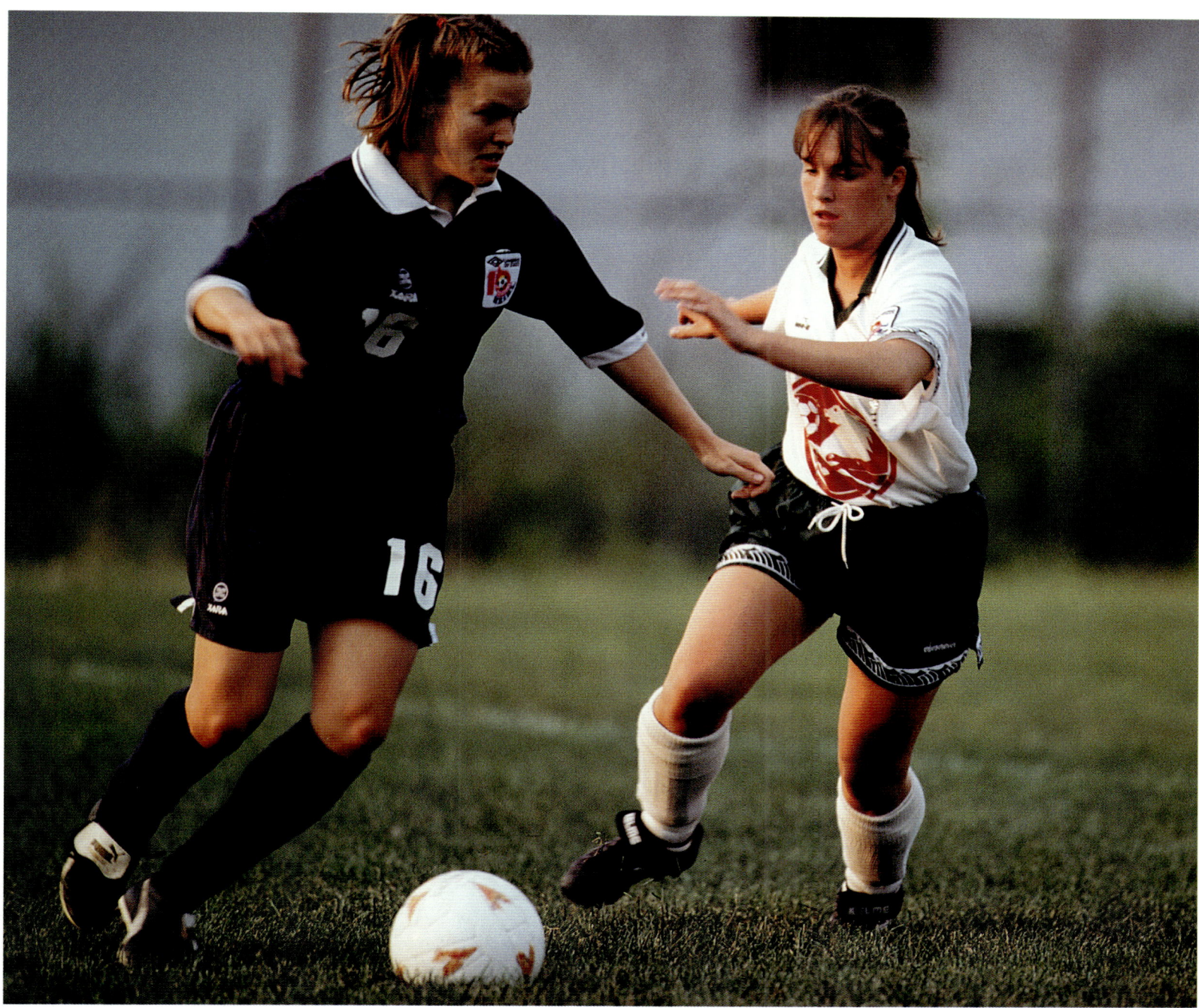

For the best of women's soccer action, fans head for the Lewiston-Porter Soccer Stadium to cheer on **the FFillies**, top-ranked collegiate and post-collegiate players who compete in a 12-game regular season schedule in the W League of the United Systems of Independent Soccer Leagues. Photo by James P. McCoy.

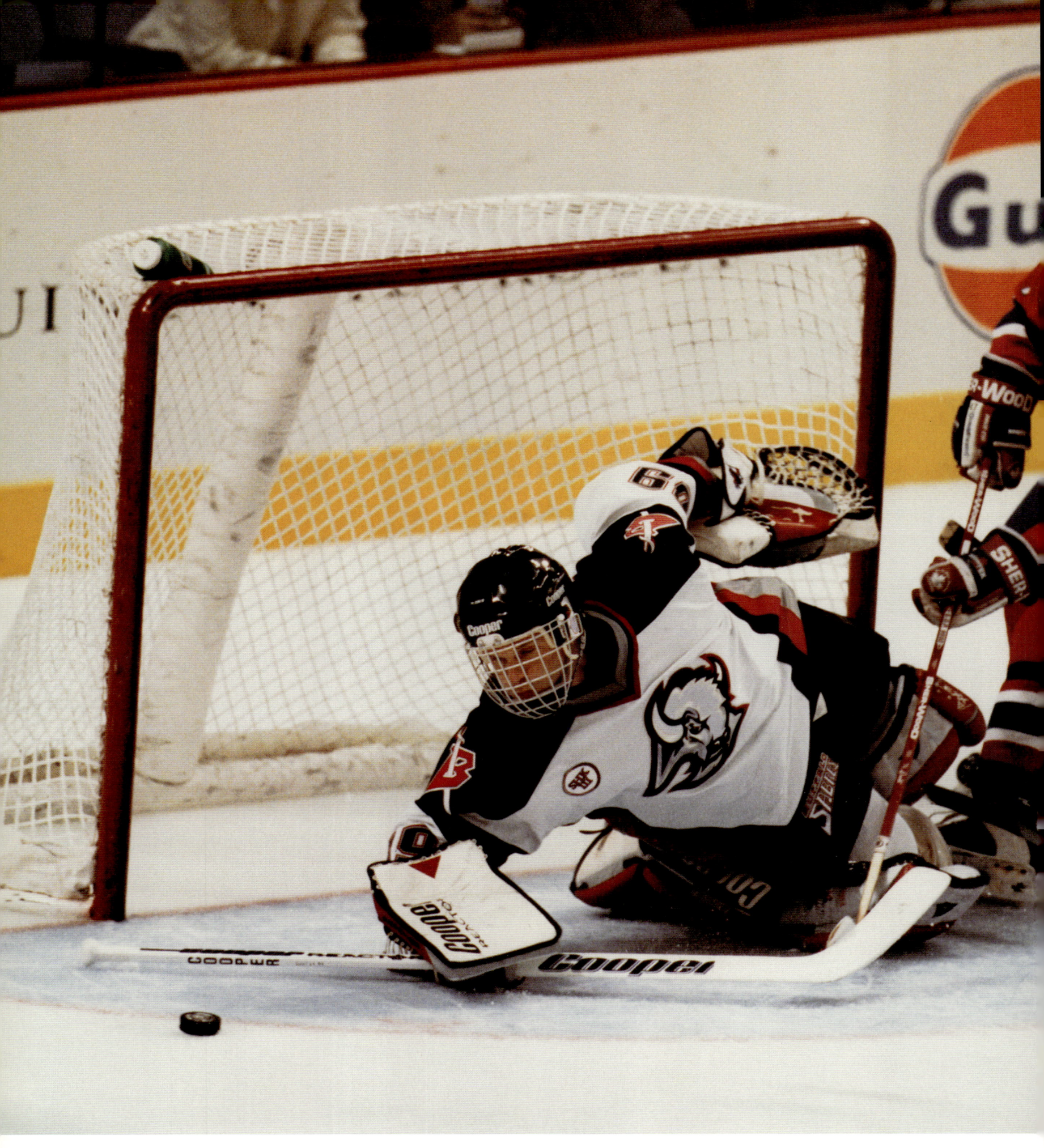

ATTRACTING THE WORLD

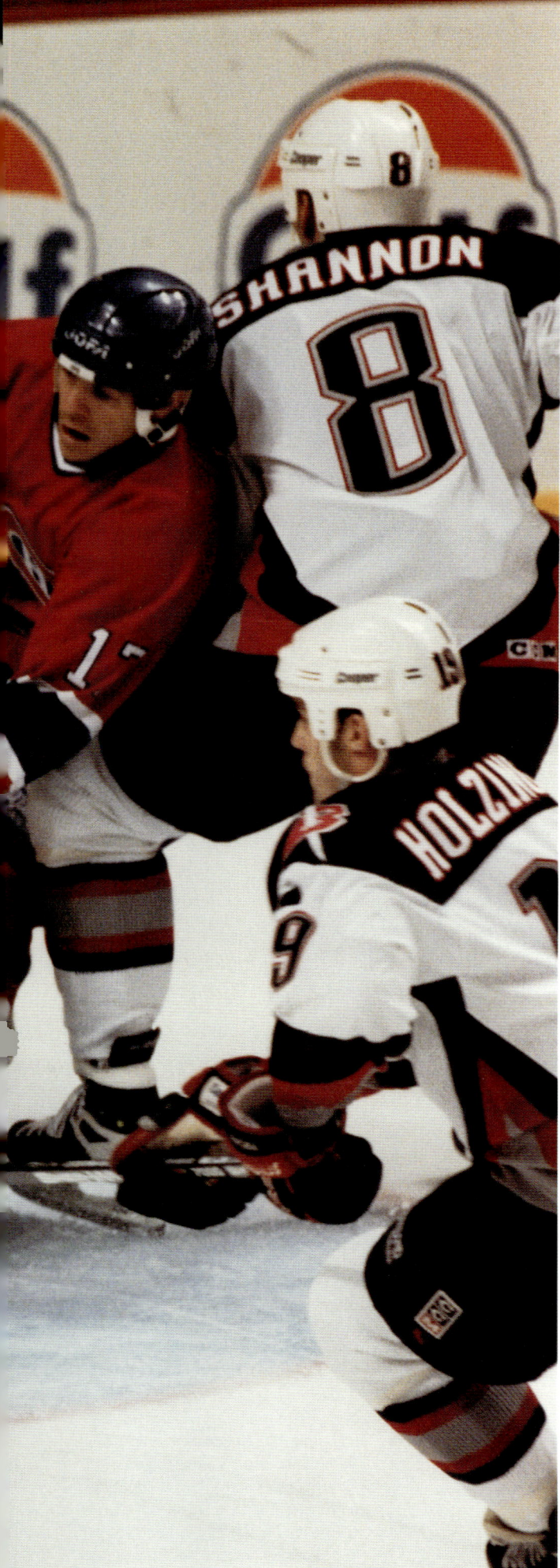

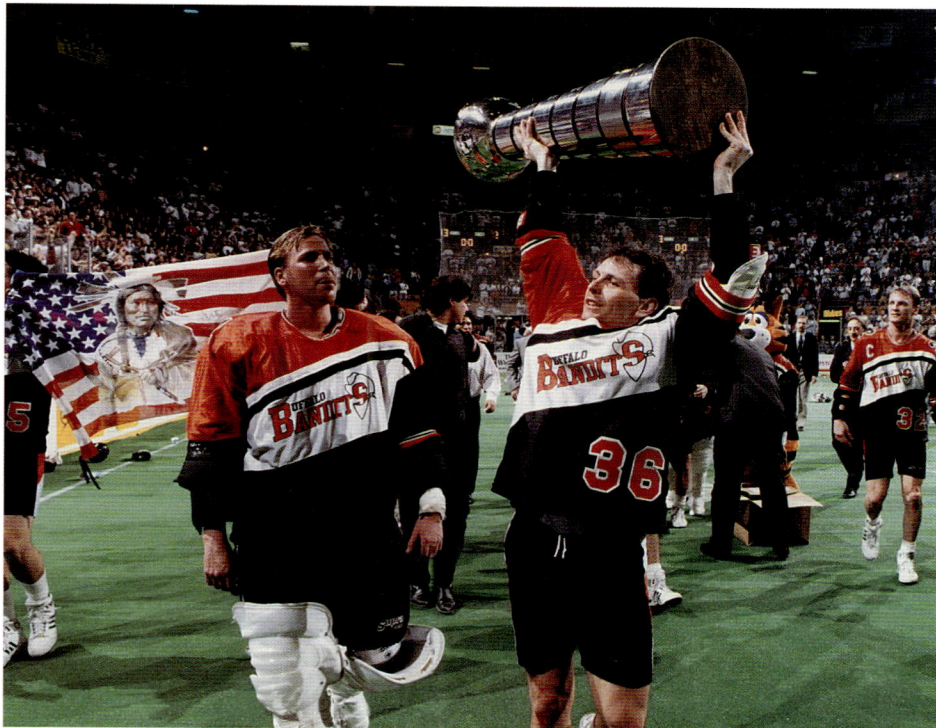

The NHL **Buffalo Sabres**, founded in 1970 by Seymour H. Knox III and his brother Northrup Knox, are at home in Marine Midland Arena, one of the best hockey facilities in North America.
Photo by James P. McCoy.

The **Buffalo Bandits** won three Major Indoor Lacrosse League (MILL) titles in five years. The Bandits have also led the league in attendance for several years, drawing over 16,000 uninhibited fans at an average home game, with several sellouts.
Photo by James P. McCoy.

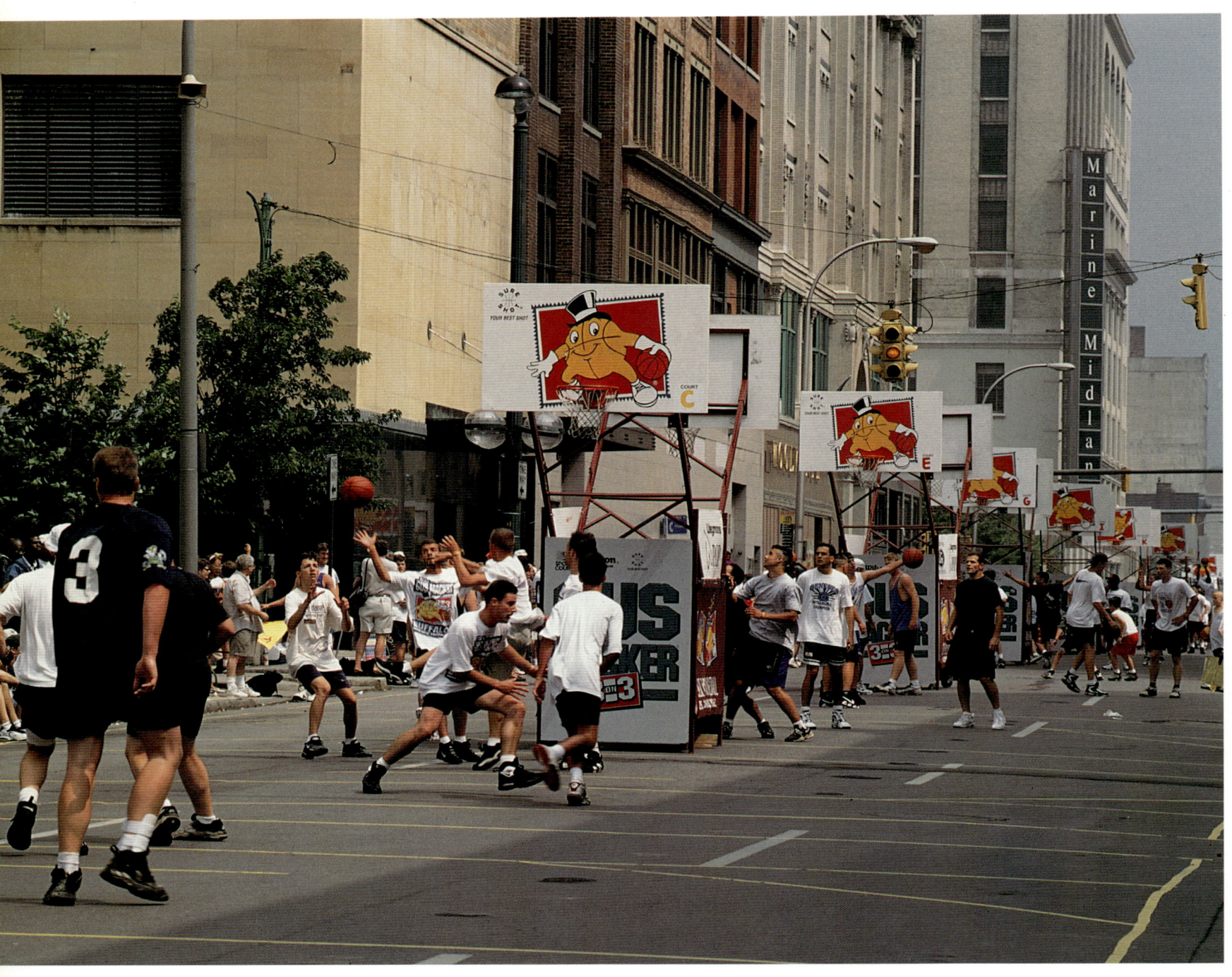

Basketball takes to the streets when the **Gus Macker 3-on-3 Tournament** hits downtown Buffalo every summer. The tournament, which travels to over 60 cities throughout the United States and Canada, comprises block after block of back-to-back half courts on Washington Street and attracts thousands of men and women players of all ages. In addition to the double elimination tournament, there's a half-court heave contest, foul shooting and three-point contests, a foul shot clinic, and a slam dunk contest. Photo by James P. McCoy.

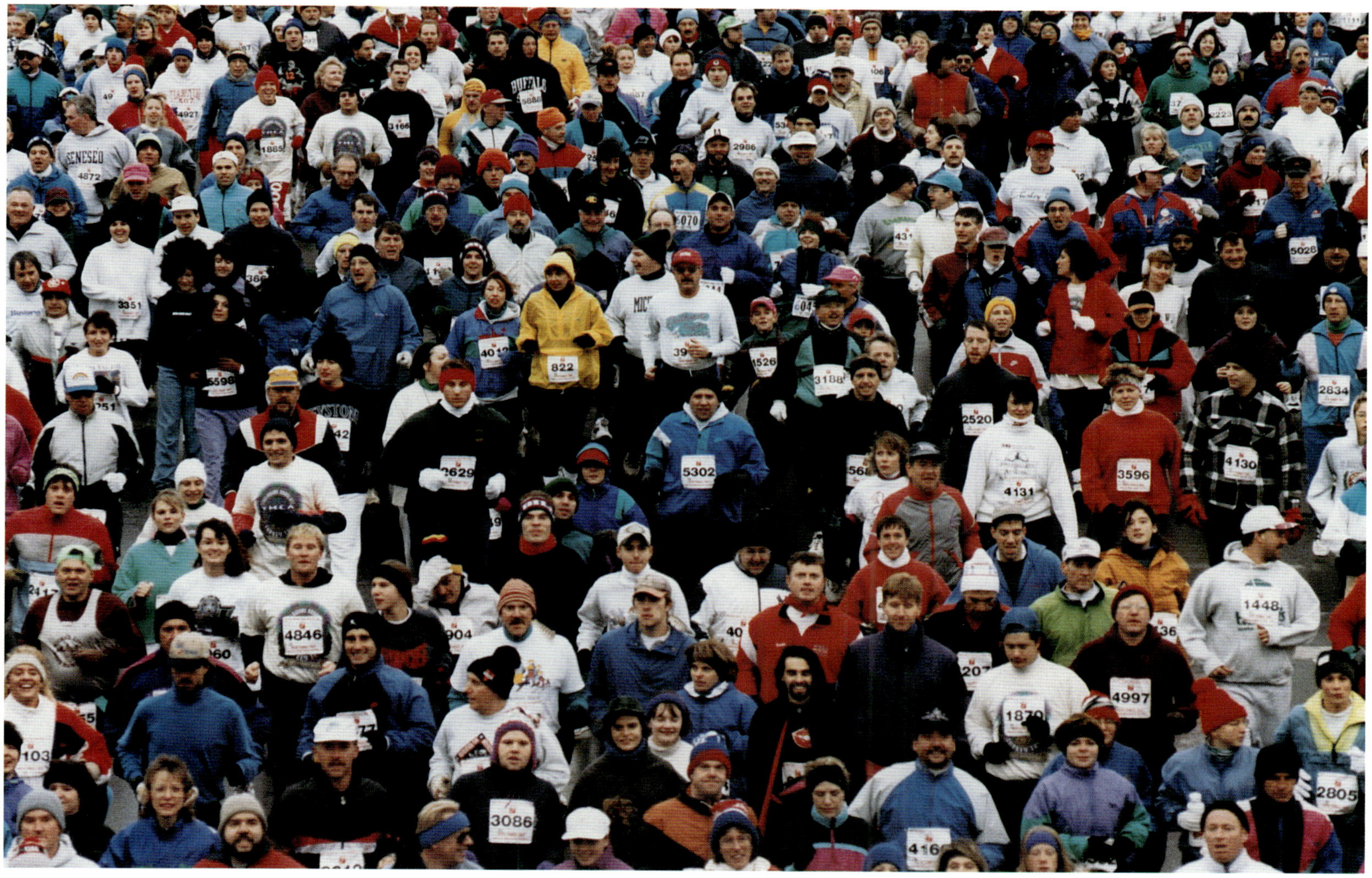

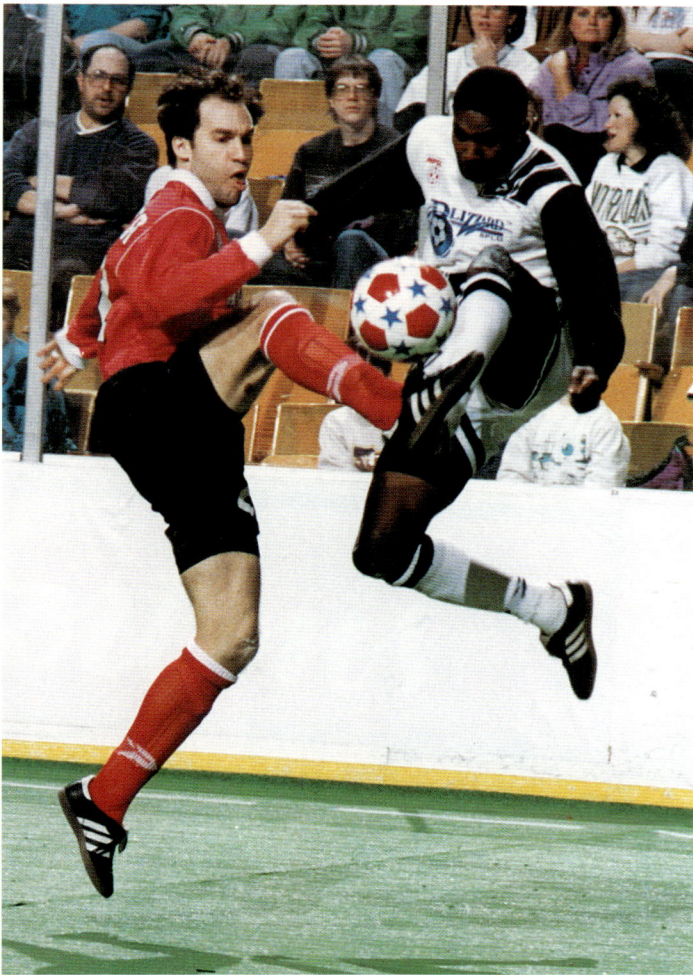

Under General Manager and Coach Jim May, the **Buffalo Blizzard** attracts fans to National Professional Soccer League (NPSL) action at Marine Midland Arena. The Blizzard generally attracts the youngest of all Buffalo pro sports fans, including young players from the area's many soccer clubs.
Photo by James P. McCoy.

Every Thanksgiving morning for over 100 years, runners have gathered in Buffalo for the J.Y. Cameron Memorial Thanksgiving Day Run, more affectionately known as the **Turkey Trot**. Six months older than the Boston Marathon, this five-mile race began in 1896 and holds the distinction of being the oldest annual road race in America. In recent years, the field has grown from dozens to thousands, with many runners dressed in whacky seasonal costumes and other creative disguises.
Photo by James P. McCoy.

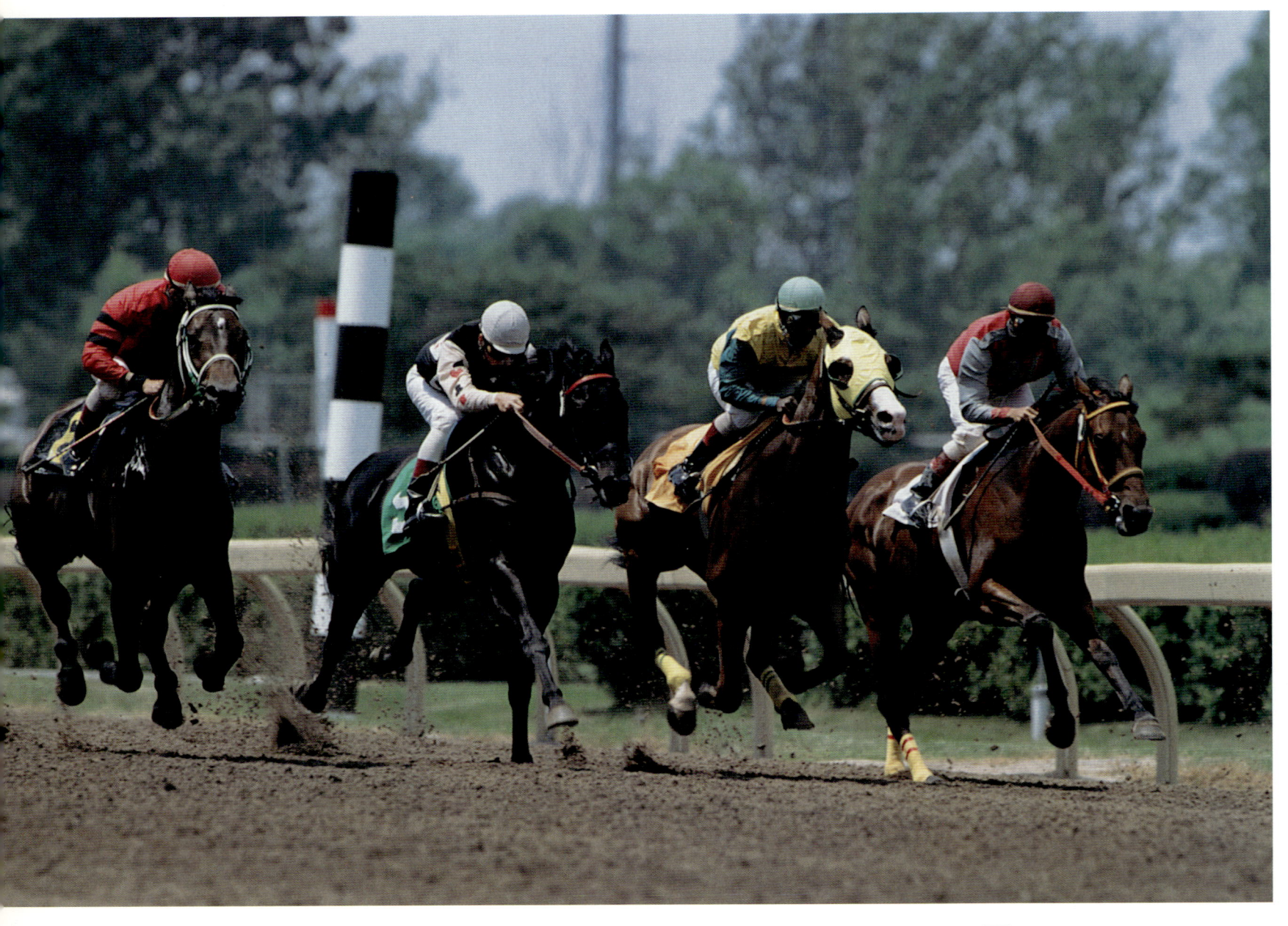

Pony lovers throughout Niagara have converged on the **Fort Erie Racetrack** for the past 100 years. Photo by James P. McCoy.

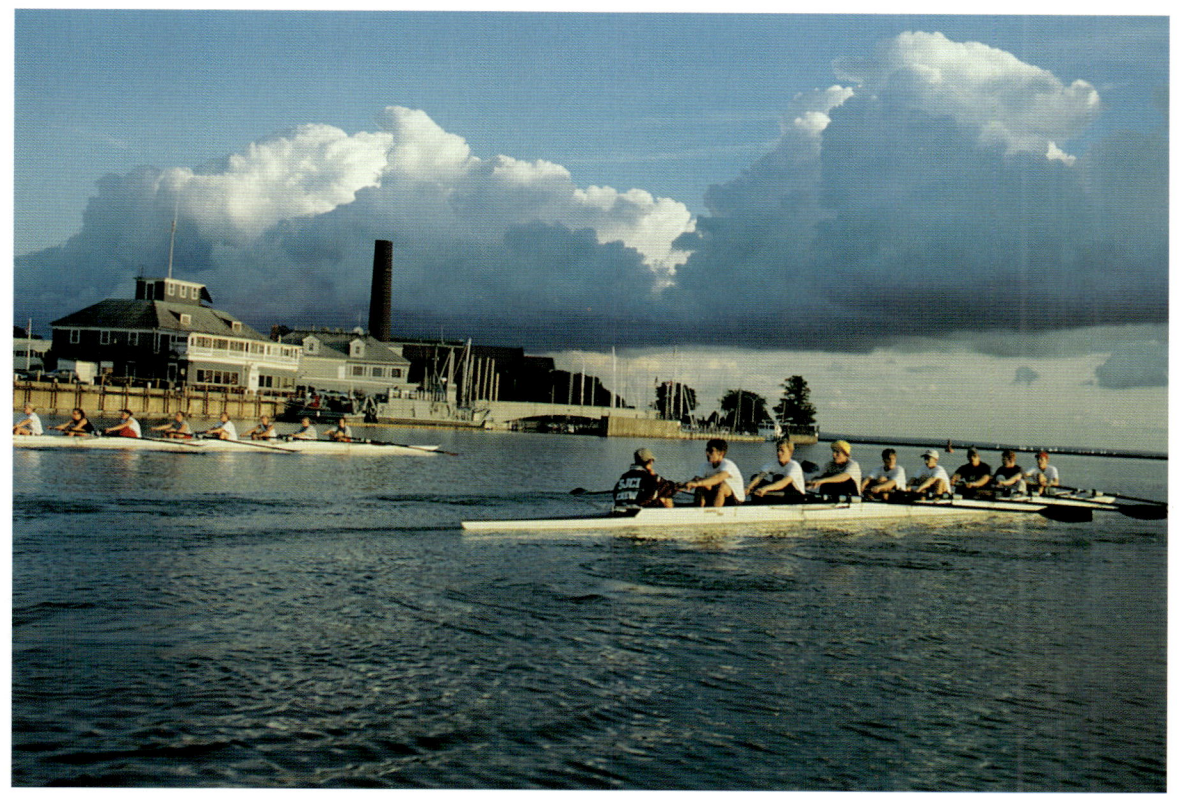

For strollers on the Riverwalk in Buffalo's La Salle Park, the smooth, rhythmic beauty of the rowers and their swift shells in the Black Rock Channel is reminiscent of a Thomas Eakins painting or an image of Henley-on-Thames. For members of the **West Side Rowing Club**, it's hard, joyous work. Founded by Michael Broderick and other Irish immigrants in 1912, the 350-member WSRC was once one of 10 rowing clubs that flourished on the West Side of Buffalo. In 1995, a WSRC eight won the North American championship at the Royal Canadian Henley Regatta in St. Catharines. Club crews also captured two national titles at Syracuse the same year. WSRC alumni have qualified for and competed in the Summer Olympics in Berlin in 1936, in Melbourne in 1956, and in Atlanta in 1996.
Photo by James P. McCoy.

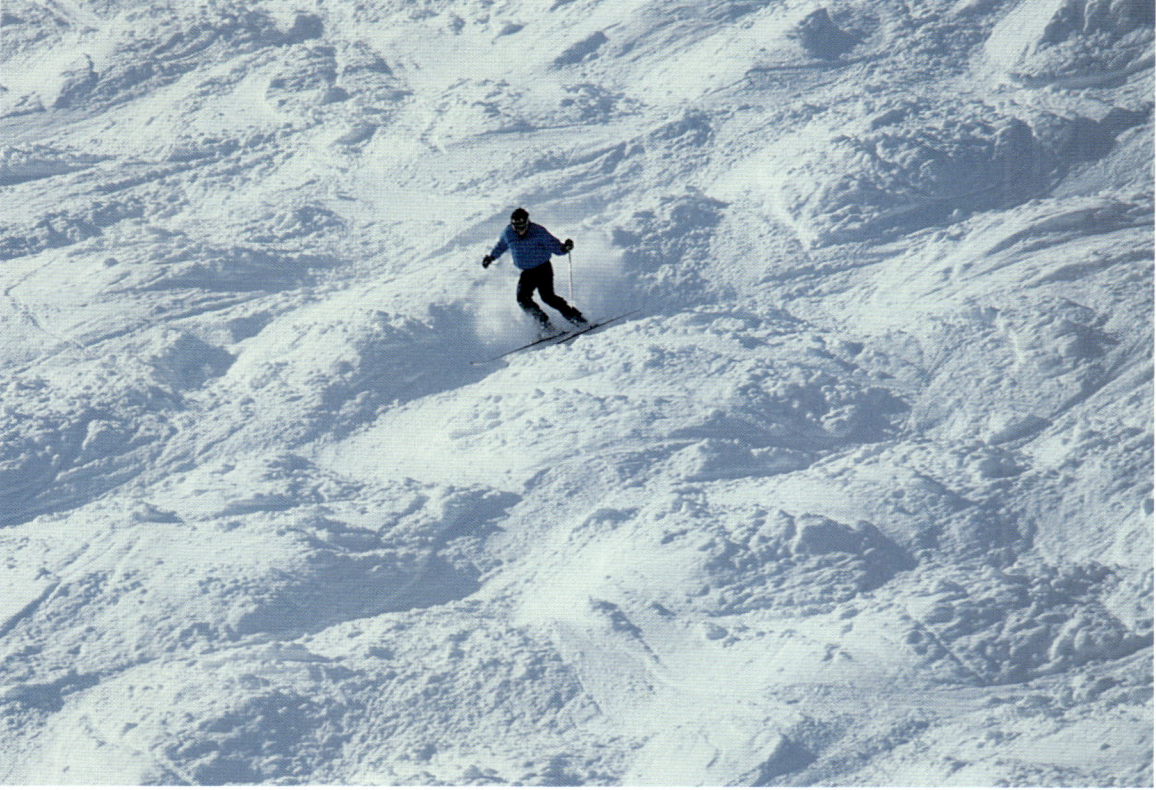

Each year, one million skiers visit **Niagara's slopes** at Kissing Bridge, Holiday Valley, Peek'n Peak, Tamarack, Cockaigne, Frost Ridge, and Swain. Skiers travel from across New York State, Ontario, and the Midwest to experience the rush of Niagara's downhill runs and to plunge into the beauty of the area's cross-country trails.
Photo by James P. McCoy.

In 1820, Buffalo founding father Samuel Wilkeson built a pier from timber cribs filled with stone and rock to create a breakwater preventing the buildup of more sand into the sandbar blocking the Buffalo River, then known as Buffalo Creek. Wilkeson then built a dam that forced the stream to remove the sandbar and create a deep, navigable channel that formed the basis of the Buffalo harbor. On the strength of this harbor, Buffalo was awarded the terminus of the Erie Canal, the key to the village's imminent growth and prosperity. Today, where Wilkeson once exhorted his workers against the elements, the Erie Basin Marina overlooks the entrance to the mouth of the Buffalo River. With over 250 boat slips, the **Erie Basin Marina** is both a haven for sailors and power boaters and favorite summer destination for downtown office workers, families, and seagulls.
Photo by James P. McCoy.

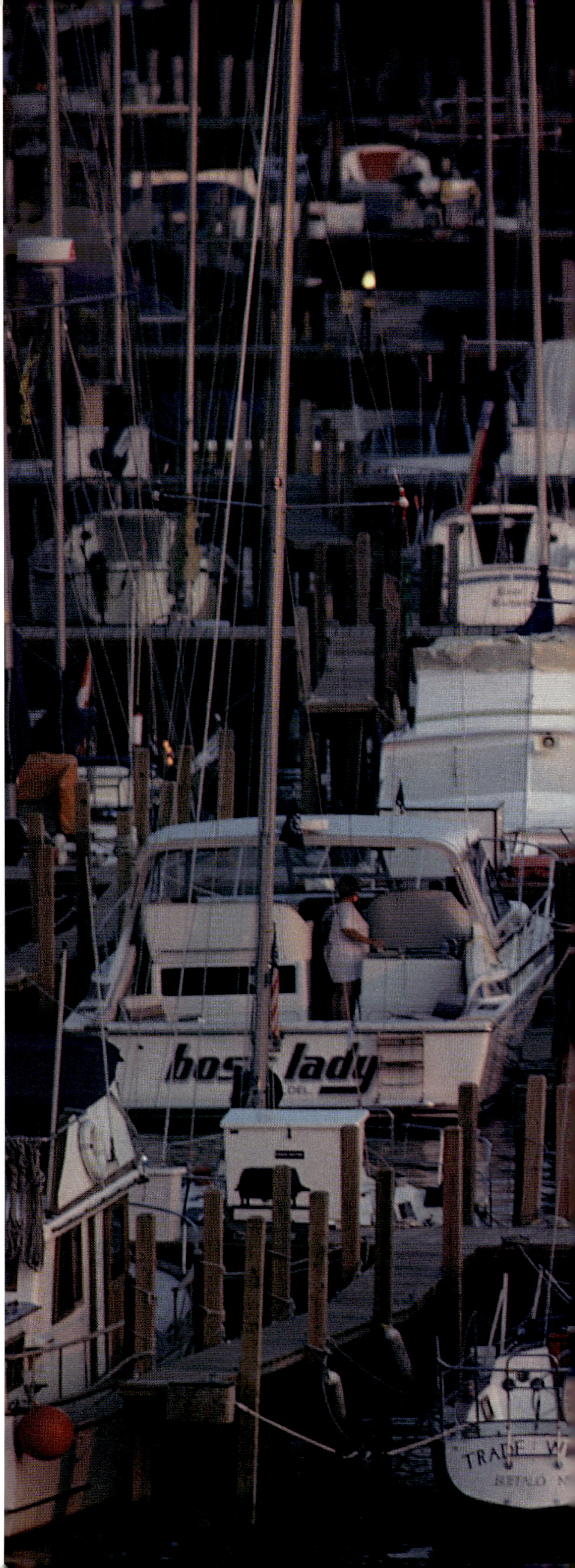

With the introduction of women's basketball competition in the 1996 Olympics and the emergence of the Women's National Basketball Association (WNBA), women's college basketball is finally getting some respect and drawing more and more fans across the region. At **Canisius College**, the **Golden Griffins** play an exciting 26-game schedule against Division I opponents from eastern and midwestern colleges.
Photo by James P. McCoy.

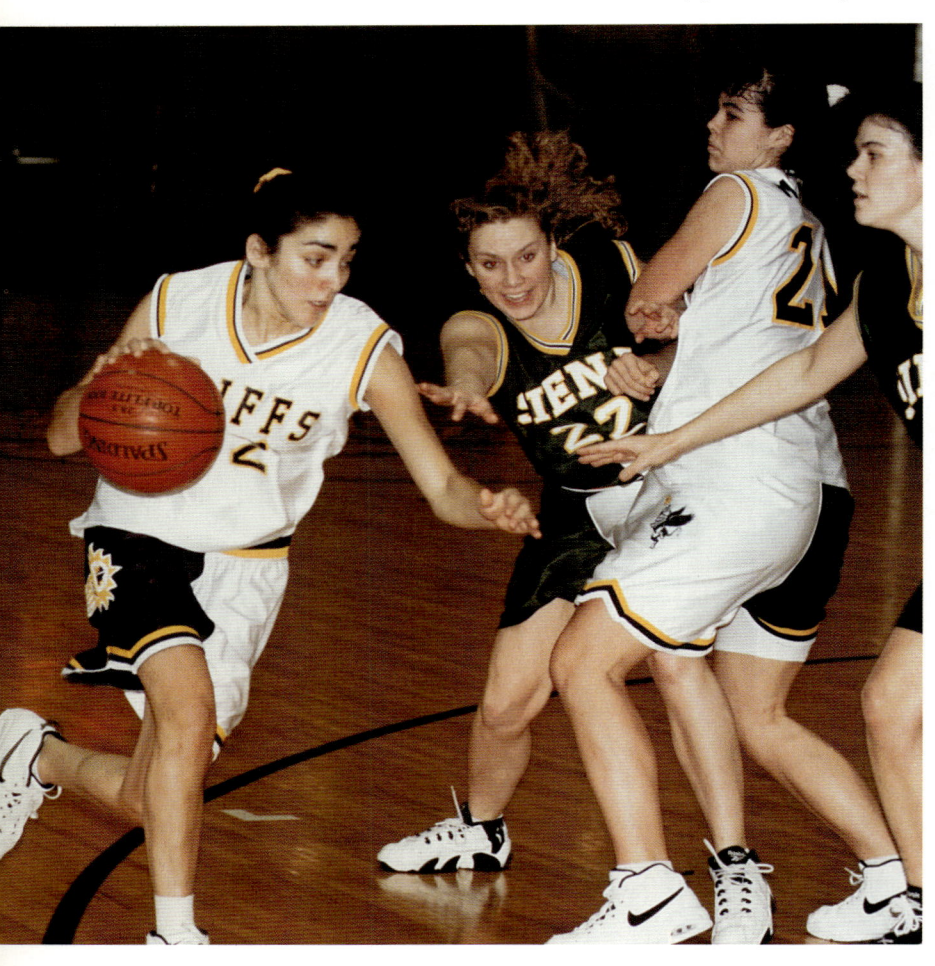

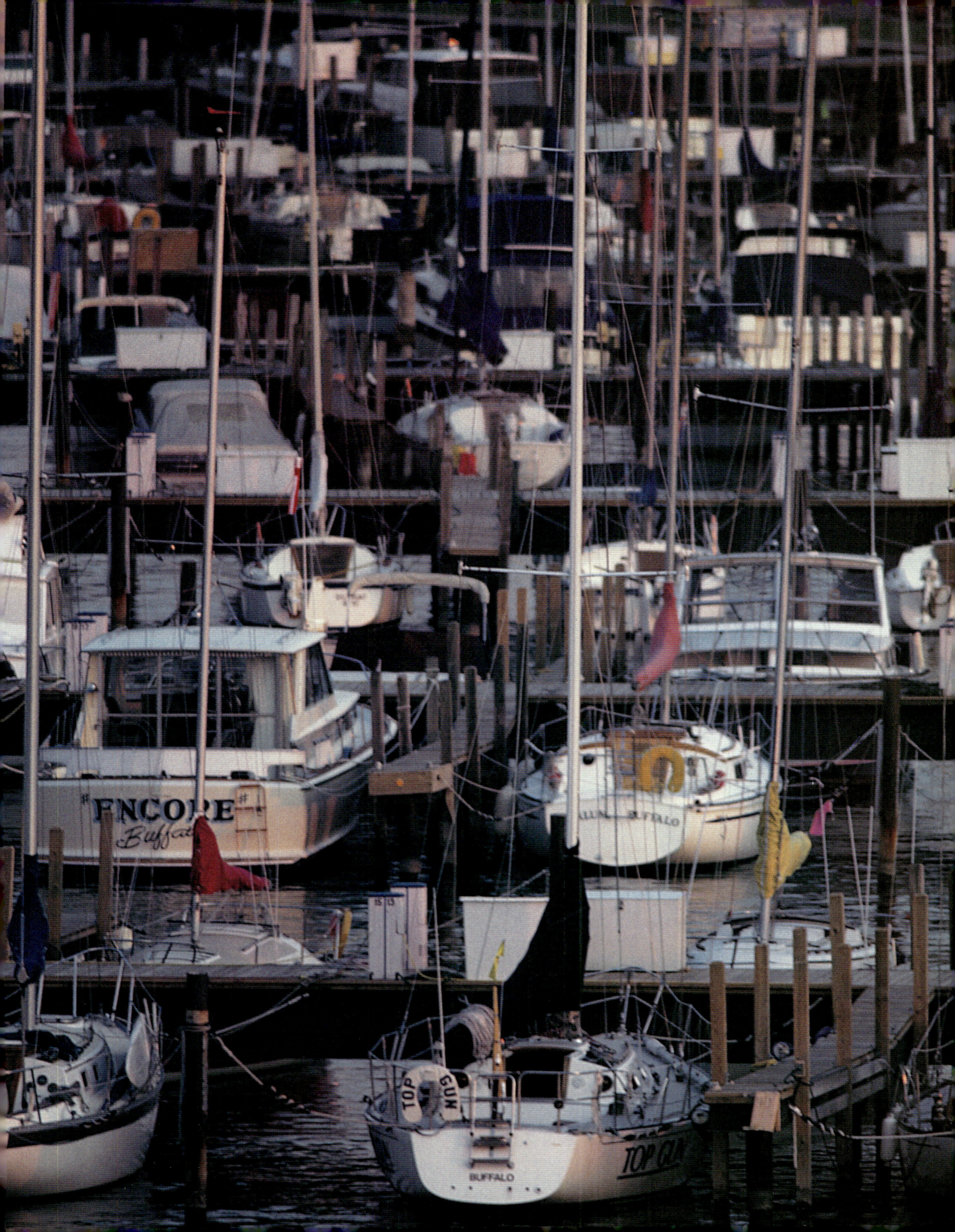

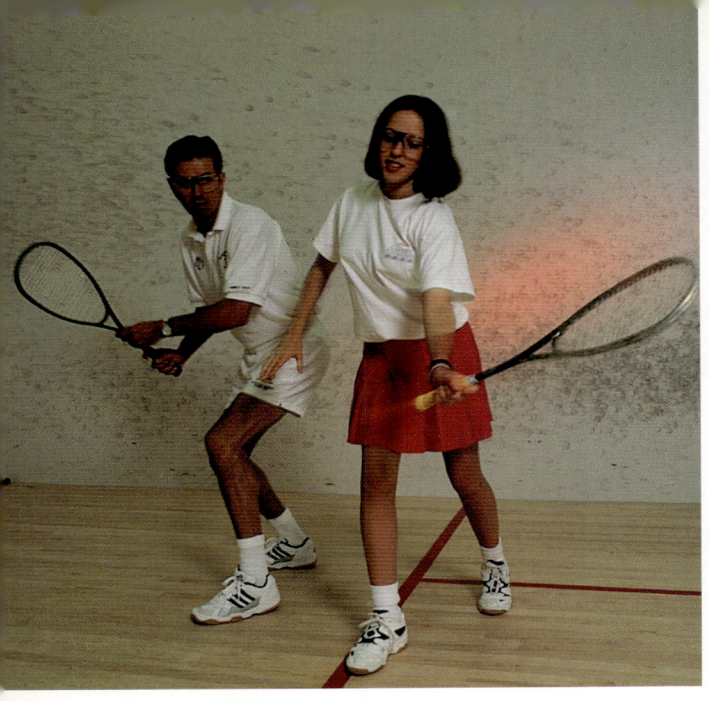

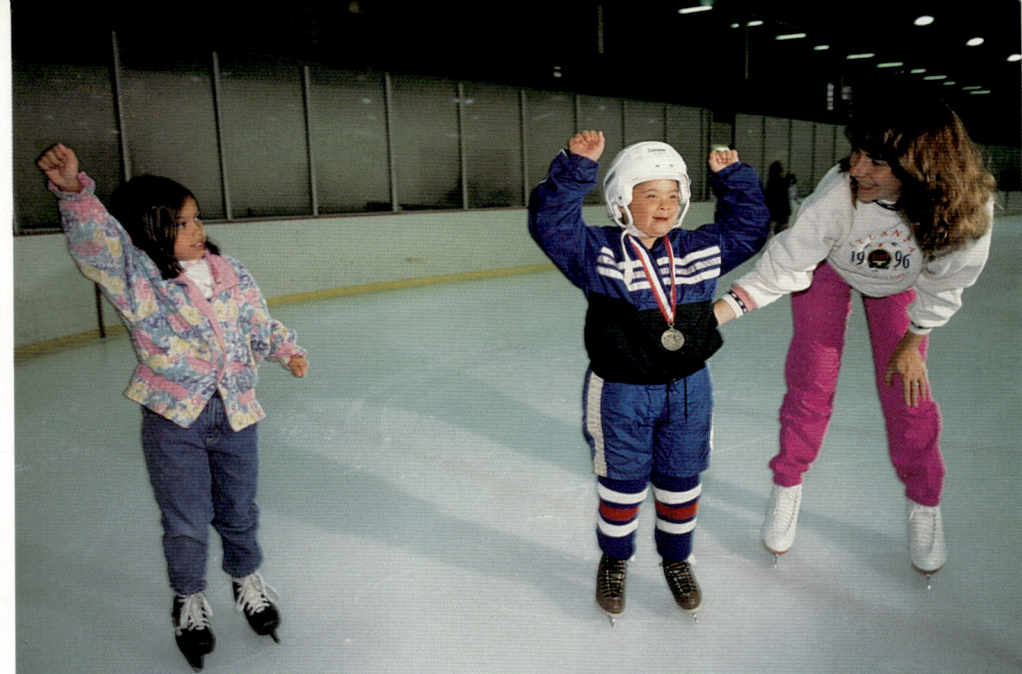

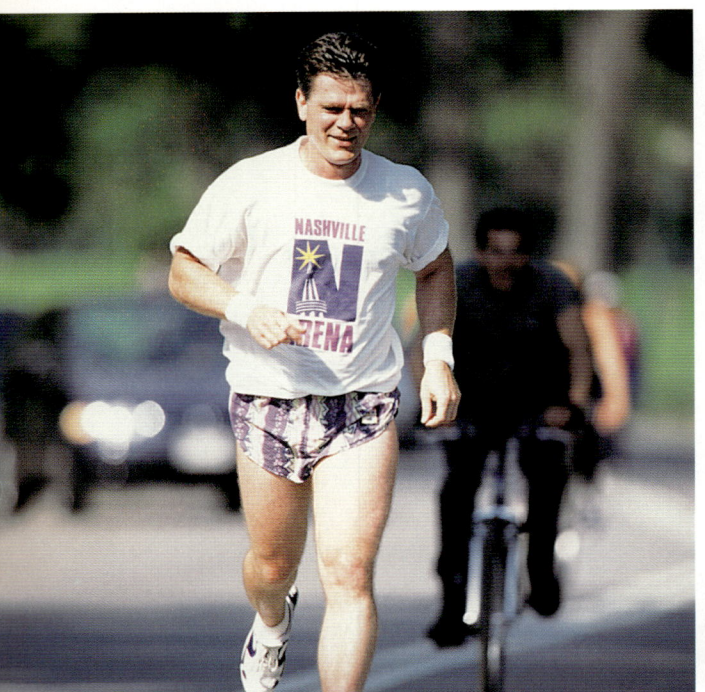

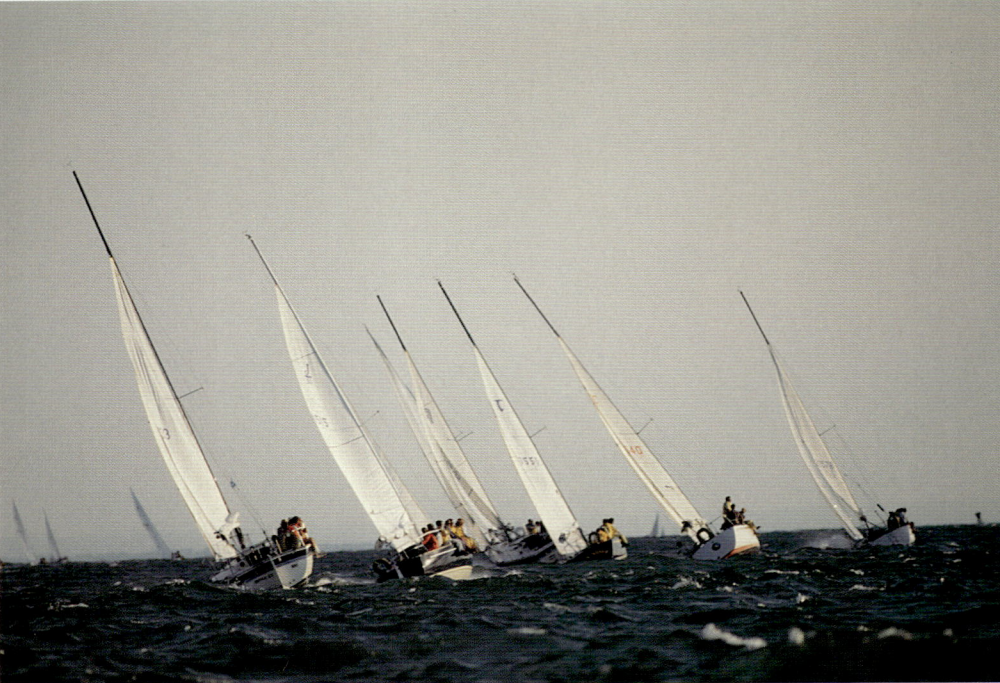

(top left) At the **Buffalo Tennis & Squash Club**, two nationally ranked players practice for an upcoming squash title match.
Photo by James P. McCoy.

(bottom left) A **choice of three running surfaces** and the company of some of the best local runners make **Delaware Park** a perennially popular training ground for both serious marathoners and recreational joggers. There's also a convenient juice bar and, for visual interest, plenty of plaid pants on the golf course and the easy-to-spot family of giraffes overlooking the far side of the zoo.
Photo by James P. McCoy.

(top right) A jewel in the crown of Buffalo's All-America City and Community Award in 1996, The **Skating Association for the Blind and Handicapped** (SABAH) began in 1977 when professional skating instructor and coach Elizabeth O'Donnell began her crusade to teach people with disabilities to ice skate. Today, with a staff of 9 and 1,200 volunteers, SABAH helps people of all ages with physical, mental, and emotional challenges gain confidence through the freedom and joy of skating. At the Annual Ice Show, costumed SABAH skaters star with other athletes and celebrities in a themed extravaganza that draws some 13,000 spectators as well as national television and press coverage.
Photo by James P. McCoy.

(bottom right) Summers are a busy season of **sailing regattas on Lakes Erie and Ontario**. At the Youngstown Level Regatta, one of the largest races in North America, some 500 boats from throughout the United States and Canada compete without handicap just offshore from the ramparts of Old Fort Niagara.
Photo by James P. McCoy.

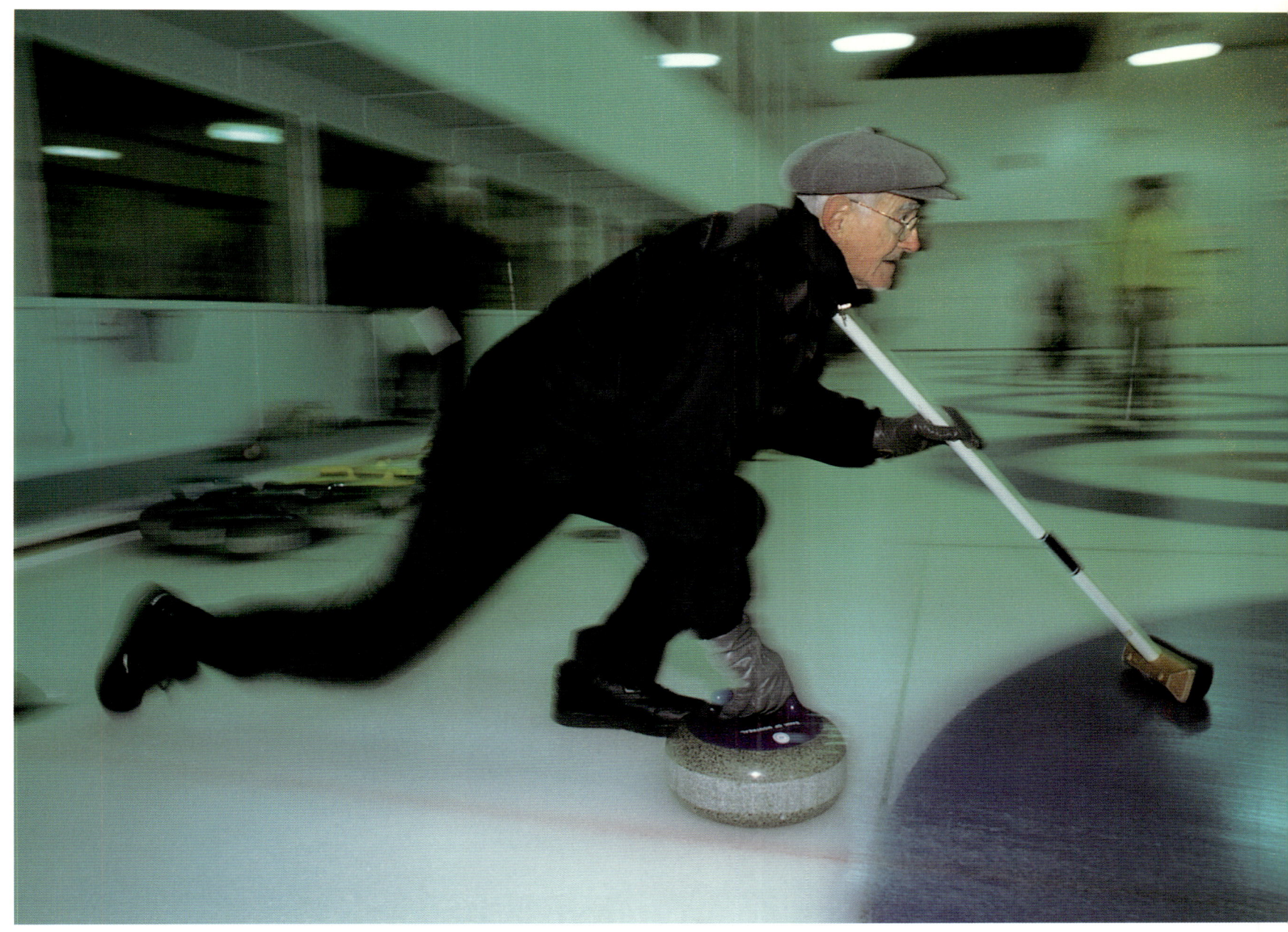

Although there is some evidence to suggest that **curling** may have had its origins in the Low Countries in the early 16th century, it was Scotland that made the game famous throughout the world. Played on ice by players without skates, flat rounded stones are slid down the ice toward a tee or button as sweepers smooth the path to assist the stone's journey to the goal.

In 1996, the World Championship of Curling took place just north of Niagara in Hamilton, Ontario.

Photo by James P. McCoy.

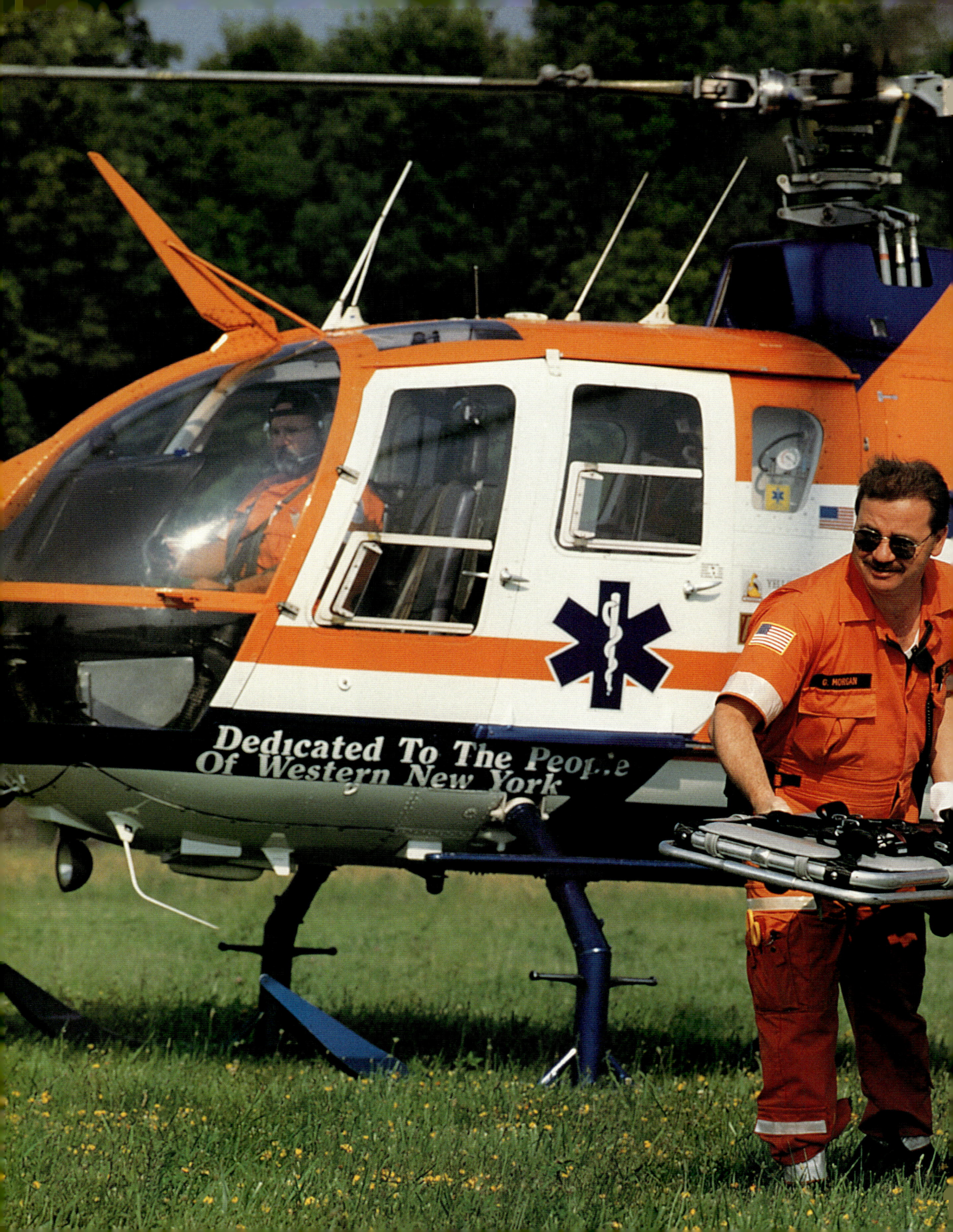

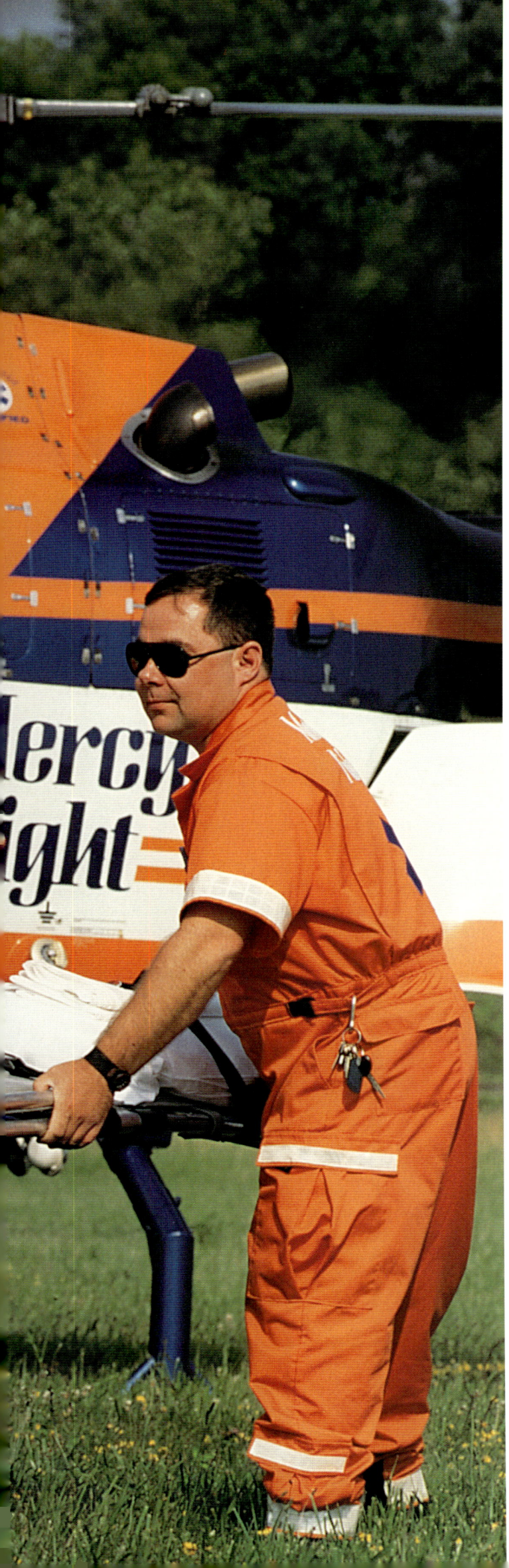

A LEADER IN HEALTH CARE INDUSTRIES

Niagara, and specifically the city of

Buffalo, is the region's medical hub, an

important center of medical treatment,

clinical research, and acute patient

care. Beginning with the founding of the

University of Buffalo Medical School in

1846, the region has continuously

attracted important physicians, scientists,

researchers, and more recently,

biotechnology companies.

In 1883, Dr. Roswell Park arrived from Chicago to join the faculty of the UB Medical School and then to become chief surgeon at Buffalo General Hospital. During the following decade, the New York legislature made the first-ever appropriation of public funds for combating cancer with a research grant to Dr. Park, whose work formed the basis for Roswell Park Cancer Institute, a leading cancer research center and hospital.

Today, Roswell Park Cancer Institute is an anchor of Buffalo's High Street Medical Campus where dramatic breakthroughs in medical research and surgical procedures are the focus of worldwide medical interest. At Roswell, a $241.5 million modernization project is under way with the building of a hospital, a diagnostic and treatment center, laboratory space, outpatient clinics and medical research labs and other support buildings. Across the street at Buffalo General Hospital, a $12.3 million operating room expansion and a $5.5 million emergency room project are under way at the region's largest hospital. The 70-acre medical campus is also home to nearly a dozen other medical and health-related organizations.

At Roswell Park, Dr. M. Steven Piver, chief of the department of gynecological oncology, is one of the institute's most visible medical heroes and a tireless warrior in the battle against ovarian cancer. Dr. Piver created the Gilda Radner Familial Ovarian Cancer Registry, named for the comedian who died of the disease in 1989 at the age of 42. The registry tracks women who have a family history of ovarian cancer, advises them of their risk of developing the disease, and suggests ways to prevent it. In addition to his articles in medical journals and television appearances where he stresses the need for early detection and prevention of ovarian cancer, Dr. Piver has collaborated with actor Gene Wilder, Gilda Radner's husband, on a book entitled *Gilda's Disease.*

During the past decades, important research at Roswell Park Cancer Institute has resulted in the PSA blood test for prostate cancer, the discovery of a genetic link to colorectal cancer, photodynamic therapy to kill tumors, and advances in anesthesiology and many other areas. Dr. Thomas Shows has mapped over 500 human genes and directs Roswell's Department of Human Genetics, which houses one of the largest collections and international repositories of human DNA libraries. Current research by Dr. Yasmin Thanavala includes the genetic alteration of common foods such as bananas and potatoes to produce a hepatitis B virus vaccine.

Genetics is also a factor in clinical research being conducted on Alzheimer's disease at Millard Fillmore Hospital's Dent Neurological Institute. Using brain scans by positron emission tomography (PET), doctors are attempting to diagnose Alzheimer's by detecting signs of mental deterioration before the onset of visible symptoms, especially in people with an inherited gene associated with the disease.

At the University at Buffalo, medical research encompasses some 40 research centers. Increasingly, these centers operate from a multidisciplinary approach as groups of scientists from several fields work together sharing skills, ideas, and resources. For example, faculty members from several schools and many departments share their knowledge in the search for new solutions to biotechnology problems at UB's Center for Advanced Molecular Biology and Immunology (CAMBI). Center researchers concentrate on developing vaccine products and new immunodiagnostic reagents to combat infectious diseases and malignancy.

One such vaccine was developed at CAMBI to combat haemophilus influenzae, a bacteria that causes meningitis in infants, middle ear infection in young children, and respiratory diseases. According to Dr. Philip T. LoVerde, a founder and former co-director of CAMBI, the dynamics of cooperative research have several advantages. "This kind of interdisciplinary organization can foster the sort of research that doesn't happen if people just stay within their own departments or school," says Dr. LoVerde. "In the long run, it makes us better scientists, our discoveries move ahead faster, and it makes the university more competitive."

Interdisciplinary is also the operative word at the Toshiba Stroke Research Center, where researchers are developing and perfecting new minimally invasive neurovascular surgery techniques using sophisticated image-guidance technology. The research center is directed by Dr. L. Nelson Hopkins, chairman of the university's neurosurgery department and a pioneer in endovascular surgery.

Elsewhere at UB, the Industry/University Cooperative Research Center for Biosurfaces brings together scientists from campuses and corporations to explore important areas of science and technology. Center research focuses on interactions between the biological and the man-made, including such phenomena as biocompatability, adhesion between dissimilar materials, corrosion of metals, and degradation of plastics and other materials in a biological environment. The center has wide experience in industrial research projects, including the assessment of medical devices.

With all of the research, medical education, and technical innovation taking place here, it's no surprise that the region is also home to over 150 medical, dental, and pharmaceutical manufacturers as well as a broad range of service industries. In a robust health care sector employing some 75,000 persons, medical manufacturers in Western New York account for 4,700 employees and more than a billion dollars in annual sales.

Medical products made by Niagara's companies include bacterial diagnostic tests, blood bank refrigerators and freezers, cleanroom equipment, contraceptives, disposable

(previous page) Since 1981, **Mercy Flight** has rescued thousands of accident and trauma victims from remote locations and choppered them to waiting emergency teams at area hospitals. With 2 full-time helicopters, 4 full-time pilots, 8 on-call physicians, and a staff of 15 skilled paramedics, Mercy Flight often means the difference between life or death for accident victims and critical care for emergency transfers from small to larger hospitals. Mercy Flight, an independent, community-based service unaffiliated with any hospital, operates with some state and county aid, private contributions, donated services, and volunteer help. Photo by James P. McCoy.

products, hospital furniture, in vitro diagnostic kits, lithium batteries for cardiac pacemakers, medical instruments, medical oxygen concentrates, monitoring systems, optical equipment, orthopedic products, patient lifts, pressure relief products, skin protection items, and veterinary products. Dental product companies manufacture orthodontic lab equipment, prosthetics, and restorative dentures and dental implants, while pharmaceutical product companies make pharmaceuticals, nonprescription medicines, and health and beauty aid products, to name a few.

The rapid growth of managed care and the deregulation of the prices insurance companies pay for patient hospital care in New York State, has created a climate of merger among the area's largest hospitals. In the mid-1990s, Buffalo General united with Columbus Hospital and formed the Columbus Community Health Center. BGH also affiliated with DeGraff Memorial Hospital and has joined with Millard Fillmore Hospitals and Children's Hospital of Buffalo to form a large health network employing 9,000 health care workers and controlling 1,673 of the region's 4,701 hospital beds. Also, the seven Catholic hospitals in the Buffalo area have joined forces. The goals of consolidating operations are always the same: to deliver higher quality health care at a lower cost to both insurers and patients.

Another indication of the increased influence of managed care is the continuing growth of home health care in the community as many hospitals expand their lower-cost outpatient care services. In 1996, home health care agencies in Western New York employed 7,651 workers, including registered nurses, health care aides, and personal care aides.

Meanwhile, there is another less celebrated health care community in Niagara that uses very different methodologies and techniques to address the problems of disease and discomfort. Among the area's many practitioners of complementary and alternative medicine, Dr. Ronald Santasiero, a physician with wide experience in family medicine, combines traditional allopathic treatment with acupuncture at his clinic in Hamburg. "We've bridged the gap by utilizing what we think is best for the patient," says Dr. Santasiero, "by choosing from the larger menu of both traditional or alternative treatments." Dr. Santasiero, who was also the area's first HMO doctor, believes that an increasing number of physicians are considering nontraditional medicine as a complementary approach to chronic illness, stress, and pain management. ◊

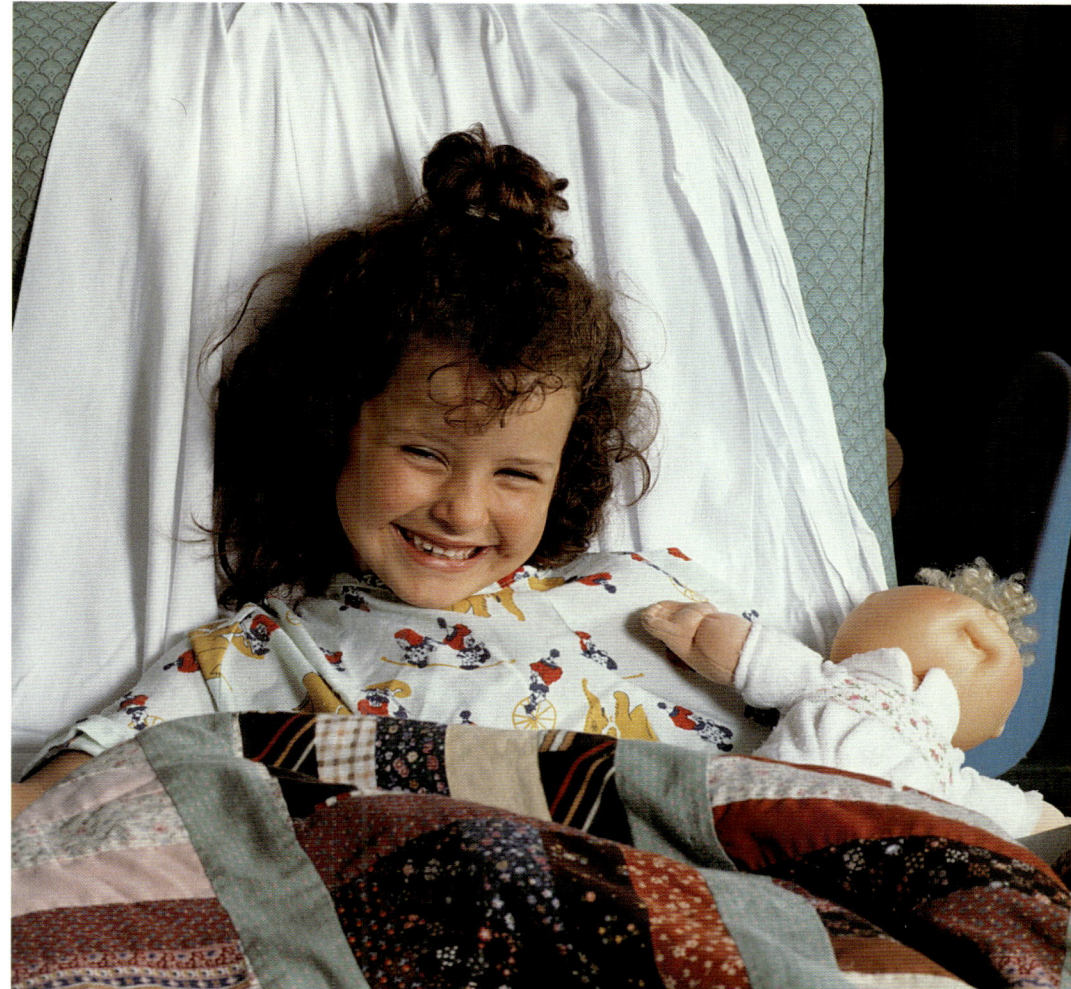

The only exclusively pediatric hospital in New York State, the **Children's Hospital of Buffalo** is the region's key provider of women and children's health care.
Photo by James P. McCoy.

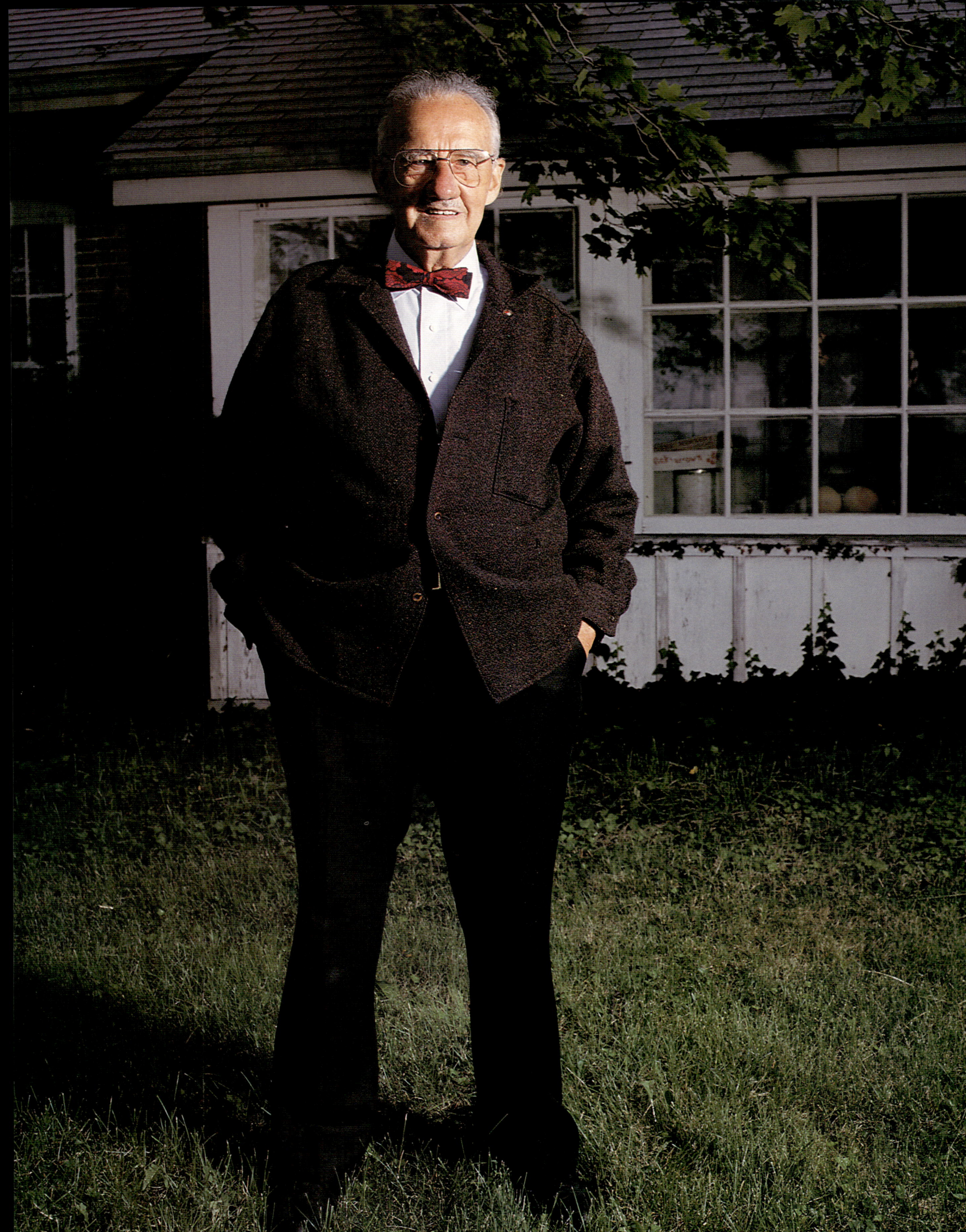

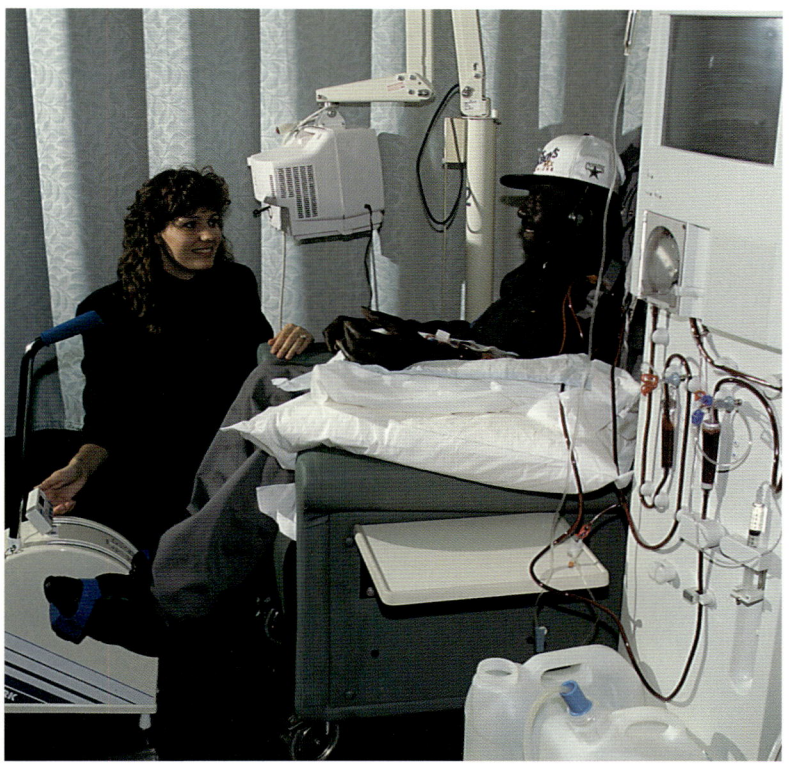

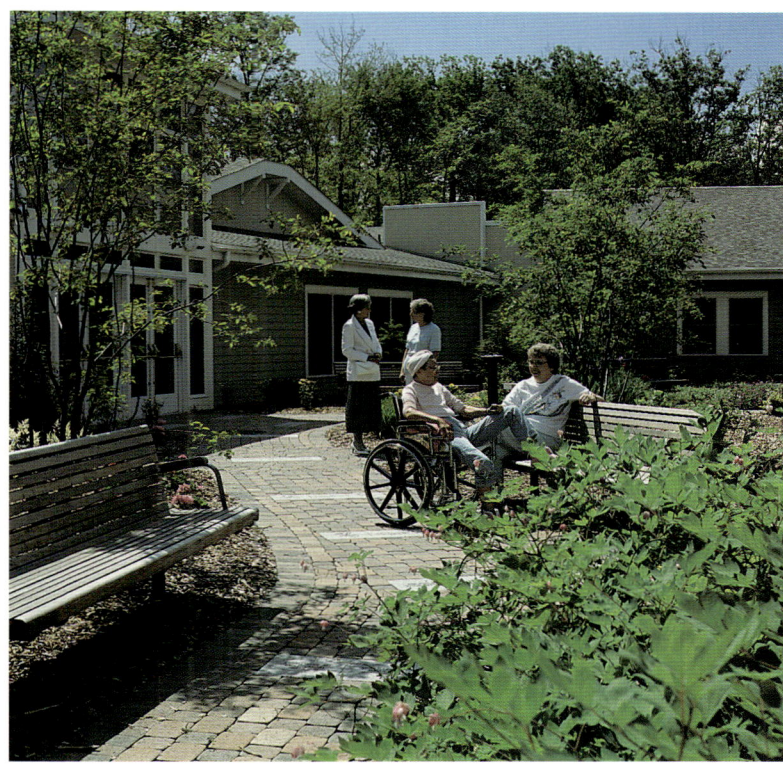

At **Mercy Hospital** of Buffalo, kidney disease patients can also receive physical therapy services during their regularly scheduled dialysis treatments. The pioneering program, called **Renal Rehab**, is the first of its kind in Western New York and one of only a few nationwide that concentrates on the physical therapy needs of dialysis patients. According to Dr. Eugene Cunningham, medical director of Renal Care of Buffalo, rehabilitation not only increases patients' stamina, but it "can also reverse or halt deterioration of muscle tissue, improve heart and lung function, control blood pressure and blood glucose, and in some cases, lower the need for certain medications."
Photo by James P. McCoy.

Wilson Greatbatch's research led to the development of the first implantable human heart pacemaker. The prolifically inventive Mr. Greatbatch, who holds 150 patents, helped launch nine companies, cloned African violets, and developed a solar-powered canoe. His research on the HIV virus has led to a patent on a process that stops reproduction of a virus similar to HIV in cats. For his work on the pacemaker, Mr. Greatbatch was presented with the National Medal of Technology by President George Bush. He is also a recipient of the Lifetime Achievement Award from the Lemelson-Massachusetts Institute of Technology Prize Program for his contributions to science and technology.
Photo by James P. McCoy.

Incorporated in 1976, **Hospice Buffalo** began home-care services and opened an inpatient unit at Buffalo General Hospital four years later. Here at the Hospice Mitchell Campus and at area hospitals and nursing homes, Hospice Buffalo provides medical care and emotional and spiritual support to people with advanced illness and their families. The Hospice Association also serves patients and families through Home Care Buffalo and through its Life Transitions Center, which offers education, counseling, and support groups for families coping with the stress and bereavement of death and dying. As the first facility of its kind in the nation, the Hospice Mitchell Campus is comprised of a residential care facility, a hospice inpatient care unit, an education center, a chapel, and administrative offices for the Hospice Buffalo staff.
Photo by James P. McCoy.

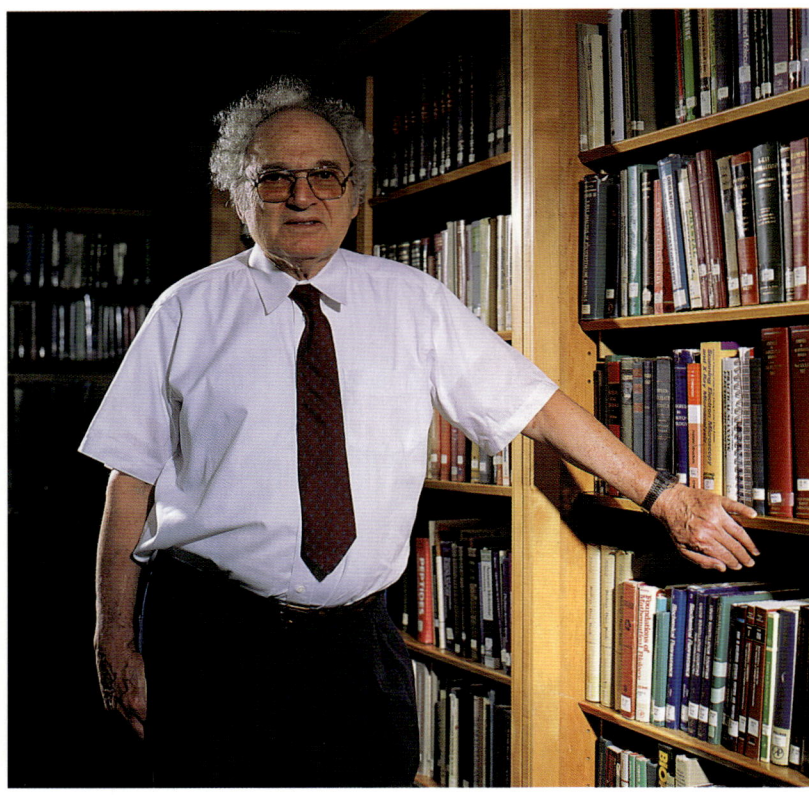

Dr. Herbert A. Hauptman received the Nobel Prize in Chemistry in 1985 for his mathematical method of determining the three-dimensional shapes of molecules. The discovery held enormous significance for chemistry and the field of drug research. Dr. Hauptman, a mathematician, is the only nonchemist ever to become the Nobel Laureate in Chemistry. Dr. Hauptman is president of the Hauptman-Woodward Medical Research Institute where research scientists have significantly advanced the understanding of the causes and potential therapies for heart disease, breast and prostate cancer, arteriosclerosis, and diabetes. Through their groundbreaking work in x-ray and electron crystallography, the institute's scientists have created scientific blueprints for the structure of thousands of molecules. These discoveries have led to the creation of more effective drugs with far-reaching implications for the treatment of cancer, heart disease, and AIDS.
Photo by James P. McCoy.

Kyu H. Shin, M.D., chairman of the Division of Radiation Medicine at **Roswell Park Cancer Institute**, checks the position of a patient about to undergo radiosurgery, a non-invasive new therapy used to treat a variety of benign and malignant brain tumors. A referral and resource center for patients throughout North America, the Division of Radiation Medicine offers cancer patients comprehensive care and innovative treatments such as photodynamic therapy, brachytherapy, contact therapy, and stereotactic radiosurgery.
Photo by James P. McCoy.

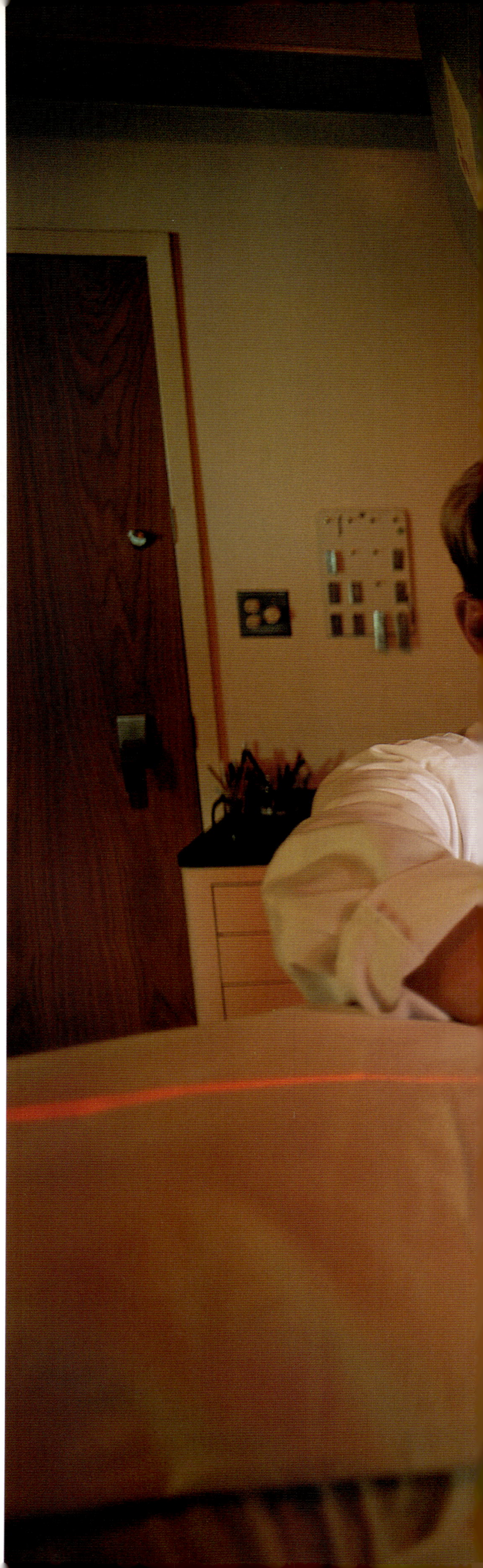

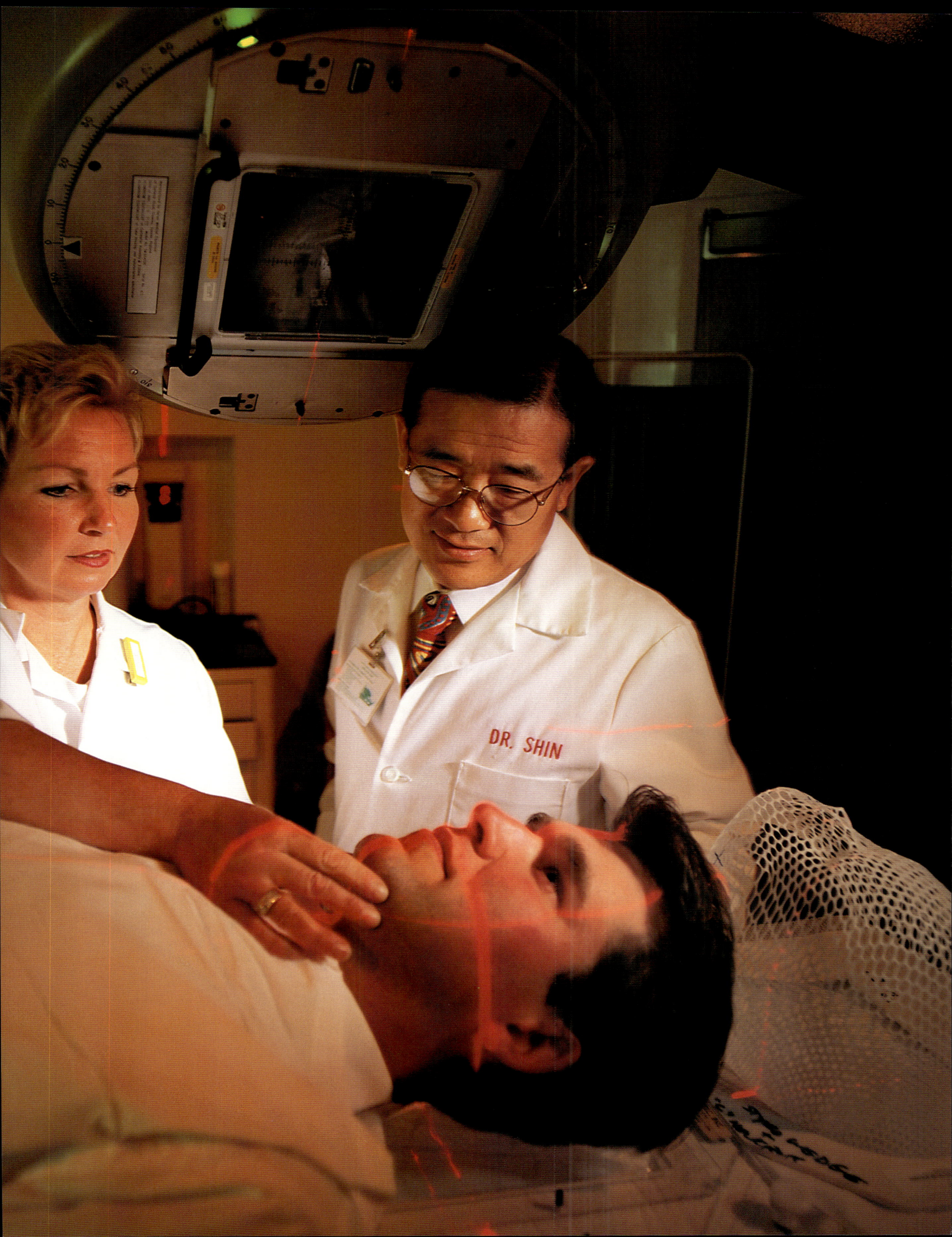

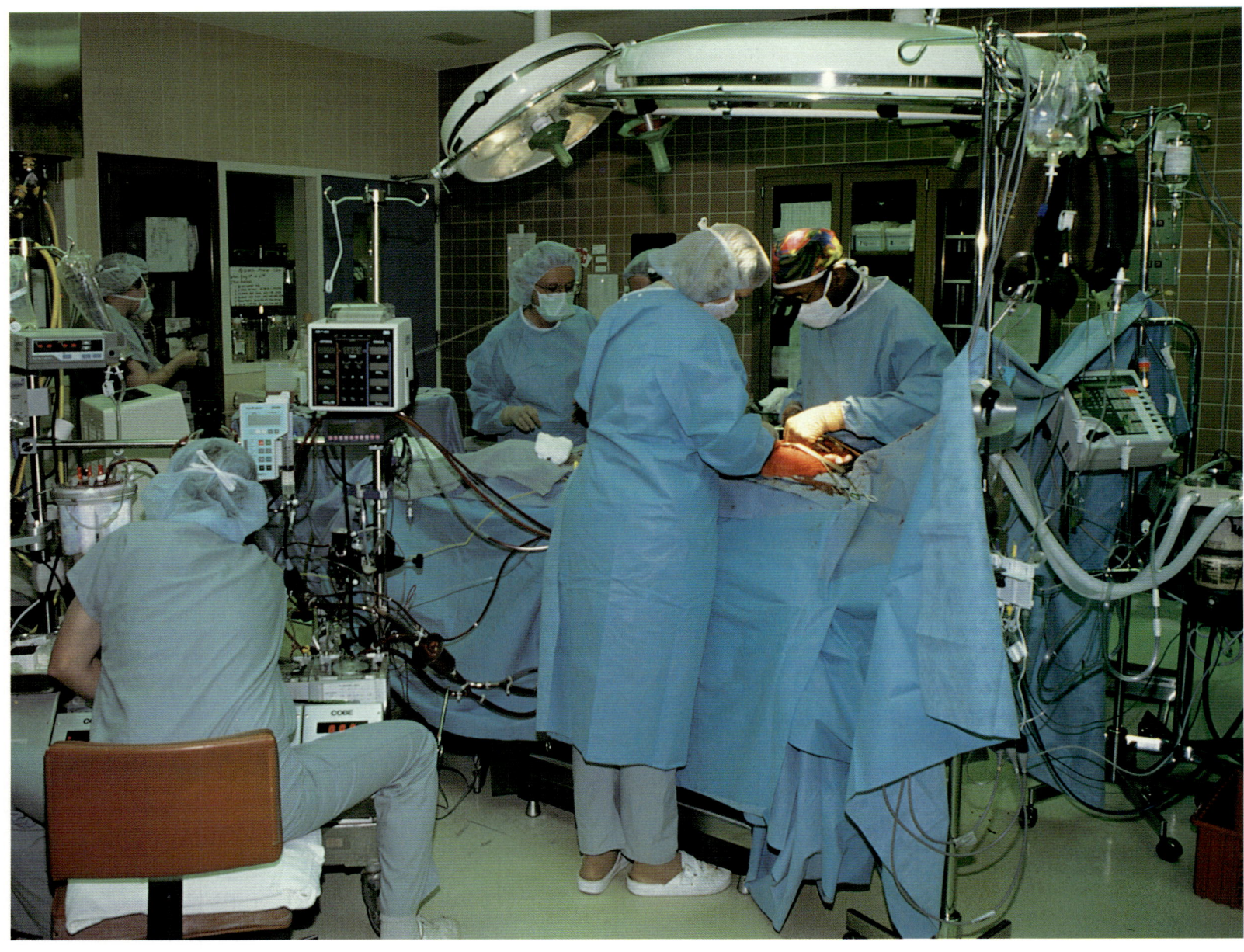

The largest hospital in upstate New York, **Buffalo General Hospital** offers medical treatments in 21 clinical inpatient departments and more than 60 outpatient programs. At the hospital's Heart and Lung Transplant Center, surgeons have developed the left anterior small thoracotomy (LAST), a minimally invasive technique to perform single bypass surgeries. Under Dr. Tomas A. Salerno, chief of heart surgery, another revolutionary cardiac surgical procedure, the partial left ventriculectomy, is also being pioneered at BGH. The procedure could provide hope to patients who might otherwise die while waiting for a heart transplant. Buffalo General also has a spine rehabilitation center, a traumatic brain injury program, bloodless medical services, and an acute-care medical psychiatric unit. During the mid-1990s, Buffalo General was the site of important research in the development of a drug for the treatment of multiple sclerosis patients. Led by Lawrence D. Jacobs, M.D., head of the hospital's Department of Neurology, Buffalo General also conducted important research in the development of a drug for the treatment of multiple sclerosis patients in the mid-1990s. Photo by James P. McCoy.

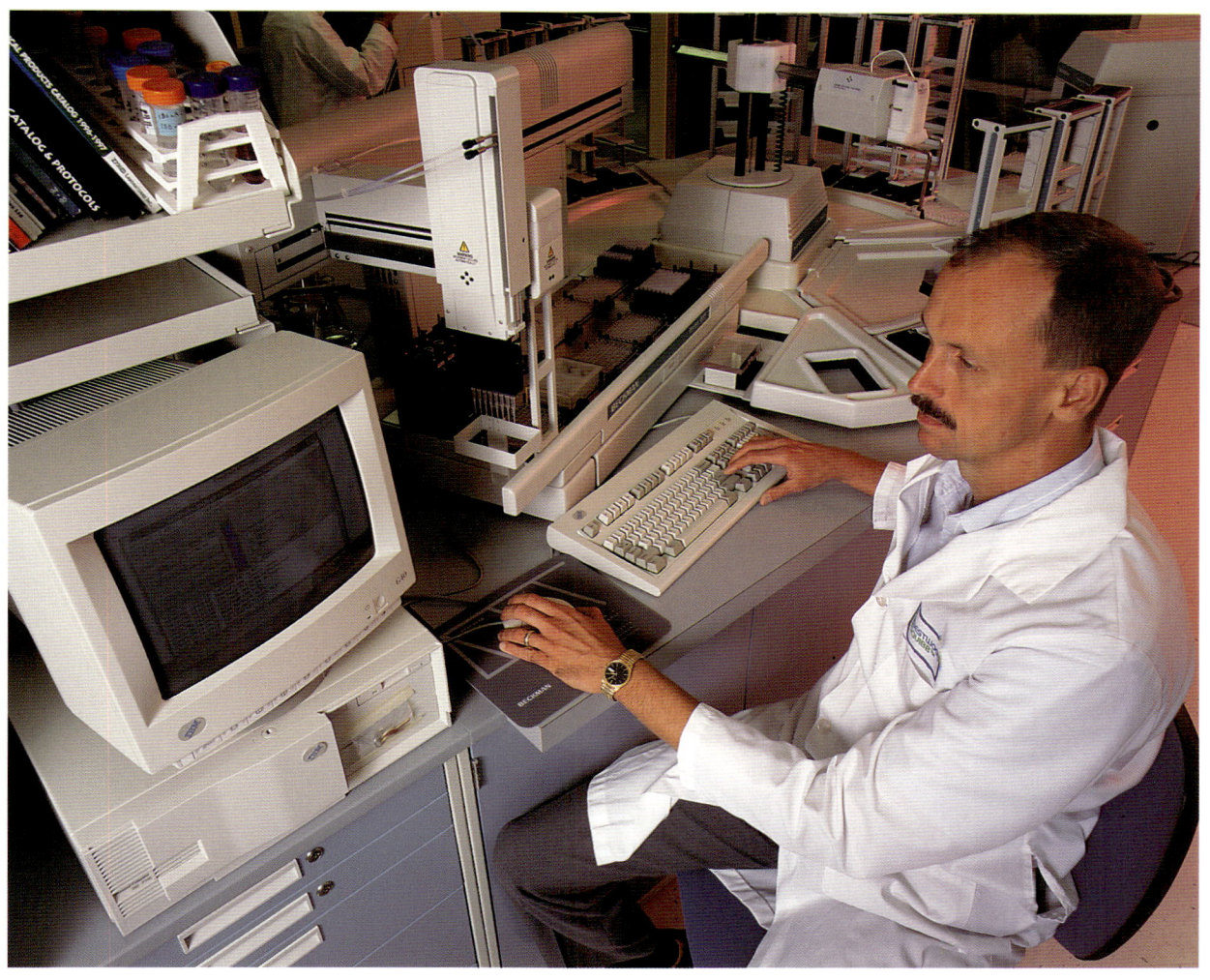

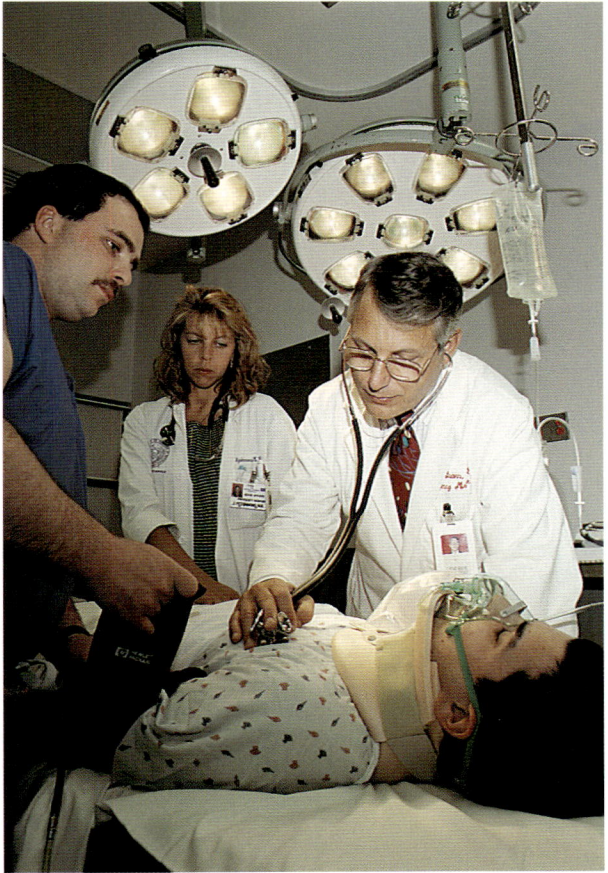

(top) At **Westwood-Squibb Pharmaceuticals**, a staff of 100 scientists and technicians works in the field of dermatology and skin care research to find remedies for afflictions of the body's largest organ. Researchers at Westwood-Squibb interact with their Bristol-Myers Squibb colleagues around the world seeking new and better treatments. Scientists here believe their findings may also have importance to the study of diseases such as cancer, arthritis, and other inflammations. Photo by James P. McCoy.

Erie County Medical Center is the regional center for trauma, burn, and rehabilitation patients and an important teaching facility for the State University of New York at Buffalo. The ECMC Healthcare Network includes an advanced clinical research hospital, off-site health centers, and the Erie County Home, a skilled nursing facility. Photo by Ronald M. Moscati.

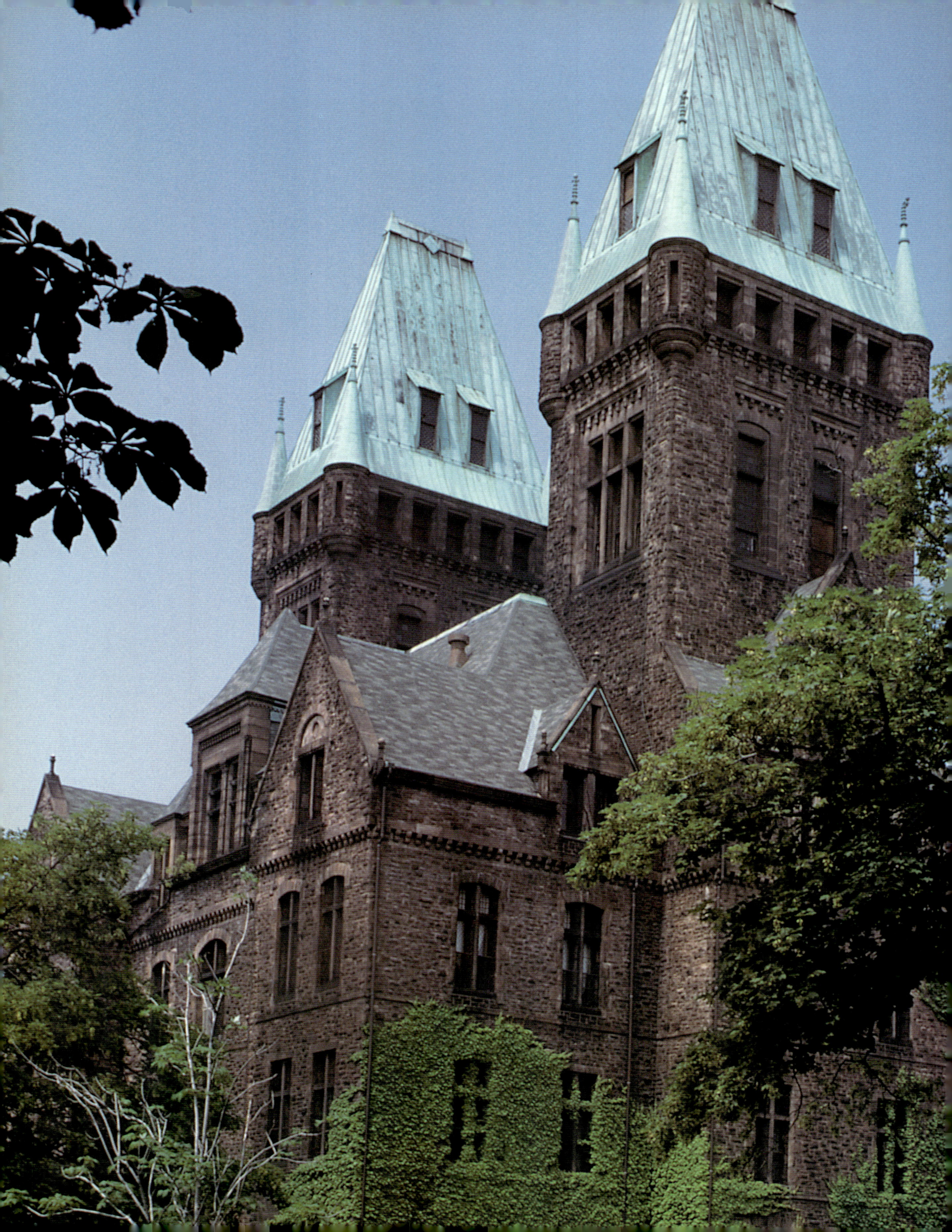

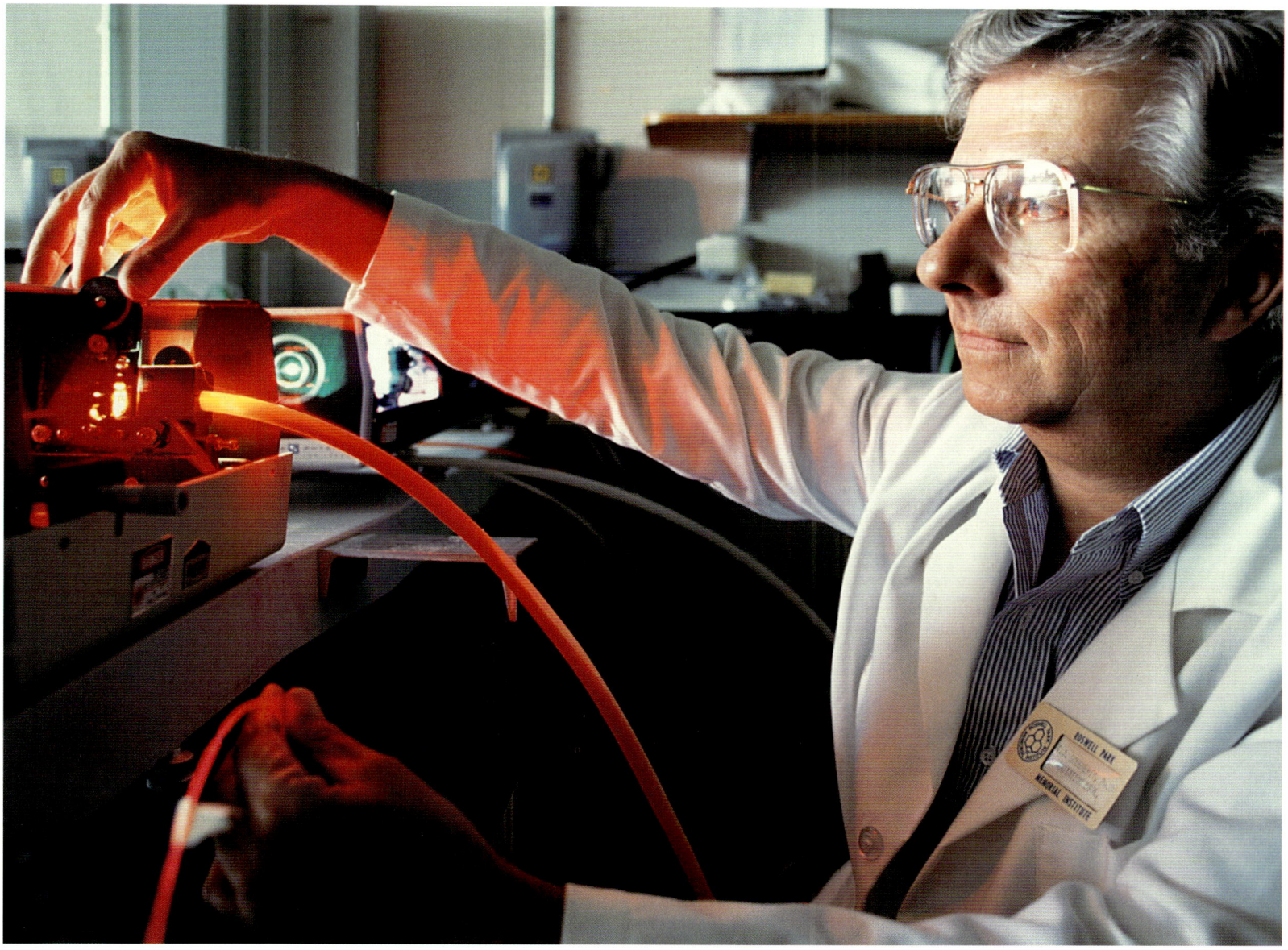

(left) When the **Buffalo Psychiatric Center** opened in 1880, it was a model for a nation committed to moving its mentally ill from poorhouses to asylums. The great gothic buildings and towers were designed by the brilliant American architect **Henry Hobson Richardson,** and the grounds and gardens were laid out by Frederick Law Olmsted. In the 1950s, nearly 4,000 patients lived in the dormitories and dayrooms of the Buffalo State Hospital, as it was formerly known. During the following decades, the hospital began a policy of "deinstitutionalization" predicated on the belief that patients could be better served in a more community-based environment.
Photo by James P. McCoy.

Dr. Thomas J. Dougherty, head of the Division of Radiation Biology at Roswell Park Cancer Institute, pioneered a revolutionary cancer treatment for esophageal cancer using a combination of drugs and lasers. In the treatment, patients are injected with the drug Photofrin, which makes the tumor sensitive to light. Next, thin fiber-optic cables are inserted into the esophagus to shine red laser light on the tumor. The drug, activated by the light, energizes tissue oxygen into a form that kills the cancer cells.
Photo by James P. McCoy.

Opened in 1996 and equipped with out-standing biomedical research facilities, the $54 million Biomedical Research Building on UB's South Campus is home to several research groups including the Center for Microbial Pathogenesis, the Center for Cardiopulmonary Biology, and the Center for Molecular Mechanisms of Disease and Aging. Research facilities include a level-3 biohazard suite for studying the AIDS virus and other dangerous pathogens, 18 temperature-controlled environmental chambers, a specific pathogen-free facility for research involving gene transfer, laboratories, offices, meeting rooms, and other workspaces. In addition to its research centers, **UB's Health Science complex** includes the university's highly ranked Schools of Medicine and Biomedical Sciences, Dental Medicine, Pharmacy, Nursing, Health Related Professions, and a 316,000-volume Health Sciences library.
Photo by James P. McCoy.

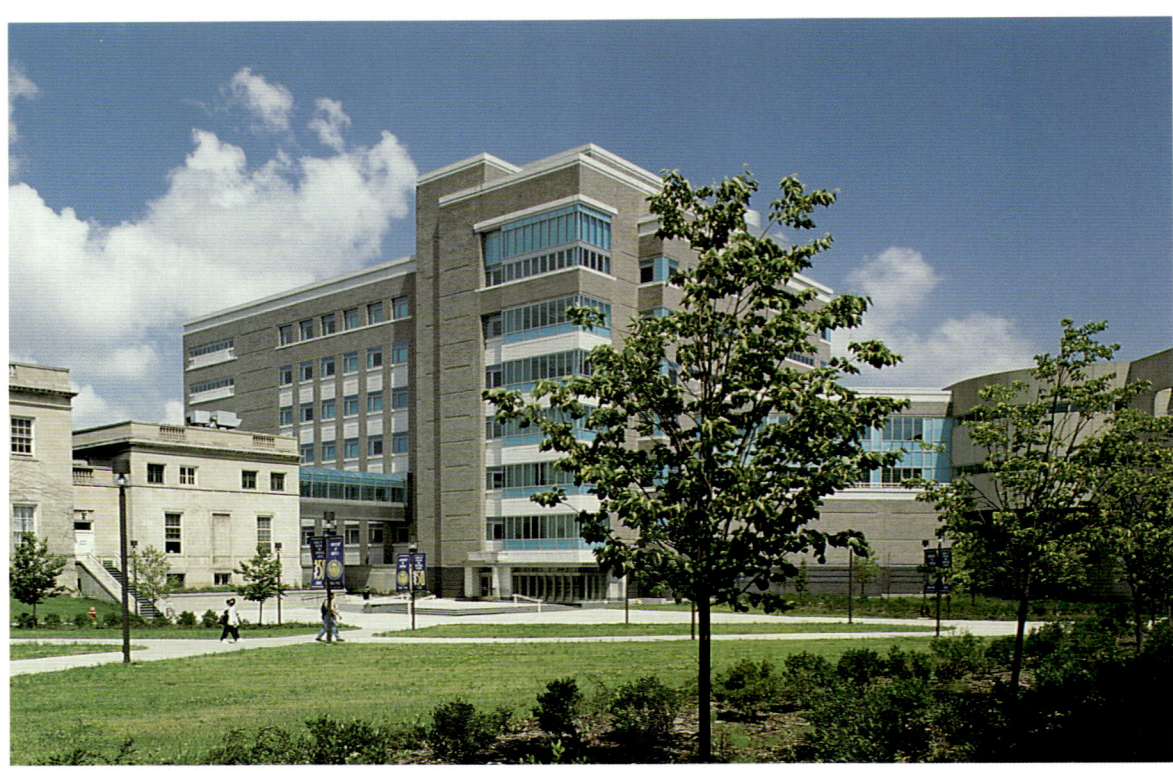

At the **University at Buffalo School of Medicine and Biomedical Sciences**, more than 800 graduate and medical students and 750 faculty work, engage in research, and study the latest advances in biomedicine. UB medical students train in clinical programs at eight university-affiliated teaching hospitals throughout Western New York. In addition to the M.D. degree, advanced degrees are conferred in anatomy and cell biology, biochemistry, biophysical sciences, microbiology, pathology, pharmacology and toxicology, physiology, social and preventive medicine, and statistics. A Medical Scientist Training Program offers a combined M.D./Ph.D. degree for aspiring clinician/scientists.
Photo by James P. McCoy.

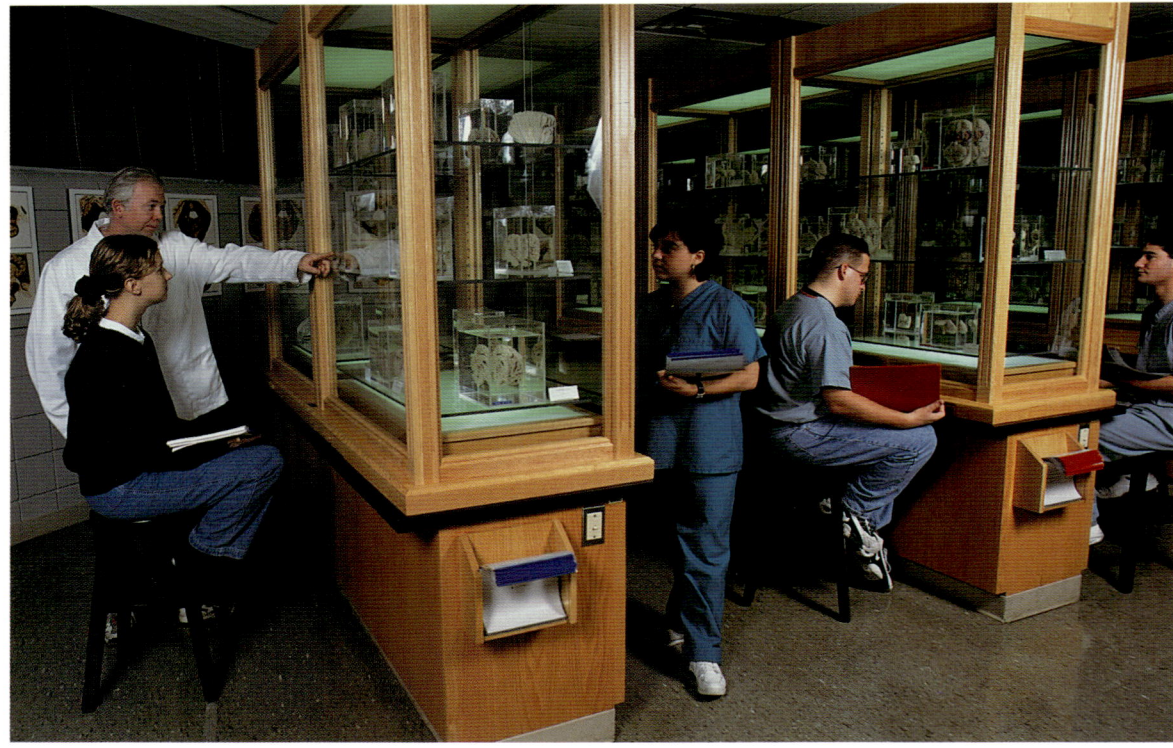

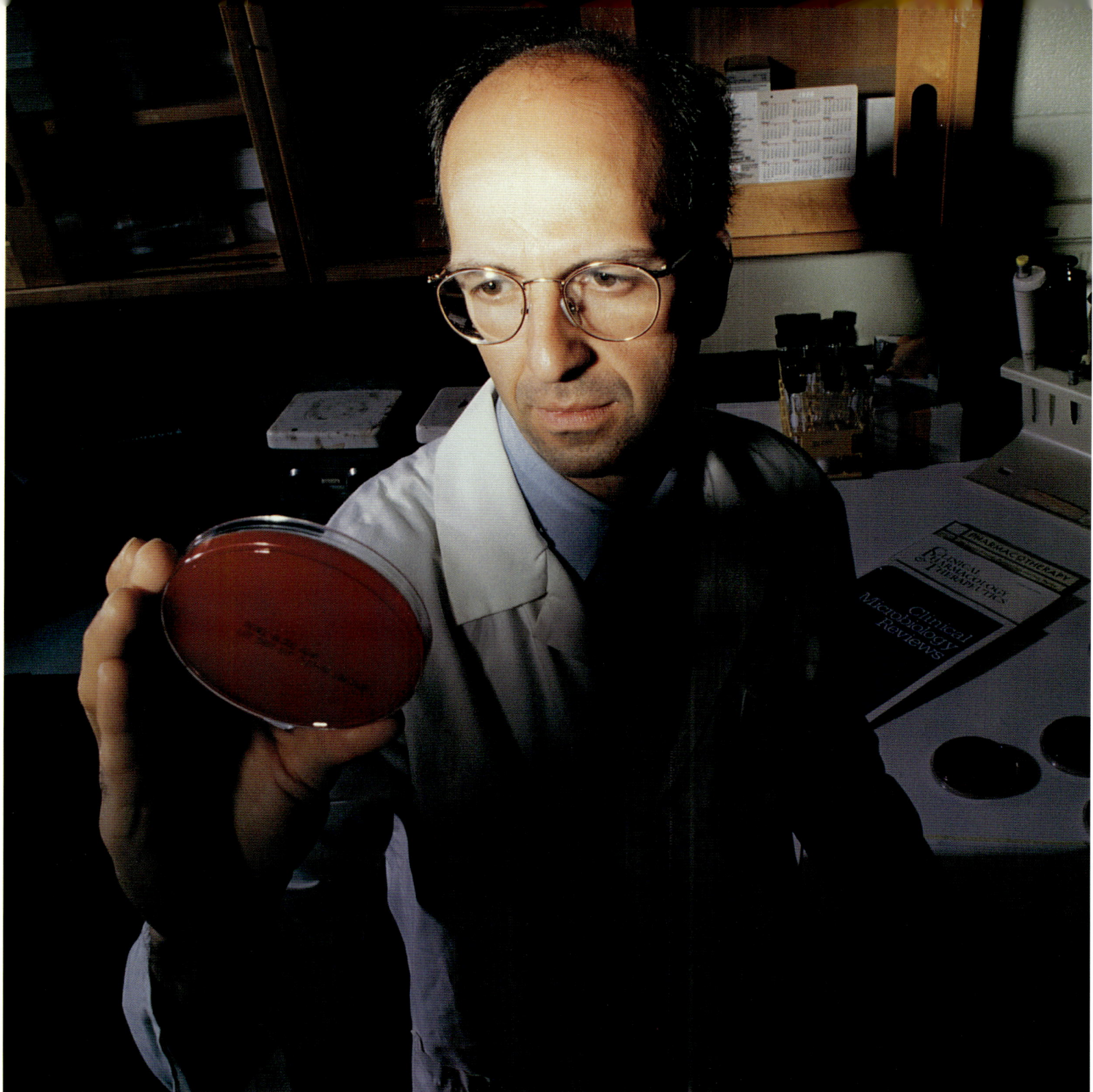

The **Clinical Pharmacokinetics Laboratory (CPL) at Millard Fillmore Hospital** is the world's oldest and largest facility dedicated to the study of medications and how they work. With three sites and a staff of nearly 100 professionals, this multidisciplinary research center conducts over 50 clinical trials a year. CPL researchers have shown physicians both how to use new drugs and use the old ones more efficiently. The laboratory has tested many commonly prescribed medications including antibiotics, asthma medications, heart medications, beta blockers, and antidepressants.

Photo by James P. McCoy.

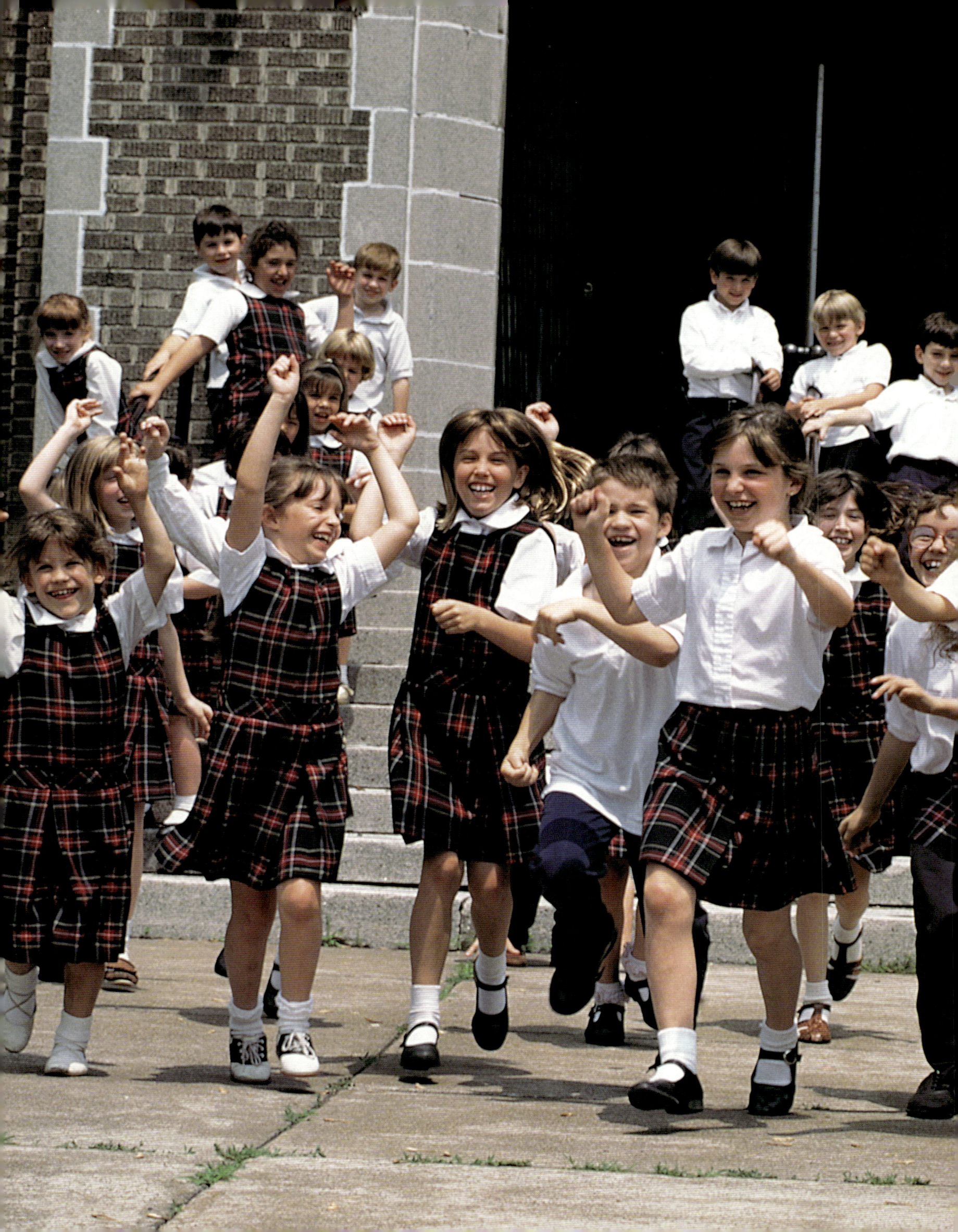

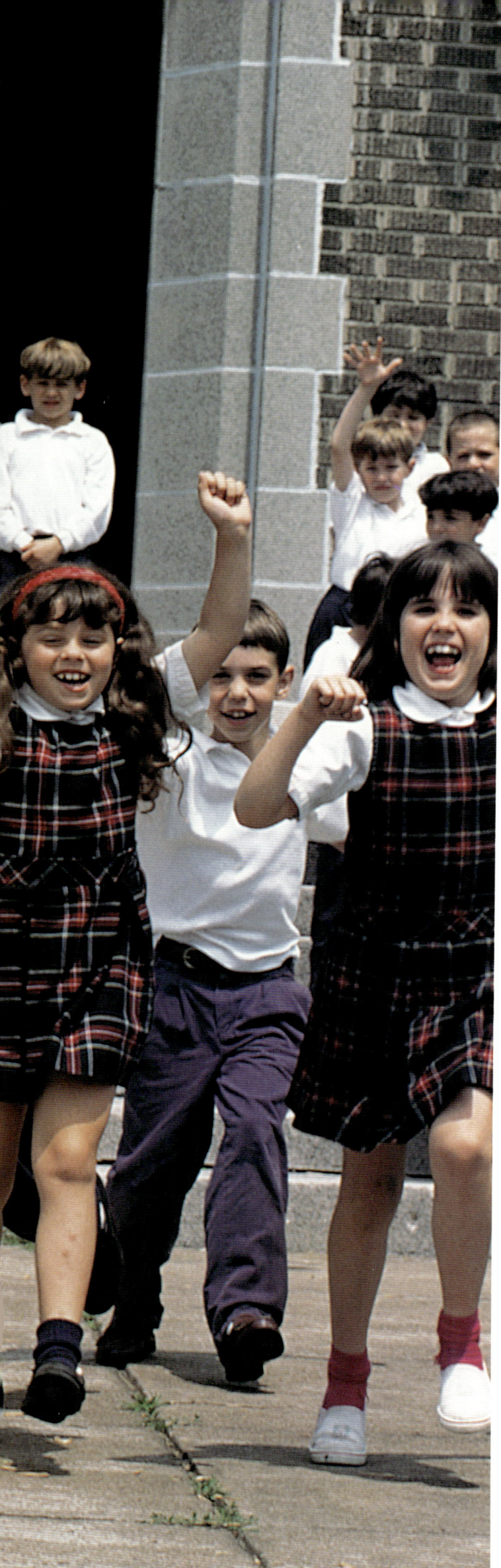

THE QUEST FOR KNOWLEDGE

A volunteer teaches city kids how to restore an old boat and lays the foundations for the restoration of a boat-building industry. A young engineering student spends a summer working with an engineering design team at a local firm. A Presbyterian minister and a Catholic nun speak to a young audience about religious tolerance. A college student teaches English to a Bosnian refugee. There are many exciting moments in education in the Niagara community, and not all of them are in a traditional classroom.

It could be curiosity, boredom, hunger, passion, or legal compliance, but all learning is driven by human need. Although its younger detractors may regard some education as merely mandated captivity, a look at the learning institutions of Western New York and the Niagara Peninsula of Ontario reveals a diverse tapestry of public, private, and nontraditional ways of imparting information and seeking new discoveries in science, technology, and the humanities. Above all, education in Niagara is distinguished by vital, and sometimes unexpected, connections—connections between students and teachers, between colleagues and disciplines, between people and machines, races and nationalities, research and performance, gown and town, science and art, money and love.

(previous page) Welcoming summer vacation with open arms, second and third-graders run from **St. Rose of Lima Catholic School** in Buffalo, one of 94 Catholic elementary schools administered by the Diocese of Western New York. With a combined enrollment of just under 25,000 elementary students, plus nearly 6,000 students in 17 independent Catholic high schools in 1996, Catholic schools are a vital force in the area's educational life.
Photo by James P. McCoy.

According to an early chronicler of life on the Niagara Frontier, in 1825 there were four "common schools," one "young ladies' academy," and one "young gentlemen's academy" in the village of Buffalo. In 1996, one hundred and one public school districts enrolled some 250,000 pupils in the eight counties of Western New York alone. That same year, the State University of New York at Buffalo, founded in 1846 as the University of Buffalo, celebrated its sesquicentennial.

For its first 40 years, the University operated solely as a medical school. Then, between 1886 and 1922, when Dr. Samuel Capen became its first full-time Chancellor, the University established schools of Pharmacy, Law, Dentistry, and its College of Arts and Sciences. On September 1, 1962, after more than a century as a private university, the University of Buffalo became the State University of New York at Buffalo, the flagship of the SUNY system. During the following decades, UB expanded rapidly as it gradually moved from its cozy but cramped Main Street campus to the vast, rural expanse and brave new architecture of its sprawling Amherst campus.

With UB's growth occurring principally in Amherst, the largest urban campus is now that of Buffalo State College, which has a total enrollment of 11,341 students. Buff State was founded as a teacher's college in 1871 and moved to its present campus adjoining the grounds of the Buffalo State Hospital on Elmwood Avenue in 1931. The college, which became part of the State University of New York system in 1948, is still an important center of teacher training with programs in early childhood education, special education, and foreign languages. In addition, Buff State offers a wide range of curricula in applied science, arts and humanities, and natural and social sciences, as well as master's degrees in criminal justice, industrial technology, art conservation, and multidisciplinary studies.

Four other SUNY colleges in Western New York provide residents with a variety of alternatives in public education. The Fredonia State University College in northern Chautauqua County began life as the Fredonia Academy in 1826, then became one of New York State's new Normal Schools in 1867. Today, the college's 266-acre campus is home to over 4,000 full-time students.

In the village of Alfred, in rural Allegany County, New York, the Alfred State College of Technology offers associate degrees in applied science, arts, science, and occupational studies; and bachelor degrees in electrical engineering, electromechanical engineering, mechanical engineering, and surveying. The college also has an auxilliary campus in Wellsville.

From the Greek word *keramos*, meaning "fired earth," comes our word "ceramics." An integral part of private Alfred University, the New York State College of Ceramics is one of the world's foremost centers of ceramic research, development, and training of ceramic artists and engineers.

For working adults seeking to earn an associate, bachelor, or master's degree, Empire State College offers guided independent study programs at 40 locations across New York State. At Empire's Western New York center in Buffalo and at units in Lockport, Jamestown, and Olean, students and their professors (known as mentors) develop learning contracts that outline a course of study designed exactly for each student's goals. Learning contracts lay out topics, learning activities, and evaluative criteria for a 16-week study term. Mentors and students can meet in person, over the phone, or online to evaluate the progress of the student's self-directed learning in business and management, the arts, interdisciplinary studies, science and technology, educational studies, and many other academic areas.

At Geneseo State College, another SUNY school located in nearby Livingston County just 70 miles east of Buffalo, undergraduate and graduate degrees are offered in education and other programs.

Brock University, a Canadian public university with 11,000 students in St. Catharines, offers both undergraduate and graduate programs in many disciplines. For aspiring creators of new ventures, Brock's Faculty of Business offers Canada's first undergraduate entrepreneurship major. With its personal atmosphere and relatively small class sizes, Brook concentrates its resources on the education of undergraduates.

Another post-secondary school on the Niagara Peninsula, Niagara College of Applied Arts and Technology, is a certificate- and diploma-granting institution with locations in Welland, St. Catharines, and Niagara Falls. Niagara College has a strong tourism and hospitality school. It also has reciprocal programs with its counterpart, Niagara Community College, in the areas of business and trade.

Cornell University celebrated its presence in Buffalo for 50 years in 1996 with ceremonies marking the founding of the Cornell School of Industrial & Labor Relations. The downtown Buffalo school offers several education and training-related undergraduate and graduate programs for both labor and management. These include supervisor training, human resource certification, and programs alerting workers to the hazards of chemicals in the workplace.

Among the area's nine private four-year colleges, six are independents founded or currently administered by members of Catholic orders—Canisius College (Jesuit), St. Bonaventure University (Franciscan), Niagara University (Vincentian), Daemen College (Sisters of St. Francis), D'Youville College (Grey Nuns of the Sacred Heart), and Hilbert College (Franciscan Sisters). Of the remaining three, two are independent and nonsectarian (Alfred University, Medaille College), and one (Houghton College) is a Christian institution affiliated with the Wesleyan Church.

For students seeking an associate degree, there are four public two-year community colleges (Erie Community College, Niagara County Community College, Genesee Community College and Jamestown Community College), two private two-year colleges (Trocaire College and Villa Maria College of Buffalo), a career-oriented business and technical school (Bryant & Stratton), and a nursing school (Sisters School of Nursing).

In the Niagara Region of Ontario, four school boards administer two public and two Catholic school jurisdictions. The Niagara South Board of Education and the Welland County Roman Catholic Separate School Board oversee their respective schools in Niagara Falls, Fort Erie, Thorold, Port Colborne, Wainfleet, Pelham, and Welland. There are 55 English language and 5 French language elementary schools, plus 12 English language and 1 French language secondary school in the Niagara South public system. The Niagara South Board also operates two skills centers with programs and facilities for students pursuing specific vocational training. Total public school enrollment was 26,358 students in 1995-96.

Towards Lake Ontario, the Lincoln County School Board and Lincoln County Roman Catholic Separate School Board run the schools in St. Catharines, Grimsby, Lincoln, West Lincoln, and Niagara-on-the-Lake. Public school enrollment in that jurisdiction also totaled around 26,000 during the same period.

In addition to its public schools, Western New York has 172 private elementary schools and 42 private high schools.

Although the great majority of these schools are Roman Catholic, there are also Lutheran and other Protestant schools as well as Jewish, Quaker, Muslim, Montessorri and Waldorf schools, and special schools for the handicapped. In Chautauqua and Cattaraugus counties, there are 20 Amish elementary schools.

The Niagara Peninsula also has 24 private non-Catholic schools. Most of these schools are affiliated with various Protestant churches, although some are non-sectarian, and three are Montessori schools.

Of course the quest for knowledge is more than the sum total of a community's students, teachers, and schools. In Niagara, education is a lifelong experience that encompasses the needs of the entire community, from neonatal care classes through nursery and pre-K programs to special skills training to adult education classes. Many of these activities take place through nonprofit organizations and the dedicated commitment of thousands of volunteers. ✣

Named for a former mayor of Buffalo, the **Stanley M. Makowski Early Childhood Center** is three schools in one. Each school, known as a neighborhood, is housed in its own instructional wing with connecting open classrooms that surround a central courtyard. In the large nature courtyard, children can water flowers, work at the weather station, or tend to the greenhouse. In an adjoining family services wing, there is a 12-month daycare center and a wellness clinic providing primary health care for students. One of Buffalo's 12 early childhood centers, each affiliated with a middle school academy, the Makowski Center is based on a child-centered curriculum that fosters learning through projects inherently interesting and captivating to children. Photo by James P. McCoy.

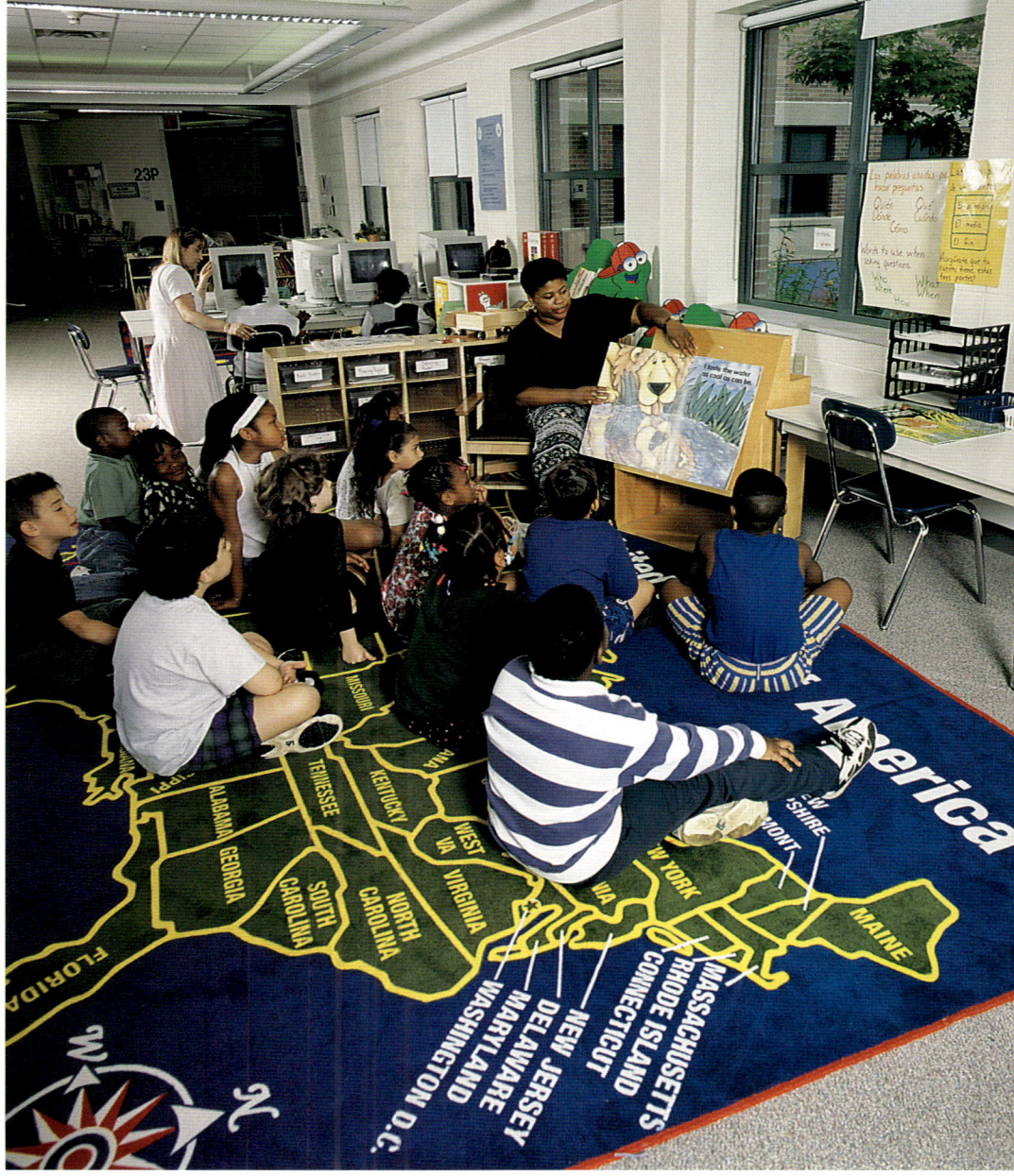

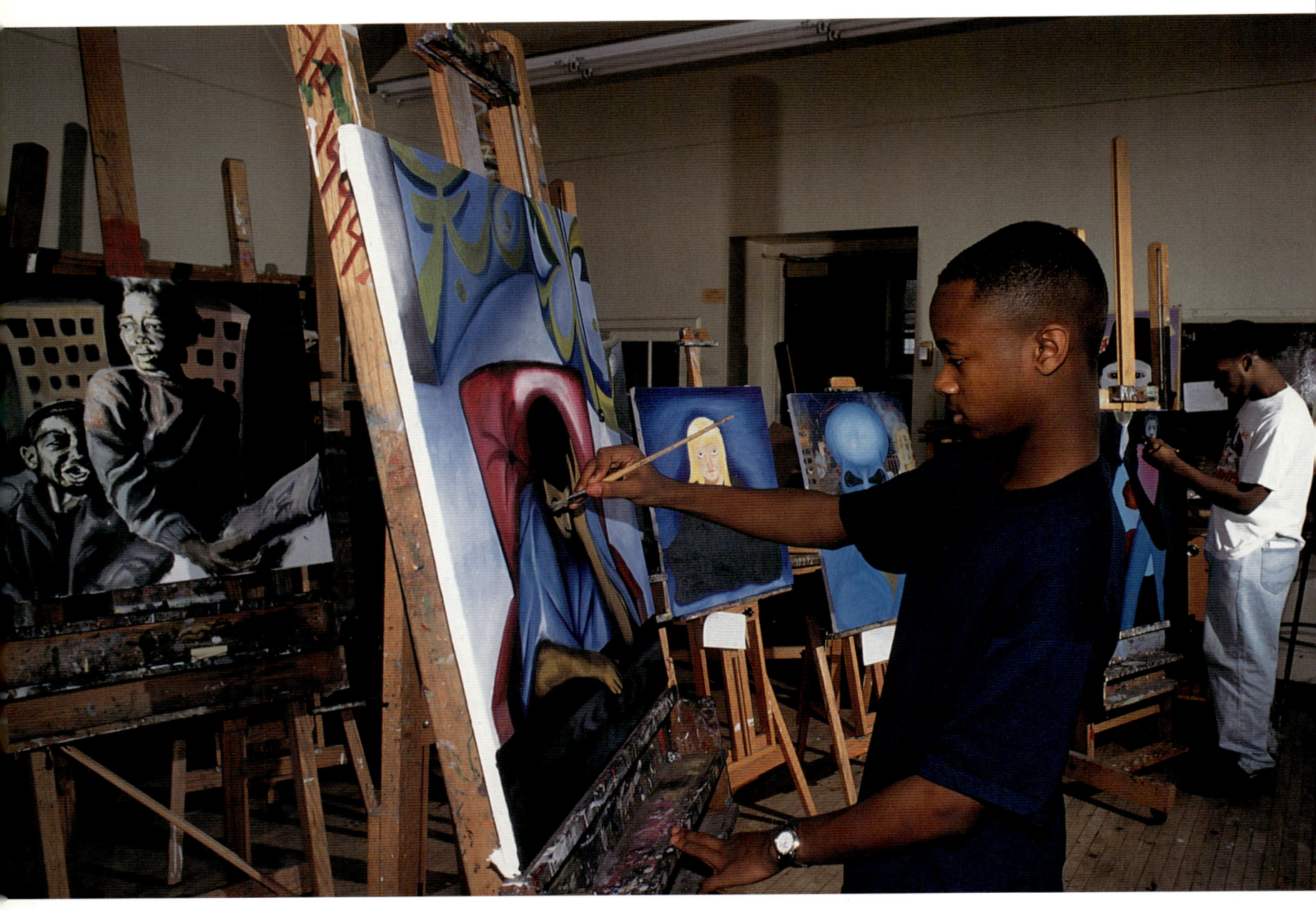

At the **Buffalo Academy for the Visual and Performing Arts**, students in grades 5 through 12 major in art, music, theater, or dance while also studying English, math, science, history, social studies, and other academic subjects. Performing Arts high school students can also major in radio and television. Regardless of their major, all students are accepted for admission to BAVPA on the basis of an audition. Photo by James P. McCoy.

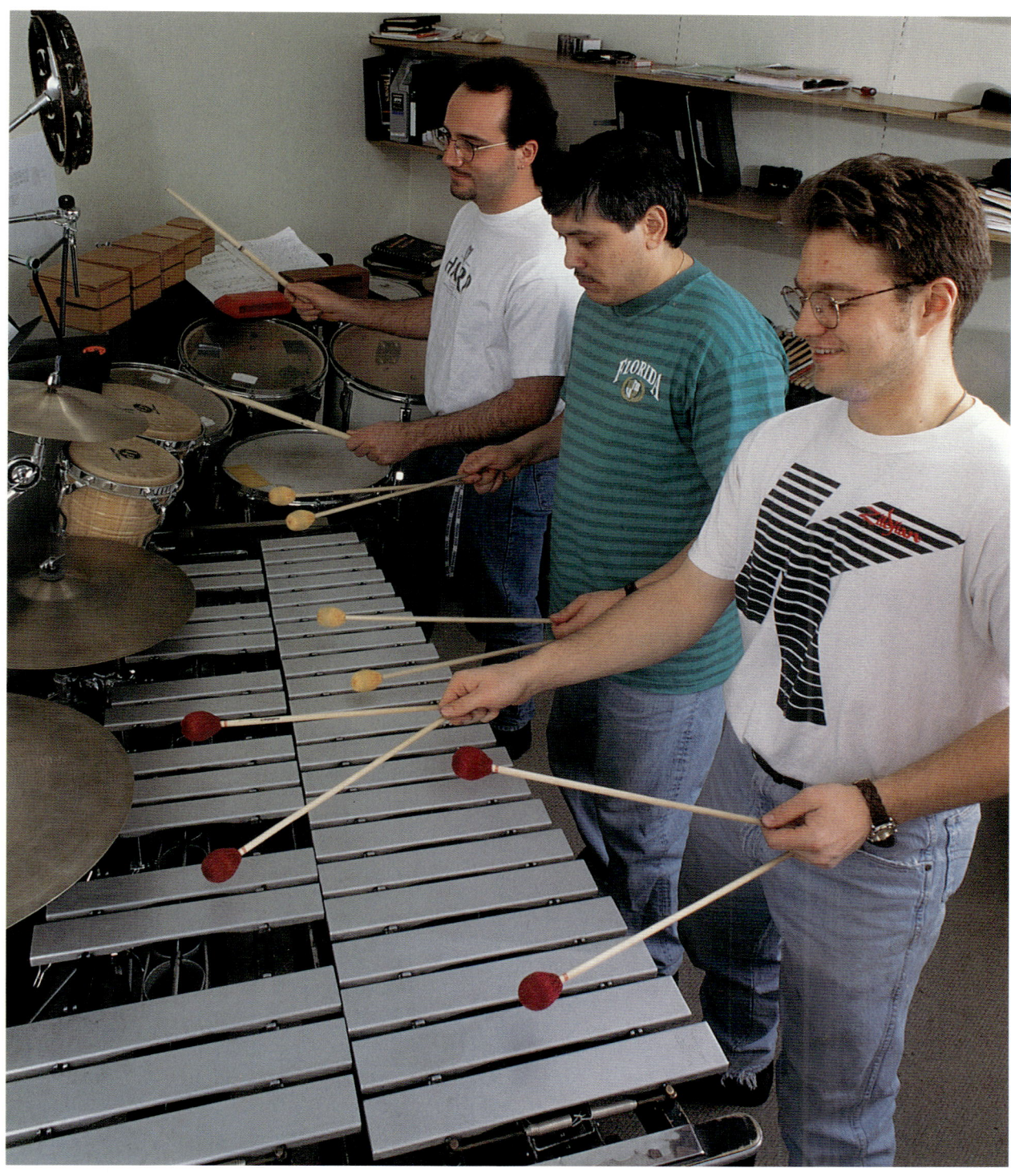

A magnet for serious music students from across the country, the **Fredonia State University College School of Music** offers programs in performance and music education as well as musical theater, composition, music therapy, and sound recording.
Photo by James P. McCoy.

The headquarters of the **National Center for Earthquake Engineering Research** was established at UB in 1986. Composed of a consortium of several academic institutions, and supported by the National Science Foundation (NSF), the center is sponsored by both the NSF and New York State. Through its Education and Technology Transfer program, the center disseminates ideas and information and helps integrate its academic research with direct industrial applications that can protect buildings, bridges, and other structures from damage during earthquakes. The center also conducts cooperative research with institutions in Japan, China, Mexico, and Taiwan.
Photo by James P. McCoy.

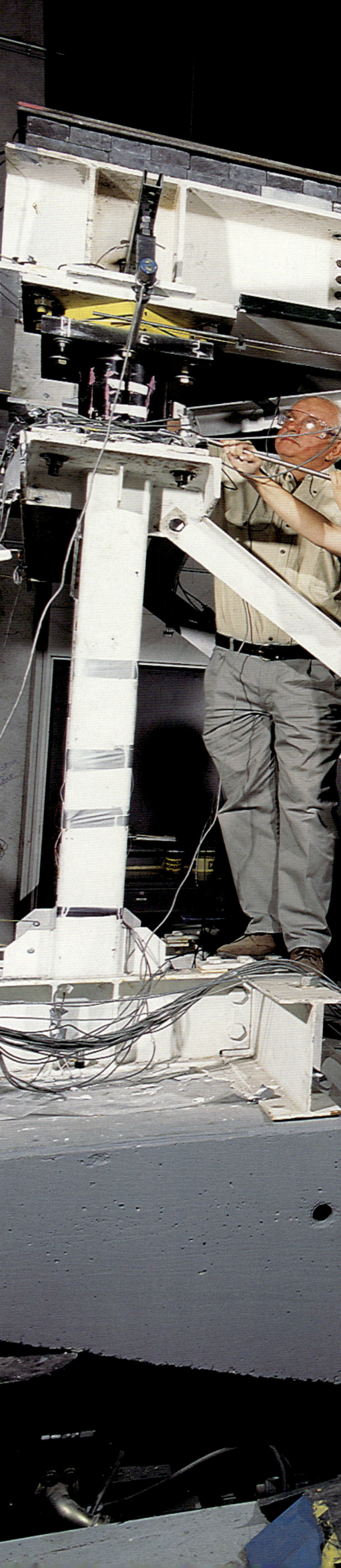

Brock University in St. Catharines offers six undergraduate degree areas, several interdisciplinary programs, and graduate degrees in eight disciplines. Total enrollment was 11,299 students in November, 1995. Named for General Sir Isaac Brock, fallen hero of the Battle of Queenston Heights in the War of 1812, Brock University is a major intellectual, cultural, and academic center in the Niagara Region of Ontario.
Photo by James P. McCoy.

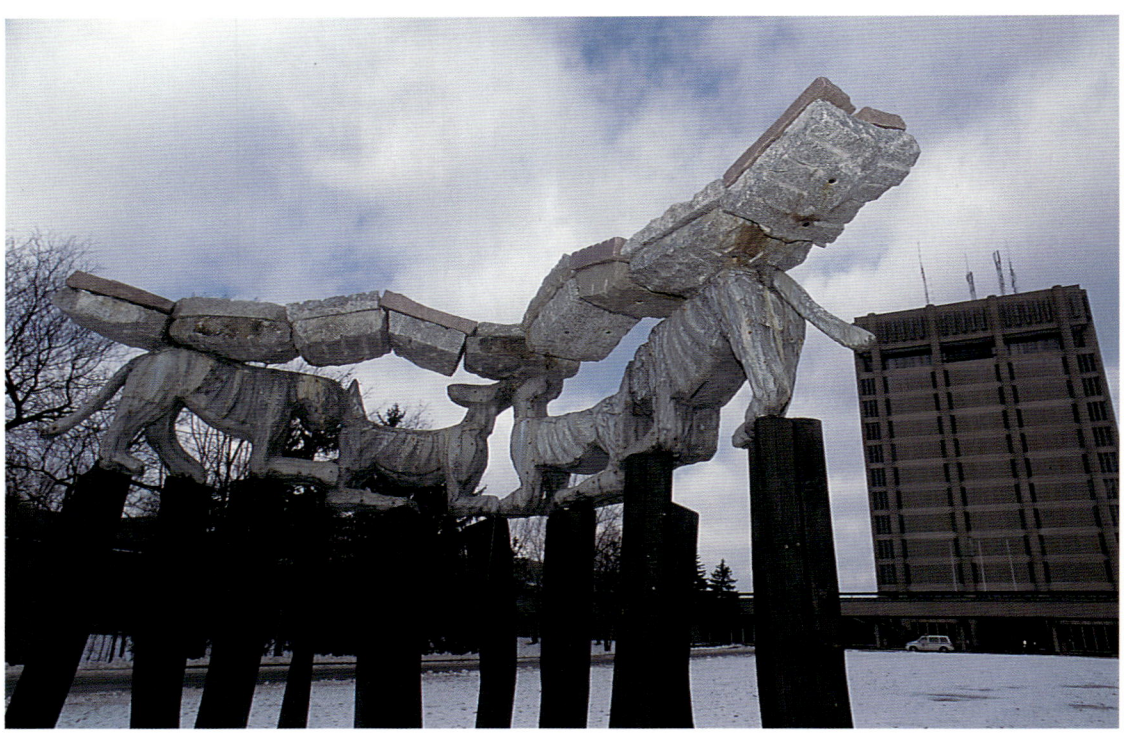

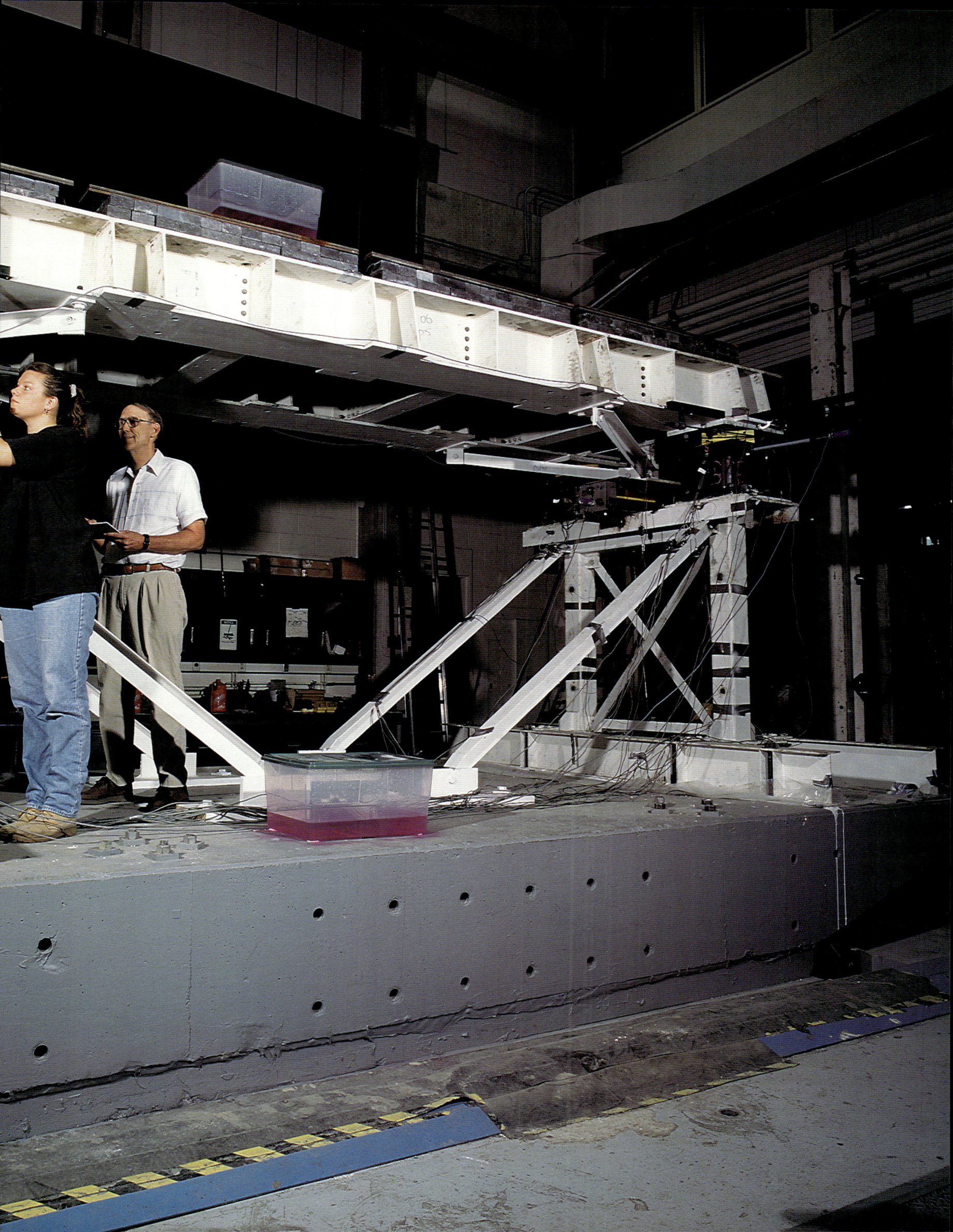

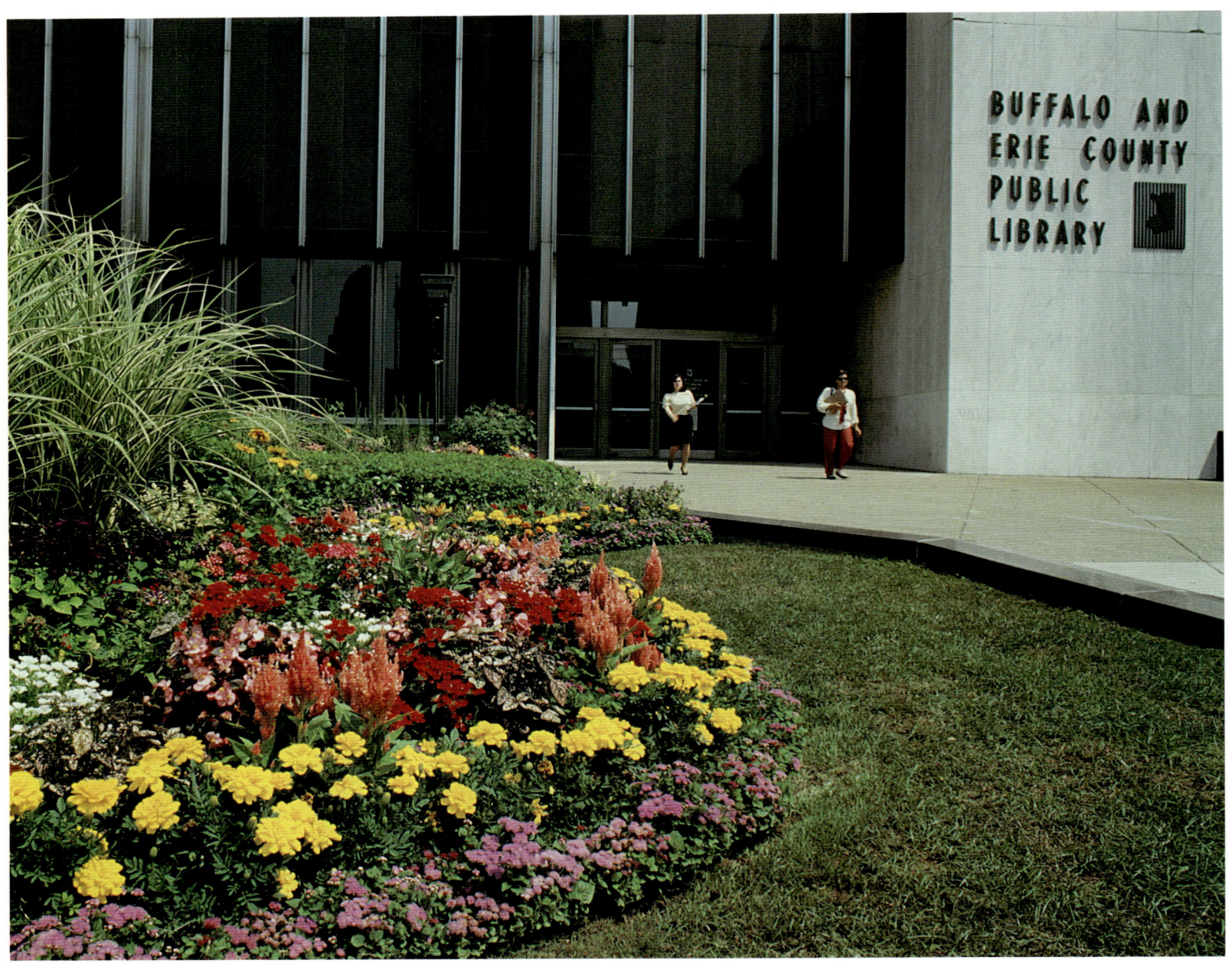

Formed from the merger of three libraries in the 1950s and 1960s, the **Buffalo and Erie County Public Library** consists of the Central Library at Lafayette Square in downtown Buffalo, 15 neighborhood branch libraries throughout the city, and 23 member libraries. One of its most treasured possessions is the complete handwritten manuscript of Mark Twain's *The Adventures of Huckleberry Finn*, handsomely displayed in its own Mark Twain Room along with other Twain artifacts and memorabilia, including many first editions in several languages. Photo by James P. McCoy.

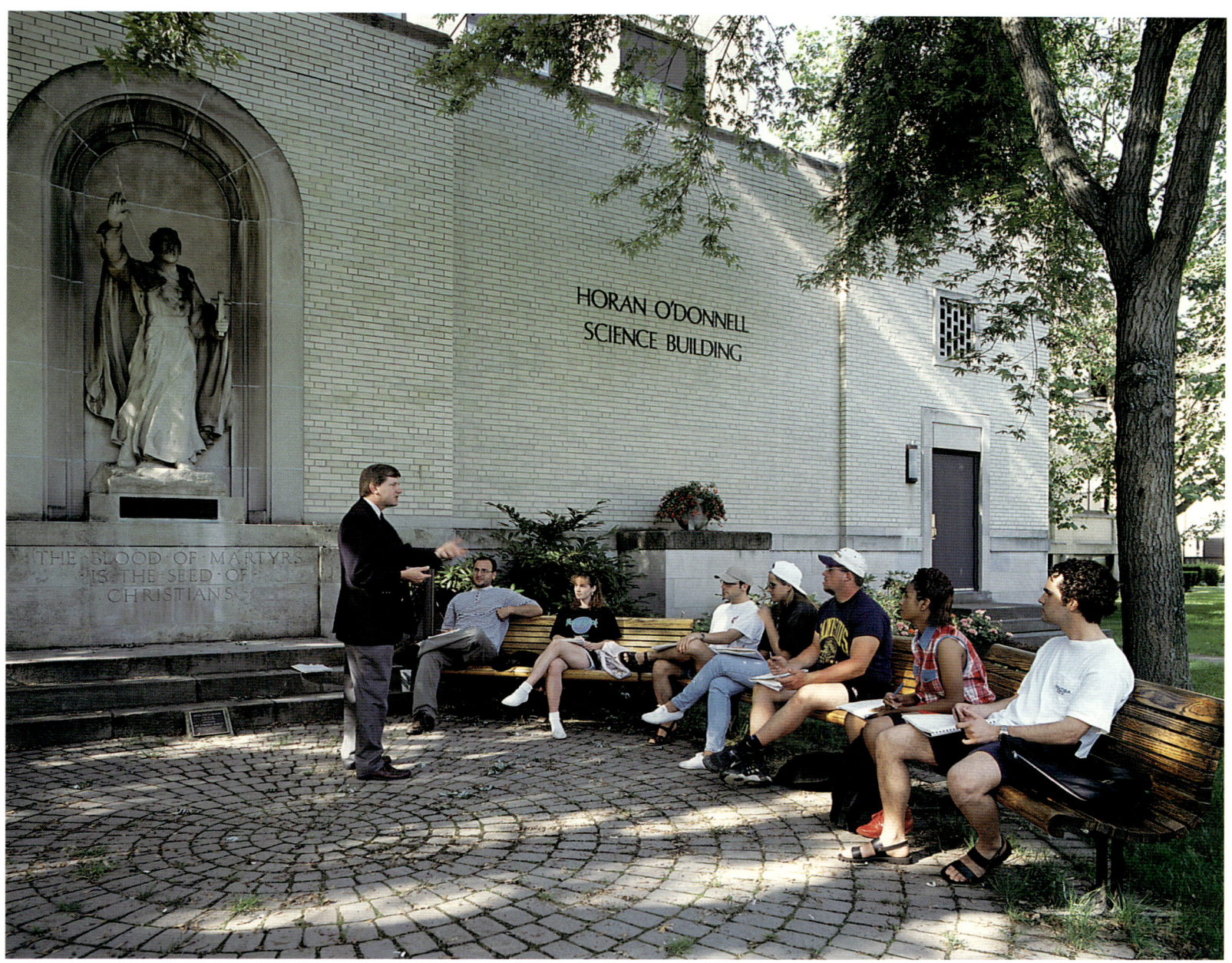

Another Main Street campus brought its classrooms to suburban Amherst in 1996 when **Canisius College** created an extension of its master of business administration (MBA) program at Uniland's University Corporate Center. The largest of Western New York's private colleges, Canisius enrolls a total of nearly 5,000 students in its college of arts and sciences, its highly regarded school of business, and its school of education and human services. Canisius, which celebrated its 125th anniversary in 1995, is consistently ranked as one of the nation's top college values.
Photo by James P. McCoy.

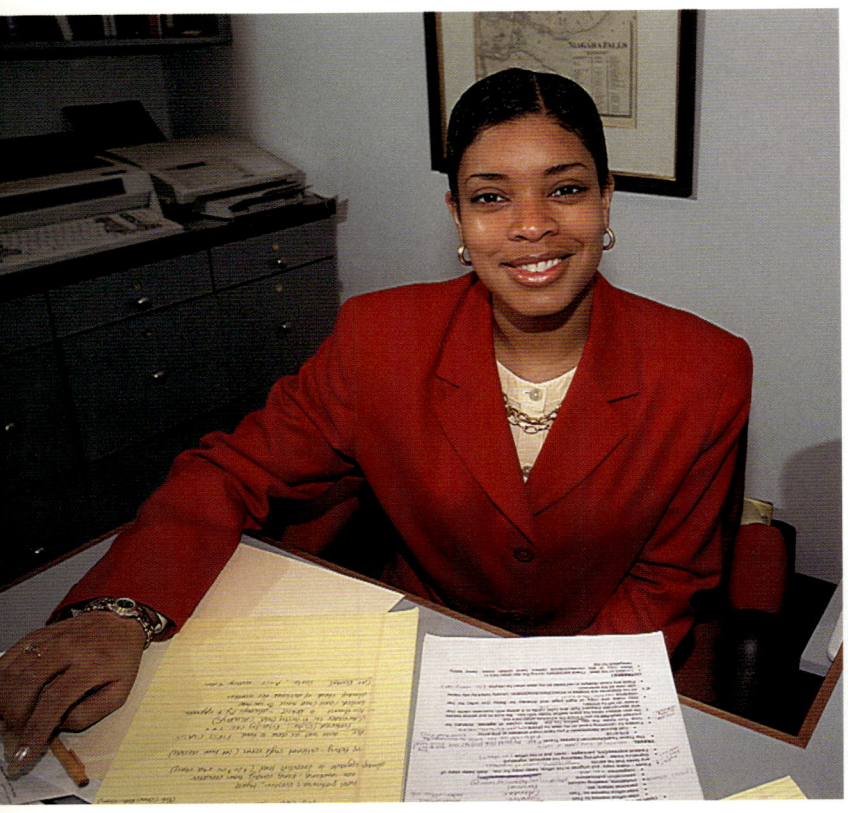

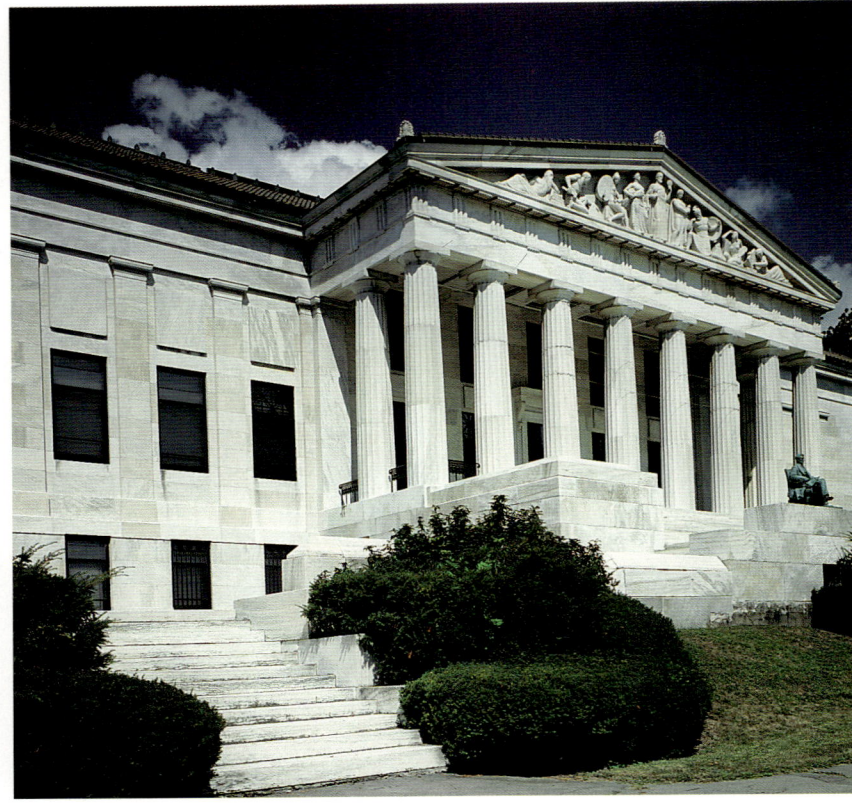

Through the Greater Buffalo Partnership's **Minority Student Internship Program**, high school juniors and seniors and college students can qualify to work as summer interns with local employers. Before interning, participating students take part in a training program that includes seminars on career planning, job seeking skills, survival skills, workplace diversity, and leadership development.
Photo by James P. McCoy.

According to Dr. William H. Siener, director of the **Buffalo and Erie County Historical Society**, the society began "by gathering reminiscences as a resource for the future." Among these "reminiscences" is the complete incoming correspondence of Millard Fillmore, 13th president and a prime mover in the formation of the society. Other items in the society's collection of 80,000 artifacts include important papers of the Holland Land Company, wine casks from the Lake Erie fleet of Commodore Oliver Hazard Perry, and the pile driver used by Samuel Wilkeson to build the Buffalo harbor. Overlooking Hoyt Lake on the northwest corner of Delaware Park, the Historical Society's building is itself a Buffalo artifact. Built on its present site as the temporary New York State Building for the Pan-American Exposition of 1901, this Neoclassical white marble temple was later converted to a permanent structure and home for the society.
Photo by Marc Murphy.

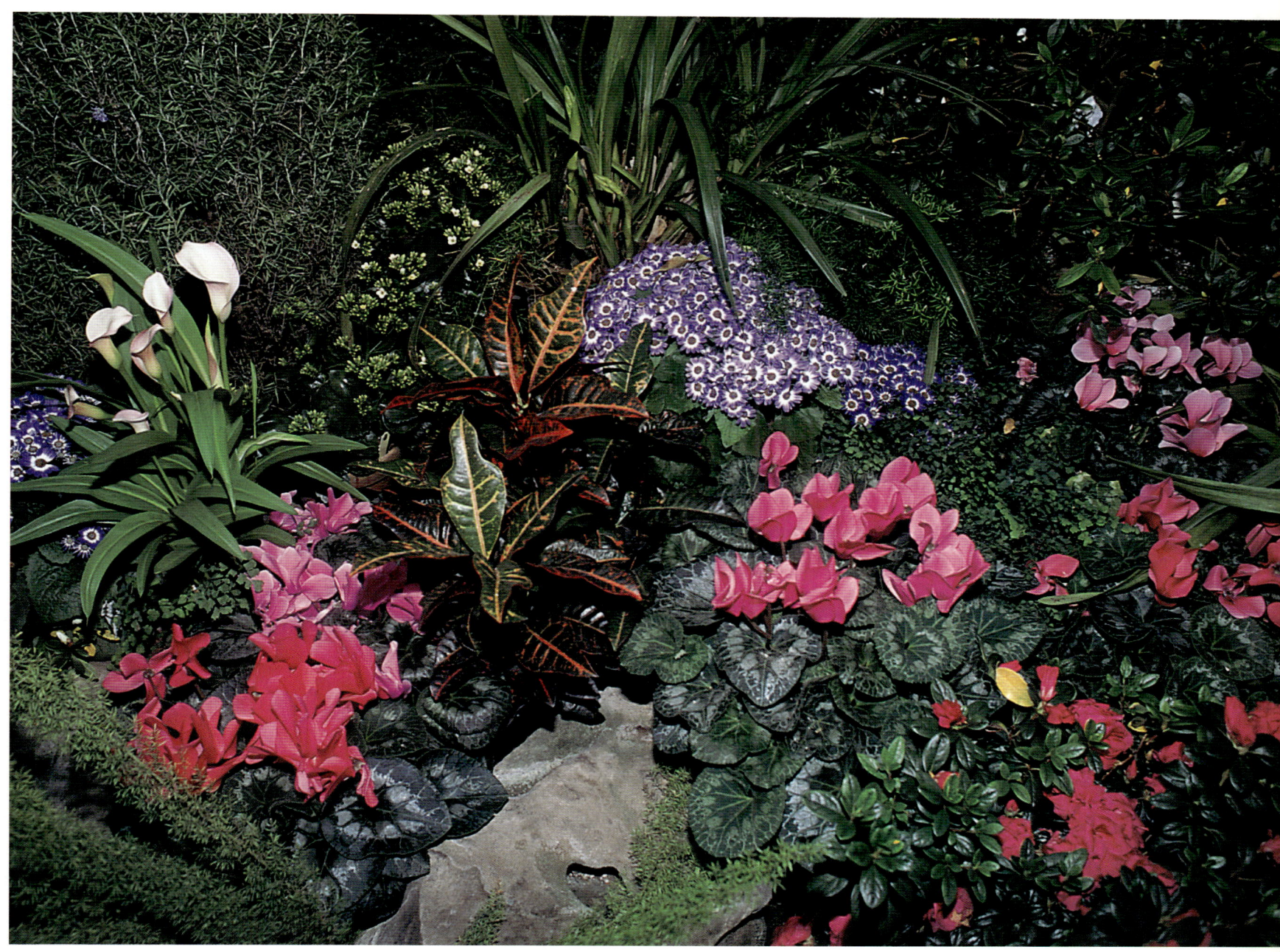

Imagine free room and board at a school with no basketball or football team! At the **Niagara Parks Botanical Gardens and School of Horticulture**, first- and second-year horticulture students receive room and board free of charge from the Niagara Parks Commission, which administers the school. Originally called the School for Apprentice Gardeners, this flourishing institution offers a three-year program that combines classroom courses such as arboriculture, botany, floriculture, entomology, and landscape design with practical experience developing and maintaining the Botanical Gardens.
Photo by James P. McCoy.

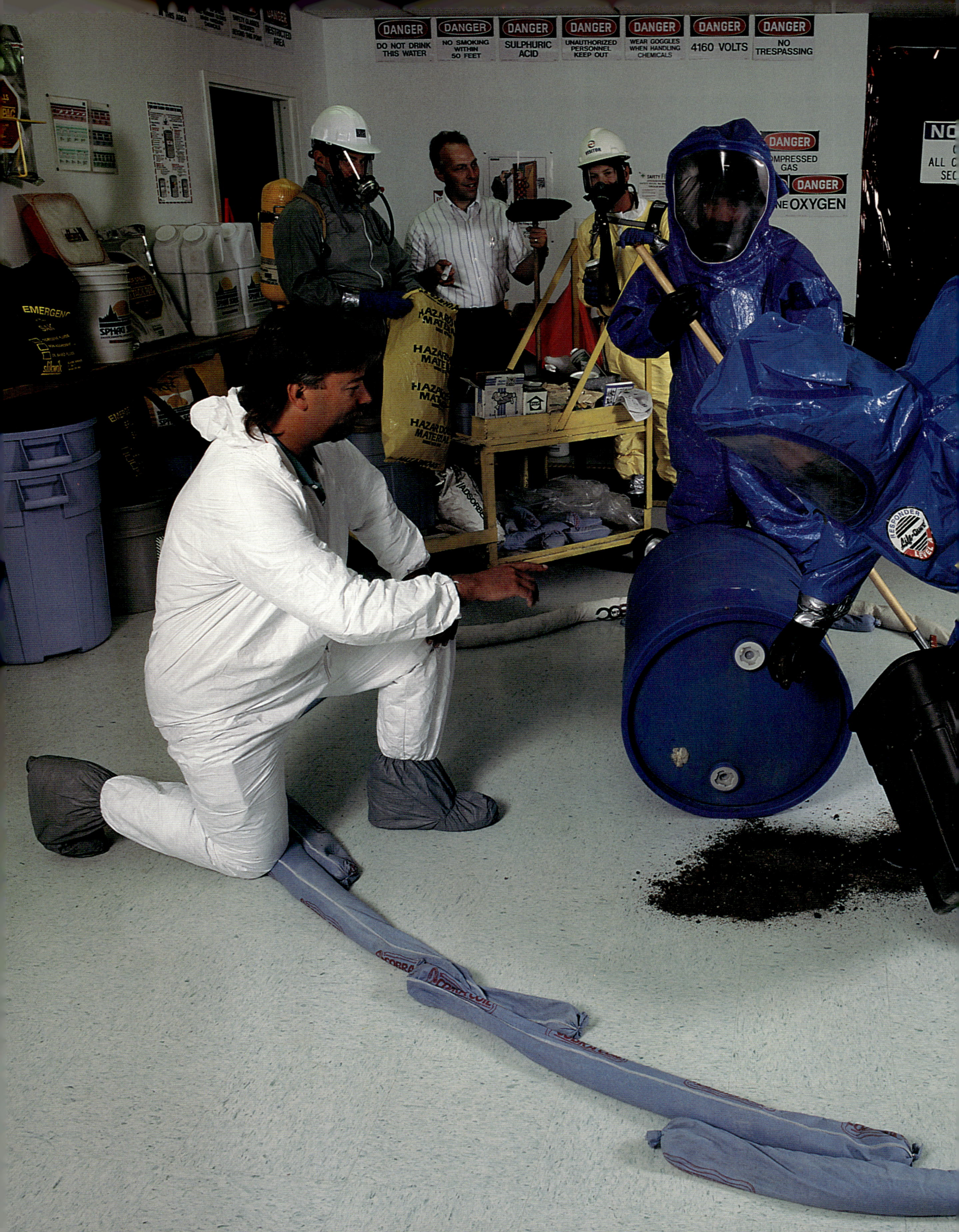

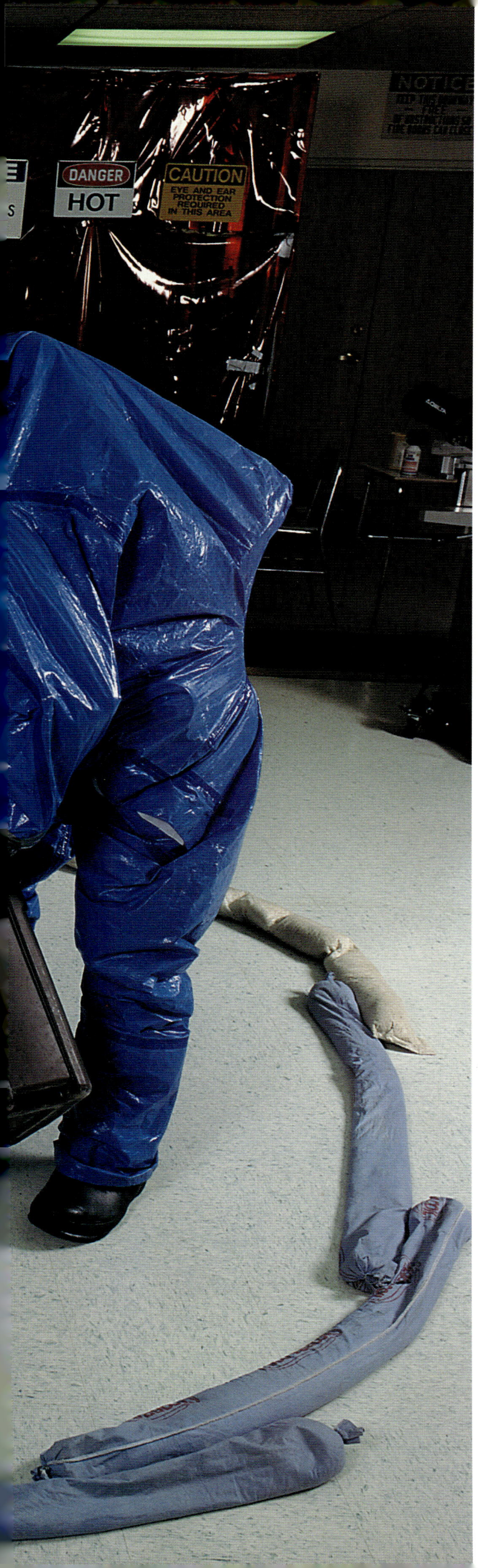

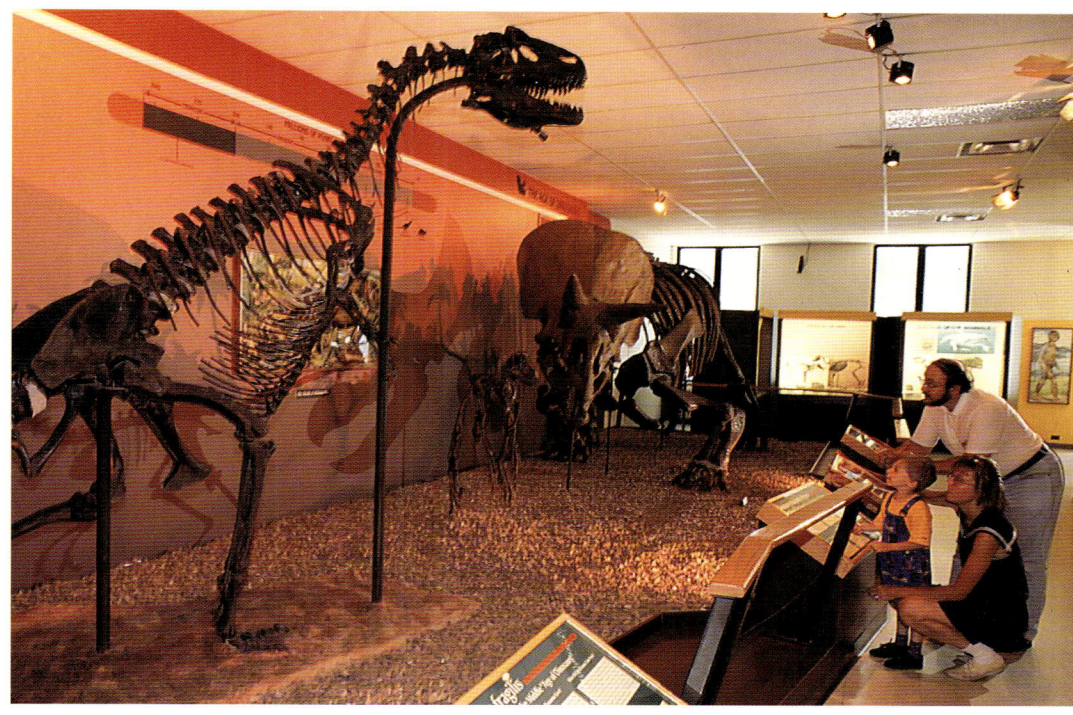

Prevention of industrial spills, explosions, and falls; asbestos abatement; and the safe handling of hazardous waste, are some of the topics covered at the **Occupational Safety and Health Administration (OSHA) Training Institute Education Center** run by Niagara County Community College at its Corporate Training Center in Lockport. Cooperative efforts between Western New York companies, unions, and local OSHA officials led to the formation of this OSHA training center, one of 12 in the nation in 1996.
Photo by James P. McCoy.

Discover the world of dinosaurs, enter the insect kingdom, take a trip down the Hall of Endangered Species or explore outer space at the **Buffalo Museum of Science (BMS)**. Under the administration of the Buffalo Society of Natural Sciences, the BMS is a fascinating repository of collections from the fields of anthropology, astronomy, botany, geology, mycology, and zoology. The Buffalo Society of Natural Sciences also administrates the Tifft Nature Preserve, a 250-acre wildlife refuge of cattail marsh, wetlands, ponds, open fields, and woodlands open to the public just south of the Buffalo River near the City Ship Canal and the Small Boat Harbor.
Photo by James P. McCoy.

The International Institute of **Buffalo** remains a beacon of hope and source of invaluable help to immigrants, refugees, and other non-English speaking newcomers seeking to build a new life in the community. Dedicated to enriching society with enthusiastic, productive new citizens representing many cultures, the International Institute offers immigration counseling, resettlement assistance, and language classes in English, Italian, French, Spanish, and German. The institute also provides translations and interpreting in more than 40 languages for corporations, government agencies, and individuals.
Photo by James P. McCoy.

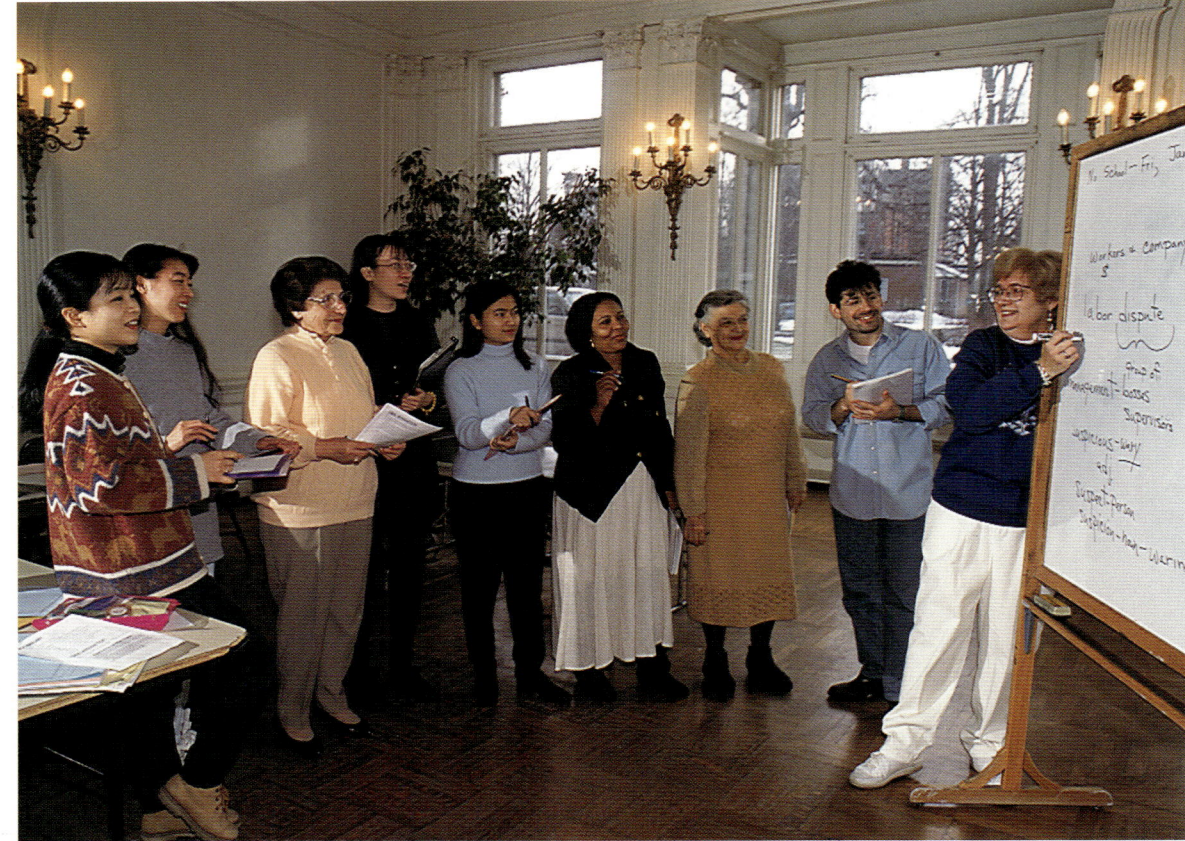

The Clarkson Center, a private, nonprofit human services agency, provides help, training, and hope to troubled youth, to abused and neglected children, to the unemployed and elderly, and to other individuals leading high-risk lives. On the center-initiated Sea Fever Project, inner-city youths learn carpentry, woodworking, mechanics, and marine repair skills. At the **Clarkson Center's Culinary Arts Institute**, students learn all aspects of food preparation and service while training for careers in food service and hospitality. Designed for unemployed youths and displaced adults in need of job retraining, the institute serves lunch twice a week at its downtown Main Street location.
Photo by James P. McCoy.

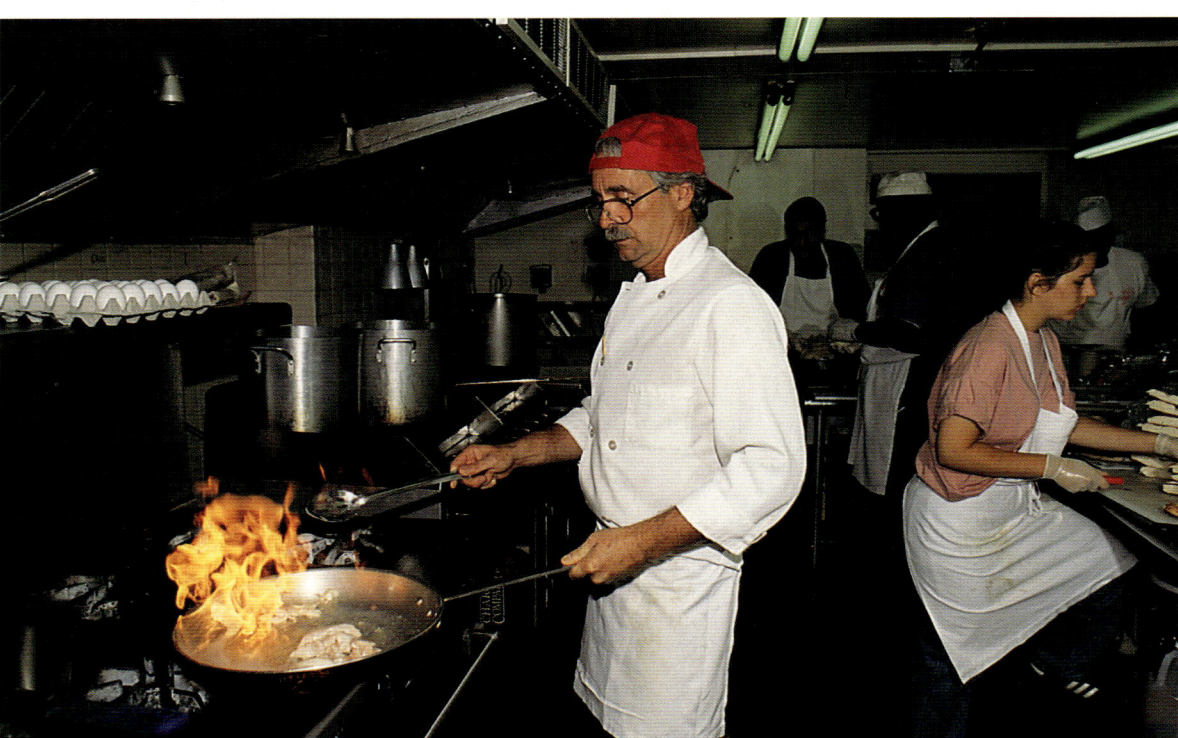

(right) At the **Center for Urban Studies** at UB, **Dr. Henry Louis Taylor, Jr.** and his staff conduct research to gain insight into the realities facing central cities and their metropolitan regions, and offer suggestions on how to restructure and rebuild neighborhoods and community institutions. Driven by a profound belief in the responsibility of the university to participate in the public discourse and to help shape social transformation, the center is both a theoretical think tank and a technical resource for individuals and groups seeking assistance in housing, economic development, neighborhood investment, and the incubation of minority-owned businesses.
Photo by James P. McCoy.

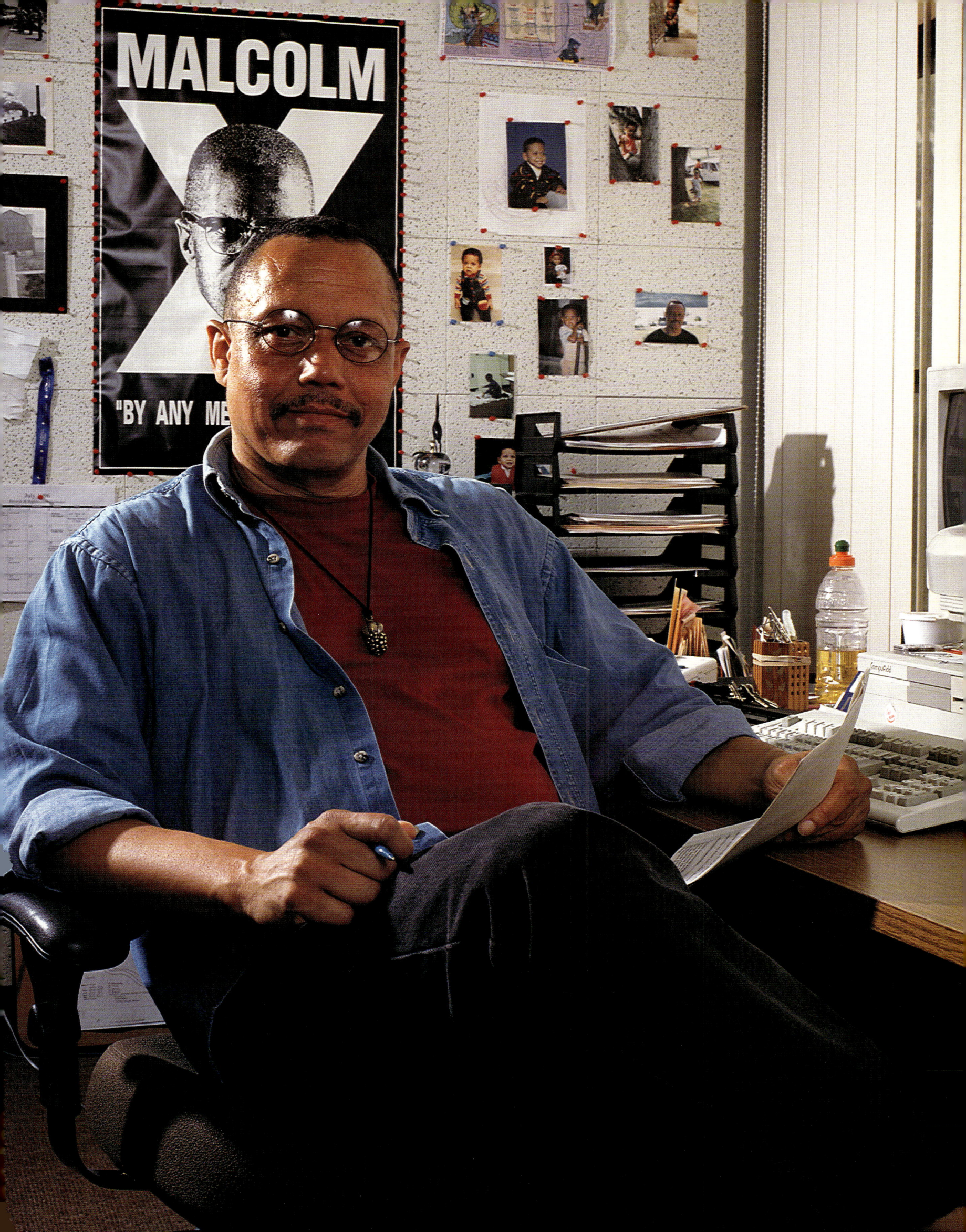

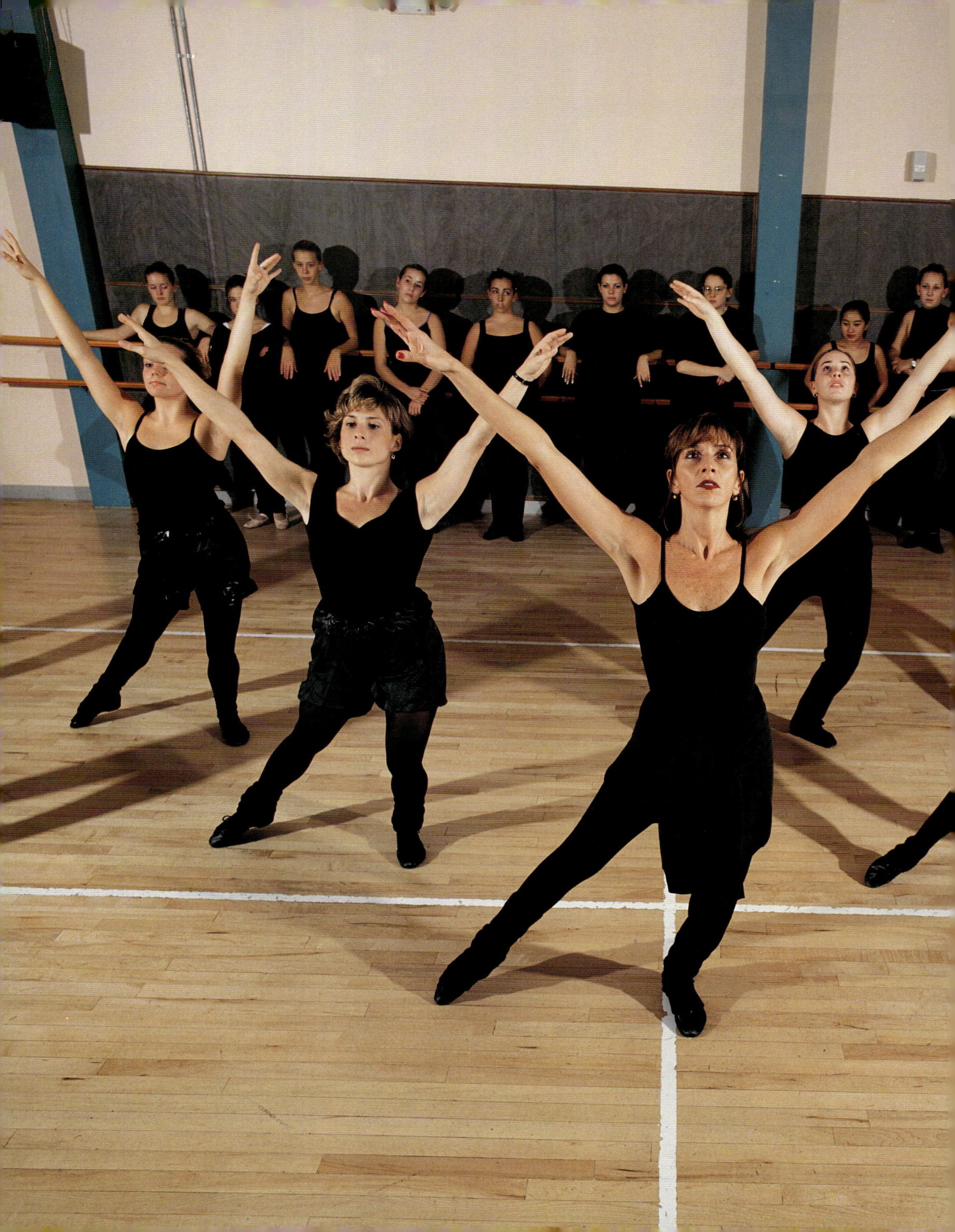

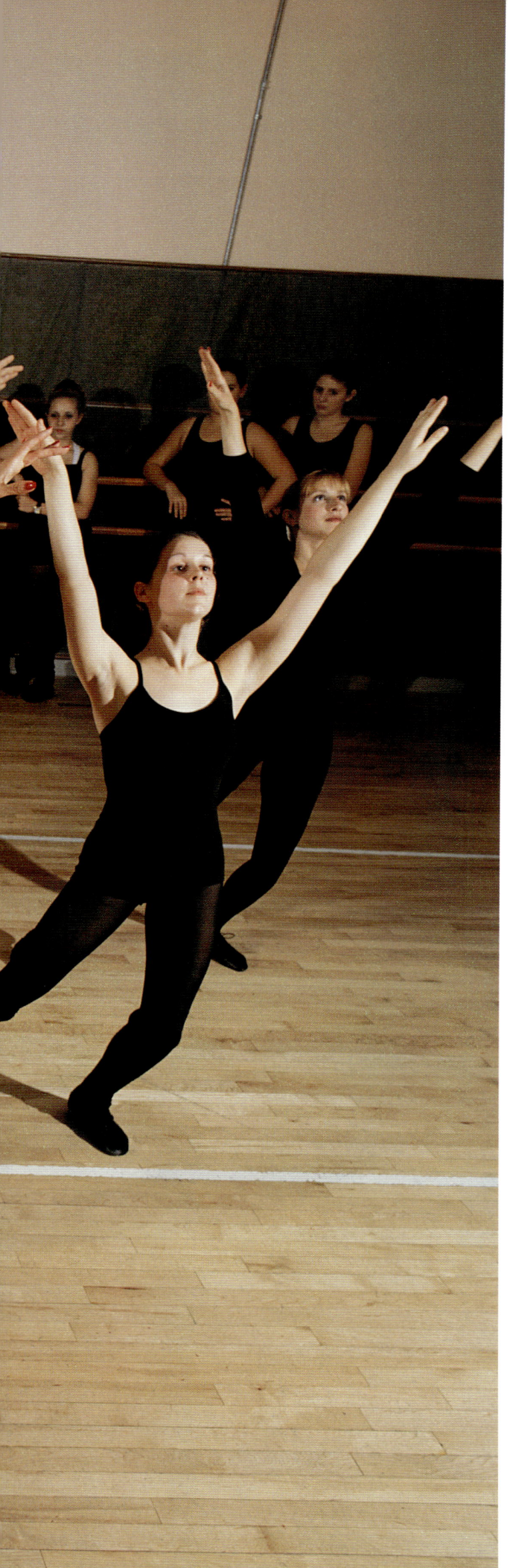

THE CREATIVE IMPULSE

For the creative artist, Niagara has often been both an attractive and supportive environment in which to live and a rewarding subject for work. The celebrated American painter Charles Burchfield roamed the streets of Buffalo on his lunch hour when he worked at the Birge Wallpaper Company in the 1920s, sketching the houses and streets of the Lower West Side. Some 50 years later, Milton Rogovin began to explore the same neighborhood to photograph residents over a period of two decades.

Darlene Ceglia's Dance Project photo by James P. McCoy.

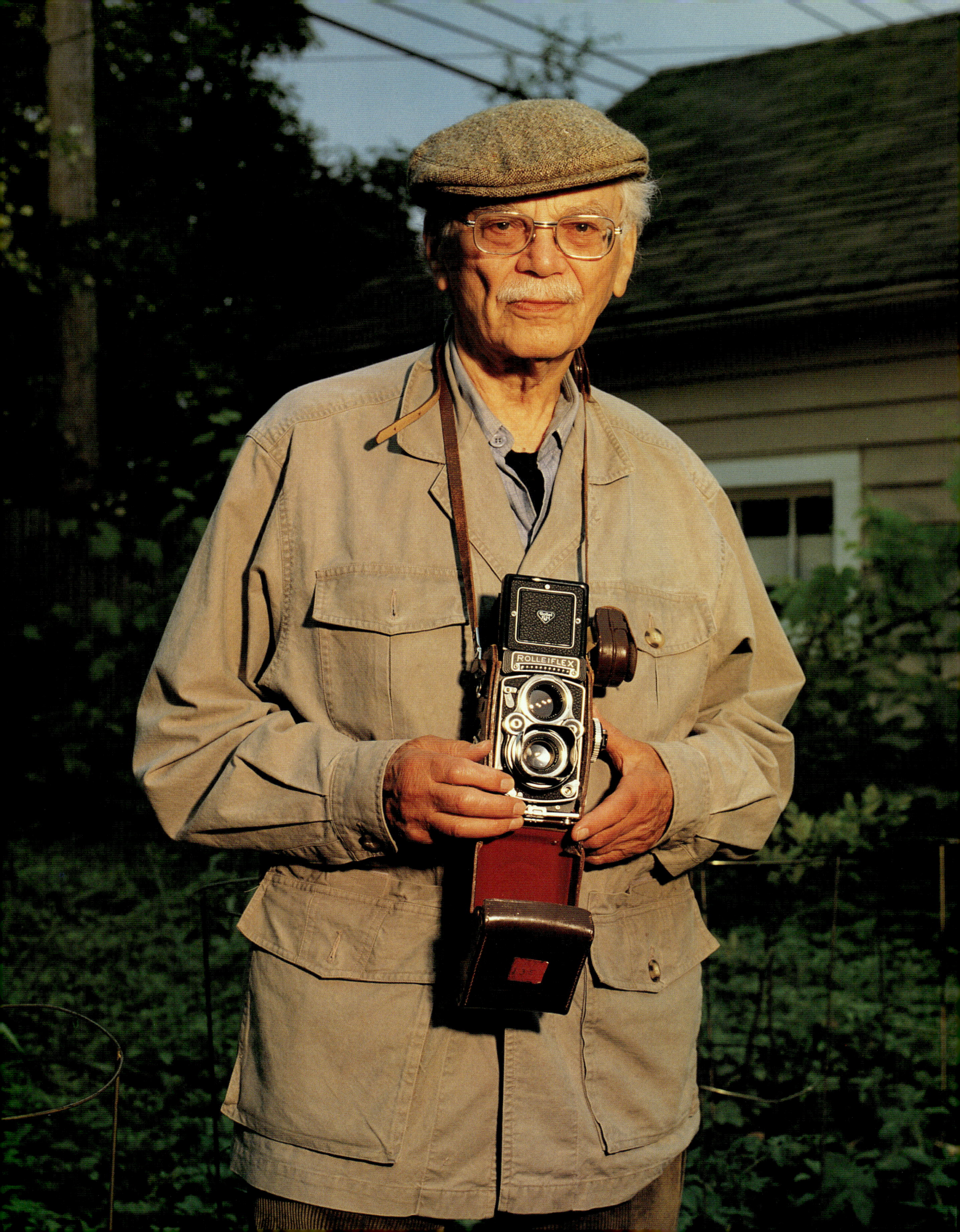

N iagara Falls has, of course, been the subject of countless artistic depictions from the early sketches based on the descriptions of Father Hennepin, to Frederick Edwin Church's definitive panoramic painting, to the photographs of John Pfahl and Preston Haskell. Poets, painters, musicians, dancers, and other creative and performing artists often cite the area's relatively inexpensive cost of living, its natural beauty and cosmopolitan character as some of the reasons for Niagara's strong and diverse artistic community.

The single most important event in the early development of Buffalo's cultural institutions was the founding of the Young Men's Association in 1836. Although the organization originally intended only to establish a library, as its interests widened it spawned several independent groups, including the Buffalo Society of Natural Sciences (1861), the Buffalo Historical Society (1862), and the Buffalo Fine Arts Academy (1862). The library, which continued under the aegis of the Young Men's Association, later became the Buffalo Public Library (1897).

The Buffalo Society of Artists, established in 1891, was neither museum nor academy but an association of artists formed to promote patronage of local and regional artists, organize group exhibitions, exchange ideas, and encourage emerging talent. In 1996, the society celebrated its 100th Annual Juried Exhibition at the Burchfield-Penney Art Center.

In 1863, the great German-born American landscape panoramist Albert Bierstadt presented his massive canvas *The Marina* Piccola, Capri to the Buffalo Fine Arts Academy. This acquisition and its display with other works launched the nation's fourth public art gallery after those already founded in Philadelphia, Boston, and Hartford. In 1900, Buffalo industrialist John J. Albright provided the funds for the academy to construct its own gallery building, a classic Greek structure designed by architect Edward B. Green, on the eastern shore of the lake in Delaware Park. Sixty years

later, Seymour H. Knox II, another prominent community leader and an astute collector of 20th-century art, provided a gift to enable the Albright Art Gallery to create an elegant new wing for the display of its growing collection of modern art. Today, you can still see Bierstadt's *Capri* along with works by van Gogh, Matisse, Renoir, Picasso, Modigliani, Leger, Eakins, Pollock, de Kooning, Warhol, Rauschenberg, Diebenkorn, Calder, Still, Motherwell, Stella, Serra and many others at the Albright-Knox Art Gallery.

Art lovers can also view exhibitions at many other important area galleries, including the Castellani Museum of Niagara University, Anderson Gallery, Art Dialogue Gallery, Benjamin's Art Gallery, Big Orbit Gallery, CEPA Gallery, El Museo Francisco Oller y Diego Rivera, Fineline Gallery, Kenan Center, Museum of European Art, and the UB Art Gallery at the Center for the Arts.

Buffalo Art Studio, founded in the early 1990s to provide artists with both exhibit and work space, has its home in the former industrial Trico building on Main Street in north Buffalo.

At Kleinhans Music Hall, the Buffalo Philharmonic Orchestra presents its annual classical series under Maestro Maximiano Valdes and a pops series led by world-famous trumpeter Doc Severinsen. The depth of Niagara's musical passion is also evident in the concerts of the area's community orchestras, including the Amherst Symphony, the Orchard

In a culture in which so many photographs reflect the images and values of the celebrated and powerful, one Buffalo photographer has taken the opposite approach. **Milton Rogovin**'s startlingly direct and revealing portraits of working and poor people from many countries have been widely exhibited throughout the United States and Europe and are held in the permanent collections of the Metropolitan Museum of Art, the Museum of Modern Art, and other major museums around the world. Mr. Rogovin collaborated with W.E.B. DuBois on a series about Buffalo's storefront churches and with Chilean poet Pablo Neruda on a documentation of the people on the island of Chiloe off the coast of Chile. Photo by James P. McCoy.

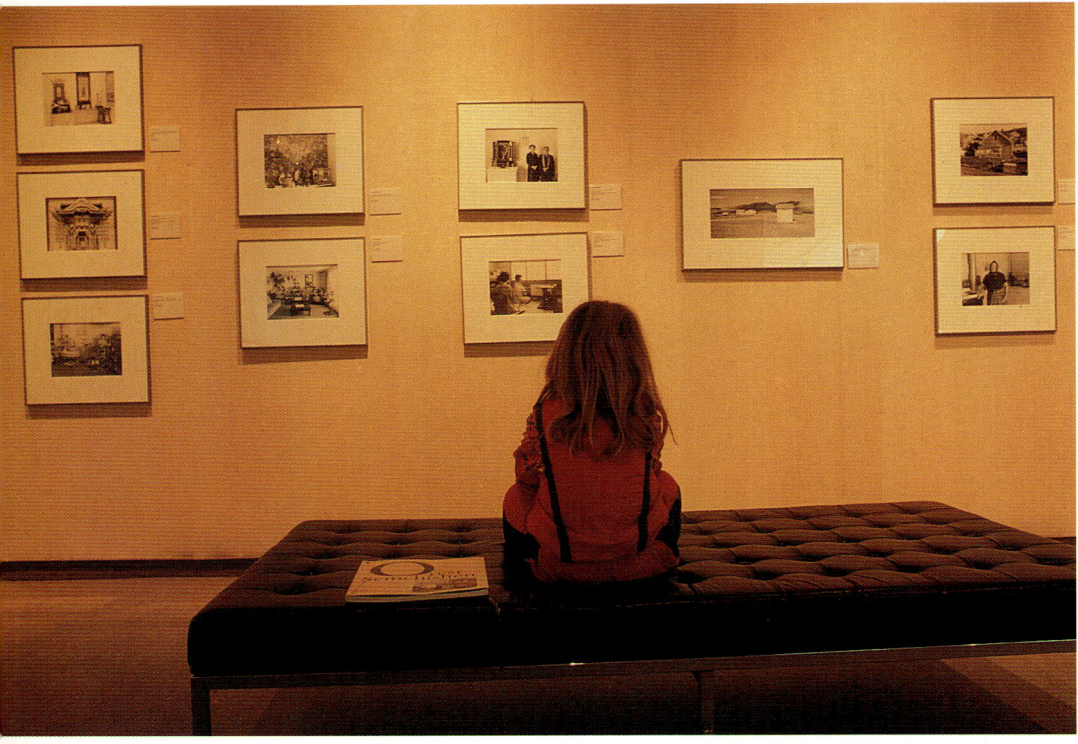

In the early 19th century, William Hamilton Merritt was a prime mover in the construction of the original Welland Canal. In 1853, William's son, Thomas Rodman Merritt, built Rodman Hall, a stately manor house on the crest of a bank overlooking the canal. Here, the Merritt family resided for over 100 years.

Today, the grand old manor is the **Rodman Hall Arts Centre**, an official Canadian National Exhibition Centre, a major gallery for the exhibition of Canadian art, and the primary focus for the visual arts in the Niagara Peninsula. On Rodman's grounds are a sculpture park and an arboretum and botanical gardens containing unusual species of plants and trees, many of which date back to Merritt's original plantings.
Photo by James P. McCoy.

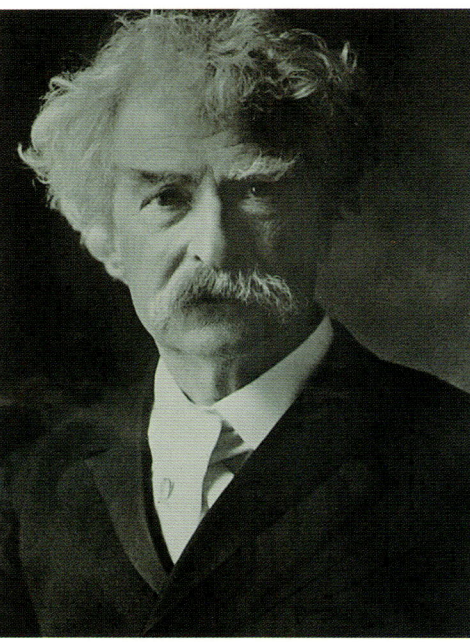

On February 2, 1870, **Mark Twain** married Olivia Langdon of Elmira, New York, and settled down in a new house on Delaware Avenue in Buffalo, a gift to the newlyweds from Olivia's father. Twain, valiantly attempting respectability to please his bride, joined Millard Fillmore, Grover Cleveland, and other worthies as a member of the high-minded Young Men's Association. Today, although Twain's house is gone, his ornate walnut mantle with the burled veneer inlays and his handwritten manuscript of *Adventures of Huckleberry Finn* can both be seen at the Mark Twain Room of the Buffalo & Erie County Library.
Photo courtesy of *Buffalo News*.

Park Symphony, and the Clarence Symphony. Performers and listeners alike are enriched by the work of the Ars Nova Musicians, Buffalo Choral Arts, Chopin Singing Society, Buffalo Schola Cantorum, the St. Paul's Cathedral Choir of Men & Boys, and many other instrumental and choral groups that regularly perform classical compositions, show tunes, folk melodies, and popular selections.

There's also a large and active theatrical world in Niagara. Downtown Buffalo's theater district is home to several live theaters, all serving a unique dramatic niche. Among the leading theaters are the Studio Arena, a professional regional theater; the Irish Classical Theatre; the Kavinoky; the Ujima; and the Shaw Festival at Niagara-on-the-Lake, which maintains three separate theaters and a professional repertory company. The Theatre of Youth, Theatre Loft, Pfeifer, Paul Robeson, Franklin Street, Alleyway, and Buffalo Ensemble theaters, along with many other venues, present classic and contemporary works, as well as plays by local playwrights.

The Shaw Festival at Niagara-on-the-Lake is a cultural jewel as well as the second-largest theater company in North America. Its season, running from April to October, showcases the plays of George Bernard Shaw and his contemporaries. Just two hours down the road in Stratford, Ontario, there's a summerlong Shakespeare Festival offering the best of the Bard, and other classic dramas. The performances of Stratford, Ontario rival those in London.

A strong literary tradition in Niagara is exemplified by the Just Buffalo Literary Center where a vital community of writers spreads the joy and power of language. The center sponsors readings and workshops conducted by prominent and emerging writers, concerts featuring poetry and jazz, and a locally produced presentation of literature on public radio station WBFO-FM.

Niagara is an incubator of artistic talent. A partial listing of homegrown artists who have distinguished themselves in their respective fields would include actors Katherine Cornell, Lucille Ball, James Whitmore, and Christine Baranski; composers Harold Arlen and David Shire; lyricist Jack Yellen; director and choreographer Michael Bennett; pianist and conductor William Eddins; flutist Carol Wincenc; pianist Leonard Pennario; jazz stars Mel Lewis, Frankie Donlop, Sam Noto, Red Menza, Joe Ford, Grover Washington, Jr., Bobby Militello, and the band Spyro Gyra; television writers Tom Fontana, Anthony Yerkovich, David Milch, Steven Bochco, and Diane English ("Murphy Brown"); playwrights A.R. Gurney, Emanuel Fried, and Elizabeth Swados; director and playwright George Abbott; novelists Taylor Caldwell and Joyce Carol Oates; historian and writer Paul Horgan; filmmaker Frederick King Keller; and former Rolling Stone illustrator Philip Burke.

In Niagara, the arts not only enrich lives, they create jobs, attract paying customers, and bolster the bottom line. The Arts Council in Buffalo & Erie County figures reveal that in Erie County alone the arts are a $33 million industry with more than a $100 million impact on the local economy. Pick up a copy of *Artvoice*, the area's weekly tabloid newspaper devoted to coverage of the arts, for an overview of the profusion of arts events, gallery openings, plays, concerts, readings, and revenues. The juxtaposition of art news, event photographs, and display advertising reveals a vibrant community of artists, citizens, and business interests linked in an artistic mosaic of mutual interest and support. ◈

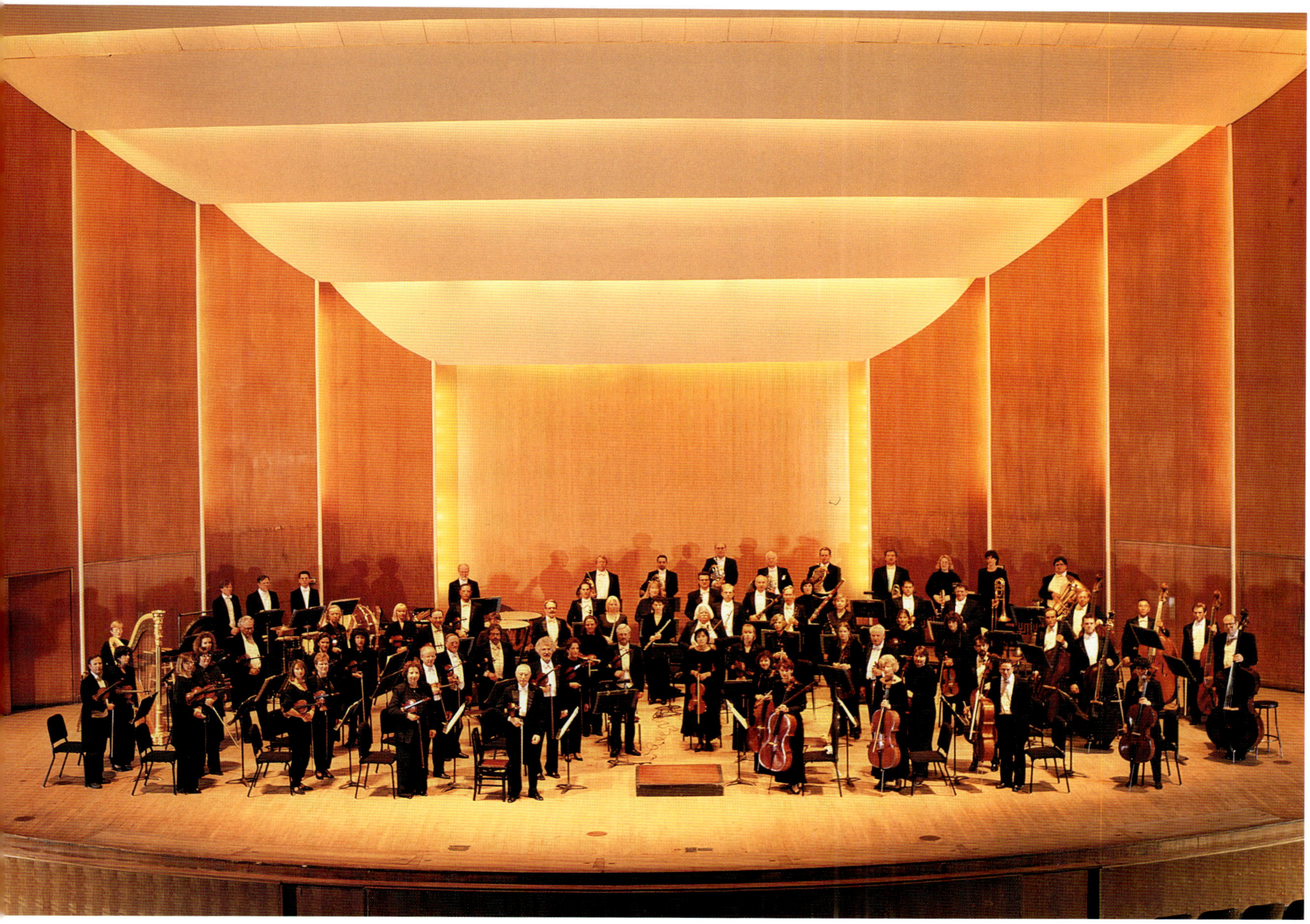

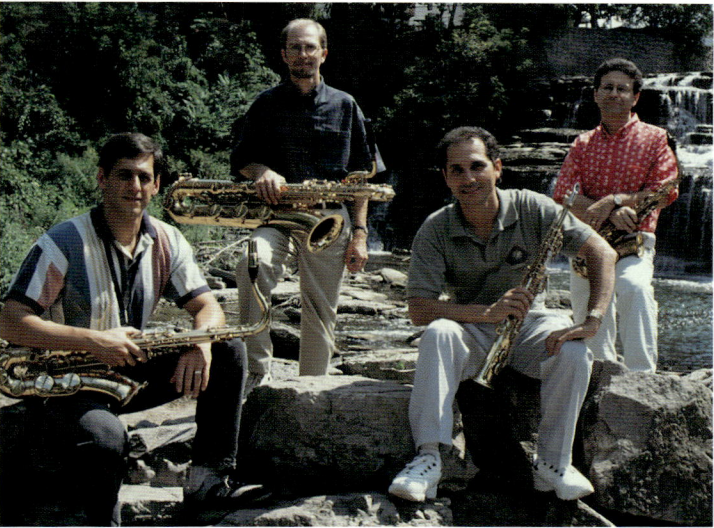

The members of the world's first full-time saxophone quartet met as students at the University at Buffalo and began performing together in early 1978. The quartet has appeared at Carnegie Hall, the Kennedy Center, Lincoln Center, Chautauqua Institution and on national radio and television programs including "The Tonight Show" on NBC. The members of the **Amherst Saxophone Quartet** are Salvatore Andolina, Russ Carere, Stephen Rosenthal, and Harry Fackelman.
Photo by James P. McCoy.

Under the baton of Music Director Maximiano Valdes, the **Buffalo Philharmonic Orchestra** presents a year-round schedule of concerts, festival appearances, and summer performances throughout Niagara. The orchestra, founded in 1935, has performed in more than 125 cities in 29 states, including over 25 appearances in New York's Carnegie Hall. Kleinhans Music Hall, its architecturally and acoustically celebrated home since 1940, was designed by Finnish architects Eliel and Eero Saarinen. The BPO also performs a rousing series of Broadway, blues, jazz, gospel, and other popular music under the direction of Principal Pops Conductor Doc Severinsen.
Photo by James P. McCoy.

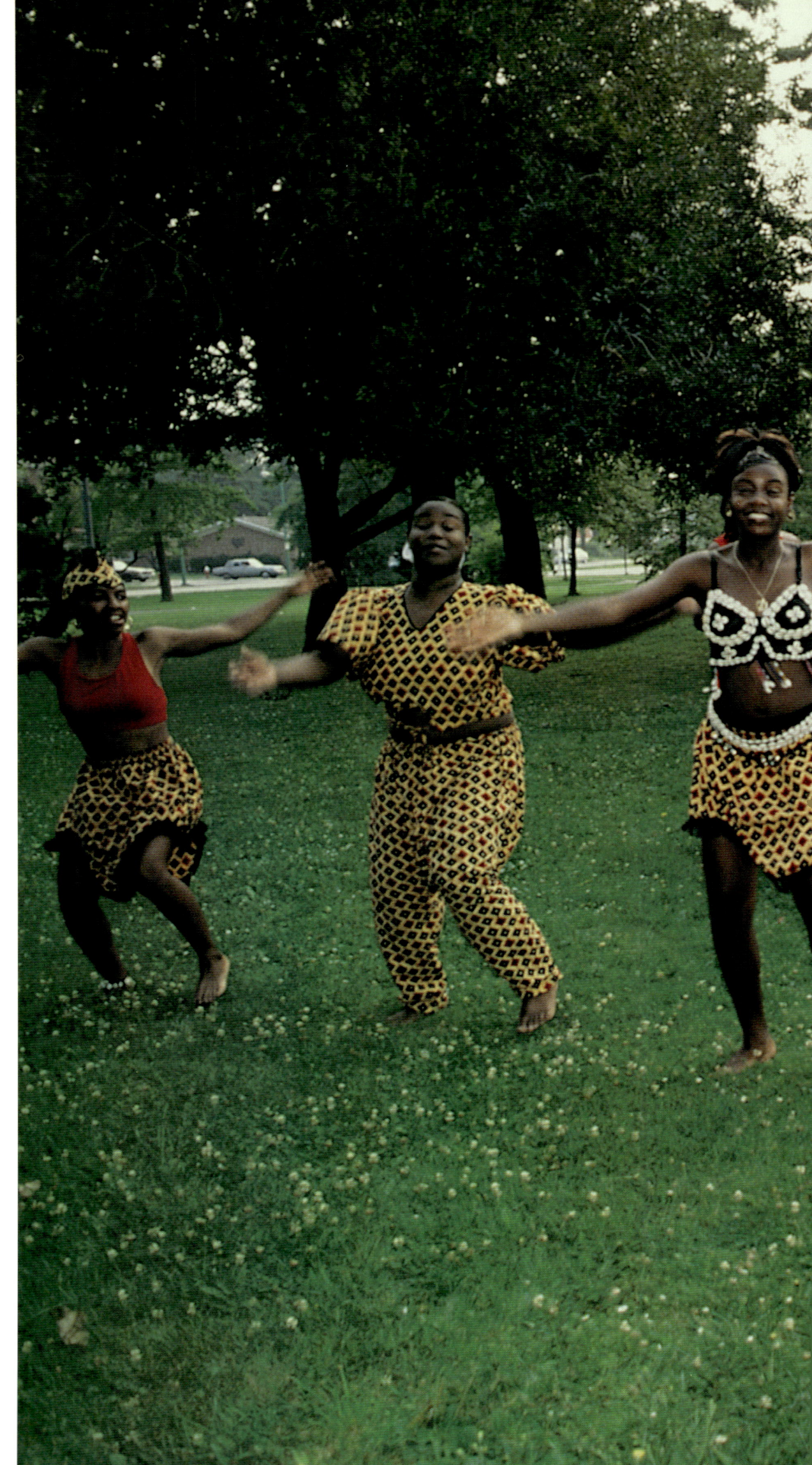

In West Africa, Kakilambe is a healing entity—the force behind the healing—that people in Guinea, Senegal, Gambia, and the Mali region have evoked for hundreds of years. In Buffalo, the **Kakilambe Dance and Drum Performing Troupe** excites audiences of all ages and chases away pain and depression with African dance and music from the Ivory Coast and Senegal, as well as dances from Haiti and other Caribbean islands. Kakilambe, a repertory company whose members also teach African dance and drumming to schoolchildren, has made numerous appearances at festivals and international events throughout the United States and Canada since its founding in 1958. Photo by James P. McCoy.

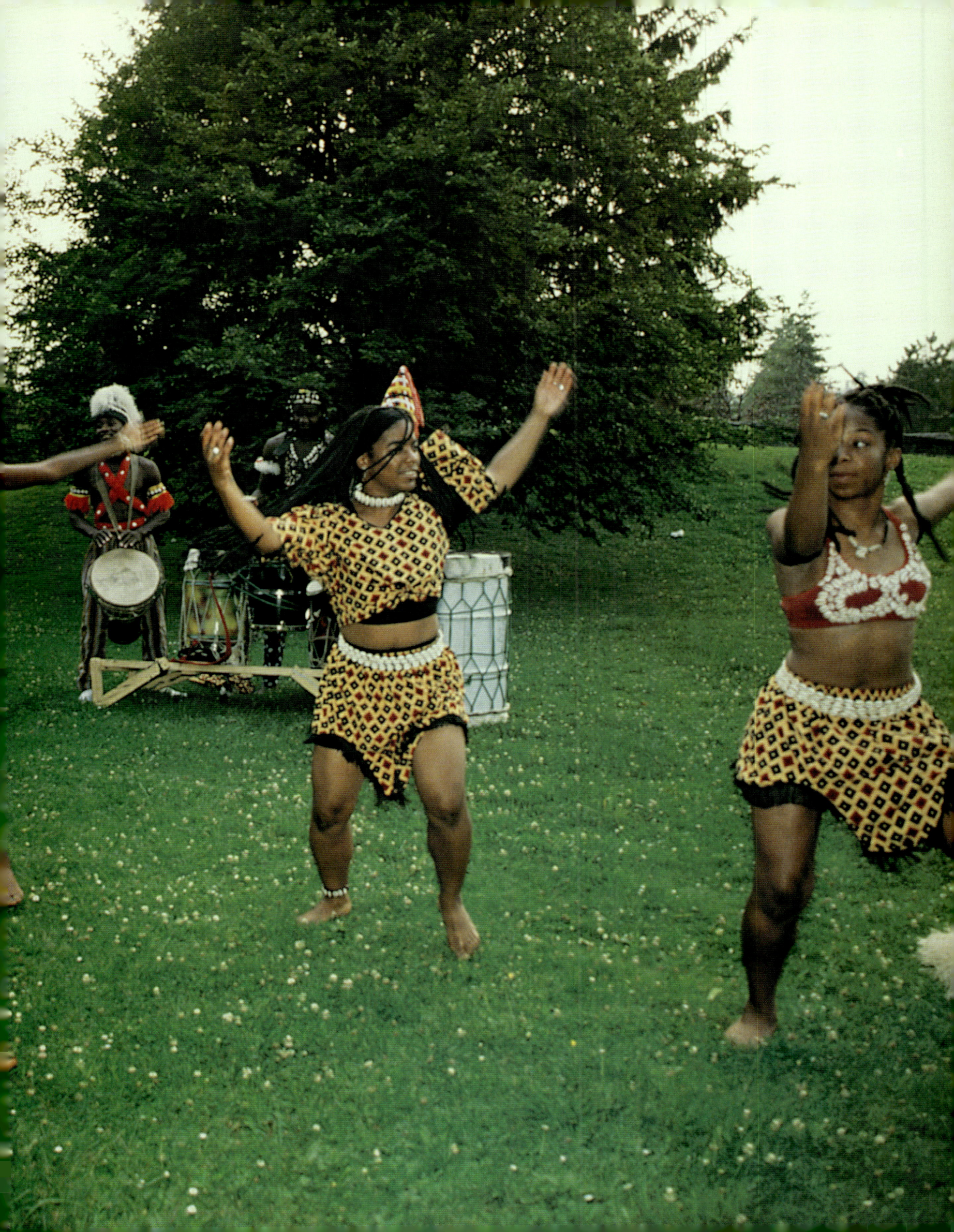

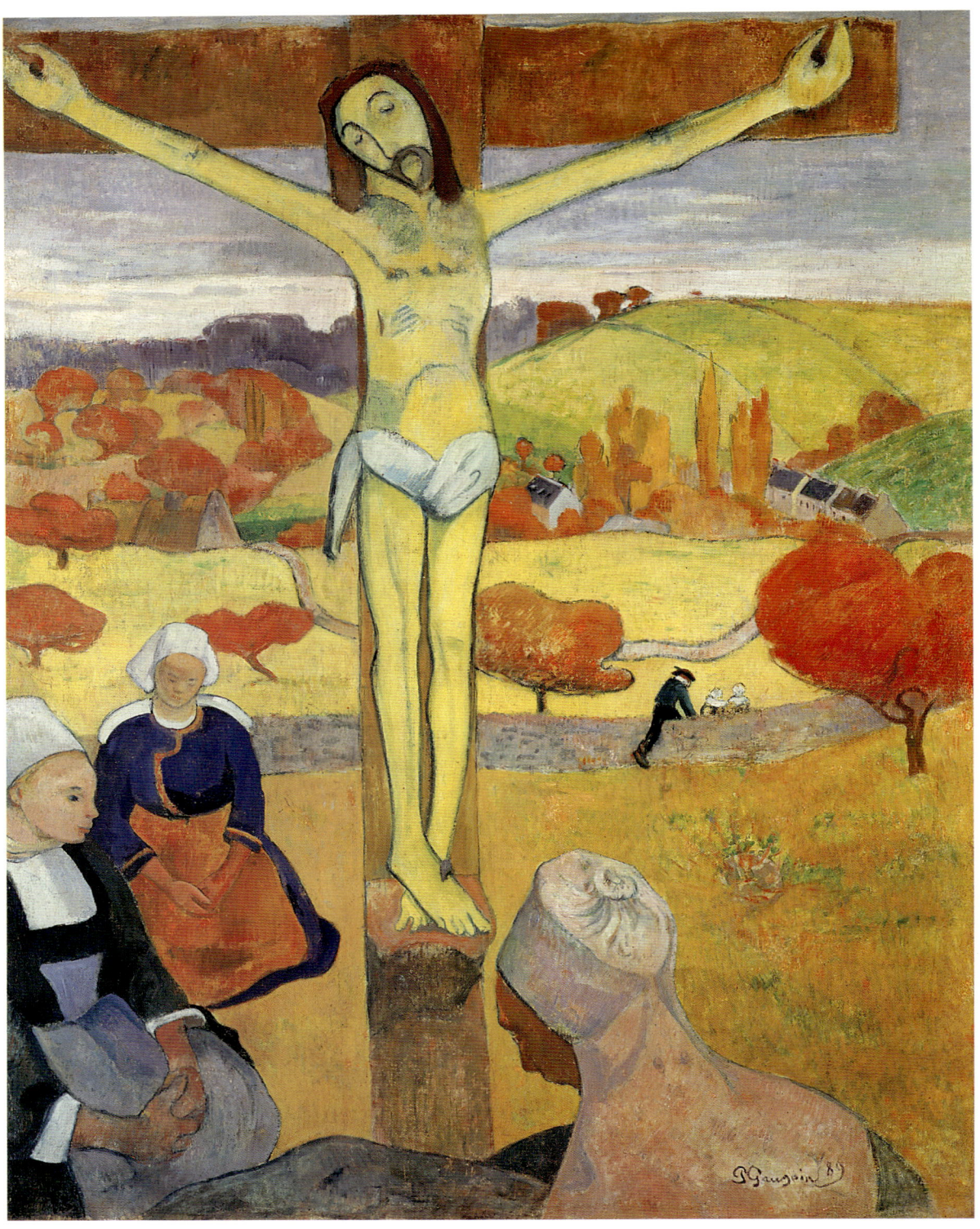

Gauguin's *Yellow Christ* is part of an outstanding permanent collection of 19th and 20th-century art at the **Albright-Knox Art Gallery**. Through the patronage of Seymour H. Knox II and his son, Seymour III, the gallery acquired notable works of abstract expressionism as well as critically acclaimed art from the 1970s and 1980s. The permanent collection contains art from ancient Mesopotamia to the leading French impressionists and post-impressionists to the work of Picasso, Braque, Matisse, Derain, Miro, Mondrian, Rodchenko, and many other important artists. Each year, the Albright-Knox loans more than 100 works from the collection to major museums throughout the world. Courtesy of the Albright-Knox Art Gallery, Buffalo, New York, General Purchase Fund, 1946.

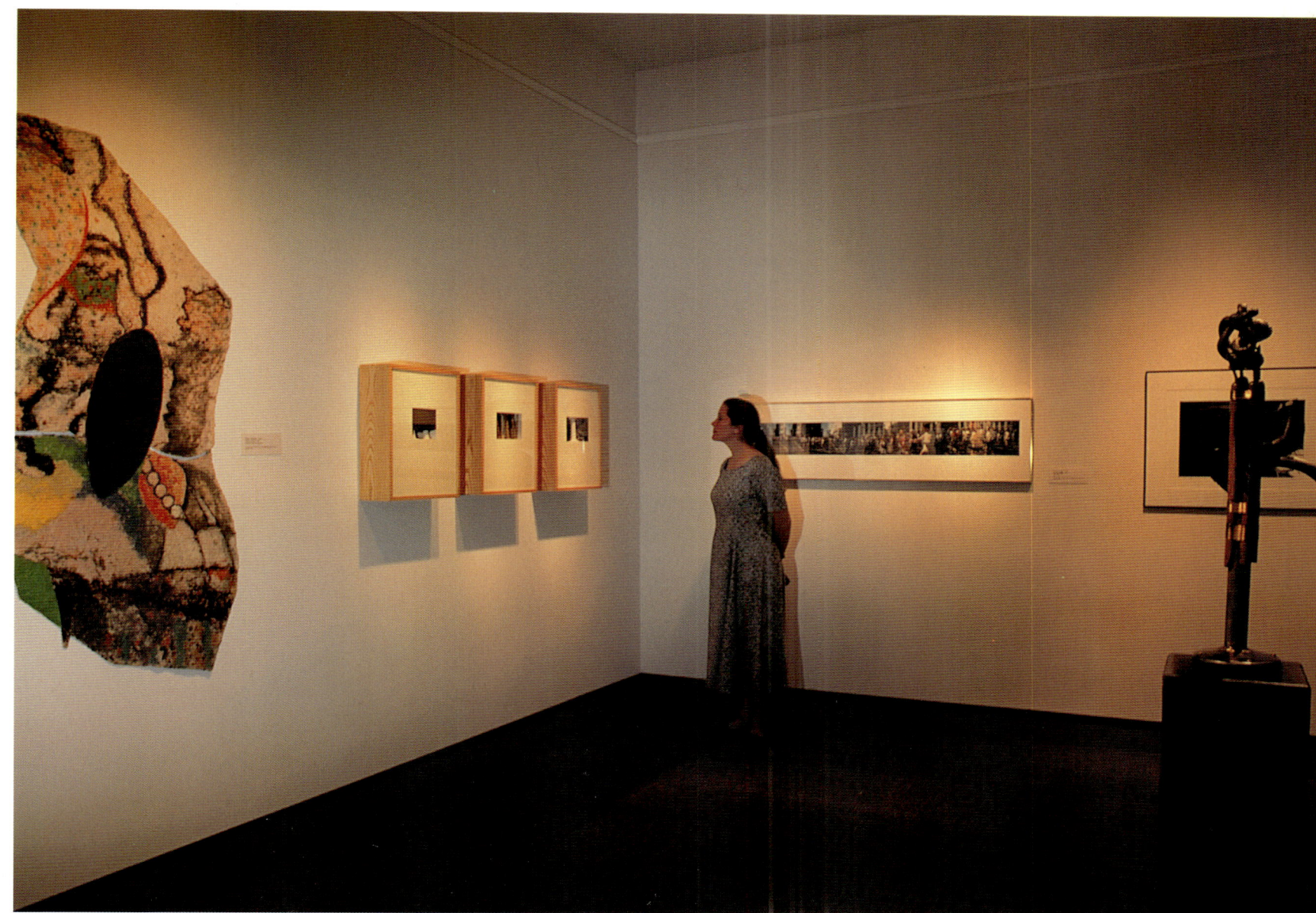

For the eminent American watercolorist Charles Burchfield (1893-1967), life in Buffalo and the nearby suburban village of Gardenville provided the conducive working environment he had sought after leaving the beloved woods and countryside of his native Salem, Ohio. At the **Burchfield-Penney Art Center**, Charles Burchfield's dazzling legacy of watercolors reflects both his love of nature and his affection for the urban landscapes of the city in which he found his artistic maturity. The donation of 183 Burchfield works by Charles Rand Penney in 1994 united the largest public and private collections of the artist's work to create the definitive collection of Burchfield art and archival materials.
Photo by James P. McCoy.

Cornerstone of Buffalo's Theatre District and acclaimed professional regional resident theater, the **Studio Arena Theatre** has an illustrious resume as a venue for notable world and national premieres, as a stage for distinguished American actors, and as home to the nation's oldest continually operating theater school (founded in 1927).
Photo by James P. McCoy.

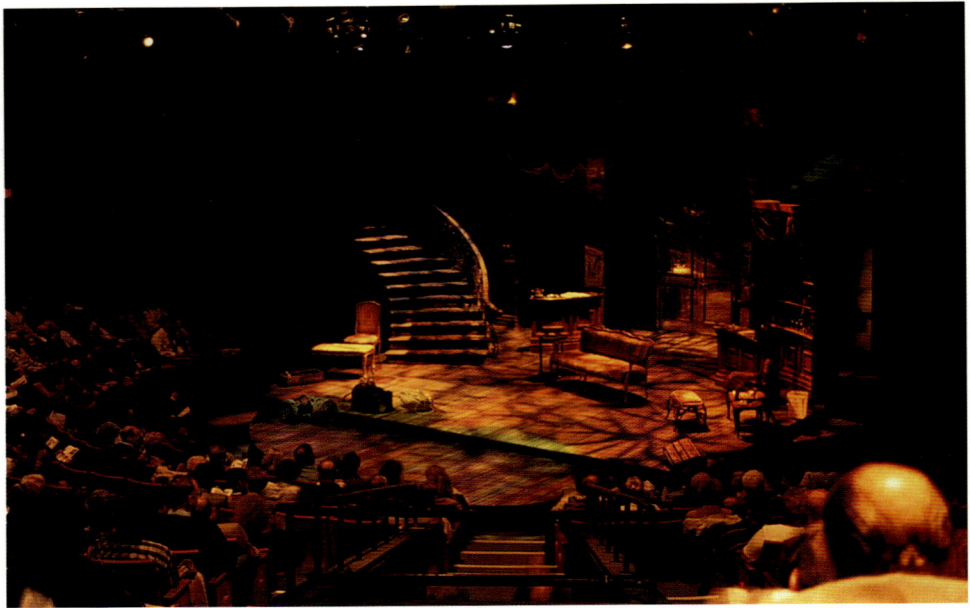

In 1968, the Buffalo Fine Arts Academy brought Buckminster Fuller, Edward Albee, Charles Olson, Allen Ginsberg, Merce Cunningham and other leading artists to town to join Lukas Foss and the Buffalo Philharmonic Orchestra in a festival celebrating contemporary music, architecture, poetry, dance, art, film, and stage design. Buffalo's natural progression from friend of leading experimental artists to a cutting edge of the new media vanguard was marked by the founding of **Hallwalls Contemporary Arts Center** in the mid-1970s.
Photo by James P. McCoy.

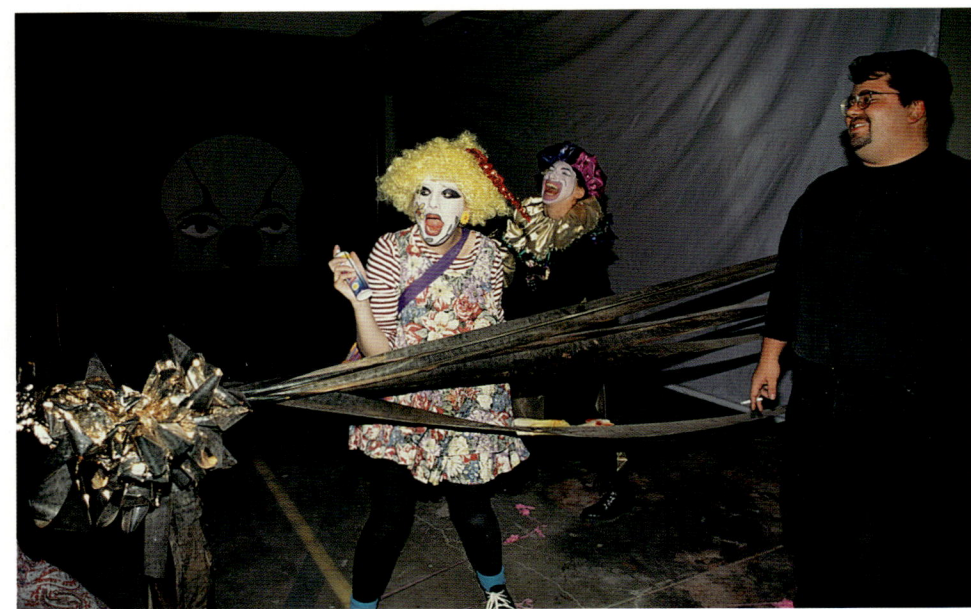

Settling onto the grassy slope behind the Rose Garden that overlooks the waters of Hoyt Lake in Delaware Park, the audience prepares for an evening of timeless theater. The second-largest outdoor Shakespeare festival in all the realm (after New York City's), **Shakespeare in Delaware Park** began in 1976 under the leadership of actor, teacher, and artistic director Saul Elkin. The professional company now produces two free outdoor plays and one indoor fall show each season.
Photo by James P. McCoy.

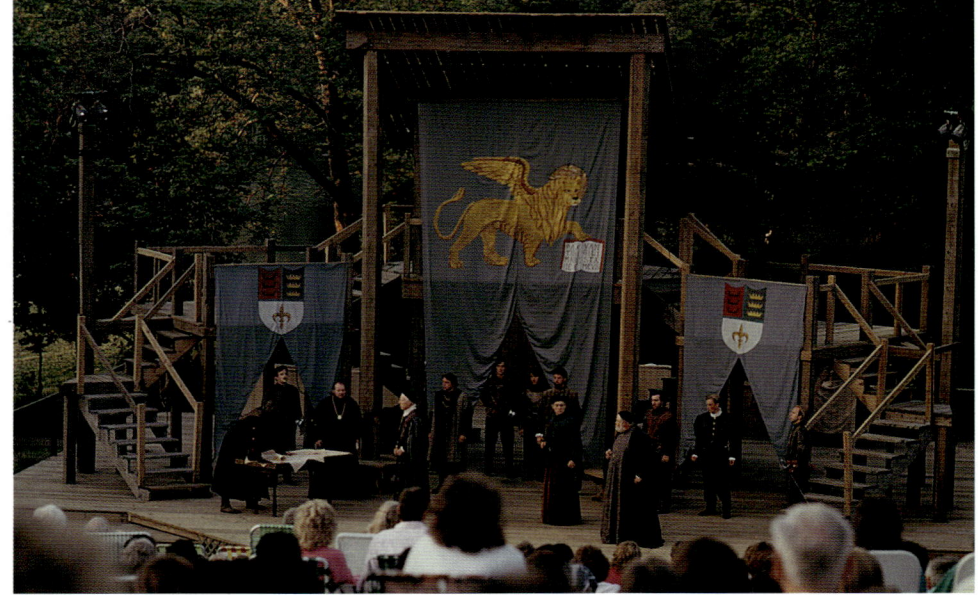

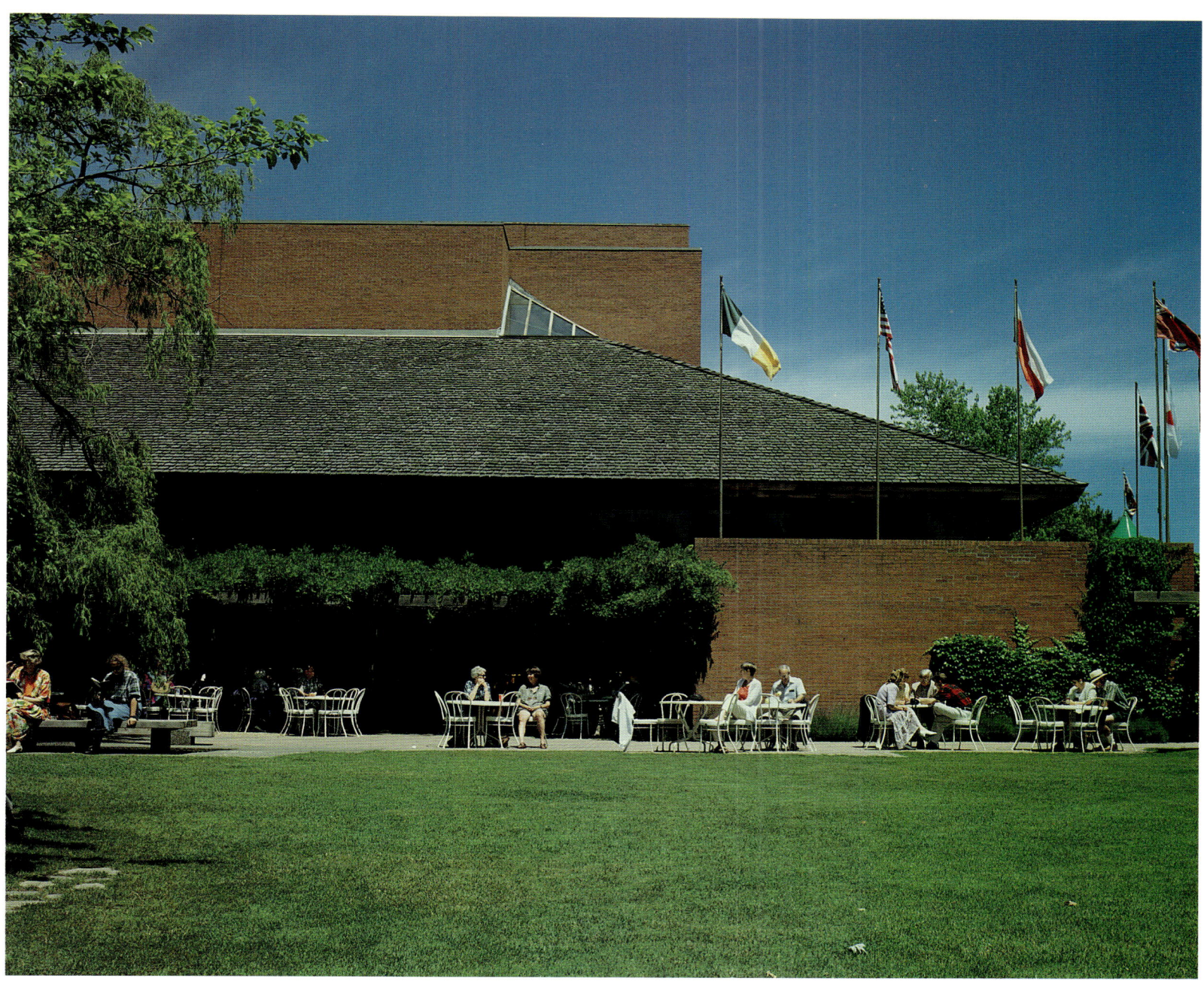

Under artistic director Christopher Newton, the **Shaw Festival** in historic Niagara-on-the-Lake, one of the largest and most successful theater companies in North America, specializes in the plays of **George Bernard Shaw** and his contemporaries. Shaw lived from 1856 to 1950 and the Shaw Festival only produces works written during those years. These include Victorian drama, plays of continental Europe, classic American drama, neglected English playwrights, classic musicals, and mystery plays, especially those of Agatha Christie. With three separate stages, a permanent international acting ensemble, breathtaking artistic design, and advanced technical facilities, the Shaw Festival is a triumph of world-class theater.
Photo by James P. McCoy.

Buffalo was blessed with the opening of a new professional theater in 1990 when brothers Vincent and Chris O'Neill, former company members of the Abbey Theatre in Dublin, and Dr. James Warde founded the **Irish Classical Theatre Company**. The company, comprised of a core group of internationally experienced actors, including artist-in-residence Josephine Hogan, presents traditional and contemporary Irish drama as well as a wide range of international theater classics. Photo by James P. McCoy.

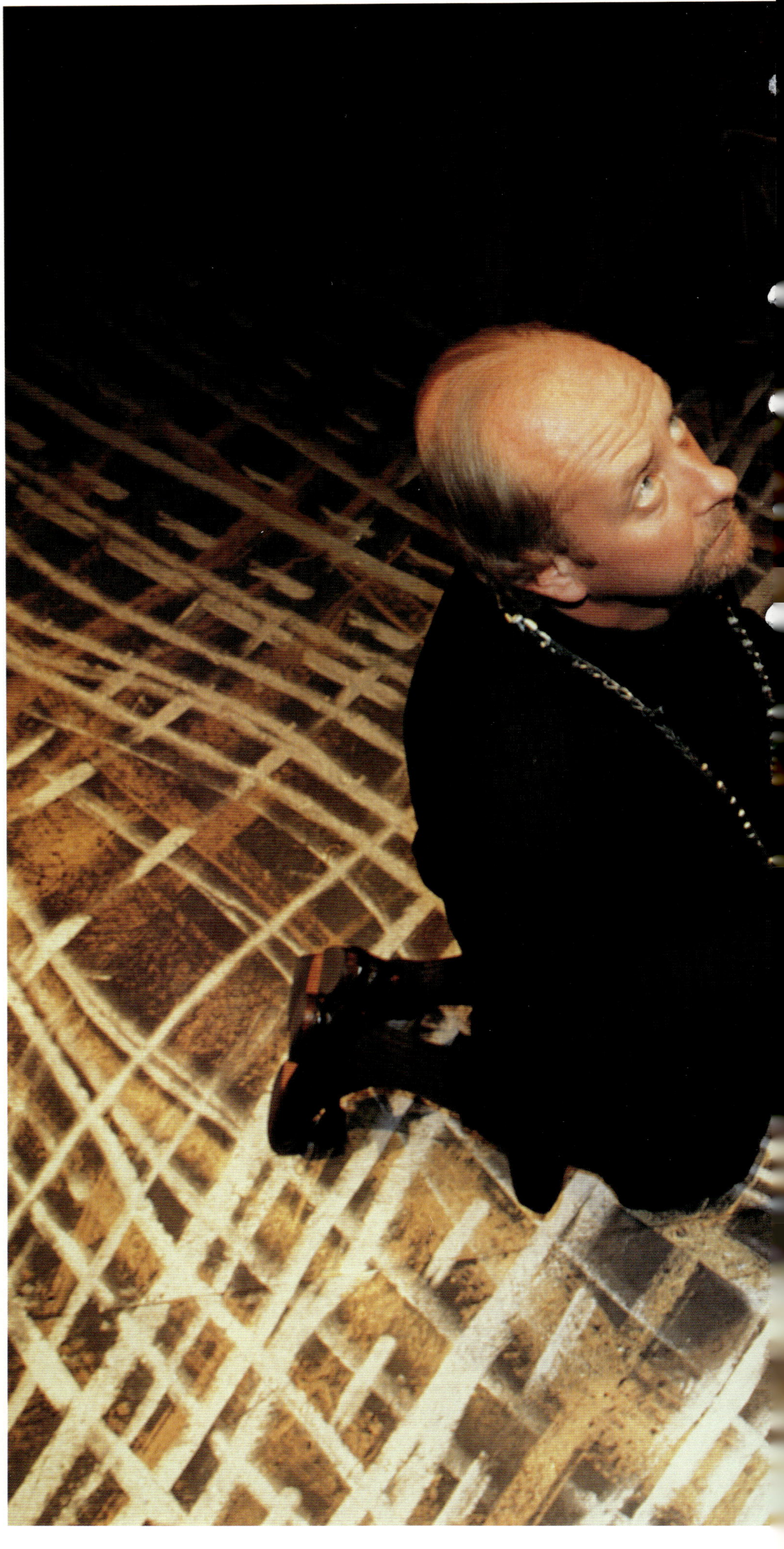

Inspired as a young man by the writing of Ezra Pound and William Carlos Williams, **Robert Creeley** in turn became one of the most influential and imitated American poets of the mid-20th century. In the 1950s, Creeley, Charles Olson, and Robert Duncan led a group of innovative poets at Black Mountain College in North Carolina to create a new, conversational poetry that departed from earlier 20th-century forms. Robert Creeley is a recipient of Fulbright and Guggenheim awards and the Lila Wallace-Reader's Digest Writer's Award. He also works with aspiring writers at the Just Buffalo Literary Center and with young poets at Buffalo's City Honors High School. Photo by James P. McCoy.

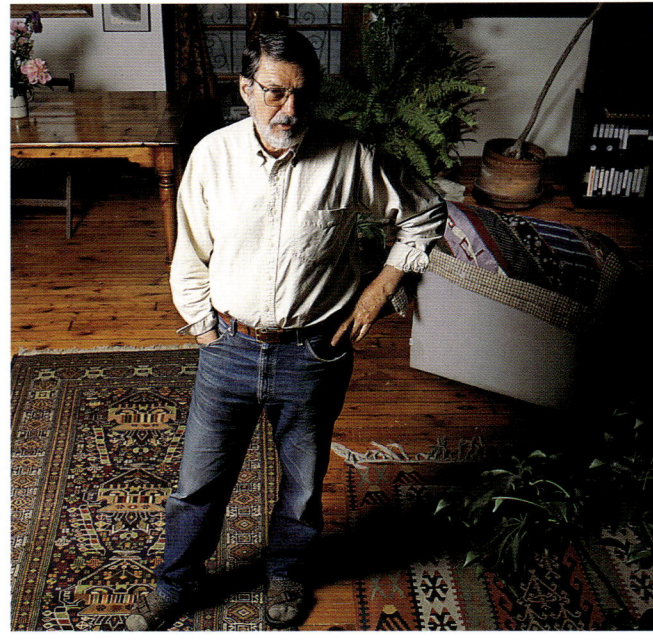

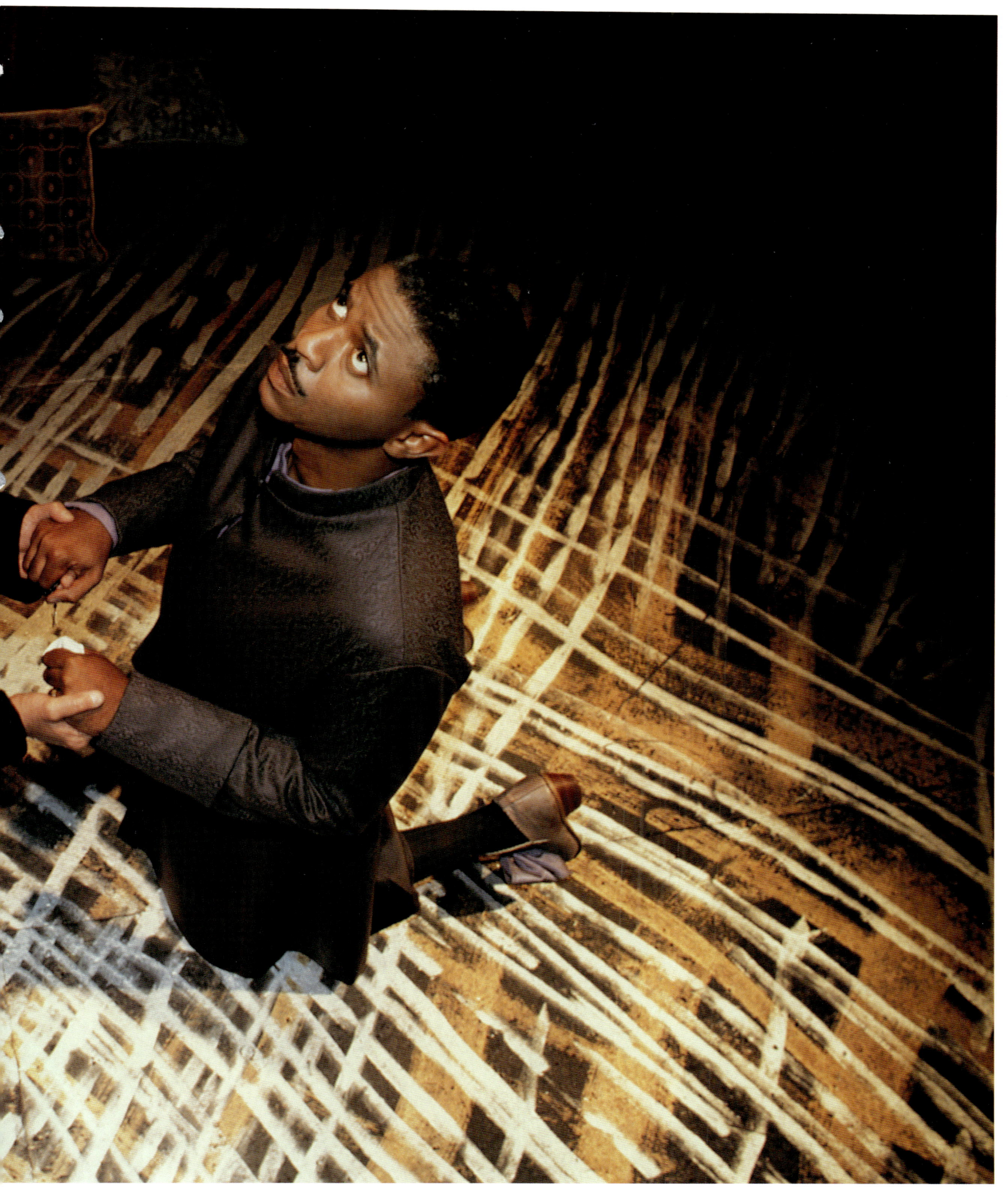

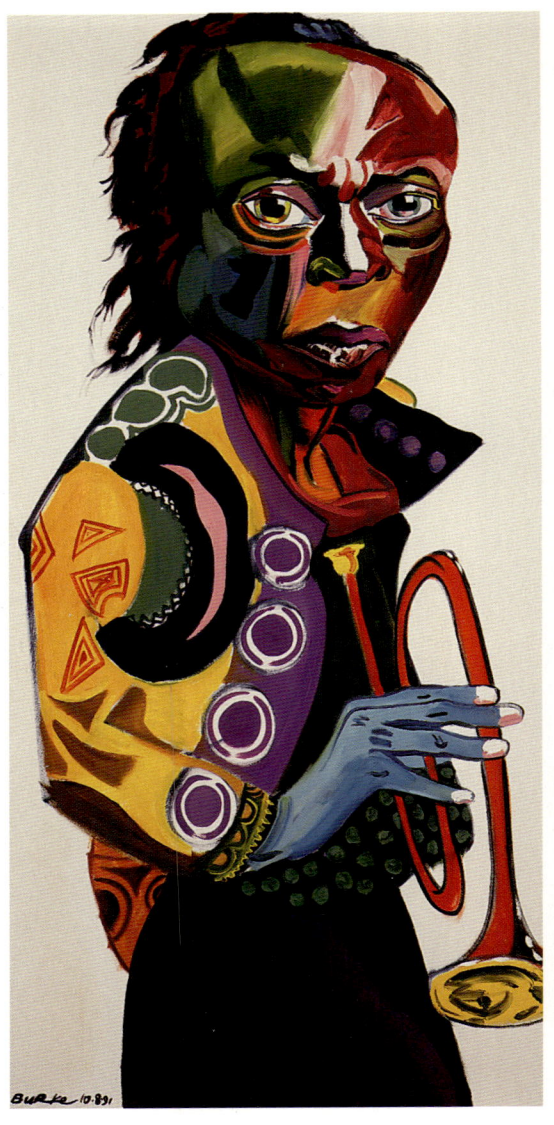

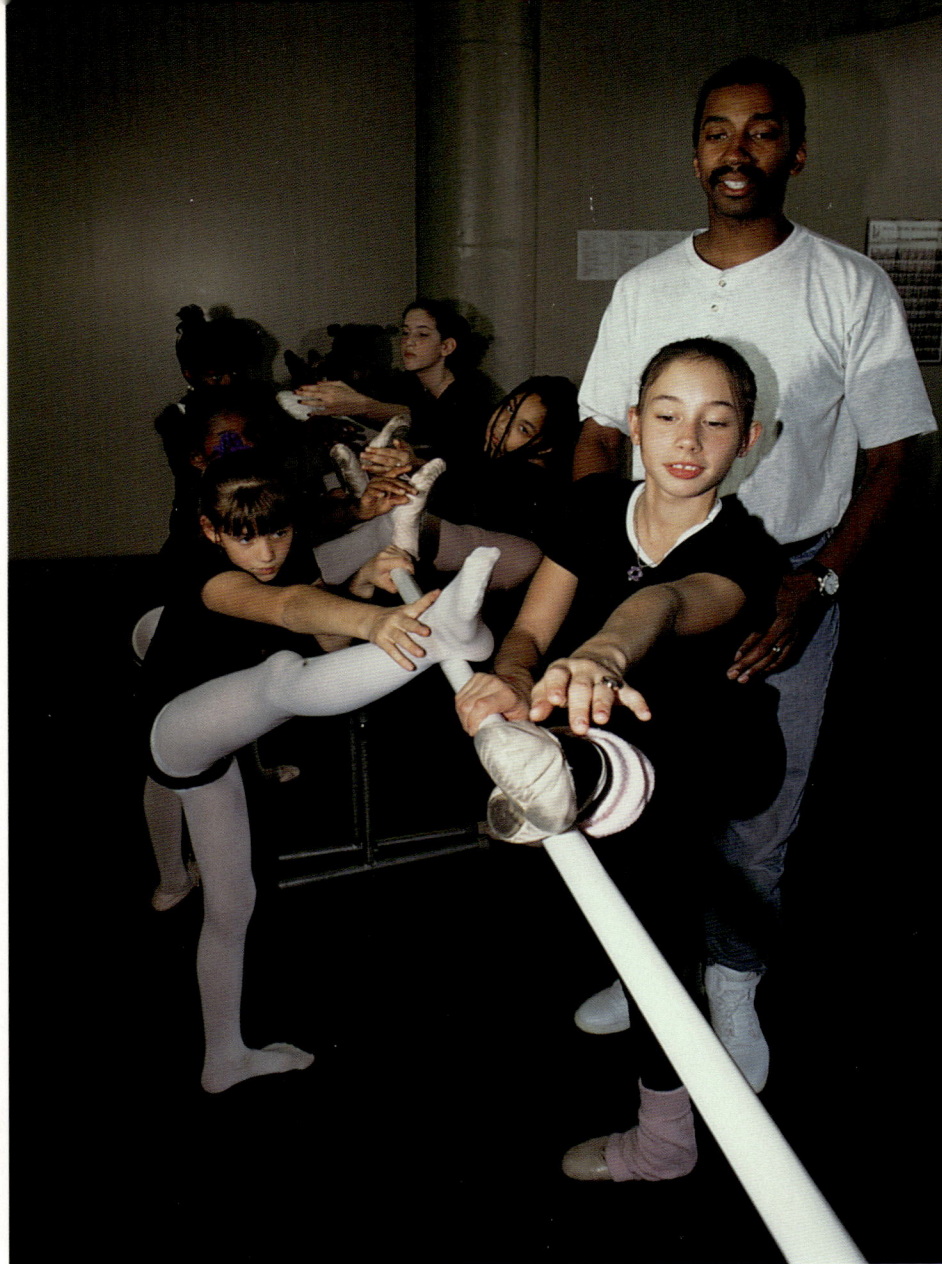

Philip Burke's colorful caricatures have appeared in *Rolling Stone, The New Yorker, Vanity Fair, Time, Esquire, Newsweek*, and many other national and international publications. Burke's loose style and technical skill create warts-and-all portraits that depict celebrities, politicians, tycoons, and even fellow artists. If it's human, it's fair game for a Burke caricature. Photo courtesy of Philip Burke.

Buffalo City Ballet is a leading dance company among many artistically acclaimed groups in the area. Under executive director Marvin Askew and artistic director Janet Reed, Buffalo City Ballet presents classic and contemporary ballet, while the company's school, **Buffalo Inner City Ballet**, offers classes in classical ballet, jazz, contemporary dance, modern dance, and other disciplines. Photo by James P. McCoy.

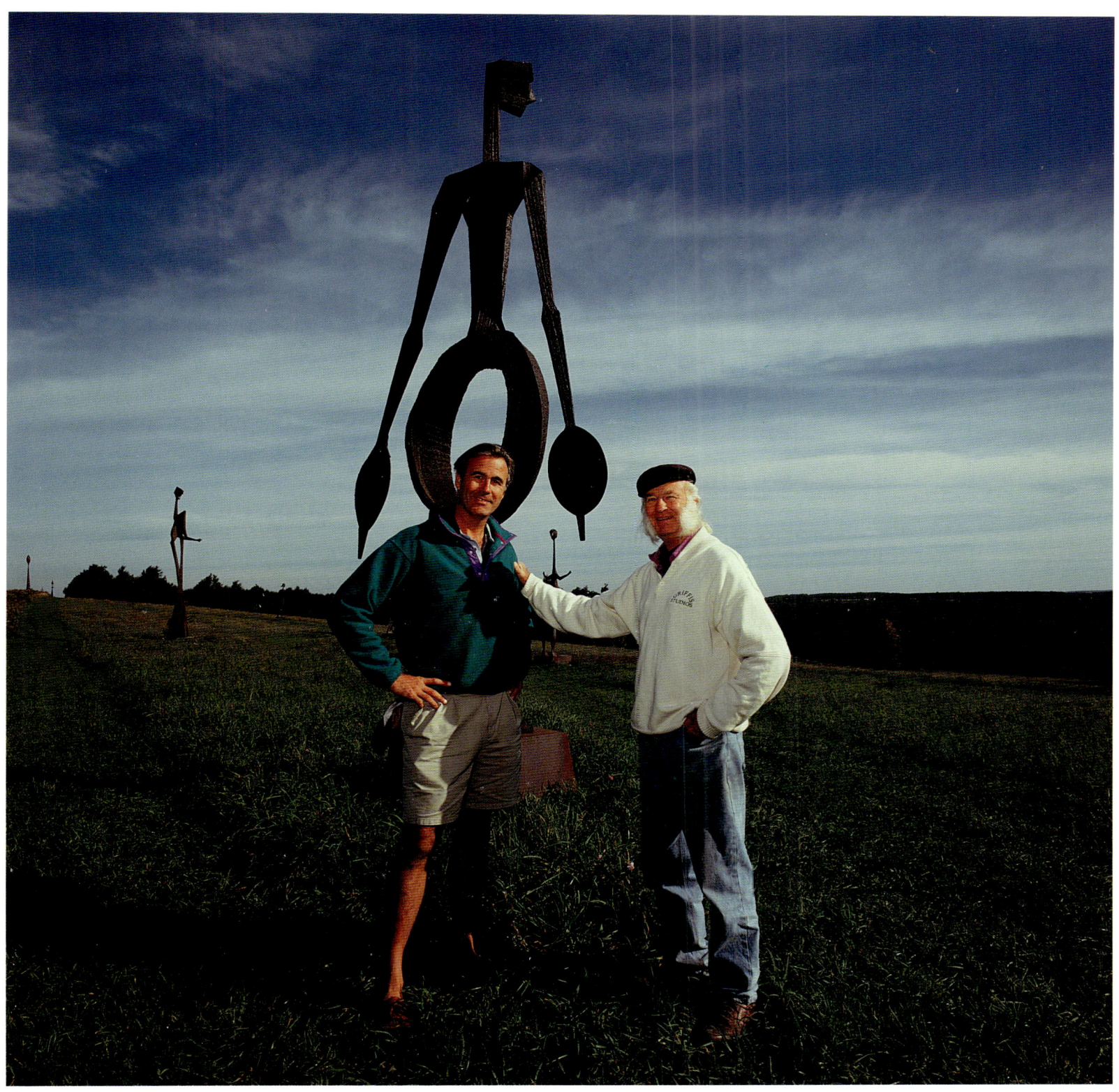

Visitors to the area are frequently surprised by the profusion of public art in Niagara. The exuberant sculptures of **Larry Griffis** are among the most prominent and notable of these works. *The Spirit of Womanhood* in Delaware Park, *Birds Excited into Flight* on Bidwell Parkway, and the towering, whimsical pieces at Griffis Sculpture Park in Ashford Hollow reveal an artistic sensibility of searching spirituality and palpable delight in the natural world.

With his son Mark, a successful designer and metal sculptor, Larry Griffis now creates commissioned works for both private and public spaces.

Photo by James P. McCoy.

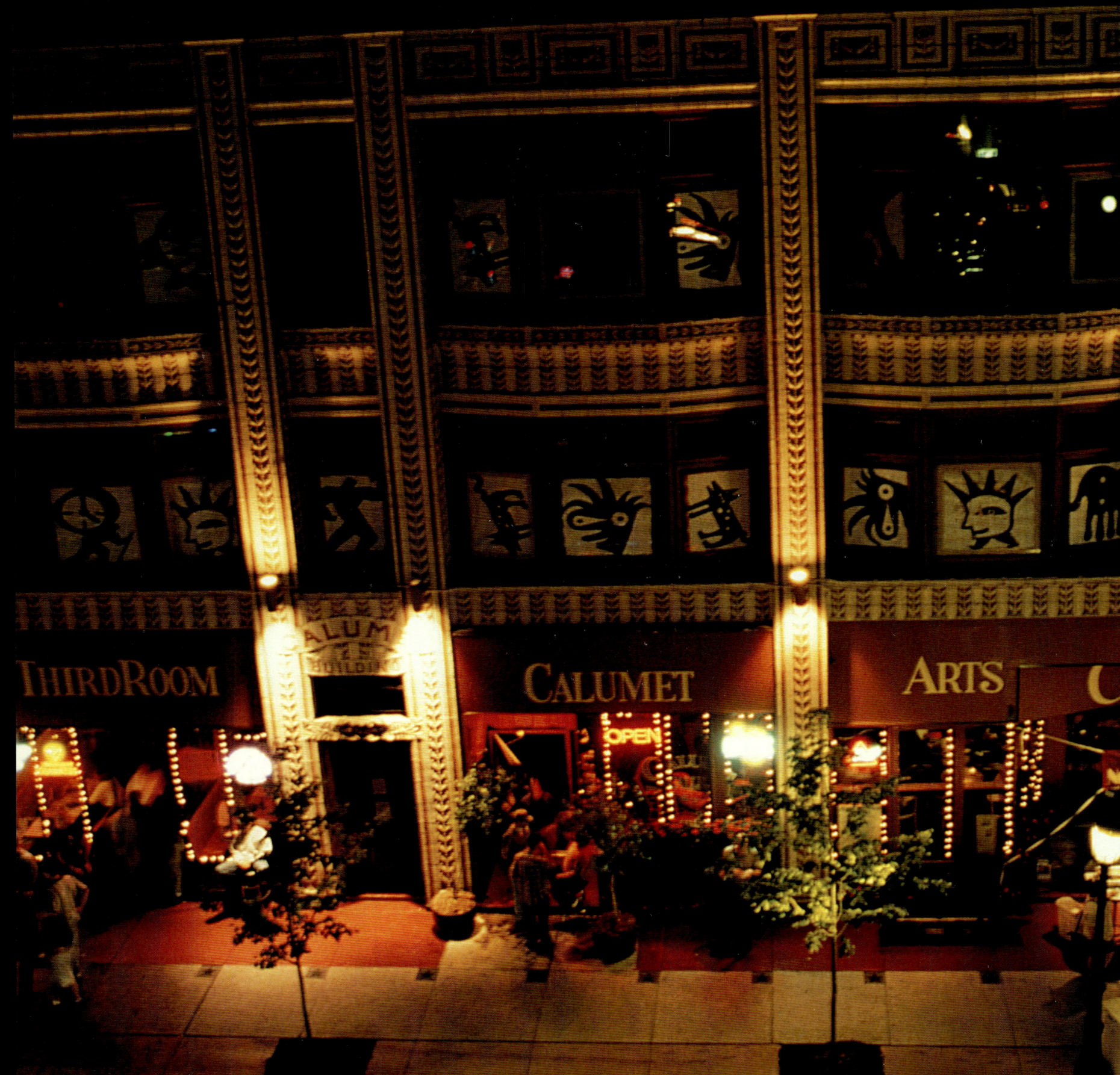

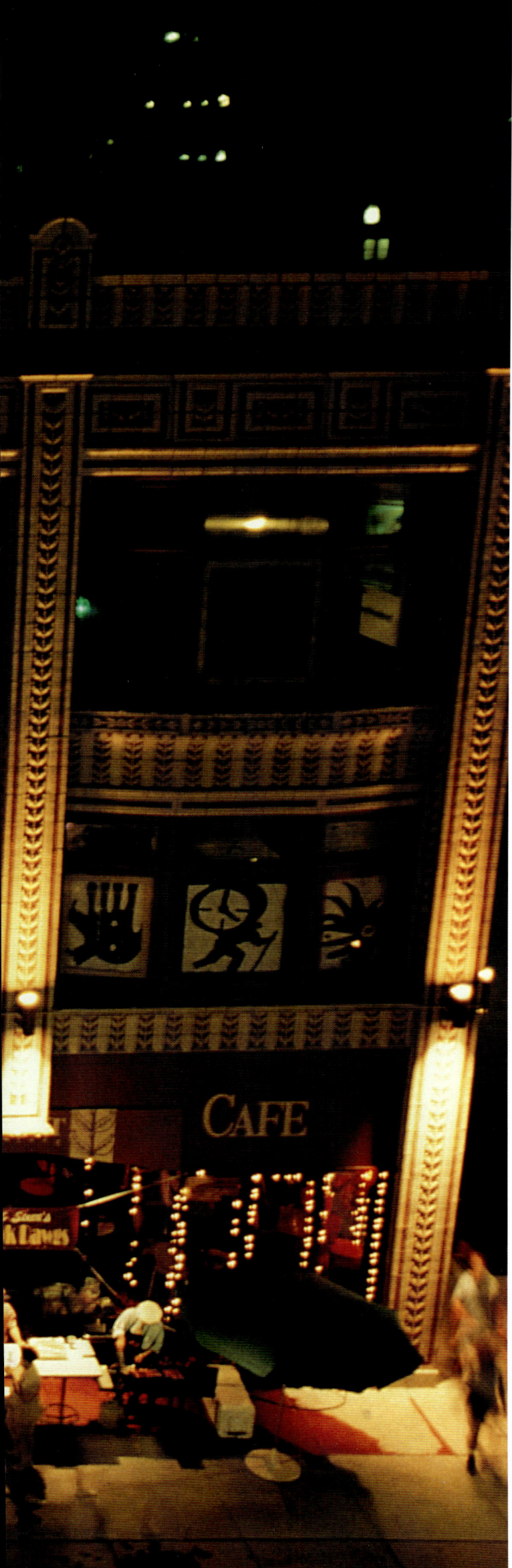

NIAGARA ATTRACTIONS

Niagara residents know how to have a good time, whether at a Sunday football tailgate party, a night out on the town, or an evening with friends at a comfortable neighborhood bar. Nightlife in Niagara is where the character and friendliness of its people shine through. The many entertainment opportunities—a sports event or a concert at Marine Midland Arena, a play in downtown Buffalo's Theatre District, a headliner at a jazz night club, dinner at Niagara-on-the-Lake, or cocktails high atop the Skylon Restaurant overlooking Niagara Falls—all finish Niagara's days in style. There's always an interesting entertainment venue, from formal affairs to easygoing get-togethers to close out the day.

N

Niagara's current wealth of entertainment options stems from the community's legacy of diversity and location.

When Dewey Michaels closed down Buffalo's Palace Burlesk in 1967 with a farewell bash starring Naja Karamusa and her two pythons—Val Lavender and Shimmy Queen—and Hal Haig (one of the original Keystone Kops), it marked the end of an era in nightlife that began in the mid-19th century with the opening of the Music Hall on Main Street and peaked in the 1920s with full houses in big, opulent theaters built for vaudeville and motion pictures. As New York's second-largest city, Buffalo was an important stop for show tryouts, road tours, traveling repertory companies, and vaudeville acts.

Buffalo's entertainment history is a mother lode of glittering lore: a theater district comprised of three stage houses and four mammoth downtown showhouses; W.C. Fields juggling cigar boxes and Will Rogers spinning yarns and lariat at Shea's Garden Theatre; Al Jolson in his first speaking role at the Teck; Bert Williams, Harry Houdini, Lillian Russell, Charlie Chaplin, Ethel Barrymore, and Lily Langtry at the Court Street Theatre; Tallulah Bankhead, George M. Cohan, Katherine Cornell, Katherine Hepburn, and Van Heflin at the Erlanger; Sammy Davis, Jr. with the Will Masten Trio at the old Plaza.

There were nightclubs with cigarette girls, gleaming banquettes, full orchestras, and potted palms. There were stock and roadshow burlesque extravaganzas, beergardens, and boxing bouts. Tommy Dorsey and Frank Sinatra were at the Towne Casino. Ted Mack was master of ceremonies at Shea's Buffalo, and the Bijou Dream was the city's premier nickelodeon. By midcentury, the "burly-cue" show (typically a washed-up comic and strippers working to a live band of bored jazz musicians) was the last gasp of the live variety show before all the paying patrons got color TV and Barcaloungers.

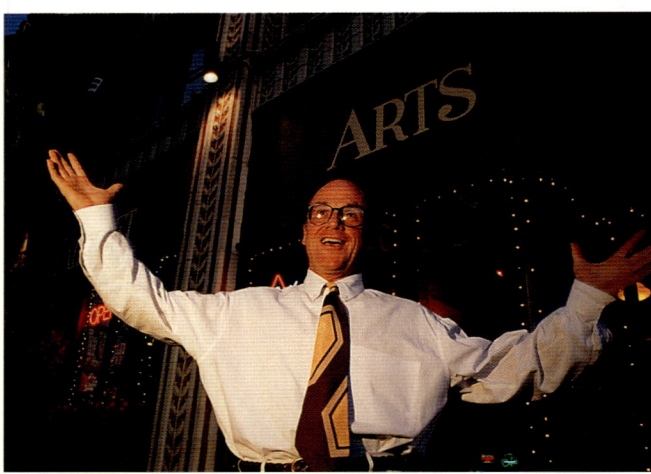

Nowadays in Niagara, there are plenty of wholesome attractions for the entire family. Each year, the area comes alive with outdoor events like the Taste of Buffalo (which draws over 400,000 aspiring gourmets annually); the Allentown Art Festival; the Juneteenth Festival; the Italian Heritage and Food Festival; the Greek Hellenic Festival; the Polish-American Art Festival; the Caribbean, Scottish, and Irish Festivals; and Thursday in the Square featuring rock, blues, alternative, country, and jazz bands in Lafayette Square, a major public space in downtown Buffalo.

At the Buffalo Zoological Gardens in Delaware Park, there's a Lowland Gorilla house, a rare Indian rhino, a white tiger, polar bears, giraffes, and a fascinating Predator Exhibit. Or take the kids to the Herschell Carrousel Factory Museum for a tour of the nation's only historic carrousel factory and a ride on a 1916 carrousel. For an even longer ride on a historic conveyance, hop aboard the Arcade and Attica Railroad for a 90-minute steam excursion through beautiful Wyoming County.

The Kenan Center in Lockport offers the chance to tour the interior and landscaped grounds of a beautiful 19-century mansion, visit its art gallery, enjoy a theater production, play soccer or volleyball at the arena, or attend one of the center's many special events.

After visiting Niagara Falls, you can catch the free family show at the Power Vista, the Visitor's Center at the Robert Moses Power Plant that describes the history of the region and the development of electric power. You'll also want to see the Aquarium of Niagara on the U.S. side and the Niagara Parks Butterfly Conservatory on the Canadian side. The Butterfly Conservatory, which opened in 1996, offers a stroll through a glass enclosed rainforest where 2,000 free-flying butterflies float among nectar-producing flowers like lantanas, pentas, and passion flowers.

While you're in Ontario, there's lots more to see by taking a drive along the Niagara Parkway to Niagara-on-the-Lake. On the way, stop for a hike at the Niagara Glen, one of the most scenic trails in the Niagara or any other gorge. Back on the parkway, don't forget to check your watch at the Floral Clock in Queenston. This 40-foot living clock is a masterwork of colorful plantings. Just up the road, you can visit historic Fort Goerge or take a tour at one of the area's many wineries. Top off the day at Niagara-on-the-Lake with shopping, dinner, and a play at the Shaw Festival.

For a bit longer theater excursion, you can head for Stratford, Ontario, to see a Shakespeare production or simply drive around the lake to Toronto for a performance. Before returning to Niagara, be sure to take the kids to the zoo and the entertaining Toronto Science Center for an amazing adventure of learning and fun. ❖

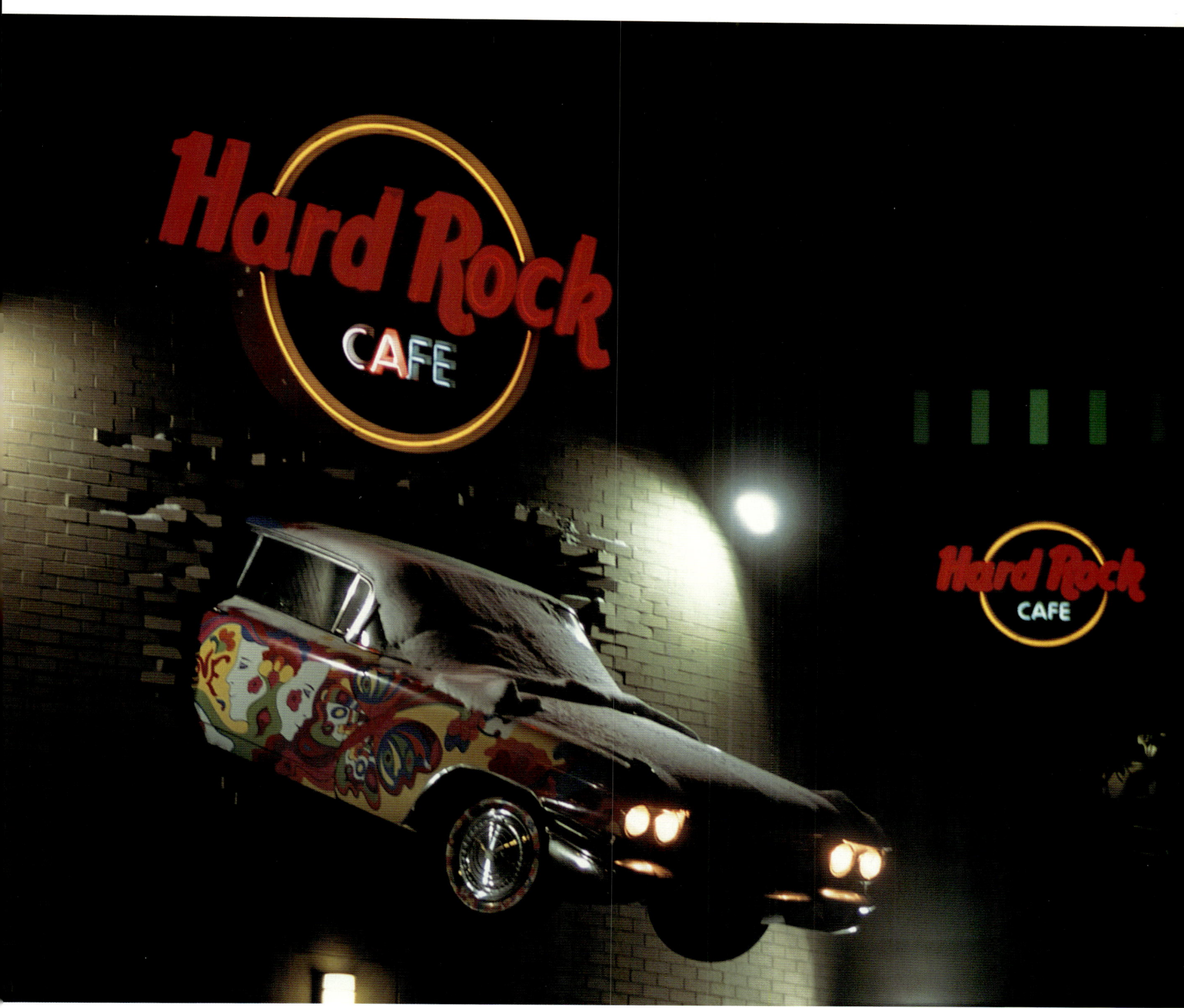

Rock 'n' roll artifacts, an all-American menu, and the allure of a hugely successful, internationally renowned theme restaurant attract residents and visitors to the **Hard Rock Cafes** in downtown Niagara Falls, New York, and Ontario.
Photo by James P. McCoy.

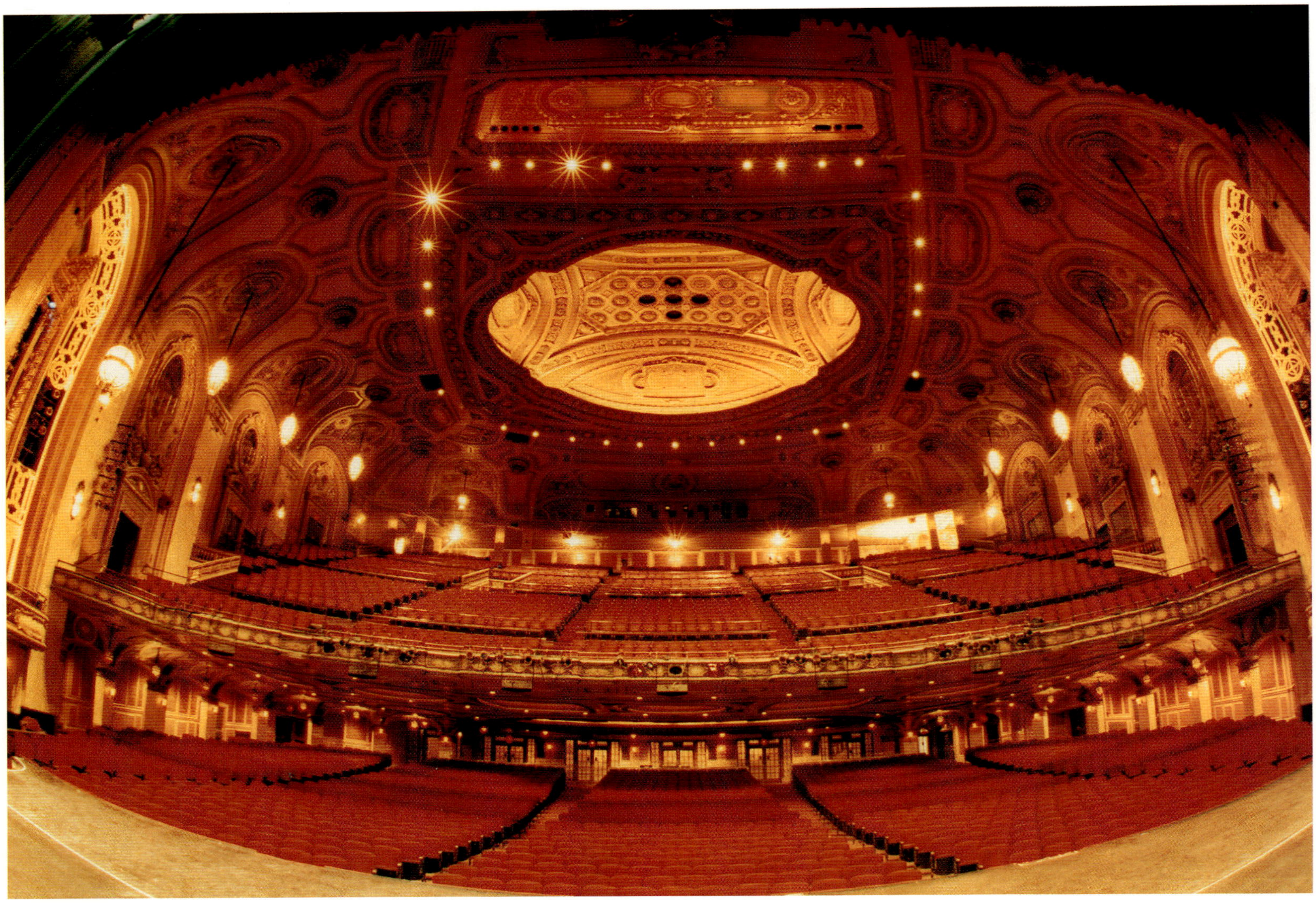

Buffalo impresario Michael Shea began his theatrical career in 1882 with the opening of Shea's Music Hall on Clinton Street, site of the present Brisbane Building. Mr. Shea opened more than a dozen theaters, most of which have been demolished. But in the heart of Buffalo's Theatre District, Shea's greatest legacy still exists in all its splendor. **Shea's Buffalo Theatre** opened on January 16, 1926, in the waning days of vaudeville and the early years of motion pictures. With Italian marble, Czechoslovakian crystal chandeliers, and an interior design by Tiffany Studios, the theater cost Mr. Shea $3 million to build. Inspired by the great European opera houses, Shea's was an extravagant movie palace that also featured a pit orchestra, a theater organ, and stage shows presenting such stars as Burns and Allen, the Marx Brothers, Bob Hope, Bing Crosby, Duke Ellington, and virtually every other headliner of the era. Since the restoration of the building and its mighty Wurlitzer organ in the mid-1970s, led by L. Curt Mangell III and the Friends of the Buffalo Theatre, Shea's Buffalo has been rechristened Shea's Center for the Performing Arts and hosts Broadway shows and many national acts.
Photo by Joseph M. Cascio.

The **Lancaster Opera House** is a magnificent old town hall and music hall built in the 1890s and restored in the mid-1970s to its original beauty. With its thick maple floor, yellow pine doors and window frames, oak rails and wainscoting, raked proscenium stage, and original gaslit (now electric) chandelier, the Opera House is one of only a few such surviving structures in the country. The Lancaster Opera House presents a 10-month season of performances.
Photo by Marc Murphy.

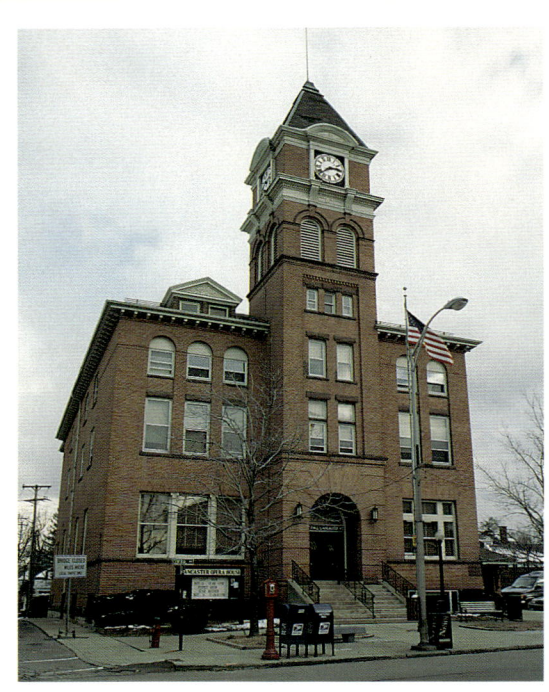

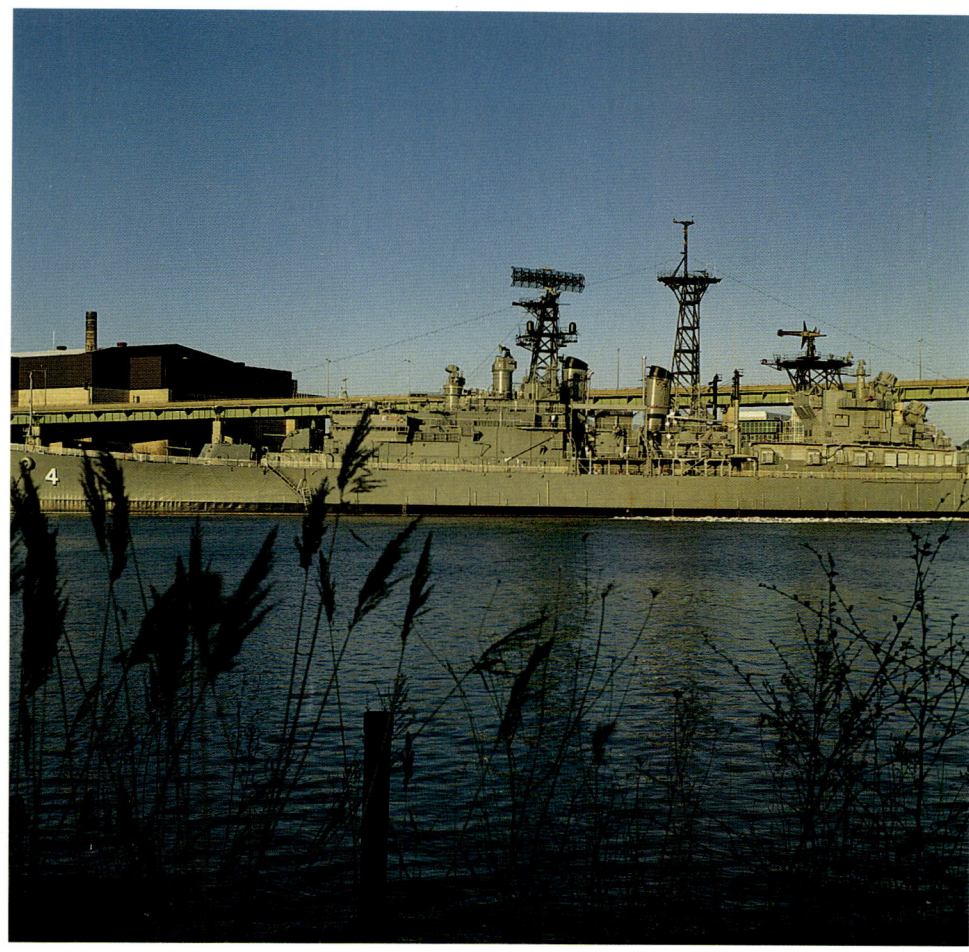

Stroll the decks of a destroyer, explore a submarine, or examine the massive guns of a guided missile cruiser at the **Buffalo and Erie County Naval and Servicemen's Park** on Buffalo's waterfront. The largest park of its kind in the nation, it honors servicemen and women from all branches of the Armed Forces and brings military history alive through a remarkable collection of ships, planes, exhibits, and artifacts. Photo by James P. McCoy.

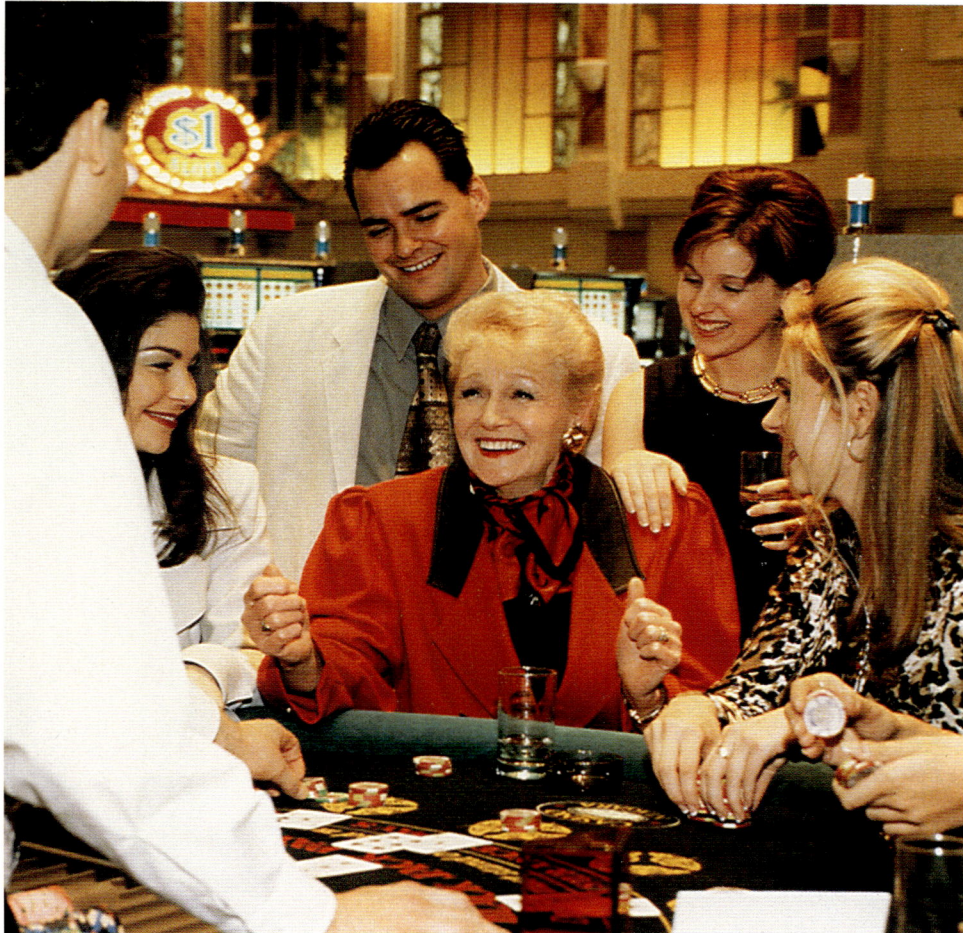

Casino Niagara, on the Canadian side of Niagara Falls, is a gaming retreat designed to offer every visitor a new level of casino excitement in an atmosphere of Canadian Empire-style elegance and ease. Inside the entrance of the 96,000 square foot facility is a spectacular three-story waterfall splashing down an 80-foot glass atrium. Publicly owned, yet privately run, this facility is one of only two casinos in North America based on this unique model. Photo courtesy of Casino Niagara.

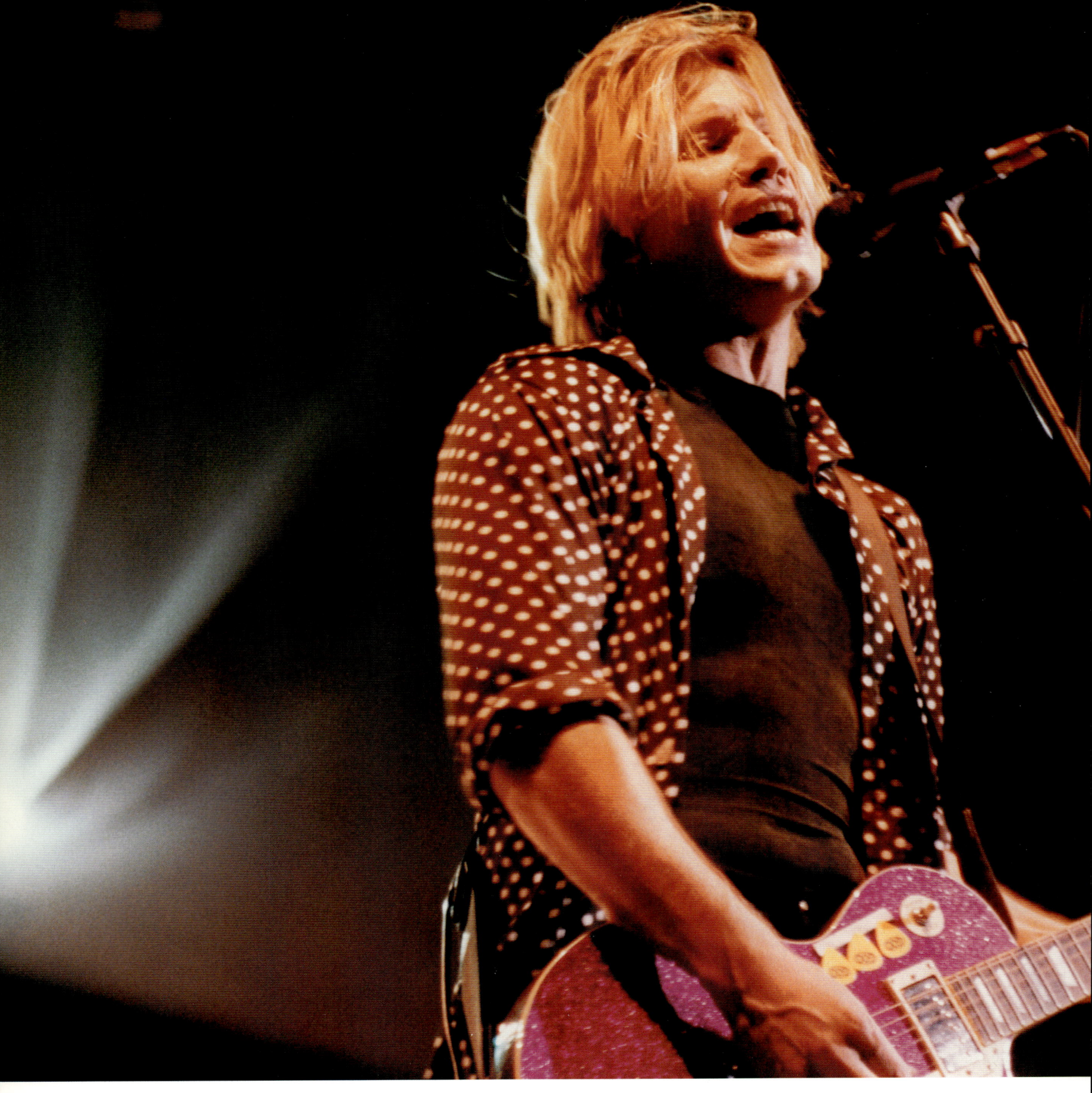

ATTRACTING THE WORLD

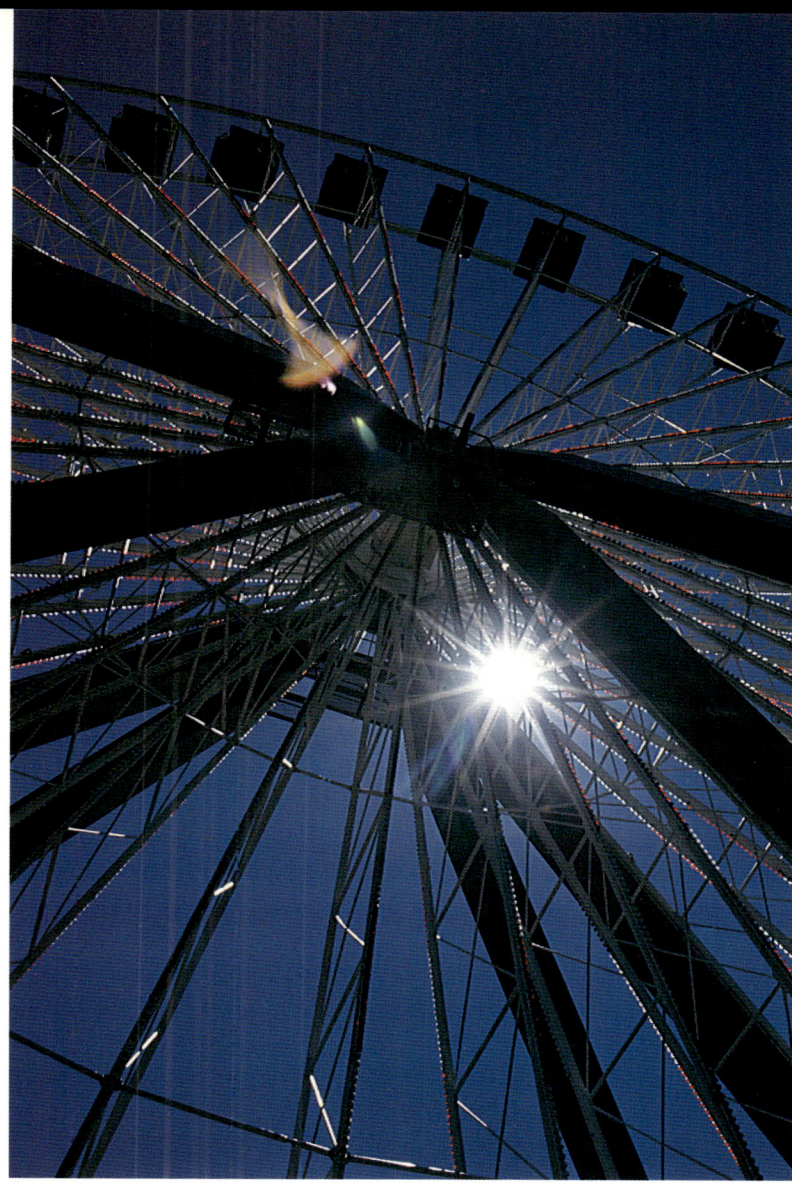

If hurtling through dark space at speeds up to 60 mph. is your kind of adventure, **Darien Lake** has your ride: Nightmare at Phantom Cave. This eight-story, 1,772-foot-long roller coaster is just one of the attractions at Niagara's premier amusement park in Genesee County. You can also splash in an aquatic playground, take the toddlers to their own minipark, or stroll the midway in search of the perfect candied apple. The musical action begins after dark, when the Darien Lake amphitheater presents national acts. Darien Lake's campground, one of the nation's largest, provides over 2,000 campsites and also rents RV campers.
Photo by James P. McCoy.

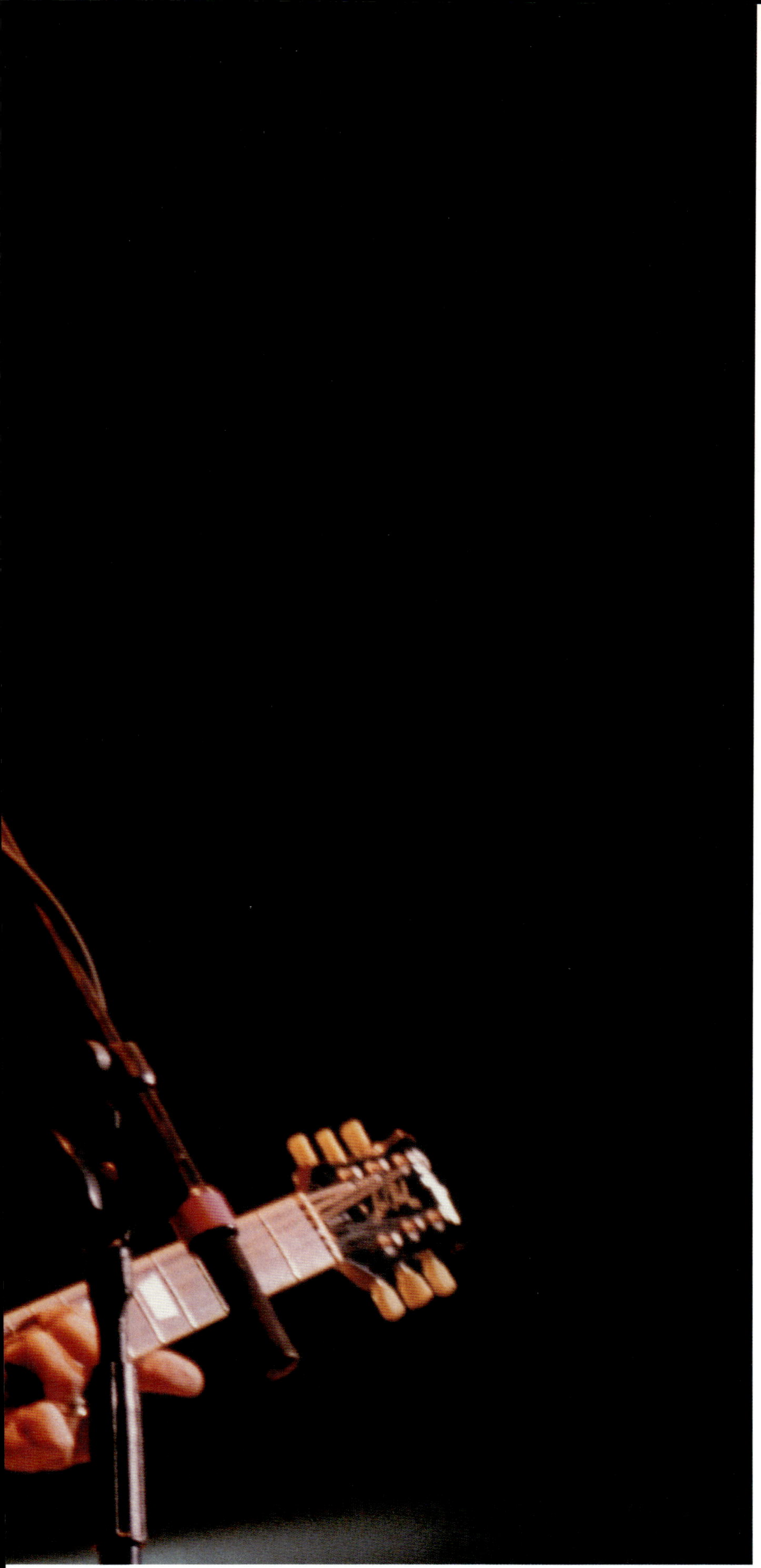

Outstanding hometown bands have always been a part of Niagara's nightlife. From the late Stan and the Ravens classic rock 'n' roll to Billy McEwen and the Soul Invaders to the perennial Party Squad to the eclectic Pine Dogs to the hip alternative band elk, Buffalo's bands are infused with energy, passion, and drive. Two bands that rocked to national prominence were Jamestown's 10,000 Maniacs and the **Goo Goo Dolls**. With their album "A Boy Named Goo" and their smash single "Name," the Goos hit the world-tour circuit but still call Niagara home.
Photo by James P. McCoy.

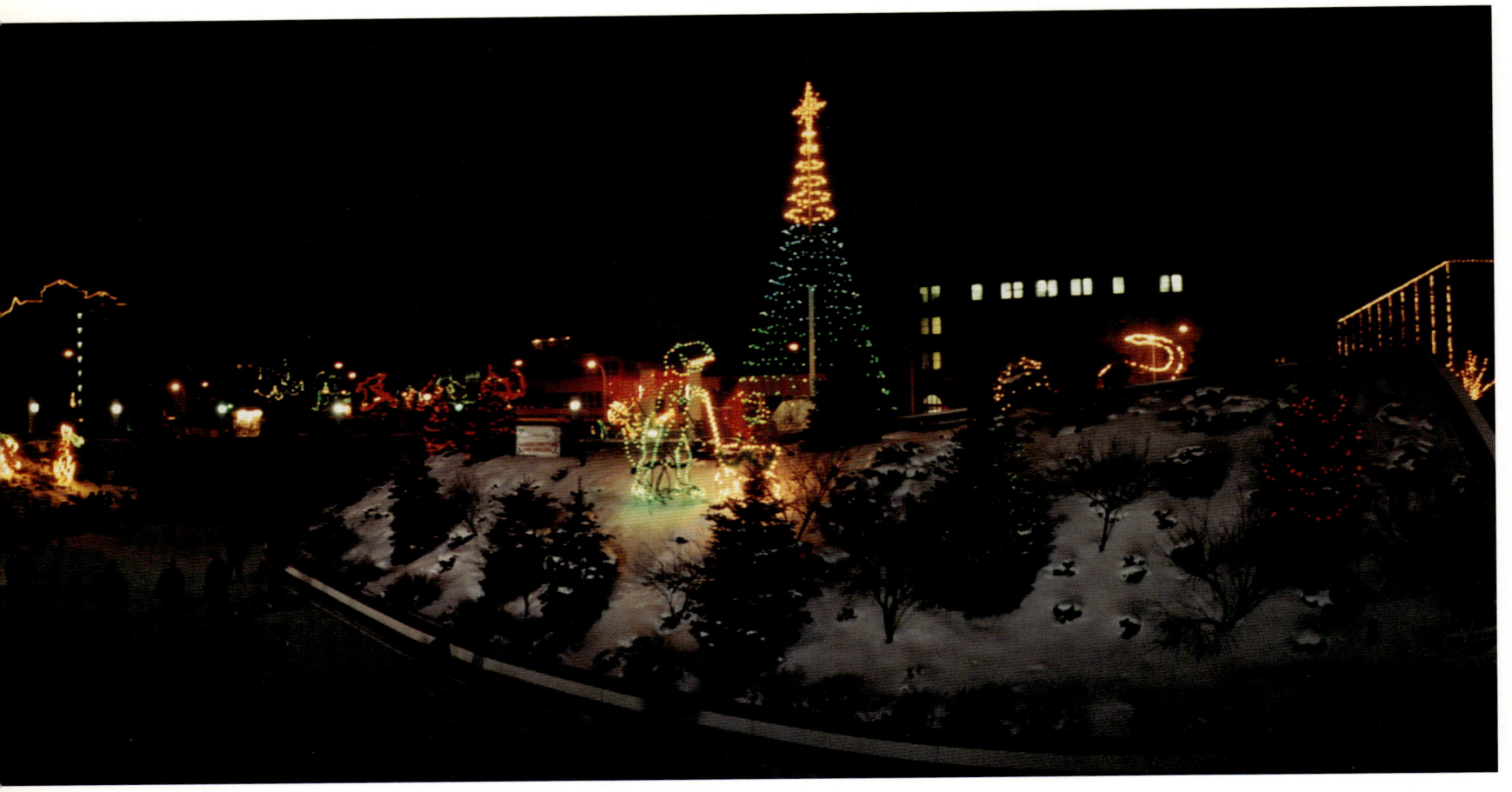

Each year, from late November until early January, spectators from both sides of the border converge in Niagara Falls for the **Festival of Lights**. This glittering festival features nightly entertainment, a gala parade, fireworks, ice skating, illuminated displays, horse and buggy rides, and many other attractions at the Niagara Falls Convention and Civic Center and its surrounding areas.

Photo by James P. McCoy.

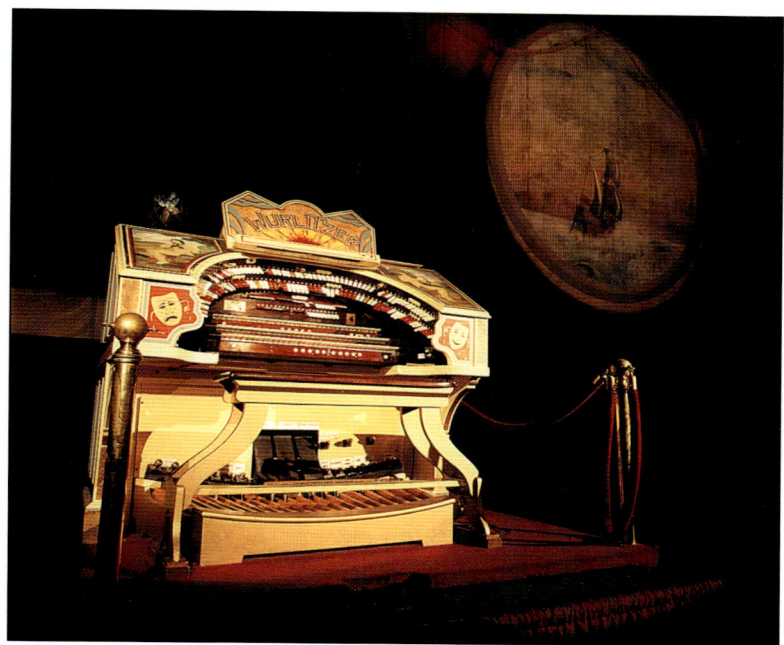

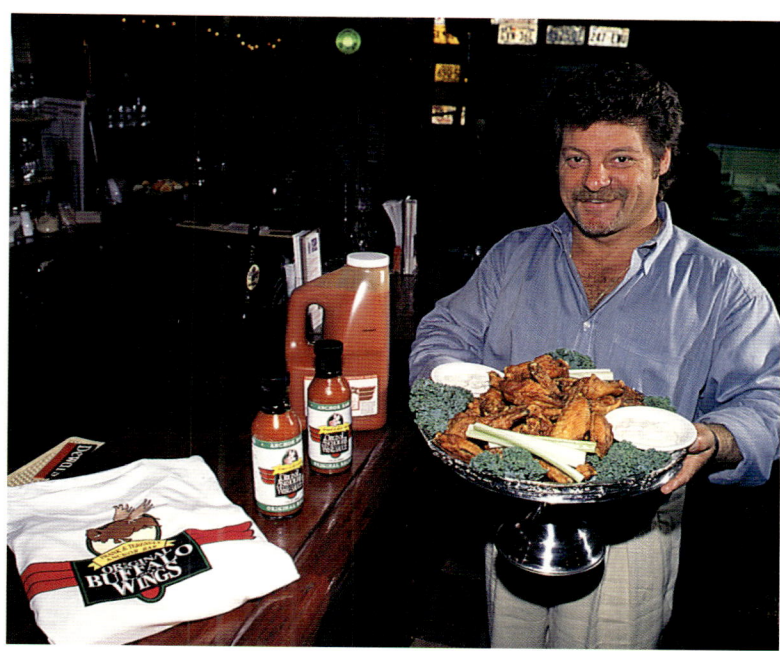

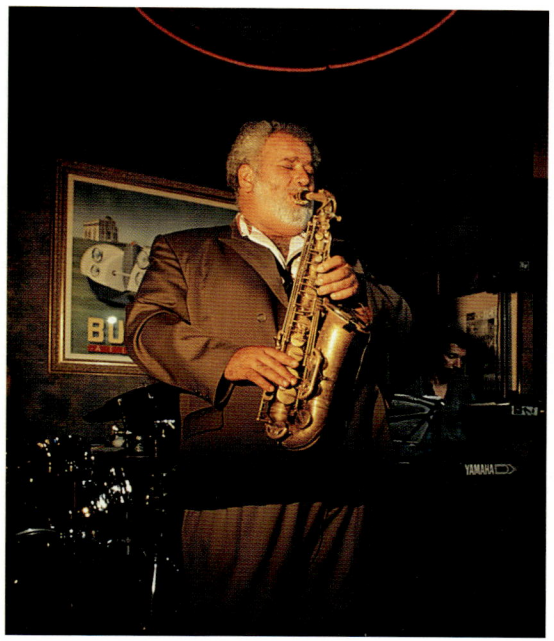

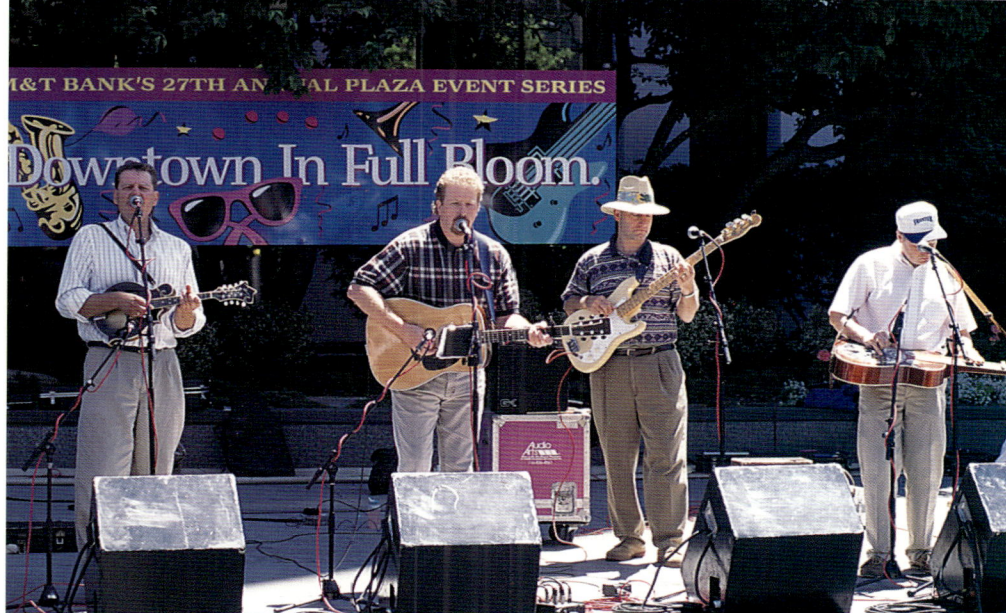

(top left) You can still hear the original **mighty Wurlitzer organ** in monthly concerts at the lovingly restored **Riviera Theatre** built in 1926. The theater, once part of Michael Shea's theater empire (which also included Shea's Hippodrome in Toronto), is now owned by the Niagara Frontier Organ Society. The organ was made by the Rudolph Wurlitzer Company of North Tonawanda, where the Riviera Theatre is located. Lavished with marble, stained glass, brass, hand-painted murals, and blazing with light from its 15,000-crystal French chandelier, the Riviera is one of the last of the great small-town movie palaces. Photo by James P. McCoy.

(bottom left) Jazz saxophonist, flutist, and vocalist **Bobby Militello** worked with Maynard Ferguson's big band in the 1970s, toiled in Los Angeles recording studios in the 1980s, and toured with Dave Brubeck and Doc Severinsen in the 1990s. A powerful and passionate player on alto, tenor, or flute, Bobby Militello frequently appears at the Bijou Grille, the downtown Buffalo restaurant he co-owns with his brother Michael. Photo by James P. McCoy.

(top right) Legend has it that Teressa Bellissimo invented Buffalo chicken wings when some hungry patrons at her family's restaurant wanted a late-night snack in 1963. Frank and Teressa's original **Anchor Bar** remains the official home of the **Buffalo chicken wing**. The Anchor Bar is also famous among jazz fans as one of the nation's oldest and most consistent jazz venues. Photo by James P. McCoy.

(bottom right) Every Monday through Friday at noon for 12 weeks during the summer, M&T Bank plays host to free lunchtime concerts and entertainment on the spacious plaza of its graceful skyscraper designed by Minoru Yamasaki. Since 1969, the Plaza Event Series has presented classical, big band, jazz, blues, rock, ballet, contemporary dance, cultural groups, international dance troupes, sports celebrities—and even the Kennel Club—in programs that have drawn more than one-and-a-half-million spectators since the series began. Winner of several awards from national and local organizations, the **M&T Bank Plaza Event Series** is one the largest corporate sponsored events of its kind in the country. Photo by James P. McCoy.

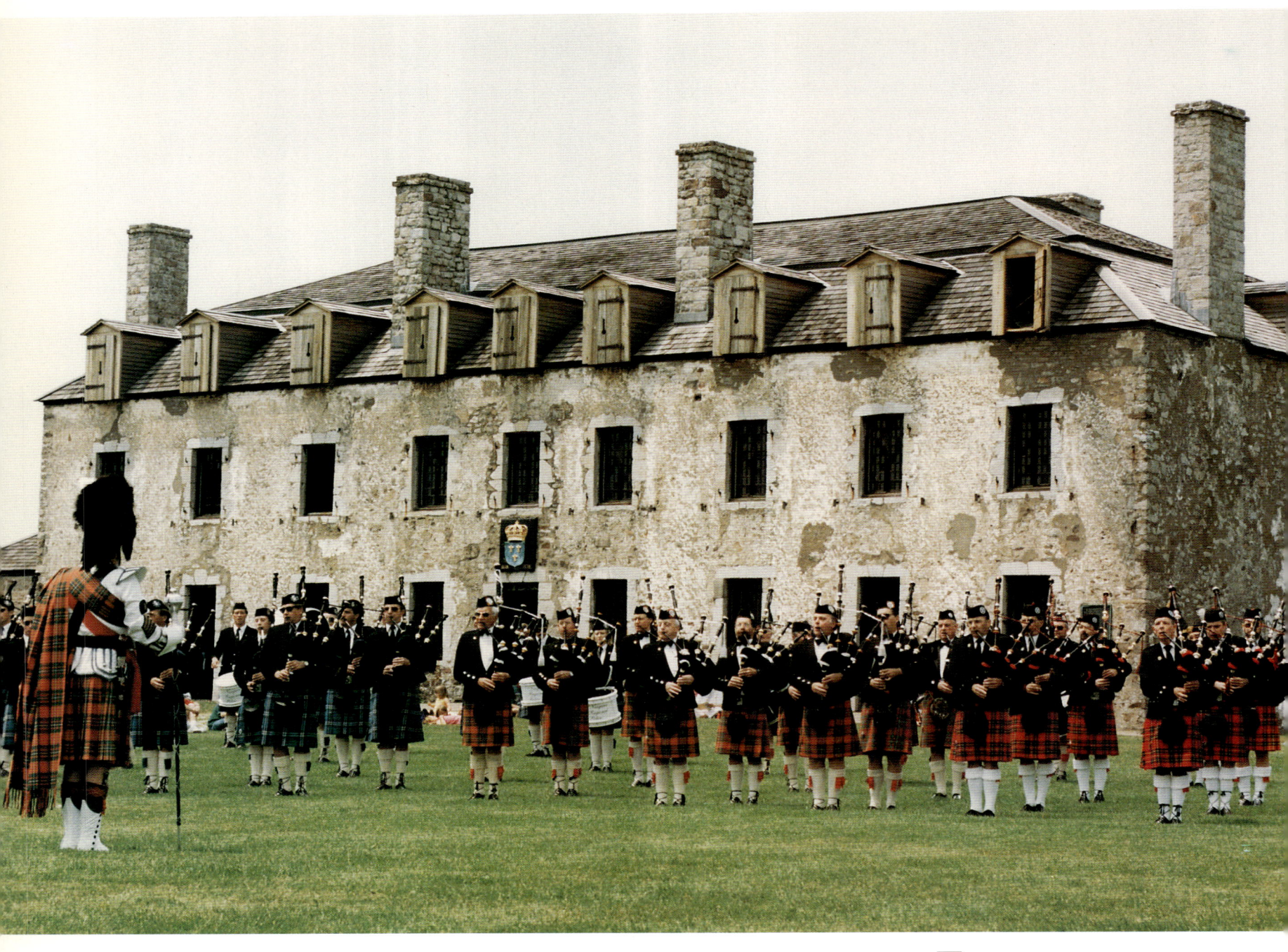

Niagara is a center of **bagpiping** and home to many bagpipe and drum bands, including the McKenzie Highlanders, the Company D Gordon Highlanders, the Caledonian Pipes and Drums, and the many outstanding street and competitive bands sponsored by police, military and municipal organizations. the Fraser Highlanders, two time winners of the international competition in Scotland, are based nearby in Toronto.
Photo by James. P. McCoy.

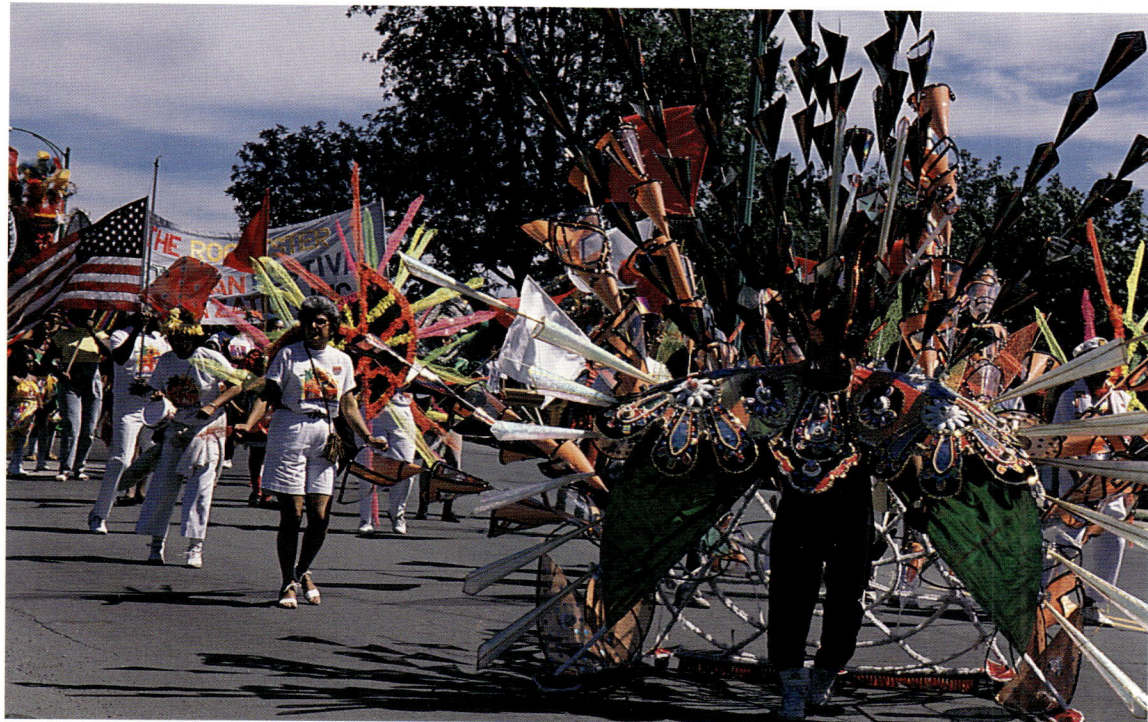

The slippery ascent of a greased pole by a determined band of youthful climbers is the highlight of the annual **Greased Pole Festival** (Festival del Palo Encebao), Buffalo's oldest community festival. The festival, founded by Agustine "Pucho" Olivencia in 1969 and held at the community center that bears his name, features games, amusement rides, traditional Hispanic dishes, and dancing to great salsa and merengue music by bands from Puerto Rico, Santo Domingo, and the eastern United States.
Photo by James P. McCoy.

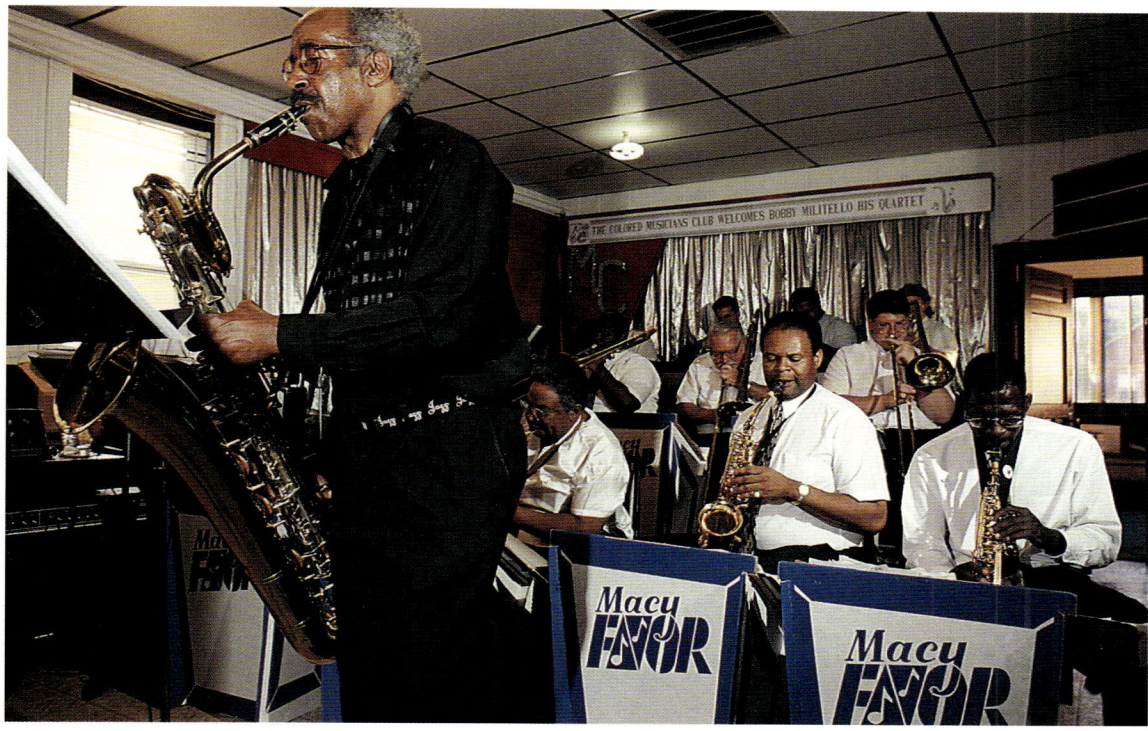

The **Colored Musicians Club of Buffalo** is just around the corner from the Michigan Avenue Baptist Church (historic underground railroad stop), on the second floor of a modest Italianate brick building. Music lovers of all races have always come here to share their love and enthusiasm for jazz and other African-American musical forms. Older club members remember the legendary jam sessions when jazz greats like Duke Ellington, Count Basie, Ella Fitzgerald, or Hank Jones, would show up with their sidemen after a gig at Shea's Buffalo, the Town Casino, or the Moonglow and play far into the night.
Photo by James P. McCoy.

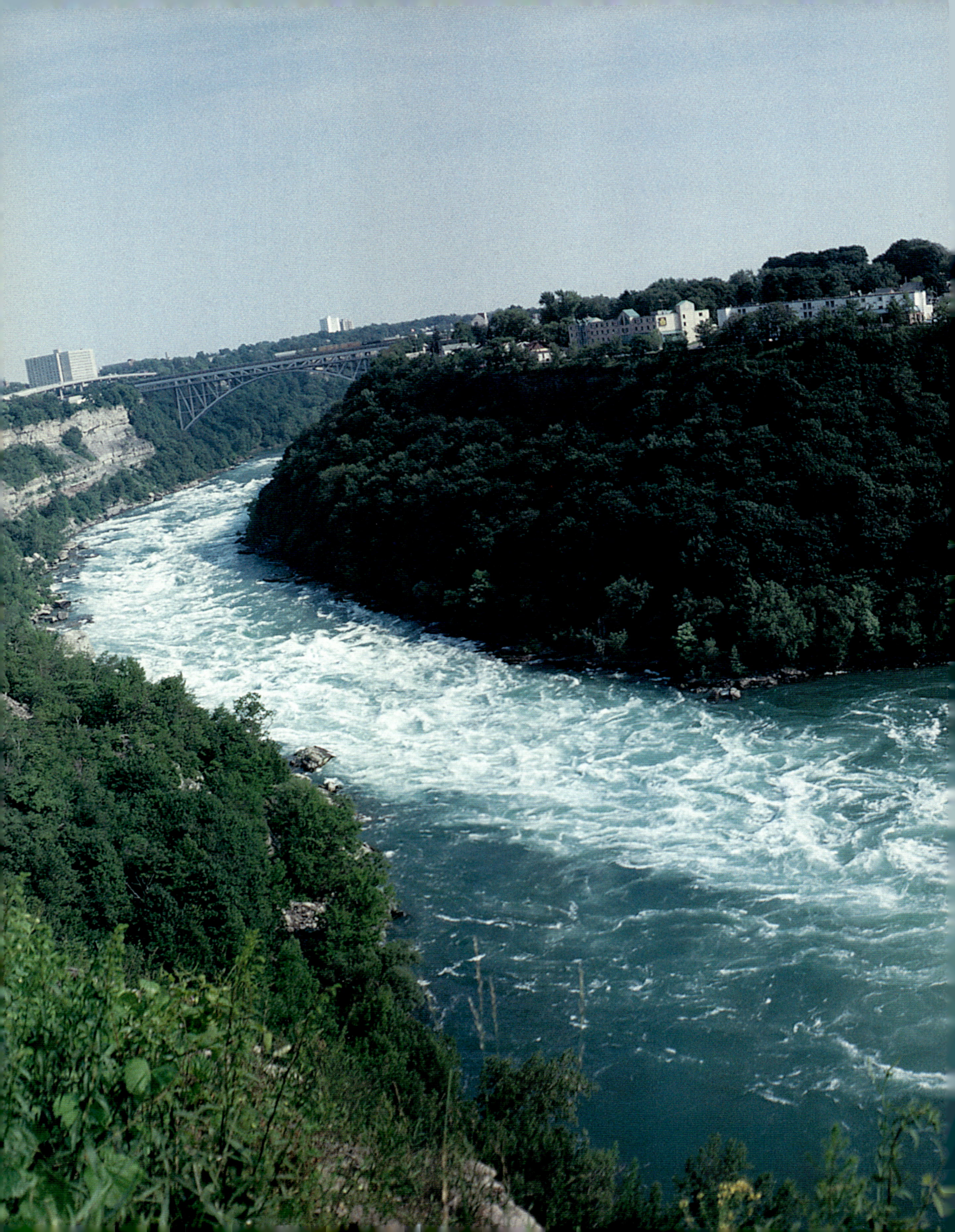

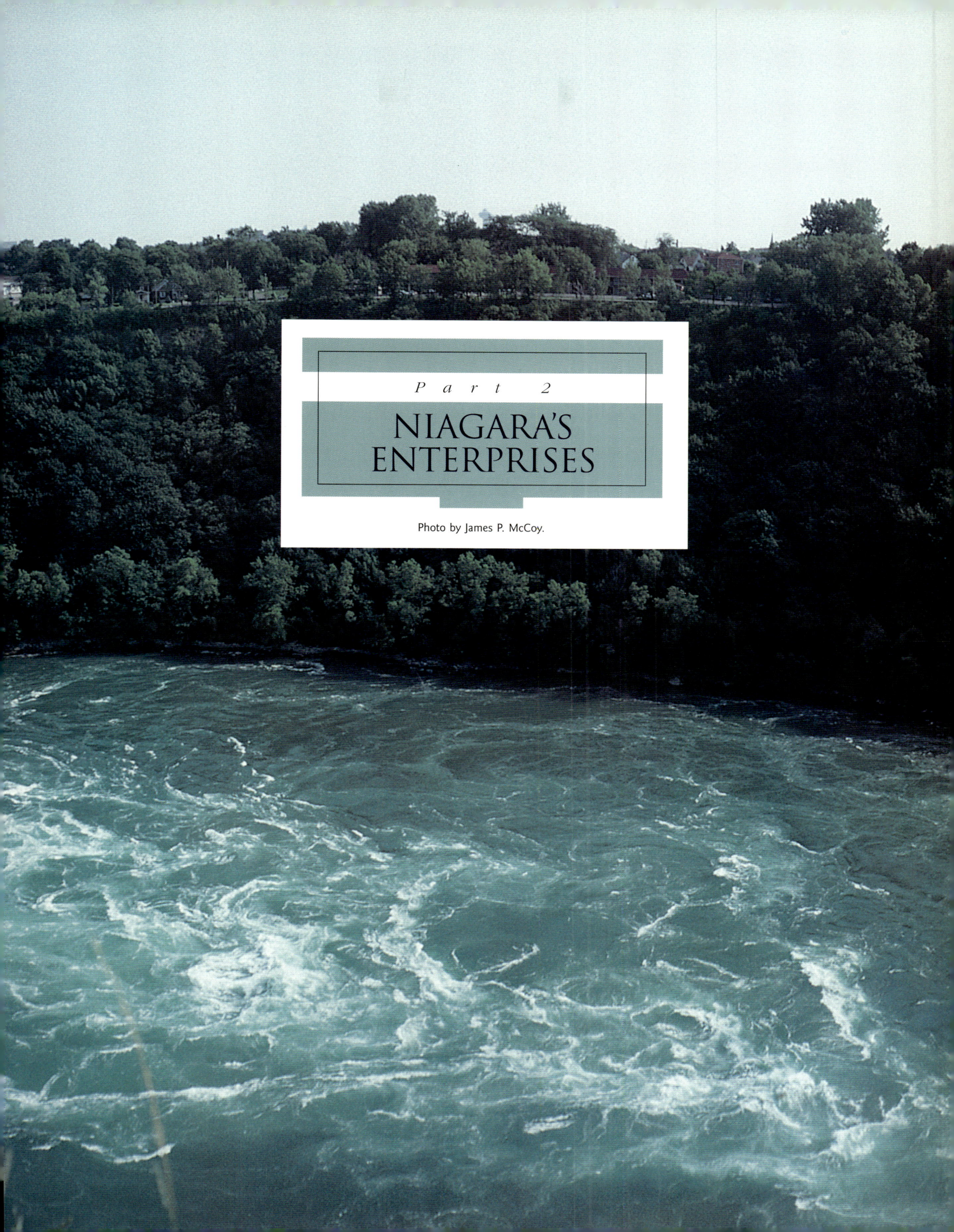

Part 2
NIAGARA'S ENTERPRISES

Photo by James P. McCoy.

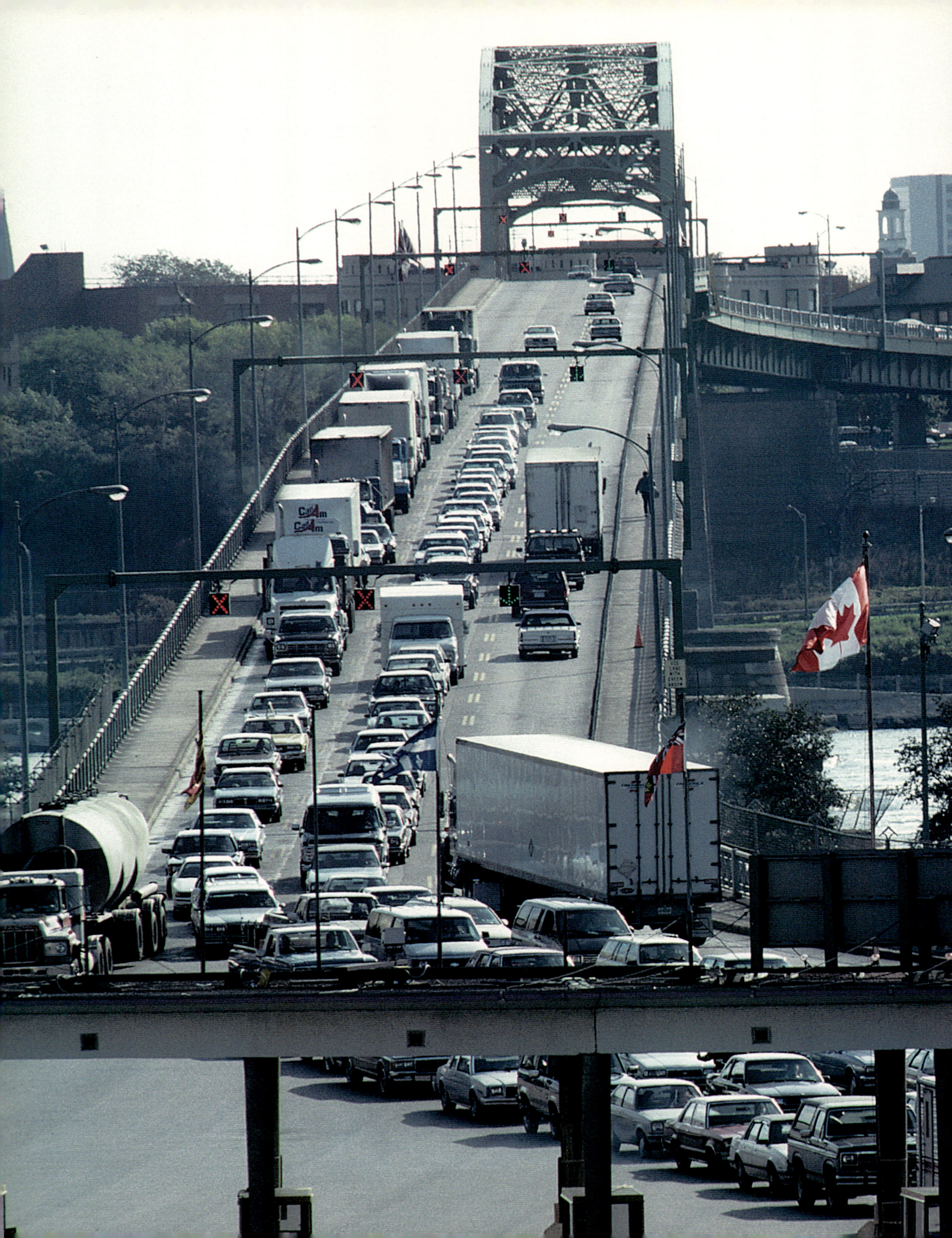

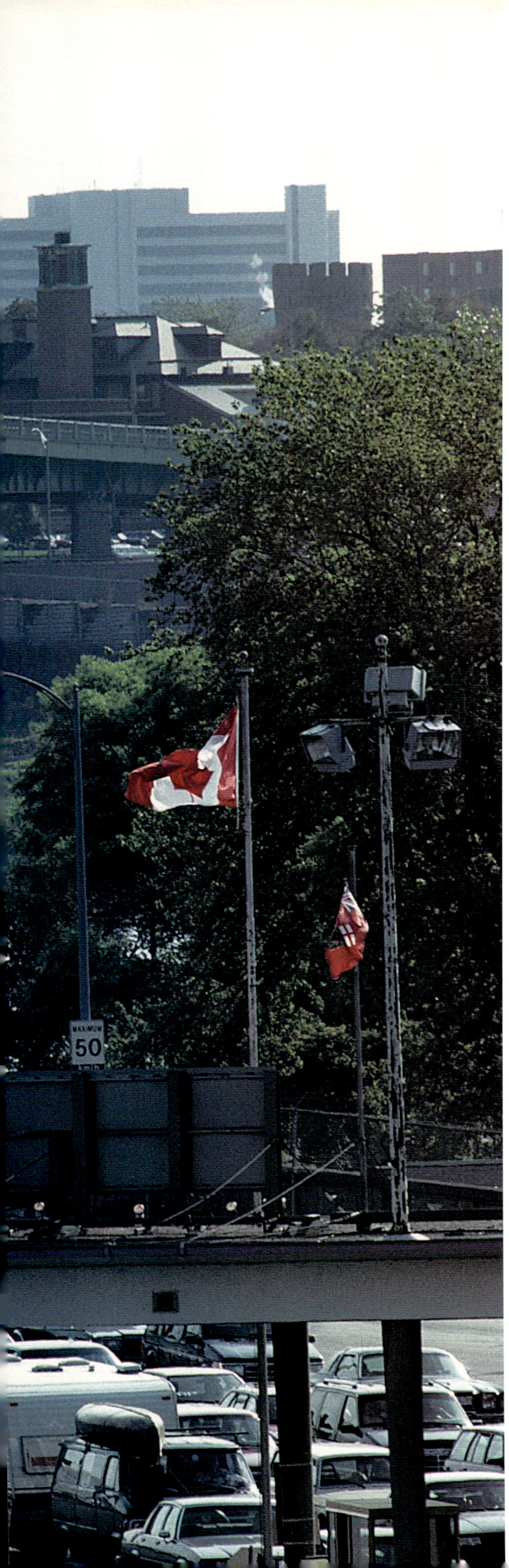

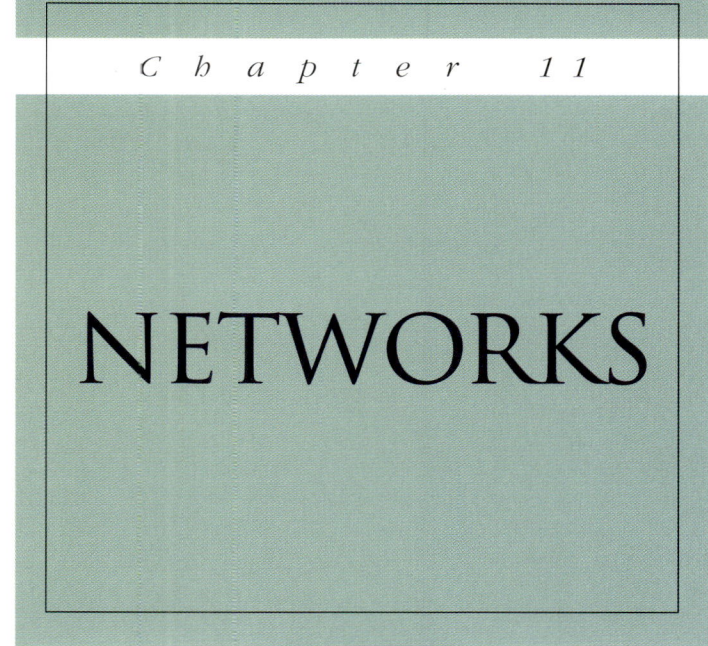

Chapter 11

NETWORKS

Photo by James P. McCoy.

WKBW

WKBW-TV is Western New York's television news channel. WKBW-TV is the ABC affiliate for Buffalo and Southern Ontario, Canada. More Western New Yorkers get their information from Channel 7's "Eyewitness News" than from any other source.

WKBW-TV is owned by the Granite Broadcasting Corporation. Granite took ownership of the powerhouse station in July of 1995, making Buffalo the largest station in the Granite Broadcasting group. The company owns nine television stations in cities across the country. The philosophy of Granite is clear—to serve the Buffalo community and maintain a dominant news voice serving our viewers and sponsors.

Susan Banks, Irv Weinstein, Kathleen Leighton, Keith Radford

The hometown team at WKBW-TV understands what hard work is all about. The people that make up Channel 7 call Western New York home and want the best for their families and viewers. It is a tradition of excellence that WKBW-TV has enjoyed for over 40 years.

WKBW-TV signed on the air on Sunday, November 30, 1958. Sportscaster Rick Azar welcomed viewers announcing that "WKBW-TV Channel 7 is on-the-air!" The station was owned by Dr. Clinton Churchill then. He was an evangelist, and the call letters stand for "Well Known Bible Witness." WKBW-TV was an offshoot of WKBW- 1520AM radio. The original studios at 1420 Main Street launched dozens of successful careers in broadcast journalism. Today, WKBW-TV is located at Church and South Elmwood streets, 7 Broadcast Plaza. Channel 7 was one of the first companies to build at Buffalo's waterfront, a shining example of the bright future ahead for Western New York.

The station was purchased by Capital Cities in 1960 and became the flagship station for that growing broadcast group through the 1960s and early 1970s. Capital Cities then bought stations in Philadelphia and other major markets, later acquiring the ABC Television network in 1985. WKBW-TV was then owned and operated by Queen City Broadcasting for the next 10 years and in 1995 joined the Granite family of television stations. Granite Broadcasting is run by W. Don Cornwell. It is recognized as one of the top broadcasting operations in the country, run by one of the country's leading minority businessmen.

Western New Yorkers have come to depend on the people they see everyday on WKBW-TV for news and information. Irv Weinstein has delivered "Eyewitness News" since 1964, after joining the television staff from radio. Tom Jolls has delivered the exclusive "Accu-Weather" forecast outside, where Buffalo's weather happens, since 1964 also. Other personalities like Susan Banks, Keith Radford, Kathleen Leighton, John Murphy, Mary Travers, Mike Randall, Linda Pellegrino, Brian Kahle, Jean Hill, Steve Boyd, Steve Brown, Sheila Mahoney, Andrew Siff, Helen Tederous, Jon Burton, Bob McKeown, Joanna Pasceri, Angie Wyatt, Vince Irby, and Jon Summers are like family.

WKBW-TV Channel 7 is the ratings leader. In

WKBW-TV Channel 7 on the Buffalo, NY Waterfront

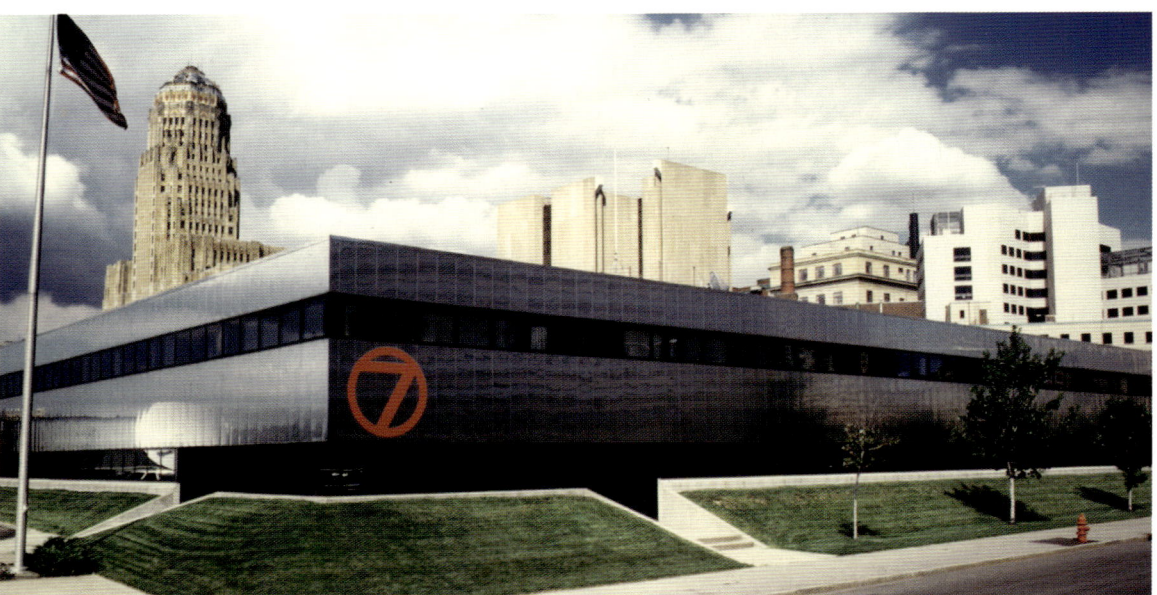

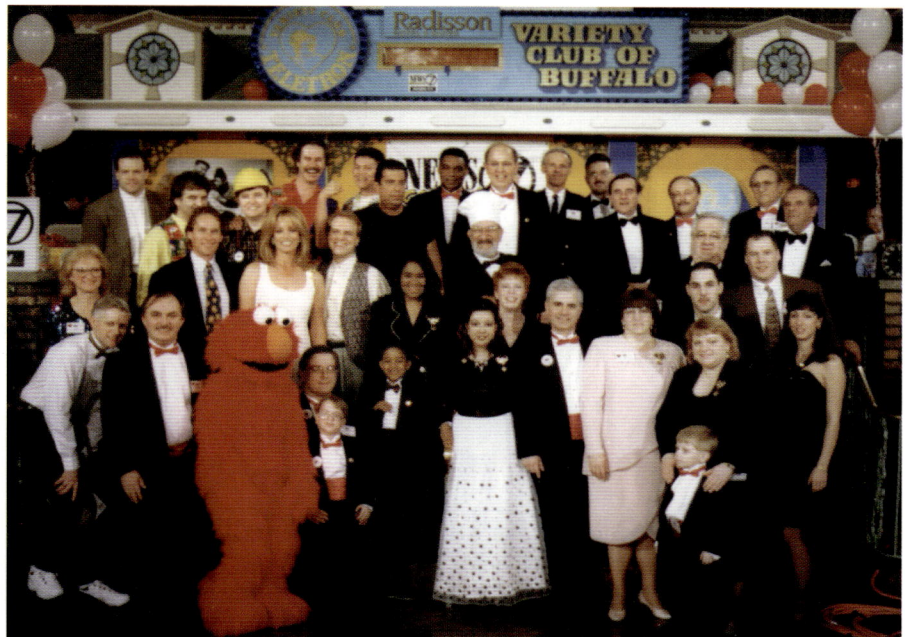

Each year WKBW-TV hosts the Variety Club Telethon to benefit Children's Hospital.

The community has a rich mix of ethnic diversity. Other locally produced programs and specials have focused on the concerns of Western New York, highlighting top students, seniors, and issues surrounding minorities. The station participates in the "Companies That Care" program featuring announcements and specials that aim to enrich the life of everyone in its viewing area.

In 1963, WKBW-TV aired the first "Variety Club Telethon." Ever since, the station has broadcast a 21-hour event each year to raise money for Children's Hospital and other children's charities. More than $1 million is raised each year!

Channel 7 also reaches out to the cultural community creating awareness of Shea's Buffalo Theater, The Buffalo Philharmonic, and other organizations. Other groups that WKBW-TV offers public service to include United Cerebral Palsy, the Buffalo Federation of Neighborhood Centers, the United Way, the Boys and Girls Clubs, Hospice, and many others.

Buffalo fans love their sports, and WKBW-TV is the place where viewers turn to for complete coverage of the area's pro teams—the Sabres, Bisons, and Buffalo Bills—every Saturday during the season, all-pro Steve Tasker hosts "Bills Scoreboard." "Eyewitness Sports" is also the place to find out about "Super 7" high school athletes and catch all the scores and highlights!

The weather changes all the time in Buffalo. The "Eyewitness News Weather Team" delivers the exclusive Accu-Weather forecast from where it happens, outside! WKBW-TV was also the first station to deliver the time and temperature on your screen every 15 minutes, with instant weather information and school closing notices on screen all morning long.

Today, WKBW-TV is poised to help bring Buffalo and Western New York into the next century. Channel 7 was the first in Buffalo and one of the first in New York State to offer a homepage on the internet with news and information 24 hours a day. The NEWStar 7 satellite truck brings the top stories from the region and the country home to you. WKBW-TV and Granite Broadcasting continue the committment to serve Buffalo with the best local news and programming available—to educate, inform, and entertain the people of Western New York. ◆

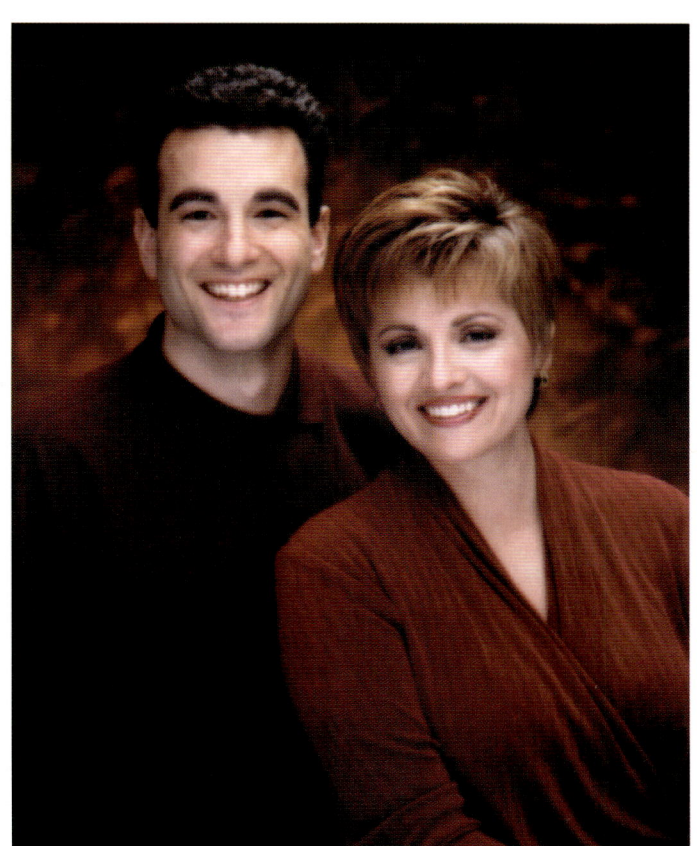

Mornings come alive with Linda Pellegrino and Drew Kahn on "AM Buffalo"

addition to "Eyewitness News," Channel 7 offers more local programming than any other station in Western New York. "Good Morning Western New York" starts the day, followed by the long-running magazine/talk program "AM/Buffalo" at 10 a.m. This program started as "Dialing for Dollars" in 1964 and changed from a game show with "jackpot calls" to an information show in 1978. It stands as one of the longest running, and most successful, local shows in the country. Many children grew up with "Rocketship 7" and "The Commander Tom Show" over the years. Those kids are adults now and continue to make WKBW-TV and ABC their television choice.

WIVB-TV

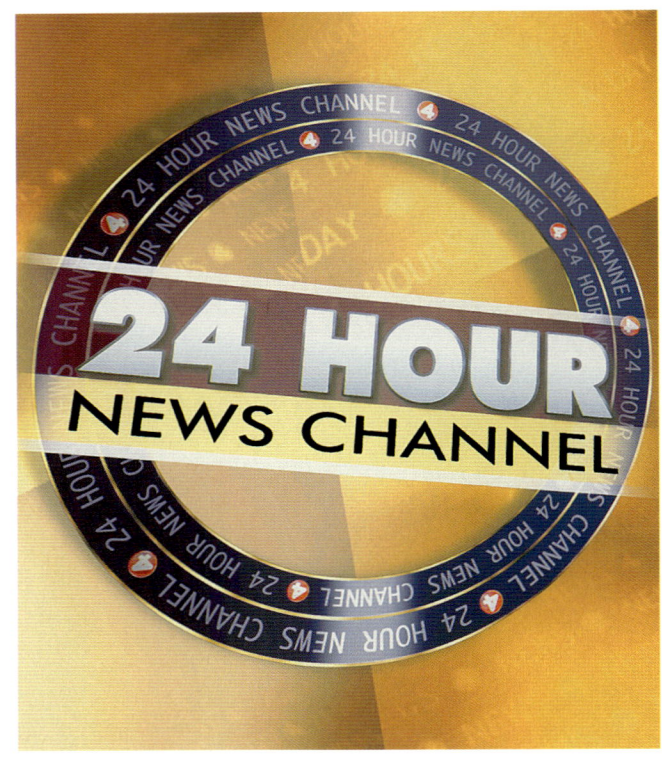

In 1948 WIVB, under the call letters WBEN-TV, signed on the air as the first television station in Western New York and only the 25th in the nation. Six years later, Channel 4 became an affiliate of the CBS network. Community service and local news coverage was the articulated mission, and from that day on, while new technology and new personnel reflect cultural change, that philosophy has been steadfast.

The station was owned by a local newspaper, *The Buffalo News*, until 1977. That year Howard Publications, Inc., purchased the station, and the call letters were officially changed to WIVB-TV. Since 1995 WIVB-TV has been owned by LIN Television. The station serves eight counties in Western New York and reaches Pennsylvania and southern Ontario, Canada.

WIVB-TV was the first Buffalo station to use a tandem anchor team in its hour-long evening news format. Today, priding itself on 24-hour news coverage, the station devotes close to five hours of programming daily to local news coverage, with hourly news updates. Its NEWS 4 team of reporters and anchors has consistently won major professional journalism awards over the years.

No newscast would be complete without a weather forecast, and WIVB-TV has been a leader in this area. Its weather team consists of three certified meteorologists, and the station has its own Doppler radar. Weathercasts are highly localized and updated continuously.

A major innovation recently is the creation of LWS, or Local Weather Stations, WIVB's unique melding of an elemental part of the newscast with an educational community project. As of the spring of 1996, sophisticated remote weather stations had been set up in 11 area schools, providing the station with local weather information from every county in Western New York.

Not only does this system enable a real-time, localized weather-gathering network that is unmatched, but it also creates a stellar educational opportunity for the students, who learn science, and other subjects, in action. The station has plans to double the size of its LWS project.

WIVB-TV likes to call itself not only first in local news reporting, but also "first in commitment to make a difference." Through the decades, Channel 4 has led the way with more than 200 locally produced drama and music specials, many featuring local actors. The station has a proud history of public service programming. Longtime local viewers recall with fondness early programs like "Meet the Millers", the first local cooking/talk show; local bowlers in action on "Beat the Champ"; and the first religious service series,

broadcast weekly from a different denomination. Still seen on WIVB is "By the People", a forum in which community service organizations can discuss their programs.

Since 1974, the station has sponsored "Call 4 Action", part of a nationwide program which trains local volunteers to take calls from frustrated consumers seeking help with complaints. This free and confidential information and referral service,

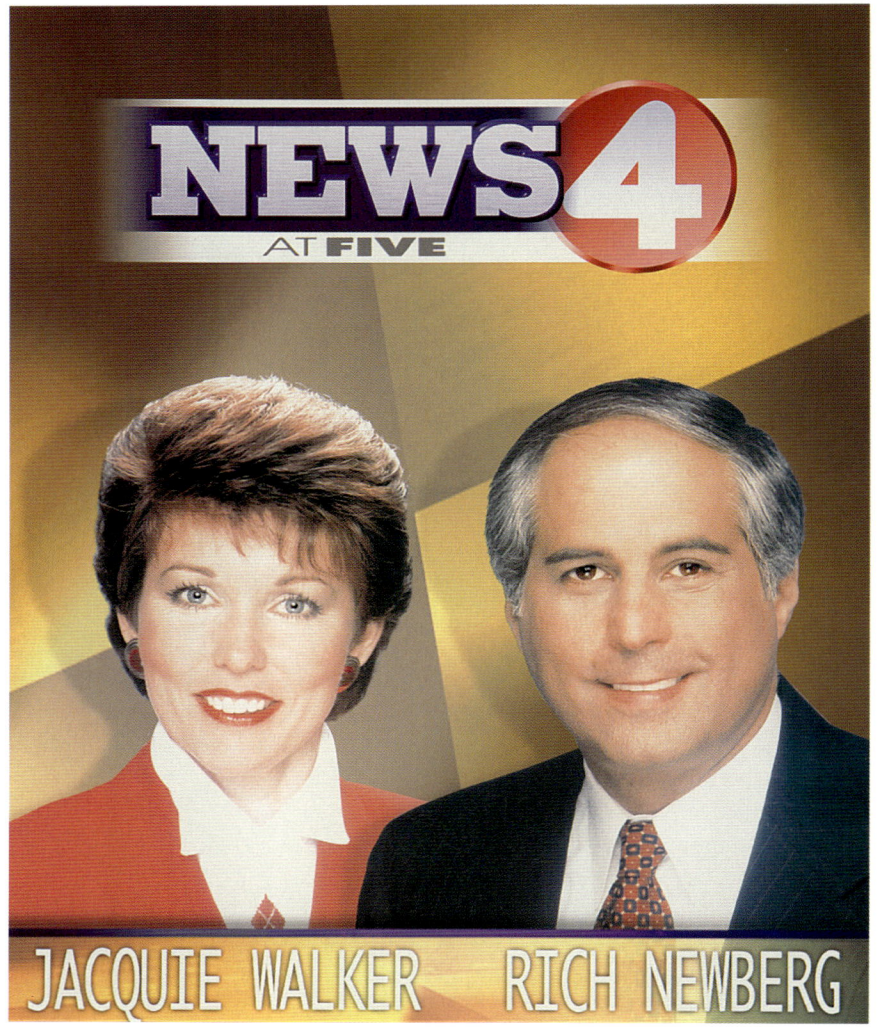

JACQUIE WALKER   RICH NEWBERG

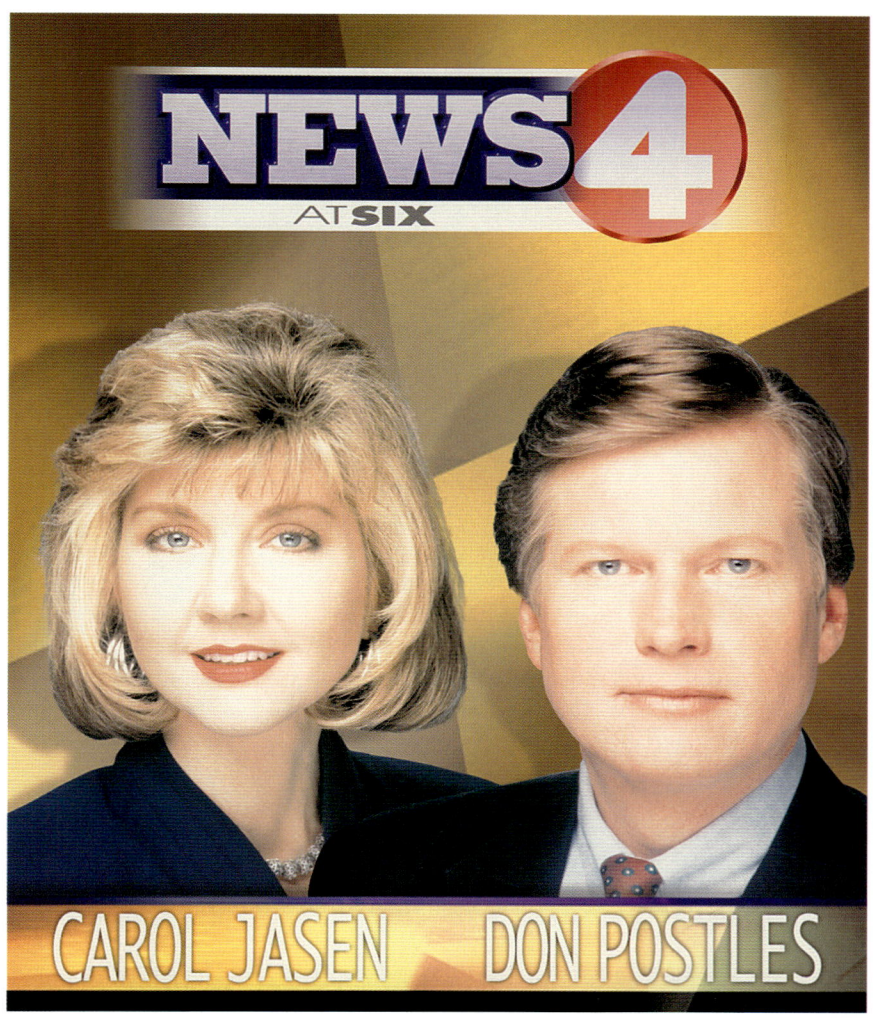

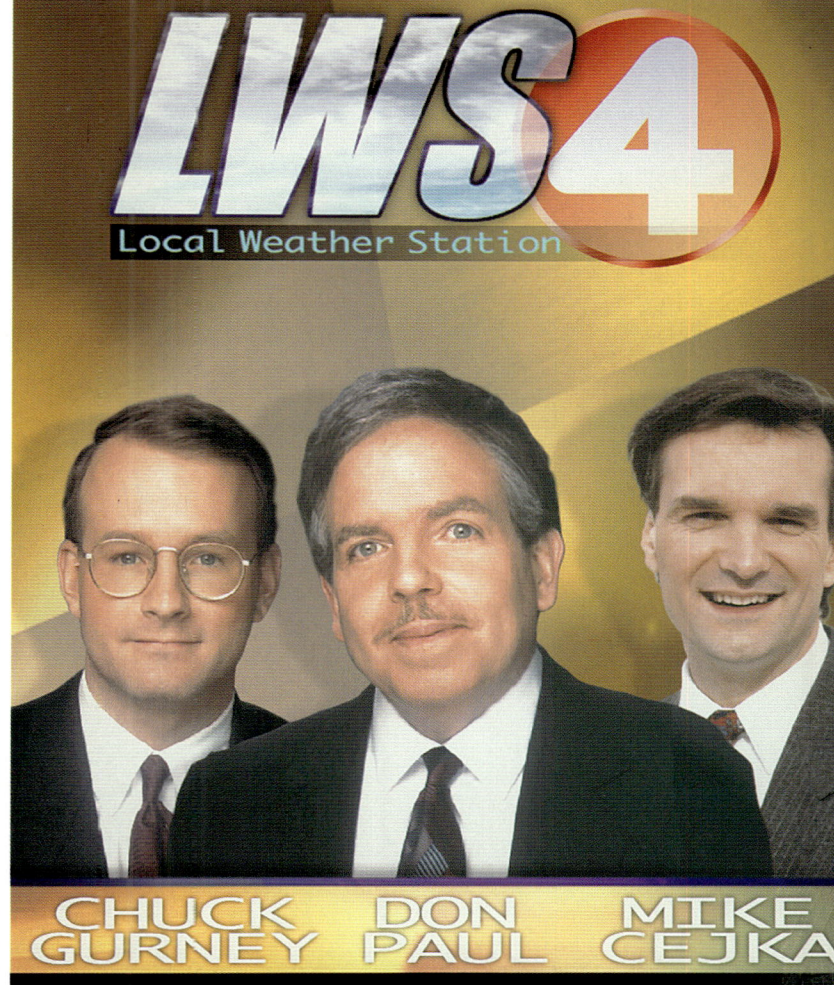

which operated as a not-for-profit affiliate of radio and television broadcasters throughout the United States, has assisted in recovering thousands of dollars on behalf of Western New York consumers. Several times a year WIVB hosts call-in nights such as "Call a Lawyer" and "Ask the Doctor" featuring free advice from area professionals.

Over the years the station has solicited millions of dollars for Western New York charitable organizations. In addition to providing extensive and valuable on-air promotion for a wide range of causes, the station's on-air talent is encouraged to donate personal time to community organizations, from emceeing events to assisting in career days and graduation ceremonies.

While factors like new technology, the cable news explosion, and societal changes have indelibly altered the business of television, WIVB-TV is determined to remain true to its heritage as a truly local station. The goal, succinctly stated, is to strive for dominance in local news coverage and local community involvement. ℕ

AMERICAN STEAMSHIP COMPANY

American Steamship Company's M/V American Republic transports the Olympic flame across Lake Erie from Detroit to Cleveland as part of the 1996 Olympic Torch Relay.

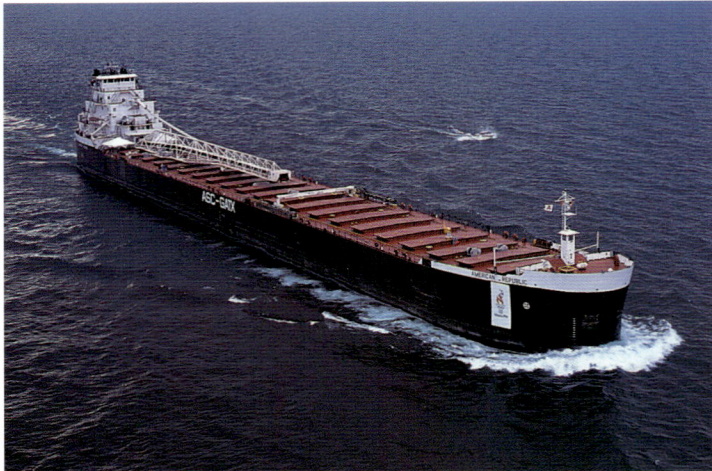

Having the honor of transporting the Olympic flame was an extraordinary task for American Steamship Company, but this Great Lakes vessel operator was equal to the challenge and proud to be a part of the pre-Olympic Games festivities in 1996. The company, a subsidiary of the Chicago based GATX Corporation since 1973, donated the use of its 635-foot vessel, the M/V American Republic, to transport the Olympic flame from Detroit to Cleveland as a part of the Olympic Torch Relay across the U.S.A. This event focused attention on the growth and prosperity that the shipping industry has brought to the Great Lakes region.

Primarily serving the integrated steel, electric utility, and construction industries, American Steamship operates the largest, most modern self-unloader vessel fleet capacity of any U.S. Great Lakes carrier. The company was originally founded as a partnership in Buffalo in 1904 by John J. Boland and Adam E. Cornelius, Sr. These men were entrepreneurs who envisioned a vessel brokerage and chartering business. By 1907, the partnership was operating three of its own vessels and the American Steamship Company was incorporated.

Thirty years later, a bold move was made to convert three of the company's vessels into self-unloader vessels. This enhancement eliminated the need for expensive onshore unloading equipment and personnel and allowed cargo to be delivered to small ports at remote locations. Today, practically all of the vessels serving the domestic Great Lakes market are self-unloaders. During the 1970's and early 1980's, American Steamship Company modernized its self-unloader fleet by taking delivery of ten new vessels at a cost of over $250 million.

American Steamship's current fleet consists of 11 self-unloader vessels ranging in size from 635 feet to 1,000 feet.

These vessels are capable of transporting individual cargoes from 17,000 net tons up to 70,000 net tons and can self-discharge cargo at speeds ranging from 3,000 to 10,000 tons per hour. The primary materials transported are iron ore, coal, and limestone aggregates.

American Steamship Company employs 48 people at its Williamsville (a suburb of Buffalo) offices and an additional 500 people are employed onboard American Steamship's vessels.

Under the leadership of President and Chief Executive Officer Ned A. Smith, the Company has continued to improve performance and efficiency through the use of state of the art technology, including onboard computers, ship to shore satellite communications and Global Differential Positioning Systems for improved navigational efficiency. American Steamship Company is committed to its progressive philosophy of providing safe, modern, efficient and environmentally responsible waterborne transportation throughout the Great Lakes. ❖

American Steamship Company's administrative office located at Centerpointe Corporate Park in Williamsville.

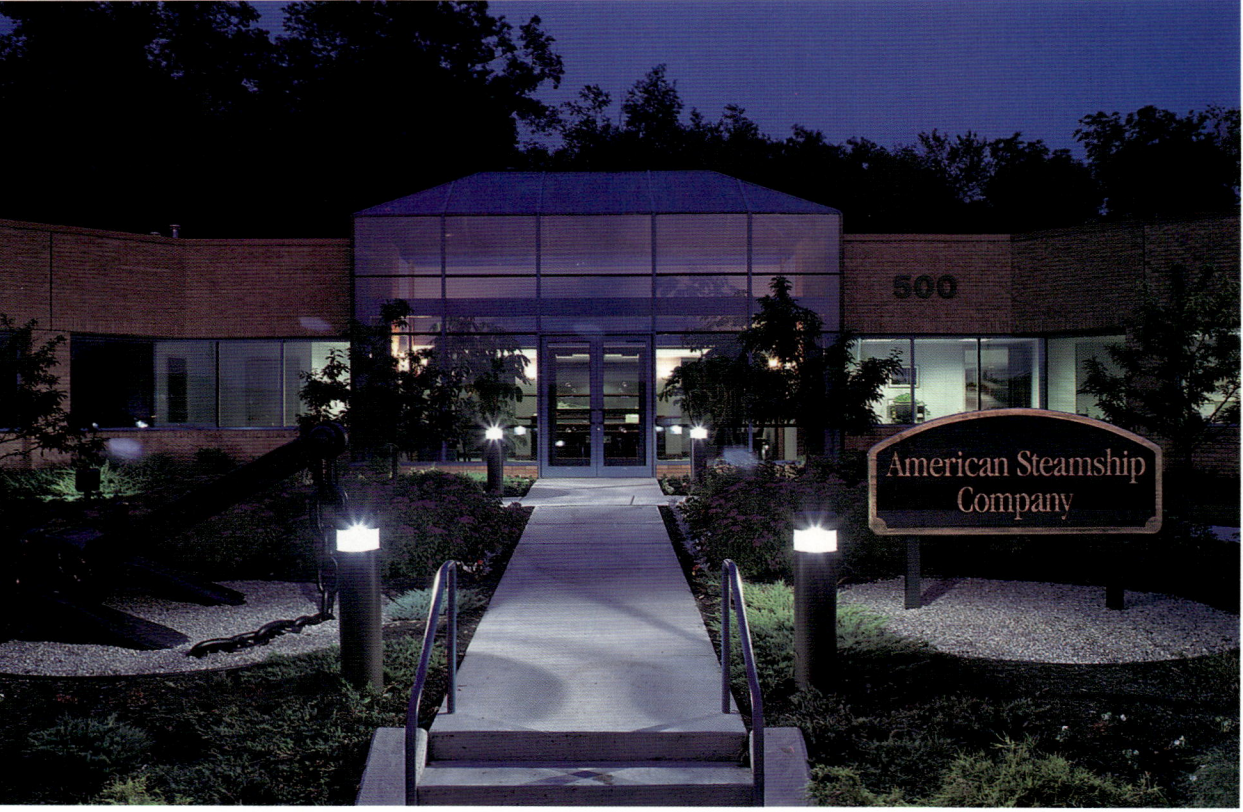

Florists Network, located in the Williamsville Place Shopping Center, 5471 Sheridan Drive in Williamsville, New York, is much more than a florist. Founder and owner Mark C. Syracuse has transformed a two telephone office into a worldwide floral and gift delivery service, offering clients around the globe superior quality flower and gift arrangements.

The Niagara region provides an ideal location for this growing international business. Florists Network is well positioned for handling both local and foreign clients, with 60 incoming phone lines, advertising in half of the major metropolitan areas in the United States, a toll-free North American telephone number 1-800-floranet, and a 20 page World Wide Web site floristsnetwork.com. With these advanced communication resources, Florists Network can take floral and gift orders from anywhere in the world, 24 hours a day, 7 days a week.

The idea of a global floral network was developed by Mark Syracuse in 1990, and in less than five years, Florists Network was thriving. The company's remarkable growth rate results from a dedication to locating the best florists in major markets around the world to serve the discriminating tastes of Florists Network customers. Today, the company has relationships with some of the finest florists in the United States, Canada, Europe, Asia, Africa, and South America, taking the Florists Network from start-up company to one of the top 10 floral services in the United States.

The Florists Network formula for success is to offer not only superior quality and service, but also custom designing with attention to individual tastes unmatched by any other floral service. A sophisticated questionnaire is used in taking orders, assuring that floral arrangements and gift baskets meet the preferences of each recipient. Color, style, type of design, and content are all recorded to ensure complete satisfaction. This personal focus and attention to quality have resulted in an outstanding success rate, and it is backed up by a three-day, 100 percent satisfaction guarantee.

Premium roses, exotic cut flowers, beautiful silk and dry floral arrangements, delicious gourmet and fruit baskets, lush green plants, and colorful balloons bouquets are just some of the gift items offered to customers. This customized service is available at the lowest service charge in the industry. Their floral showroom has an array of silk and dry floral arrangements expressing the finest in floral art.

Florists Network handles large volume corporate orders easily with its fax service and the company's emphasis on quality and service have made it the choice of many of western New York's leading corporations.

VIP Gold discount cards are available to all customers and are especially popular with high-volume corporate clients. VIP cards offer a 10 percent discount on all orders and express overnight delivery is guaranteed at no extra charge.

Building on its proven formula for success, Florists Network will extend its advertising throughout the United States and continue to expand its global network of floral specialists. From Bangkok to Buffalo, Nairobi to Niagara Falls, customers will always be assured of receiving only the finest arrangements and gifts from the world's best worldwide floral service, Florists Network. ◈

FLORISTS NETWORK

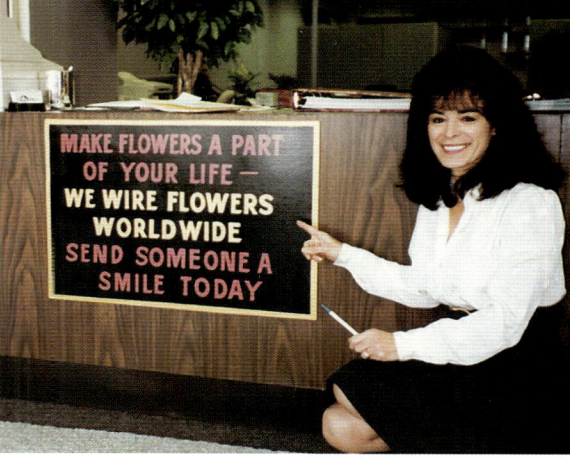

The idea of a global floral network was developed by Mark Syracuse in 1990.

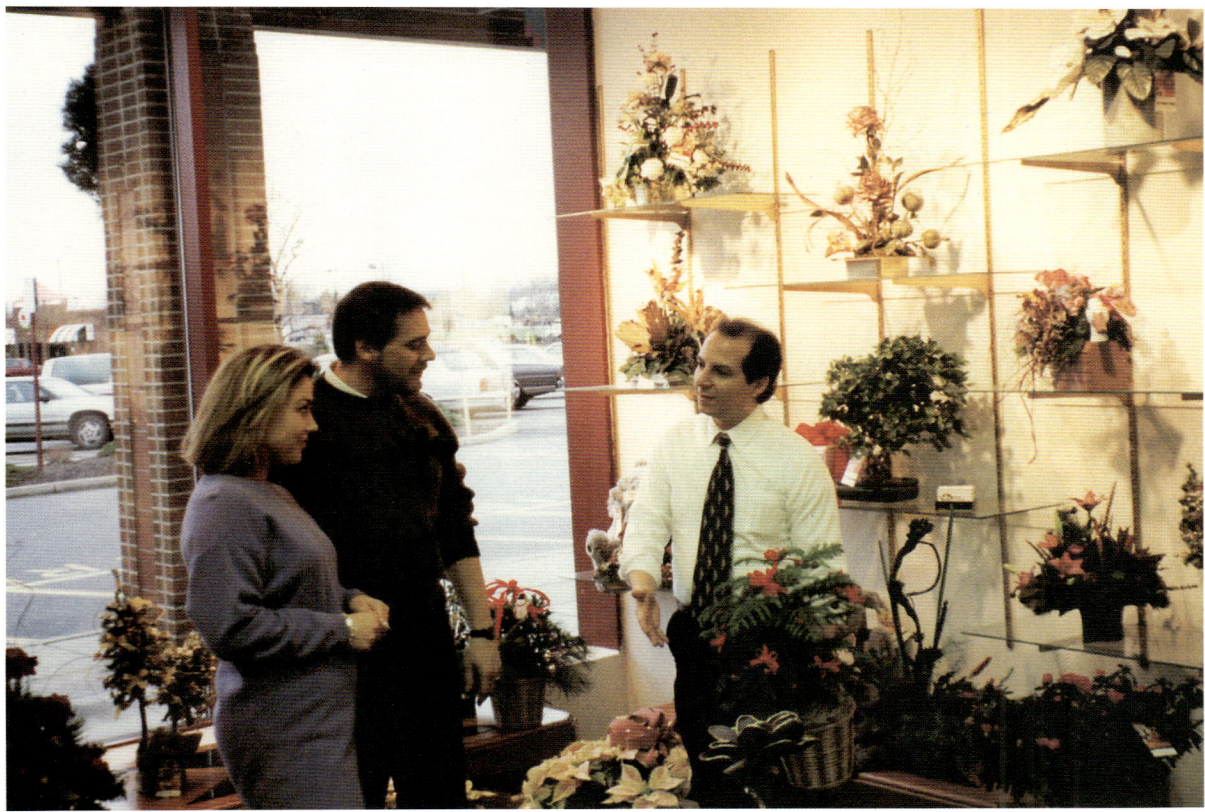

(left) Florists Network is much more than a florist.

MARKETING & ADVERTISING SERVICES CENTER (BUFFNET)

As the world embraces the technology of the Internet, Marketing & Advertising Services Center (MASC) Corporation and its subsidiary, BuffNET, are leading the way to make sure the Niagara region is kept up to date, providing Internet solutions, telemarketing, fulfillment, and marketing support services. The West Seneca company, in operation since 1993, is the brainchild of Gary N. Bacchetti and Michael D. Hassett, president and vice president, respectively. A third partner, Stephen L. Hovey, chief engineer, joined the corporation in 1996.

The corporation was established when GTE Marketing Services Center, a local division of GTE Products Corp. (Stamford, Connecticut), closed its West Seneca office.

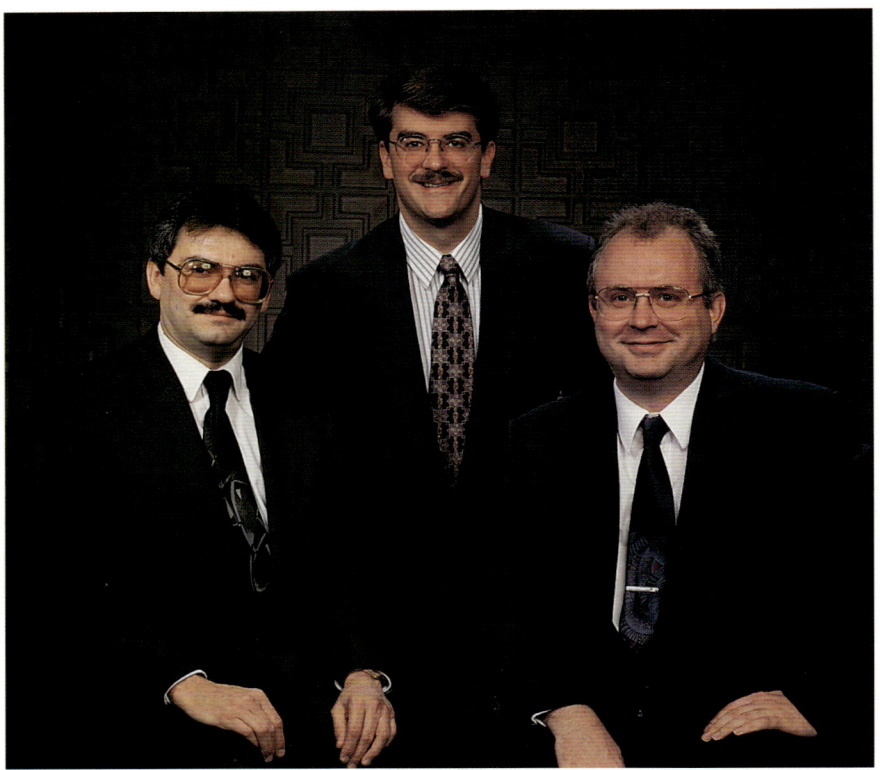

Owners are (left to right): Gary N. Bacchetti, Michael D. Hassett, Stephen L. Hovey.

"Bessie" as the goodwill ambassador.

Hassett, who had supervised the telemarketing and rebate clients for GTE, and Bacchetti, manager of GTE's prepress services, both Western New York natives, pooled their resources to fill the gap and help revitalize their hometown. They founded MASC as a new service provider of telemarketing and rebate fulfillment for such former GTE clients as Molson U.S.A., Corning Food Services, Osram-Sylvania, and others, including the Canadian market.

BuffNET, a subsidiary of the parent company, has made the most impact on the Niagara area. As a local provider of Internet Access, as well as a global provider of Usenet News, the company has had a significant role in educating the local market on what the Internet is and setting the standard for both products and services.

The most profound developments in MASC's service offerings take place in the BuffNET division. It was an innovator to the local market when it started offering preconfigured software to subscribers, enabling them to get online quicker. It's next major innovation was to be the first local Internet provider to establish a global Internet service, BuffNET News.

This was designed for those people who are satisfied with their current provider yet want access to more Usenet news groups. Offering over 34,000 newsgroups, BuffNET News is one of only four global providers (at the time of this writing) and most cost-effective as well as the most robust.

MASC has acquired a reputation for innovation, including its commitment to giving users such value-added services as free personal Websites, reasonable pricing, and constant communication regarding their service. For its business clients, MASC has hired marketing and communications people who use and understand the Internet and know how to integrate this technology into a traditional marketing plan.

Its Website reporting provides clients with the details needed to ensure the effectiveness of their on-line efforts, and their value-added service of providing high-quality Interactive elements also makes BuffNET stand out. MASC answers the needs of businesses seeking results-oriented marketing, not a hardware and software vendor. The company views itself as an extension of a client's marketing department, bringing in an "a la carte" menu of marketing support services.

The MASC management team is acutely aware of the constantly changing environment, from competition with cable and phone companies, to the demands of improving the bandwidth of the Internet. The company pledges to continue providing quality services and launching high-quality content, training services, and banner ads to provide clients with the marketing data they need.

Equally important is the company philosophy of giving back to the community. MASC/BuffNET has provided free public demonstrations, financial support to the Buffalo Freenet, and donations of Internet services to organizations that shed positive light on the region, including Western New York International Trade Council, BorderNet, and Empire State Development Agency. The company has also donated services to Variety Club, Allentown Village Society, Friendship Festival Foundation, United Way of Buffalo and Erie County, Buffalo Music Hall of Fame, Erie County Agricultural Society, Hamburg-Eden Animal Rescue Team, SPCA, Western New York Public Broadcasting, YMCA-Delaware, and MercyFlight. ℕ

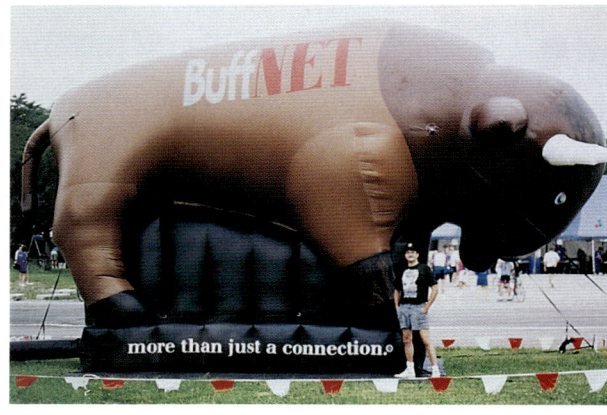

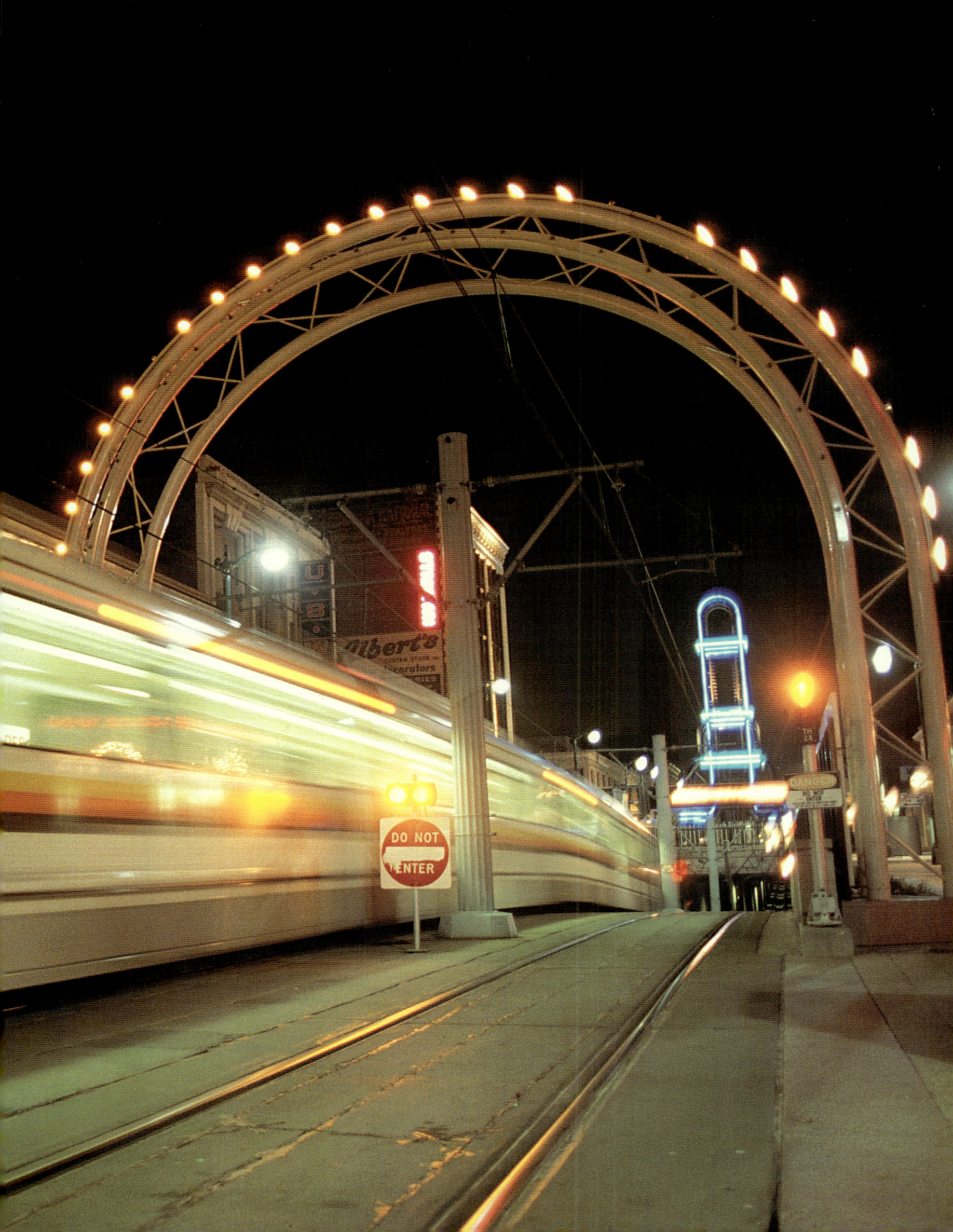

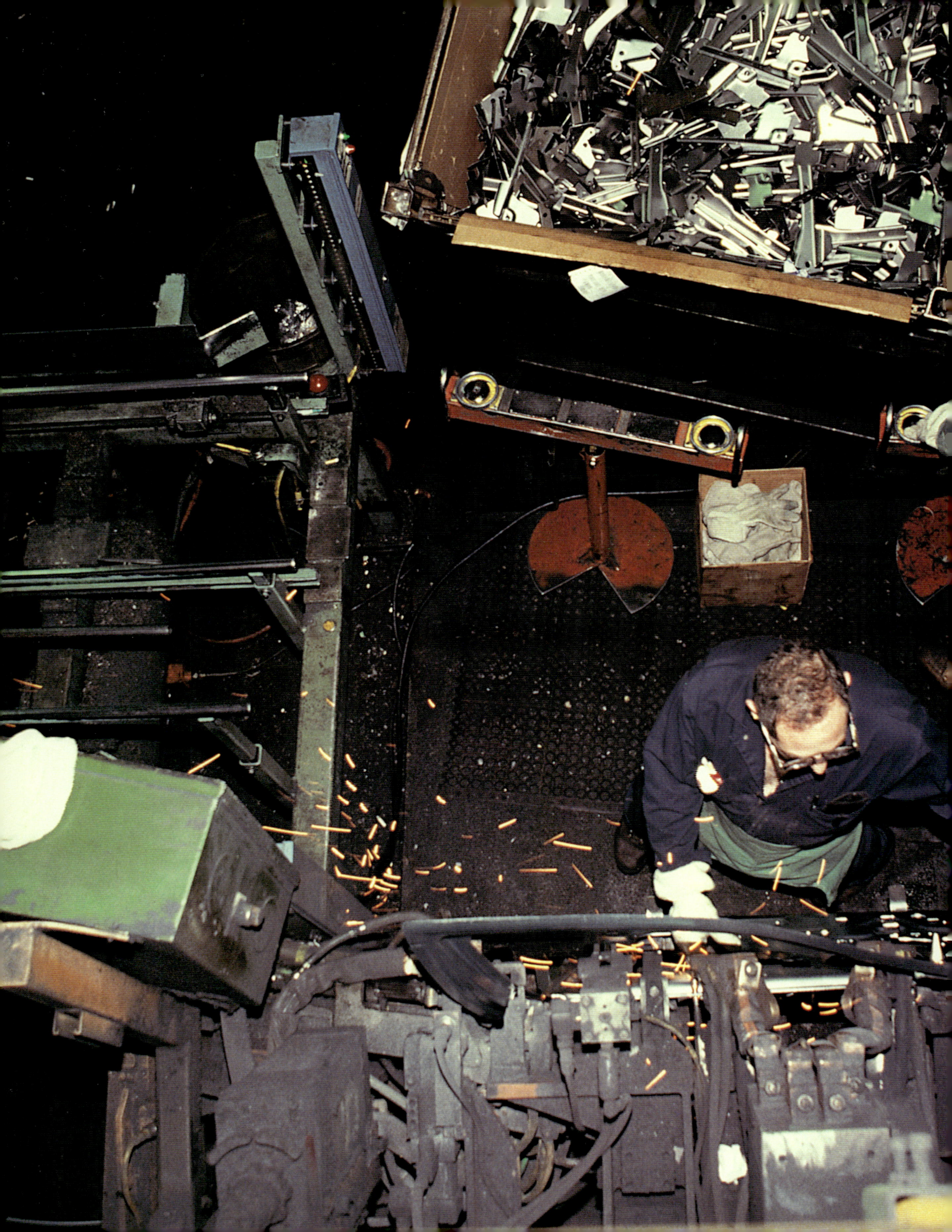

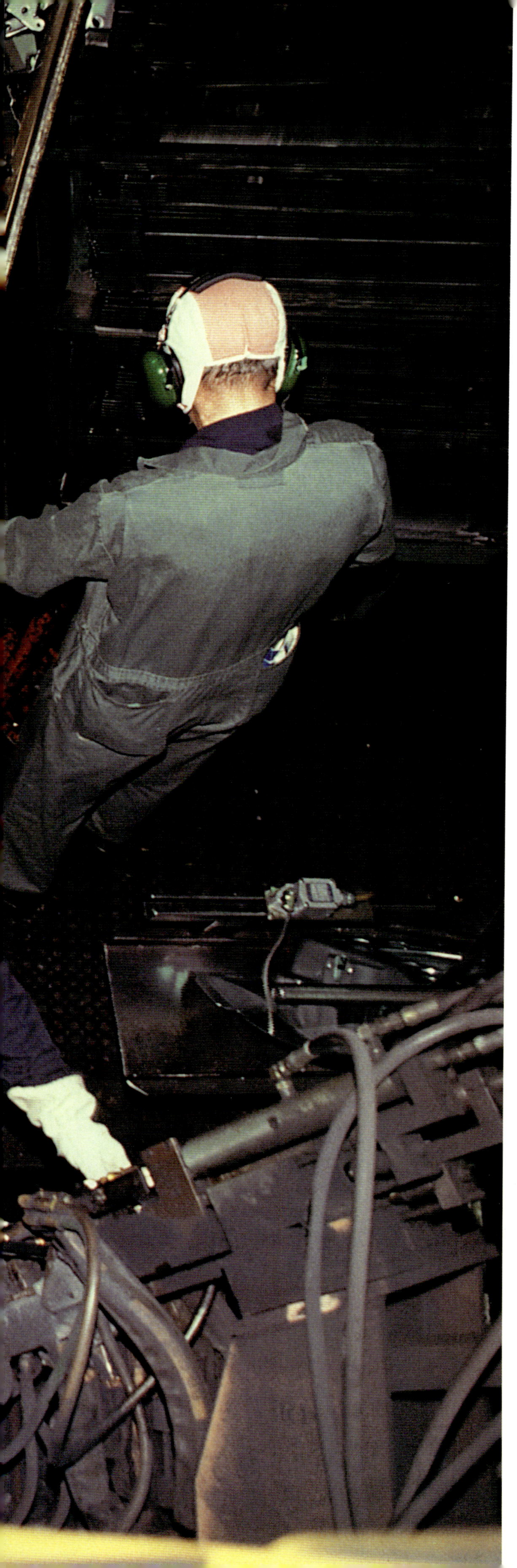

C h a p t e r 12

MANUFACTURING

Photo by James P. McCoy.

GENERAL MOTORS

General Motors Powertrain Tonawanda

The world's largest volume manufacturer of engines is located on a 130-acre site overlooking the Niagara River in the town of Tonawanda. The GM Powertrain Group's three-plant complex, covering more than 2.5 million square feet of floor space, produces four engine lines for use in GM automobiles as well as commercial truck chassis and marine and industrial applications.

The facility was constructed in 1937, with initial production at what was then the Chevrolet Motor and Axle Plant starting a year later. In the early 1940s, wartime needs resulted in a shift to aircraft and jet engine assembly. By the late 1940s, production had resumed on engines for commercial use. Through the boom years of the 1950s and 1960s, technological developments were implemented as engine design was refined and physical plant facilities were expanded. Nineteen sixty-two marked the first year one million engines were built. A decade later, over 1.7 million engines were assembled.

In 1984, as part of a General Motors reorganization, what was by then known as Chevrolet Tonawanda Engine Became Chevrolet- Pontiac-Canada Group Tonawanda Engine. Six years later, the "Powertrain" appellation was adopted, a reference to the engine plus transmission combination.

Today, the Powertrain facility produces a family of four engine lines—the L-4 (2.2 liter), V-6 60 degree (3.1 liter), V-6 90 degree (4.3 liter), and the Mark V, V-8 (6.0/7.0/7.4/8.2

liter). In the record-breaking production year of 1994, a total of 1,875,846 engines was built. The facility also holds the distinction of a world's record for the most engines produced in one day—8,832.

The Tonawanda facility was chosen in August, 1996 as the site that will be manufacturing General Motor's new "world machine." The initial design is a 2.2-liter, four-cylinder overhead cam engine for the new midsized Innovate from GM's Saturn Division. The new engine is part of the corporation's overall long-term global strategy. The engine meets GM's need for flexibility requirements in their domestic and world-wide market. This reflects the commitment of both management and labor and a dedicated plant workforce. As a result, the positive growth of the Tonawanda Engine Plant will continue well into the 21st century.

With over three shift operations, GM Powertrain employs nearly 300 salaried workers and more than 4,000 hourly employees. The latter are represented by United Auto Workers Local 774.

Innovative leadership on the part of union and management, GM Powertrain received the Work in America Institute Award for productivity and labor-management relations. Founded in 1975, the institute is a workplace change catalyst, striving to improve U.S. productivity and the quality of working life through its national research and diverse member relationships. comprised of leaders from labor, management,

The main administration building for the three-plant complex is located on River Road in the Town of Tonawanda.

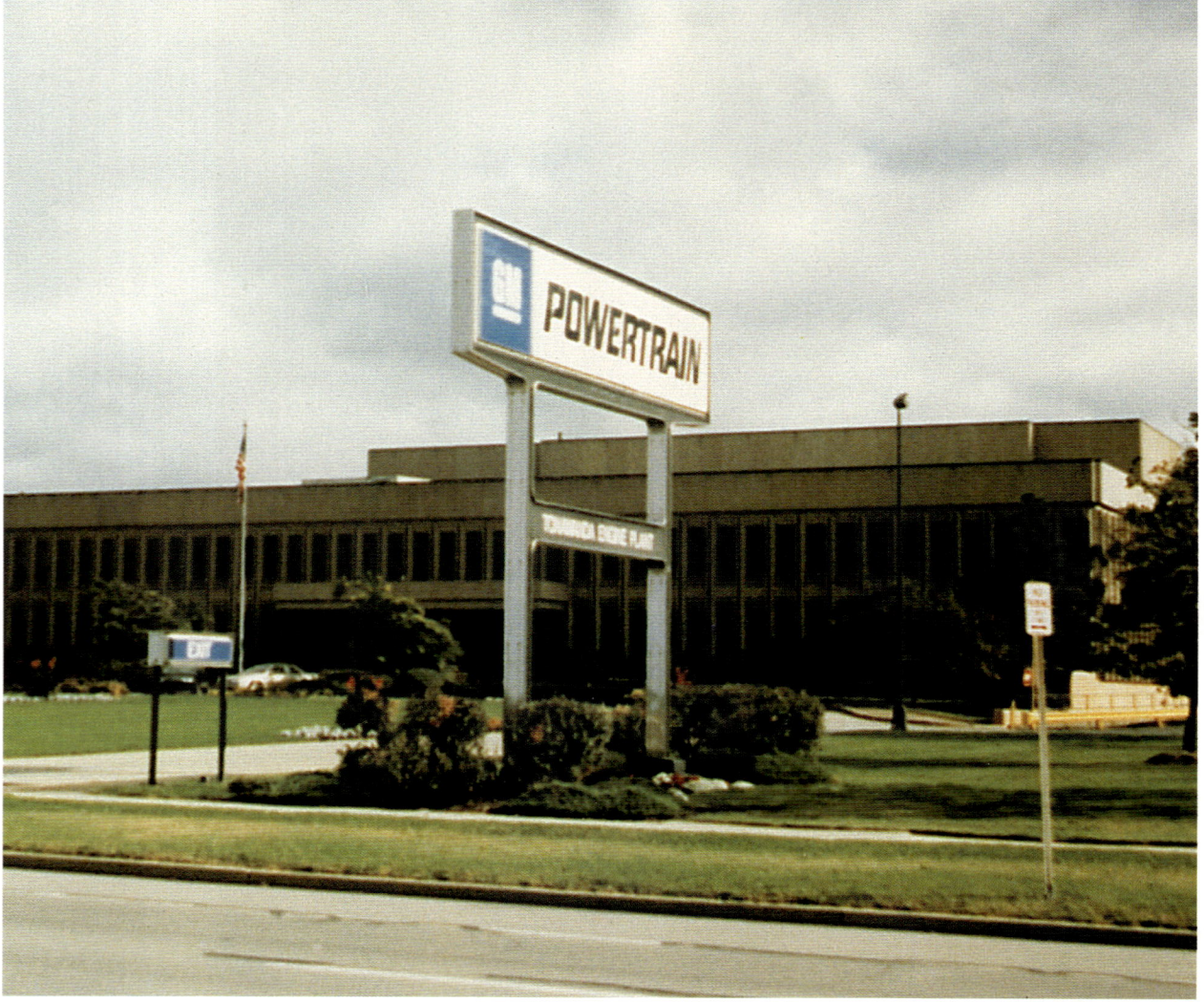

ATTRACTING THE WORLD

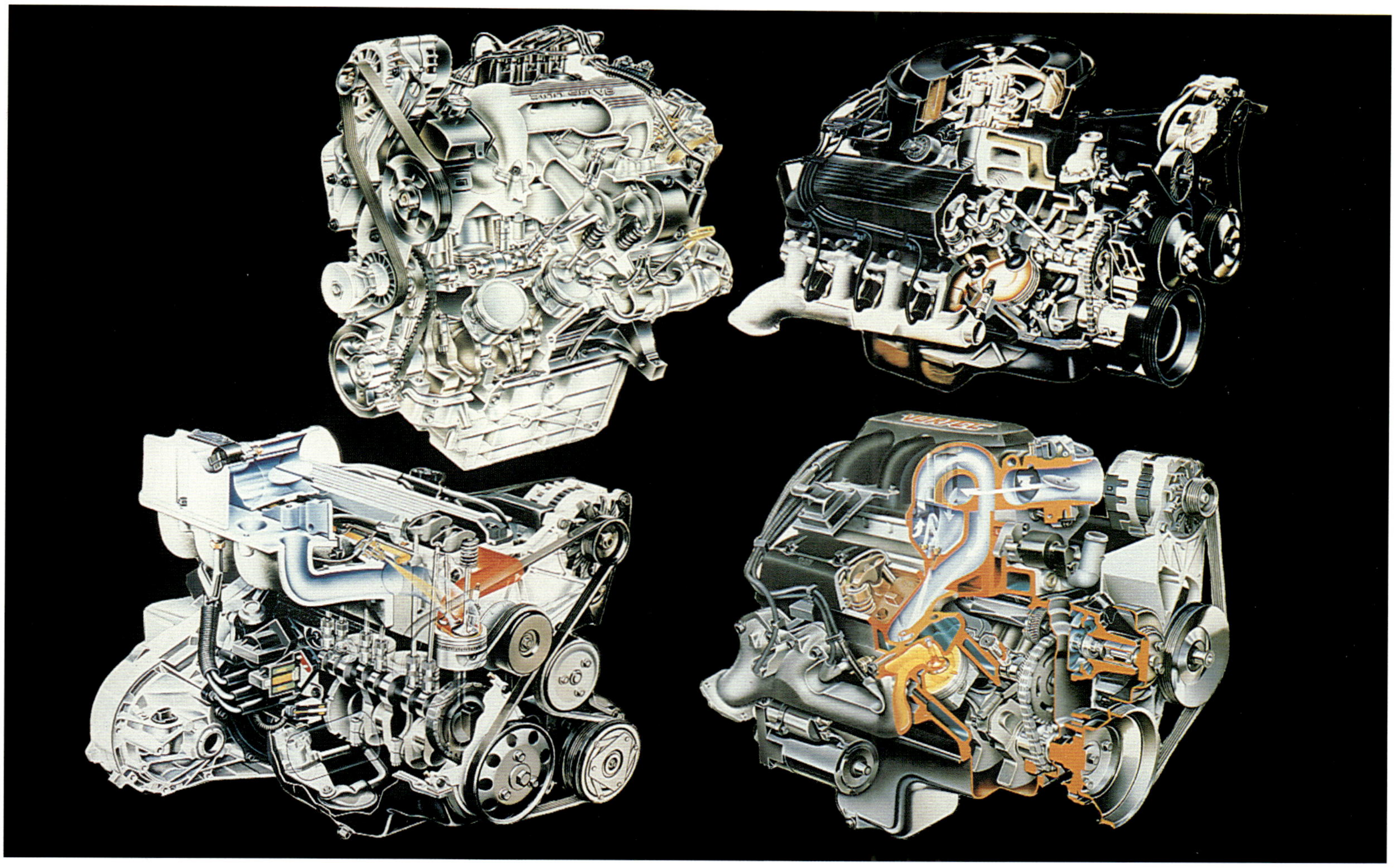

government, and academia, the institute recommends practical solutions and constructive policies in response to a wide range of workplace issues.

The Tonawanda Engine Plant is a leader in the community as well as its industry. Plant activities open to the public include the annual Classic Chevy Show & Auto Expo, started a decade ago as a Corvette show. today, it's a much-anticipated summertime event at the facility that attracts classic car aficionados from all over the country. Some 400 General Motors vehicles are displayed, with awards in more than two dozen categories, including "Best Custom," "Best Antique," and "Best Engine," given by experts in the fields.

General Motors was a major sponsor of the 1996 Summer Olympics in Atlanta, and the Tonawanda facility reaped benefits from that. The UAW/GM Olympic Spirit Tour visited

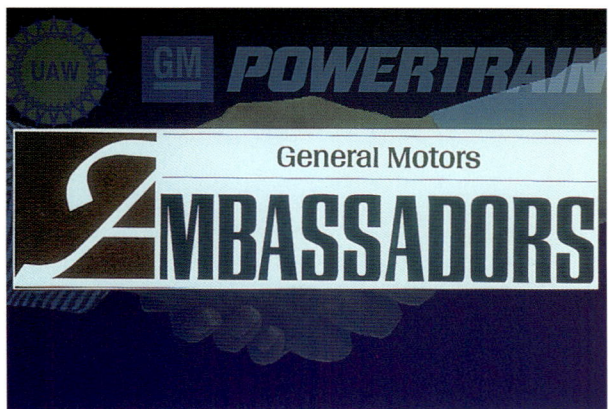

the plant that summer, featuring demonstrations of athletic prowess by Olympic hopefuls and appearances by former Olympic athletes.

GM Powertrain and UAW Local 774 have jointly supported the concerns and needs of the community by encouraging workings to actively participate in charitable endeavors benefiting such organizations as The United Way of Buffalo and Erie County, the annual Crippled Children's Telethon, Camp Good Days and Special Times, the Buffalo News Neediest fund, and the Town Boys and Girls Club.

An innovative program that started at the Tonawanda Engine Plant in the mid-1980s has been adopted company-wide. The UAW GM Ambassador Sales Referral Program encourages all active and retired employees to become "sales ambassadors" for General Motors products. "creating lifelong customers one handshake at a time." Friends, neighbors, and family members put their trust and confidence in the knowledge that GM employees have about the vehicles they help build, resulting in new sales, increased market share, and added job security.

Delphi Harrison Thermal Systems

Delphi Harrison Thermal Systems, a division of General Motors' Delphi Automotive Systems, is a world leader in the research, development, and production of automotive climate control and engine cooling systems. Founded as Harrison Radiator Division in 1910 by English entrepreneur Herbert Harrison, the company has grown to be part of the world's

GM Powertrain Tonawanda currently manufactures four high-quality engines for GM: (upper row) 3.1-liter V6 60 degree and the Mark V, V-8; (bottom row) the 2.2-liter L-4 and the 4.3-liter V6 90 degree.

The GM Ambassadors program stated at the Tonawanda Engine Plant in 1985. It helps our employees create lifelong customers one handshake at a time.

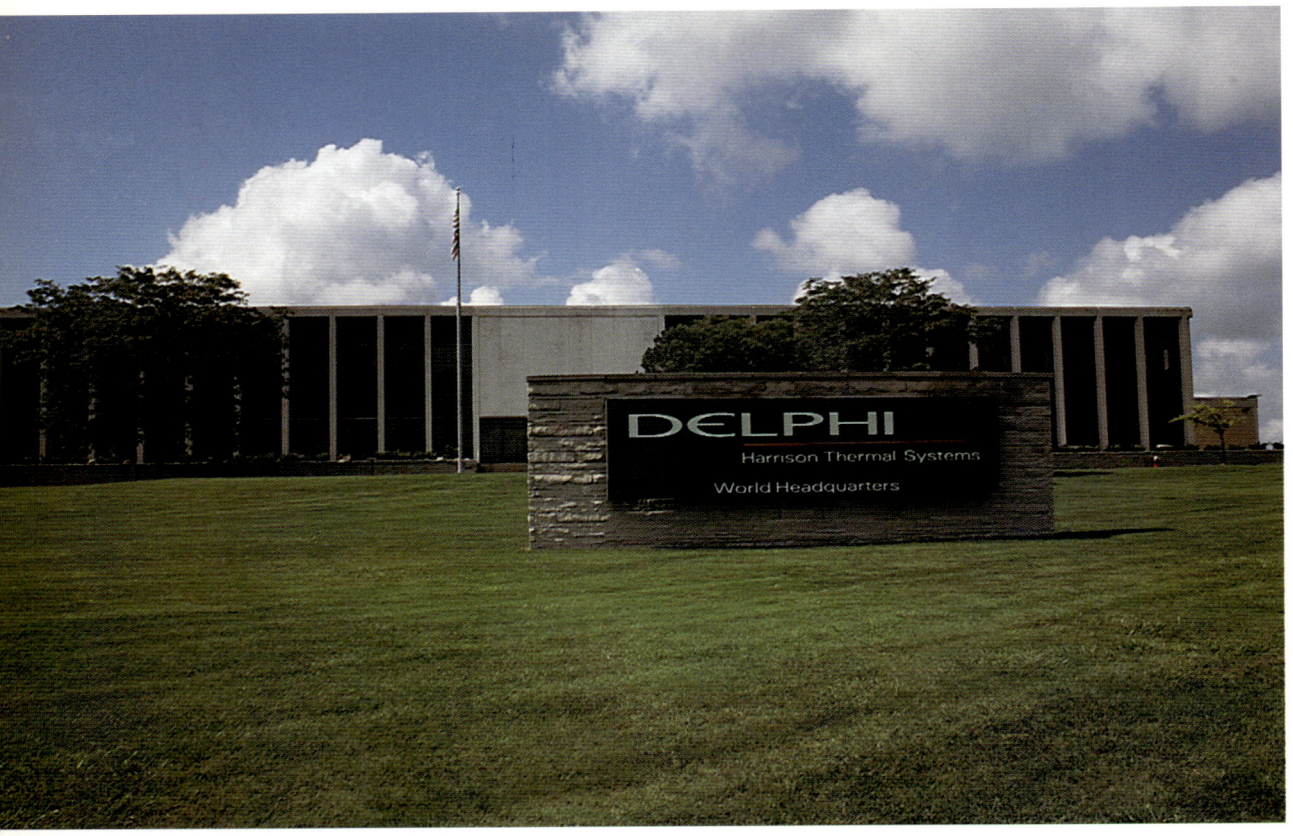

In 1987, Harrison Radiator opened a manufacturing operation in Tuscaloosa, Alabama. Three years later, the company's name was changed to Harrison Division to reflect the diversity of the products manufactured.

Another name change followed in 1995, when in a move to convey a fresh global identity, Harrison division became Delphi Harrison Thermal Systems—simplifying for the customer and symbolizing a stronger unified image. It also closer aligned the company's systems and organizations. Delphi Thermal produces with the most advanced manufacturing processes a variety of thermal management products, and its expertise in producing complete systems provides customers with timely solutions for each vehicle. As a result, Delphi Thermal is finding its way into new markets every, year producing high-quality, competitively-priced products and providing customer support the world over. That customer base includes 8 of the top 10 vehicle manufacturers worldwide.

In February 1995, the former Harrison Division became Delphi Harrison Thermal Systems.

largest, most comprehensive automotive components supplier. With 6,800 employees at its world headquarters in Lockport, Delphi Thermal is the leading private sector employer in western New York.

Herbert Harrison's ingenious solution to the early automobile's overheating engine problem was a ribbon cellular-type radiator featuring what became famous as the Harrison Hexagon Core. It was more efficient and cheaper to make than any other radiator then in use, and a classic business success story ensued.

In 1916, Harrison became part of the United Motors Corporation, which two years later merged with General Motors Corporation. In 1981, the merger of Delco Air Conditioning with Harrison Radiator resulted in the establishment of manufacturing operations in Dayton and Moraine, Ohio. Dayton has since consolidated into the Moraine facility.

Delphi Thermal traces its rich history back to 1910.

Delphi Thermal's heating, ventilating, and air condition (HVAC) and engine cooling systems are engineered to meed specific vehicle requirements, with the increasingly complex technical and environmental changes mandated today, changes not even the visionary Herbert Harrison could have foreseen. New, innovative technologies have spurred the move from discrete, manual heaters and air conditioners to fully automatic HVAC systems that maintain comfortable interior temperatures with the touch of a button. Advanced technology has resulted in the development of aluminum radiators with an industry-leading, performance-to-weight ratio. Today, the division designs, analyzes, manufactures and packages every component into a fully integrated system capable of efficiently maintaining passenger comfort in all climates and weather conditions. Delphi Thermal has been an international leader in the research, development, and usage of the alternate refrigerant R-134a and its associated lubricant. The company is also a past winner of the New York State Governor's Award for Pollution Prevention, cited for its solvent degreaser elimination program.

The Lockport word headquarters site includes three manufacturing facilities spread out on 500 acres, producing everything from radiators and oil coolers to HVAC units and condensers. The Lockport complex also features state-of-the-art advanced climatic wind tunnels, rapid product prototyping.

It takes a large and diversified components supplier to meet today's global systems requirements, and Delphi Thermal is committed to maintaining its industry lead. Delphi thermal's global footprint in continuously expanding, with employees strategically positioned to work closely with customers and meeting their stringent vehicle requirements. At the close of 1996, Delphi Thermal had 17 manufacturing

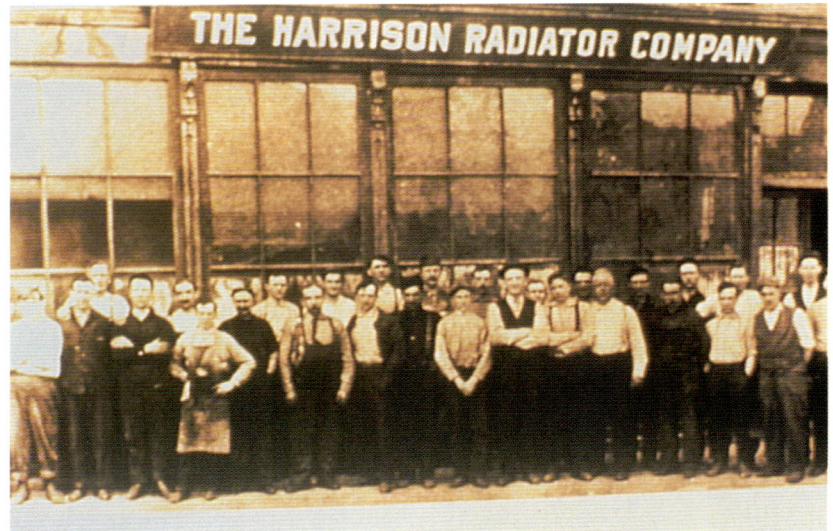

facilities and 28 engineering locations. And with more than 1,000 employees worldwide located in 18 different countries, roll call at Delphi Thermal truly is an international experience.

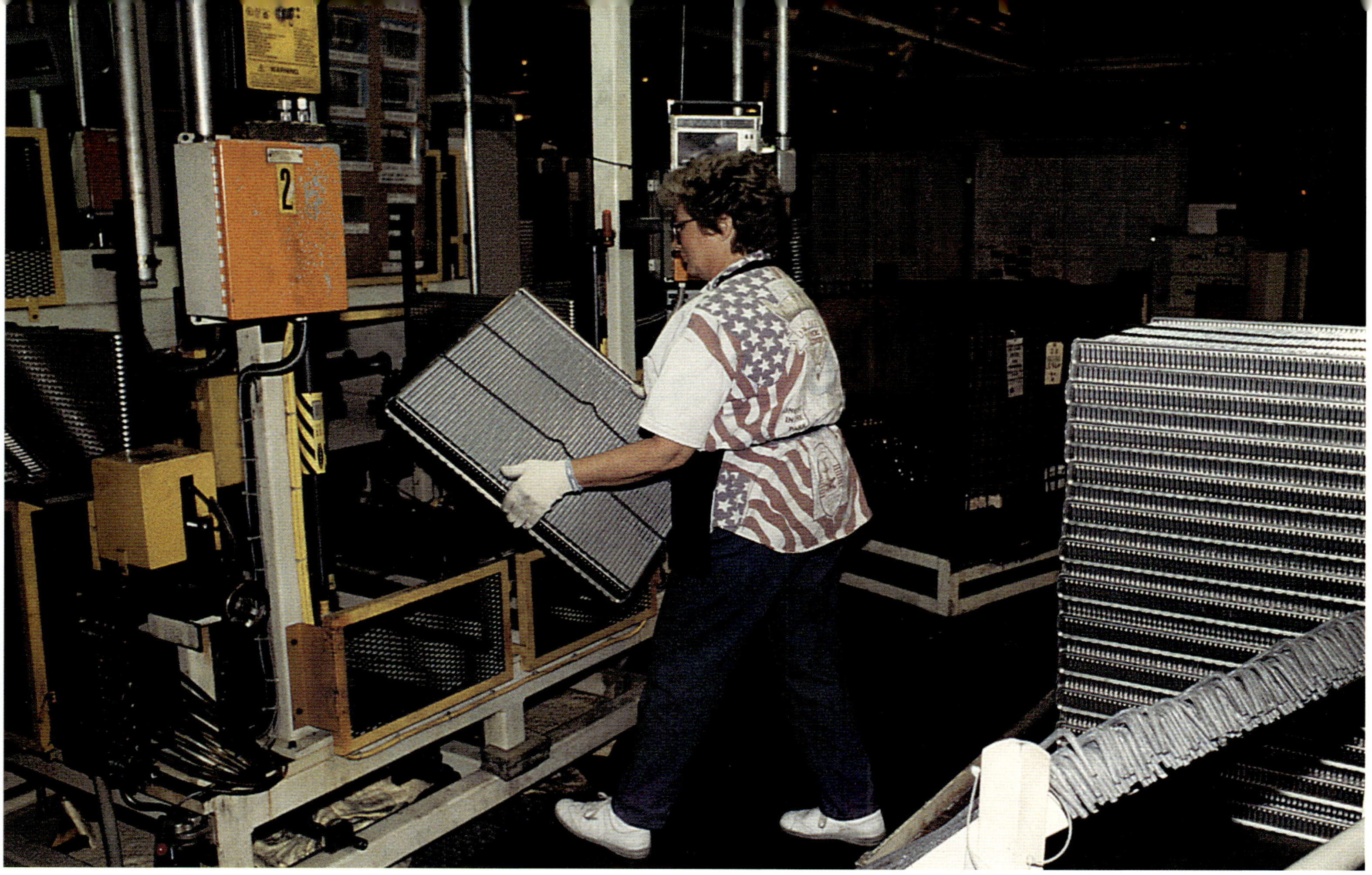

Delphi Thermal continues to expand its presence in Europe, where the automotive air conditioning market is expected to balloon by the year 2000. Three new manufacturing facilities have recently been added to the Delphi Thermal European lineup, including two in France and one in Poland. All three are supported in part by Delphi Thermal employees at the Luxembourg Technical Centre. Meanwhile, further east, Delphi Thermal's presence in the Asia-Pacific region has increased significantly, a trend that should continue well into the 21st century. Engineering and support staff can be found in China, Japan, Korea, and Singapore.

The company's global vision hasn't diminished its local Niagara Frontier presence, where with the members of UAW Local 686, a firm commitment to support and enhance the region remains in place. Working with GM Powertrain's Tonawanda Engine Plant in General Motors Western New York community Relations committee, Delphi Thermal has been able to recently initiate several programs in local schools the past few years, exposing junior and senior high school students to career opportunities and boosting the arts in elementary schools. Delphi thermal also remains strongly tied to the collegiate ranks, having received the Buffalo State College Corporate Employer of the Year Award and Niagara County Community College's Partnership Award. Employees also staunchly support the United Way, volunteering for activities, leading initiatives, and comprising more than half of the donations made to Eastern Niagara Untied Way's annual campaign.

With world-class people products and process, Delphi Harrison Thermal systems continued to be the company towards which automotive manufacturers look. And with its ever-increasing world presence and continued growth, they don't have to look far. ⚜

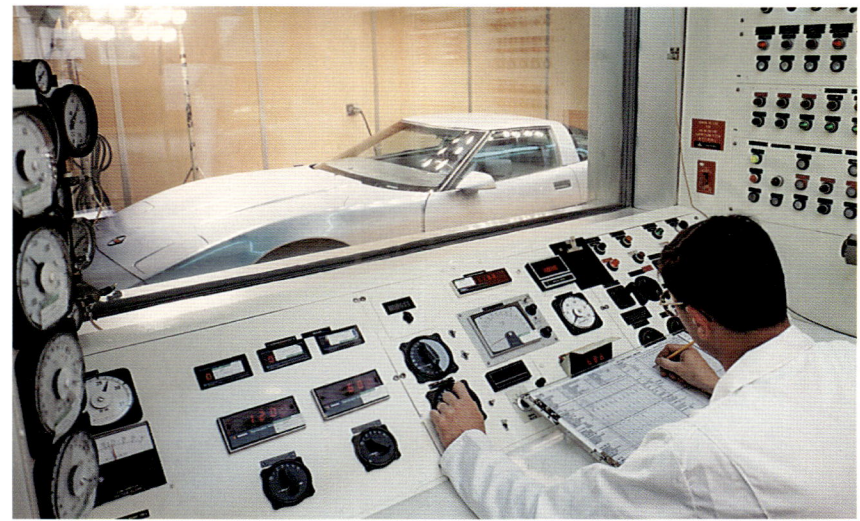

(top) Delphi Thermal has three manufacturing plants located at its Lockport site.

(bottom) There are several advanced climatic wind tunnels located within Delphi Thermal Lockport's test labs.

GIBRALTAR STEEL CORPORATION

BUILDING ITS FUTURE ON A ROCK-SOLID FOUNDATION

Gibraltar is proud of its reputation in the industry for having the closest tolerances as well as 97 percent on-time delivery.

Gibraltar Steel Corporation, headquartered in Buffalo, New York, is a solid force among the Greater Niagara industrial community. In 1972, the current organization was founded by the late Dr. Kenneth E. Lipke, who devoted his ingenuity and foresight to the development of an entity with international influence. At all levels, an innovative focus has guided Gibraltar through the turbulent period of the 1970s and 1980s, and helped position the company on a solid foundation for future growth.

The current management team (pictured), headed by Chairman and CEO Brian Lipke, has further accelerated the growth of the company, taking it well beyond its Buffalo roots. While expanding its geographical coverage, the management team has also expanded the company's product range and capacity by adding new equipment at existing facilities, building new plants, forming joint ventures, and acquiring other companies.

Over the years, Gibraltar's products and services have been heavily relied on by many manufacturers in industries such as automotive, steel fabrication, appliance, communication, electrical, machinery, office equipment, recreation, and construction. "Our products probably wind up in some way, shape, or form in most automobiles and homes in the U.S.A.," one company executive recently indicated.

Without a doubt, Gibraltar is known in its industry as an aggressive-growth company, with a sharp focus on quality and customer service. Its many customers, including several world giants in

the automotive industry, recognize this fact and have consistently given the company preferred supplier awards and special recognitions.

Clearly, Gibraltar has emerged as a leader in its industry, not by its own admission but by that of leading third-party observers. Maintaining such a high profile in today's dynamic and aggressive steel industry is seen as both a challenge and an opportunity by the entire Gibraltar organization. Everyone at Gibraltar is part of "The Team," and the cornerstone of the Gibraltar philosophy is that every member of that team shares in the results of the organization's achievements through the company's profit-based reward programs. This progressive "people" emphasis is clearly responsible for unifying the

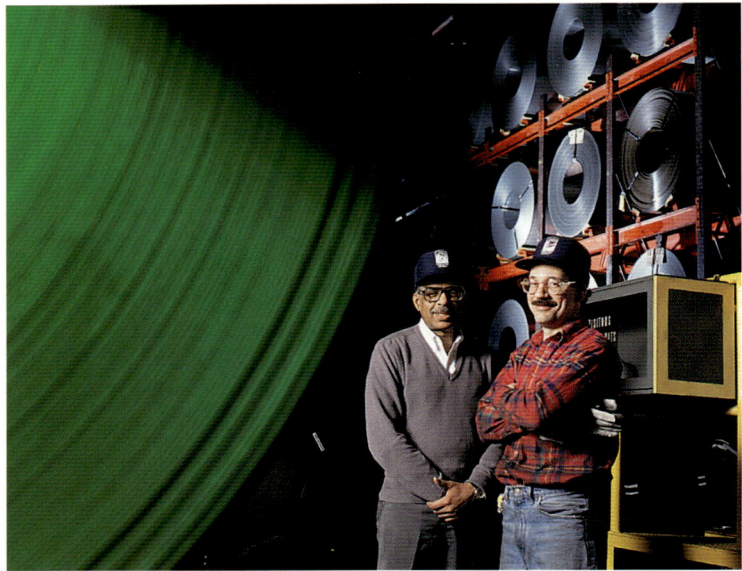

Gibraltar's executive management team includes from left: Joe Rosenecker, Neil Lipke, Brian Lipke(Chairman and CEO), Carl Spezio and Walt Erazmus.

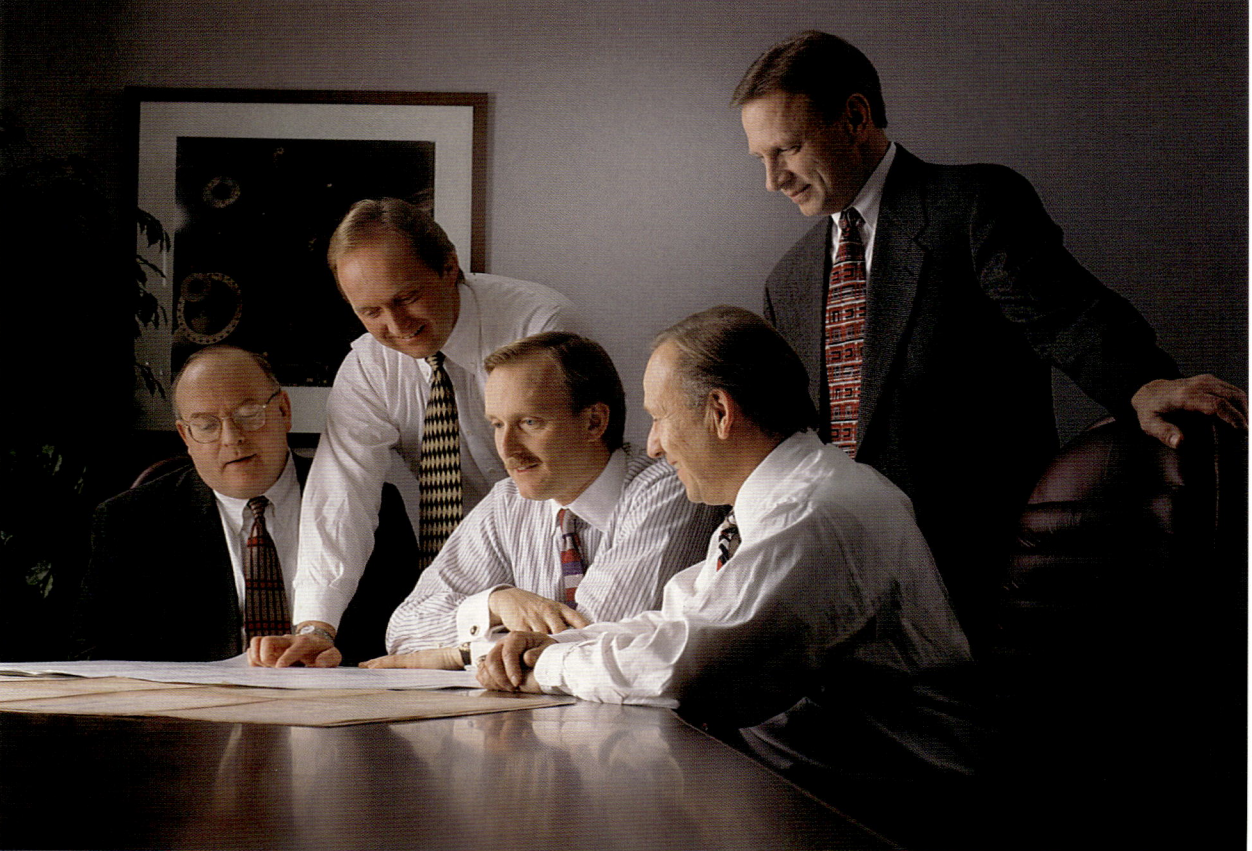

efforts of the entire organization and for sparking its focus on relevant growth opportunities in its industry.

Today, Gibraltar's management is looking to the future with a clearly articulated goal of becoming a billion-dollar corporation early in the new millennium. To achieve this objective, the company's leadership, at all levels, is continuously searching for solid "synergistic" opportunities that will provide for both product and geographic diversification. As a clear example of their already achieved successes in this endeavor, corporate facilities currently extend throughout much of the eastern U.S.A.; from the Canadian border, south into Mexico; and from the Atlantic seaboard, west to the Mississippi River, and beyond. Also, corporate strategic plans currently being developed will even further extend the company's domestic presence and its international participation as well.

In addition to its keen operational focus, Gibraltar also believes in being a good corporate citizen and has consistently displayed this commitment by actively supporting the various communities in which it has an established presence. For example, at its home base in the Niagara region of Western New York, the late Dr. Lipke's daughter, Meredith, oversees the awarding of the Kenny Award in order to recognize area high schools for excellence in theatrical productions. This coveted honor is presented each year in conjunction with Shea's Performing Arts Center, the region's premier entertainment focus.

No doubt about it, Gibraltar is an organization on the move. And with its "home base" well-established in Western New York, it is all the more reason why Niagara will be "attracting the world" for many years to come. ✧

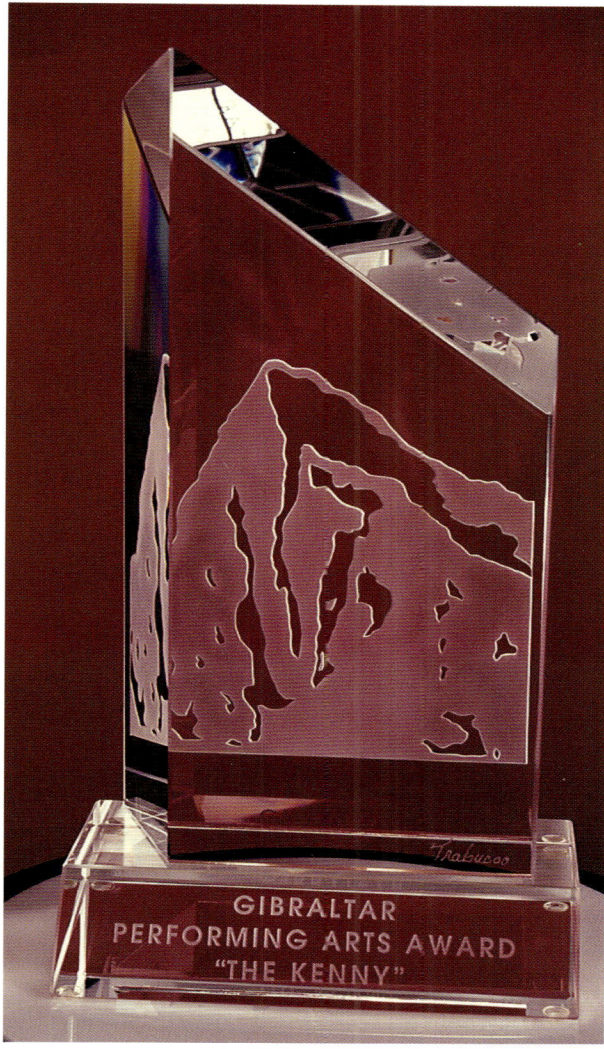

Established by the Shea's Performing Arts Center of Buffalo and the Lipke Foundation, "The Kenny" award recognizes excellence in local schools producing Broadway shows.

Gibraltar's value-added processing helps product manufacturers to remain competitive on a global level.

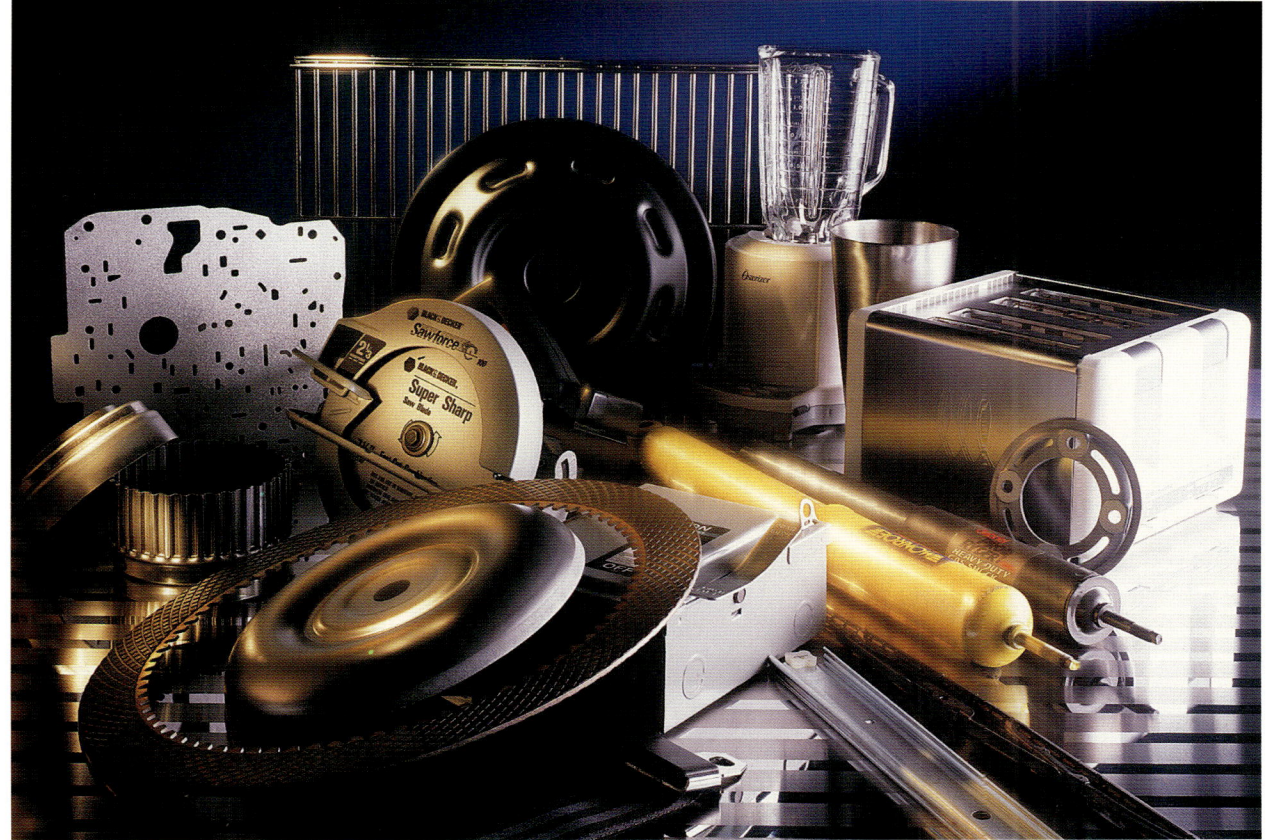

COLUMBUS MCKINNON

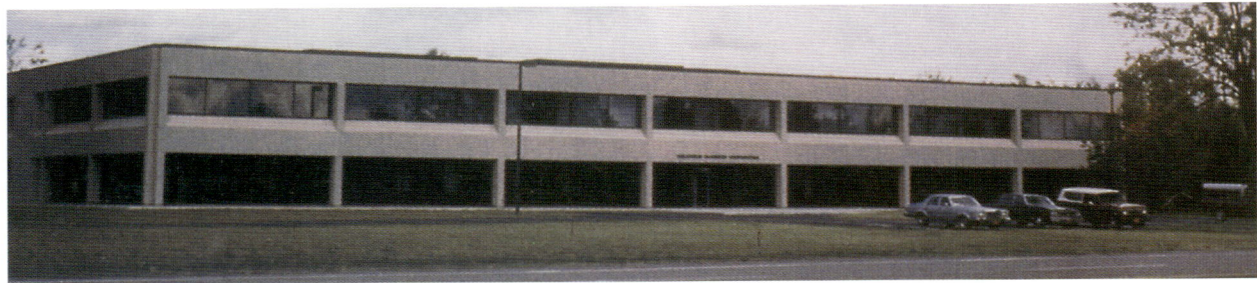

Columbus McKinnon world headquarters in Amherst, New York, USA.

Columbus McKinnon Lodestar - # 1 seller in the USA.

Columbus McKinnon Corporation has been in the "moving" business—helping people and products to move—since 1875. That was when Lachlan Ebenezer McKinnon first started selling horse harnesses and a patented adjustable buggie dash in a small shop in St. Catharine. His company progressed to making a top- quality line of welded link chain using hydropower from the Niagara Region.

Columbus McKinnon, with headquarters in the Buffalo area of the Niagara Frontier, is a diversified manufacturer and a market leader in the material handling industry. Its products, used in industry, transportation, agriculture, construction, and health care, are sold and serviced in more than 65 countries through a network of more than 4,000 distributors.

In addition to its premier line of hoists and chain products, Columbus McKinnon manufactures manipulators, below the hook lifters, air powered load balancers, actuators, jacks, circuit breakers, lift tables, patient transfer systems for the health care industry, and tire shredders. The latter, a waste-management, environmentally friendly, innovation in which tires of up to 48-inch diameter are reduced to 2-inch or 1-inch square chips, eliminates unsightly, and dangerous tire piles providing raw material for tire-derived fuel.

With standard or custom designs and tooling, CMConco® and CMPositech® ergonomically correct manipulators provide the capacity to lift, move, maneuver, position, reach or transfer loads, in tight spaces or unfriendly environments, thus reducing the risk of back injury. CM Cady® heavy duty lifters provide power below the crane hook.

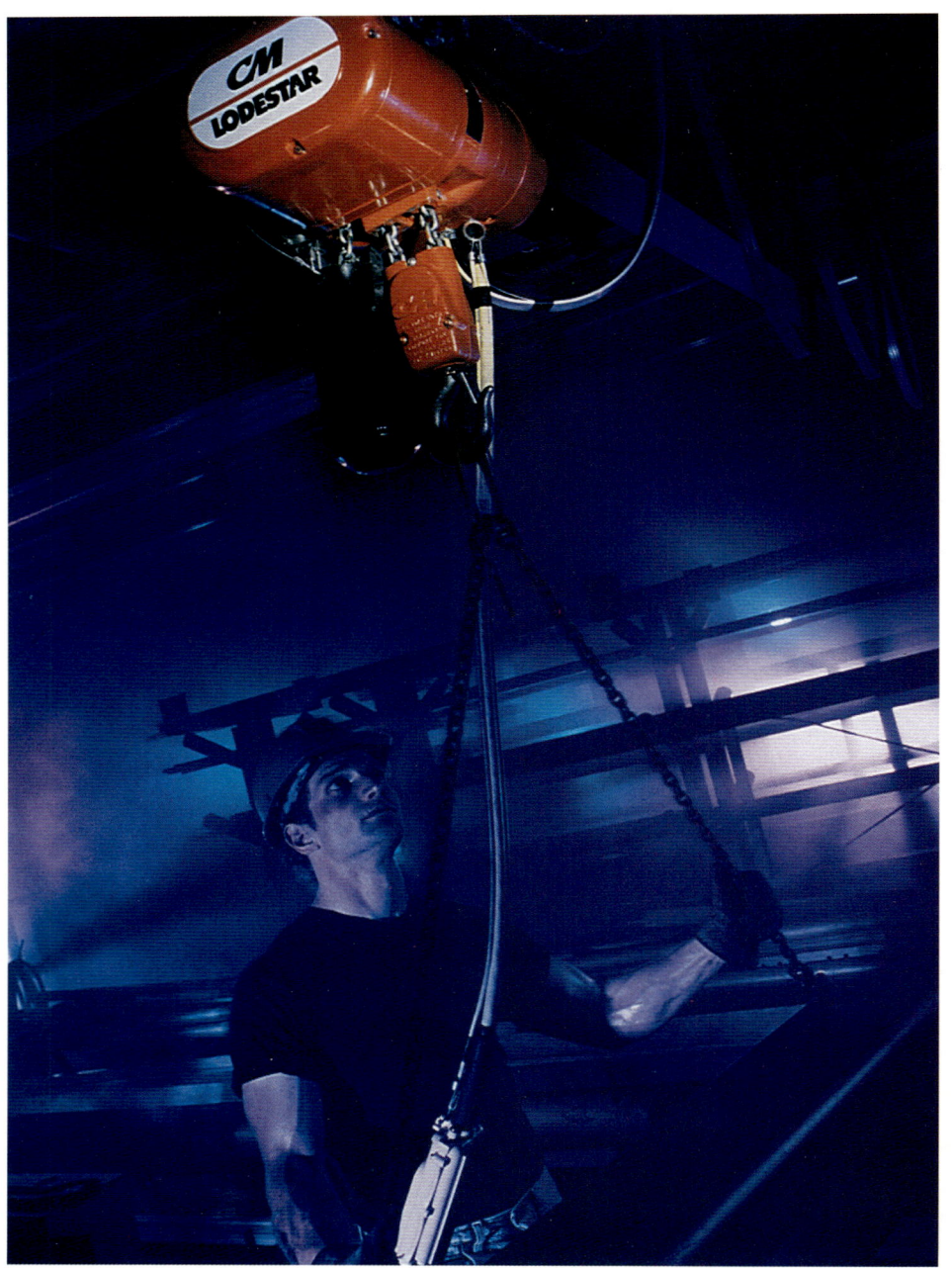

In recent years, Columbus McKinnon has extended its product lines and penetrated new markets through a series of acquisitions that have been successfully integrated into the company. A significant move was made late in 1995, when the company acquired LTI International. The addition of Lift-Tech's electric wire rope and air-powered hoists gave the company the broadest hoist line in North America.

In 1996 the company gained the dominant share of the North American hoist market by acquiring both the Yale and Coffing hoist lines through acquisition of Yale International. It also increased its capacity to make high quality chain, up to 3 1/4" in diameter via the acquisition of the Lister Group headquarterd in Vancouver B.C.

The company's strategic plans call for pursuing additional non-dilutive acquisitions of businesses whose operations and product lines are complementary to its own, with an emphasis on enhancing its international presence.

With over 3,600 employees in Canada, Germany, China, Mexico, and the United States, Columbus McKinnon has 20 manufacturing facilities and warehouse locations in most major markets.

Approximately 200 people are employed in Western New York at the Amherst headquarters and a Tonawanda manufacturing facility.

The company's domestic growth has been achieved through its ability to respond to the demands of the marketplace. Close communication with its distributor network has facilitated anticipation of end-users' product needs, and the industries largest installed base of hoists and other products provides a large market for repair and replacement parts. The company continues to develop and introduce new products that take advantage of the increased emphasis by end-users on worker productivity, workplace safety, and ergonomics.

By strengthening its international distribution network and making further strategic acquisitions and alliances, Columbus McKinnon has positioned itself to grow internationally.

Columbus McKinnon stock is quoted on the NASDAQ under the symbol CMCO.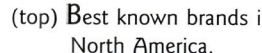

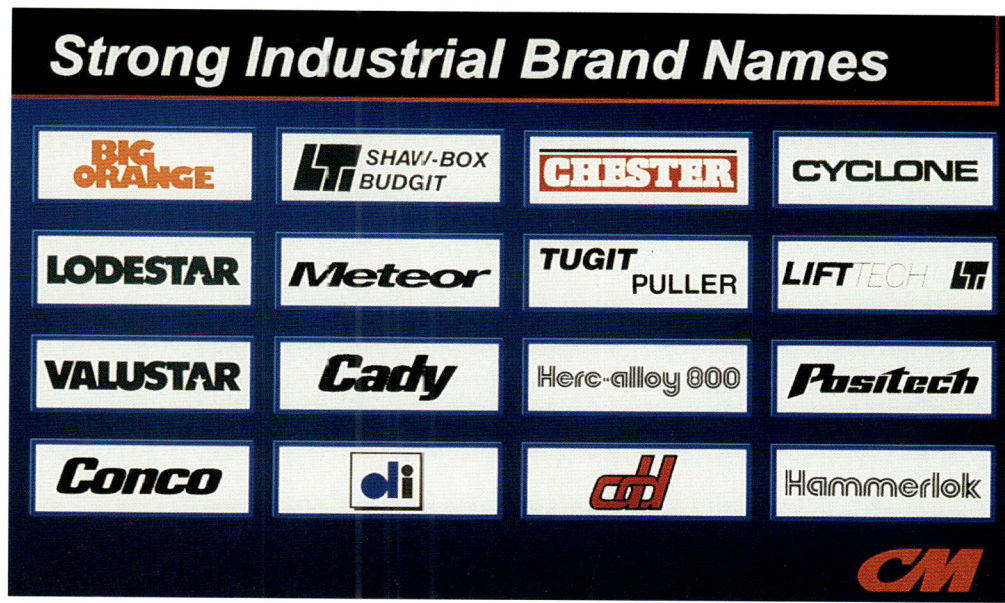

(top) Best known brands in North America.

(left) Columbus McKinnon Cady 12 Ton Lifter.

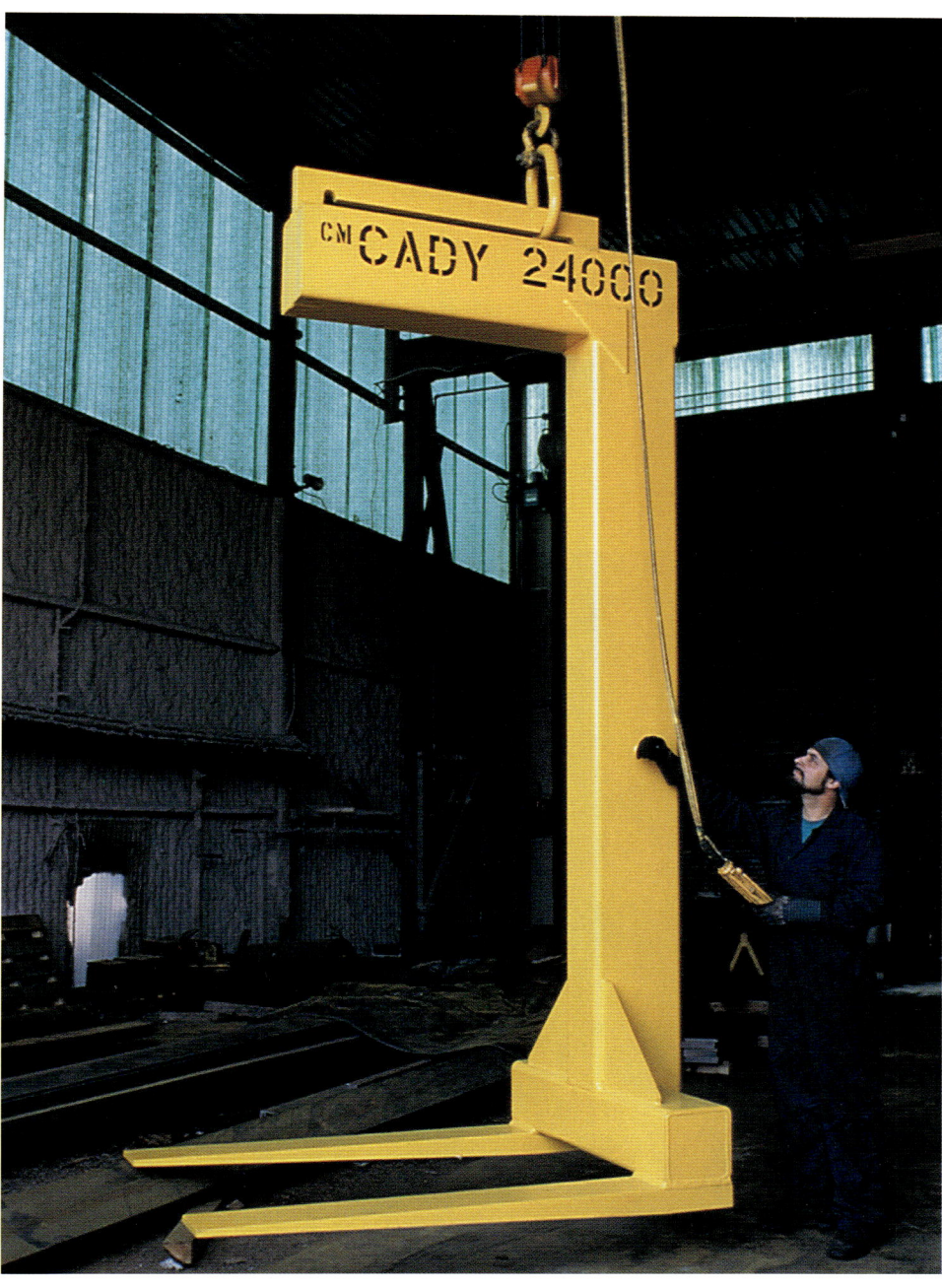

CURTIS SCREW CO., INC.

A commitment to craftsmanship has been the sustaining theme of Curtis Screw since its turn-of-the-century beginnings as a manufacturer of screw machines. The company is still headquartered in its original location in the heart of Buffalo's Niagara Street industrial corridor.

It was here that Frank O. Curtis, who held a U.S. Patent on an early five-spindle screw machine, founded the company in 1905. Nearly a century later, Curtis Screw is a world leader in the manufacture of high-volume, custom-machined precision metal components and a major supplier to the global automotive market.

Through the middle part of this century, the company expanded its facilties from 9,000 to 25,400 square feet, eventually adding a 50,000-square-foot building. By 1970, Curtis Screw was ranked as one of the nation's leading manufacturers of machined metal components. In the mid-1980s, a decision was made to focus on the automotive industry, resulting in significant growth.

Today, Curtis Screw operates three facilities, two in Buffalo, with 90,000 and 155,000 square feet respectively, and a third, a 50,000-square-foot plant in North Carolina. The company employs more than 400 people, with some 300 in Western New York.

Ranked among the nation's top five industry leaders in the manufacture of high-volume, value-added, screw machine products, Curtis Screw is constantly acquiring the leading-edge machine tool technology needed to produce the complex parts required by its primary market, the automotive industry.

To enhance its position of leadership within the industry, Curtis Screw has merged a team of experienced, quality-oriented people, all conversant in statistical process control, automatic gauging systems, and the most recent quality-assurance technology, with a high-volume, Hydromat-based manufacturing capability.

A Hydromat, which is a 16-station rotary transfer machine, can be tooled to produce hundreds of complex finished components hourly, without the need for a secondary setup. The company currently operates an arsenal of 17 Hydromats. Other highly specialized state-of-the-art equipment in use includes Guildemeister Screw Machines, which are multispindle automatics; and the Swanson Assembler, used to assemble several components and perform six separate inspections and two functional tests, all within three seconds.

The latter operation is so cost-effective and efficient that customers have specified Curtis Screw assemblies, exclusively, worldwide. From a GM-certified metrology laboratory and an impressive manufacturing capability to a fully equipped quality lab, Curtis Screw is superbly structured to perform well into the 21st century. Adhering to the principle that

This bank of Hydromat multiple spindle automatic screw machines adds depth and dimension to Curtis Screw's manufacturing capability — Located at Curtis Screw Company's Roberts Street plant.

Curtis Screw Company Inc. headquarters and 90,000 sq. ft. manufacturing plant on Niagara Street in Buffalo, New York.

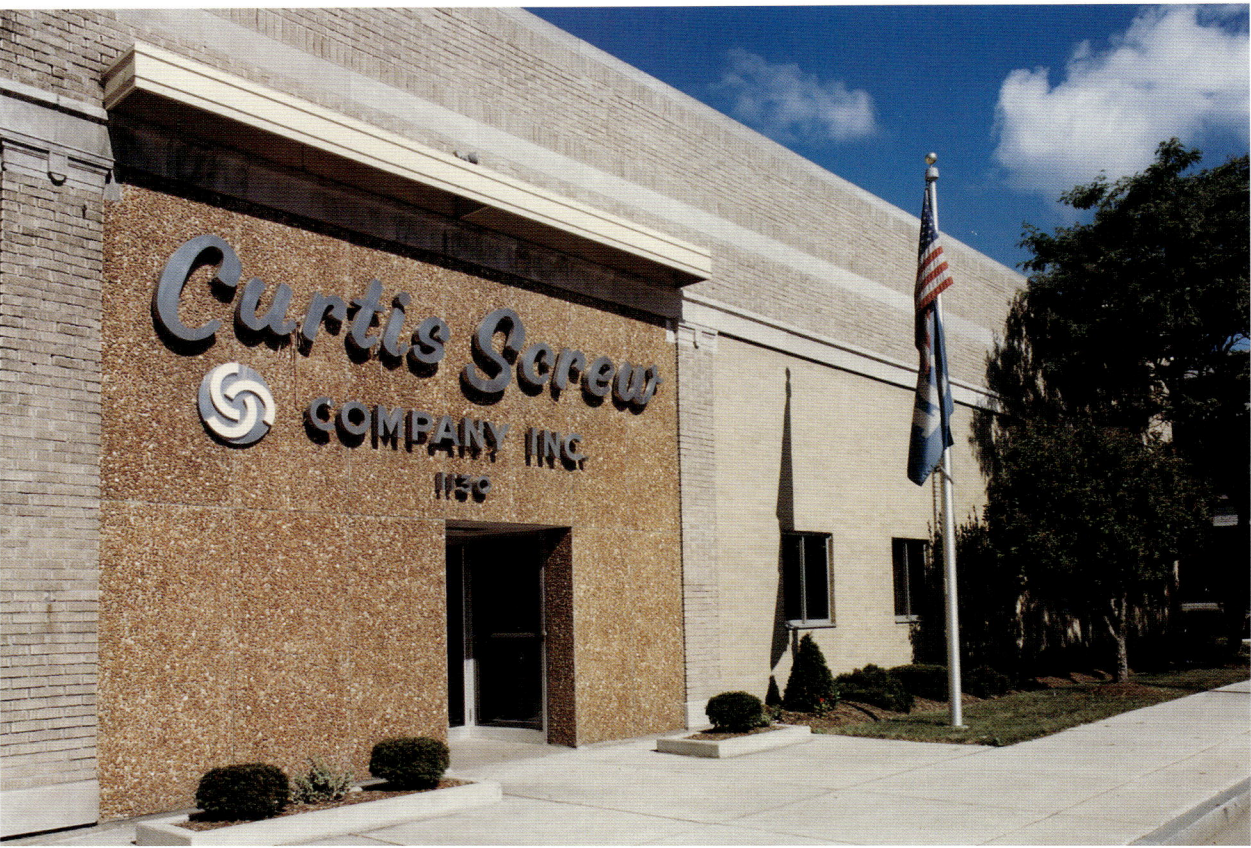

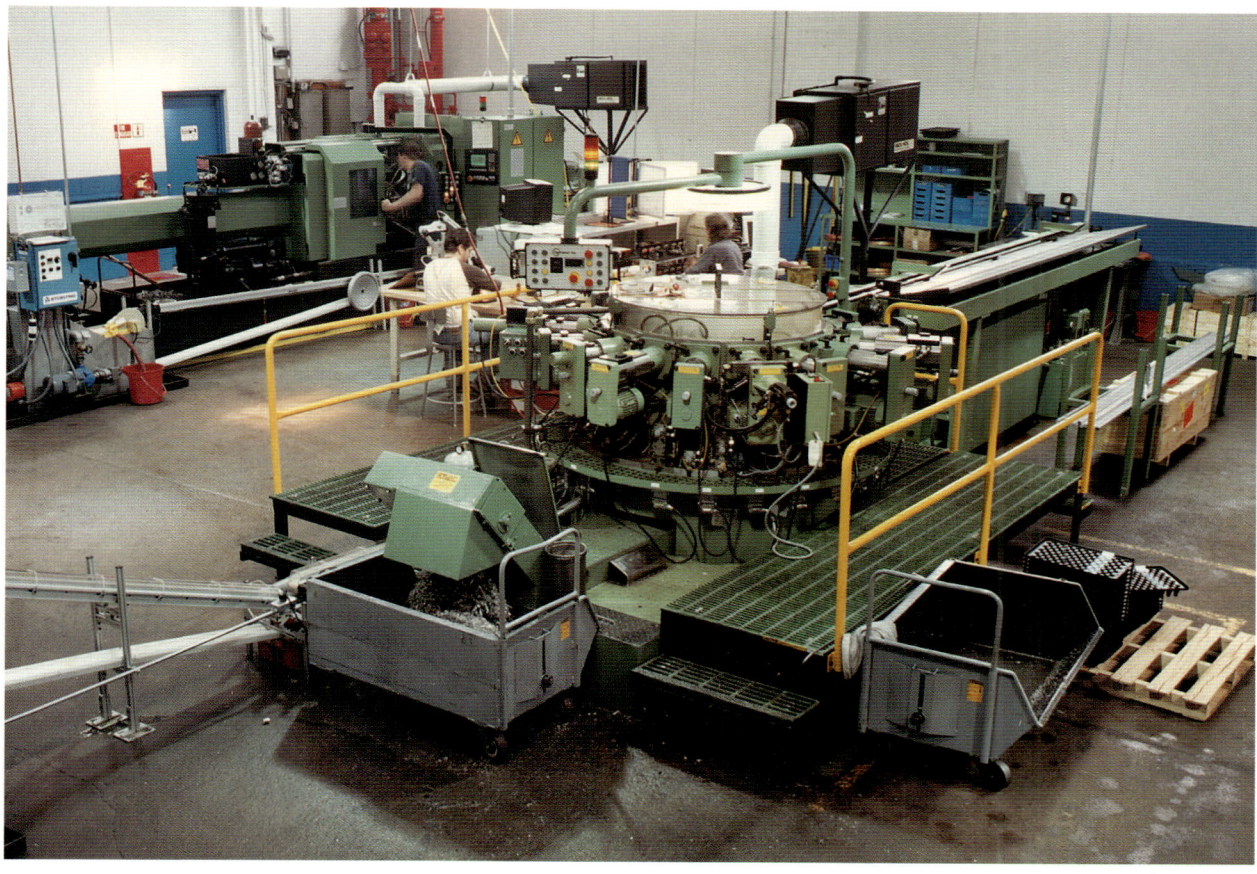

This new manufacturing cell was brought on line in April of 1996. Machining, cleansing, deburring, quality control and packaging operations take place within the cell maximizing efficiency and maintaining quality.

quality is its key competitive advantage, the company has stated its goal as setting the "bench mark" for its industry.

Curtis Screw has also been a standard-bearer for community involvement in the Greater Buffalo/Niagara Region. From participating in United Way fund drives and assisting in youth sports programs to signing on as a corporate partner for Buffalo public schools, the company encourages hands-on volunteer work from its employees.

Curtis Screw is also an active promoter of Western New York business. Company executives like to point out their proud heritage and speak glowingly of the future of this community. In all company literature one phrase stands out as emblematic: "At Curtis Screw, quality and pride stand side by side." ❧

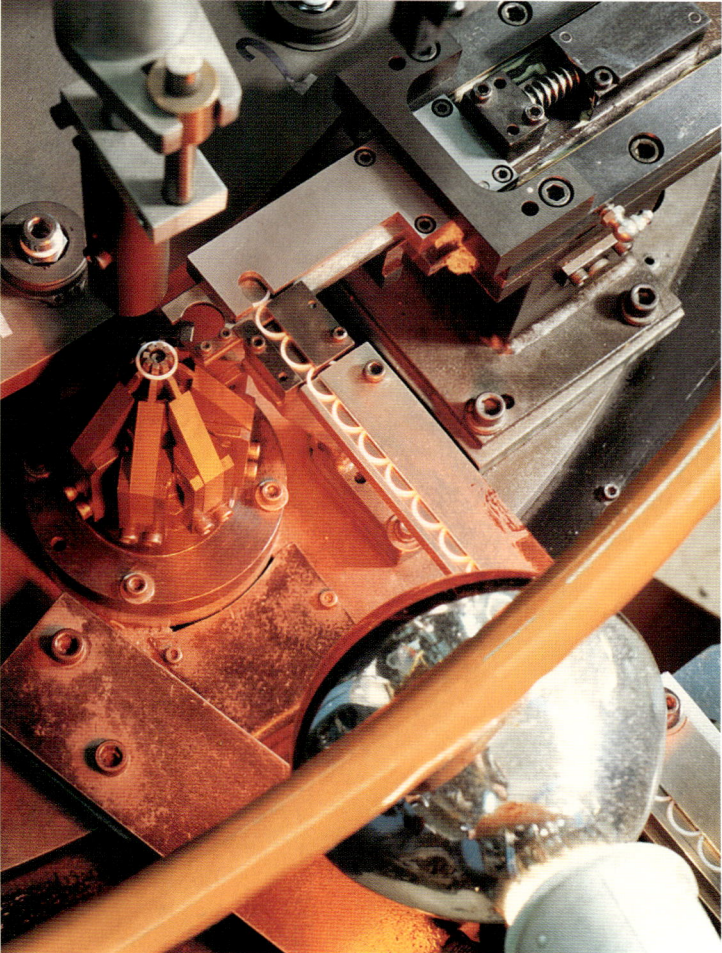

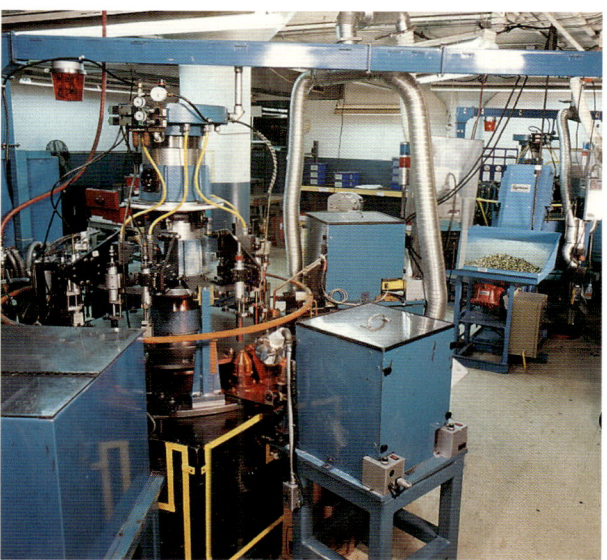

Quick-connect assemblies represent an area of specialty for Curtis Screw Company. Utilizing Swanson assembly machines, Curtis Screw has developed a new breed of automotive connection components for fluid power systems.

PERRY'S ICE CREAM

For many people, one of their fondest childhood memories is of enjoying rich, creamy, delicious ice cream on a warm summer afternoon. And for almost everyone in the Niagara region, that memory was supplied by Perry's Ice Cream of Akron, New York.

Founded in 1918 by Morton Perry, Perry's grew from a small local dairy to one of the most successful regional makers of ice cream and other frozen desserts in the United States. Today, the company is still owned by the Perry family, now in its fourth generation. And they carry on the tradition of quality that has been the key to Perry's success.

That tradition is summed up in the advice founder Morton Perry gave to his grandson and the company's current CEO, Tom Perry: "Make sure you put enough of the good stuff in it." Following that advice, Perry's combines the freshest milk and rich, buttery cream from local dairy farms with choice flavorings and ingredients from around the world, from vanilla beans grown in Madagascar to juicy ripe strawberries from Oregon.

Along with the finest ingredients, Perry's special manufacturing process assures that consumers can taste Perry's distinctive quality in every bite. For example, Perry's uses the more expensive vat pasteurization process to give its ice cream a richer, custardy feel on the palate. And to lock in that special goodness, Perry's flash freezes all its frozen desserts to an unbelievably cold 40 degrees below zero, then stores them in its own warehouse at 20 below—colder than industry standards, and more expensive, but worth it in the superior quality consumers enjoy in every Perry's product.

Perry's combines this emphasis on traditional quality with a commitment to innovation. A leader in new product development, Perry's now offers more than 350 frozen desserts, from ice cream to yogurt to sherbets to novelty treats including cones, ice cream sandwiches, fudge bars, dixie cups, and more. Among the company's taste innovations is Free and Fruity, a fat-free sherbet loaded with chunks of delicious fruit and one of a complete line of low-fat, nonfat, and sugar-free ice creams, yogurts, and other frozen desserts developed to meet changing consumer tastes. In its traditional ice cream lines, Perry's has pleased the public's palate with fun flavors such as Muddy Sneakers for kids, Monday Nut Football for sports fans, Death by Chocolate for chocolate lovers, and a host of other inventive flavors.

The company's modern facility, located at One Ice Cream Plaza in Akron, makes possible both the high-quality standards and the tremendous variety of products. Designed by Tom Perry and constructed in 1982 to accommodate the company's rapid growth, the facility's flexible, efficient production capabilities earned industry recognition as one of the most modern and innovative plants in the United States. Complementing the modern facility is a superb local work

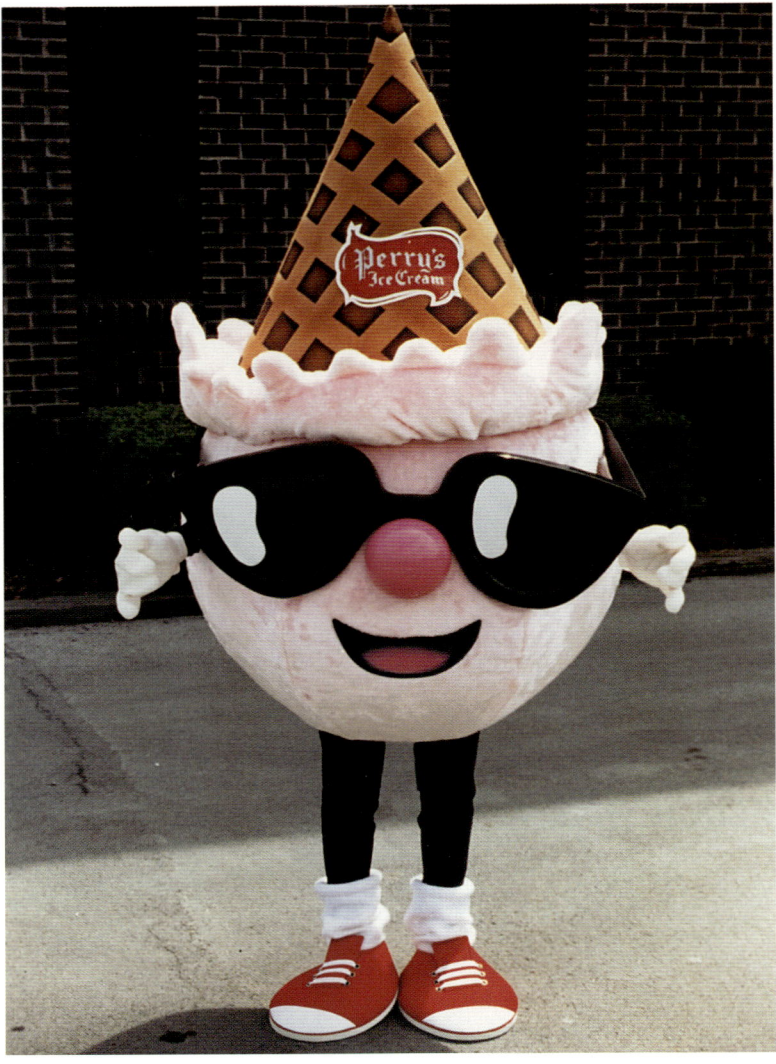

Perry Winkle, beloved mascot of Perry's Ice Cream.

force. Experienced and dedicated to the Perry's philosophy of quality, many of the firm's more than 250 employees have years of experience and are themselves second or third-generation Perry's people.

Along with the Perry family and the local work force, Perry's has a young and enthusiastic management team assembled to help the company grow into the 21st century. This combination of traditional family-oriented values and modern management has Perry's on target to become a $100 million company by the turn of the century.

The dominant brand in Western New York for many years, the company is now taking the Perry's brand name to a larger market. The company's distribution area now includes most of upstate New York, as well as significant portions of Pennsylvania. Within that area, Perry's serves many customers through many different distribution channels. Again building on tradition—the first Perry's ice cream was made especially for the local high school —Perry's is served in more than 1,200 school cafeterias across New York State, ensuring that the great taste of Perry's will be a fond memory for generations of schoolchildren to come. Along with other institutional sales and restaurants, Perry's main markets are grocery stores and roadside ice cream stands, where Perry's is a favorite summer attraction for kids of all ages.

In addition to Perry's brand products, the company is a major private label ice cream maker as well as a co-packer for branded frozen desserts. It also leverages its strengths in cold storage and distribution—the company operates a fleet of more than 90 trucks—by partnering with selected national brands, serving as a reseller and distributor.

Maintaining Perry's image in the national and international arenas, Tom Perry serves in many industry organizations, including terms as vice-chairman and chairman of the International Ice Cream Association and as a member of the board of directors of the International Dairy Foods Association. There he has worked to lift trade restrictions on dairy products, especially with regard to the expansion of the North American Free Trade Agreement to include dairy products. Opening the Canadian market will not only allow Perry's to expand to markets only minutes from its headquarters, but will also let Canadian consumers find the quality and goodness of Perry's right in their neighborhood stores.

Even as Perry's expands, it remains deeply committed to the community where it was founded. The company has earned many awards and honors locally, including recognition as a Family Business of the Year in Western New York, and was a recipient of the John Lafalce Community Service Award given to companies that have made outstanding contributions to the local community and community organizations. In addition to corporate and individual gifts, event sponsorships and volunteer service, Perry's maintains a high community profile through many public appearances of the Perry's Antique Ice Cream Wagon and Perry Winkle, the company's beloved mascot.

Continuing the tradition of quality that began in 1918, the Perry family intends to maintain Perry's Ice Cream as a strong regional company with growth sufficient to provide the critical mass to compete successfully in the 21st century, assuring that consumers who "pick Perry's" can enjoy old-fashioned ice cream taste and goodness for generations to come. ❧

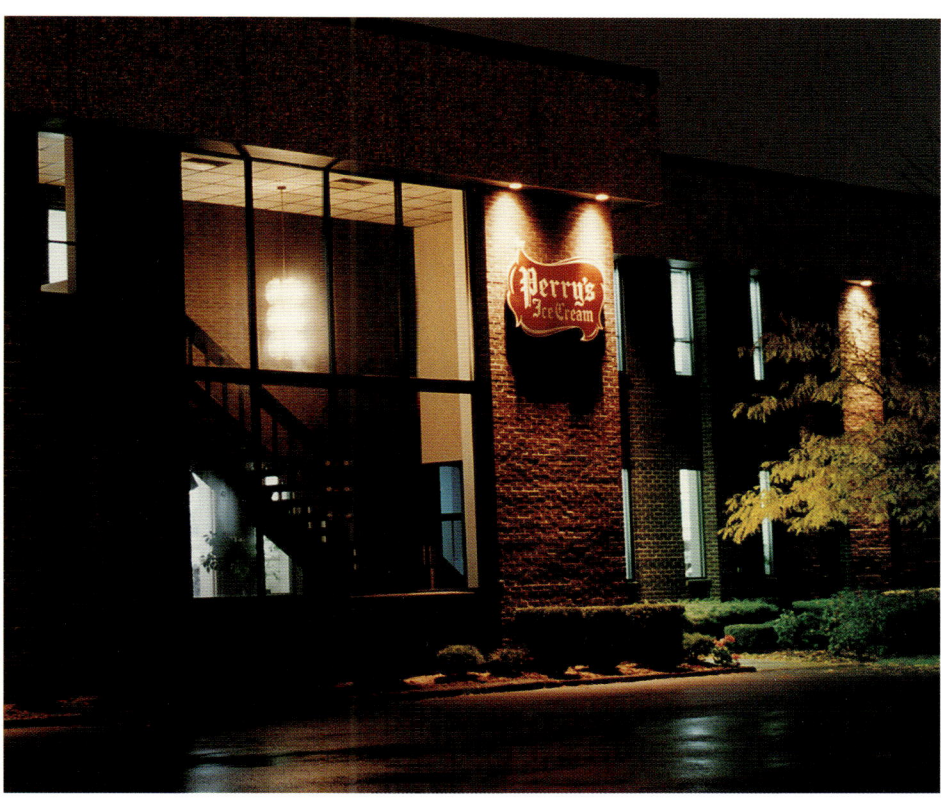

Perry's Ice Cream plant and headquarters located at One Ice Cream Plaza, Akron, New York.

Perry's on-site freezer warehouse stores 400,000-500,000 gallons of ice cream and other frozen desserts.

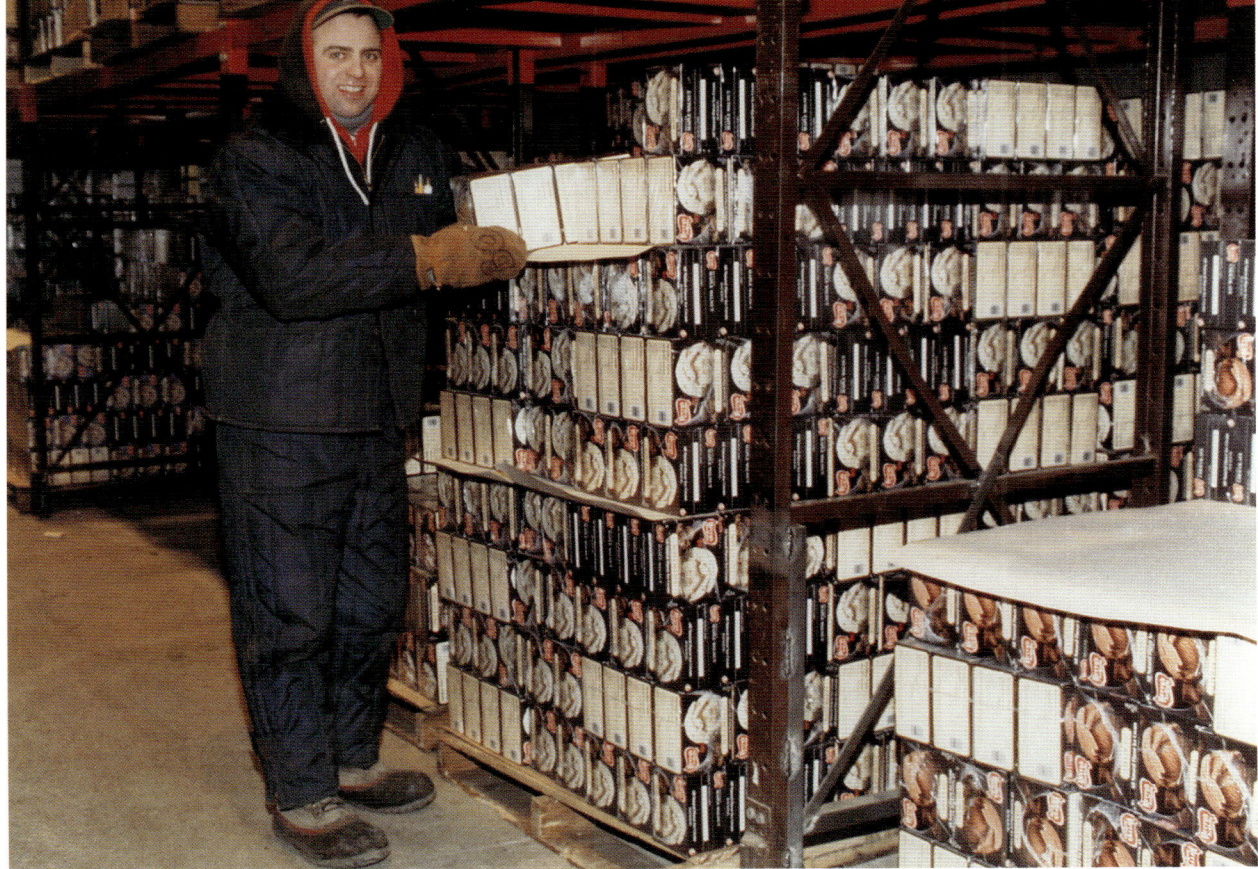

RUSSER FOODS

From a provisions route started in Brooklyn, New York, in the 1920s, Russer Foods has grown into a national leader in deli meats. Headquartered in Buffalo since 1969, the company remains family owned and operated, with Howard Zemsky serving as president. Today, following strong growth throughout the 1970s and 1980s, and a $10,000,000 expansion in 1997 raising annual capacity to 120,000,000 pounds of ham, bolognas, franks, cooked salami, braunschweiger, and assorted luncheon loaves, Russer is well on its way to making Buffalo the deli capital of the United States.

The company has achieved much of its growth through innovative niche marketing. A nationally recognized leader in the deli industry, Russer maintains its competitive edge by combining innovative product development, modern technology, and a tradition of quality.

One of Russer's most successful innovations is the Lil' Salt line of deli meats. Introduced in 1982 to capitalize on the nationwide trend toward healthier foods, this successful product line was revamped in 1988 into the Russer Light line of low-fat, low-salt foods. Offering consumers 25 percent less salt and 50 percent less fat, Russer Light products provide a healthy alternative in deli meats while preserving the traditional taste and quality consumers' demand. And, like all Russer products, the Russer Light line contains no fillers,

extenders, or MSG, and only all-natural spices. Now sold at more than 15,000 supermarket and convenience store delis, Russer Light deli meats have been an extraordinary success, allowing the company to expand into new markets.

Continuing to anticipate market demands, in the 1990s the company introduced self-serve deli meats to meet the needs of consumers who want deli quality but need the convenience of prepackaged products. Working with supermarkets, Russer offered consumers their favorite meats in convenient 8 ounce pre-packaged sizes. Only three years after being introduced, the Self-Serve line comprised 15 percent of Russer's overall sales, another remarkable achievement in a very competitive market segment.

Russer's dedication to teamwork and customer support is expressed in its mission of being "the highest-quality supplier of products, merchandising, and service to the in-store supermarket delicatessen." Russer's support for in-store delicatessens includes merchandising and point-of-purchase displays, with consumer giveaways such as free recipes, discount coupons, and nutritional information. In addition, the company provides training to the supermarkets' in-store deli workers. And it helps stores with new deli openings and remodelings. A result of this close partnership and support is that Russer deli meats are now found in more than half the

Russer is well on its way to making Buffalo the deli capital of the United States.

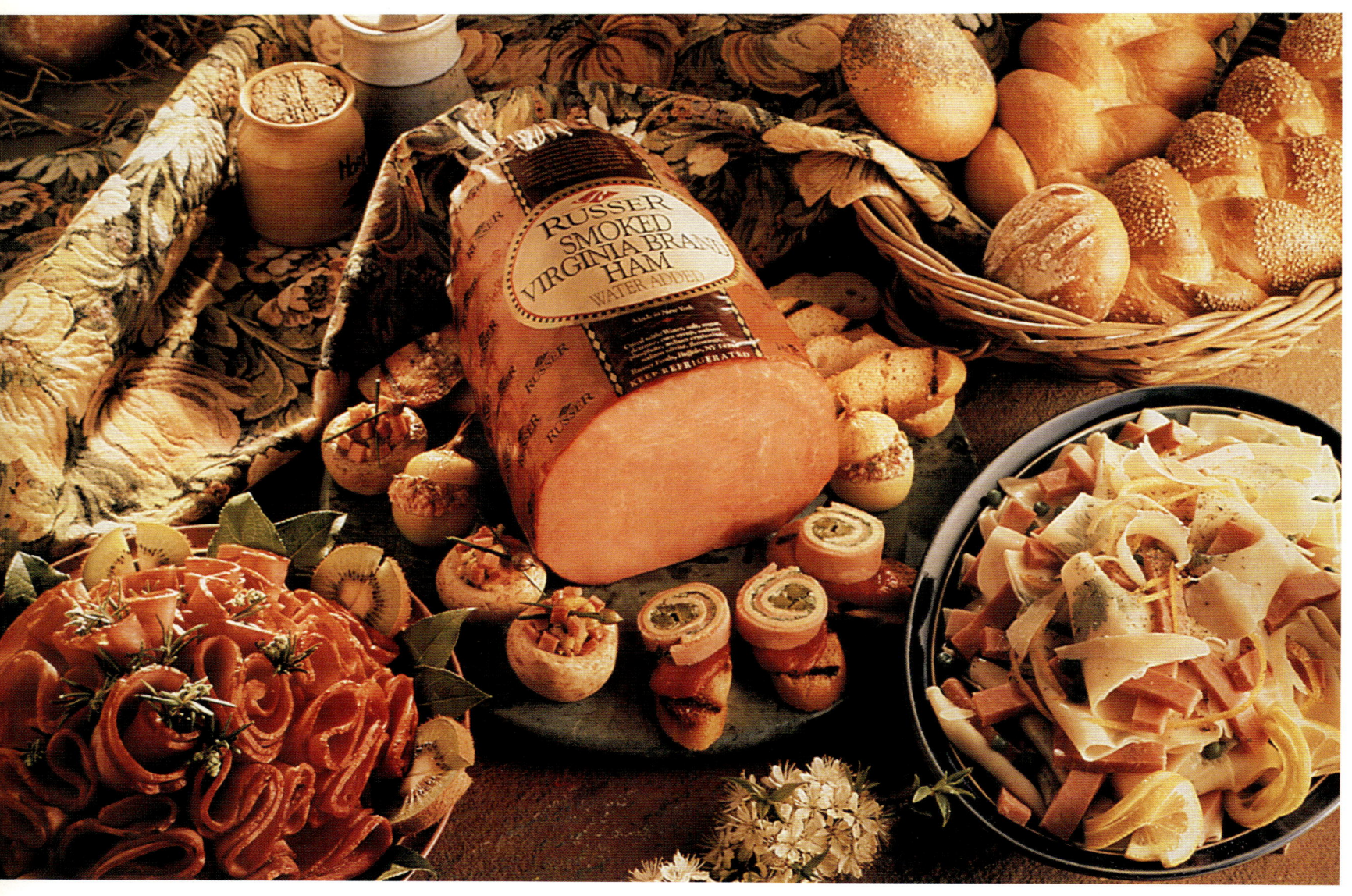

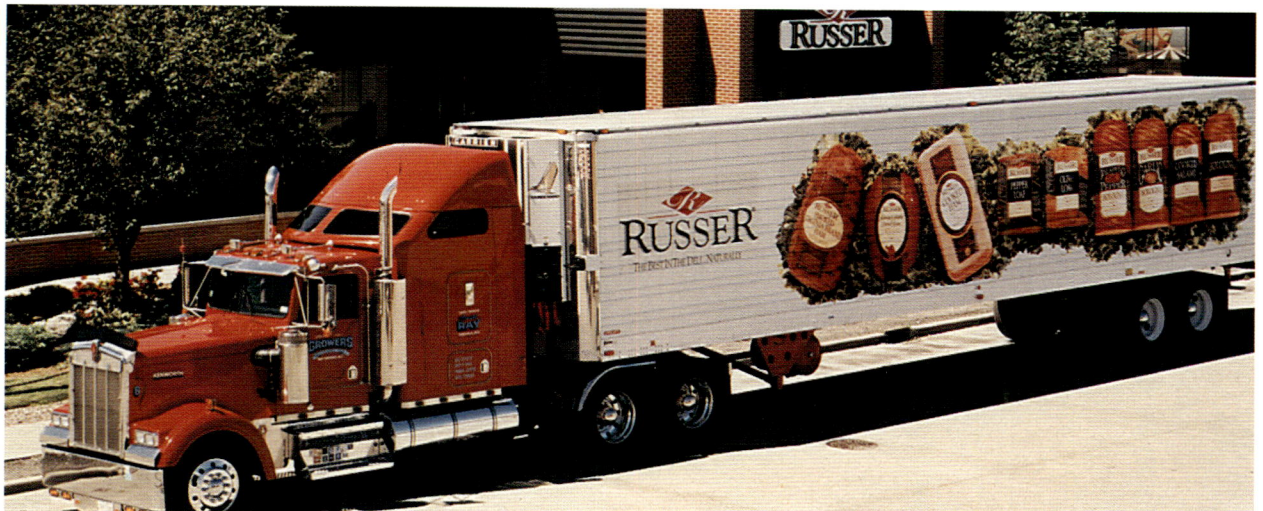

supermarket and convenience store deli counters in the United States.

The company has contributed to the industry in other ways as well, sponsoring deli-industry research through several trade associations.

Yet, along with an innovative approach to product development and marketing, the company has remained focused on traditional quality. Even after investing tens of millions of dollars in major renovations and modern equipment, Russer is one of the few meat processors that still smokes its hams rather than adding artificial "smoke" flavoring. The company also oven-cooks its loaf products, uses no starch, flour, or cereal extenders, and insists on using all-natural spices and seasonings.

This combination of progressive thinking and old-world values has made Russer products a favorite with consumers in all 50 states. And, in existing product lines, Russer continues to innovate with product line extensions such as Canadian Brand Maple Ham, assuring that within the company's wide variety of products there will be something to suit almost any taste.

Another key factor in Russer's success is the superior quality of its management and its work force, which the company believes to be the finest in the industry. The company has more than 250 employees, and the number continues to grow. At Russer, quality of work life for all employees has been a shared tradition since the company's beginning. Everyone is in the same profit-sharing and health plans. Open offices and a flat, non-hierarchical organization encourage teamwork. Although committed to modern technology to achieve efficiency, Russer has avoided some automation in order to preserve the human touch necessary to produce a superior product.

Russer is also firmly committed to the Niagara region. One of the original signatories of the Niagara Compact promoting the area among local executives, Russer president Howard Zemsky cites the superior work force, excellent transportation, and strategic location within a day's drive of more than half the U.S. population as key factors in Russer's success and its long-term goals.

Along with creating jobs for the region, Russer works hard to improve the overall quality of life in the area. The company

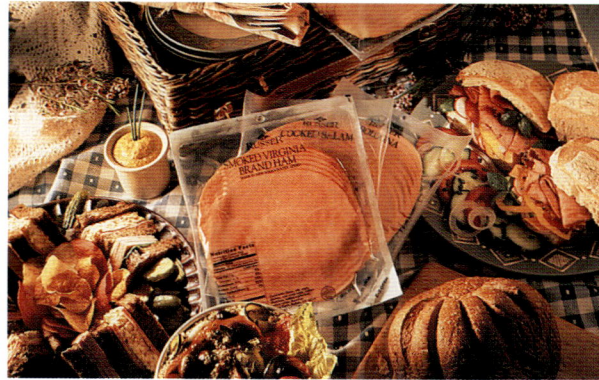

regularly supports the Buffalo Philharmonic Orchestra, Studio Arena Theater, Children's Hospital, the United Way, Boy Scouts of America, the Western New York Food Bank, the Buffalo Museum of Science, the Albright-Knox Art Gallery, and many other organizations that give Buffalo its cultural and community identity.

In addition to generating internal growth through its innovative products, Russer has participated in a trend of industry-wide consolidation through strategic acquisitions, acquiring Deutschmacher Brand meats in Boston, Massachusetts, in 1992, and Frey's Brand in Buffalo in 1994. Along with expanding Russer's product offerings to include the specialty frankfurter and German-style specialty niches, those acquisitions brought with them familiar regional brand names that provided access to important new markets. The company also operates a processing facility in Boston, acquired with the Deutschmacher operation, and a distribution facility in Brooklyn, New York. In the future, Russer will continue to look for growth opportunities through acquisitions in order to maintain the critical mass necessary for success.

Innovative product lines. An aggressive business strategy. Dedicated workers. With these ingredients, Russer has become a national leader in the production and distribution of premium deli meats and, in the process, moved Buffalo and the Niagara region to the forefront of the deli industry. ◆

Russer deli meats are now found in more than half the supermarkets and convenience store deli counters in the United States.

One of Russer's most successful innovations is the Lil' Salt line of deli meats.

BUFFALO TECHNOLOGIES CORPORATION

Theodore E. Dann, CEO Buffalo Technologies Corporation.

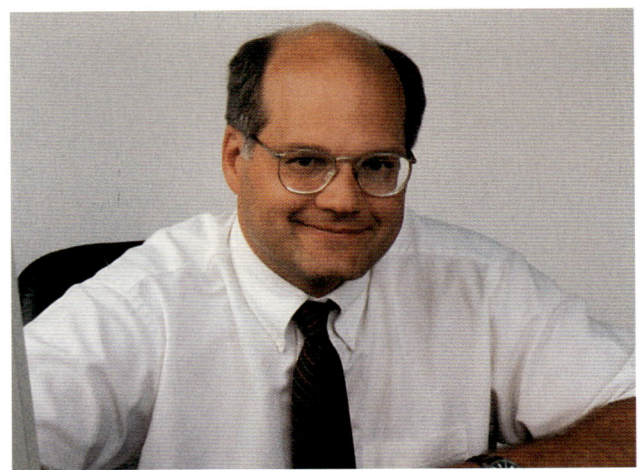

With its roots in the great Buffalo industrial tradition and its future in innovative, technology-driven products and services for the food, chemical, pharmaceutical, and waste treatment industries, Buffalo Technologies Corporation is a model success story in the vibrant new economy of the Niagara Region. Recognized in 1996 as the Turnaround Company of the Year for upstate New York in the National Entrepreneur of the Year Awards sponsored by Ernst & Young, *USA Today*, and NASDAQ, Buffalo Technologies Corporation today is a growing and thriving player in the international marketplace.

Founded in 1901 as the Buffalo Foundry and Machine Company, the company grew to include four divisions. The company's Buflovak division designs and manufactures evaporators, dryers, flakers, reactors, kettles, and total systems for customers around the world. The Jabez Burns division designs, manufactures, and installs coffee, nut, and grain processing plants, equipment, and systems, also for the international market. The design and manufacture of atmospheric and pneumatic screeners/sifters, feeders, packers, compactors, flask shakers, and systems is performed by the Gump division. The BKE division serves the metals industry, designing, manufacturing, and servicing Heppenstall handling equipment, including buckets, water-cooled panels, and hot blast/reversing valves.

The company is one of only a few worldwide offering product research and testing, the design and engineering of process equipment and systems, and manufacturing of complex one-of-a-kind and first-of-a-kind equipment and systems all at a single location. Occupying 17 acres in Buffalo, the company's facilities include a pilot testing laboratory, sales and engineering offices, and more than

250,000 square feet of manufacturing space. A skilled and dedicated work force includes production employees represented by the International Association of Machinists and Aerospace Workers, as well as a technical staff representing virtually every engineering discipline.

Working together, the company's employees have built an enviable reputation for offering customers value-added services, state-of-the-art technologies, and superior technological development. Their success in providing quality products, services, and on-time delivery is reflected in an impressive customer list that includes many of the Fortune 500 companies along with firms in more than 60 countries worldwide.

To meet the evolving needs of its diverse and growing customer base, and to develop new technologies for emerging industries, Buffalo Technologies Corporation is adapting many of its core technologies to new and exciting applications. One of the most important new applications is the adaptation of Buflovak dryers for waste treatment. Used for more than

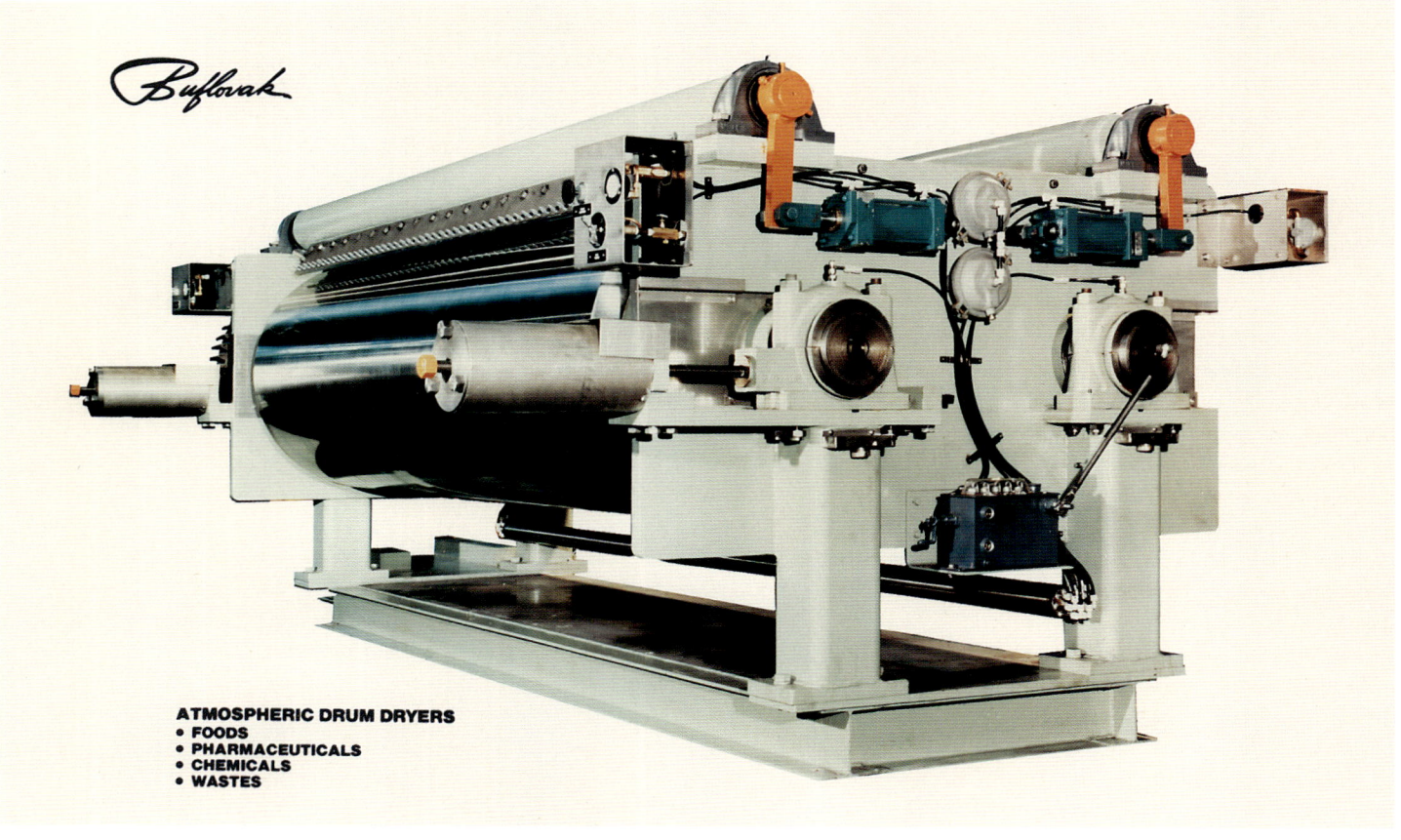

ATMOSPHERIC DRUM DRYERS
- **FOODS**
- **PHARMACEUTICALS**
- **CHEMICALS**
- **WASTES**

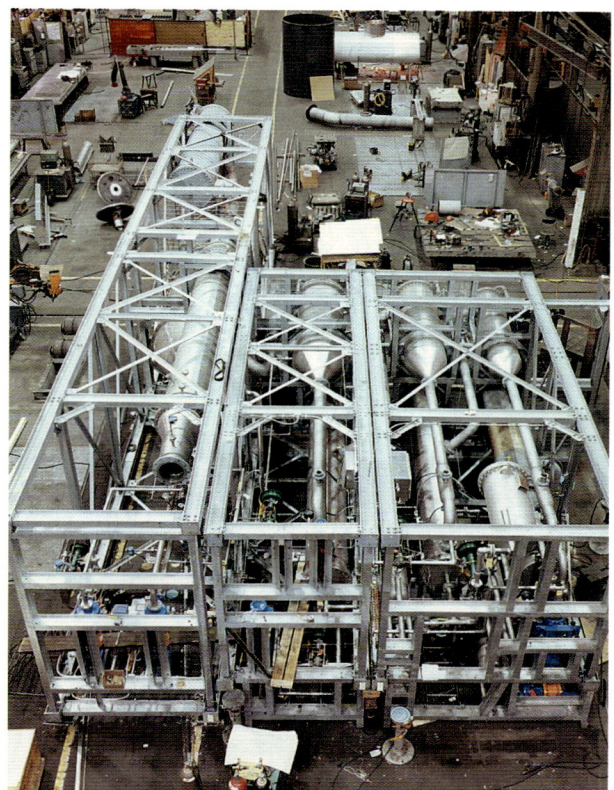

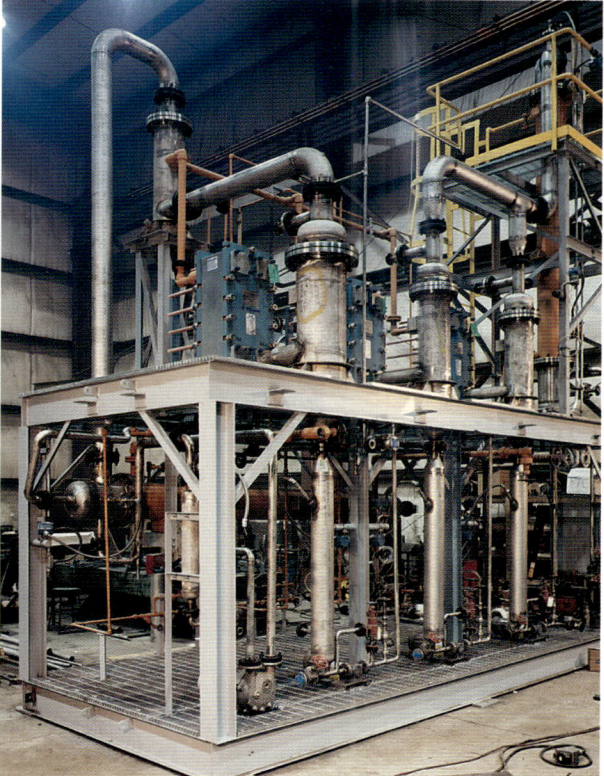

70 years in the processing of food products, chemical, and pharmaceuticals, Buflovak dryers and evaporators have now been adapted to the treatment of industrial and municipal sludge. Samples for drying are tested at the company's laboratory, and Buffalo Technologies Corporation engineers and product managers then work with customers to develop innovative solutions to waste disposal problems.

Another example of the company's success in adapting its technology to environmentally friendly processes is a method developed for extracting caustic soda from the waste stream of plants making prewashed denim jeans. Using the Buffalo Technologies Corporation process, jeans makers can reclaim the caustic for reuse in the manufacturing process while rendering the waste water more easily treated for release or reuse. And in a contribution to the post-Cold War economy of the United States, Buflovak dryers are being used as part of the complex process of eliminating the nation's arsenal of nerve gas.

The company is also exploiting the Gump division's expertise in separating and particle sizing, applying this technology to environmental uses for the efficient handling of chaff and other particulate wastes. In one application, Gump technology is used to size packaging waste generated by an internationally known fast food company to the ideal size for recycling. As companies in the United States and abroad increasingly view sound environmental practices as good business, Buffalo Technologies Corporation will continue to expand its role in this growing market niche.

Enhancements to existing product lines and technology are also playing a large role in the company's resurgence. In the Jabez Burns division, a new patented technology for coffee roasting promises to revolutionize the way coffee beans are roasted around the world. Using high velocity, low temperature for true "packed bed" roasting, this proprietary process assures a completely uniform roast in far less time than can be achieved with conventional roasters. The system offers coffee roasters of all sizes, a wide range of benefits, including a higher quality roast, lower fuel consumption and lower operating costs, for greater control over the roasting

process, a low maintenance system with very few moving parts, and higher yields. In addition, the roasting system can be coupled with Burns granulizers, offering coffee roasters and packers a complete system that meets all their needs. As an added benefit, the equipment takes up far less space than conventional roasters, offering another cost savings. Proven in tests in the Burns laboratory and in customers' plants, the new system is attracting interest and orders throughout the United States and overseas.

In addition to enhancing current designs and developing new products, Buffalo Technologies Corporation is in the business of providing ideas and technical solutions for its customers. As more companies are upgrading existing facilities rather than building new ones, Burns offers special expertise in reengineering process systems and system controls for greater efficiency and higher performance. With the company's new emphasis on system engineering and waste stream handling solutions, it can often supply a complete process system solution for its customers.

To compete effectively as a full-service, technology-oriented problem solver, the company has undertaken an aggressive program to upgrade the skills of all employees. Problem-solving teams engage employees in the company's decision-making process. Profit sharing gives workers a stake in the firm's success and a recognition program rewards creative thinking and hard work. The company firmly believes that its people are its greatest asset, and that a highly motivated, highly qualified staff is the key to its future success.

While continuing to recruit and nurture the best and brightest workers for its work force, the company will also look for potential business partners and acquisition prospects with complementary business lines that can provide the synergies needed to fuel growth, strengthen its position in its existing markets, and capitalize on new opportunities.

By incorporating the best of its past with a clear vision of the future, Buffalo Technologies Corporation has staked its claim as one of the leaders in the twenty-first century's economy in the Niagara region. ❧

UNITED ALLOYS & STEEL CORP.

Industrial scrap: A byproduct of manufacturing processes.

Recycling, long before it became a trend, was the genesis of United Alloys & Steel Corp. The Buffalo-based business was begun in 1946 by Edward Linder and Leonard "Bud" Frank, entrepreneurs who started out with a borrowed pickup truck collecting scrap and surplus steel from local manufacturers for sale to larger steel processors. From two employees and $50,000 in sales in the first year, the company has grown to over 50 employees with annual sales of $25 million as it now celebrates its 50th anniversary.

In the early days, the partners leased space on Lower Terrace Street and then Market Street in downtown Buffalo. The company's current home on Hannah Street was purchased in the late 1950s, and in 1990, a second plant was acquired on Clinton Street. Today, United Alloys operates in nearly 100,000 square feet of space on 10 acres of land. The company also maintains a trading\brokerage office in Pittsburgh, Pennsylvania.

Originally involved in the ferrous (iron) recycling business, United Alloys later moved into the purchase and sale of new and/or used structural shapes and, finally, the recycling of nonferrous surplus and scrap (such as copper, brass, aluminum). The current focus is a complementary integration of all aspects of recycling, including a more recent foray into non-metallics (paper and plastics). Eighty percent of the scrap United Alloys purchases and processes comes from the manufacturing sector; 15 percent is from other scrap dealers, and 5 percent comes from what are known in the industry as peddlers.

The processing phase of United Alloys' operations begins with the picking up of production, maintenance, or obsolete scrap from the manufacturing sector and bringing it to one of United's processing facilities. Here the scrap is identified, sorted, sized, and packaged to the strict specifications of consumers in the remelting phase. This material is then marketed and ultimately sold to well-screened, environmentally sound companies and converted into raw materials such as sheet, plate, or ingots. To complete the recycling "loop," this product is then used in the manufacturing area.

While the primary service provided by the firm is to collect the scrap and surplus material on the manufacturer's site, it also works with those customers to increase their revenues and contain costs through better scrap handling methods. United Alloys helps their "partners in recycling" realize hundreds of thousands of dollars annually through its scrap recycling expertise and consultation.

The environmental benefits of recycling are paramount not only in this industry, but the broad economy as well. Ultimately, United Alloys is a private enterprise in the public interest. Recycling scrap keeps a valuable resource from being wasted in landfills; currently, recycling saves the United States more than $2 billion each year in solid waste disposal costs. The remelting of scrap is also much more energy efficient than melting virgin material—it takes four times as much energy to make steel from virgin iron ore as it does to make the same steel from scrap. Therefore, utilizing scrap metal reduces the amount of raw material that would otherwise be mined. In this way, United Alloys & Steel's operation can be best appreciated as an aboveground mine. At United Alloys, the continued investment to handle scrap in an environmentally responsible manner is critical to its employees, customers, and the community.

Urban forest: America's ready resource - scrap.

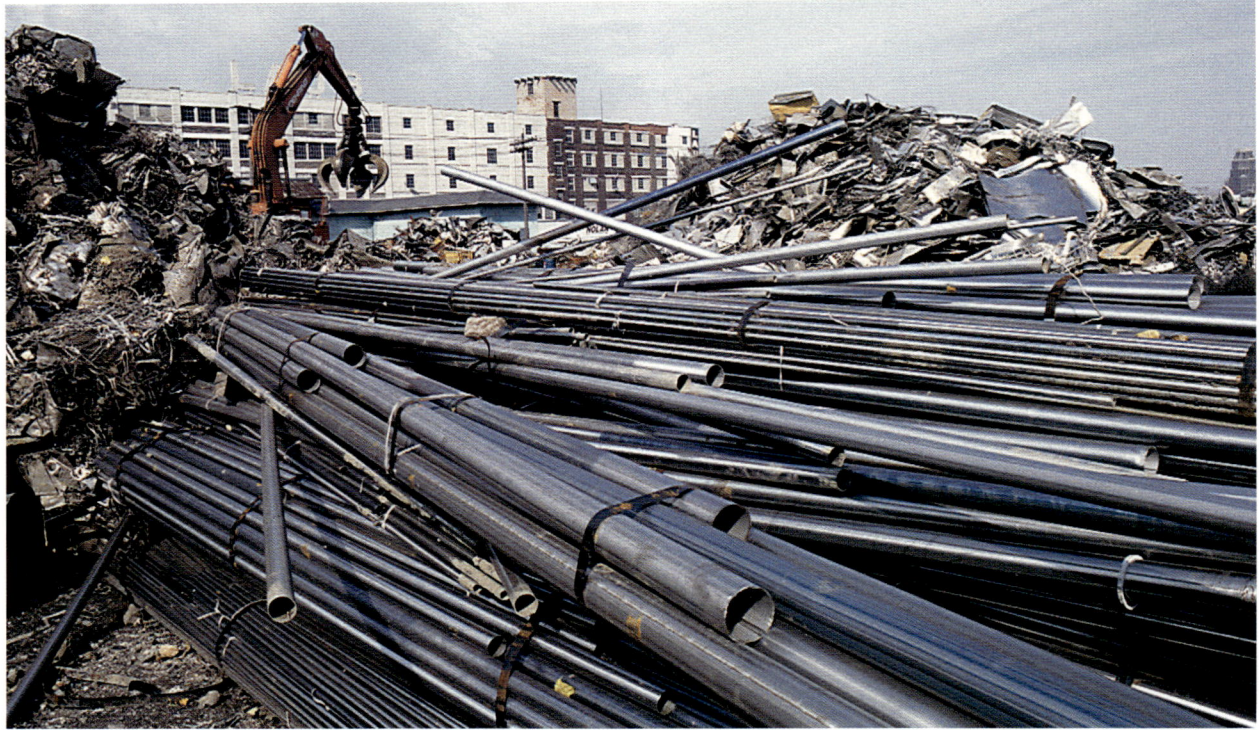

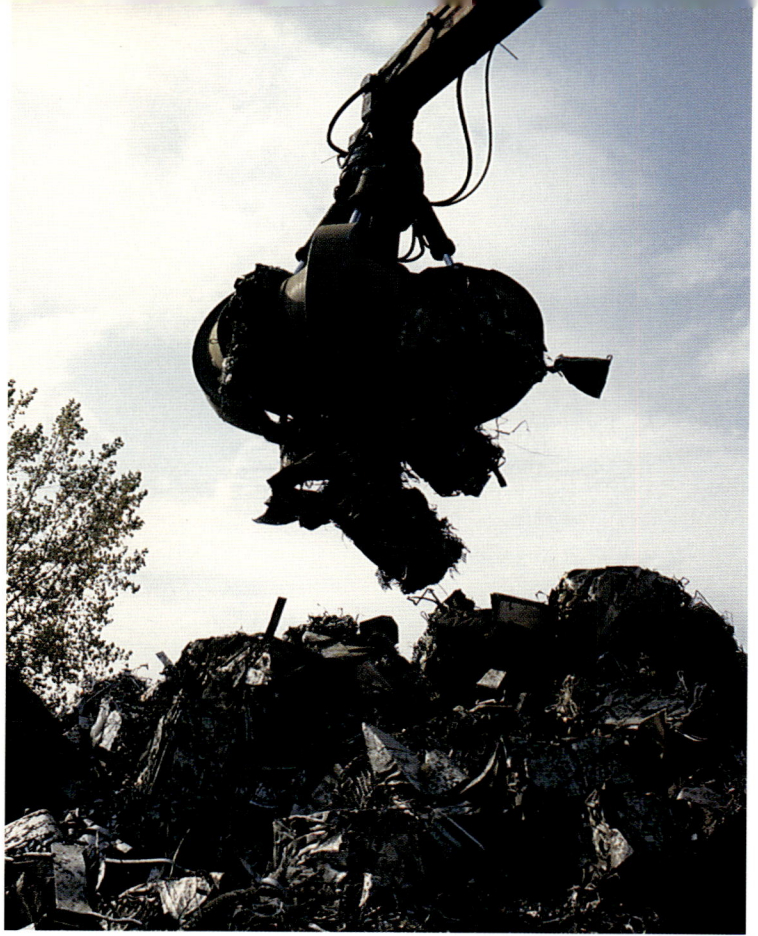

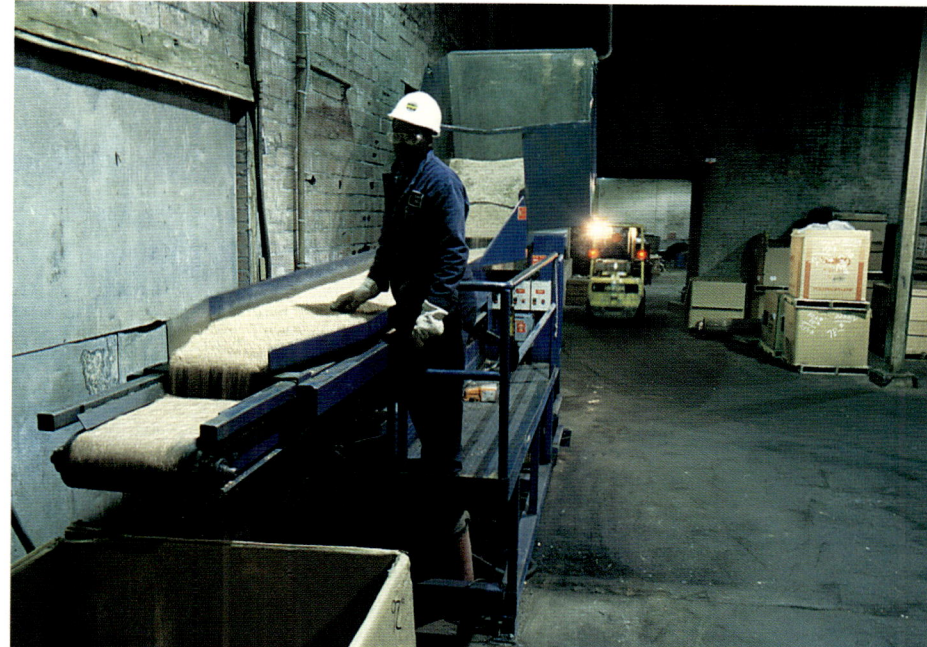

Another aspect of the company's work is in the trading and/or brokerage business. United Alloys acts as a middleman of sorts, coordinating the purchase, marketing, and shipment from its customers (the source of production or obsolete scrap) to its consumers (the melt shops—steel, aluminum, or brass mills).

The success earned in 50 years in the scrap recycling industry has given a second generation the springboard to continued growth. The company plans not only to capitalize on opportunities within its current customer base and expanding brokerage activity, but also to integrate other industry innovations and technology to attract new business.

Several joint ventures are currently under way. One operation was funded in 1993 with a friendly competitor in Western New York. Its primary function is to melt down obsolete aluminum products for shipment into the secondary market. The unqualified success of this cooperative effort led to the creation on Integrated Recycling Services, L.L.C.; its primary focus is the on-site management of a recycling facility at Eastman Kodak Co. in Rochester, N.Y

Another venture involves United Alloys working in a brokerage coalition concentrating on the production and marketing of speciality steel products. Other partners in this enterprise are located in Toronto, Chicago, Columbus and Los Angeles.

Additionally, United Alloys is also acting in concert with a local software developer to market industry-specific inventory software under the acronym SMARTS (scrap management and recycling tracking systems). The last joint venture is a foray into the global realm, working with an international trading group in managing a small foundry operation in Tunisia. Here they melt aluminum and copper for shipment into the European market.

The company continues to explore and invest in opportunities from precious metals and nonmetallics to new product research. As an example, it is one of eight companies involved in a consortium of steel mills and manufacturers working with a major university to research and develop new, more environmentally friendly raw materials. United Alloys is

the only recycling concern working on this proprietary project.

With a future holding so many bold new projects, company officials are confident the next decade will see staff expansion as well as physical plant development. In addition to its' internal development, the company is actively involved in and has held key leadership roles, locally and nationally, in its industry trade association, the Institute of Scrap Recycling Industries (ISRI).

Today, Ed Linder remains involved in the company he founded as chairman of the board. Though Bud Frank retired several years ago, he is still a familiar face on the premises, serving as a consultant. Peter A. Linder, son of the cofounder, provides the day-to-day leadership as the company's president and CEO. Peter states the company's mission very succinctly: "Recycling under the highest ethical, safety, and environmental standards, to provide support for our customers, our employees and their families, and the community at large. He continues: "What we do takes expertise about markets, manufacturing, and solutions to environmental challenges. It also takes a willingness to roll up our sleeves and get the job done."

Community involvement has long been a cornerstone of United's profile. The Linders and Franks have made a significant contribution of time and other resources to enhance the general quality of life in the Western New York community. Now a second generation is committed to continuing this legacy of civic service that seems to be a professional, as well as familial, tradition.

"We are committed to growing the business in Western New York and continuing to be involved in the fabric of the community," said Ed Linder. Family members have held, or currently hold, trusteeships and other leadership positions with such organizations as Millard Fillmore Hospital, Salvation Army, National Conference of Christians and Jews, United Way, Buffalo Zoological Society, SPCA, Kids Escaping Drugs Campaign, Boys and Girls Clubs of Buffalo, Irish Classical Theater, Artpark, Hallwalls, Nichols School, and Nardin Academy. ◆

Processing: Safety, efficiency, environmental compliance.

(above left) Scrap metal recycling: An above ground mine.

ALLING AND CORY

It was big business news in the spring of 1996 when Alling and Cory Company was acquired by a New Jersey-based forest products giant, Union Camp Corporation. As one of the nation's oldest and largest independent wholesale paper distributors, Alling and Cory, headed by President Tom Hubbard, hastened to reassure its customers and shareholders that business would continue with the same high quality as usual, even as the company expanded into new markets.

The merger is emblematic of the kind of vision that underlies Alling and Cory's hardiness in a very competitive important product line. In the 1960s and 1970s, Alling and Cory was one of the first distributors to stock a wide selection of business products for automated offices, including paper, toners, and developers for copying machines; rolls and tapes for business machines and telecommunications equipment; and supplies for word- processing equipment.

Throughout Alling and Cory's history in Buffalo, the company has adapted to the needs of the area. To assist in the city's World War II effort, paper stock distributed by the firm was used by local companies to manufacture military

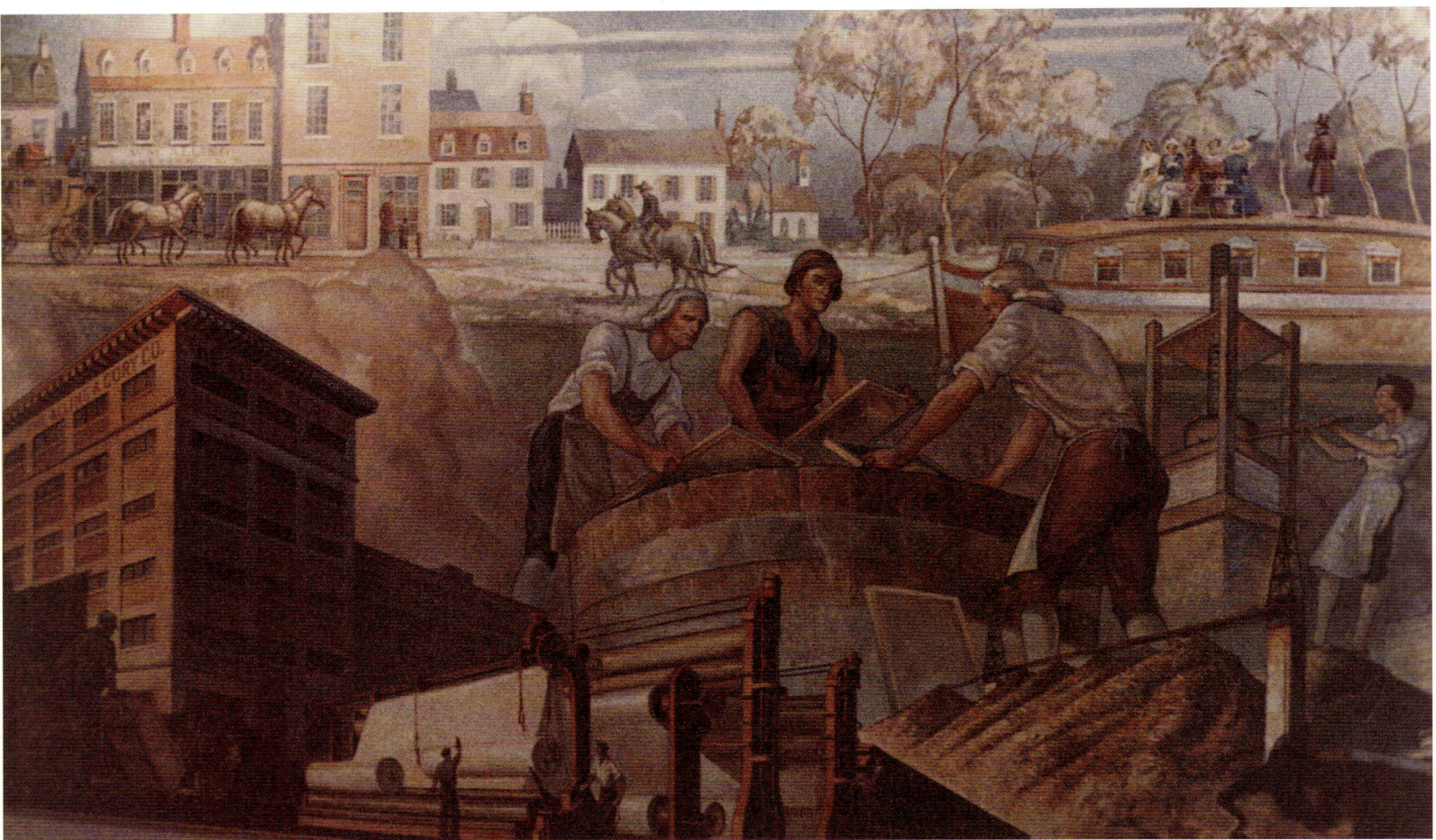

Alling and Cory is one of the nation's oldest and largest independent wholesale paper distributors. Pictured here is the beautiful mural located in the lobby.

industry. Its Western New York history dates all the way back to 1819, when Elihu F. Marshall, a cousin of Chief Justice of the Supreme Court John Marshall, founded a small stationery and book shop in Rochester, New York. In 1834, Marshall sold the store to one of his clerks, William Alling. Upon his death in 1890, Alling's son, Joseph T. Alling, and Harvey E. Cory took over. The firm was incorporated as the Alling and Cory Company in 1908. Its Buffalo office on North Division Street was opened in 1911. Today, the company, still head-quartered in Rochester, operates 15 distribution centers and 20 retail paper shops in the Northeast.

As the printing industry has expanded across the Lake Erie corridor through New York, Pennsylvania, Ohio, and West Virginia, the name Alling and Cory has become synonymous with high-quality printing papers. Printers, graphic designers, artists, advertising agencies, and other printing professionals look to the firm for all their printing paper needs.

Over the years, packaging materials, from wrapping films to containers and protective covers, have become another manuals, maps, and food and munitions packing for soldiers overseas. During the area's postwar heavy-industrial economy boom, the company expanded its maintenance products division. And, as Buffalo has moved into the information age, Alling and Cory has moved right along, providing not only computer supplies but also a full line of technical and specialty papers.

The future looks bright as Alling and Cory, infused with capital from its new parent Union Camp, plans to expand aggressively into new markets. ❧

The global industrial company known as Varity Corporation became LucasVarity plc, one of the top 10 automotive component suppliers in the world, in the fall of 1996, the result of a merger with Lucas Industries plc of the United Kingdom. The company, with its world headquarters in London and North American headquarters in Buffalo, designs, manufactures, and supplies advanced technology systems, products and services in the world's automotive, diesel engine, aftermarket and aerospace industries.

LucasVarity comprises seven divisions:

♦ Light vehicle braking systems (Lucas car braking systems and VarityKelsey-Hayes): the world's number two supplier of light vehicle braking systems, with particular strengths in foundation brakes, actuation, rear-wheel and four-wheel anti-lock braking systems.

♦ Heavy vehicle braking systems (Lucas heavy-duty braking systems and VarityDaytonWalther): a leading manufacturer of heavy-duty foundation brakes, wheel and brake components for medium- and heavy-duty trucks and trailers.

♦ Diesel systems (Lucas Diesel Systems) the world's second-largest manufacturer of diesel fuel injection systems.

♦ Diesel engines (VarityPerkins): a global supplier of diesel engines to more than 600 original equipment manufacturers.

♦ Electrical and electronic systems (Lucas Electrical and Electronic Systems and VarityZecal): a world-class supplier of advanced electronics, wiring systems, body systems and electrical systems.

♦ Aftermarket operations (Lucas Aftermarket Operations and the aftermarket operations previously within the Varity automotive businesses): a leading provider of comprehensive parts, service, technical and diagnostic support to both vehicle manufacturers and the independent automotive aftermarket. Its global distribution network spans 120 countries.

♦ Aerospace (Lucas Aerospace): provides the global aerospace industry with high-integrity systems in flight controls, engine controls, electrical power generation and management and cargo handling, all backed by a worldwide customer support operation.

LucasVarity is the world's second-largest producer of light vehicle braking systems and the number two worldwide manufacturer of diesel fuel injection systems.

Victor Rice, former chairman and chief executive officer of Varity, is chief executive of LucasVarity.

The company's North American headquarters offices are situated in an architectural treasure, a historic mansion on Delaware Avenue in Buffalo. The building, completed in 1899 as a private residence, was designed by the celebrated New York City architects Mead, McKim and White. Interior and exterior renovation of the site has netted LucasVarity a number of prestigious design and historic preservation awards. ◆

LUCASVARITY

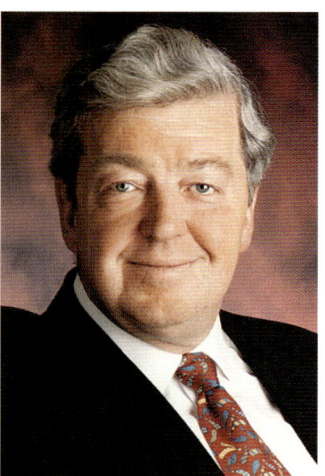

Victor Rice, LucasVarity Chief Executive

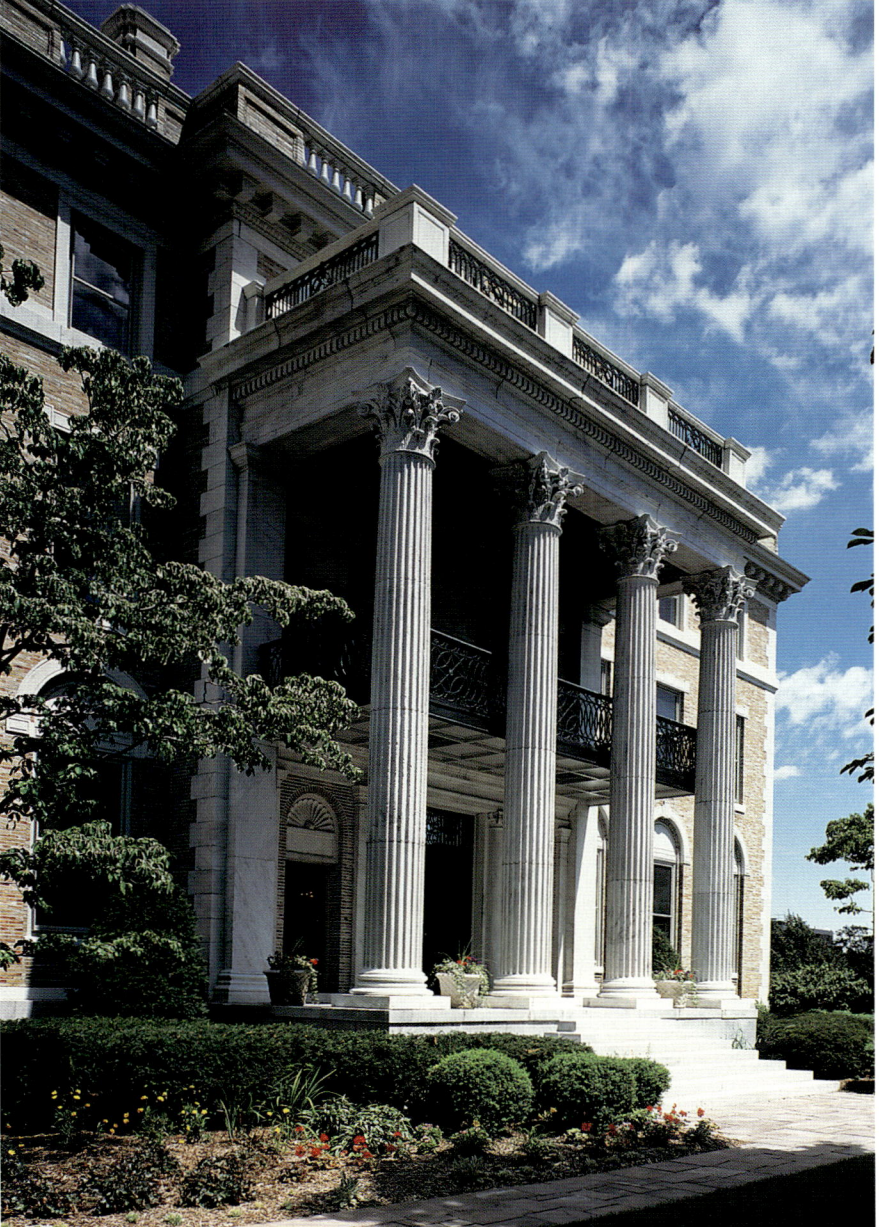

LucasVarity's North American headquarters, a historic architectural treasure in Buffalo.
Photo by James Cavanaugh.

COOPER TURBOCOMPRESSOR

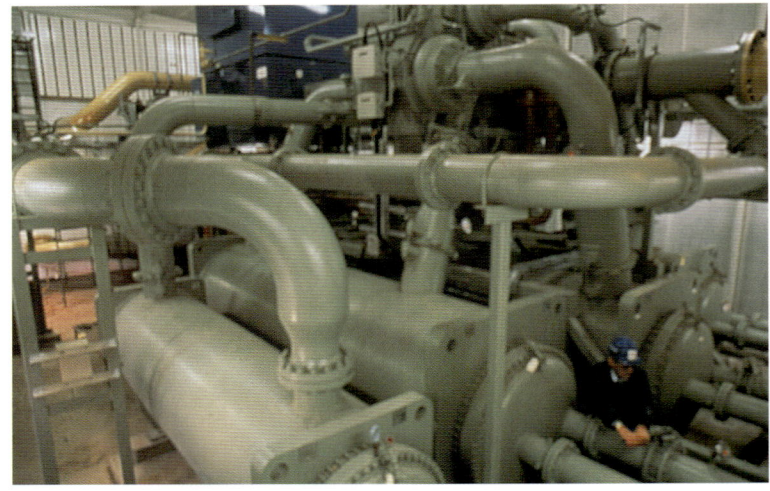

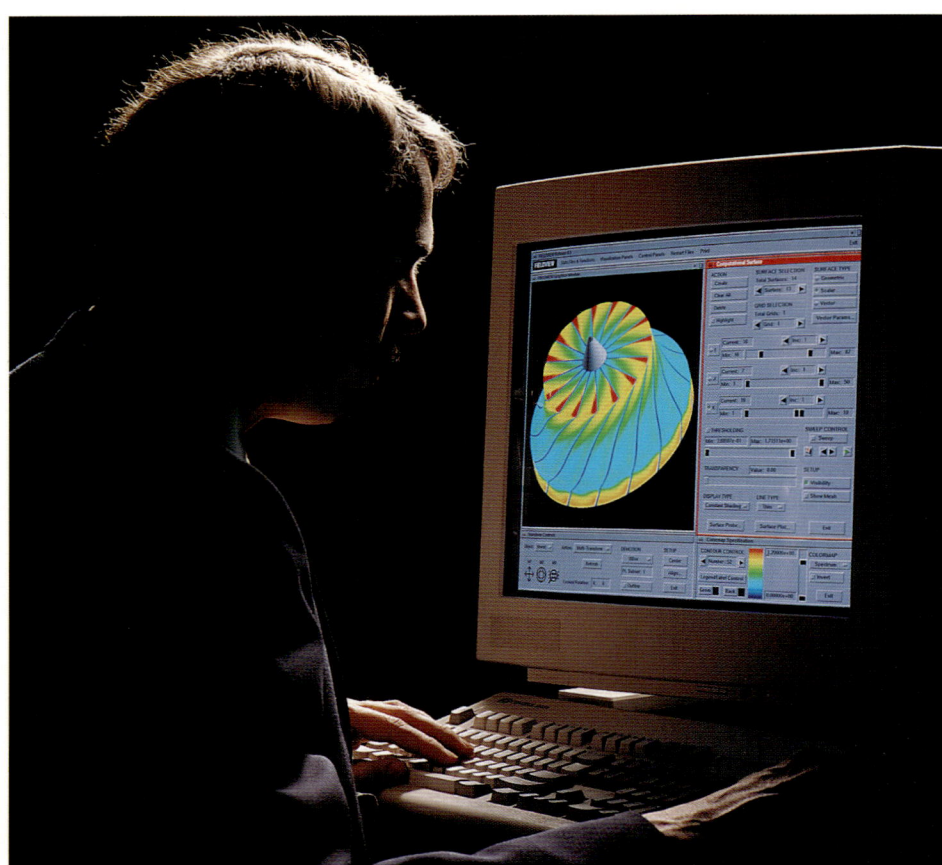

customer interest in a clean environment with the use of oil-free compressed air, lower energy consumption, and ease of automation with high operating reliability. The compressors today span a range of 150 to 20,000 horsepower in standard and customized configurations.

In custom process applications, Cooper Turbocompressor TA and MSG Models are used by the air separation, pharmaceutical, petrochemical, refining, and electric utility industries. The same attributes of oil-free air, efficiency, and reliability make the more standard Turbo Air 2000 and Series C-8 models a leading choice for plant air applications in automobile, food and beverage, glass and metal container, textile, electronics, and general manufacturing facilities around the world. Cooper Turbocompressor machines can be found in Western New York providing oil-free compressed air for snowmaking, water treatment, and automobile production.

As the company's headquarters and manufacturing center, the engineering, financial, marketing, manufacturing of proprietary components, assembly, packaging, and testing activities take place here. The Buffalo operation has an ISO-9001 certified quality system. Recent investment in the facility includes a $12 million test facility that is equipped with several test stands (the largest being 11,000 horsepower), new precision machine tools, and a 24,000-square-foot compressor assembly building addition. The plant also has a dedicated repair facility and customer training center.

A high-technology company, Cooper Turbocompressor employs engineers in disciplines such as aerodynamics, mechanical engineering, and heat transfer. The company's commitment to research and development continues to yield advances in compressor design. Sophisticated CAD/CAM and finite element analysis computer systems are used to support the engineering effort.

In addition to attracting engineering and other high-technology professionals, Cooper Turbocompressor contributes significantly to the regional economy by sourcing many non-proprietary components such as castings, heat exchangers, and selected machined parts in Western New York and Southern Ontario.

Today, the company employs more than 500 employees and continues to enjoy strong growth. To continue that growth into the 21st century, Cooper Turbocompressor will offer a growing product line with continued innovation. The company is also working to strengthen its worldwide marketing and service network. With established markets in Asia, Latin America, and Africa, growing new markets in Central and Eastern Europe and the republics of the former Soviet Union, as well as manufacturing and technology licensees in Japan and India, Cooper Turbocompressor is bringing new economic growth to the Niagara region and demonstrating that U.S. technology and manufacturing can compete in the global market. ◈

In 1955, four engineers from Buffalo were given a challenging assignment by Joy Manufacturing: design a line of high-speed centrifugal compressors for air and gas applications. The result was an integral gear centrifugal compressor, a design so ingenious and efficient that even today it is the defining standard for oil-free centrifugal compressors.

The company has been headquartered at the 3101 Broadway location since 1960 although its name has changed over time. Known as Cooper Turbocompressor, Inc. since 1995, it is a wholly owned subsidiary of Cooper Cameron Corporation, a worldwide leader in oil, gas, and industrial equipment headquartered in Houston, Texas. The synergy created by the company's strong engineering tradition and the global reach of parent Cooper Cameron make Cooper Turbocompressor one of the most innovative and successful manufacturers of high-technology industrial compressors in the world, with over 60 percent of its products going to the international market.

The worldwide strength of the market for the company's centrifugal compressor products is based on the growing

American Precision is a diversified manufacturing company serving the industrial equipment market with the highest-quality products available in heat transfer, motion control, and electronic components. Founded in Amherst, New York, in 1947 the company's success is a testament to the responsiveness and talents of its dynamic engineering team and highly skilled labor force.

Since 1992, Kurt Wiedenhaupt has presided as the CEO of American Precision, now headquartered on Walden Avenue in Buffalo. Through selective acquisitions and investments in research and development, revenues grew from $50 million to $120 million in a four-year period. In recognition of that achievement, *World Trade* magazine named American Precision Industries to its list of the Top 100 Fast-Growing High-Tech Manufacturers in America.

The company operates nine strategic business units in its three core technologies of heat transfer, motion control, and electronic components. As the top industrial heat transfer manufacturer in the United States and the largest supplier of heat exchangers to the compressor industry, American Precision designs, engineers, and manufactures a broad range of products used in a wide variety of thermal applications including cooling of water, oil, air, and other gases; steam condensing; vapor recovery; and refrigeration. The Heat Transfer Group is composed of the Basco, Ketema, and Air Technologies divisions.

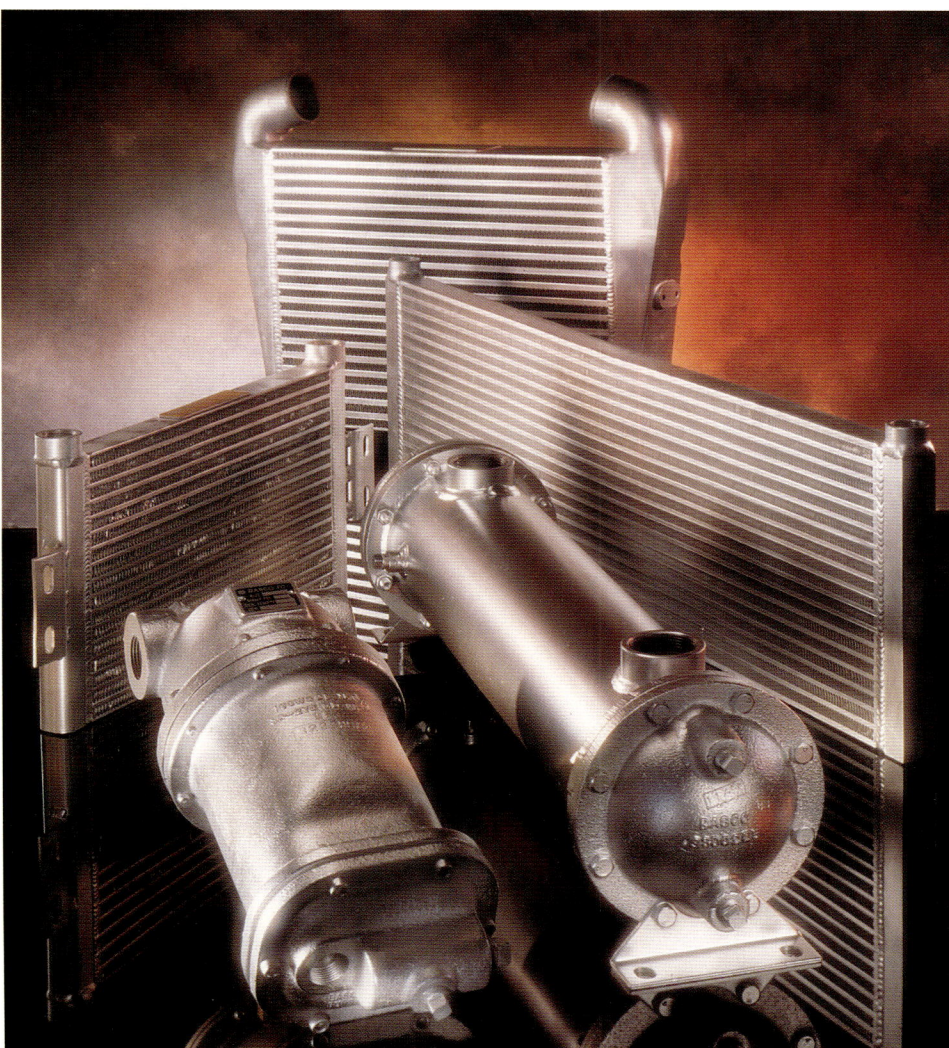

AMERICAN PRECISION INDUSTRIES

Products from the Motion Technologies Group.

The Motion Technologies Group, including Deltran, Controls, Gettys, and Harowe, produces high-end electromagnetic clutches and brakes, power amplifiers, controls and position feedback devices, in addition to stepper motors, AC synchronous motors, and high-performance DC servo motors.

The Electronic Components Group is composed of Delevan and the Surface Mount division. These divisions manufacture an extensive product line of inductors, chokes, and coils used in a variety of electronic applications including telecommunications, avionics, diagnostic medical equipment, computers, and military/defense applications.

The management team of American Precision Industries plans to aggressively expand and build upon these core technologies. The company is actively seeking acquisitions in Europe to broaden its channels to market and add complimentary product lines. Through applied research and development, acquisitions, and joint venture, American Precision is committed to be a leader well into the 21st century. ❖

Products from the Heat Transfer Group.

MOLIN AUTO PARTS

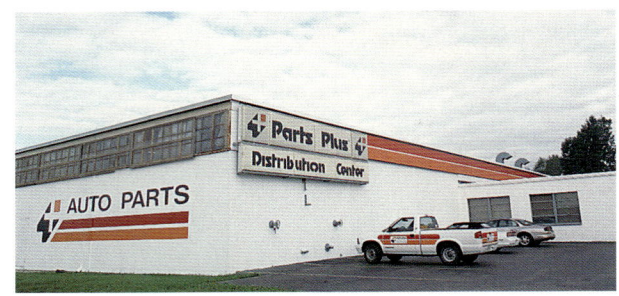

From its beginning as the Home and Auto Supply Store on Grant Street in Buffalo, Molin Auto Parts has grown into one of the largest parts distributors in upstate New York. And 75 years after its founding by Carl Molin, the company is family-owned and operated by a third generation of the Molin and Brown families.

The company's growth followed the rise of the automobile in American life, with its greatest period of expansion occurring in the 1960s and 1970s. Today, the company has warehouses in Buffalo and Syracuse and owns 18 retail outlets. In addition, it distributes parts through more than 40 independent outlets across upstate New York.

In 1976, Molin joined the Association of Automotive Aftermarket Distributors. Comprising more than 35 companies located across North America, the Association—better known to consumers and automotive professionals as Parts Plus—is now the second-largest auto parts distribution group in the United States. Through its Parts Plus affiliation, Molin is able to offer its customers many programs and benefits, including marketing assistance, training, improved product acquisition, and more.

Selling primarily to auto dealerships, garages, body shops, and other professional automotive service outlets, Molin provides its customers with fast, dependable delivery and superior customer service. The company takes particular pride in the expertise and professionalism of its more than 200 employee associates. Through extensive training, attractive incentives, and open communication throughout the organization, Molin maintains a stable and loyal work force. In turn, Molin's customers benefit from dealing with people the company truly believes are the best in the business.

One of Molin's greatest strengths is in inventory management. With more than 100 different product lines and more than 80,000 parts numbers in its warehouses, Molin has acquired the expertise to provide superior inventory management skills for other companies as well. Parts Plus nationally provides complete auto parts, and inventory management to 750 Goodyear outlets across North America. Molin supplies 29 Goodyear Service Centers in Western and Central New York State. In New York, inventory management customers include utilities such as Niagara Mohawk Power Corporation and New York State Electric and Gas. Molin's inventory management expertise also helps its wholesale customers stock and sell the right parts to meet the ever-changing demand cycles in the car and light truck markets. The company is also bringing its expertise to new market niches, including the heavy duty truck market.

As a family-owned, community-oriented business, Molin has played an important role in many local organizations, especially the United Way, the YMCA, and the American Cancer Society. In addition, the company provides significant support to local police and fire companies and volunteer groups in the communities where it does business.

Most importantly, the company enjoys an enviable reputation among area businesses as an open, reliable business partner. Many customer relationships have spanned almost the entire history of the company, with many customers who are themselves in the second or third generation of family ownership. By providing both its customers and its associates with solid working relationships built on trust and professionalism, Molin is positioned to continue growing into the 21st century. ◈

Molin provides its customers with fast, dependable delivery and superior customer service.

Founded by Carl Molin 75 years ago, Molin Auto Parts is family-owned and operated by a third generation of the Molin and Brown families.

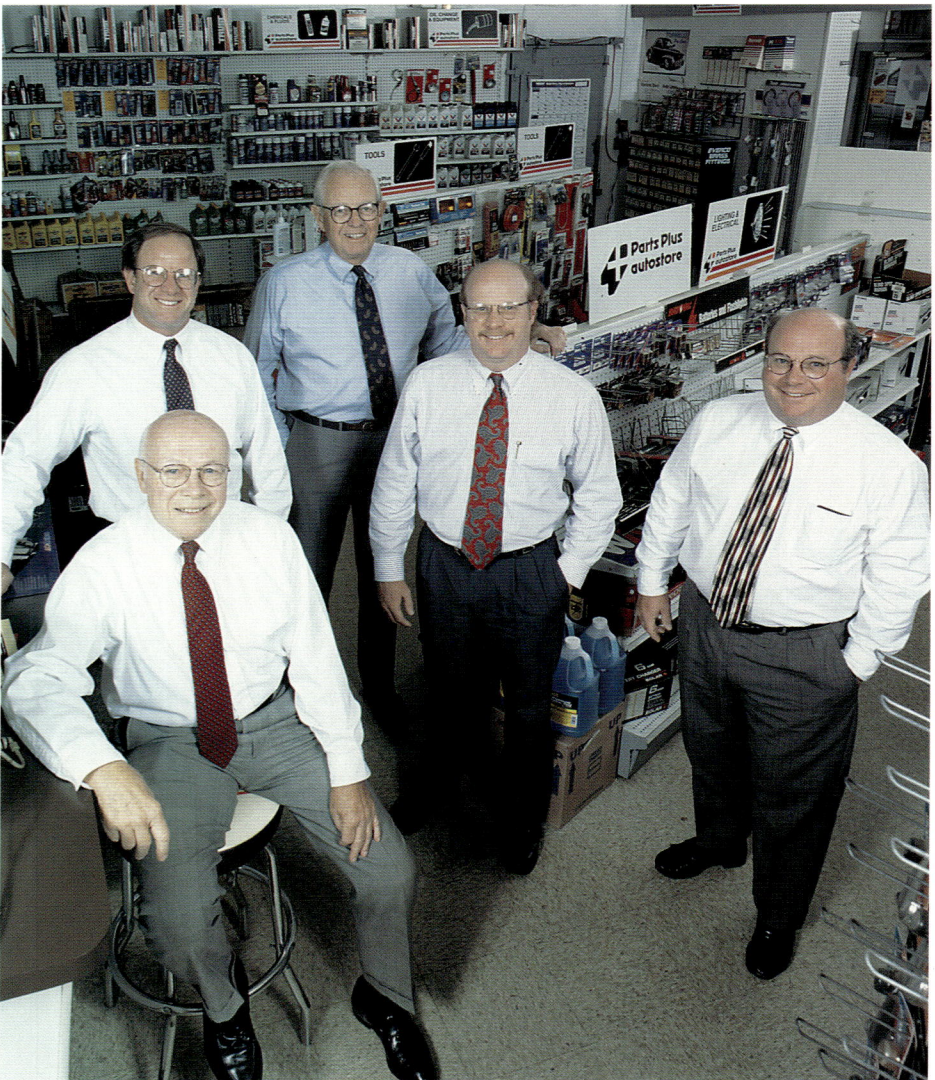

The most visible Osmose products can be found in backyards throughout the United States and Canada. From decks to gazebos to hot tub enclosures, from picnic tables to lawn chairs to landscaping timbers, from retaining walls to playground jungle gyms, lumber treated with Osmose preservatives has changed the face of American architecture and landscaping.

A leader in wood preserving since the 1930s, Osmose was one of the first to identify the tremendous potential for pressure treated lumber in the consumer market. Through promotion to architects, designers, building code officials, and innovative consumer marketing, including advertising and now a popular television show, Backyard America®, Osmose has made what was once strictly an industrial product into one of the most popular and widely used outdoor building materials in North America.

The company's Wood Preserving Division sells Osmose brand wood preservatives, treating equipment, and customized marketing services to wood preservers throughout the United States. Product innovations include SunWood® and Wood Shades™ coloring systems and WeatherShield® water repellent and stabilizer, an exciting new technology that promises to be as revolutionary as decay prevention by allowing consumers to purchase wood treated to help prevent warping, checking and cracking, as well as fungal decay. Through its Consumer Products Group, the division also offers a complete line of sprayable or brush-on clear and tinted protective coatings, and deck screws sold through retail lumberyards and paint stores.

Another significant part of Osmose is the company's Utilities Division which serves utility pole owners throughout the United States and Canada. This division has more than 300 mobile, highly trained crews working in remote locations across the continent, inspecting power and telephone poles, providing on-site decay remediation through both booster treatments or strength restoration programs, or recommending replacement where necessary. In addition to providing highly effective on-site treatment programs, the company offers sophisticated survey services that capture a wide array of information. Using advanced satellite technology such as the Global Positioning System (GPS) and high speed data transmission links, crews record and transmit data from the field to the company's Buffalo headquarters, where complete site inventories can be stored, analyzed, and reported to the utility for use in Geographic Information System (GIS) databases.

The company's Railroad Division provides on-site inspection and supplemental treatment of the continent's wooden railroad trestles and bridges. Along with repairing existing structures, Osmose offers complete engineering, design, and construction services for wood, steel and concrete railroad bridges.

Other Osmose divisions include Timber Specialties International, Ltd., organized for international timber trading, and Timber Specialties, Ltd., responsible for servicing treating plants and sales of preservatives to treated wood producers in Canada. Osmose International, staffed by the company's international experts, is responsible for sales of Osmose wood preservatives and treating plant equipment to customers throughout the world outside North America.

Growing and thriving, Osmose is an innovative manufacturer, distributor, contractor, and marketer. Privately held, a significant portion of the company is owned by its employees through an Employee Stock Ownership Plan. As Osmose continues to grow with its customers, it will seek more skilled and dedicated people on the Niagara Frontier and around the world with the vision to take wood preserving into the 21st century. ❖

OSMOSE WOOD PRESERVING, INC.

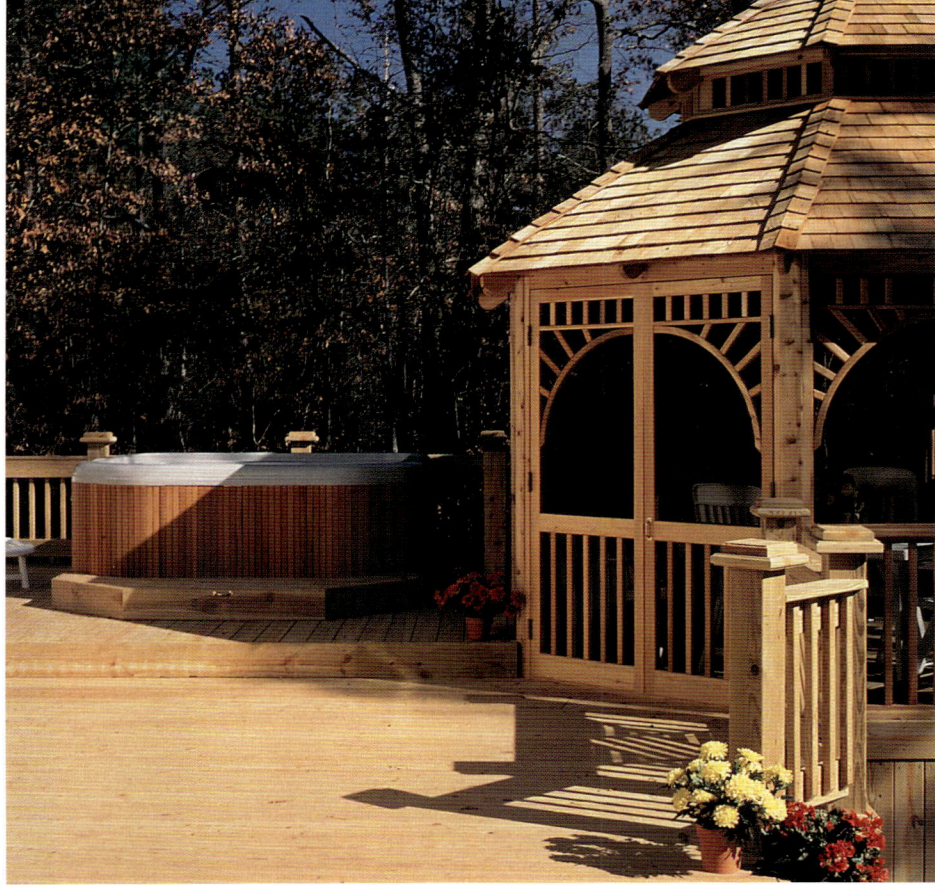

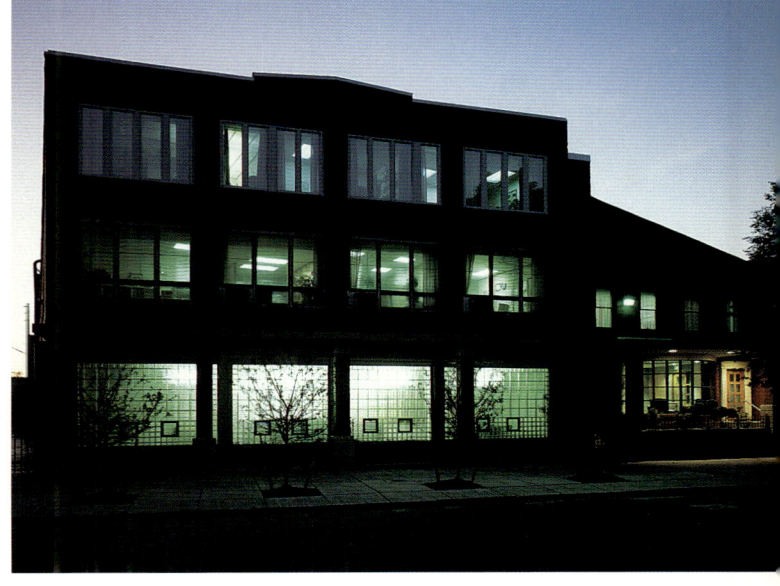

Osmose treated lumber at work in a beautiful backyard environment.

Osmose World Headquarters

GRAPHIC CONTROLS

Graphic Controls Corporation is a world leader in the design, manufacture, and distribution of products that make possible the accurate recording of vital data for medical diagnoses and industrial processes, as well as safeguarding health care professionals and patients. With international distributors and over 130 direct sales personnel, the company manufactures and markets its products worldwide, employing nearly 2,000 people.

Started in 1940 as a company that made charts for recording instruments, Graphic Controls has evolved into a major medical products manufacturer, having successfully adapted to changing societal needs via strategic acquisitions of additional health care product lines and companies.

Graphic Controls is a world leader in the design, manufacture, and distribution of products that make possible the accurate recording of vital data for medical diagnosis.

Some 650 employees work in Buffalo, site of the company's corporate headquarters. Its headquarter's facility houses corporate product development, finance, systems, logistics, marketing, sales, customer service, warehousing, and chart manufacturing.

Graphic Controls products are used throughout the hospital, as well as in ambulatory and alternate care settings. Its MEDI-TRACE® product line includes cardiology and neurology products such as diagnostic and monitoring electrodes, ECG and EEG recording charts, cables and leadwires, diagnostic imaging media, and telemetry kits. Its LIFE-TRACE® obstetrical

products include the new SOFTRANS™ Intrauterine Pressure Catheter Monitoring System, used to monitor contraction frequency, duration, intensity, and resting tone within the mother's uterus during labor. The system is revolutionary for its easy use and minimal patient disturbance features. Other LIFETRACE® products include fetal spiral electrodes, fetal recording charts, abdominal belts and straps, and disposable leg plates.

In 1996, Graphic Controls acquired Devon Industries, Inc., a California company that makes disposable medical products, in a move that broadened the company's product line. Devon products are used during surgery and to control infection. They include sharps collection and disposal systems, containers designed to hold used needles and syringes and other sharps that are used in the health care environment. Devon's major product lines also include needle blade counting and collection systems, sterile light handle systems, instrument protection systems, patient positioning products and safety straps, chemotherapy waste collection containers, and surgical kits.

In addition to Buffalo, New York; Rock Hill, South Carolina; and Chatsworth, California, Graphic Controls has manufacturing locations in Cherry Hill, New Jersey, where disposable medical devices and other products are produced. The facility includes a controlled medical manufacturing area and a chemical laboratory for development and testing. The Methuen, Massachusetts plant is responsible for electrode product development and equipment design, in addition to manufacturing a complete line of disposable monitoring and diagnostic electrodes used for EKG and EEG. Tronomed, a subsidiary headquartered in San Juan Capistrano, California, is a leading domestic and international supplier of custom-design interconnect systems for the medical marketplace.

Graphic Controls' international plants are in Canada (ECG fetal electrodes, fetal belts and straps, monitoring electrodes, medical mounts and EEG charts, and video printer film), and Spain (roll and circular charts and accessories, and fax and wax-coated rolls, electrodes, cables, bulbs, batteries, gels, and accessories for EEG and ECG).

Graphic Controls continues expansion in the medical products line, with company officials aiming for 15 percent annual growth. By the beginning of the 21st century, Graphic Controls is projected to be a $500 million company.

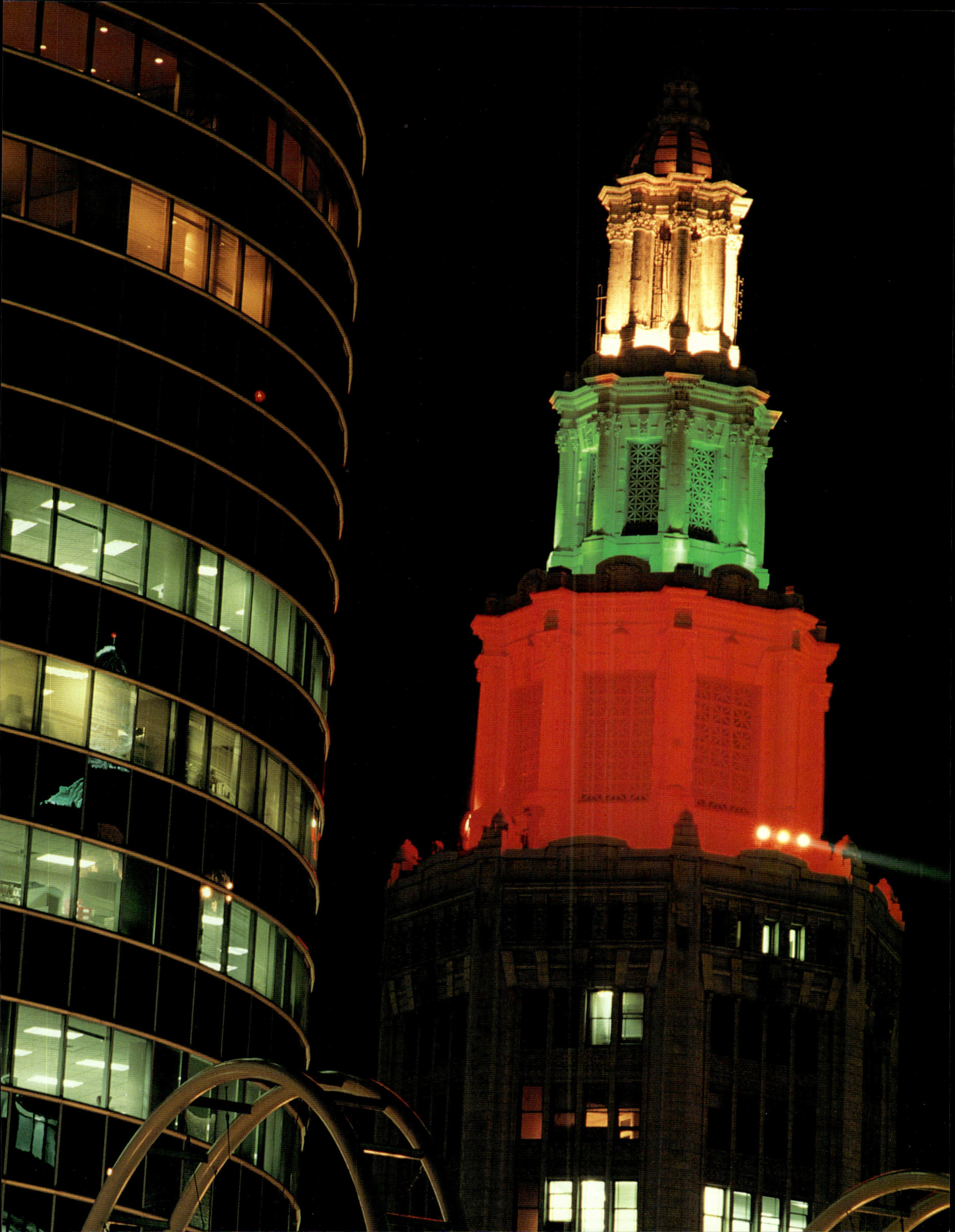

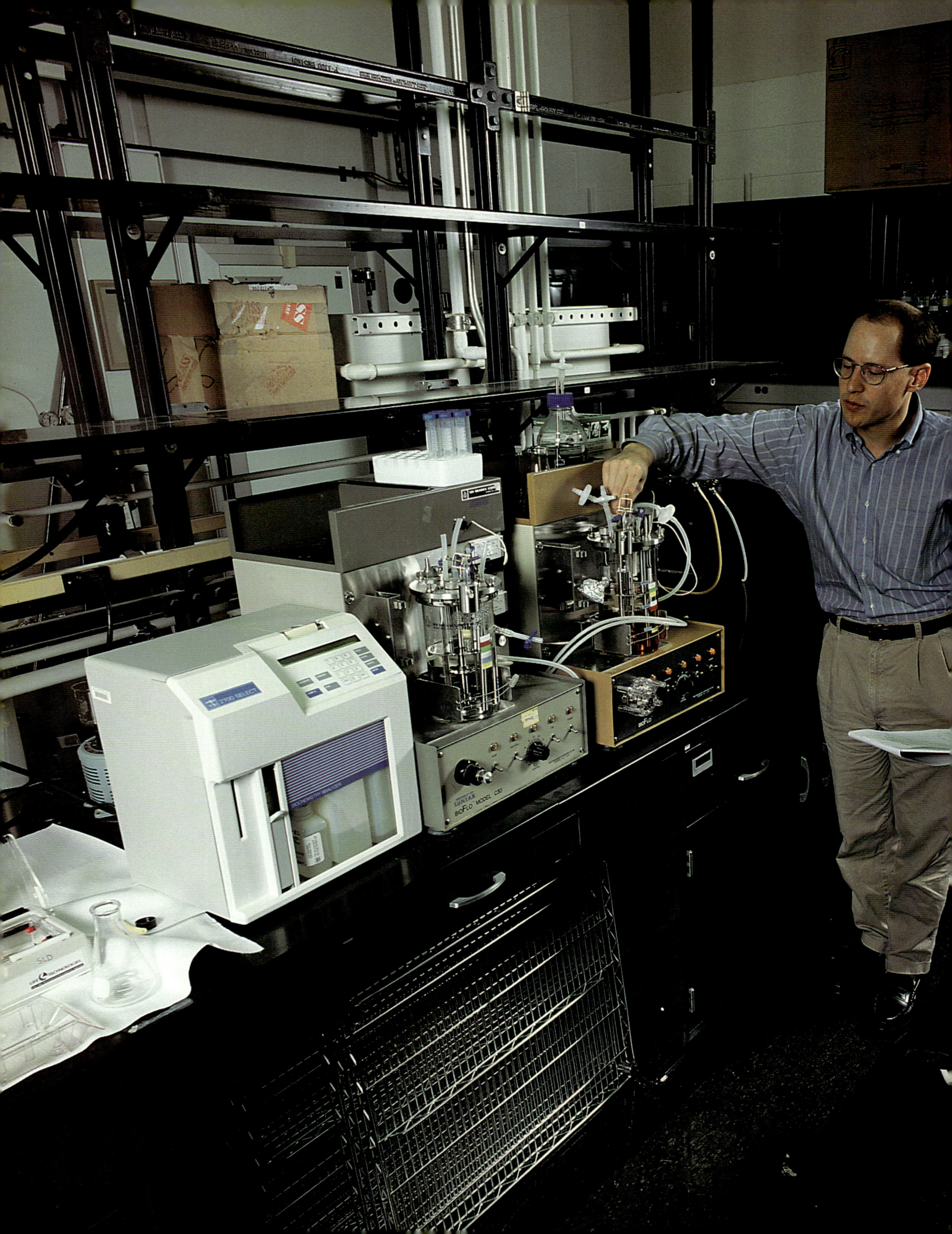

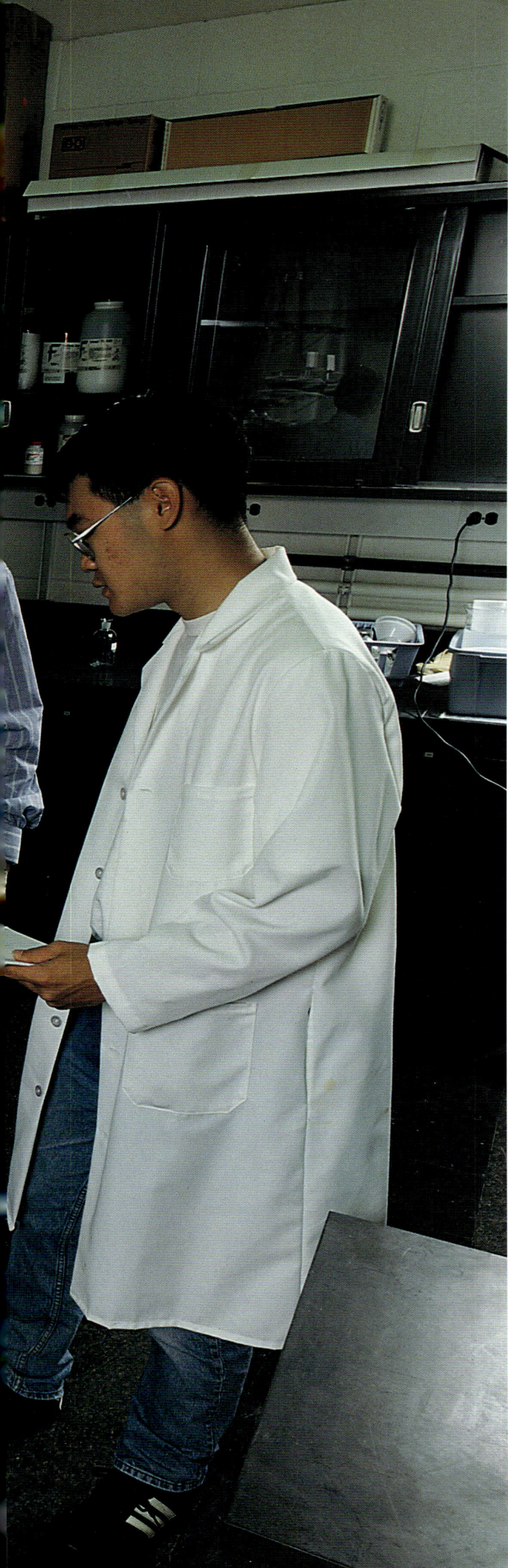

HIGH TECH

Photo by James P. McCoy.

SERVOTRONICS, INC.

From advanced medical devices to supersonic aircraft to the NASA space telescope, the innovative products of Servotronics, Inc. have played a vital role in some of the most important achievements of the age of technology. And just as the company has operated on the frontiers of high technology throughout its history, today it is poised for new milestones in the 21st century.

Servotronics was founded in 1959 by Dr. Nicholas D. Trbovich, Sr., who continues to guide the company as president, chairman, and CEO. Holder of more than 20 U.S. and foreign patents in electromagnetic technology, fluid power, and consumer products, Dr. Trbovich has been the driving force behind the company's ascent to the top rank of high-technology companies.

Convinced there was a better way to design and manufacture electromagnetic actuators, the then 24-year-old Trbovich put together a business plan that included innovative product designs, attracting private investors. Only four years later, in 1963, the growing technology company offered shares for sale, becoming a public corporation that is currently listed on the American Stock Exchange. This combination of strong business and engineering skills—Trbovich holds both an M.B.A. and a doctorate from the University of Rochester—has been a hallmark of the company's operation throughout its history.

Servotronics pioneered the application of single-stage servocontrols and proportional solenoids for high-temperature, high-radiation environments. One of the firm's early major advances was the development of a new electromechanical actuator that could operate continuously at 1,200 degrees

Fahrenheit in a nuclear radiation environment. The device garnered the first of many awards for excellence and helped establish the company as a leading-edge competitor in high technology.

Today, Servotronics is known for its design, development, and manufacture of high-quality components, systems, and subsystems for use wherever precise control, reliability, and cost containment are required. The company's product line includes servocontrol valves, torque motors, actuators, check valves, pressure regulators, metallic seals, and a wide range of additional products for applications in space flight, military and commercial aircraft, ground vehicles, test equipment—wherever state-of-the-art precision controls are required.

Servotronics products are found on some of the world's most sophisticated and technologically advanced devices. For example, the Hubbell Space Telescope, which can probe the far reaches of the universe, used an electromagnetic actuator manufactured by Servotronics that helped to calibrate the 12.5-ton telescope after it reached orbit. A Servotronics pneumatic valve in the thrust reverse system provides deceleration during landing for the world's only supersonic commercial transport, the Concorde. Other commercial aircraft depending on Servotronics components includes business aircraft such as the Cessna Citation 3, the Gulfstream 3 and Lear Jet, and commercial jetliners, including the Airbus, the McDonnell Douglas DC-10, and the Boeing 747, 757, 767, and 777.

Servotronics has also played a major role in the U.S. defense program, where its devices perform critical functions on many weapons systems. Since 1966, a Servotronics component has been used on the U.S. Navy's Standard Missile series, one of the world's most reliable tactical air defense missiles. The company also manufactures the coil assembly for the laser-guided Maverick missile.

The company's products are also found on a wide variety of high-performance military aircraft, including the F-18, F-14, F-15, and F-16 fighters and the B-1B bomber. Many military helicopters also use Servotronics valves, and the company's pneumatic servovalves are incorporated in the General

(bottom right) Dr. Nicholas D. Trbovich, CEO, Founder, Chairman and President.

A world class company.

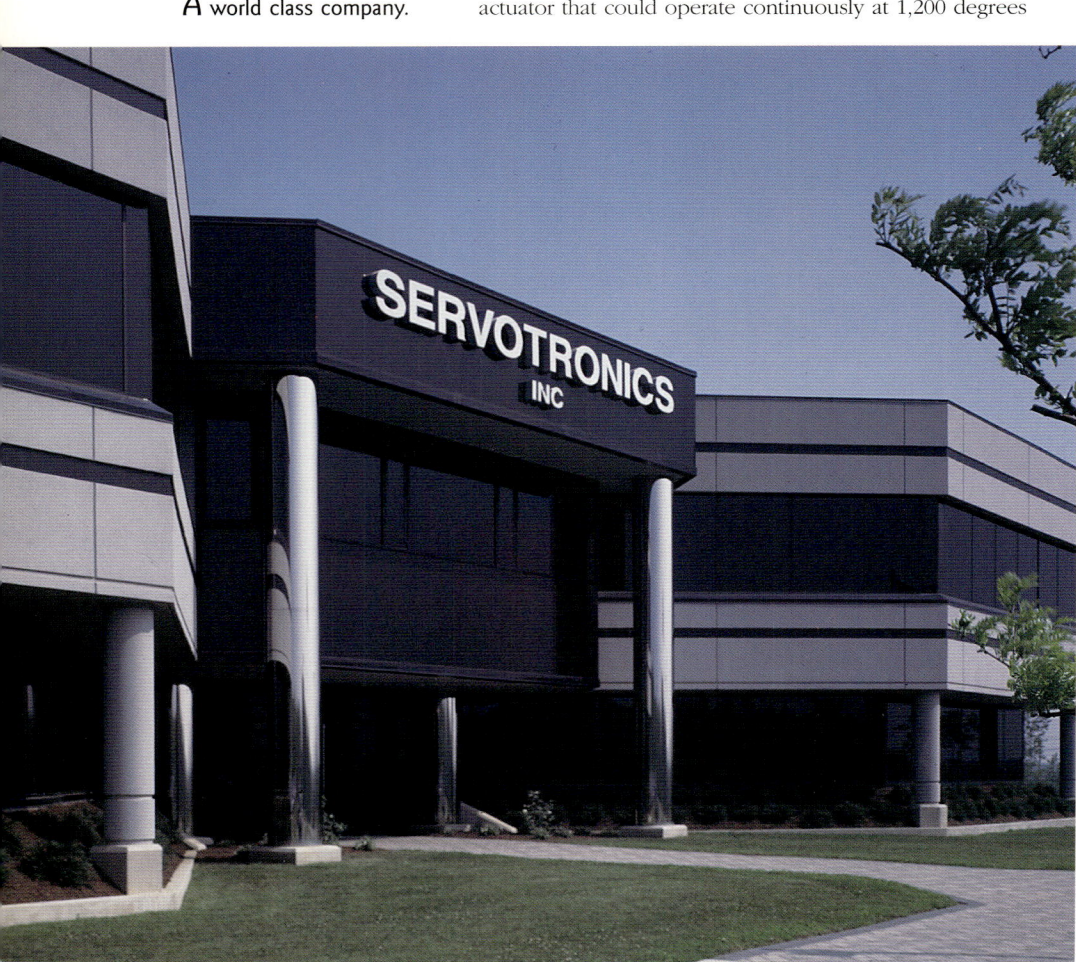

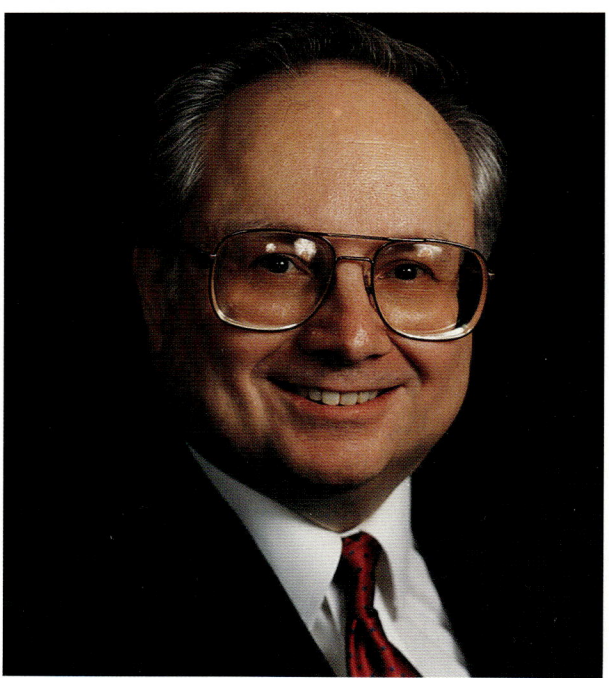

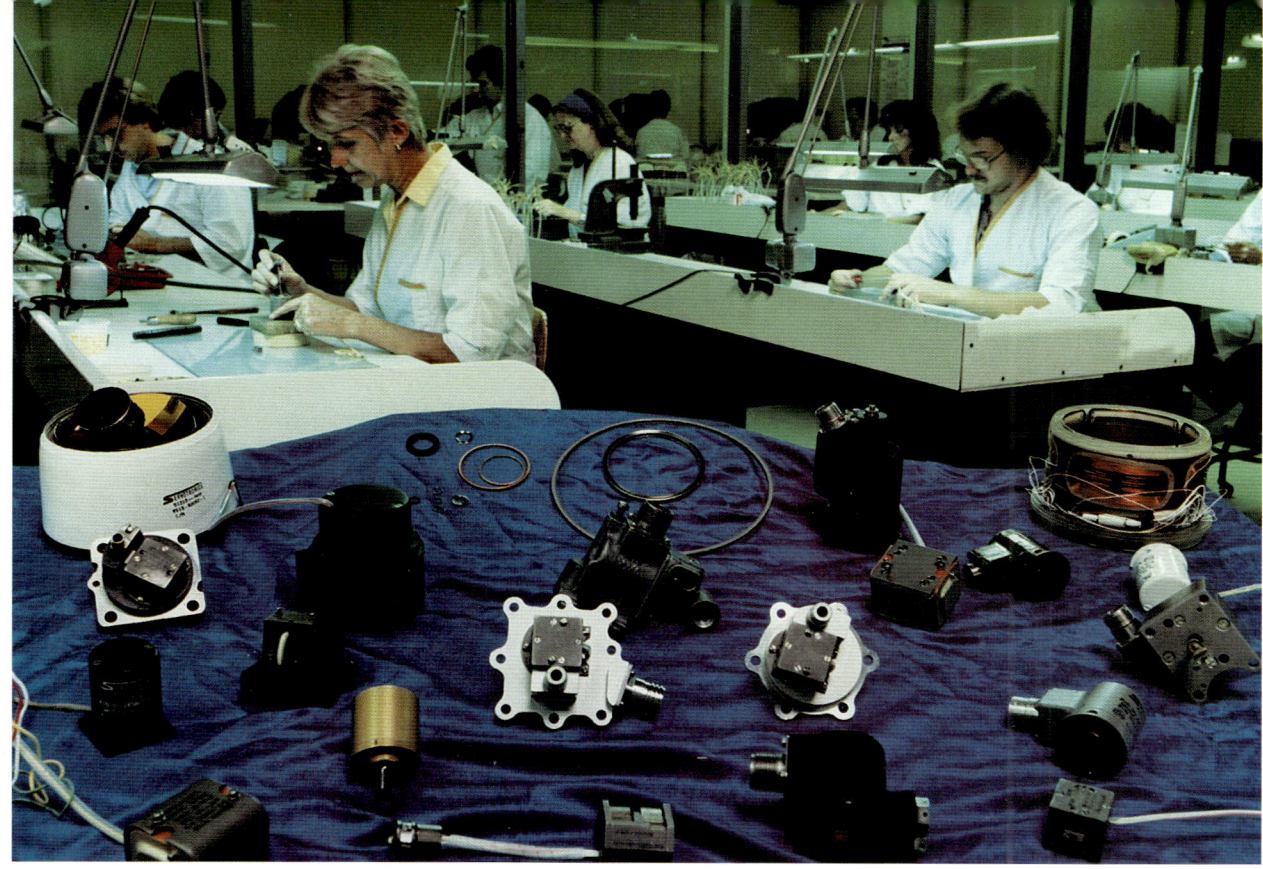

Various Servotronics' advanced technology products.

Electric rapid-fire Gatling gun drive. Servotronics technology has also played a key role in the development of the turbine drive systems for the U.S. Navy's sophisticated "super-silent" torpedoes.

To maintain the stringent quality standards required by its demanding customer base, Servotronics has continuously upgraded its resources, from computer-aided design to numerically controlled machining centers to fully equipped "white rooms." As a tribute to its success, the company has received many awards in a wide variety of quality categories, including technical excellence, supplier of the month and supplier of the year, 100 percent delivery and quality, key supplier and certified supplier, and many more.

The company has also adapted successfully to changing markets. As defense spending has declined, Servotronics has broadened its product line and customer base, applying its leading-edge technology and expertise to develop products with many commercial applications. At the same time, the company has maintained its competitive edge as many of its customers have significantly reduced the number of their approved suppliers. Servotronics continues to be a preferred vendor for many of the world's leading technology companies, and it will continue to aggressively expand its facilities, equipment, and capabilities to meet the growing demands of being a successful high-technology company in the 21st century.

As part of its strategic expansion, Servotronics moved into a new 82,000-square-foot facility in 1994. After a nationwide search, the company once again chose to locate its business in the Niagara region. Throughout its history, the company's strong belief in the advantages of the region has been rewarded over and over again. Among the many advantages the company has found is its highly skilled and dedicated work force. An employee-oriented company, Servotronics has enjoyed excellent relations with its work force and has made its employees part owners of the company through an Employee Stock Ownership Plan.

For the future, Servotronics will continue to look for opportunities worldwide. The company currently has customers in Europe and Asia, including Japan, and is aggressively seeking to expand its overseas business. The company is also engaged in a record number of programs and has expanded its capabilities to produce a substantially wider range of products, forming a solid base for future growth and expansion. Offering a unique synergy of engineering expertise and production capabilities, Servotronics is positioned to remain on the leading edge for years to come. ❖

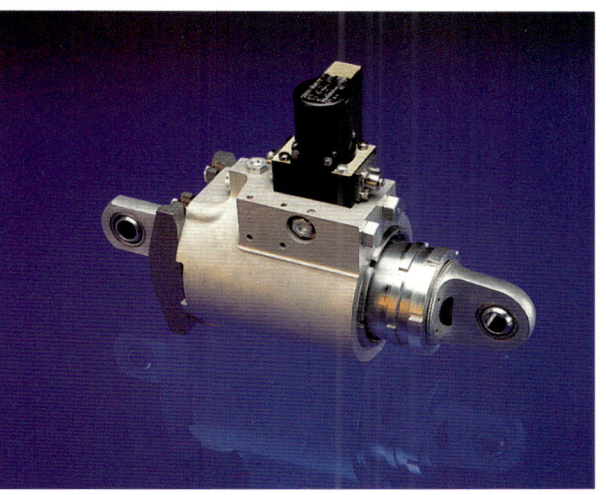

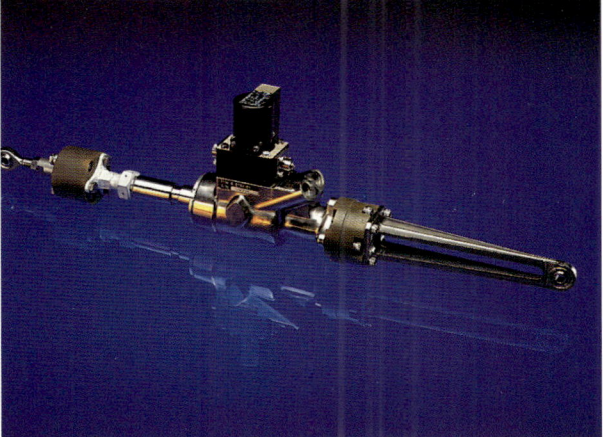

Steering control actuators and servovalves for satellite launch vehicles.

MOOG INC.

In 1951, William C. Moog founded the company that still bears his name on an idea good enough to propel the business into the 21st century. The inventor of the electrohydraulic servovalve, a control device originally used in guided missile systems, had a vision that has exceeded anyone's dreams. Today, Moog, still headquartered in East Aurora, New York, employs some 3,500 people worldwide, manufacturing precision control components and systems for a wide variety of aerospace and industrial customers.

Moog continues to meet the challenges of an evolving global marketplace, applying leading-edge technology to the solution of motion control problems in all the industries requiring precision performance.

Moog's broad array of products includes flight controls for military and commercial aircraft, attitude controls for satellites, and precision controls for high performance industrial machinery. Moog's fly-by-wire flight control actuators are part of most modern military aircraft. And, in the commercial

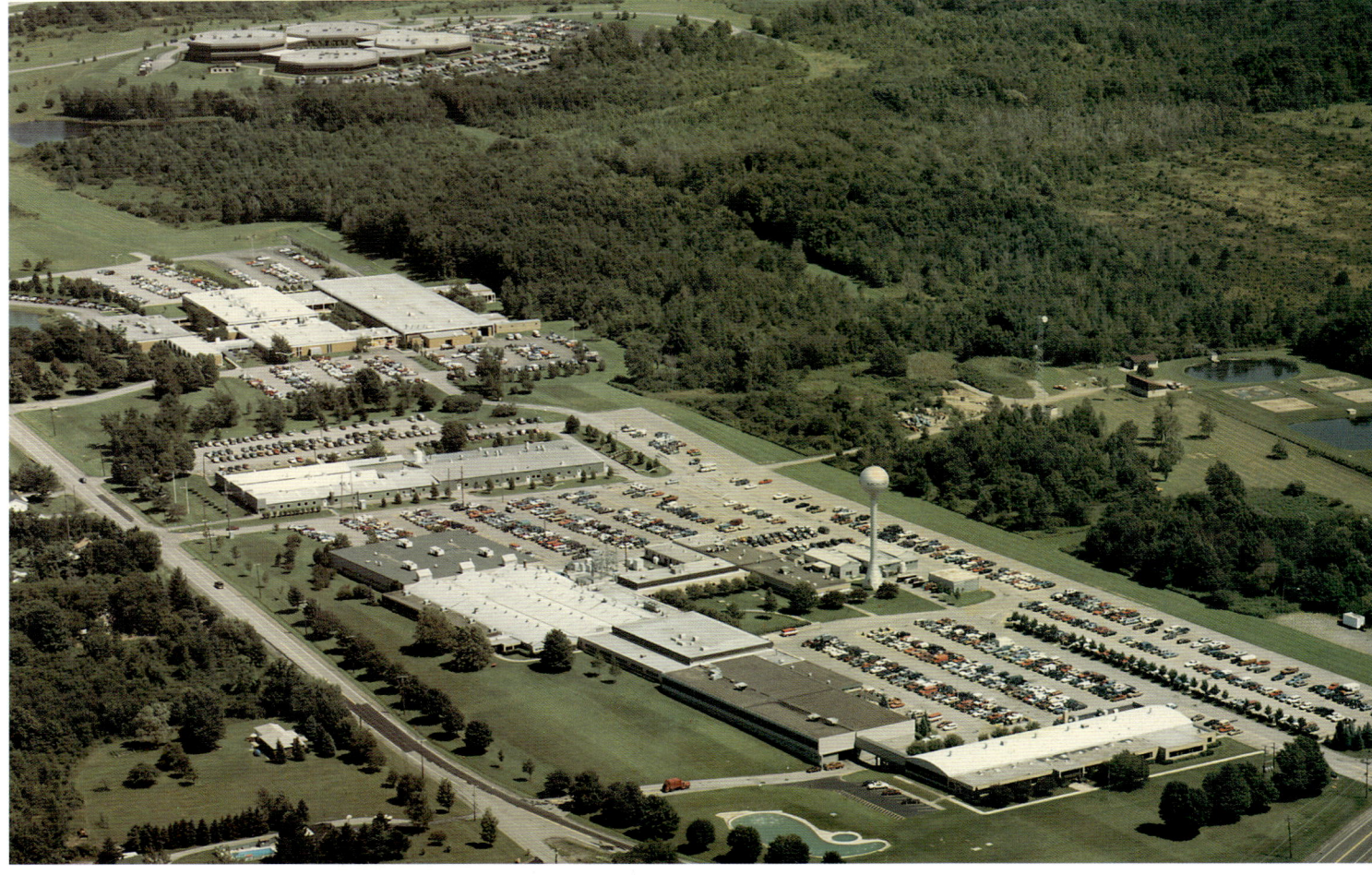

In 1951, Moog began its operations in an abandoned aircraft hangar. Today, Moog has its facilities in 20 countries spanning the globe. Its largest campus is in Elma, New York.

Over half of Moog's business comes from commercial and military aircraft markets in the United States and overseas. Its flight control systems are considered by pilots to be the "eighth wonder of the world".

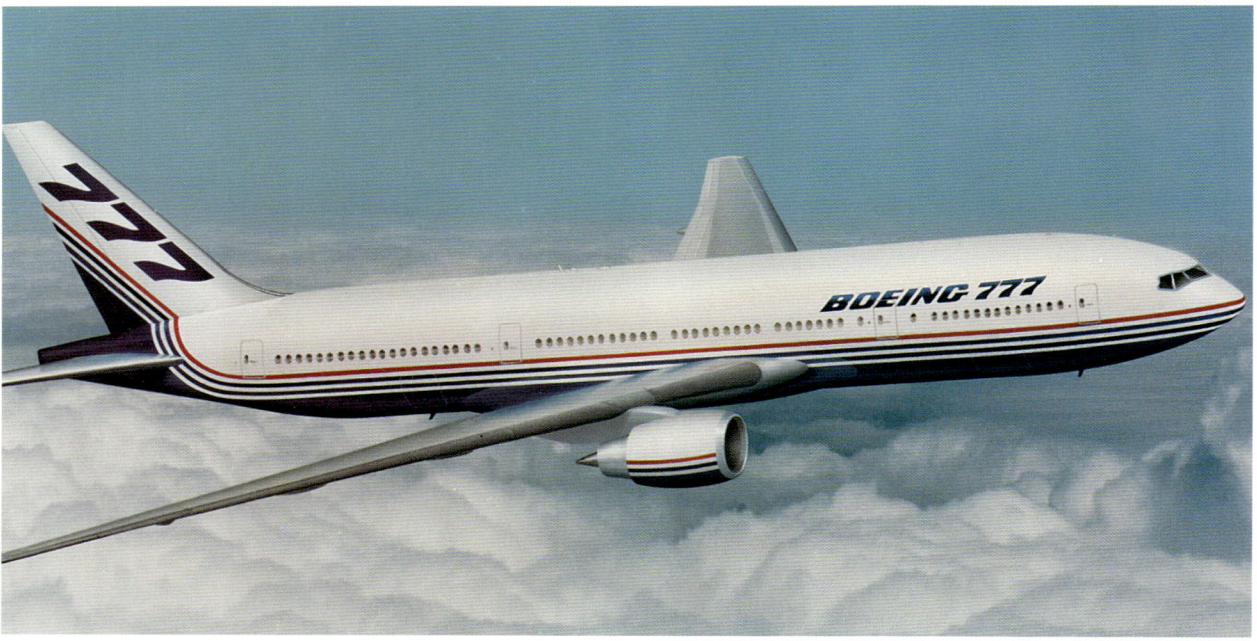

aircraft market, Moog is Boeing's number one flight control actuator supplier. Moog's contribution to the missiles and space programs include four decades of work on components and systems for the Titan family of launch vehicles as well as participation on nearly every satellite launched today. In the industrial machinery arena, highly automated steel mills throughout the world use Moog servovalves to control the steel's final form. In addition, Moog's brushless D.C. electric drives power ISI's shuttle and gantry robots in the world's most advanced automotive manufacturing centers. This is one of hundreds of applications that include carpet tufting, robotics, mining machines, and entertainment platforms.

Moog has a proud history of providing advanced technology to defense agencies in the United States and around the world. In the late 1980s and early 1990s, defense industry cutbacks necessitated a serious downsizing at Moog, but the company has rebounded nicely. Currently, industrial and commercial customers provide nearly 60 percent of revenues.

Moog is proud of its inclusion among the elite in the book, *The 100 Best Companies to Work For in America*. The listing is largely attributable to a workplace atmosphere of evident "mutual trust and respect," a legacy of the founder's philosophy. The visionary Mr. Moog was also ahead of his time in employee empowerment. He provided his employees an opportunity to participate in the management of their activities 30 years before it became fashionable. To this day there are no time clocks at Moog, and quality control is self-monitored by individual workers who inspect their own work and mark each product with their own personal stamp. The emphasis is on individual responsibility within a supportive, stimulating environment. Motivation thus becomes a natural by-product.

In the words of Moog Chairman and CEO, Robert T. Brady, himself a 30 year employee, "We build products that launch astronauts into space. . . .It's very reassuring for them and for me to know that these products are built by people who feel personally responsible for everything made at Moog." ⋈

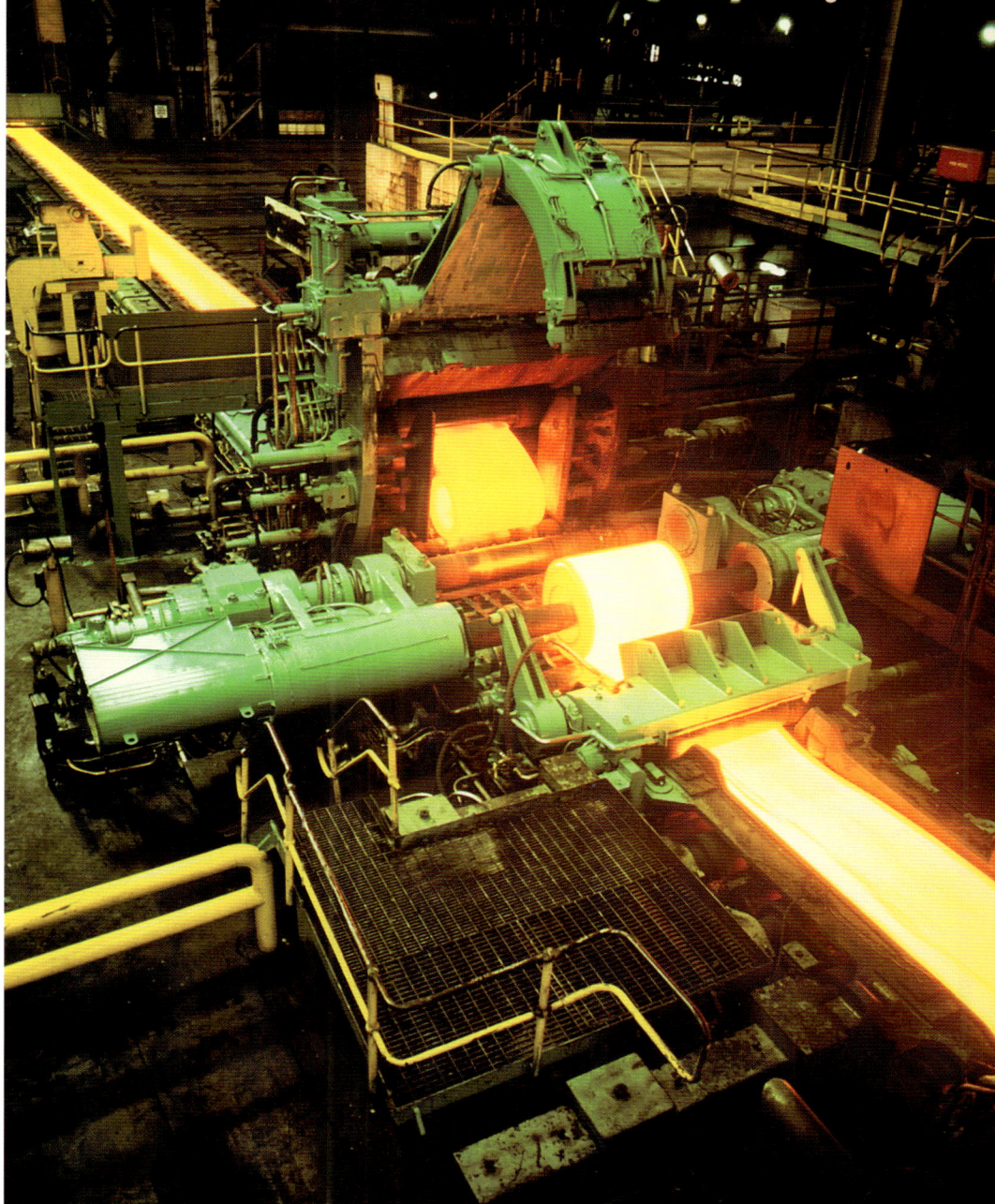

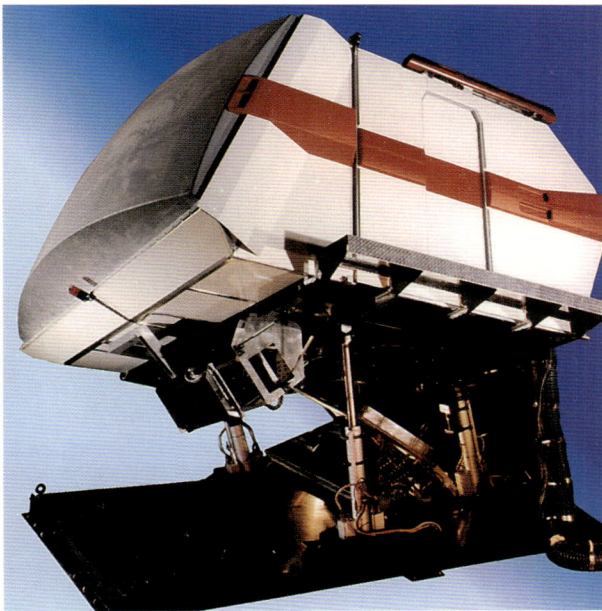

Moog's all electric entertainment motion simulator platforms set the performance standards in this rapidly growing industry.

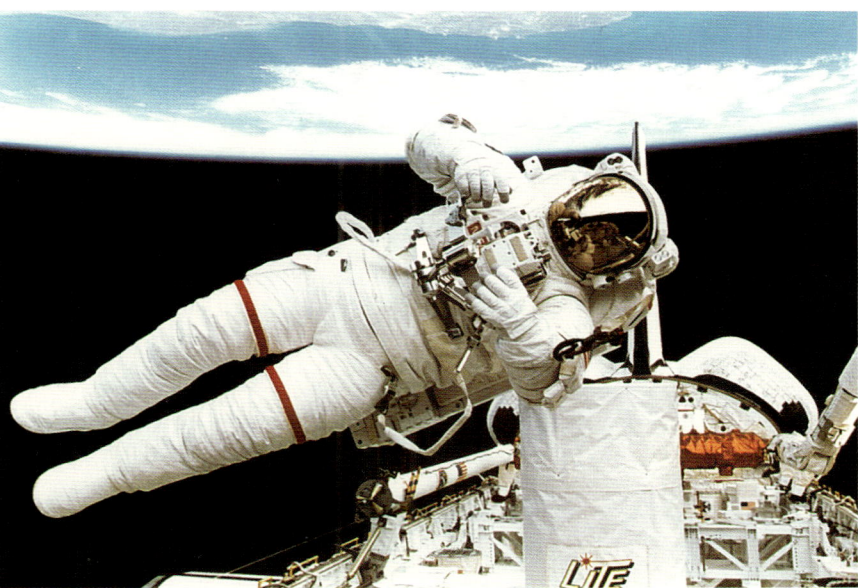

(top) In 1959, Moog adapted the aerospace servovalve for use in high performance industrial machinery. Today, Moog's technology is used on such diverse equipment as steel rolling mills and entertainment motion simulators.

Twenty-four of Moog's miniature cold gas thrusters provide U.S. astronauts with the control capability to perform self-rescues while wearing the SAFER self-propelled space life jacket.

SIERRA TECHNOLOGIES

Somewhere around the world cargo aircraft fly in close formation in zero visibility conditions, linked only by a unique technology called Stationkeeping Equipment (or SKE). SKE is developed and manufactured by the Sierra Research Division of Sierra Technologies. The system not only makes formation flying possible in adverse weather, but also permits communication of essential flight command information without voice transmissions. This provides military transports with an extra measure of security during hazardous missions over hostile territory.

Sierra Technologies, the world's only supplier of SKE airborne systems, is a global leader in the design, integration, and manufacture of a wide variety of sophisticated electronic products and systems for military and civilian customers. Founded in 1957 by a group of entrepreneurial engineers, Sierra continues that innovative tradition by adapting existing technologies to new markets while continuously developing new ideas, products, and services.

In addition to its Stationkeeping Equipment, Sierra is an acknowledged leader in Electronic Warfare Simulators and Radar, Flight Inspection Systems, Aircraft Systems Integration and Data Link Technology. This data link technology offers a variety of data communication products used both for communicating essential data between ships and aircraft as well as for shipboard data communications.

In Electronic Warfare (EW) Sierra is a leading supplier of simulated enemy air defense systems. Developed to meet the

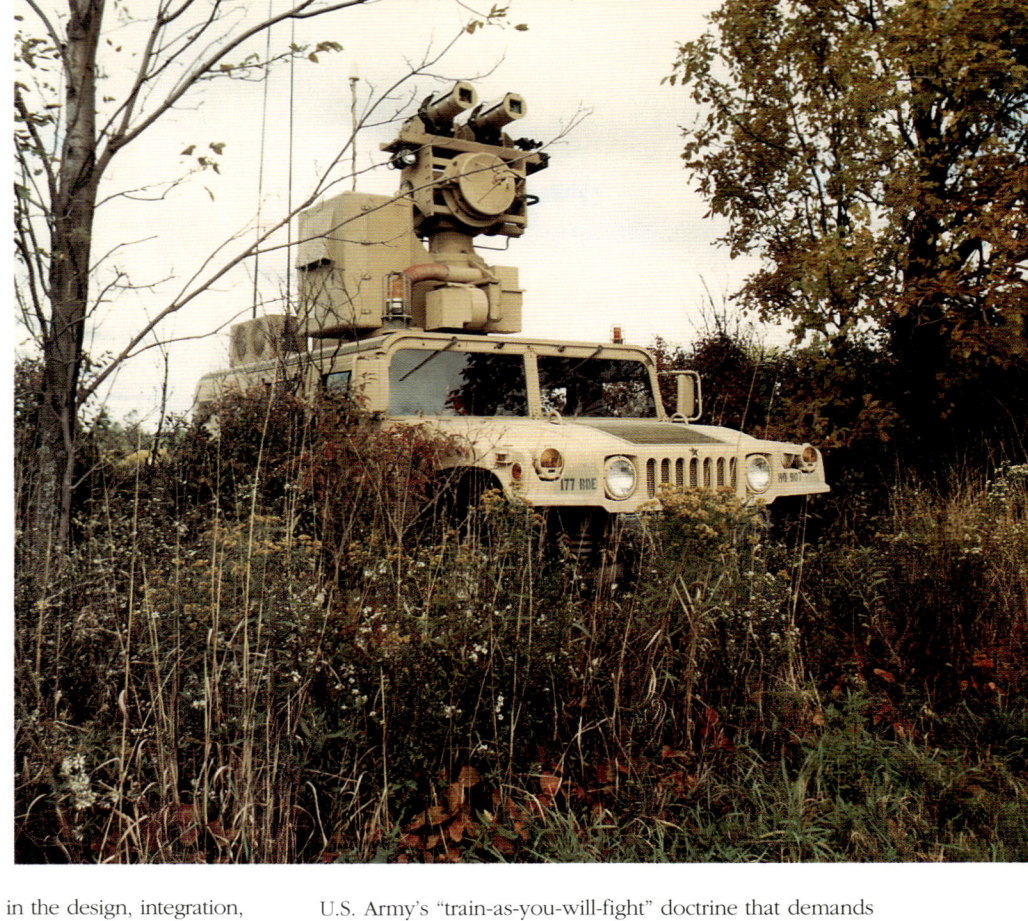

Deployment of U.S. Army Aircraft Survivability Equipment Trainer (ASET IV) system.

Integration of flight inspection systems in worldwide aircraft at Sierra's hanger facility.

U.S. Army's "train-as-you-will-fight" doctrine that demands highly accurate threat representation, training realism, and tactical mobility, Sierra's Aircraft Survivability Equipment Trainer (ASET) IV is used to train U.S. Army helicopter pilots for true battlefield conditions. Other EW systems include the Unmanned Threat Emitter (UMTE), used in training U.S. Air Force fighter pilots, and the Mobile Threat Emitter Systems (MoTES), used to keep Air National Guard fliers at peak combat readiness. Sierra is one of only a handful of companies worldwide offering EW training systems that incorporate both mobile and interactive features.

In Flight Inspection Systems Sierra is the world leader with systems installed on more than 31 major aircraft types used by 40 countries. More than 85 percent of all Flight Inspection Systems worldwide have been built, installed, and maintained by Sierra Technologies. These sophisticated systems analyze

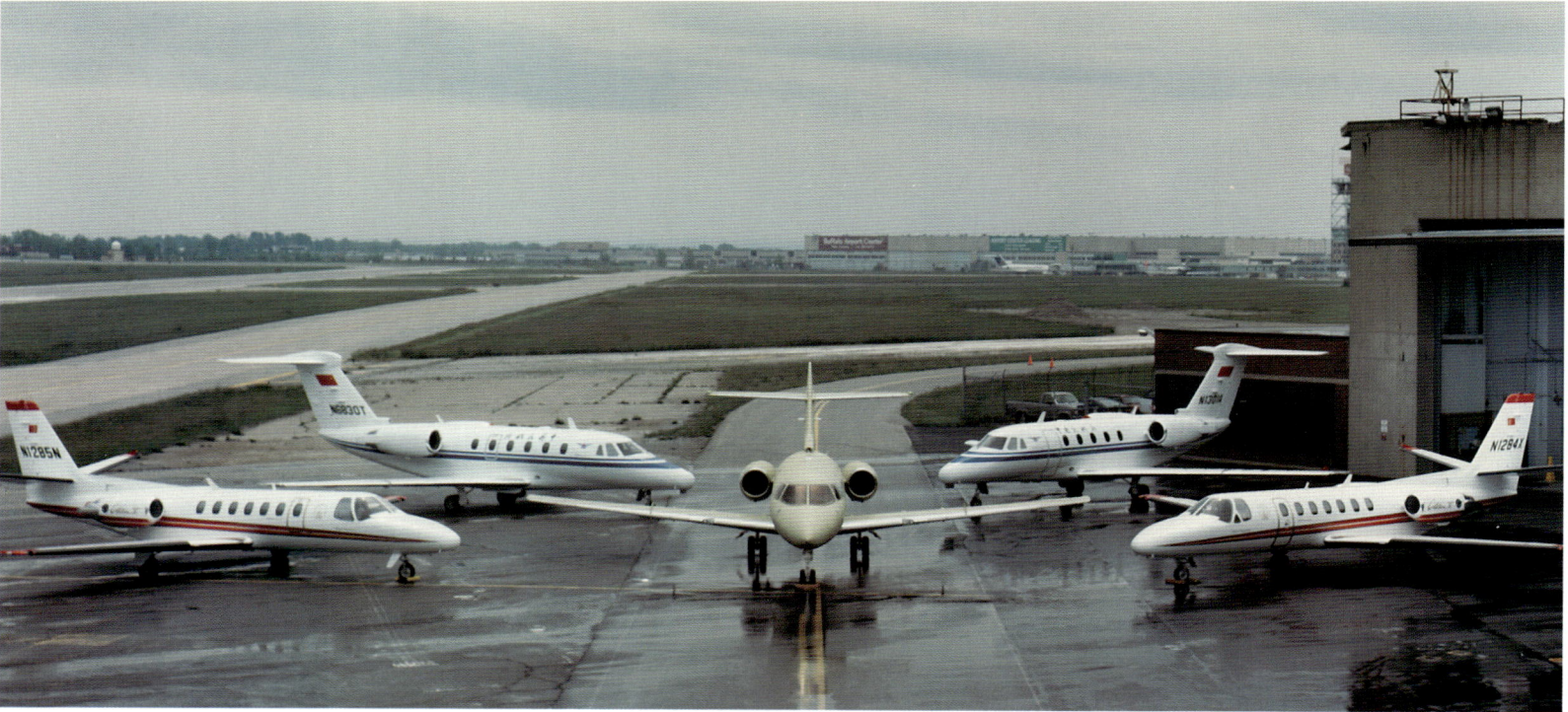

the accuracy and performance of land-based air navigation aids and airport instrument landing facilities, critical components of flight safety for commercial passenger and cargo aircraft. Sierra has recorded a number of firsts in Flight Inspection Systems, including being the first manufacturer to have six aircraft in its facility simultaneously for system updating and integration.

Aircraft Systems Integration is another area where Sierra offers a leadership role. Drawing on a wide range of engineering, manufacturing, and system integration disciplines, Sierra upgrades existing aircraft avionics with new digital equipment and structural modifications. Sierra is the only manufacturer in the world to have successfully upgraded F-5 fighter aircraft with F-16 avionics, including the F-16 Heads-Up Display, transforming the F-5 into a trainer for pilots prior to flying the F-16. This upgrade to the F-5 aircraft was accomplished for the Royal Norwegian Air Force. Additional upgrades have been completed for the U.S. Air Force and NASA T-38 aircraft. Sierra has also developed and delivered several aircraft systems designed for special missions.

Sierra's expertise in communication technology is significant. Data communication systems, such as the LAMPS MK III (better known as the Hawk Link), provide secure full duplex communications between U.S. Navy warships and the Navy's Seahawk helicopters. Wireless data communication using sophisticated spread spectrum technology is finding increased use as the company discovers new and exciting civilian and commercial applications.

In fact, examples of Sierra's technological innovation can be found locally in emergency road service vehicles. The Digital Dispatch System designed for the American Automobile Association delivers a number of benefits for any fleet management application, including enhanced safety, efficiency of operation and faster response time. The system has the capability to use the Global Positioning System—another U.S. Department of Defense technology now providing benefits for civilian markets—for computer-aided dispatching and automatic real-time vehicle location. Vehicle positions are continuously monitored and can be displayed on-screen at dispatch headquarters using the system's computer mapping capabilities. The system allows new information and instructions to be transmitted to vehicles already dispatched, saving time and, in the case of rescue vehicles, providing a critical margin of safety.

Identifying opportunities such as these and using the company's leadership in electronics and engineering is key to providing quality products and services to a multitude of customers. In addition to research and development supporting this objective, the company is a full-service electronics manufacturer with a reputation for superior testing and quality control. Sierra is ISO 9001 certified. Capabilities include printed wiring assemblies and subassemblies, backplanes, cables and harnesses. An in-house metalworking shop provides a wide array of fabrication capabilities. Extensive computer-aided engineering, software laboratories and testing resources are also available.

Located adjacent to Buffalo International Airport, Sierra offers 400,000 square feet of manufacturing, research, testing and systems integration space. Aircraft can taxi directly into

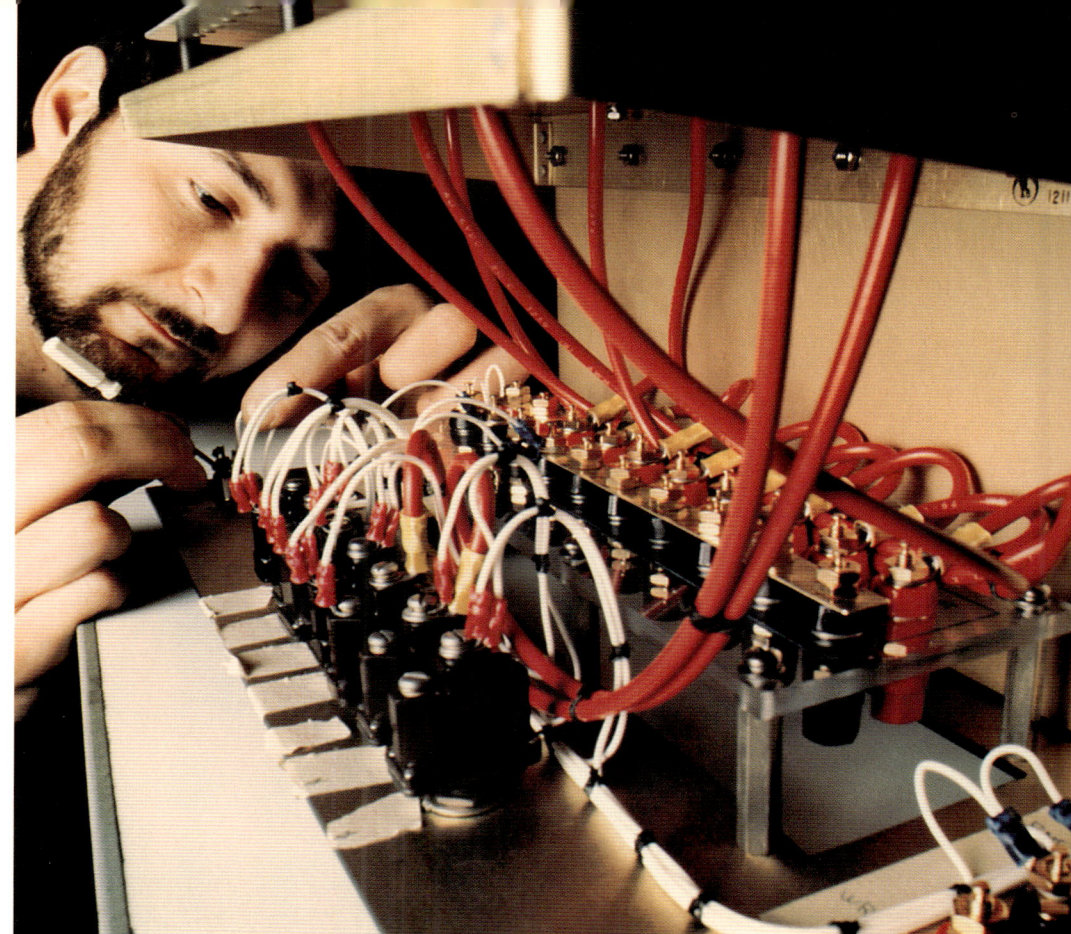

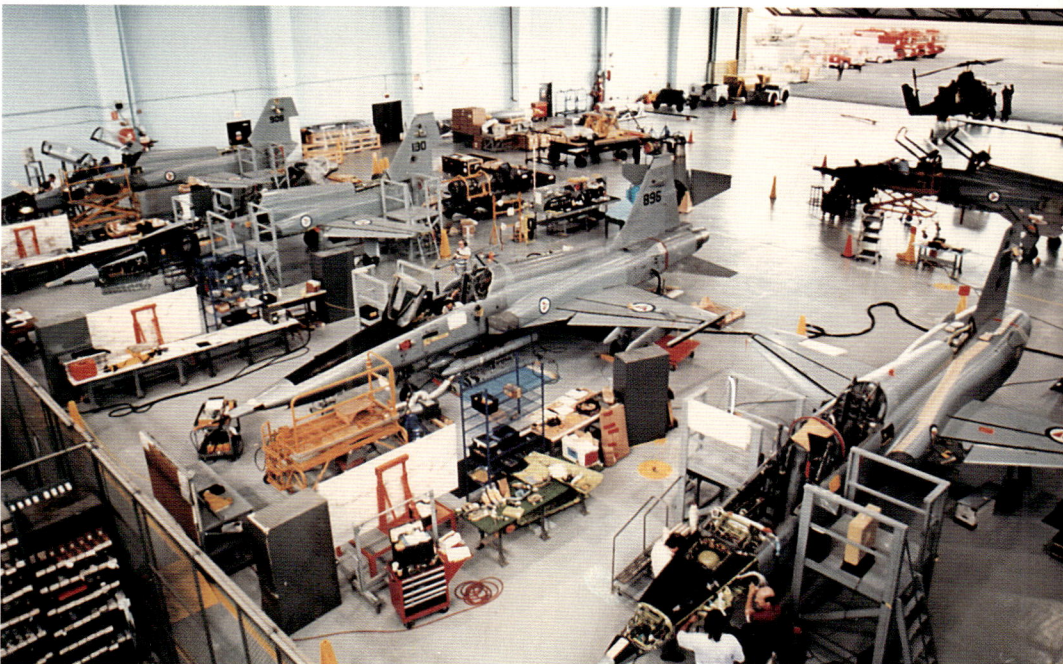

hangars equipped with integration and test labs for hot bench testing and equipment staging. The hangar is also equipped to perform structural modifications and repairs and is an FAA certified repair station for avionics system repair, installation and integration. The facility also offers environmental testing to both military and commercial specifications, including temperature, altitude, humidity, shock and vibration testing.

Sierra maintains the entrepreneurial spirit of its founders, encouraging innovation and experimentation in the pursuit of new technologies and new applications that meet the needs of the marketplace. Building on its record of engineering excellence and expertise, Sierra will continue to be a leader in developing efficient, cost-effective technology solutions for customers around the world. Sierra is proud to be part of the Niagara Frontier region. ✿

(top) Complex electronic manufacturing.

F-5 aircraft undergoing integration of digital avionics in Sierra's integration facility.

CALSPAN SRL CORPORATION

For more than 50 years, Calspan SRL Corporation has been attracting the best and brightest researchers from across the United States and around the world. Drawn by the company's advanced research projects, unsurpassed facilities, and international reputation for excellence, Calspan scientists, engineers, and designers have made ground-breaking advances in aerospace, transportation, human systems technology, information systems and electronic warfare, chemical defense and demilitarization, specialty sciences and products, and more.

(top) Vista Aircraft
(bottom) Transconic Wind Tunnel

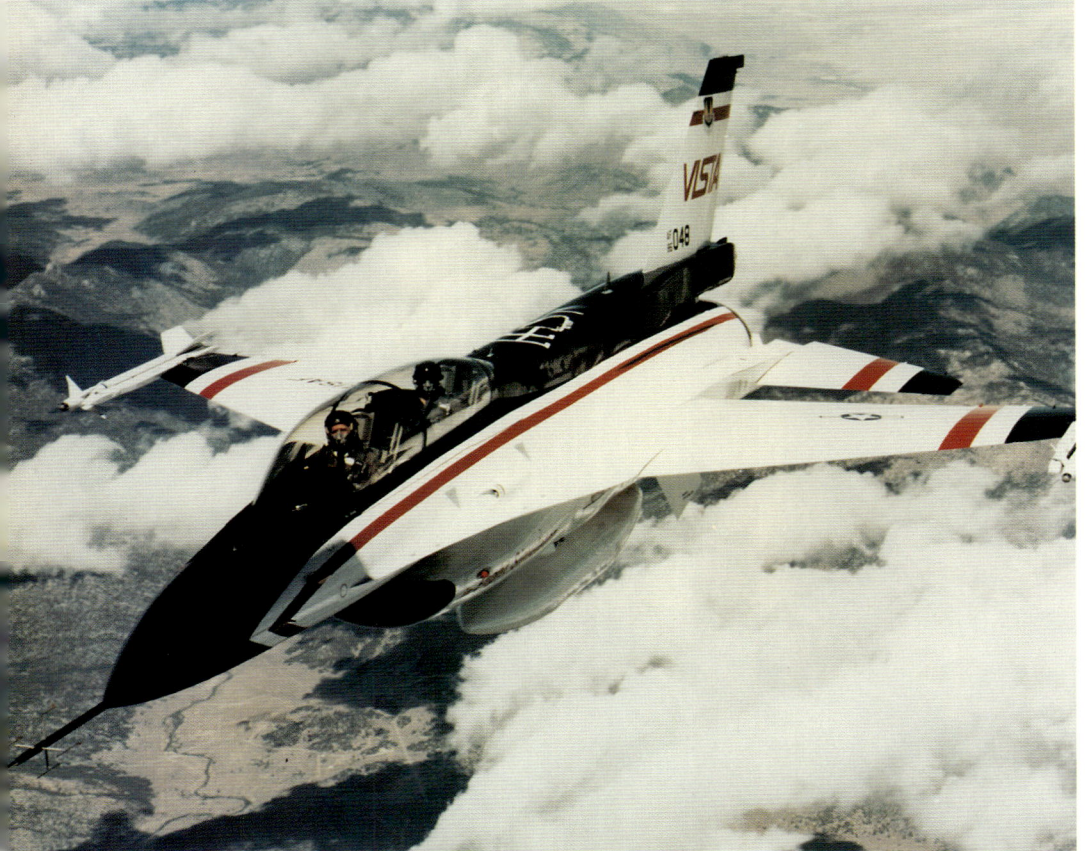

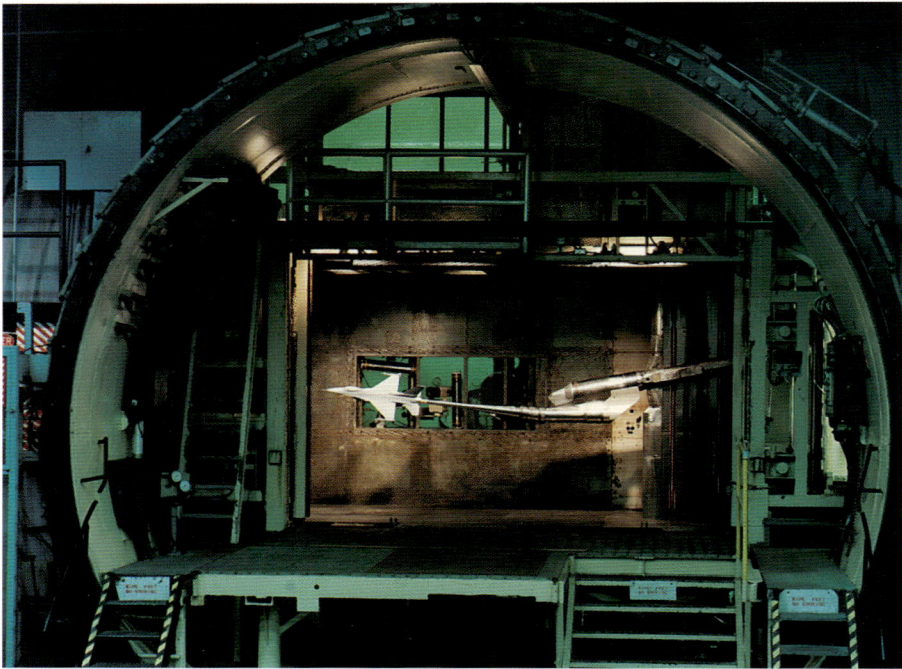

One of the country's premier organizations for defense research, development, testing, and evaluation (RDT&E), Calspan is now bringing its technological expertise to industrial and consumer markets. With a goal of $500 million in annual sales by the year 2000, Calspan is focusing on aggressive product development, marketing, manufacturing and distribution, and forming alliances with other technology leaders to achieve growth in both domestic and international markets.

One of the company's most exciting new technologies is its intelligent transportation systems. A marriage of military command and control technology with automotive safety advances— two traditional Calspan strengths—these systems promise to make it safer and easier for drivers to reach their destinations. The company's MAYDAY system uses a Global Positioning Satellite (GPS) receiver, cellular phone, modem, and special-purpose computer system to aid stranded drivers. When a breakdown occurs, the driver simply presses a button to transmit the car's location to Calspan's message center so help can be dispatched. In the event of an accident, an automated collision notification system automatically transmits notification of the accident regardless of the driver's condition.

Throughout much of its history, Calspan has been a leading test site for automotive safety features, performing tests for the Big Three U.S. automakers, many foreign manufacturers, and several U.S. government agencies. Calspan developed the first crash test dummies in 1948, and its accelerator sled, also used for testing airplane equipment, determines the effectiveness of various types of seat restraints. Other Calspan safety innovations include the box beam guardrail and median barrier now in use across the country. The company also operates a unique automotive tire-testing facility that includes the world's largest flat-roadway test machine capable of testing tires at speeds of over 200 miles per hour. To meet growing international demand, Calspan has also begun manufacturing and marketing automotive test equipment, selling turnkey testing systems to customers in Korea, South America, and around the world.

Another promising technology transfer was originally developed by Calspan for defense in chemical warfare. Using a technology based on fluorescent polymers, the company is developing a cost-effective package the size of an identification badge that can detect hazardous substances in extremely minute quantities—down to one-half part per billion. The detectors can be manufactured to detect a wide range of substances. An inherent "memory" capability allows the detectors to provide information on exposure to substances even after the exposure occurs.

While the company is moving defense technology to commercial markets, a significant portion of the company's activities are still closely related to Calspan's military background. Founded during World War II as a research facility devoted to making planes safer and more effective in combat, Calspan continues to play a leading role in both military and civilian aerospace research and testing at its Flight Research Group facilities, also in Buffalo. Among the company's resources are wind and shock tunnels providing extremely cost-competitive testing for defense and commercial customers. More than 1,000 aircraft from around the world have been tested here by Calspan engineers. A hypersonic shock tunnel

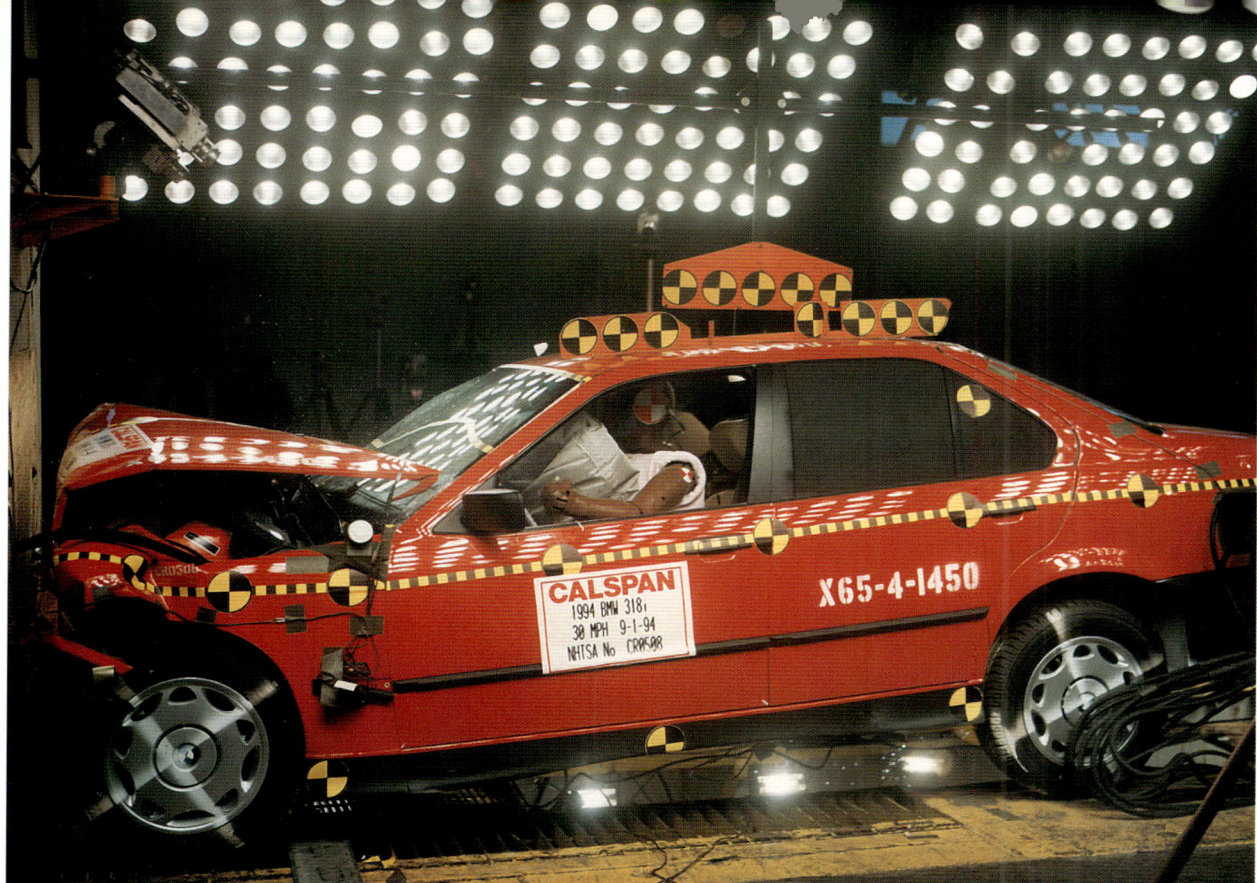

capable of speeds up to Mach 20 is used for testing missile and vehicle re-entry into the atmosphere, including models of the U.S. space shuttle.

The company is also a leader in in-flight simulators. It maintains four aircraft that can be used to simulate the flight characteristics of a wide array of different aircraft and for pilot training as well. Along with flight simulators, Calspan provides realistic models of enemy air defense systems, such as REDCAP (Real-Time Digitally Controlled Analyzer Processor), which trains pilots by creating an artificial combat environment.

Since its dedication as a research laboratory in 1943, Calspan has had a major impact on the economy of the Niagara region, producing two dozen spin-off companies that have remained in Western New York. Calspan also supports the University at Buffalo (UB) through the Calspan University at Buffalo Research Center (CUBRC), where Calspan engineers work with faculty and students to combine pure research and application opportunities in the areas of molecular physics, biomechanics, hypersonics, and other disciplines. The company's ties with UB date back to the company's first director, Dr. Clifford C. Furnas, who later became the university's chancellor.

Calspan's record of innovation is testimony to the creative atmosphere the company affords its researchers. Over the years, Calspan engineers have applied their skills to a wide variety of problems, including using lasers to measure gas density, developing the first Doppler radar system, studying oil pollution in U.S. rivers, developing the first fully automatic terrain-following flight system, working with the FBI to create an automated fingerprint reading system, and developing advanced security systems for banks.

Today, Calspan is working to enhance the environment that produced these and many other innovations. The company aspires to become an organizational model for companies throughout the Niagara region as it moves from a hierarchical management structure to a flatter, more flexible organization depending on high-performance teams. In an industry where unique ideas and the ability to implement them are the

driving force, Calspan offers its employees the resources and freedom to work on ground-breaking projects in a stimulating, creative environment.

Unique facilities. A tradition of innovation. A corporate culture that encourages creativity and diversity. These are the qualities that have attracted more than 430 of the best and brightest technicians, researchers, designers, and managers from around the world to join Calspan SRI's Buffalo operations. Their talents, ideas, and discoveries will take Calspan and the millions of people in the United States and around the world who benefit from the technologies developed here into the 21st century. ❧

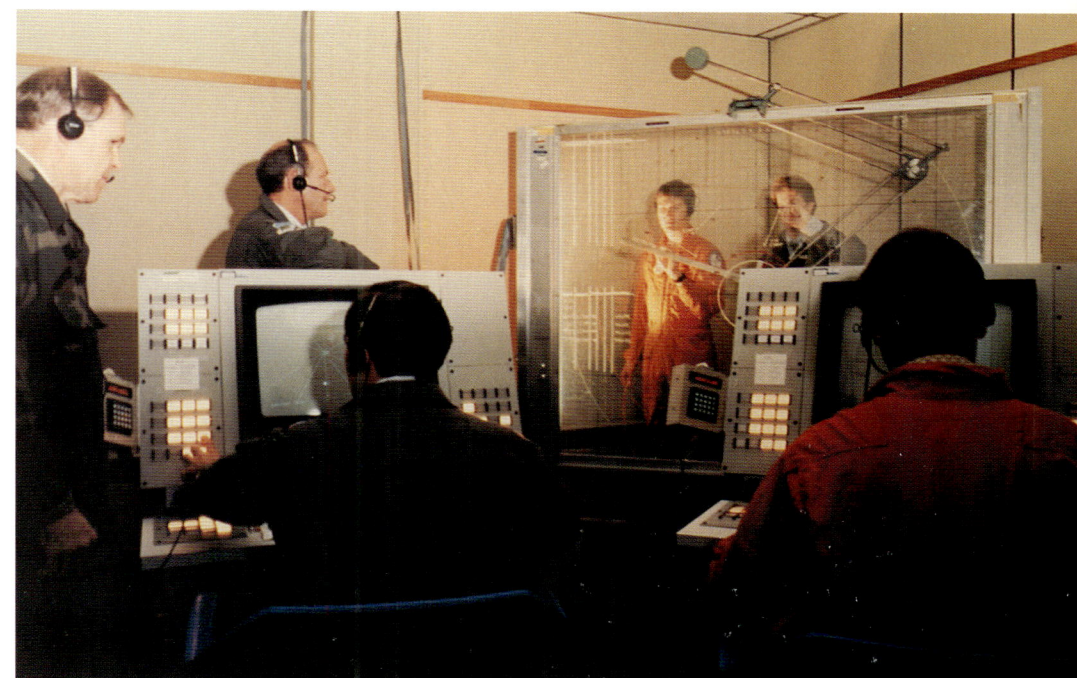

AIRSEP CORPORATION

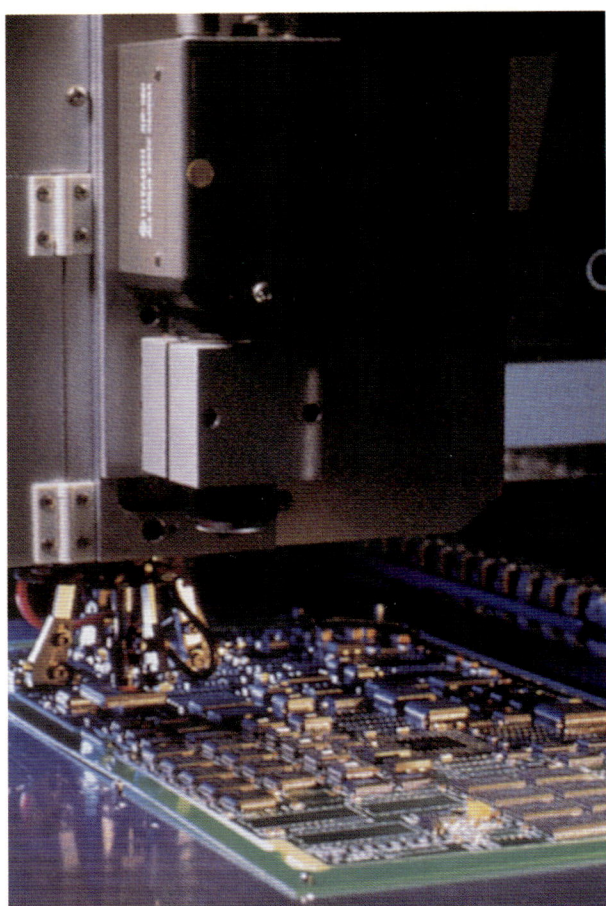

After more than a decade of solid growth, market expansion, and international recognition, the success of AirSep Corporation is a testimonial that the entrepreneurial spirit is as vibrant as ever in Western New York.

Founded in 1987, AirSep entered the marketplace as a manufacturer of medical and industrial oxygen generating systems. The medical oxygen concentrator line is used primarily by the home health care industry. The industrial product line supplies oxygen from the most basic to the most sophisticated thermal and chemical oxidation processes. Today, AirSep's name can be found on oxygen generators for everything from central hospital supply to aquaculture, ozone generation to coal gasification, in paper mills and sewage treatment plants, on oil rigs, at mini steel mills, health clinics, veterinary, hospitals and homes, around the world.

It was obvious, early on, that AirSep's commitment and responsiveness to its customers, employees, and the environment were key in making this company so successful, here and abroad. The corporate commitment to research and development, improving and expanding its product lines, and exploring new opportunities is reflected in numerous acquisitions, office and manufacturing plant expansions, and the development of new products.

Currently, the organization is divided into three divisions—medical, industrial, and OEM/electronics. The medical division manufactures both diagnostic and therapeutic medical products. The therapeutic products address issues of respiratory disease and sleep disorders requiring supplemental oxygen,

This surface mount component placement machine is used to assemble precision electronic circuit boards.

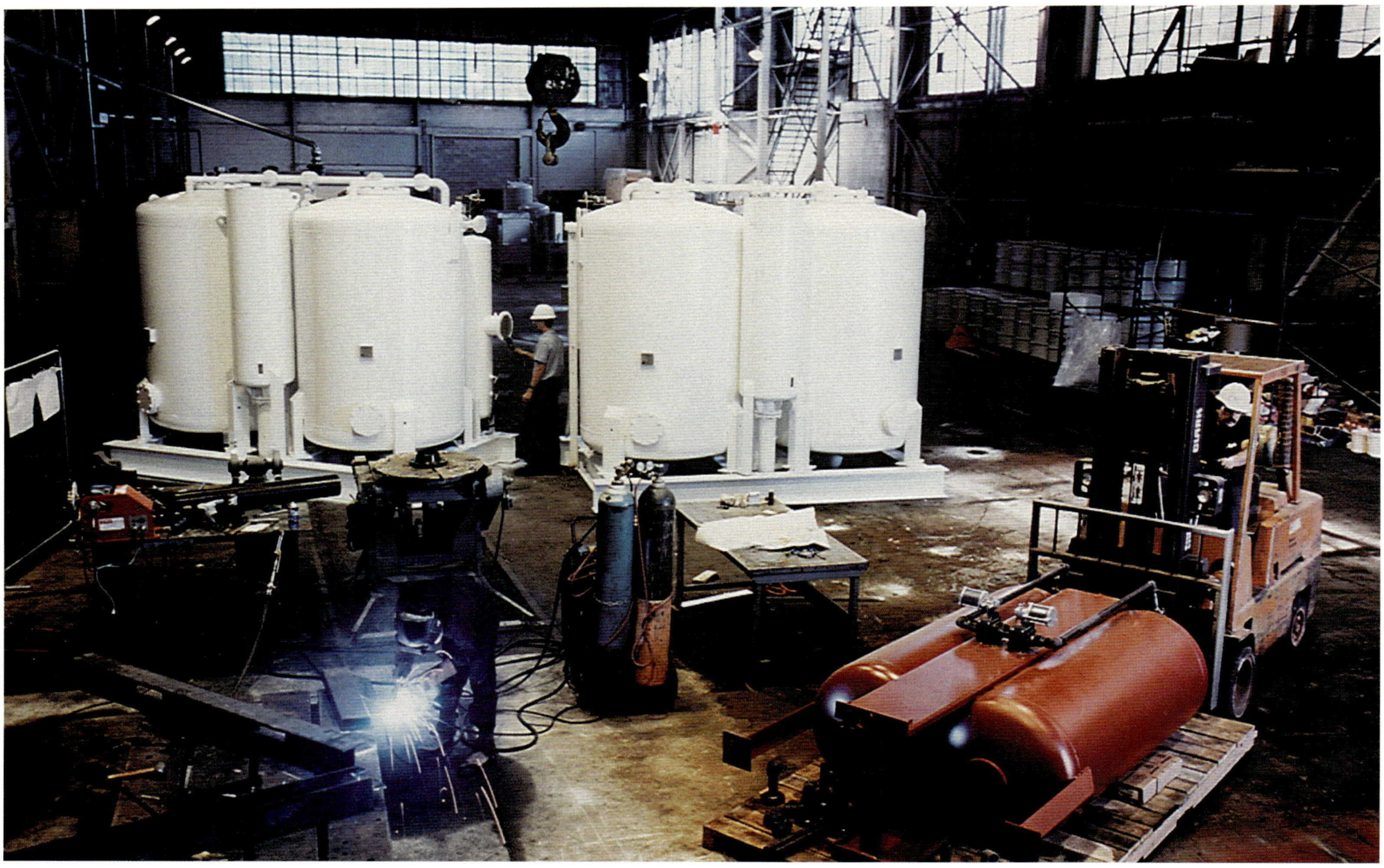

In-house fabrication ensures timely delivery.

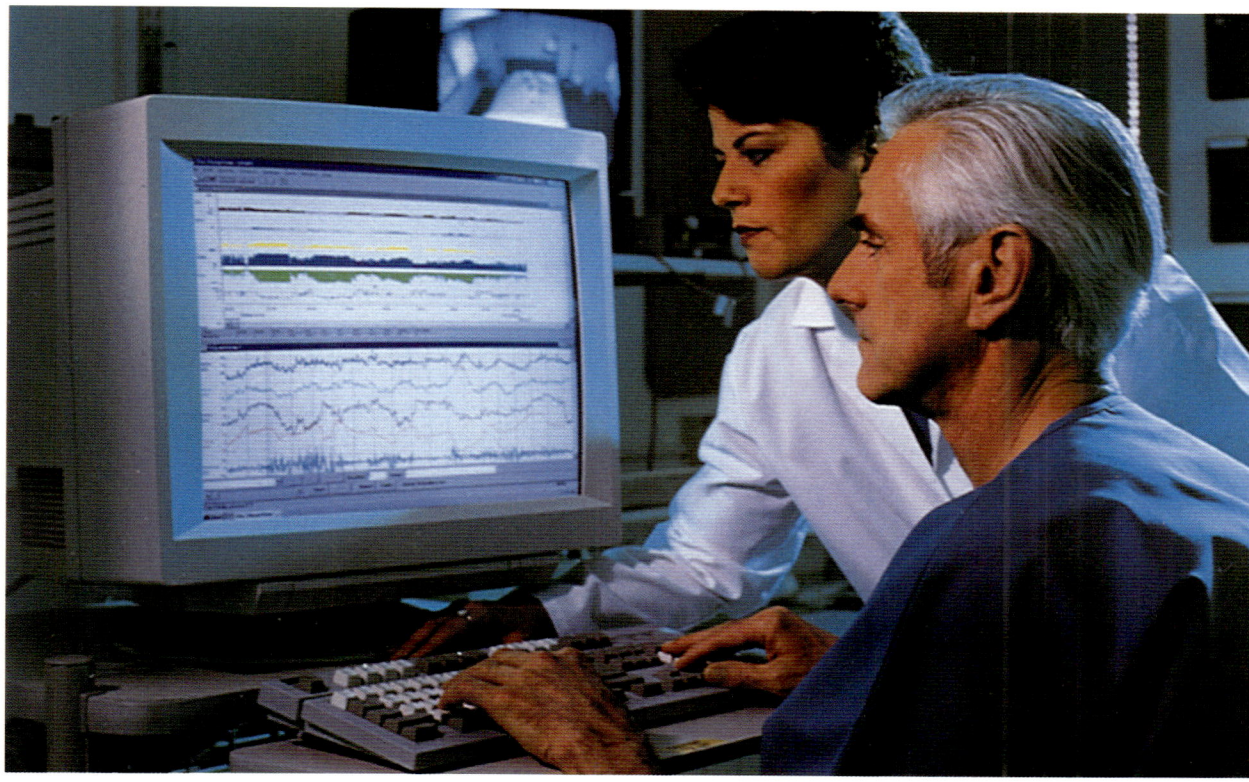

The Rembrandt™ sleep monitoring and analysis software package offers a flexible, cost-effective system for the computerized collection, evaluation, and archiving of sleep data.

ventilation, and aerosol therapy. The diagnostic products, including both software and hardware, provide sophisticated tools for the clinical evaluation of both sleep and neurological conditions. AirSep's industrial division continues to be a world leader in the oxygen generator industry, with a product line unequaled by any manufacturer. AirSep built the world's largest two-bed PSA (pressure swing adsorption) oxygen system, which is used for oxygen delignification and bleaching at a New Zealand pulp and paper mill. The acquisition and integration of EJE Research, AirSep's OEM/electronic division, has further solidified the company's investment in the future. As automation and electronic sophistication races forward, EJE Research designs and manufacturers electronics for the high-tech demands of a wide range of industries from medical products to aerospace and telecommunications. EJE provides its customers with expertise, capabilities, and products that inspire innovative solutions for virtually every aspect of industry.

AirSep's corporate offices are headquartered in a campus-like setting, located in Amherst, a suburb of Buffalo. This dynamic company, led by an aggressive management team, is now one of the major employers in the Western New York area. With distribution in more than 80 countries and regional, national, and international sales offices and service centers, the company's management focuses on strengthening its position as a market-driven, quality conscious manufacturing and service organization.

AirSep believes it is the attention to detail that separates this company from the competition. Whether in quality control and assurance, documentation, customer service, or technical support, AirSep concentrates its efforts to ensure the very best and most sophisticated response to its customer's needs. The emphasis on technical expertise extends to all areas of the business. As a technology-driven business, it is imperative that the company brings highly qualified teams to each of its projects. AirSep continues to be an avid supporter of employee development, training, and advancement within the organization, strengthening its commitment to quality teams.

Welcoming the challenge of strong global competition, AirSep remains dominant in the marketplace. Despite vigorous growth in the company and vast changes in the many facets of this organization's respective markets, AirSep has remained steadfast in its dedication to excellence and its approach to the workplace.

From its roots in on-site oxygen production, AirSep Corporation has grown and prospered by cultivating strengths that are synonymous among successful companies—market leadership, benchmarks in quality, and technical sophistication. These strengths enable AirSep and its subsidiaries to be dominant players in their respective fields. ◊

AirSep's medical product line is used for the home health care market throughout the world.

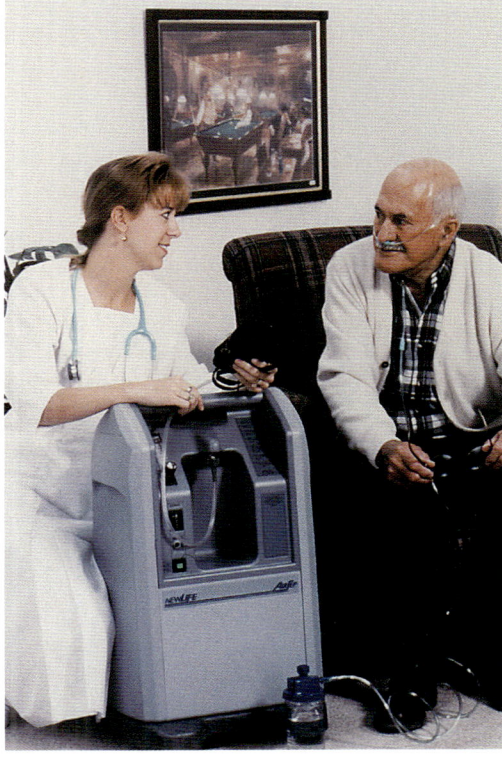

WILSON GREATBATCH LTD.

Imagine a manufacturing facility set in a wooded area where motivated and committed workers make precision products— including some that offer life-saving medical technology—for critical industries. Imagine ergonomically-designed work stations and employees taking regular "flex-breaks" to avoid fatigue. Imagine a place where everyone is on a first-name basis, and family-friendly benefits like a generous college tuition- reimbursement program are status quo.

That such a utopia exists is a tribute to the vision of one gentleman, Wilson Greatbatch. The Buffalo native started his company, based in rural Clarence, New York, in 1970, 12 years after having invented the world's first successful implantable cardiac pacemaker. The Greatbatch dream spawned not only a company, but an entire industry.

Today, Wilson Greatbatch Ltd. (WGL) is the world's leading manufacturer of lithium batteries and other components for implantable medical devices. The company makes or licenses more than 90 percent of the world's pacemaker batteries. According to a manufacturer of Greatbatch's pacemaker design, more than three million lives have been saved since the first pacemaker was implanted.

WGL's growth over more than a quarter-century has included the development of batteries for other medical devices, including implantable cardiac defibrillators, drug delivery systems, and neurostimulators. Numerous commercial applications for its battery products have been developed over the years.

WGL batteries are used in the defense and aerospace industries, including NASA's space shuttle program, as well as in oil and gas exploration, geophysical surveying, and emergency locator beacons.

Additional product applications rely on the company's micromechanical manufacturing and assembling expertise. Through its Engineered Components Division, WGL provides a custom manufacturing service specializing in the manufacture of precision miniature components and assemblies used for medical, aerospace, and similar technically demanding applications.

Progress of this magnitude might have been unthinkable even for an inventor the likes of Wilson Greatbatch—still, the success of WGL is largely due to the thinking and tinkering of this septuagenarian who calls Thomas Edison his personal hero. Among the projects of his storied life are a solar-powered canoe (in 1991, at age 72, he set a world record by traveling 130 miles in such a canoe through part of New York's Finger Lakes); cloned African violets; engines that run on alcohol; and nuclear-powered batteries. In 1988, Greatbatch was inducted into the National Inventors' Hall of Fame in Akron, Ohio. In all, he has over 140 U.S. and foreign patents, including the one for the implantable pacemaker.

That invention was incubated during Greatbatch's post-World War II employment at an animal behavior farm run by the Cornell University Psychology Department. There he spent lunchtimes talking with two surgeons who were on sabbatical and puzzling over how to treat an ailment called heart block, which occurs when natural electrical impulses from the heart's upper chambers (atria) fail to reach the ventricles in adequate quantity. The result is irregular heatbeats that can cause shortness of breath and, in extreme cases, loss of consciousness and even death.

"When they described it, I knew I could fix it," Greatbatch recalls, "but not with the vacuum tubes and storage batteries we had then." By the mid-1950s, back at home in the Buffalo area, Greatbatch put his inquiring mind to work on the problem. He helped found the first chapter of the Institute of Radio Engineers' Professional Group in Medical Electronics, which is now the IEEE Engineering in Medicine and Biology Society (EMBS). The group sought to attract equal numbers of doctors and engineers, and had a standing offer to send an engineering team to assist doctors on any instrumentation problem.

Greatbatch was on one such team called to aid the chief of surgery at Buffalo's Veteran's Administration Hospital. Dr. William C. Chardack needed help with a blood oximeter. While the inventor was unable to solve that particular problem, he had finally found an ally in the medical community: Dr. Chardack was enthusiastic about prospects for an implantable pacemaker. Such a device might save 10,000 lives a year, the surgeon estimated.

In May, 1958, Greatbatch brought what would become the world's first implantable cardiac pacemaker to the animal lab at Dr. Chardack's hospital. There Dr. Chardack and another surgeon, Dr. Andrew Gage, exposed the heart of a dog. Greatbatch touched the two pacemaker wires to the heart, causing it to beat in synchrony with his device. In a lab book entry, the inventor reflected on that moment: "I seriously doubt if anything I ever do will ever give me the elation I felt that day when my own two cubic-inch piece of electronic design controlled a living heart."

Early pacemaker designs specified wrapping modules in electric tape as a sealant. It soon became clear that the

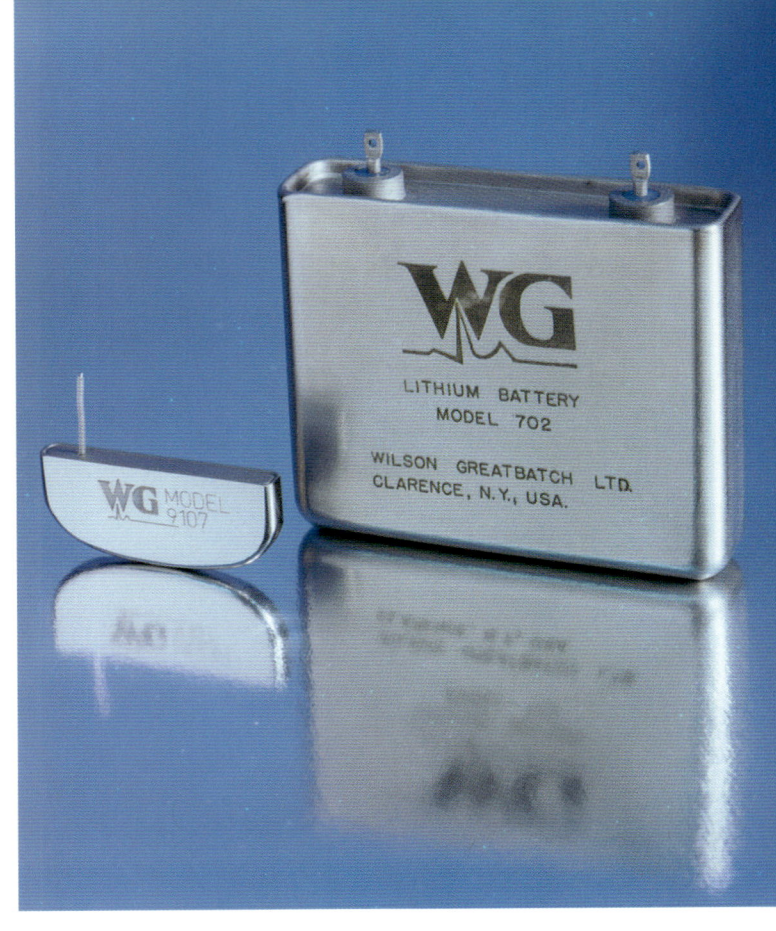

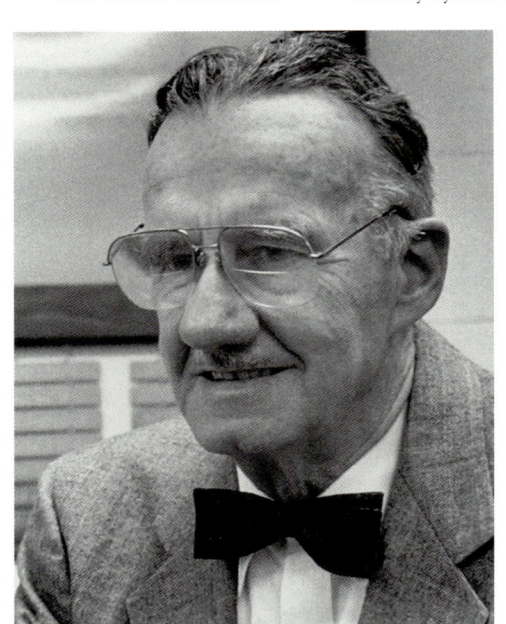

Lithium iodine cell, Model 702P—first lithium iodine cell implanted.

Our founder, Mr. Wilson Greatbatch.

slightest void in the wrapping would fill with fluid and short out the circuit. First implants lasted a matter of hours. Within a year, survival time rose to four months, as units were encased in a solid block of epoxy, replacing the ineffective tape.

Greatbatch, by then working independently in his barn workshop on the invention that was the goal of several other groups in the late 1950s (from General Electric Company to Swedish researchers), made several basic discoveries. He learned that uninsulated wires bond better with epoxy. In two years' time, working with his own savings of two thousand dollars, he made 50 pacemakers by hand.

Most of these went into animals, but Dr. Chardack and his associates implanted 10 of the devices in humans. All the patients had complete heart block; without pacemakers they had perhaps a 50 percent chance of living more than a year. The first patient lived 18 months. Another in the initial group lived with a pacemaker for 30 years.

In early 1961, Greatbatch signed a license for the implantable pacemaker with Medtronic, Inc. of Minneapolis. As remuneration for his design, he agreed to accept stock shares. It was the beginning of Medtronic's Chardack-Greatbatch Pacemaker, which would dominate the field for the next decade, in spite of many competitors' innovations. Medtronic is still the world's top producer of therapeutic implantable devices, with sales of $1.4 billion in 1994. Pacemakers accounted for 67 percent of that revenue.

Throughout the years of improving his device, Greatbatch subjected component parts to rigid reliability testing, a prime tenet of the current corporate philosophy of WGL. Initial corrosion problems with electrodes plus the difficulties attendant with cardiac surgery on high-risk patients were gradually overcome. Greatbatch was dedicated to improvement and sharing ideas, traits he retains today.

In the early 1970s, after numerous experiments, Greatbatch and his colleagues adapted a new lithium iodine power source, recently invented by James Moser and Allan Schneider, to the high-reliability demands of pacemakers. Greatbatch's confidence in this lithium battery was so great that he created a company to manufacture them.

Today, Wilson Greatbatch Ltd. is a rapidly growing company chaired by the founder's oldest son, Warren. According to WGL President and CEO Edward F. Voboril, the company is currently "poised for major market expansion." Greatbatch Surgical was recently formed to develop and market unique instrumentation for use in minimally invasive surgical procedures. In 1992, the company completed a facility expansion to keep pace with increased business and now has developed new plans to again expand its Clarence world headquarters, adding some 70 new jobs. The company has also instituted a quality improvement process, resulting in the achievement of ISO 9001 certification. This certification, an internationally recognized quality standard for documenting total quality management, is essential for doing business in the European marketplace.

Reflecting the founder's continuing commitment to social responsibility, WGL recently established the Direct Community Action Program to benefit tax-exempt charitable, educational, and scientific organizations in Western New York. Funding the work of others is just part of the

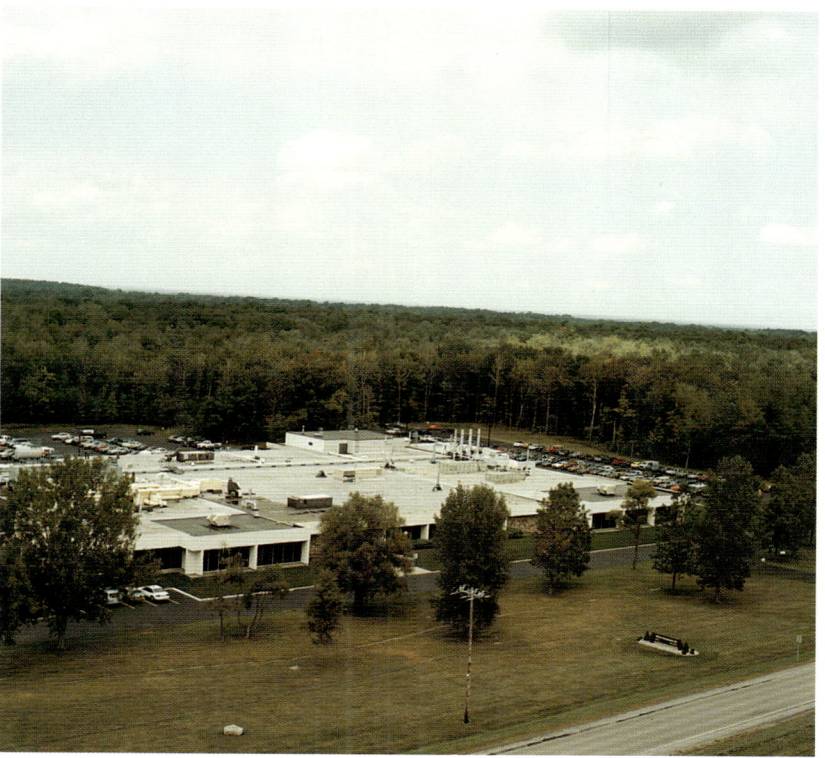

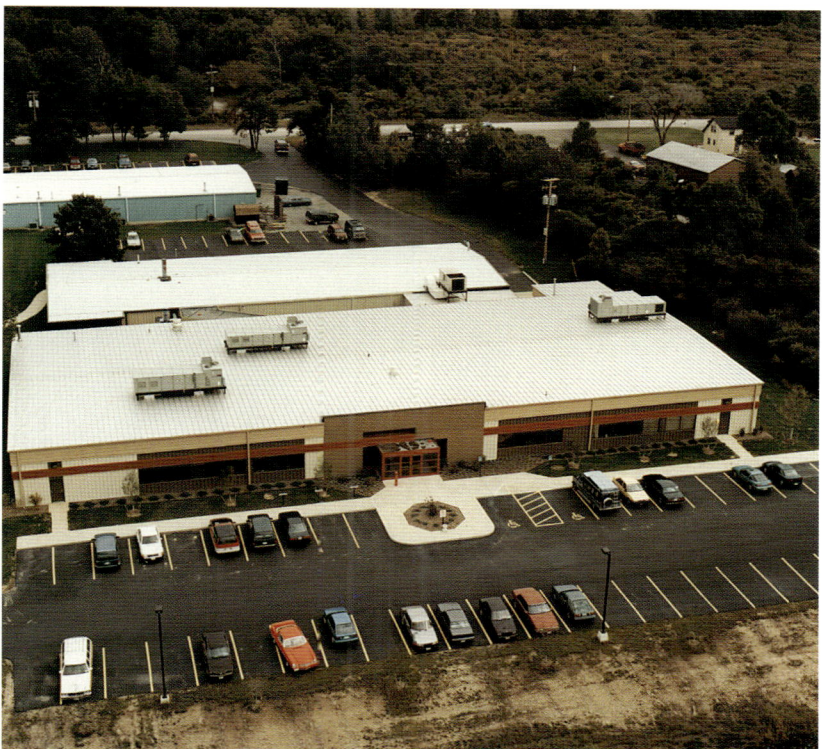

Greatbatch vision, and the inventor continues to develop his own projects. His latest venture is in the field of genetic engineering where he is pursuing AIDS research, as well as an innovative cancer screen and also a 21st century fuel source involving nuclear fusion of helium-3 which is completely free of nuclear radiation. ❧

The Wilson Greatbatch Ltd. facility (top) and Engineered Components Division (bottom) are located in Clarence, New York.

INGRAM MICRO, INC.

Ingram Micro's 1,500 East Coast-based associates have called Buffalo home for over a decade. The company traces its Western New York roots back to 1982, when Buffalo entrepreneurs Ronald Schreiber, Irwin Schreiber, Gerald Lippes, and Paul Willax founded Software Distribution Services (SDS). In 1985, SDS was acquired by Nashville, Tennessee-based Ingram Industries, and through the merger of Ingram Computer, Inc. and Micro D, Inc. in 1989, became Ingram Micro, Inc. Today, Ingram Micro is the world's largest wholesale distributor of microcomputer products in the United States, with an inventory of 36,000 products and a worldwide workforce of more than 9,000 associates. The company is headquartered in Santa Ana, California, and recorded 1996 revenues in excess of $12 billion.

In addition to leading the way in worldwide distribution, Ingram Micro is also a principal provider of advanced and value- added services, including technical support, electronic programs, and financial options, as well as basic services and support programs. These services are provided by 114 of the most experienced support specialists in the industry, of which 87 are based on the East Coast. Furthermore, Ingram Micro supports more than 105,000 resellers in 120 countries through 19 affiliates from strategically located offices throughout the globe.

Ingram Micro's Buffalo operations center provides sales, credit, and technical support, as well as management information systems, and customer service support to our vendors and reseller partners. "Our Buffalo operations center has seen tremendous growth over the last couple of years, and we are now one of Erie County's largest employers," says Alan S. Cherbow, vice president of Ingram Micro. He added, "We are also proud of our long tradition of service. Our associates freely volunteer their time and money to education and community service projects that enrich the quality of life of every citizen in Erie County."

Ingram Micro associates give Erie County an international perspective that comes from working with 1,000 of world's leading hardware and software companies.

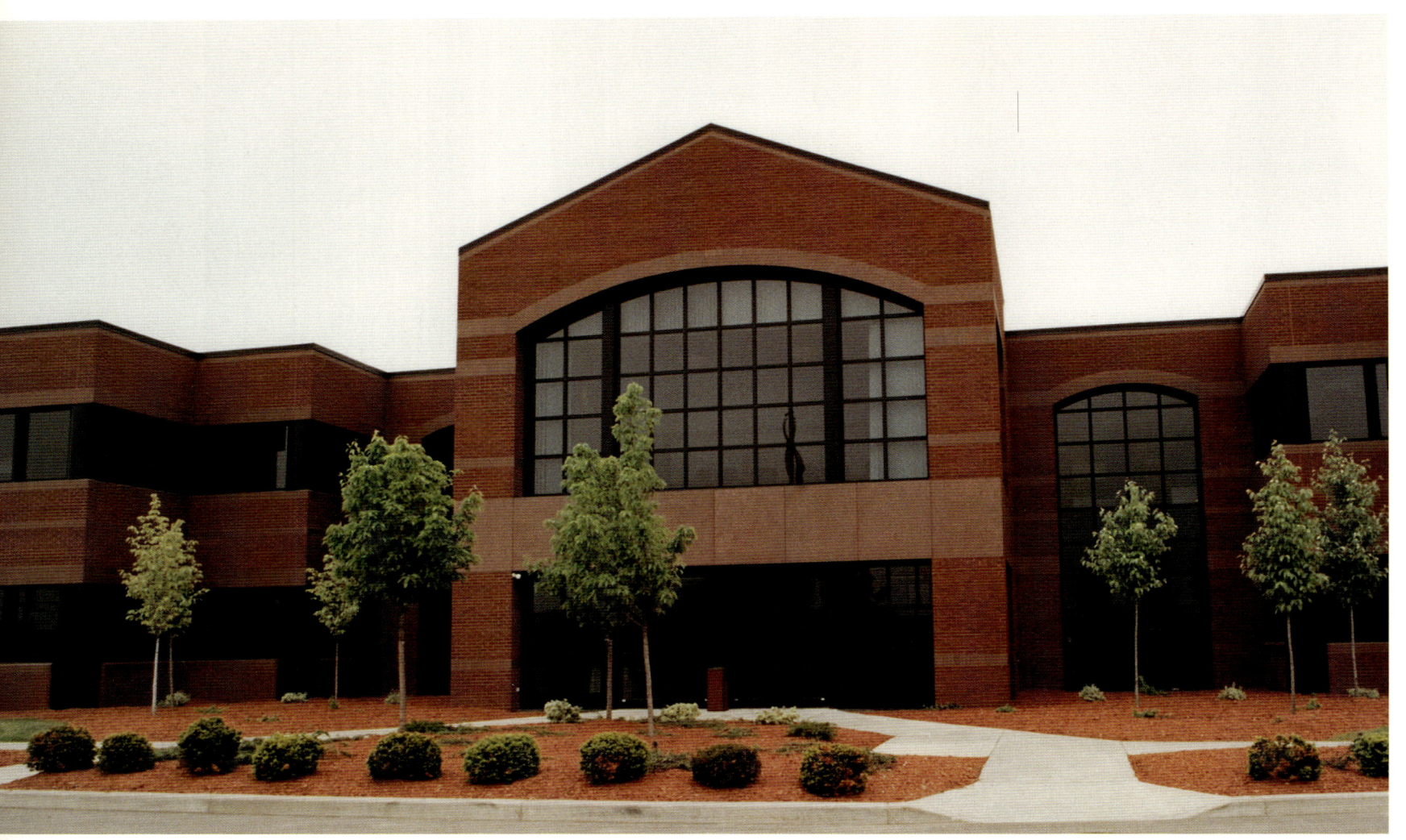

Ingram Micro's Buffalo operations center provides sales, credit, and technical support, as well as management information systems, and customer service support to our vendors and reseller partners.

From a late 19th-century manufacturer of automated punchcard tabulating machines, IBM has grown into the world's largest and best-known computer manufacturer, software publisher, and provider of information technology services. At home in more than 156 countries around the globe, the company truly lives up to the "International" in its name, International Business Machines.

The company's roots in Buffalo go back to 1896, when Dr. Herman Hollerith, a Buffalo native, founded the Tabulating Machine Company, one of the predecessors of today's IBM. The first local office was established in 1916. After several moves, today the company has offices in Buffalo's Waterfront Village Complex on Buffalo's scenic Lake Erie waterfront. The regional headquarters for Western New York, the office oversees operations throughout the eight-county area, including satellite offices in Olean and Jamestown.

Offering sales, service, and consulting, IBM provides services to many local businesses, including banks and other financial enterprises, manufacturing, food services, education, and retail organizations. The company also serves many government and municipal agencies.

The Buffalo office is also ideally located to assist IBM Canada, providing services and technical assistance as required to IBM Canada customers and business partners, especially in Toronto and throughout southern Ontario. Located less than five minutes from the Peace Bridge, the local office is also superbly positioned to serve companies involved in international trade, such as customs brokers and other cross-border trade specialists.

Today, as information technology continues to be the driving force in economic development throughout the world, IBM is committed to maintaining its international leadership. In 1995, the company was issued more U.S. patents than any other organization for the third consecutive year.

A key strategic component in IBM's blueprint for the future is network computing. From interoffice computer networks to the global reach of the Internet, IBM is dedicated to providing new solutions that allow people to collaborate, share ideas, and solve problems using information technology.

To make that technology accessible to the widest number of people, IBM provides major support to education, especially in the use of computers and information technology. The Buffalo office offers a full range of customer training, support, and education for the complete line of IBM products, both in its offices and on-site where its customers work.

To support education within the local community and throughout the region, the Buffalo office has made significant donations of both computer equipment and the skills of IBM employees to schools and to many other organizations. Along with sharing its information technology expertise, the company has also provided training in sales techniques to volunteers for local charitable organizations such as the United Way.

Offering a unique combination of global size, strength, and expertise with a commitment to the local and regional communities it serves, IBM is dedicated to bringing the benefits of information technology to both its customers and the communities where its employees live and work, today and throughout the 21st century. ❖

IBM

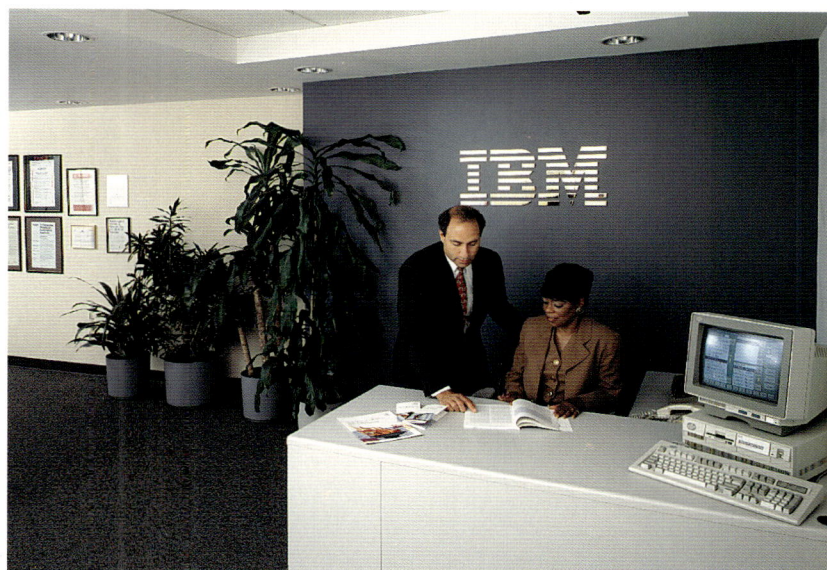

The Buffalo office offers sales, service and consulting to many local businesses and is ideally located to assist IBM Canada. Photo by Marc Murphy.

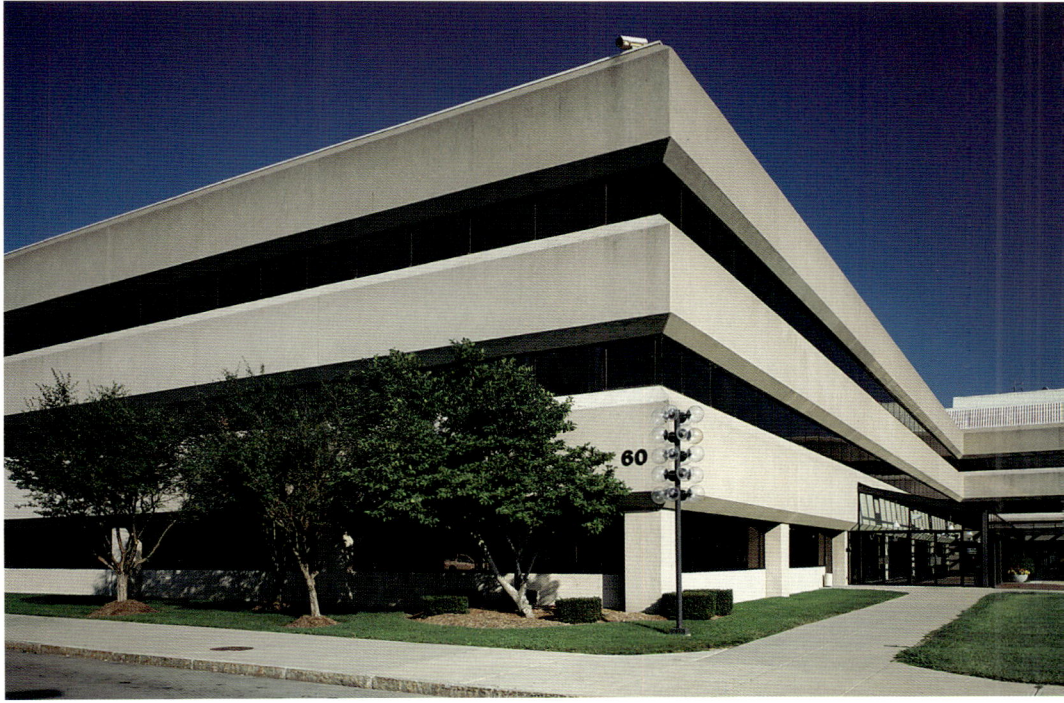

IBM has grown into the world's largest and best-known computer manufacturer, software publisher, and provider of information technology services. Photo by Marc Murphy.

TRANSCONTINENTAL PRINTING

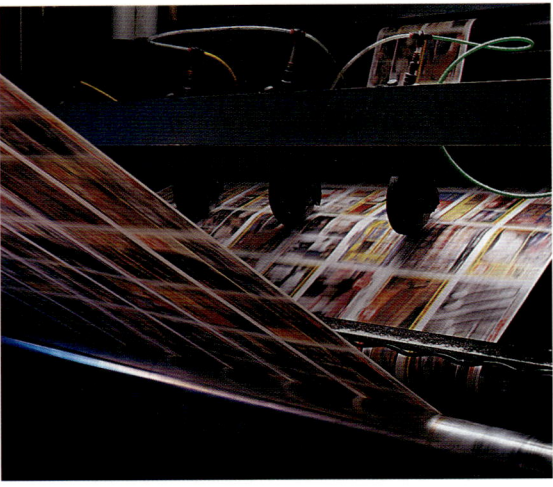
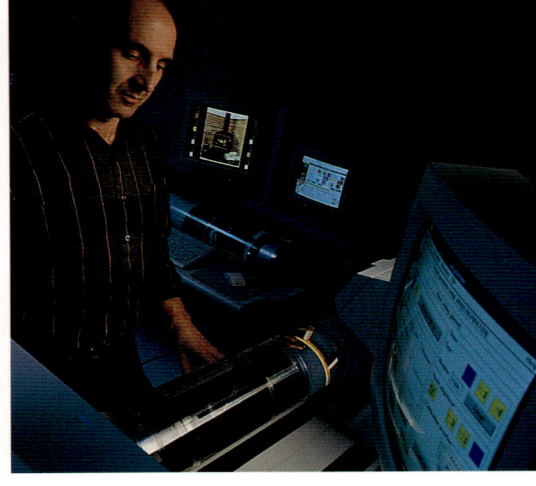

Skilled, experienced operators, high speed and high tech equipment are consistent throughout all 28 Transcontinental printing facilities.

Transcontinental Printing is one of the four business sectors of GTC Transcontinental, Group Ltd., headquartered in Montreal, Quebec. Formed in 1976 through the amalgamation of several companies, the organization's printing heritage reaches back more than 140 years. Through an aggressive growth strategy, total corporate revenues have increased from $1 million in 1976 to over $1.2 billion in 1996, the company's 20th anniversary. Today, Transcontinental Printing is Canada's leading printer of advertising inserts and circulars, the second-largest printer in its home country, and one of the top 10 printers worldwide.

Transcontinental Printing's Buffalo sales office was opened in April of 1991 to develop a retail market customer base in the northeastern United States, part of a larger expansion plan that has seen Transcontinental's North American Network grow to include 28 plants, including a state-of-the-art printing plant located in Fairborn, Ohio, and several United States-based sales offices. The Buffalo office, staffed by three of the company's more than 7,000 employees, generates $25 million annually in sales revenues from U.S. customers from New York to Tennessee.

The company's focus is on high-end, high-quality, high-volume printing needs, including magazines, catalogs, direct mail, case-bound books, and retail newspaper inserts. A few

Transcontinental's sales and management team are proactive in meeting customer's needs.

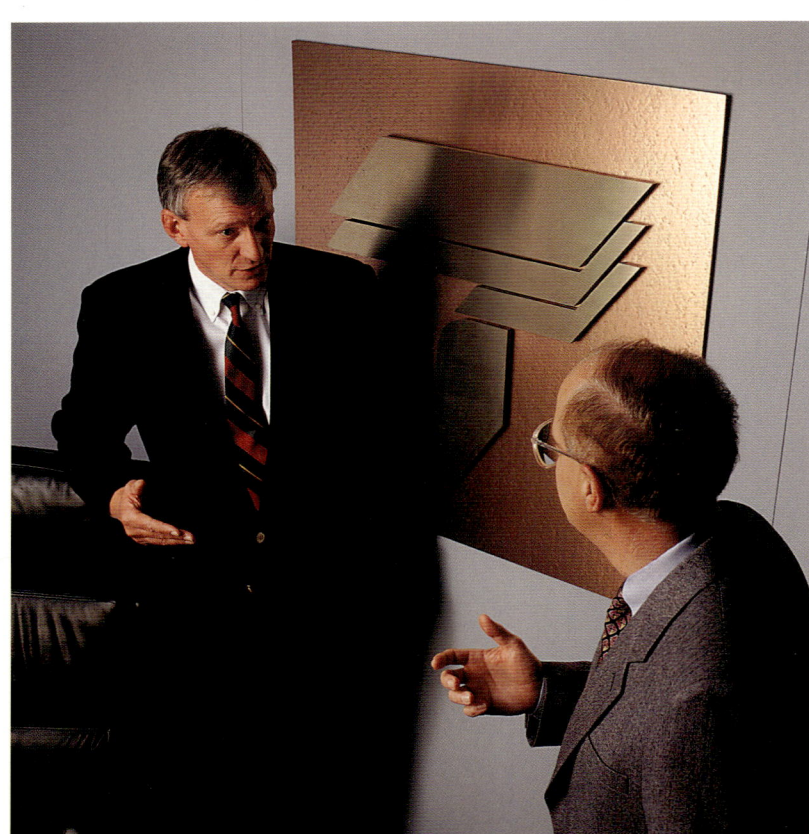

of the national customers served by Transcontinental Printing include Sears, K-mart, WalMart, Fisher-Price, and Avon. The Buffalo office services the quality printing needs of numerous retail, commercial, book, catalog, and newspaper accounts including weekly printing of the *New York Daily News* TV magazine, as well as the high quality printing needs of the *Buffalo News* and *Tops* markets locally. The forementioned serves as a testament to the company's unlimited capability to handle every customer's need regardless of size, shape, or quantity. From pre-press services to heat-set web printing, Transcontinental Printing offers excellent service and competitive pricing for all its customers.

Key to that service and pricing is the company's network of plants extending across North America. By completing work in the plant best suited to a customer's particular needs, the company assures reduced costs, faster turnaround, the flexibility to fill large orders, and employee participation and development. This cooperation in turn fosters an innovative and creative environment that makes the customer part of a partnership, allowing specific needs to be met, future needs to be anticipated, and last-minute changes to be completed more easily.

Electronic transfer of files between plants via modem and the Internet further streamlines the production process. Fully electronic pre-press is combined with direct output to plate-ready film or plate, accelerating the printing process even more. Add automated bindery, distribution capabilities, and state-of-the-art computer design and imaging equipment, and Transcontinental's high-tech approach to meeting customer needs provides in-house capabilities unrivaled in the printing industry.

The company's commitment to forging effective partnerships with its customers also goes beyond print technology to a wide array of value-added services, including hand finishing, inserting, poly bagging, direct mail, and folding. In addition, Transcontinental provides innovative consumer promotional print vehicles such as Touch & Sniff, CD-ROM technology, internet website services, telemarketing, and highly targeted customer loyalty programs such as magalogs offered as a turnkey service.

Dedicated to maintaining its remarkable growth and continuous improvement in the years to come, Transcontinental Printing will continue to provide leadership in the communications industry while achieving maximum value for customers, employees, and shareholders alike.

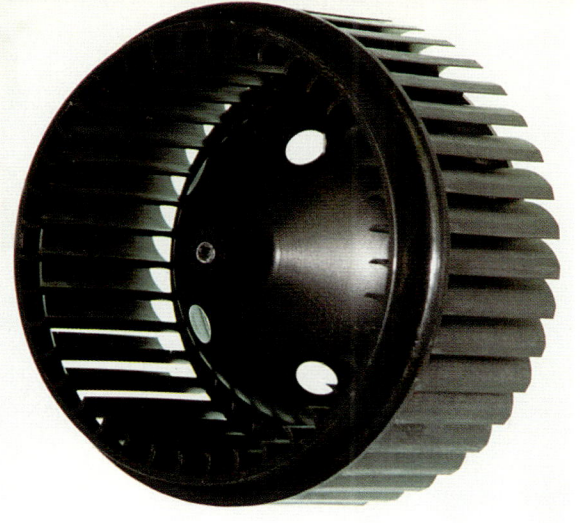

PALMA TOOL & DIE

Palma Tool & Die began in 1962 with one employee, a single mill and a single lathe, and one job making parts for tire display racks in local gas stations. A year later, founder Anthony Palma hired his first apprentice, Bill Tate, who moved up to toolmaker, tool designer, shop foreman, general manager, and, in 1986, after buying the company, president and chief executive officer. Today, with his partner Tom Owczarzak, the company's executive vice president and another former Palma apprentice, Tate oversees a thriving tool, die, and moldmaking operation with more than 23,400 square feet and a staff of more than 80 highly skilled employees.

Palma Tool & Die has grown in capabilities as well as size. Today, the company offers in-house design and engineering, including full CAD/CAM capabilities; tool and diemaking capabilities, including machining and assembly of complex dies up to 12,000 pounds; production sheet metal stamping; wire and sinker EDM; inspection services, including SPC and a video probe- equipped coordinate measuring machine; and growing capabilities in moldmaking.

Dedication to quality and service is the hallmark of Palma's operations. A teamwork attitude, solid managerial skills, and the ability to operate 24 hours a day allow Palma to provide fast turnaround and competitive pricing.

The company's exceptionally high standards for quality are seen in its certification for the ISO 9001 and ISO 9002/QS 9000 standards. The company was not only one of the first in the world to obtain the rigorous ISO 9002/QS 9000 certification, but also achieved certification on its first attempt, a remarkable accomplishment and a testimony to the teamwork and dedication of all the firm's employees.

Superb quality and service have garnered Palma an impressive customer list, including manufacturers in the automotive, aerospace, food processing, equipment manufacturing, and plastics industries. Palma not only produces machine parts for customers in western New York, Ohio, and Pennsylvania, but handles orders via a World Wide Web site from as far away as Hawaii, Canada, Mexico, Brazil, France, and the Middle East.

Palma is also an industry leader in education and training. The company developed the United States' first apprentice program in wire EDM and hired the program's first graduate. Currently in the planning stage is a moldmaker apprentice program, another first for the company. The company has offered a tool and die apprentice program for many years. Palma also plans to cross- train moldmakers and diemakers, something rarely done outside the largest manufacturing organizations. The company's principals and employees are also active in industry associations, including the Metalworking Institute of Western New York, the Machine Shops Association of Western New York, the Machine Tool Advisory Committee of BOCES, the National Tooling and Machining Association, the Society of Manufacturing Engineers, the Society of Automotive Engineers, American Society for Quality Control, and the American Society of Mechanical Engineers.

As the company continues to seek new opportunities for growth in technology, equipment, education, and personnel, it recognizes that the machining and managerial skills of its people, which it believes to be the best in the industry, are the key to the company's success as it meets the challenges of the future. ❧

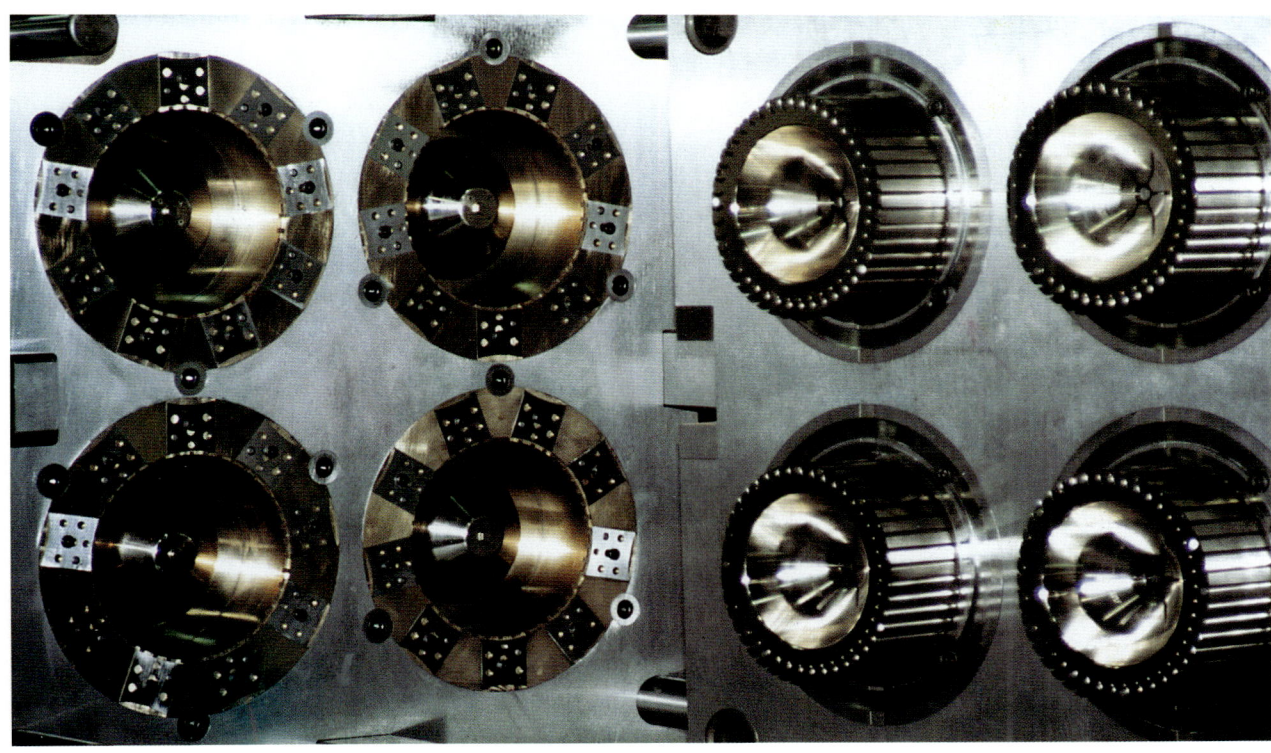

Palma Tool & Die is a thriving tool, die, and moldmaking operation with more than 23,400 square feet and a staff of more than 80 highly skilled employees.

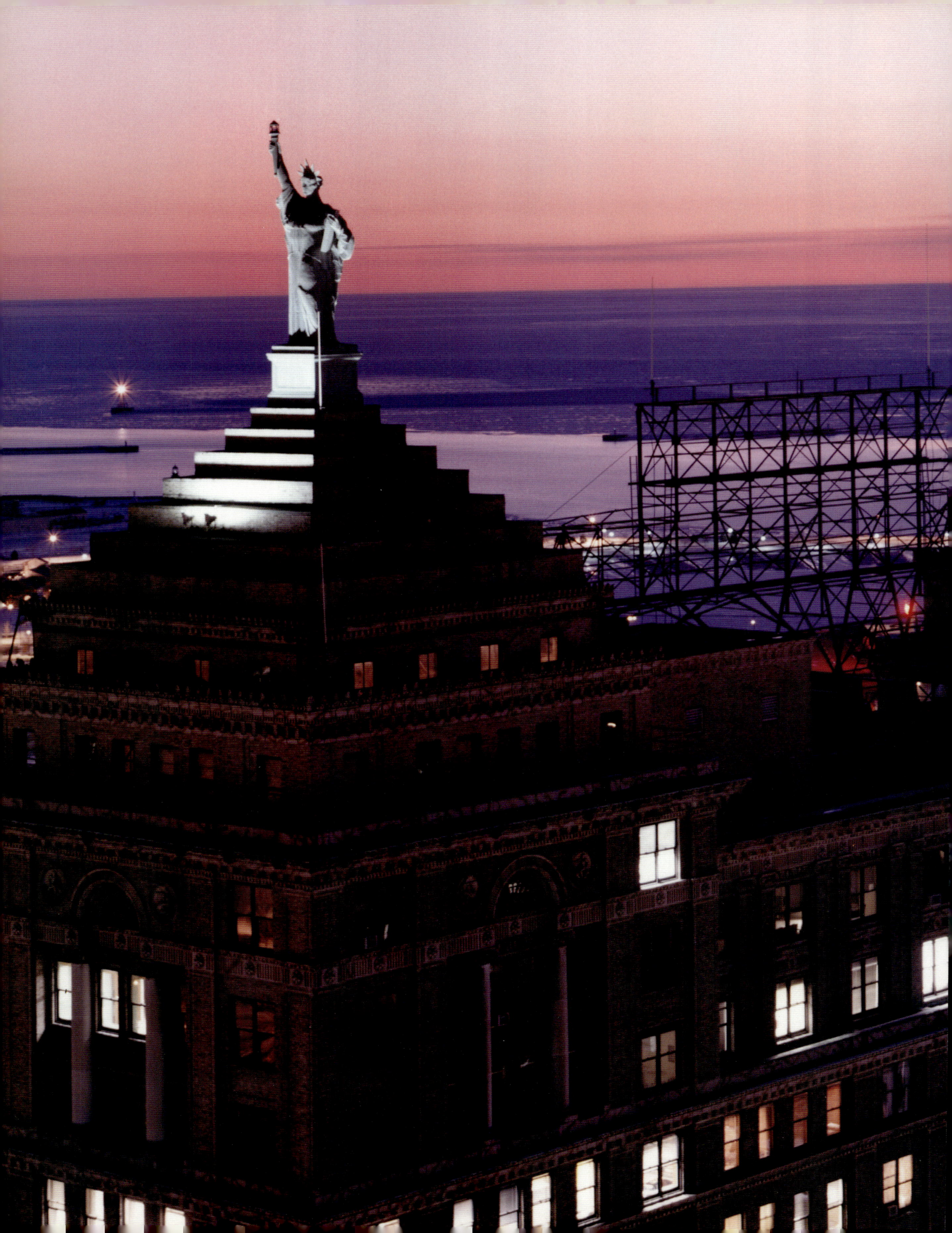

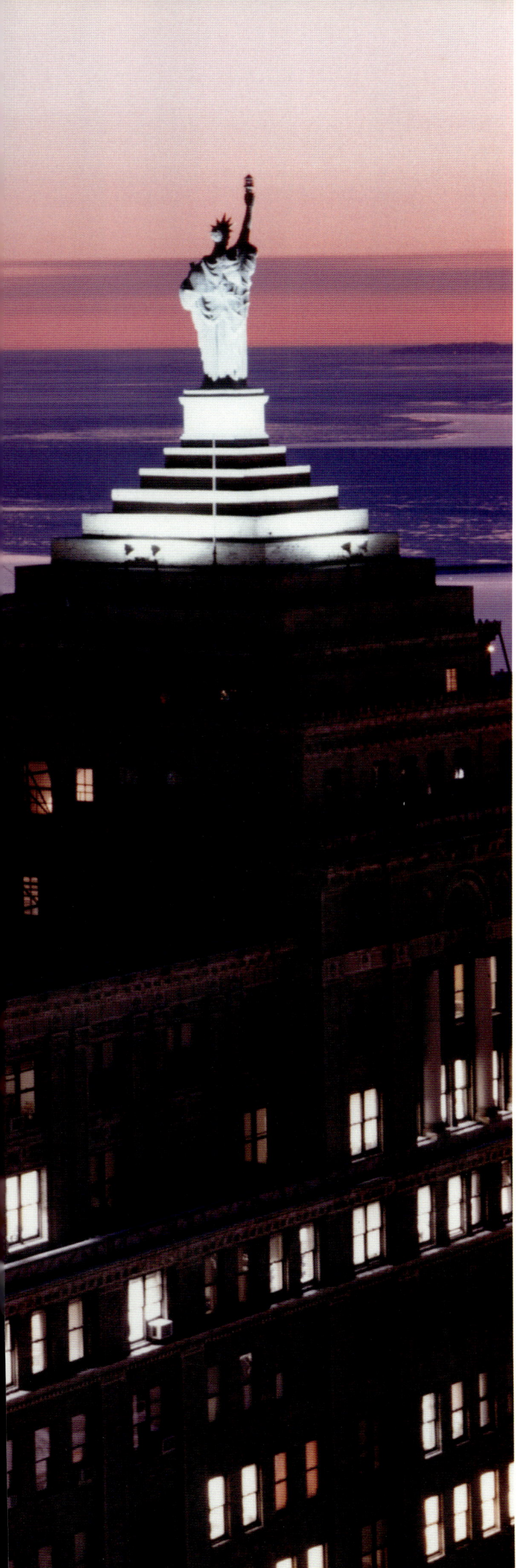

BUSINESS COMMUNITY

Photo by Marc Murphy.

GREATER BUFFALO PARTNERSHIP

Just as the binational region of Niagara occupies a unique position in the global marketplace, the Greater Buffalo Partnership, too, plays a unique role to improve this area and promote it to the world.

Formed in 1993, through the merger of the Greater Buffalo Development Foundation and the Greater Buffalo Chamber of Commerce, the Partnership today is the largest employer organization in Western New York and the eight counties of Western New York and the Niagara Peninsula of Ontario, with more than 3,300 member firms representing nearly a quarter of a million employees. Members range from multinational corporations to individual entrepreneurs and represent virtually every employment sector.

The Partnership is also unique in the breadth of its membership—including leaders from labor, higher education, the community, and religion leaders on its board of directors along with business leaders. This active broad-based involvement by community leaders is crucial to maintaining a holistic view of issues that affect virtually all residents of the region.

Broad-based membership and extensive staff capabilities also create a synergy that gives the Partnership a unique strategic role. Along with fostering a regional identity, the Partnership has identified three major strategic industry clusters for growth that capitalize on the region's unique geographical and economic strengths: trade and distribution, tourism, and medical manufacturing and services. For each of these three clusters, the neccesary infrastructure already exists

to provide extensive opportunities for growth and development well into the 21st century.

Committed to expanding business activity and enhancing community vitality throughout the region, the Partnership brings together public and private-sector resources to strengthen the economy and quality of life for the region's two million residents. By focusing on three primary functions—business development and regional marketing; government relations and public policy; and member services, products, and discounts—the Partnership creates an environment for business and individuals to succeed.

For business development, the Partnership has taken the lead role in creating and marketing a regional identity for Western New York and the Niagara peninsula of Ontario. The result is the "Niagara: Attracting the World" umbrella concept. Along with recognizing the region's world renown natural feature, Niagara Falls, the identity highlights the close geographical, economic, and political relationships enjoyed by businesses and residents of the area.

A related key achievement is the Niagara Compact, a commitment by business leaders to keep their businesses in Niagara, promote the marketplace to other executives, encourage relocation to the region to their peers and provide a CEO to CEO network to assist firms with various business climate issues.

The Partnership is also very active in enhancing infrastructure improvements, especially in transportation, an important

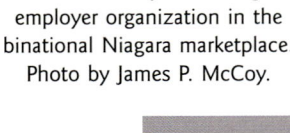

The Partnership is the largest employer organization in the binational Niagara marketplace. Photo by James P. McCoy.

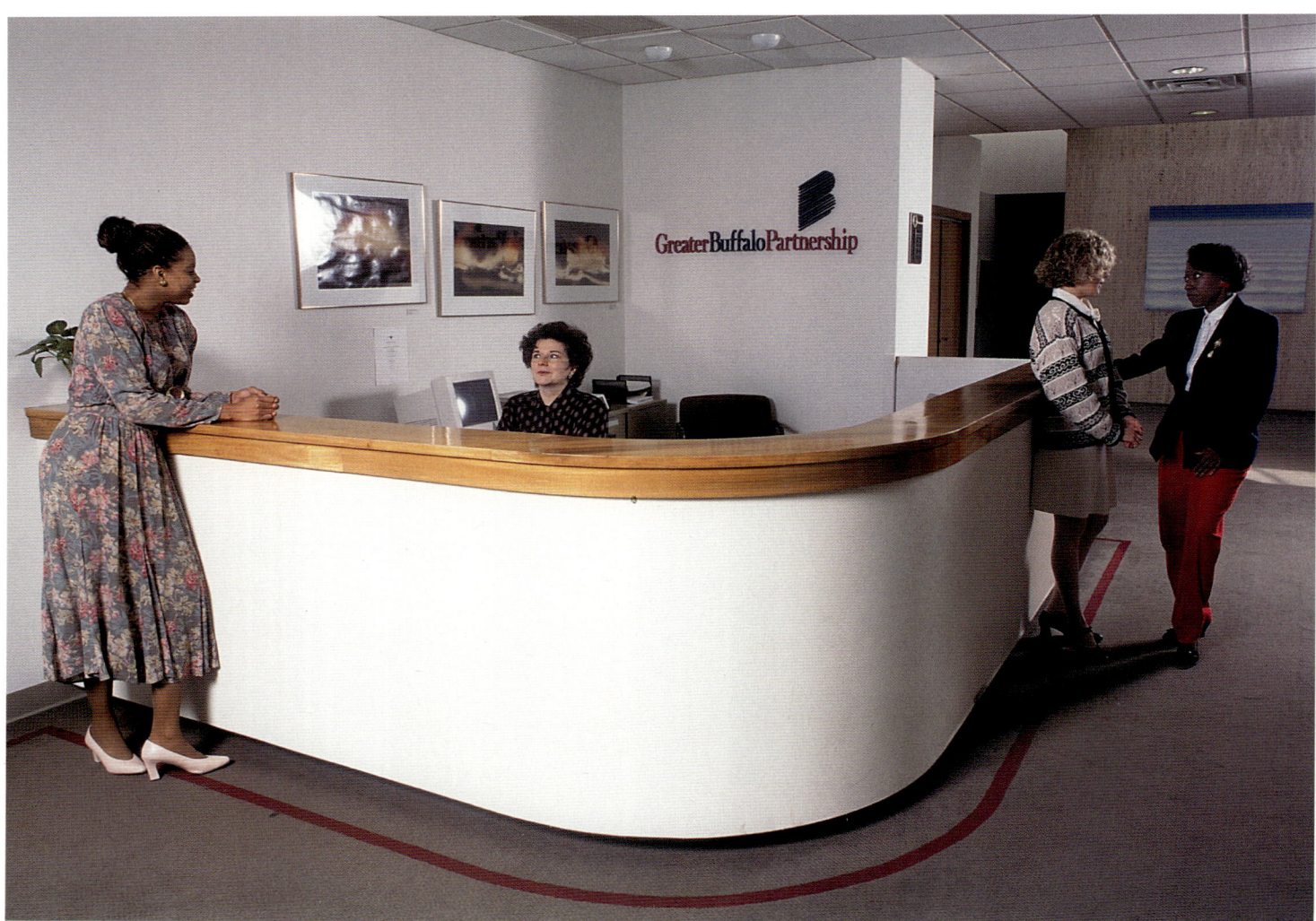

element in the marketplace's competitive advantage. Among the strengths the Partnership has identified and actively markets is the area's role as a transhipment point for almost one-third of the more than $270 billion (U.S.) in annual trade between the United States and Canada, the world's largest trading partners. With six international bridges, the region provides easy access to the major population and industrial centers of both countries.

Both sides of the border offer highly skilled and motivated work forces. One indicator of the close cross-border economic ties promoted by the Partnership is that the largest private-sector employer on both sides of the border is General Motors, which finds the right combination of factors in Niagara to make it a major manufacturing center.

On government relations and public policy, the Partnership serves as a liaison between private-sector interests and local, state, provincial, and federal governments. In addition to serving as an advocate for business interests, the Partnership brings private-sector expertise to aid governments in dealing with the challenges of economic growth in today's rapidly changing markets.

In Buffalo, hub of the region and New York State's second-largest city, the Partnership has provided critical private-sector expertise on a number of development projects, including the Buffalo Financial Plan Commission. Such public-private partnerships help local governments provide better services while using public funds in the most efficient manner. The Partnership has also played a leadership role in regional cooperation among local governments, helping municipalities increase their financial leverage through joint purchasing agreements and other innovative options for financing public projects.

On the state level, the Partnership represents the Niagara marketplace's collective concerns for New York State's legislative and budget activities, particularly issues related to taxation and regulatory reform.

For member services, the Partnership takes a market-based approach that identifies and develops services tailored specifically to member needs. Along with operational services, such as group purchasing and access to health insurance, cellular and long distance telephone service, payroll, package delivery, transportation and other services, the Partnership offers customized research capabilities on market data, demographics, and other business information. Members also receive free and discounted publications, including member and general industrial directories, mailing lists, wage and salary surveys, maps, and relocation kits.

The Partnership acts as a clearinghouse for information about the marketplace. The Partnership refers each inquiry to the appropriate agency or organization in Western New York or Southern Ontario, including many affiliated organizations and agencies in tourism, education, and development that have a more specialized role in promoting Niagara.

According to the Partnership's president, Andrew J. Rudnick, the Partnership fulfills the role of a "21st-century employer organization," serving not only immediate member interests, but also providing a strategic vision for the region's future. That vision includes continuing to improve the business climate by reducing those regulations and mandates that raise

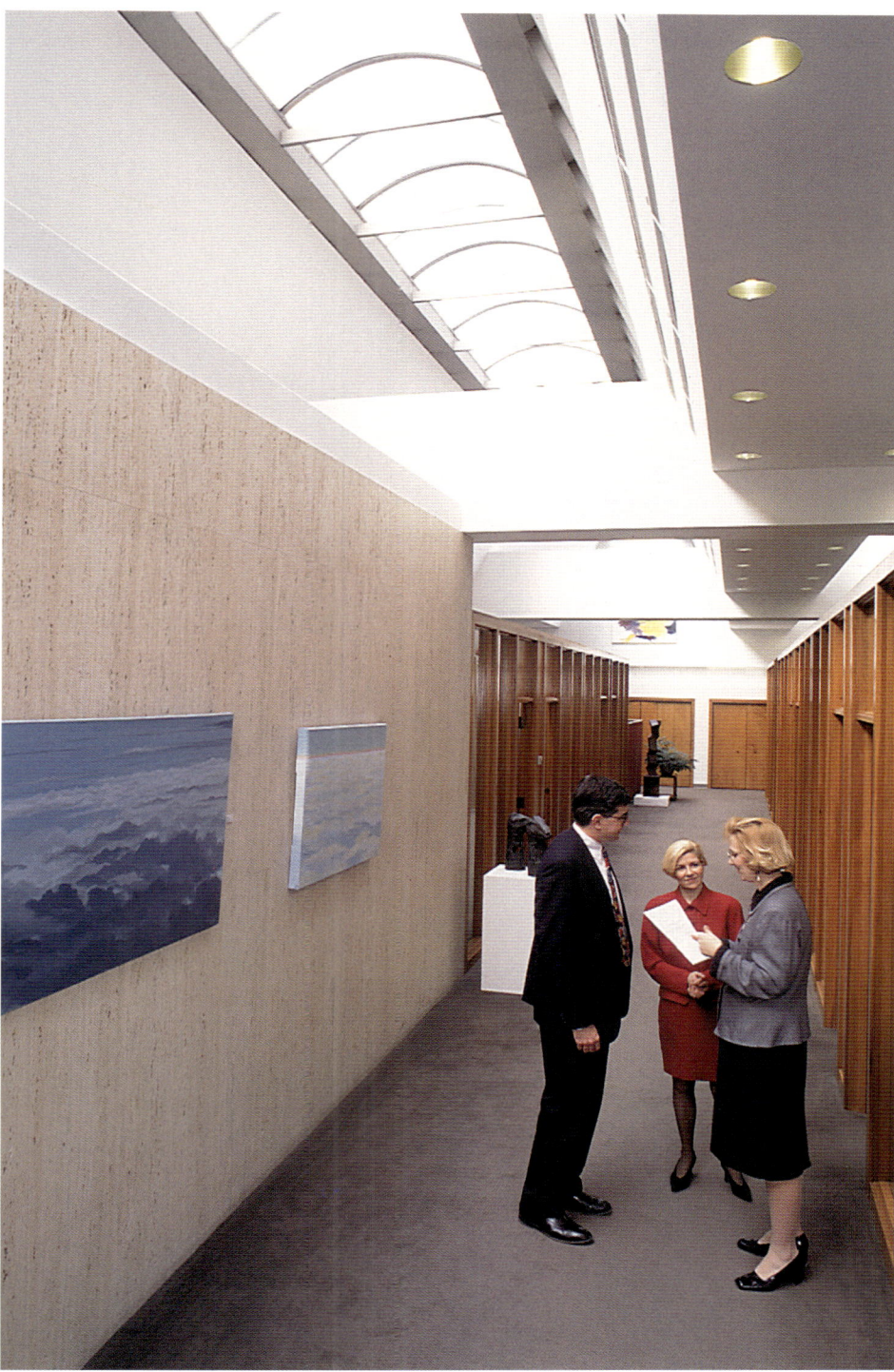

the cost of doing business. The Partnership will also continue to foster greater cooperation and improve operating efficiencies among local and regional governments. Most important, it will continue to be the leading advocate for a regional and binational approach to developing and marketing the binational Niagara marketplace. ◆

The broad-based membership and extensive staff capabilities create a synergy that gives the Partnership a unique strategic role. Photo by James P. McCoy.

MERCHANTS INSURANCE GROUP

Merchants Insurance Group is the largest Buffalo-based insurer of personal automobiles in Western New York.

In 1918, merchants on the West Side of Buffalo got together to seek insurance protection for their delivery vehicles. Today, Merchants Insurance Group protects thousands of business owners and their vehicles in Buffalo and throughout the Northeast.

Founded in Buffalo in 1918 as an insurer providing coverage for local merchants' delivery vehicles, Merchants Insurance Group has grown from a small mutual insurance company to a regional insurer providing property and casualty insurance in 13 states. Established to meet the needs of small businesses and individuals, the company has remained true to its mission, operating as a customer-oriented underwriter that identifies the need for new and innovative insurance coverage, then moves to fill those needs with affordable, quality insurance products.

Today Merchants provides insurance to more than 120,000 customers through two companies, Merchants Mutual Insurance Company and Merchants Insurance Company of New Hampshire, Inc. Merchants Mutual continues to operate as a mutual insurer owned by its policyholders, and Merchants Insurance Company of New Hampshire, Inc. is the wholly owned subsidiary of Merchants Group, Inc., a publicly traded company listed on the American Stock Exchange. Marketed together as Merchants Insurance Group, the companies have more than $150 million in annual premiums, placing Merchants Insurance Group among the top 200 insurers in the United States.

The two companies maintain separate underwriting guidelines, pricing, and products while sharing the same facilities and employees. Merchants of New Hampshire insures preferred risk customers, while Merchants Mutual insures standard risks, allowing agents to offer coverage to a wider range of customers.

The core of Merchants' commercial customer base includes artisans and contractors such as plumbers and electricians, small retail and mercantile businesses, and

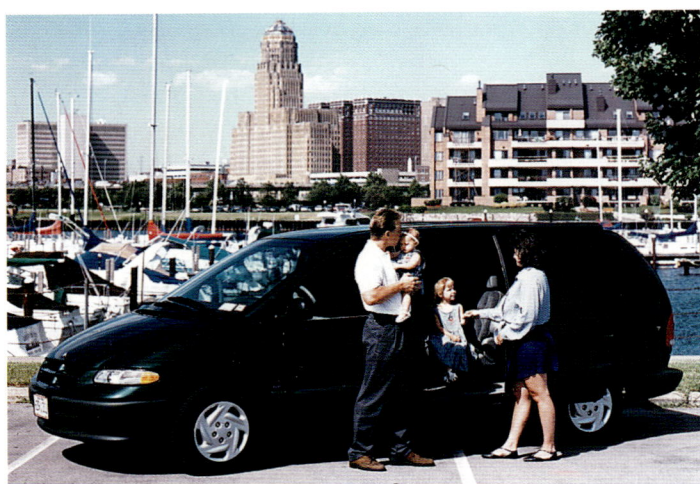

midsized business such as light manufacturers. Merchants provides these customers with a full line of commercial coverage, including property, liability, commercial automobile, and workers' compensation. In addition to its commercial lines, Merchants offers homeowners, personal automobile, and personal umbrella coverages in many of its market areas.

The company's network of more than 670 independent agents is essential to its success. Responsiveness to agents' needs is key to Merchants' growth strategy for the future—a strategy that sees the company in the top 100 U.S. insurers within 10 years.

As a regional insurer, Merchants is uniquely positioned to meet the needs of both its insureds and its agents. For insureds, Merchants offers a better understanding of local and regional economic conditions. That permits Merchants to offer products designed specifically for local conditions, often priced more competitively than products offered by larger insurers.

Similarly, Merchants emphasizes close ties with its agents, taking a proactive approach to identify and meet their needs. Unlike larger companies, Merchants is able to place senior management in the field on a regular basis, talking with agents and insureds to make sure the company is responding to their needs. Merchants actively solicits information from its customers, using focus groups and other formal surveys in addition to regular informal contacts.

Merchants' regional base also allows fast and personal response to everything from routine policy or billing inquiries to claims. Through its network of regional business centers in Albany, Buffalo, and Central Islip, New York; Manchester, New Hampshire; and Moorestown, New Jersey, the company is able to maintain a closer relationship with customers than many national firms.

For agents, Merchants offers a team approach to doing business. Locally based Business Assistance Teams are empowered to quote, underwrite, and accept business in an agent's office, helping agents provide timely and competitive responses to requests for coverage and pricing from existing customers and prospects. Similarly, Claims Assistance Teams work with agents and insureds to provide fast, equitable claims service. A special litigation unit handles most third-party claims, allowing the Claims Assistance Teams to expedite more routine claims.

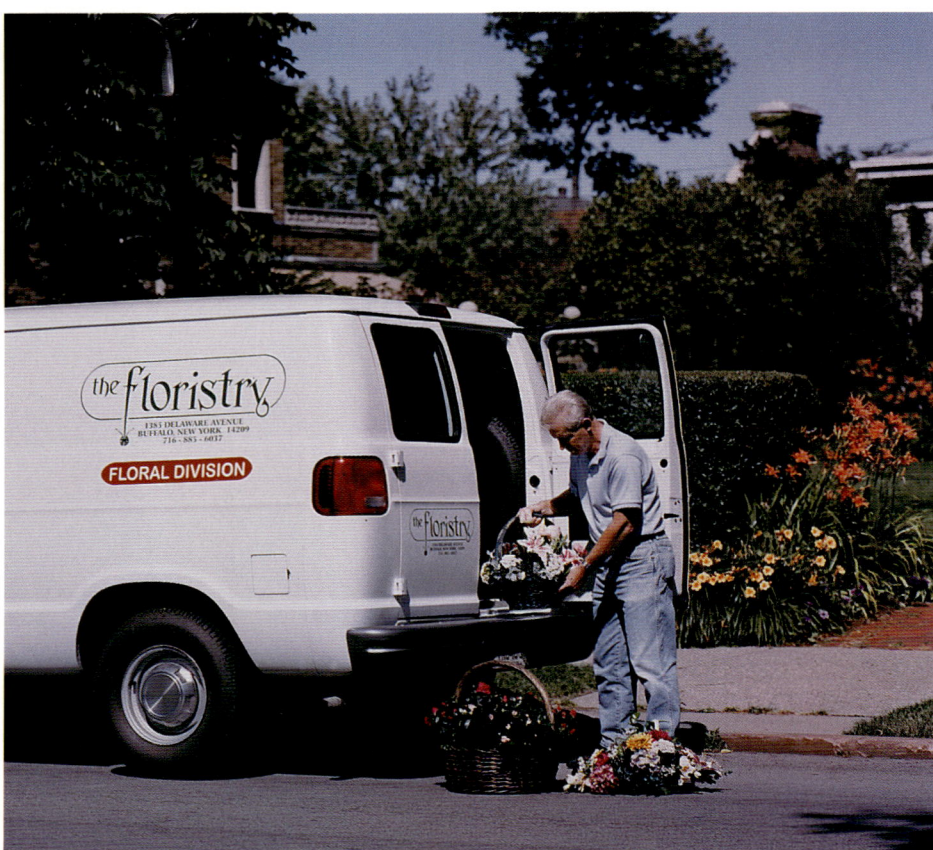

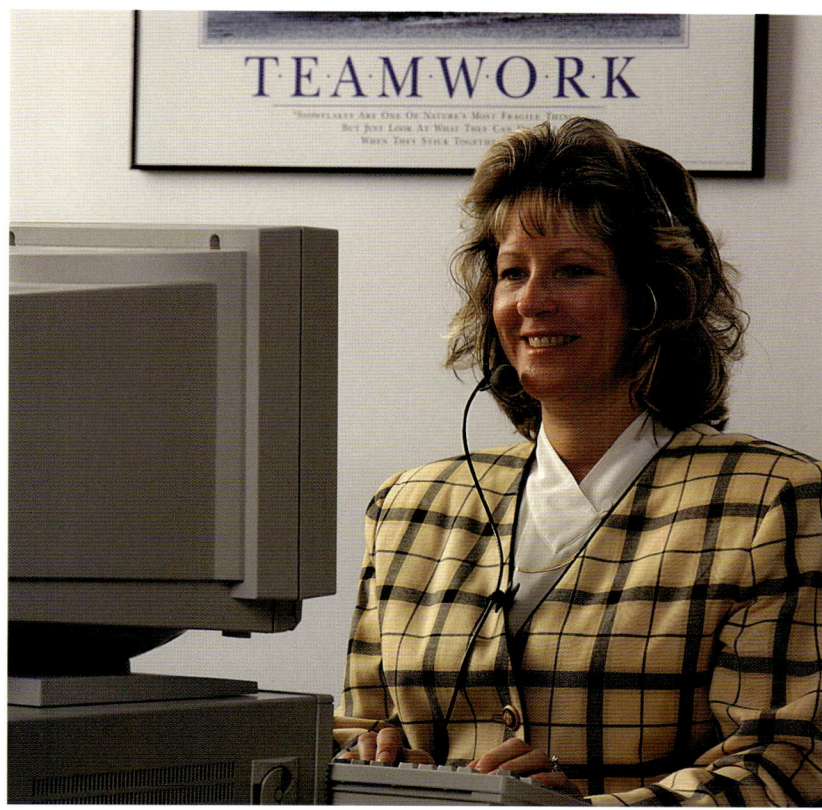

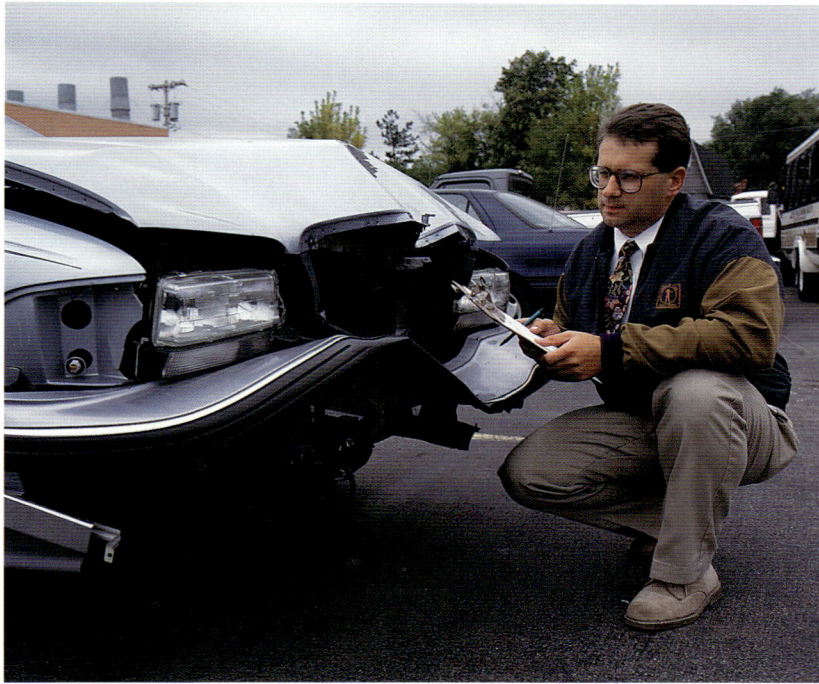

Along with superior service, Merchants' commitment to identifying and responding to customer needs has produced innovative products. For example, the company offers a general liability policy for contractors for which premiums are based on the number of employees rather than payroll amount. Not only does this approach potentially reduce paperwork for the contractor; in many cases it can provide lower premiums, rewarding customers that may have highly paid and skilled workers.

Another area of emphasis for Merchants is expanding its competitiveness and tailored coverage for various classes of business. Expanding the number of classes allows Merchants to tailor coverage specifically to each type of business, often providing better coverage at more competitive premiums. And as economic and business conditions change, Merchants continues to offer new coverage to meet its customers' evolving needs.

Merchants' financial condition is excellent and it has often outperformed the property and casualty insurance industry as measured by the combined ratio, the industry's standard for operating performance.

Another measure of Merchants' industry leadership is its participation in industry groups such as the Coastal Market Assistance Programs, a voluntary program designed to provide affordable insurance to customers in high-risk coastal areas in certain states.

The company participates in the communities it serves. A contributor to many charities, Merchants encourages employee participation through an employee organization called Colleagues In Action (CIA), with a board of directors comprised of employees who evaluate, select, and plan volunteer efforts. Activities have ranged from corporate sponsorship of a multiple sclerosis fund-raising walk to distribution of free smoke detectors during National Fire Prevention Week. The company is also a major contributor to Buffalo's annual United Way fund drive.

As Merchants improves its efficiency and responsiveness, it plans to grow regionally. Expansion plans target the near Midwest, especially Ohio, where Merchants is already positioned to bring its unique blend of personal service and innovative, custom-tailored property and casualty insurance products to individuals and businesses who need affordable protection for their homes, automobiles, and businesses.

This focus on service has resulted in a loyal group of agents who work closely with Merchants to provide insureds with the products and service they need. In addition to a close working relationship, Merchants offers its agents attractive incentives such as bonuses of policy premiums to insureds and profit sharing, and time-saving services such as direct billing.

Merchants has also embarked on an aggressive automation campaign to streamline internal work flows for greater efficiency and better customer service. Because of its size, the company is uniquely positioned to combine the most modern computer technology with a human touch. Along with improving internal efficiency, the company sees new and exciting applications for technology, including assisting its agents in using the Internet to capture and disseminate information, generate and pursue leads, and deliver quotes.

There are over 300 colleagues behind every Merchants insurance policy. The company prides itself on the service its colleagues provide to independent insurance agents and policyholders.

A Merchants Claim Adjuster inspects a damaged automobile. Fast, equitable claims settlements have helped Merchants earn consistently high customer satisfaction ratings.

LOCKPORT SAVINGS BANK

The only savings bank headquartered in the Niagara region, Lockport Savings Bank has both a proud tradition and a promising future. Incorporated in 1870 as the Farmers and Mechanics Savings Bank, the bank has grown and prospered through late 19th-century money panics, two world wars, the Great Depression, and the financial turmoil of recent times when many savings banks disappeared.

Throughout its history, the bank has been distinguished by conservative financial management and a strong commitment to the community it serves. That commitment is reflected in everything from the bank's name change in 1967 to its current name, Lockport Savings Bank, to its customer service philosophy, *"Experience the Person To Person Commitment."*

The success of this philosophy is evident in the bank's growth in recent years, precisely when many other banks were struggling to survive. In 1971, the bank's assets were $100 million; today, assets top $1 billion and continue to grow. The bank has received numerous commendations from state and national banking associations, including recognition as one of the safest banks in the United States, and it ranks in the top 300 savings banks in both size and profitability.

Today, the bank has branches throughout the Niagara region, with plans for continued expansion locally. A further indication of the bank's commitment to the area is its new 76,000-square-foot administrative center in Pendleton, on the border of Niagara and Erie counties. Slated for completion in 1997, the building will provide space for more than 300 employees, increasing the bank's growth capabilities and

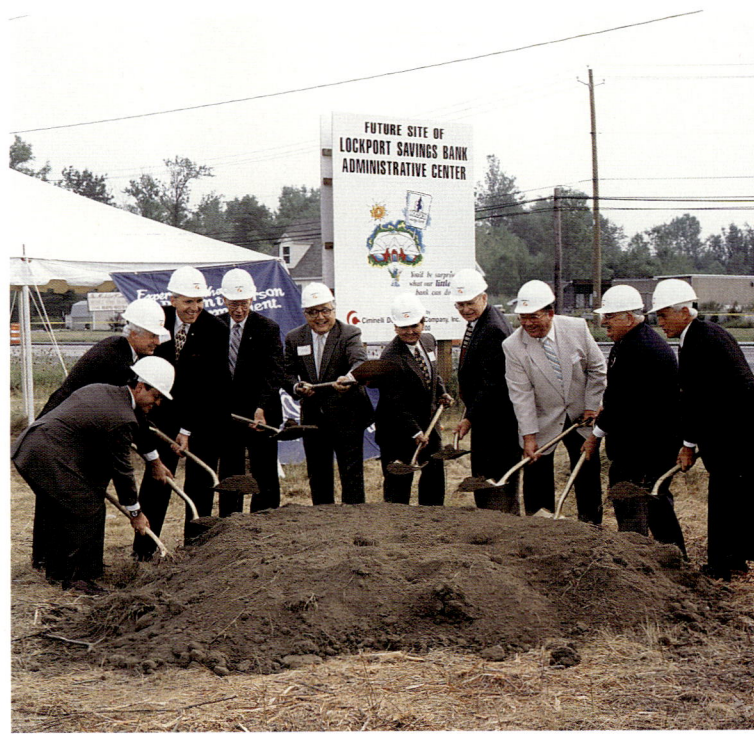

Bank management, government officials, and project developers break ground for the bank's new Administrative Center scheduled for completion in 1997.

High tech equipment increases speed and accuracy, allowing customer questions to be answered more efficiently.

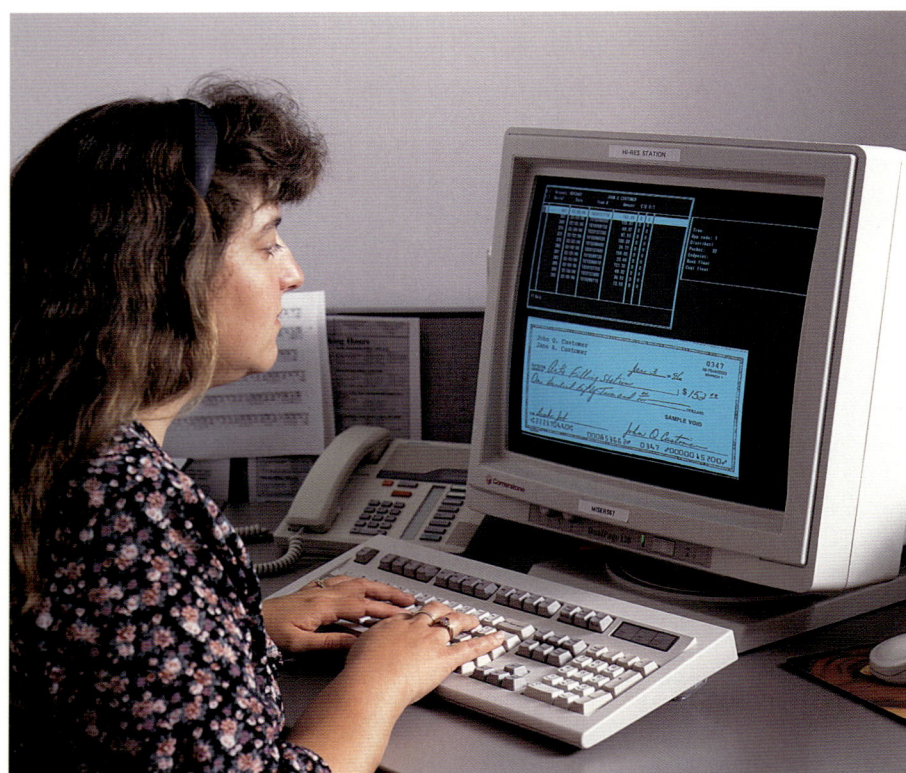

adding jobs to the local economy. The bank's president and chief executive officer, William E. Swan—only the 10th president in the bank's history—is also a signatory of the Niagara Compact, committing the bank to promoting job growth and attracting new business to the Niagara region.

While Lockport Savings Bank's growth is impressive by any measure, even more remarkable is that it has been generated internally. Instead of pursuing a strategy of acquisitions, the bank has dedicated itself to attracting new business by providing superior customer service and banking products in its home market, Western New York.

Labeled a "plain vanilla bank" by competitors, Lockport Savings Bank has proven that community banking based on solid customer service and core banking products not only can succeed but thrive. The hallmark of the bank's service is the combination of "high touch" personal service with "high tech" sophistication, providing competitive products delivered with warm, friendly service.

In addition to earning the bank a reputation for stellar customer service, this combination has made Lockport Savings Bank a local innovator in selected products and services. It was the first local bank to offer a check imaging service to its checking customers in lieu of returning cancelled checks. It was also one of the first to offer in-store banking in area supermarkets seven days a week.

Along with traditional savings bank products, such as savings and checking accounts and home mortgages, the bank offers consumer loans, student loans, commercial loans, credit and debit cards, special savings plans for pensions, payroll and education, telephone banking service, and more. It also has extended banking hours at many branches, as well as 7-day-a-week, 24-hour-a-day banking access through its Customer Connection phone line, and with Mastermoney™ at Automatic Teller Machines (ATMs). The bank is also one of the largest Savings Bank Life Insurance (SBLI) providers in New York State.

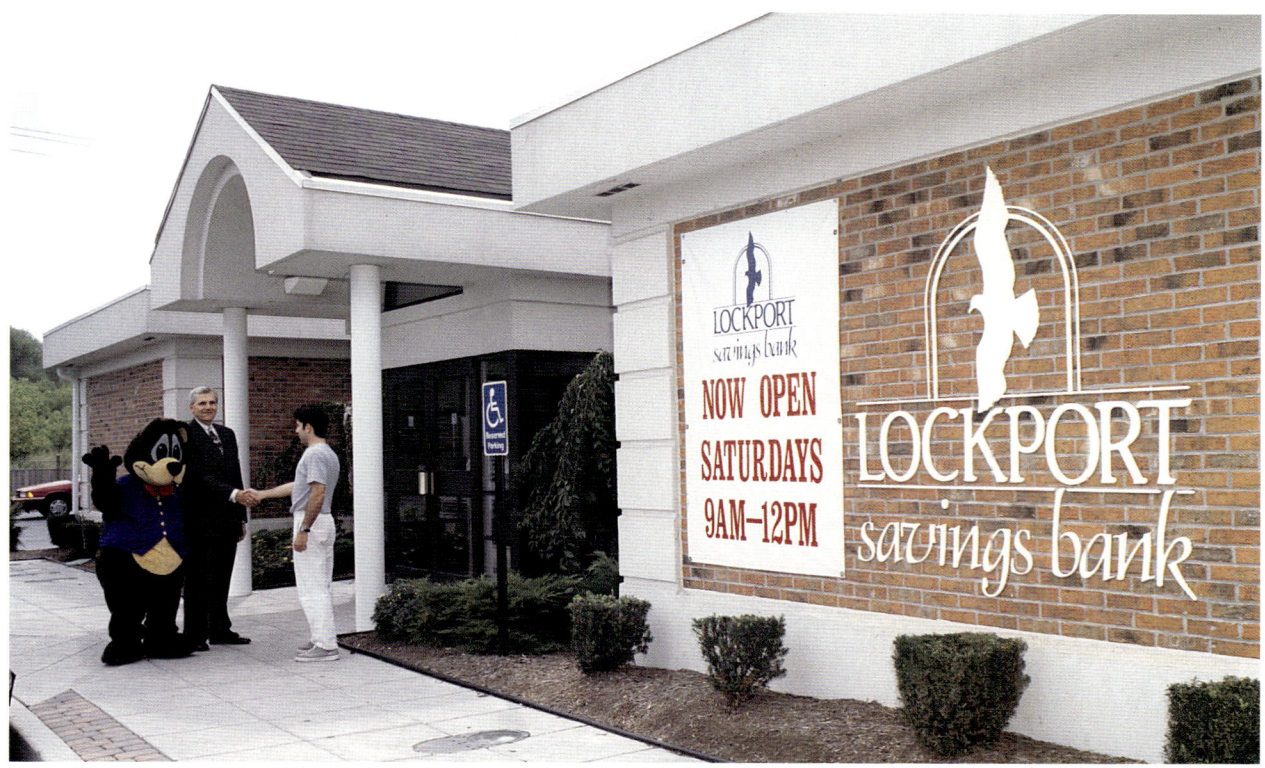

William E. Swan, President and Chief Executive Officer and Ellis B. Bear, the bank's mascot, greet a customer at Lockport Savings Bank's North Tonawanda location.

Another important ingredient in the bank's success is its responsiveness to customer needs. The bank has performed extensive surveys of both customers and non-customers to learn what the local market wants in a bank, then has moved aggressively to meet those needs. Along with in-branch surveys, every customer receives "Person To Person" surveys each year. Every customer recommendation leads to direct action, providing the bank with an opportunity to improve service for all its customers.

Most important of all is the commitment of everyone at Lockport Savings Bank to shared values that include not only the "Person To Person Commitment" to provide superior service to all customers, but also a strong commitment to enhancing the quality of life in the communities the bank serves. Through employment opportunities, contributions to and participation in community organizations, and reinvestment in the Niagara region through lending activities, Lockport Savings Bank contributes to a stronger economy and a better quality of life for the entire region.

This commitment to the community is found at every level, from the teller lines to the executive offices. Both as an organization and through the efforts of individual employees, Lockport Savings Bank supports more than 550 local, regional, and national organizations. As part of the activities commemorating the bank's 125th anniversary year in 1995, the bank's employees increased their already strong community involvement to provide an average of 125 hours a week of community service to local organizations.

One of the most visible symbols of the bank's community involvement is its ever-popular mascot, Ellis B. Bear, whose appearances at community events, schools, hospitals, and nursing homes delight everyone from the very young to the region's senior residents. Lockport Savings Bank also runs one of the few remaining School Saver plans, collecting savings from elementary school children throughout the area

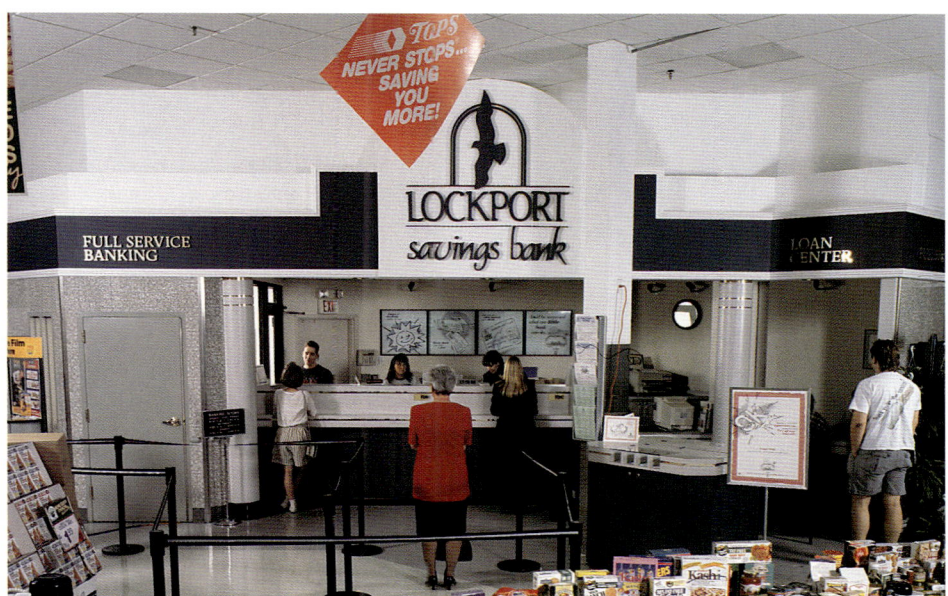

Supermarket locations provide customers with the convenience of seven day-a-week, full service banking and extended hours.

and helping to develop good financial habits in the next generation of Western New Yorkers.

Combining traditional values with a strong appreciation of its home market and an openness to change, Lockport Savings Bank has grown and adapted to become one of the most successful savings banks in the United States. Conservative without being complacent, strongly capitalized and superbly positioned for continued regional growth, Lockport Savings Bank will continue to thrive as a community-oriented institution committed to exceeding the expectations of its customers and to meeting the needs of future generations. ❖

INTERNATIONAL MOTION CONTROL, INC.

In its brief lifetime, International Motion Control (IMC), Inc. has already become a world leader in motion control. Headquartered in Orchard Park, New York, IMC was established in 1994 to make acquisitions of companies with technologies and product lines synergistic to a particular area of expertise in motion control. These four operating groups include Energy Absorption and Vibration Isolation, Fluid Power, Controls, and Distribution.

By 1996, IMC had quintupled its size and purchased several companies, all manufacturers of engineered motion control products. The company's philosophy is to seek out new products, new markets, and acquisitions that will add to the mix already in place. According to one company official, "We look for new products, technologies, or businesses that give us the opportunity to expand our core competencies."

Every company in IMC's four operating groups is a proven market leader (including the flagship company, Enidine Incorporated). Working together as a Global Solutions Team, their collective expertise enables them to custom engineer the best solution for virtually any motion control challenge, for any customer, anywhere in the world.

Enidine, the IMC Energy Absorption and Vibration Isolation Group, is headquartered in Orchard Park, New York, with a manufacturing facility in Germany, a sales office in California and Japan, and sales distributors all over the world. Since 1966, Enidine has achieved a worldwide reputation for quality engineering solutions, and offers the world's most comprehensive range of standard and special products for energy absorption and vibration isolation, including shock absorbers, rate controls, seismic dampers, air springs, wire rope isolators, and elastomeric mounts. Markets include industrial manufacturing, material handling, communications, seismic, power generation, commercial aviation, and defense. The company's custom engineering, manufacturing, and testing capabilities can solve virtually any challenge. Enidine attributes its success to its ambitious research and development programs and its commitment to understanding and responding to specific customer needs.

In 1996, Enidine was awarded $3,370,000 as part of the Technology Reinvestment Project to develop a semi-active isolation system for seismic protection on structures and shock protection on submarines. Enidine and partners matched the federal award to fund the project at a total of $6,740,000 and are working on the 24-month program in partnership with the State University of New York at Buffalo, the National Center for Earthquake Engineering Research, the Naval Surface Warfare Center CARDEROCK, and Hydro-Line, Inc.

IMC's Fluid Power Goup includes Hydro-Line, Inc. of Rockford, Illinois; Reno, Nevada; Charlotte, North Carolina; and Midland Pneumatic, Ltd. of Wolverhampton, England. Its markets include motor vehicle production, plastics, packaging, pulp and paper, textiles, lumber and wood products, power generation, material handling, agriculture, marine, medical, entertainment, mining, and process control equipment.

High-quality and exceptional product performance have led Hydro-Line to the forefront of fluid power actuation technology. Continually innovative since its inception in 1946, Hydro-Line has been responsible for the development of the HLT electronic linear positioning probe for systems actuators, specially designed injection and blowmolding actuators for the plastics industry, seismic and low-friction cylinder designs, and Rapid Advance Cylinder Technology. Its products include hydraulic, pneumatic, and custom actuators; linear actuator sensing and feedback systems.

Founded in 1956, Midland Pneumatic provides a full range of noncorrosive stainless steel and brass pneumatic products. The firm has built an international reputation for its ability to respond quickly with special solutions to meet unique customer requirements, especially those resulting from stringent government and environmental regulations. Midland pioneered the use of PTFE material in the construction of valve slides and developed a total dry run actuator for the food and beverage industry. Its products include stainless steel and brass pneumatic actuators, valves, filters, regulators, and ancillaries.

IMC's Controls Group is comprised of Cleveland Motion Controls (CMC) and Dynact, Inc. and Motion Science, Inc.

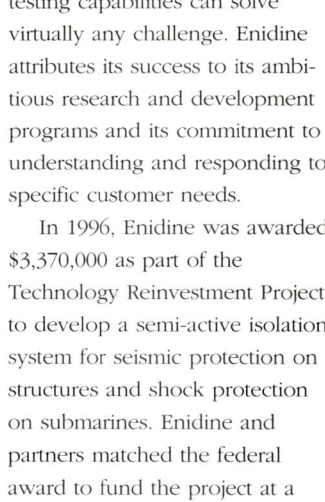

IMC Leadership:
(standing) Patrick P. Lee, Chairman & CEO;
(seated) John Burgess, President & COO; Richard Ryan, CFO.

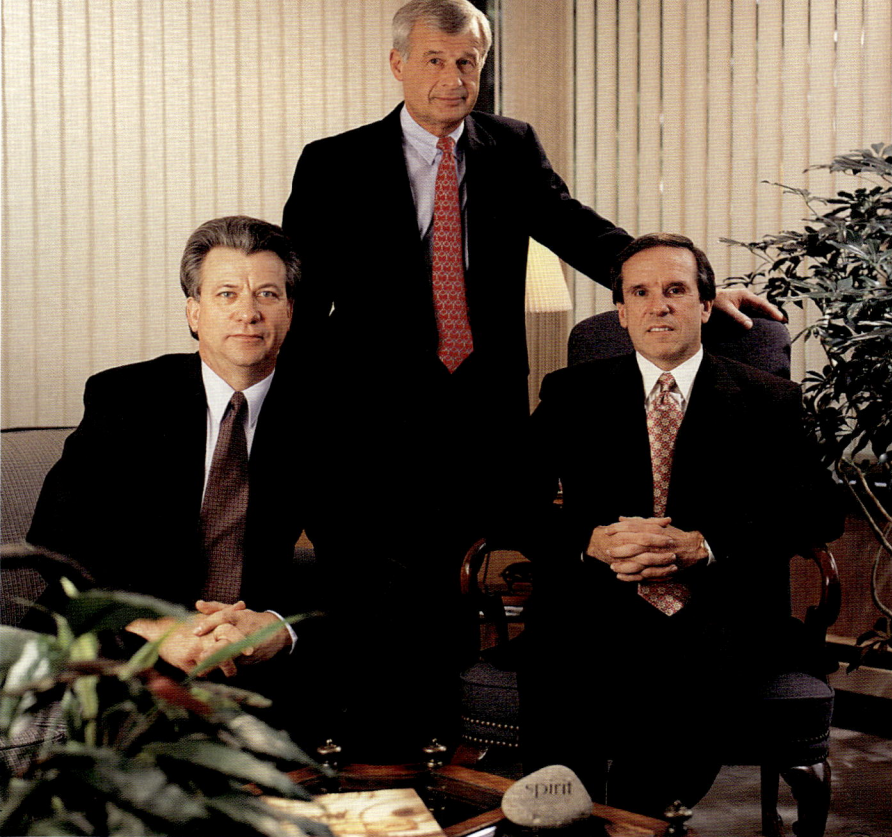

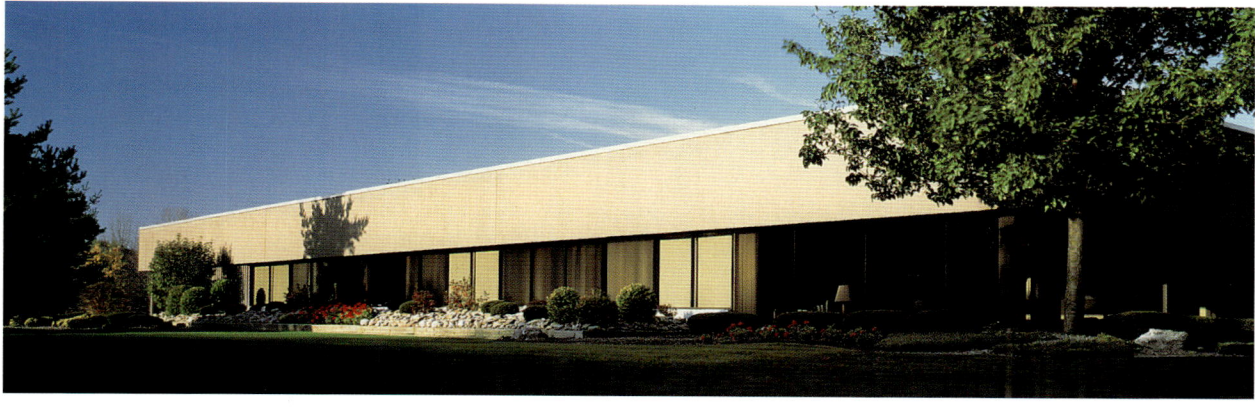

Founded in 1958, CMC manufactures and markets high-performance electronic motion control products worldwide. It currently has several product groups: the Servo Group in Boston, Massachusetts; Applied Technology Group in Pittsburgh, Pennsylvania; and the Industrial Products Group, Engineered Drives and Systems Group, and Burny Group in Cleveland, Ohio.

CMC markets through an extensive network of distributors, manufacturer's representatives, and a direct sales force throughout the United States, Canada, Europe, and the Far East. CMC's product line includes adjustable-speed AC and DC drives, brush and brushless servo drives and motors, encoders, CMC controls for shape cutting, controls for regulating tension in moving webs, and distance measurement systems. CMC Groups serve diverse markets such as printing, converting, packaging, material handling, steel processing, papermaking, welding and flame cutting, as well as machine tools, automotive, and health care. Much of the success of the organization has been the company's ability to design and engineer complete motion control systems.

Dynact, Inc. the Actuator Products Group of Orchard Park, New York(electromechanical), and the Motion Science Group of San Jose, California(servo amplifiers and motion controllers) was founded in 1979, and are well known for their capability to design and manufacture standard and custom solutions that employ electromechanical linear actuators and electronic drives and controls. Their products deliver exceptional field performance, exceeding customer requirements for accurate positioning, velocity control, setup flexibility, and ease of use. The products are designed to peak performance and reliability in the most demanding of applications.

Products include electromechanical positioning devices, servo amplifiers, and motion controllers. Their markets include semiconductor equipment, machine tools, plastics machinery, packaging, factory automation, and medical equipment.

IMC's distribution strategy leverages marketing strength through selective partnership and ownership arrangements. IMC's Distribution Group, Credimex A.G. of Switzerland, specializes in the sale of motion control products and specialty antifriction materials and processes. Delta Rail S.A. of France markets Enidine railroad products to the European rail markets. Located in Brussels, La Dynamique Appliquee distributes Enidine products in Belgium. Enidine S.A. distributes IMC products to Spain and Portugal, and Enidine S.A. de C.V. represents IMC products in Mexico.

IMC companies maintain close working partnerships with some 275 independent distributors and sales organizations in 45 countries across the globe. This strategy has resulted in the finest international distribution network in the motion control industry.

IMC firms have set a standard of excellence. For its outstanding export business, Enidine was recognized by the governor of New York State with a Governor's Award for export. The firm is also the recipient of a national President's "E" Award for Excellence, given to those few outstanding companies and individuals who have excelled in their efforts to increase United States exports.

IMC's current mix of sales is about 75 percent domestic and 25 percent in the export market. The company's primary objective has been to build an organization offering the broadest range of resources available, including products, engineering assistance, and service, to respond to customer needs as quickly and efficiently as possible.

For IMC, leadership means achieving a synergy of products, services, resources, and expertise no other corporation can match. In the future, its strategy of developing new technologies, new products, and new markets will continue to strengthen this synergy. ❧

Synergy in motion.

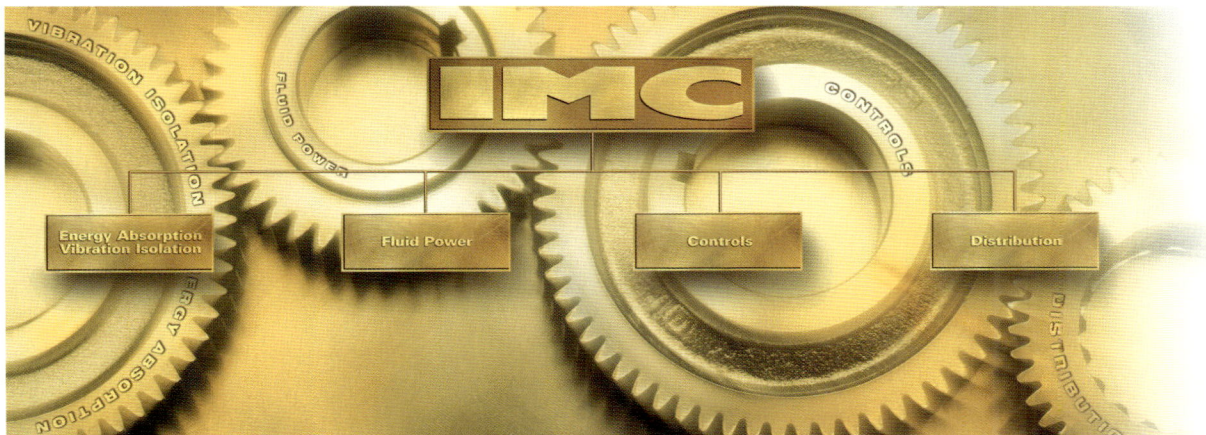

CIMINELLI CONSTRUCTION COMPANIES

In New York State and northern Pennsylvania, Ciminelli translates as "can do." Comprised of the Louis P. Ciminelli Construction Company, Inc. and Ciminelli-Cowper Company, Inc., respective experts in general construction and construction management, the firm has acquired a reputation for getting large, complex building projects done within budget and on time.

In a business where delays and spiraling costs are just another occupational hazard, that's quite a claim, but Ciminelli has the public accolades—not to mention solid structures of steel and concrete—to prove it. The firm is the winner of an unprecedented four Build New York awards, bestowed by the General Building Contractors of New York State to honor excellence and quality in building construction. The following projects were honored: Pilot Field, now called North AmeriCare Park, Buffalo's minor league ball park, where Ciminelli-Cowper was particularly commended

for managing the difficult site conditions and challenging schedule; Key Center at Fountain Plaza, Buffalo's "twin peaks" office/retail complex; North Atlantic Regional Office of State Farm Mutual Insurance Company in Malta, New York, which Ciminelli completed ahead of a very aggressive schedule; and Menorah Campus, now known as the Weinberg Campus, a 72-acre gerontological complex in Eggertsville that offers a full range of housing and health services to the community's elderly population.

The Ciminelli Construction Companies are in a continuous state of building, managing or completing the construction of some of the area's most prominent structures. High-volume facilities such as the Airport Parking Ramp, the U.S. Plaza at the Rainbow Bridge in Niagara Falls, Target Stores, and Marine Midland Arena are in good company with industrial and manufacturing projects at General Motors, Dunlop Tire Corporation, American Ref-Fuel, Outokumpu American Brass, and Russer Foods. In addition, the firm is proud of its involvement with school districts such as West Seneca Central, Hamburg Central, East Aurora Union Free, Phelps-Clifton Springs, and Oakfield-Alabama Central.

The history of the Ciminelli Construction Companies is the story of two successful firms joining forces. The Frank L. Ciminelli Construction Company was founded in 1961 by Frank Ciminelli, a concrete contractor. By 1972, the firm had expanded to provide general contractor services, with "self perform" capabilities in concrete, site, and carpentry work. Ciminelli grew throughout the 1970s and 1980s, developing an excellent reputation for high-quality work, provided on time and within budget.

In 1989, the construction management division of the John W. Cowper Company (a firm incorporated in 1915) was purchased by Ciminelli, thus forming a separate company, Ciminelli-Cowper Company, Inc. The firm is now the largest 100 percent construction management company based in upstate New York and has been cited as the 10th-largest health care construction manager in the nation by *Modern Healthcare* magazine.

A major project recently completed by Ciminelli-Cowper's management team was the $65 million Tops Supermarket Distribution Center in Lancaster. At slightly under one million square feet, the mammoth facility is emblematic of the latest development in food distribution technology, as well as having presented new construction challenges to Ciminelli-Cowper.

The year 1996 was a landmark for the general construction side of Ciminelli. The Frank L. Ciminelli Construction Company, Inc. became the Louis P. Ciminelli Construction

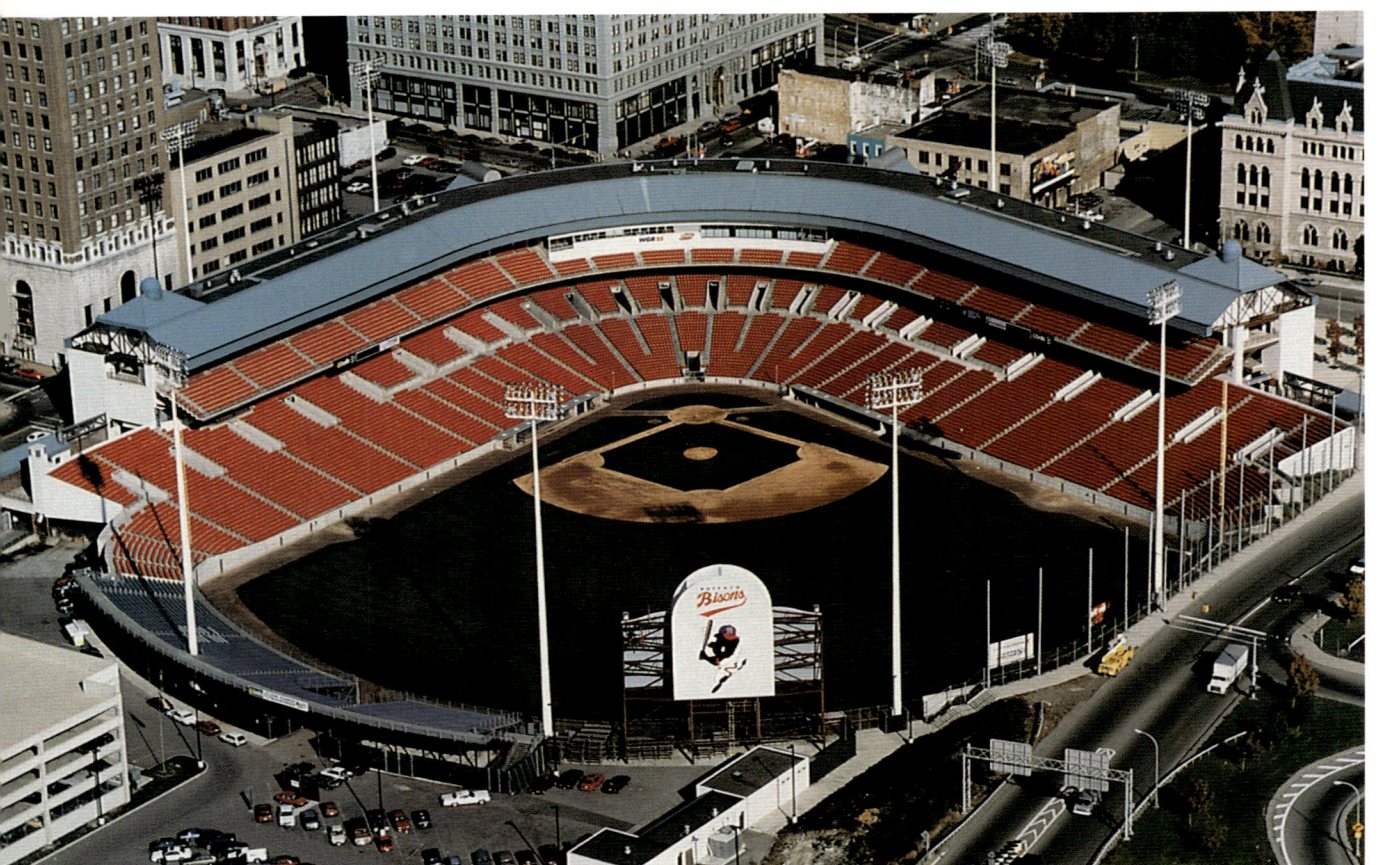

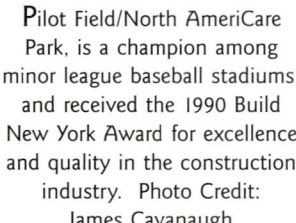

Pilot Field/North AmeriCare Park, is a champion among minor league baseball stadiums, and received the 1990 Build New York Award for excellence and quality in the construction industry. Photo Credit: James Cavanaugh

Sisters of Charity Hospital in Buffalo features state-of-the-art medical facilities, built during a major addition/renovation program while hospital operations continued. Photo Credit: James Cavanaugh

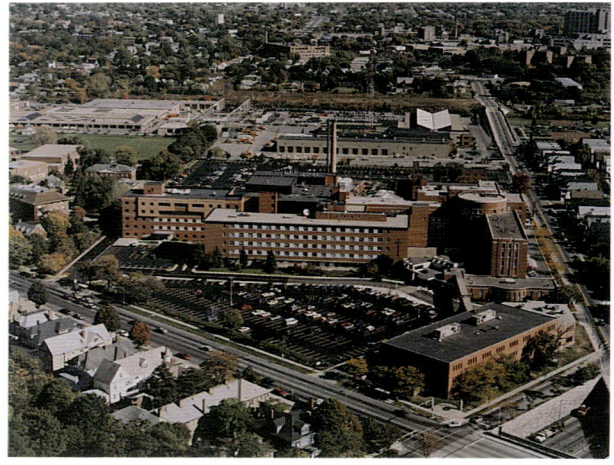

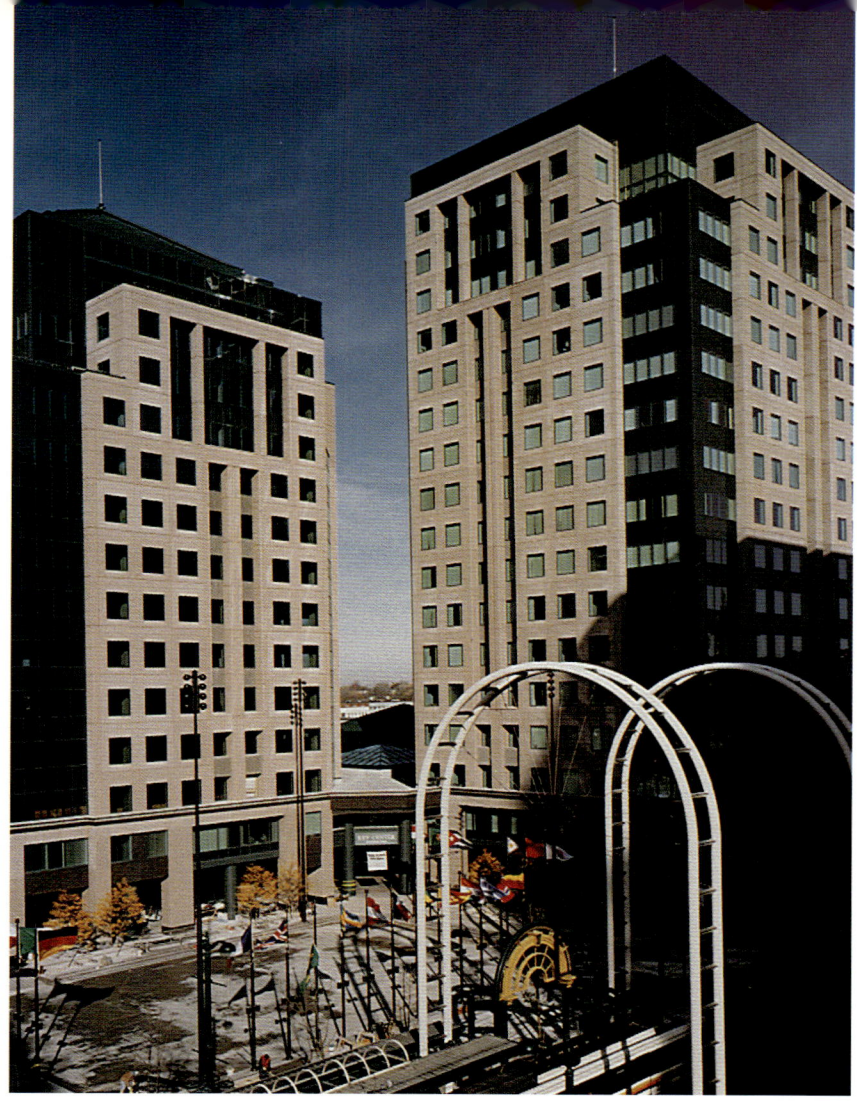

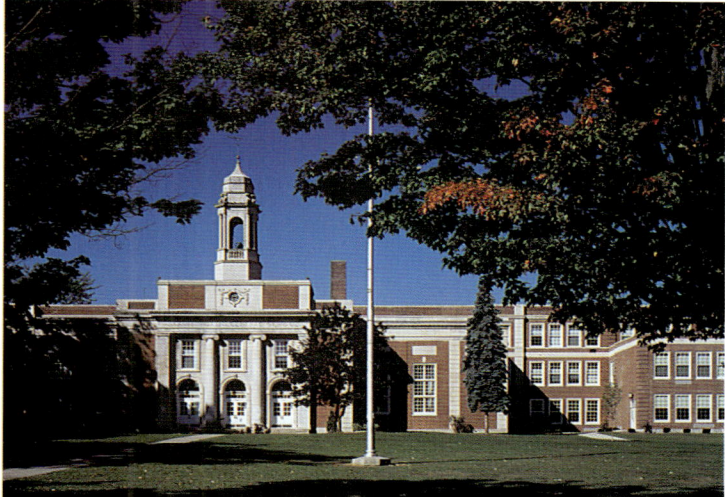

at the achievements across New York State in stone, steel, and glass.

In a fitting tribute to the vision of Frank Ciminelli and the enduring reputation of the company he founded, the Ciminelli Construction Companies opened new corporate offices in the restored Cyclorama Building in downtown Buffalo in 1989. The architectural treasure is one of only two extant cycloramas in this country and dates back to 1888 when immense oil paintings were hung in great round temples as entertainment. When the cyclorama fad ended, the building was used as a roller skating rink, then as a livery stable, a garage, and in 1913, it was deeded to the Grosvenor Library. After being condemned, the Works Progress Administration remodeled the old rotunda for use as a main reading room. The building served scholarly pursuits until the 1960s when the local libraries merged to form the Buffalo and Erie County Public Library. After another decade of disuse, the dilapidated building went up for auction in 1985. Frank Ciminelli bought it and, with designs from George Lukaszewicz Architects and lengthy negotiations with historic preservation officials, renovation began in 1988.

Today, this unique corporate headquarters is a showpiece and an apt symbol of the kind of dedication and perseverance that characterizes the work of Ciminelli Construction Companies. ✤

North Rose-Wolcott Central Schools recently completed a $27 million dollar capital improvements program and relied on construction managers Ciminelli-Cowper to ensure the massive project was completed on target. Photo Credit: Tim Wilkes.

Key Center at Fountain Plaza, the premier office and retail complex in downtown Buffalo, was honored with the 1991 Build New York Award. Photo Credit: James Cavanaugh.

Company, Inc., when Louis bought out the remaining interest in the general contracting company held by his father. The passing of the torch from father to son resulted in changing the company's name, but not its philosophy.

"My father and I have been carefully planning and preparing for this day to ensure a smooth buy-out process," said President and CEO Louis Ciminelli. "He's put his life's energy into building this company, and I think the results of his diligence are more than evident. What he started back in 1961, I'm here to take into the next century."

The combined full-time staff of both companies numbers approximately 140, and together they specialize in educational, industrial, health care, commercial, public, and correctional facility work. In addition, each company has been annually ranked as one of the largest firms in the nation by *Engineering News Record.*

Firm officials expect a large part of the Louis P. Ciminelli Construction Company's future work to continue in the industrial sector with additions and plant renovations, and also the retail market and public work. A major advantage for the construction firm is its ability to do its own concrete, site, and carpentry work, and pull in subcontractors as needed. Round-the-clock work forces are always available to complete tough projects on target.

Ciminelli-Cowper's construction management services to K-12 schools and health care facilities is reputed across upstate New York. Ongoing activities at these institutions require careful planning to overcome the scheduling and phasing challenges, which the company continually meets and exceeds.

Each with its own area of expertise and market niche, the Ciminelli Construction Companies grow by building success upon success, with quality and stability measured by looking

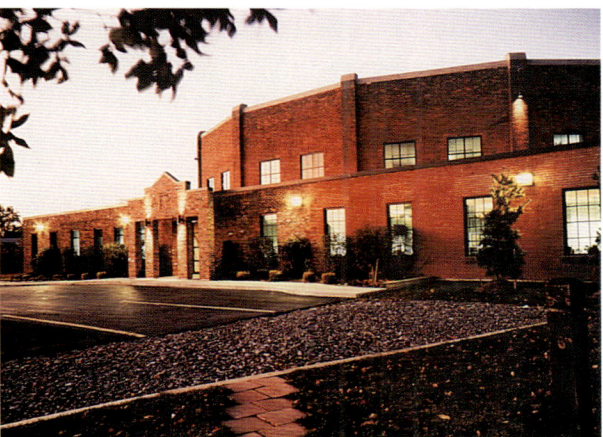

The once derelict Cyclorama Building was saved from demolition when Ciminelli bought the historic structure and worked with preservationists to make the architectural treasure into exceptional office space, and the Ciminelli Construction Companies' central office. Photo Credit: Paul Maze.

NIAGARA ECONOMIC AND TOURISM CORPORATION

The Niagara Economic and Tourism Corporation (NET Corp.) is a nonprofit organization charged with advancing through investment and visitation the economic prosperity of the Niagara region in a globally competitive marketplace. The agency serves the Regional Municipality of Niagara, which is made up of the following cities, towns, and townships: Fort Erie, Grimsby, Lincoln, Niagara Falls, Niagara-on-the-Lake, Pelham, Port Colborne, St. Catharines, Thorold, Wainfleet, Welland, and West Lincoln.

Niagara, Canada—from which one hour's travel accesses the major metropolitan markets of Toronto and Buffalo, and one day's travel reaches 120 million consumers and almost 60 percent of the North American industrial market—is uniquely situated at the center of an international profit zone that offers unlimited opportunities for business.

among the private sector and other government offices and agencies in a binational region.

Its services include site selection assistance for business clients expanding in or relocating to the Niagara region. Destination marketing includes coordinating cooperative marketing programs for the tourism industry, operating information centers, and answering mail and telephone and Internet inquiries. The staff also provides statistical and market data on Niagara's economy, including industrial land and building information, economic indicators, manufacturing/service business contacts, and human resource/training support.

NET Corp. coordinates promotional programs to attract new business, tourism, and investment, including advertising, newsletters, trade shows, and travel to target markets. Consultation and referral to appropriate local businesses, government officials, and other sources for further assistance; support and promotion of regional tourism events; and business assistance program information and support for Niagara companies developing new export markets are also available.

Niagara's business community has a diverse economic base in a broad range of economic sectors. The 1996 Niagara Business Directory documents 847 manufacturing firms and 1,454 companies in selected business service sectors. Overall there are approximately 13,000 businesses in the Niagara Region, including commercial, retail, and industrial companies.

Bounded by the waters of Lake Erie, Lake Ontario, and the Niagara River, the region offers excellent marina facilities and hosts many world-class fishing derbies annually.

Niagara is known for special events and festivals, including the Niagara Grape and Wine Festival, the Friendship Festival, Winter Festival of Lights, the Welland Rose Festival, the Niagara Food Festival, Port Colborne International Week, Grimsby Festival at the Forty, and the St. Catharines Folk Arts Festival.

Niagara Falls remains a premier destination, but the Niagara Region is also famous for many unique attractions, including the Welland Canal, where people can view the ships of the world as they pass through this marvel of modern engineering; historical Niagara-on-the-Lake, the Niagara Wine Route; and the Niagara Parks Commission Butterfly Conservatory, featuring 2,000 free flying butterflies.

The Queen Elizabeth Highway connects much of the region, from Grimsby to Fort Erie, to Southern Ontario and the Northeastern United States. Niagara is also connected to New York State via four international bridges. ✒

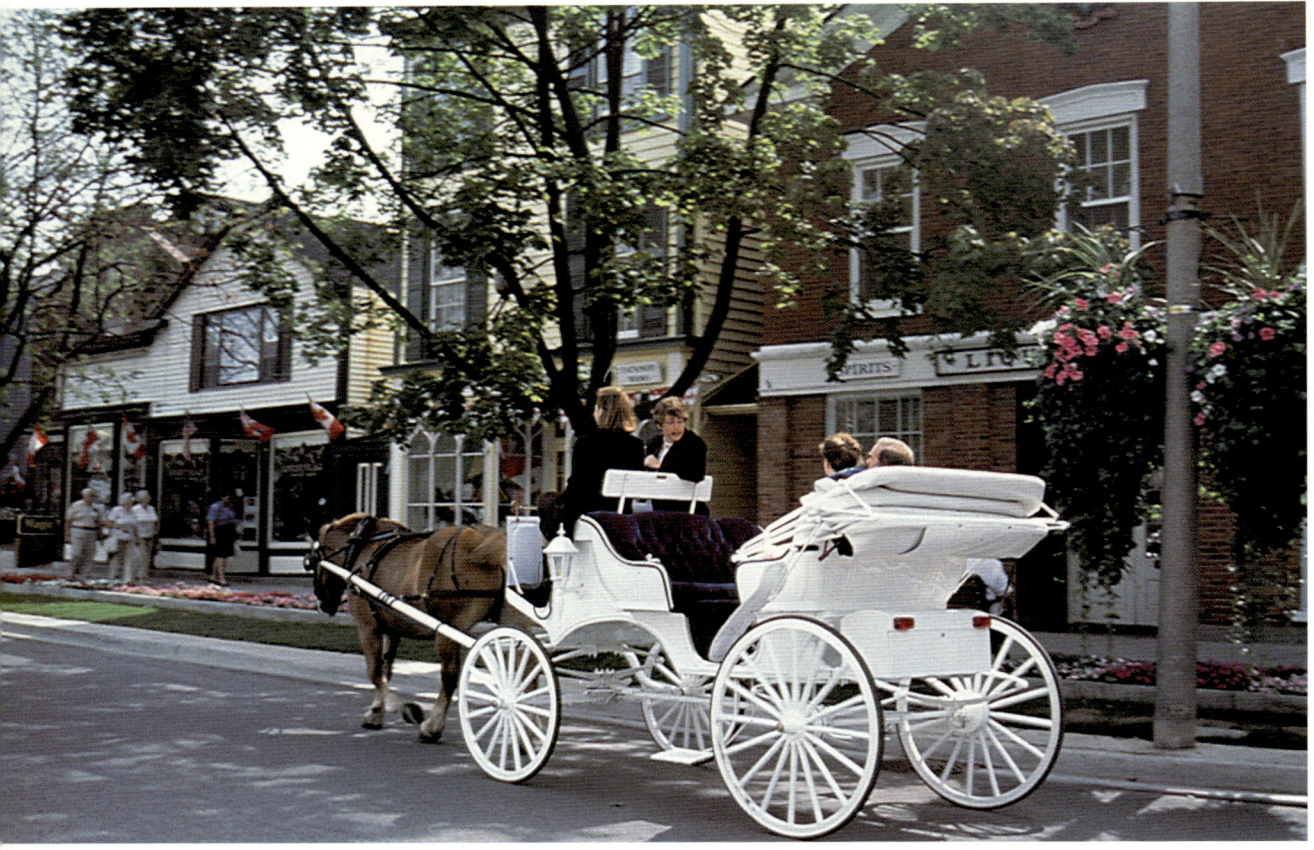

Carriage rides are just one way to enjoy the history and ambiance in Niagara-on-the-Lake, named "Canada's Prettiest Town" in 1996.

The region, which borders on major U.S. markets, is also posited as a vibrant "leisure zone," with an unparalleled diversity of fitness, sporting, social, artistic, historical, theatrical, educational, sightseeing, dining, and shopping opportunities. Niagara is home to the world-famous Shaw Festival, featuring the plays of George Bernard Shaw and his contemporaries; Casino Niagara, golfing on dozens of professionally designed courses; thoroughbred racing at Fort Erie; sailing on the Great Lakes; professional sports venues; and more than 25 wineries producing award-winning vintages including internationally known ice wine. The area draws 14 million visitors annually.

NET Corp., funded by the Regional Municipality of Niagara, is the recognized authority in the business of providing cost-effective, innovative service delivering economic and tourism information to customers, and facilitating decision making

Just as the Niagara region plays a growing role in international trade, so Tower Group International is a leader in global trade services throughout North America. From logistics to information management, Tower Group is one of the preeminent providers of trade services to companies in the U.S. and Canada, and around the world.

Backed by more than 125 years of experience and the resources of The McGraw-Hill Companies, one of the world's leading information and publishing firms, Tower Group has both the size and flexibility to meet the needs of more than 25,000 customers. Clients that range from the world's largest manufacturers to midsized companies to small entrepreneurial firms. As the largest northern border customs broker in North America, Tower Group covers all leading trade gateways on the U.S.-Canada border.

Tower Group offers importers and exporters a wide range of services, including customs brokerage, freight forwarding, transportation, warehousing and distribution, duty drawback, and consulting. In addition, the company offers software products that help international traders manage their logistics channels more efficiently.

Throughout its history, Tower Group has been a pioneer in the use of information and automation. The company filed the first computer-prepared entry with U.S. Customs and was the first to pay duties electronically through the Automated Clearing House. Tower Group was also among the first in the industry to use electronic data interchange. Other innovations include the development of Line Release, the first high-volume use of the Automated Broker Interface, and using imaging technology to enhance customs compliance.

Building on that imaging expertise, Tower Group worked with Federal Express to develop a paperless system that allows FedEx International Priority shipments to be cleared through U.S. Customs without traditional paperwork. The first of its kind, this new method links Tower Group associates in Toronto, Ontario, with the FedEx air hub in Indianapolis, Indiana, and the U.S. Customs Cargo Selectivity computer system in Newington, Virginia. By eliminating document handling, this state-of-the-art system speeds the flow of packages and enhances customs compliance, improving efficiency for FedEx.

The combination of information technology and customs expertise makes Tower Group an attractive business partner that can help companies of all sizes reach new markets and become more profitable in the rapidly changing world of international trade. With 1,200 associates in more than 60 offices across North America, Tower Group provides both personal attention and the resources of a leading logistics services provider.

In the Niagara region, Tower Group has played a key role in facilitating trade under the North American Free Trade Agreement. The company has worked with both U.S. Customs and Canada Customs to develop programs and processes that enable its customers to trade more efficiently while complying with the regulations of both countries and Mexico. Offering true "one-stop shopping" for all import, export, and logistics services, Tower Group has helped many small and midsize companies enjoy the benefits of the world's largest trading relationship, enhancing the Niagara Region's status in international trade in North America and around the world. ❖

TOWER GROUP

Tower Group International provides regulatory compliance and transportation services to North American importers and exporters.
Photo by Marc Murphy.

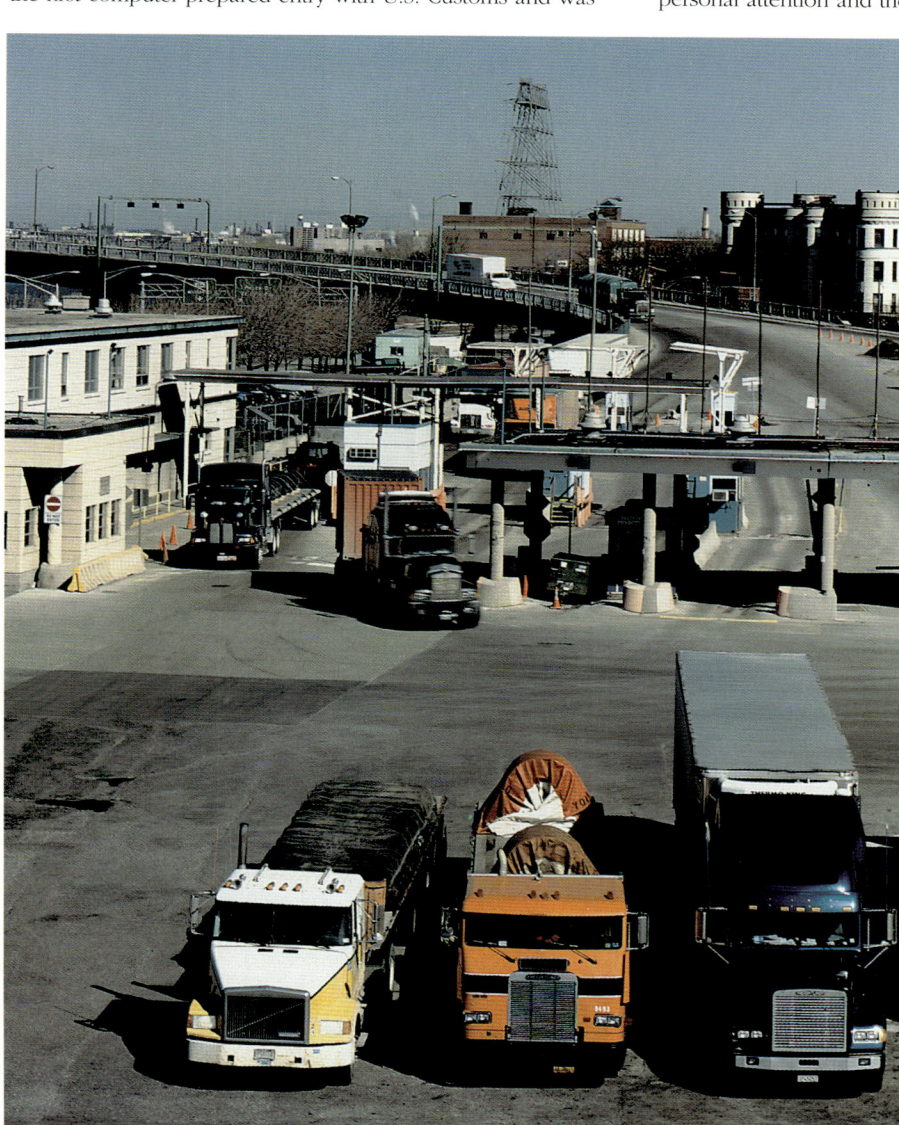

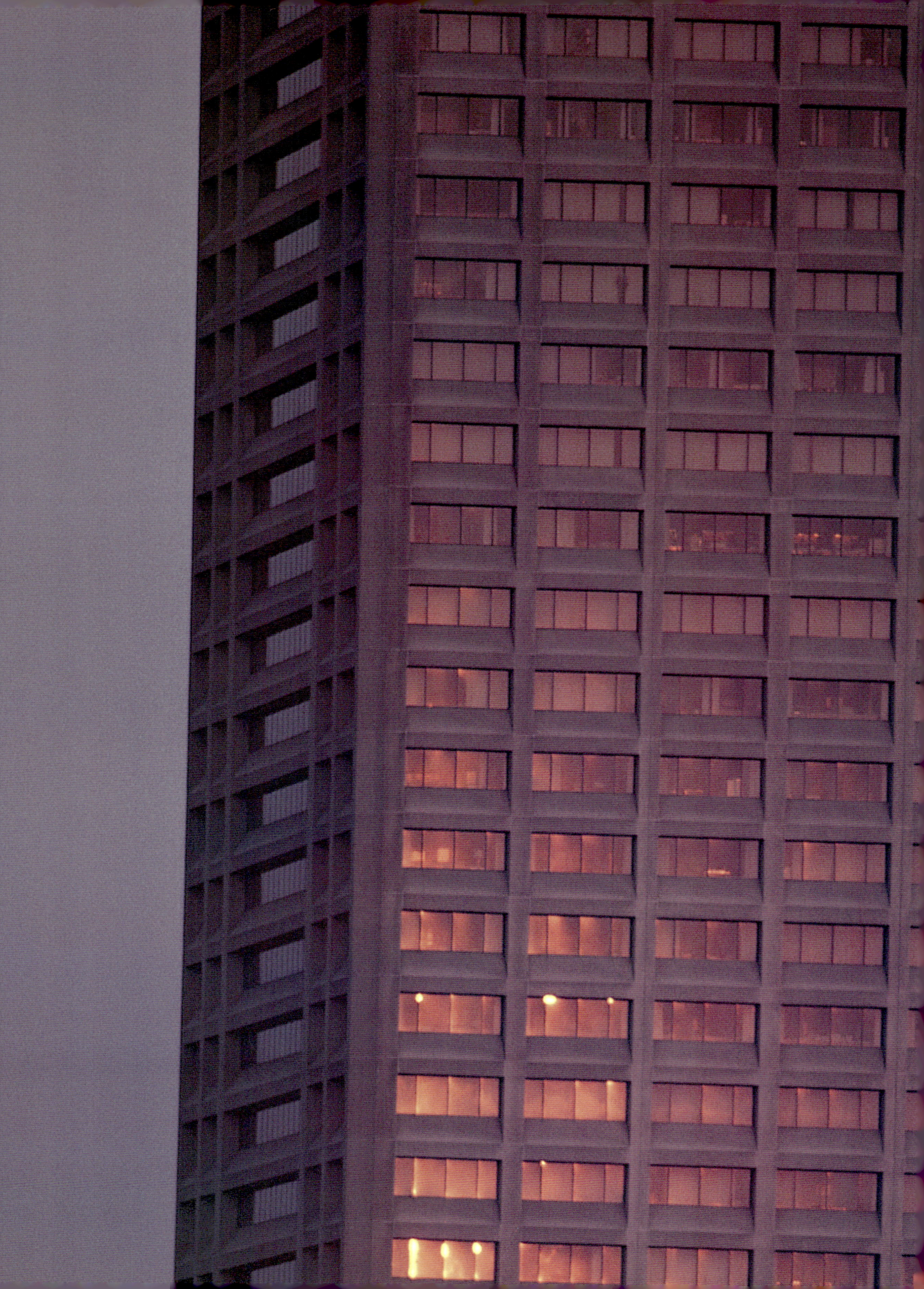

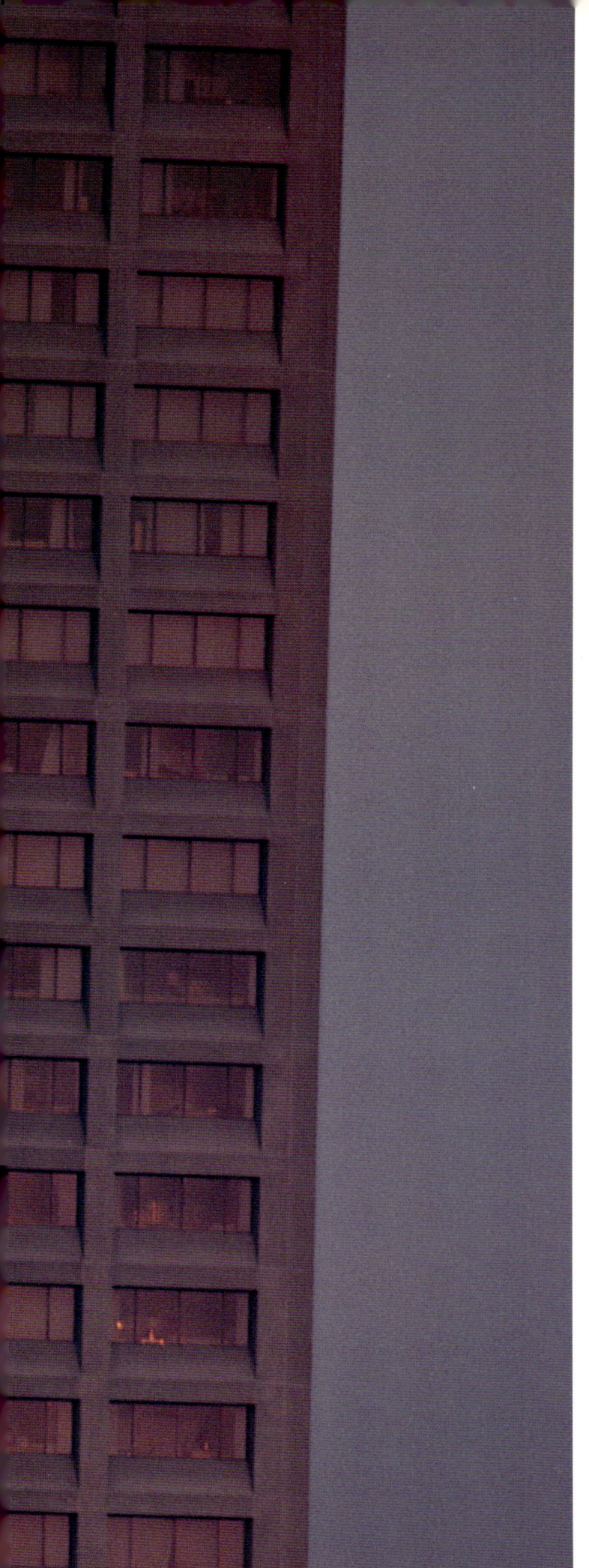

PROFESSIONS

Photo by James P. McCoy.

HODGSON, RUSS, ANDREWS, WOODS & GOODYEAR, LLP

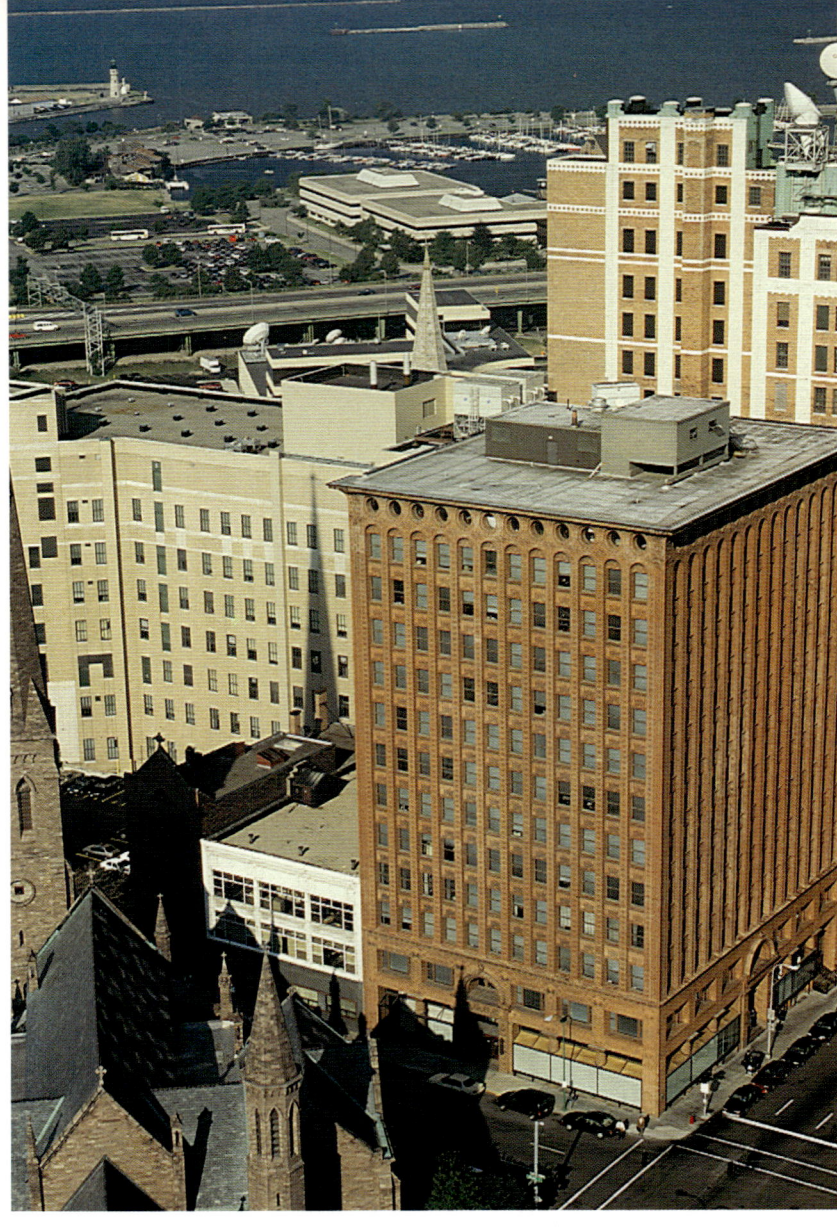

After working to preserve and restore Louis Sullivan's world-renowned Guaranty Building(1896), the Firm occupied the top three floors of the building for many years.

Home of the Firm's principal offices, One M&T Plaza adds distinction to the Queen City skyline.

Hodgson, Russ, Andrews, Woods & Goodyear, LLP is the oldest law firm in Buffalo, tracing its roots to a firm opened in the then frontier town in 1817. Today, it is the largest law firm in Buffalo and one of the three largest in upstate New York. The firm has more than 100 attorneys in its downtown headquarters, as well as offices in Mississauga (Toronto), Ontario; Rochester, Albany, and New York, New York; and Boca Raton, Florida.

Notably, the Firm is distinguished by much more than size and longevity. Firm members have included two U.S. presidents, five U.S. congressmen, a president of the World Bank, an assistant secretary of the U.S. Treasury for Tax Policy, and three Buffalo mayors. Hodgson Russ was also the first area firm to have a woman partner and the first to have a minority partner. In short, Hodgson Russ is a regional law firm with national stature earned through the leadership and dedication to excellence of the attorneys who have practiced with it for more than 175 years.

Today, Hodgson Russ is taking that leadership to an international arena as its practice expands to include the thriving cross-border business and professional relationships transforming the Niagara region into a center of international trade and commerce. The Firm counts dozens of Canadian companies as clients, along with many more U.S. businesses involved in international trade with Canada and countries around the world.

Hodgson Russ is exceptionally well positioned by its size and location at the crossroads of the Niagara Frontier to provide all the legal services required by both corporate and personal clients on a regional, national, or international level. The Firm's five departments of Business and Banking, Estates and Trusts, Labor and Employment Law, Litigation and Taxation are staffed by teams of experienced lawyers, each offering a particular specialty or area of expertise. These teams or practice groups offer clients both the wide array of skills and the depth of experience required to handle the complex issues confronting every business today.

Among the areas or practice groups receiving particular emphasis as the Firm's international practice grows is tax planning, an area of particular importance as businesses expand into local, state, provincial, and national jurisdictions, each with its own complex tax code. For both businesses and individuals, expert legal counsel can significantly reduce potential tax burdens through careful planning. The Firm's tax practice is the largest in upstate New York and is increasingly recognized by publications such as *The Best Lawyers in America* as one of the most distinguished in the United States. Another indication of this national reputation was the appointment of the former head of the Firm's tax practice to the position of assistant secretary of the U.S. Treasury for Tax Policy, the highest position in the U.S. government for tax policy matters, in both the Carter and Clinton administrations.

Another growing practice area is intellectual property. As raw materials and manufactured goods are superseded in international trade by communications, biotechnology, com-

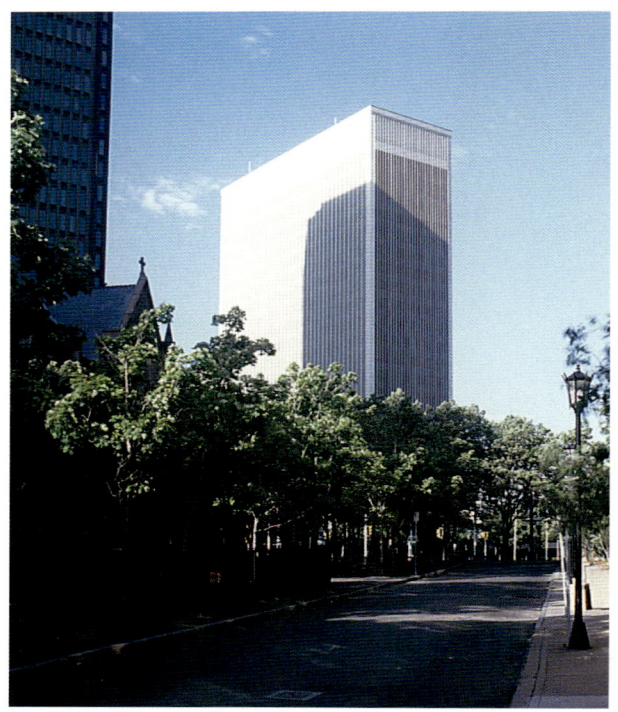

range of employment-related issues. The firm is also engaged in plan design and administration of employee benefits packages.

Health Care Law

The firm's client base also includes many of the area's hospitals, nursing homes and other health care providers, as well as medical technology companies. The firm also offers wide-ranging experience in medical device liability litigation. Additional services to the regional health care industry include an annual seminar presenting the latest legal issues in health care.

Intellectual Property Law

Another growing practice area is intellectual property. Phillips, Lytle has extensive experience in the prosecution of patent applications in virtually all technical disciplines and regularly files and processes foreign trademark applications. The firm has close working relationships with foreign counsel in Europe, Asia, and across North America.

International Trade Law

The firm also has significant international experience in Canadian practice. As the North American Free Trade Agreement opens many new business opportunities between the United States and Canada, Phillips, Lytle's Canadian practice group has served as counsel on a wide variety of issues to many firms on both sides of the border.

Client Service

Dedicated to full service to its clients, Phillips, Lytle attorneys maintain the high practice standards through ongoing education of associates and staff, giving the firm exceptional strength in navigating an ever-changing legal landscape that is increasingly international in scope.

Community Service

Phillips, Lytle partners and associates also take a leading role in the community, sitting on the boards of more than 90 regional, charitable, cultural, and social service institutions, including the local public broadcasting network, Shea's Performing Arts Center, Artpark, the Greater Buffalo Partnership, Zoological Society of Buffalo, Buffalo Philharmonic Orchestra, and many others. The firm also provides thousands of hours of pro bono work to the community each year.

The Phillips, Lytle Difference

While Phillips, Lytle was founded in a time when a client could rely on a single lawyer to handle any legal concern, today clients from large corporations to small businesses and individuals are more efficiently and effectively served by the combination of resources available from a large firm. Phillips, Lytle continues to offer its clients traditional personalized service while providing the resources necessary to accommodate the varied needs of its diverse and growing list of clients.

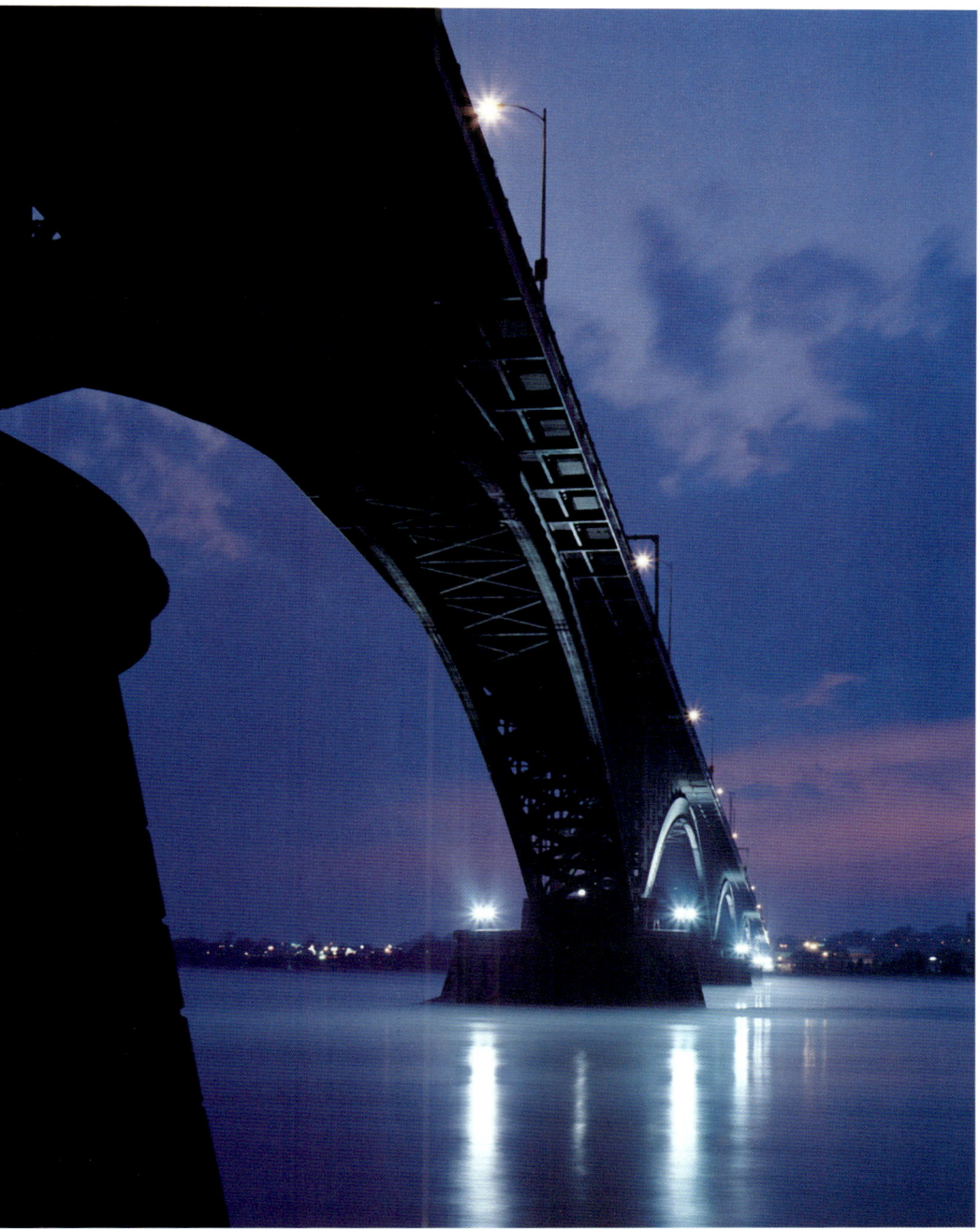

Of course, the firm's key resources are the skills and expertise of its attorneys. Throughout its history, Phillips, Lytle has remained young and vibrant, recruiting promising younger attorneys from the nation's top law schools and firms to complement the experience and wisdom of its partners. Backed by a support staff of more than 200, the attorneys of Phillips, Lytle are superbly equipped to provide the client with the close relationship that has always been, and always will be, the heart of this distinguished firm's success. ❖

Buffalo's Peace Bridge is one of the most travelled gateways into the United States. Linking with Canada at Fort Erie, Ontario, the span over the Niagara river is symbolic of the uniquely close relationship between the two international communities of the Niagara region. Phillips, Lytle is another vital link betwen these international communities, serving the business, commercial and legal needs of clients on both sides of the border. Photo by Marc Murphy.

KPMG PEAT MARWICK

KPMG Peat Marwick LLP is the U.S. member firm of KPMG International, The Global Leader in providing a wide range of value-added assurance, tax, international, and performance improvement services. The Buffalo office of KPMG, one of the "Big Six" national public accounting firms, commenced operations in the early 1950s, under the aegis of what was then Peat Marwick Mitchell.

The firm's origins date back to 1897, when two Scottish chartered accountants opened their first office in the financial district of New York. In 1904, offices were opened in Minneapolis and Chicago, with Pittsburgh and Philadelphia added in 1905 and 1906, respectively. In 1911, to keep pace with the growing international scope of its practice, Marwick, Mitchell and Co. merged with the London firm of Sir William B. Peat, Keeper of the Privy Purse.

In 1987, Peat Marwick International merged with Klynveld Main Goerdeler. As a result, the firm has access to offices in more than 800 cities in 140 countries around the globe. KPMG audits nearly one-third of Europe's most respected companies and provides professional services to 310 of the world's 1,000 leading commercial and industrial companies.

The firm has 130 U.S. offices, including a significant presence in upstate New York with full-fledged operations in Buffalo, Rochester, and Syracuse; the only Big Six accounting

firm with offices in all three cities. KPMG Peat Marwick is located in the Fleet Bank building in Fountain Plaza, in the heart of Buffalo's downtown financial district.

Locally, some 60 employees provide services in the five market areas in which KPMG excels: financial services; manufacturing, retailing and distribution; health care and life sciences; information, communications and entertainment; and public services. This restructuring along industry lines, a KPMG innovation, enables custom-tailored client service. In the Buffalo region, for example, the key areas of service are in the financial and manufacturing, retail, and distribution markets.

KPMG has been an industry leader in many other respects. The firm introduced Business Measurement Process, an audit process tailored to specific industries that helps companies identify ways to improve business performance as part of their annual financial statement audit. The move was touted as one of the biggest advances in the $6 billion auditing business in nearly 100 years.

The PhD Project, a KPMG-led landmark effort to systemically improve the diversity of business school faculties, was a first among the Big Six firms. KPMG also entered into the International Internship Program, one of the first of its kind in private industry in the nation, helping to create tomorrow's global financial leaders.

KPMG is a professional leader, serving many of the region's most respected firms.

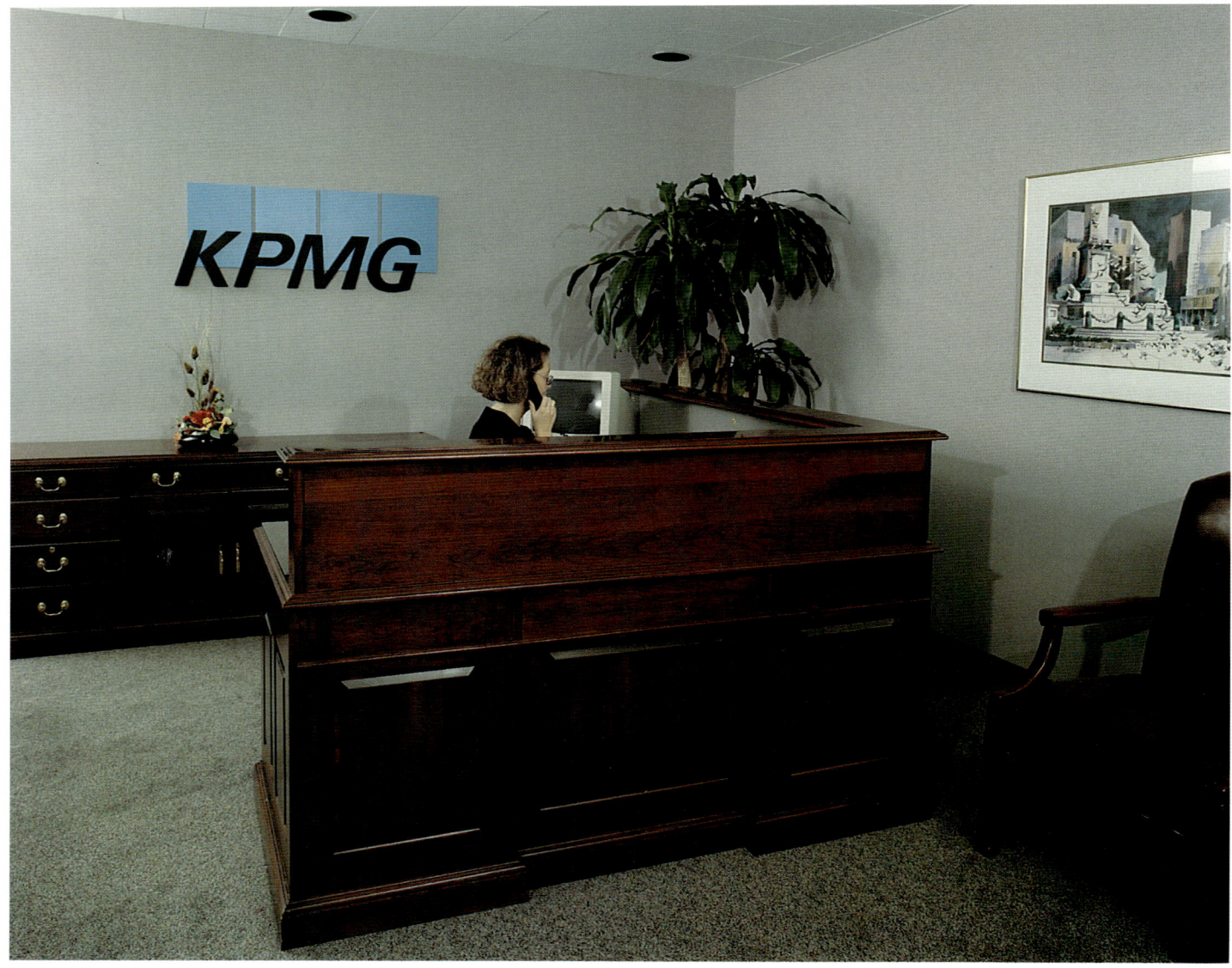

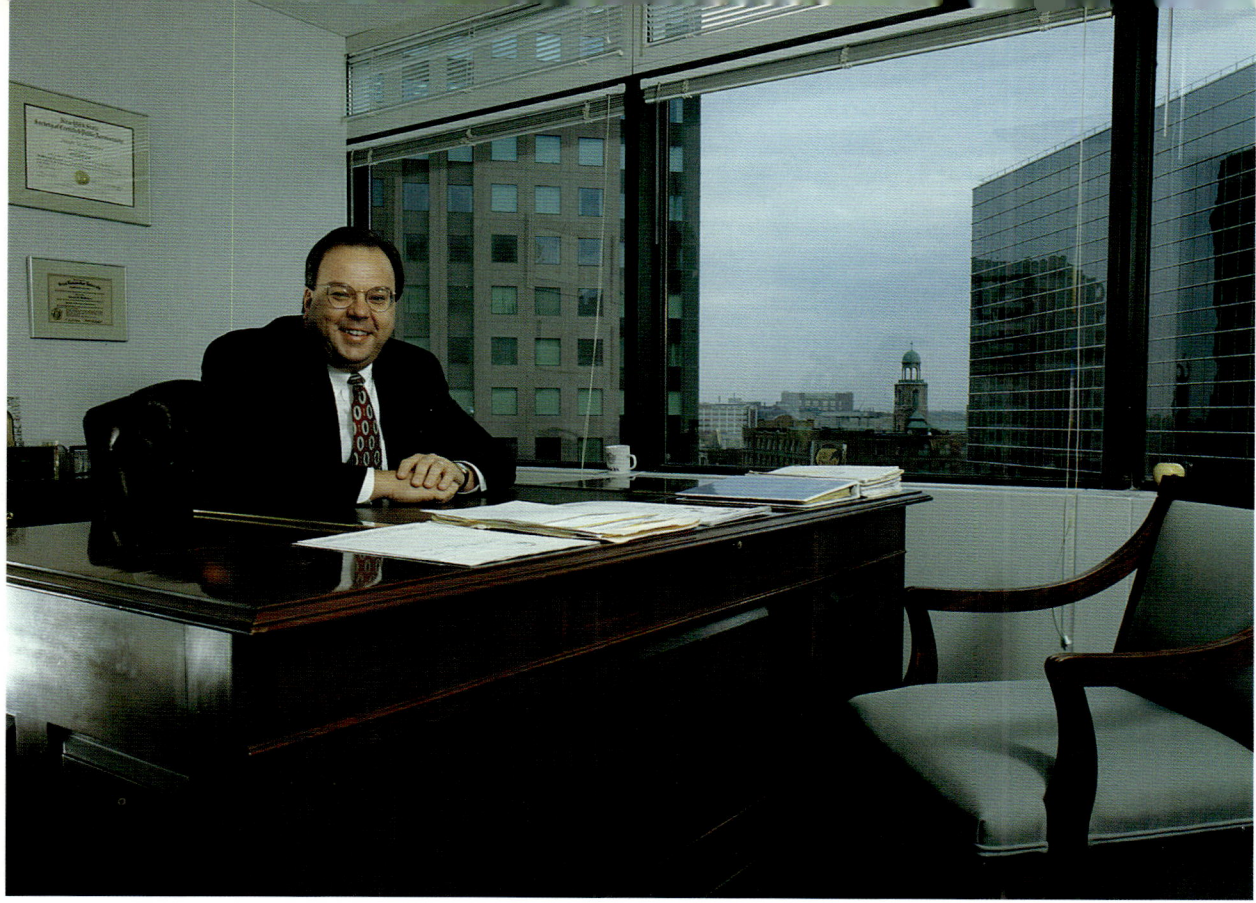

John R. Koelmel.

It's all part of the company's progressive outlook and focus on continued growth and development in areas outside the traditional accounting realm of basic compliance work. As the market changes and technology advances, a responsiveness to individual client needs has been the KPMG formula for success. The opportunities ahead lie in the consulting arena, with value- added services offered to a broader array of clients.

Emulating its parent, the Buffalo office of KPMG has been a professional leader, serving many of the region's most respected firms, from the beginning. Most of the partners are natives of the area, people who grew up here and are deeply committed to maintaining the vitality of Western New York.

That translates to community involvement on many levels, and KPMG has always been a key player in this regard.

Company executives have held leadership positions on the boards of organizations such as the United Way, the Buffalo Philharmonic Orchestra, Children's Hospital, and Studio Arena Theatre, to name a few. Volunteer work—giving back to the community—has emerged as a KPMG tenet that extends all the way down to entry-level employees. Fostering the continued growth and development of the city makes good business sense, but it's also a personal belief shared by KPMG staff members. "We've long taken pride in our history here and involvement with Buffalo," says partner John R. Koelmel.

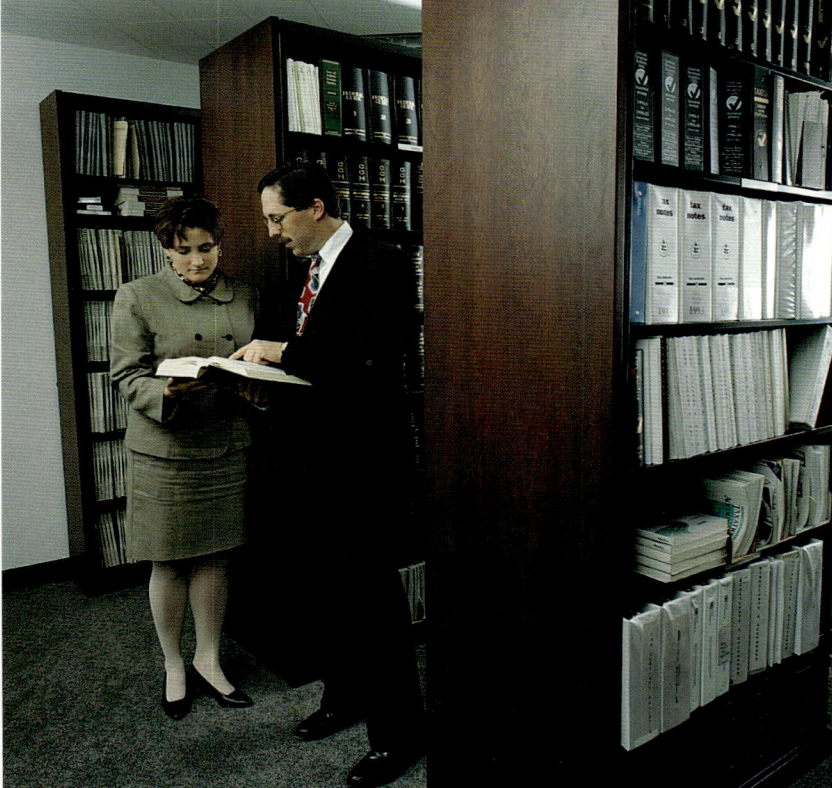

Locally, some 60 employees provide services in five market areas.

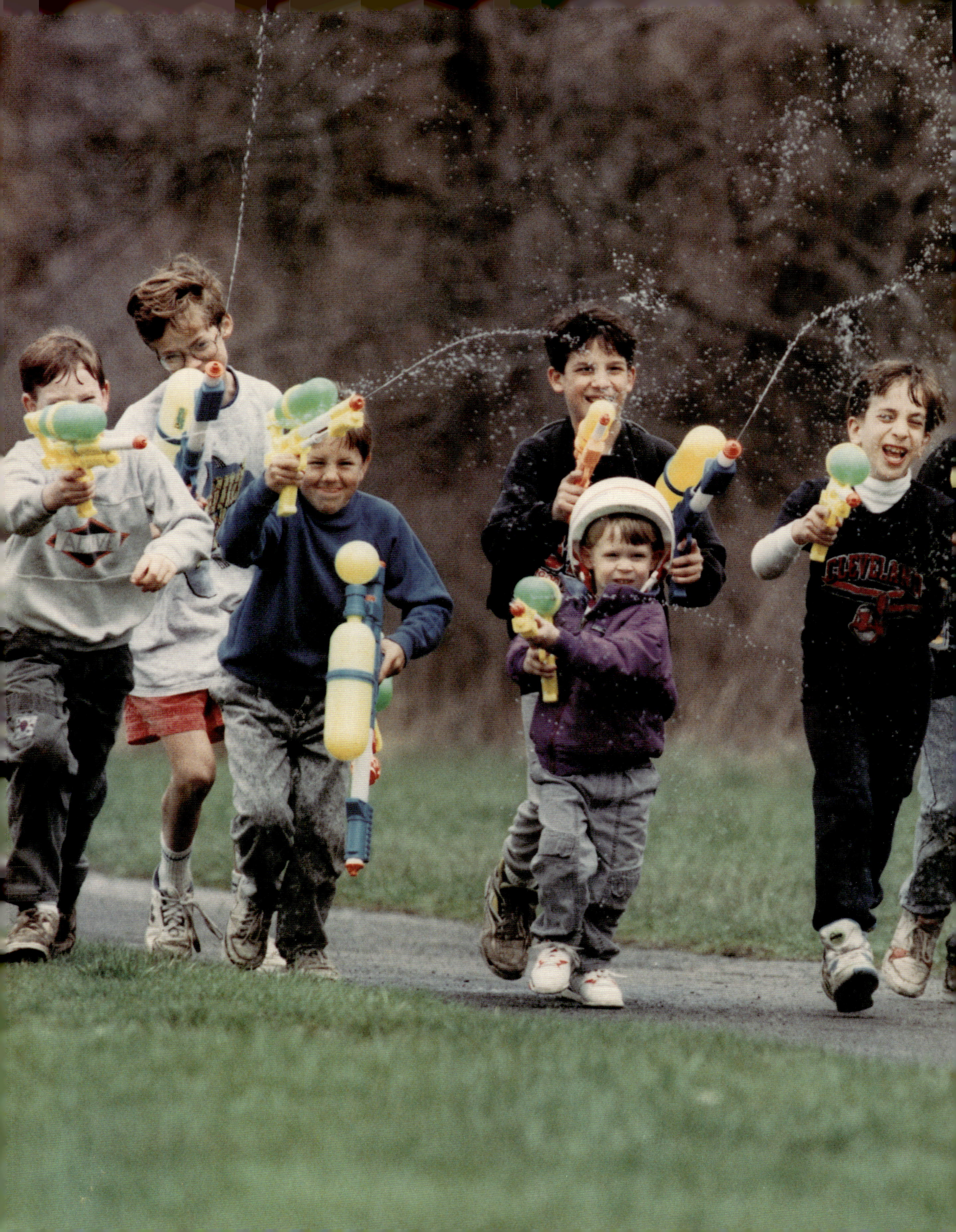

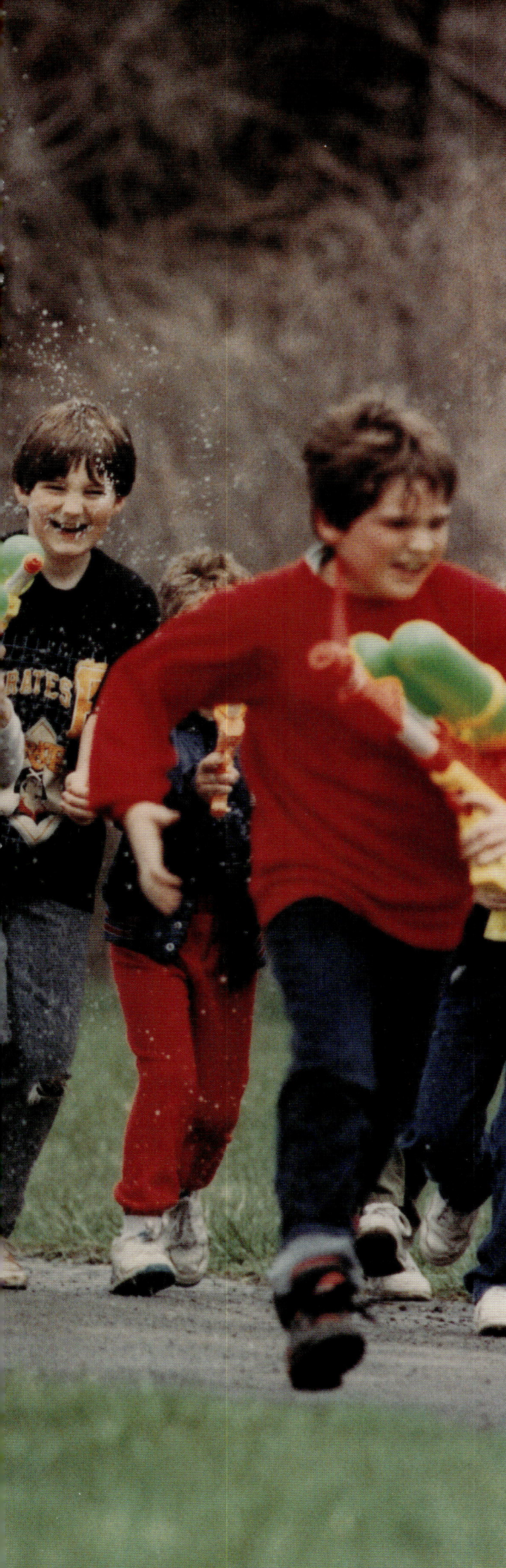

EDUCATION

Photo by James P. McCoy.

UNIVERSITY AT BUFFALO

The State University of New York at Buffalo is New York's premier public center for graduate and professional education and the state's largest and most comprehensive public university. The university offers more undergraduate and graduate degree programs than any other public university in the state. It is an international presence, with strong programs and affiliations from Korea to Southeast Asia on the Pacific Rim and in eastern Europe. It is a nationally prominent center for pure and applied research with many industrial partners. And it is a local economic powerhouse with an annual billion-dollar-plus regional impact.

UB, as it is known to its students, alumni, faculty, neighbors, and friends, is both venerable and brand new. Founded in 1846 as a private institution, the university was reborn in 1962 when the already highly regarded regional institution merged with the State University of New York and, as a public university, gained national reach and stature. Since that time, a billion-dollar public investment has endowed UB with some of the most modern research and teaching facilities of any major university in the nation.

From its original classrooms in a renovated church in downtown Buffalo, the university has grown to occupy two campuses: Its South Campus, in the northeast corner of the city, is UB's health sciences center and the home of its architecture school; its 1250-acre North Campus, in Amherst, houses UB's other schools and its athletics facilities. The university is engaged in vigorous construction and renovation programs on both campuses.

UB offers more than 300 undergraduate and graduate degree programs through its schools of architecture, dental medicine, education (graduate), engineering and applied sciences, health related professions, information and library sciences, law, management, medicine and biomedical sciences, nursing, pharmacy, and social work; through its faculties of arts and letters, natural sciences and mathematics, and social sciences; through Millard Fillmore College, its continuing education division; and through a graduate affiliation with Roswell Park Cancer Institute. UB enrolls 24,000 students a year (15,000 undergraduates and 9,000 graduates) and has a full-time teaching faculty of some 1,800.

The professional schools at UB share an unusually research-intensive orientation with their counterpart faculties in the arts and sciences. And the interactions among these schools and faculties, especially in cross-disciplinary research centers, give education and training at UB a particular

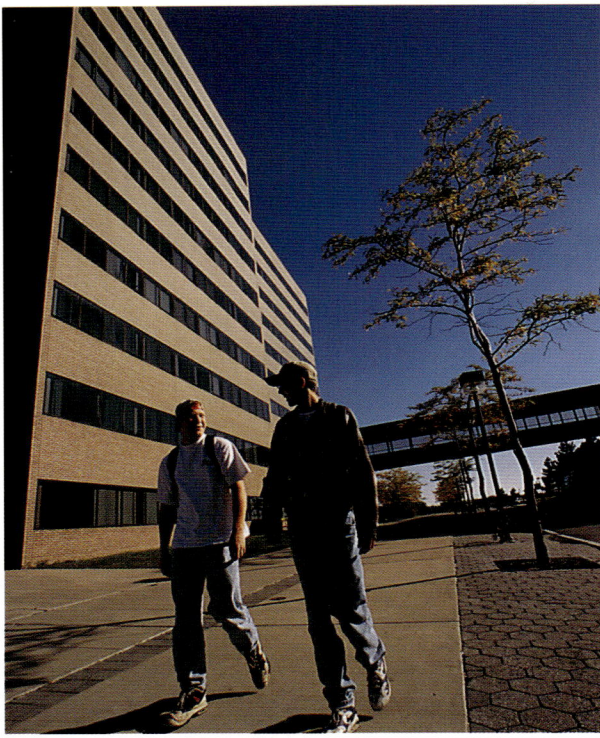

UB is New York's premier public center for graduate and professional education. Photo by Bob Walion.

UB offers more than 300 undergraduate and graduate degree programs. Photo by Doug Levere.

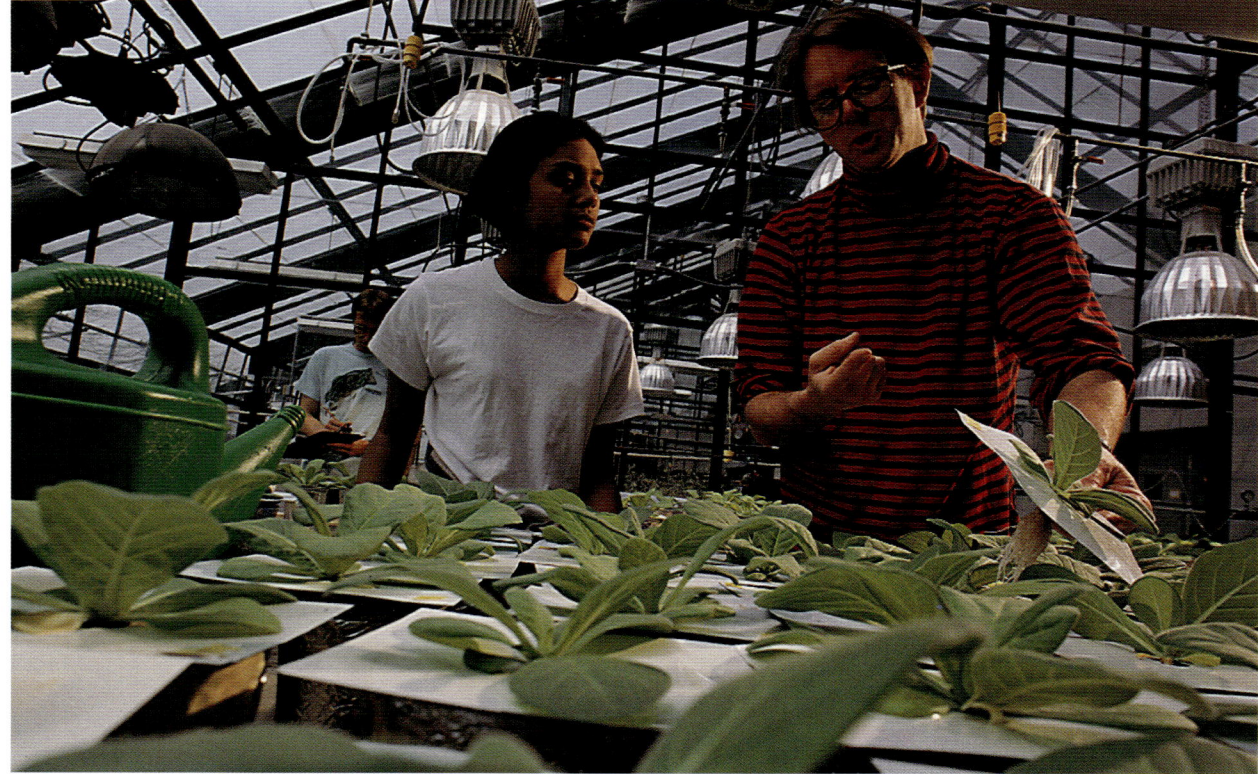

richness and depth. In addition to national ranking for several of its professional schools, UB consistently ranks among the top universities in the nation for the educational value of its undergraduate offerings.

While UB has always been an integral part of Buffalo and the Niagara region, today its beneficial social, cultural, and economic impact on life in the community has never been greater. More than half of the university's students are Western New Yorkers, and about one-third of its 152,000 alumni reside in the Niagara region. In addition to serving as the area's foremost center of higher education, UB is also a bridge to the rest of the world. About one-quarter of the student enrollment comes from the New York City metropolitan area, and the rest from else-where in New York State, the United States, and around the world. Nearly 2,000 international students are attracted to the university each year, enriching the region's diverse ethnic blend.

Beyond its educational enterprise, UB participates in the life of its Western New York community in a myriad of ways. The university is involved in numerous projects with local school systems; its Educational Opportunity Center offers training in critical job skills; its Center for Industrial Effectiveness is a vital partner with regional industry; its medical school is a mainstay of the regional health-care system; its students involve themselves in community life with projects ranging from Habitat for Humanity to legal clinics; and UB's theater, music, and NCAA Division I sports programs offer cultural enrichment and fun for all.

The university has a tremendous direct impact on the local economy. Its nearly 12,000 full- and part-time employ-ees make it Western New York's fourth-largest employer, and it is estimated that UB's local economic activity supports almost 8,000 jobs outside the university. In the mid-1990's, total annual expenditures by the university approached $700 million, with 85 percent of that amount spent in Western New York. In addition to tuition and fees, UB students spend more than $130 million in the Buffalo area annually, and visitors to the university spend $10 million for food and lodging each year.

A major university goal in recent years has been to achieve recognition as the premier public research-intensive university in the Northeast. In 1989, UB was invited to join the Association of American Universities, an exclusive group of North America's 62 most influential private and public research universities. In 1995 alone, UB won more than $250 million in federal, state, corporate, and private grants and contracts for research and training.

Research at UB is conducted within and among the university's eighty academic departments. Among its more than fifty research centers, UB is home to the National Center for Earthquake Engineering Research, the National Center for Geographic Information and Analysis, the Center of Excellence for Document Analysis and Recognition (applica-tions of artificial intelligence to document processing), the New York State Center for Hazardous Waste Management,

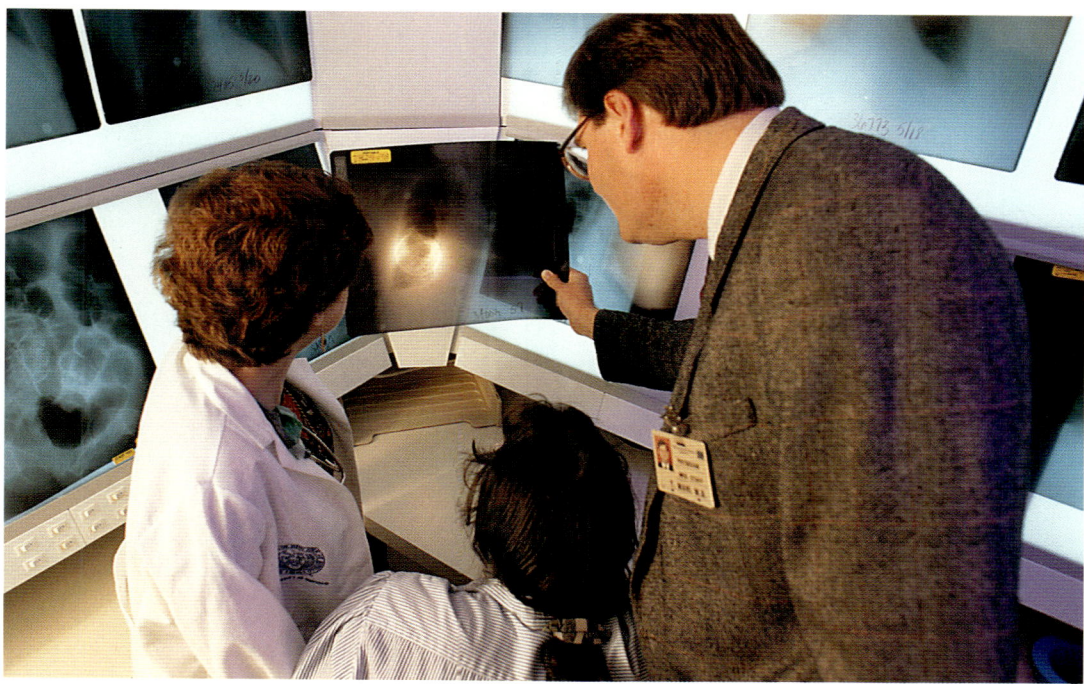

the New York State Institute on Superconductivity, the Rehabilitation Engineering Research Center on Aging (devel-oping assistive devices for older persons), the Canada-United States Trade Center, the Industry/University Center for Biosurfaces, and the Great Lakes Program.

UB has become increasingly involved in nurturing university-industry partnerships for research and the transfer of university-developed technologies to local industries. One such collaboration converted technology originally conceived to protect missile silos from nuclear explosions into equipment that will protect buildings during earthquakes. UB has signed more licensing agreements and initiated more connections to local industry than any other State University of New York campus.

As the University at Buffalo grows and evolves, it will continue to serve the Niagara region, New York State, and the world in new and exciting ways. While UB's founders might not recognize the institution they established more than a century and a half ago, they would no doubt applaud the quest for excellence and the spirit of innovation that have prepared the University at Buffalo to be a national center of excellence in higher education for the twenty-first century. ❧

UB's medical school is a main-stay of the regional health care system. Photo by Doug Levere.

The South Campus, in the northeast corner of the city, is UB's health sciences center and home of its architecture school. Photo by Doug Levere.

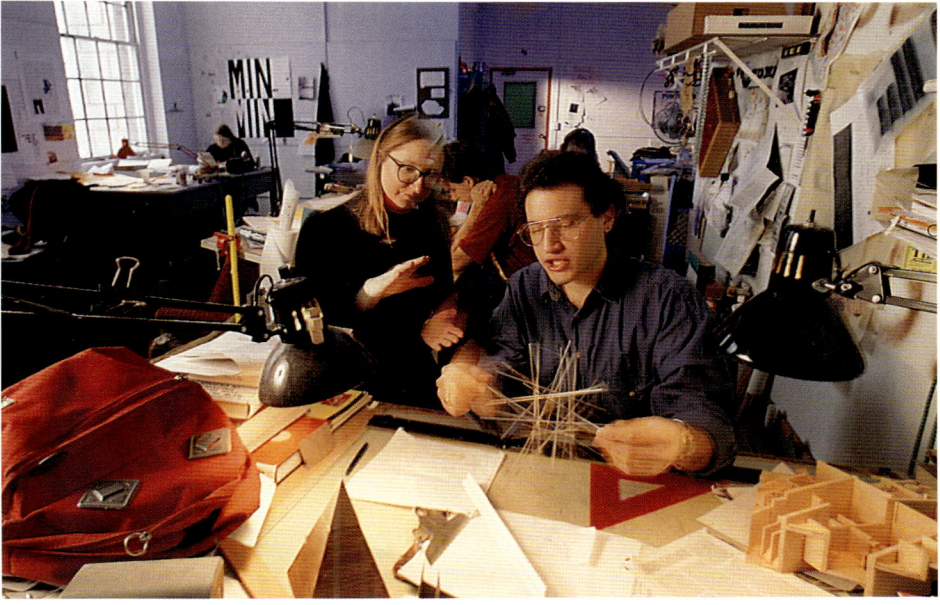

NIAGARA UNIVERSITY

Niagara University was founded and is sponsored by the Congregation of the Mission, the order of priests and brothers more commonly known as *Vincentians*.

Ivy-covered Clet Hall is one of the landmarks of the picturesque Niagara University campus.

Niagara University, a comprehensive university in the Catholic tradition, is imbued with the progressive spirit inspired by its historic geography. Located on the northern edge of the city of Niagara Falls, the 124-acre main campus overlooks the Niagara River gorge just four miles north of the world-famous Falls. Here, adjacent to the international border between the United States and Canada, the university carries on its nearly 150-year-old tradition of preparing students for success in their professional and personal lives.

Niagara University traces its roots to 1856, when two priests established a seminary in Buffalo. They were members of the Vincentian order, a name derived from their founder, Saint Vincent de Paul. By the following year, the Vincentians had moved their school, called the College and Seminary of Our Lady of Angels, to a 100-acre farm just north of the Village of Suspension Bridge, now Niagara Falls. The farm was set on Monteagle Ridge,

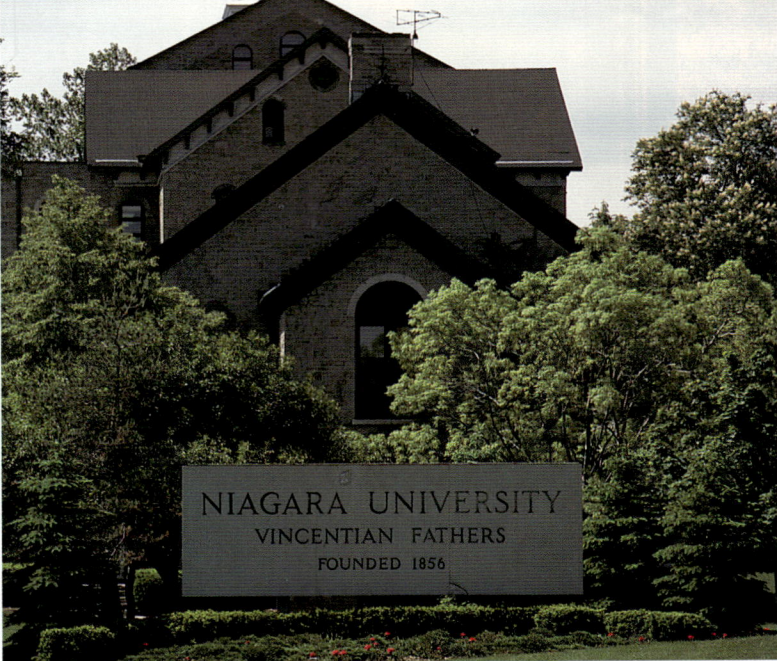

the current home of what is now known as Niagara University, so called since 1883 by charter of then-New York Governor Grover Cleveland.

Over the years, Niagara has evolved into a comprehensive university with an enrollment of approximately 3,000 students. They choose from over 800 undergraduate and graduate courses offered through the university's five academic divisions, including the colleges of Nursing, Business Administration, Arts and Sciences and Education, and the Institute of Travel, Hotel and Restaurant Administration.

Since its founding, Niagara University has presented a balanced curriculum. In the 1860s, the university provided a curriculum in "the learned languages and in the liberal and useful arts"; as the 21st century approaches, Niagara offers to every undergraduate student a liberal arts education coupled with career and professional education. Each undergraduate degree program consists of general education and major courses, with the goal of providing students with a threshold of common knowledge, as well as the opportunity to explore several subject fields in the selection of a major.

Niagara's high-quality academic programs have set a standard for excellence. One of the first universities to award a bachelor's degree in accounting, Niagara was also the first university in the nation to establish a bachelor's degree program in travel and tourism.

If academic excellence is the heart of Niagara University's tradition, its soul is service to those less fortunate, a legacy of Saint Vincent de Paul, the 17th-century French priest revered for his ministry to the poor. As its mission statement proclaims, "Niagara University feels called to emulate the altruistic spirit of Saint Vincent de Paul. It seeks to instill in its students a deep concern for the rights and dignity of the human person, especially for the poor, the suffering, the handicapped, and the outcast." Students, faculty, and administrators are encouraged to volunteer their time to any of the many charitable service programs established on campus, including the Niagara University Community Action Program and a program through which university students tutor at-risk pupils from Niagara Falls city schools.

Social and cultural activities are not neglected at Niagara University, where students can choose to attend sports events, theatrical productions, and festivals on campus or in the nearby cities of Niagara Falls, Buffalo, and Toronto. One of the finest art museums located on any college campus in

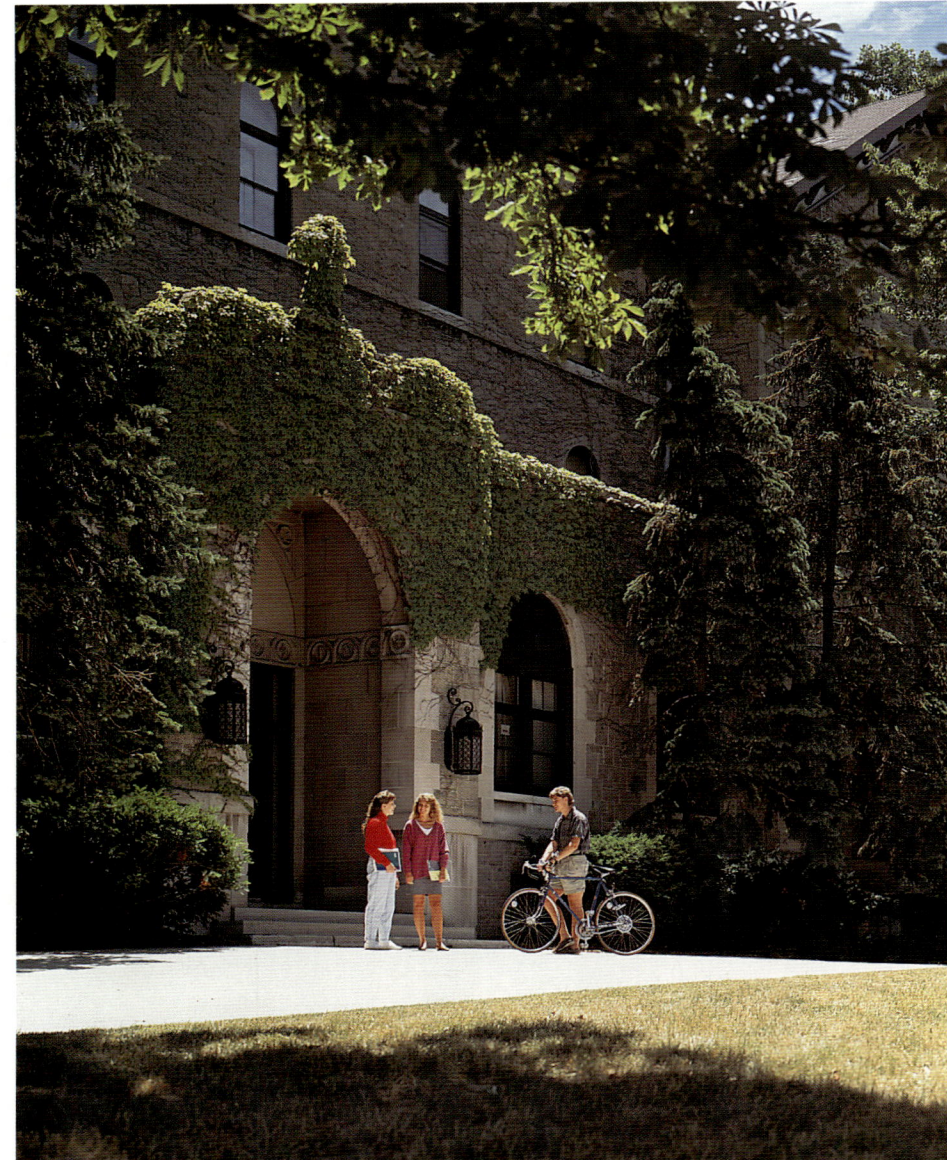

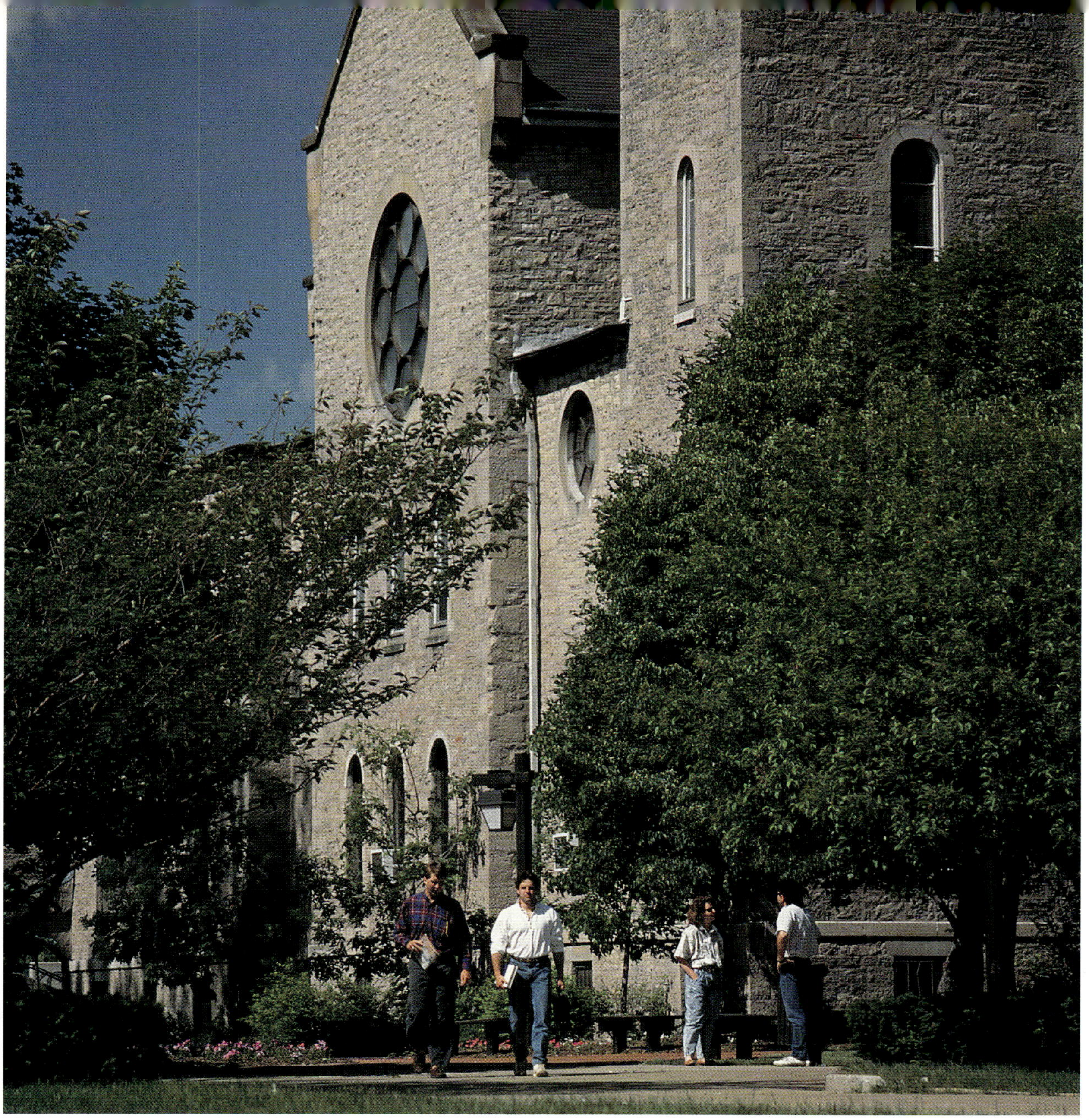

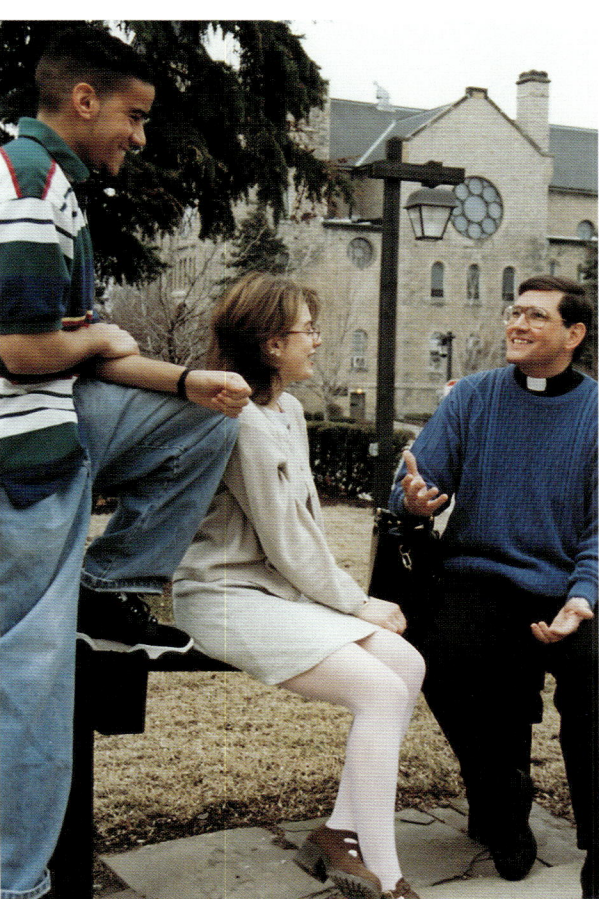

Niagara University Alumni Chapel/Hall houses the main administration building.

the world is right at Niagara—the Castellani Art Museum, including works by Picasso and other masters as part of its collection of more than 3,000 paintings, sculptures, drawings, and prints from the 19th century to the present.

Athletes and sports fans enjoy a state-of-the-art facility in the Niagara University Ice Hockey Arena, opened in the fall of 1996. The twin-pad, 76,000-square-foot facility offers seating for 2,000 spectators, with expansion capabilities for another 2,000. It is in use by community groups as well as the university's Division I men's and women's hockey.

Under the leadership of the Reverend Paul L. Golden, C.M., the Vincentian who is serving as the 24th president of Niagara, the university is poised to surge into the 21st century with new vision nourished by tradition. "We will be a bridge to excellence," Father Golden has said, pledging to bring to Niagara University a national reputation in the field of community service, as well as the development of quality teaching, scholarship, and creative work in an increasingly diverse university population. ℵ

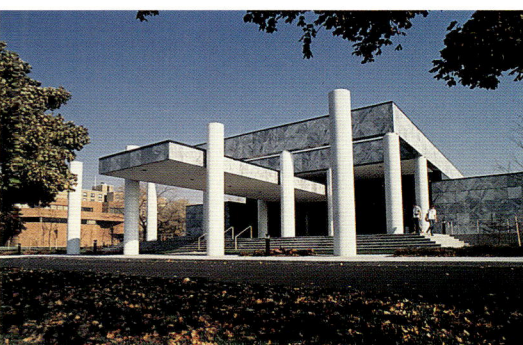

Castellani Art Museum is one of the treasures of the Niagara campus.

Availability of faculty enhances the education experience.

BRYANT & STRATTON

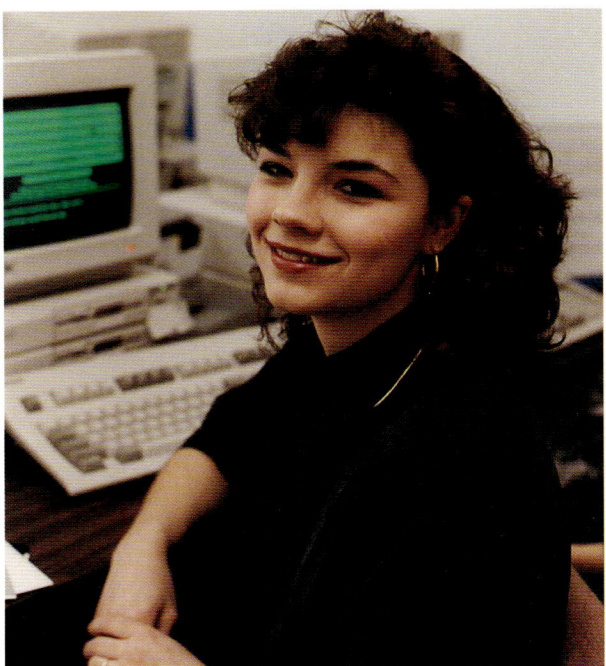

Founded in 1854, Bryant & Stratton Business Institute is one of the oldest businesses in Buffalo and one of the first business colleges in the United States. While the first of the organization's current 15 schools was founded two years earlier in Cleveland, Ohio, it was the Buffalo campus that quickly set the standard for other developing business schools across the country. Today, this family-owned company has expanded to include three convenient, decentralized Western New York locations, as well as campuses in Syracuse, Rochester, and Albany, New York; Milwaukee, Wisconsin, Richmond and Hampton Roads, Virginia.

Bryant & Stratton's 1,300 employees currently serve approximately 8,000 students, providing an extremely low student-to-faculty ratio better than that of most four-year colleges and universities. The school graduates approximately 40 percent of its students, and has, over the past decade, consistently placed over 90 percent of its students in jobs within six months of graduation, outperforming both community colleges and four-year colleges and universities. In 1995 alone, Bryant & Stratton placed an impressive 92 percent of its 2,144 graduates at an average salary of $17,250, representing nearly $37 million in added tax base wages to the economy.

Bryant & Stratton's impressive placement and graduation rates are the direct result of an aggressive and innovative two-year degree program that promotes a fast-track entry into the workplace. By offering associate degrees and diplomas in 33 business and technical disciplines highly desired by employers, the school trains its students to meet the specific

Bryant & Stratton has always kept its students on top of current trends in today's business world. Photo by Jim Bush.

Bryant & Stratton Business Institute is the first business college in the United States.

needs of the community. As the workplace changes, the curriculum changes accordingly, adapting to new technology and trends on a continuous basis.

The school's adaptability is passed on to its students as well. Bryant & Stratton graduates are provided not only with the skills necessary to succeed in their chosen field, but also with the ability to apply those skills in real work situations, and to adapt to new and changing conditions in the workplace. Students are taught a three-tiered foundation of basic, thinking, and personal skills, and are instructed in five areas of competence: resources, information, systems, technology, and interpersonal relations. These skill sets, identified as critical to success by the U.S. Department of Labor, take Bryant & Stratton beyond the limitations of the ordinary college classroom and into the workplace.

Not only do the schools' evaluation processes require students to apply their skills in simulated work situations, but the instructors themselves are also a part of that workplace.

Externships take students directly into that workplace to learn through hands-on training, and an emphasis on performance-based teaching encourages students to achieve success in the business world before they've even entered it. This style of teaching creates students who are capable and efficient with the latest technologies, tools, and practices used in today's workplace and in the workplace of tomorrow.

Bryant & Stratton has always kept its students on top of current trends. Double-entry bookkeeping, the Spencerian style of shorthand writing, and many other practices now standard in today's business world were invented at Bryant & Stratton. As more women began to enter the workplace at the turn of the century, the school immediately developed a comprehensive secretarial program to meet the growing demands

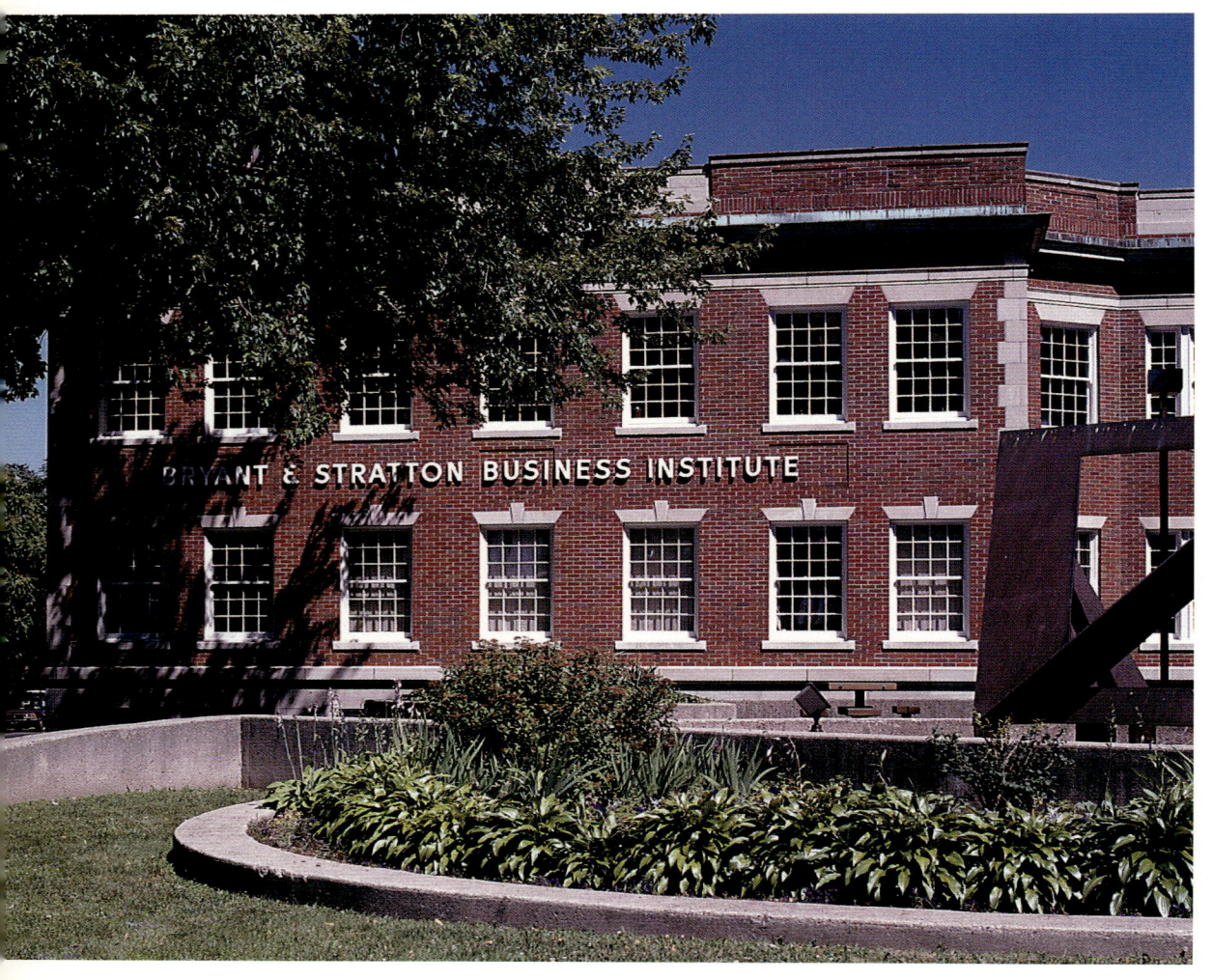

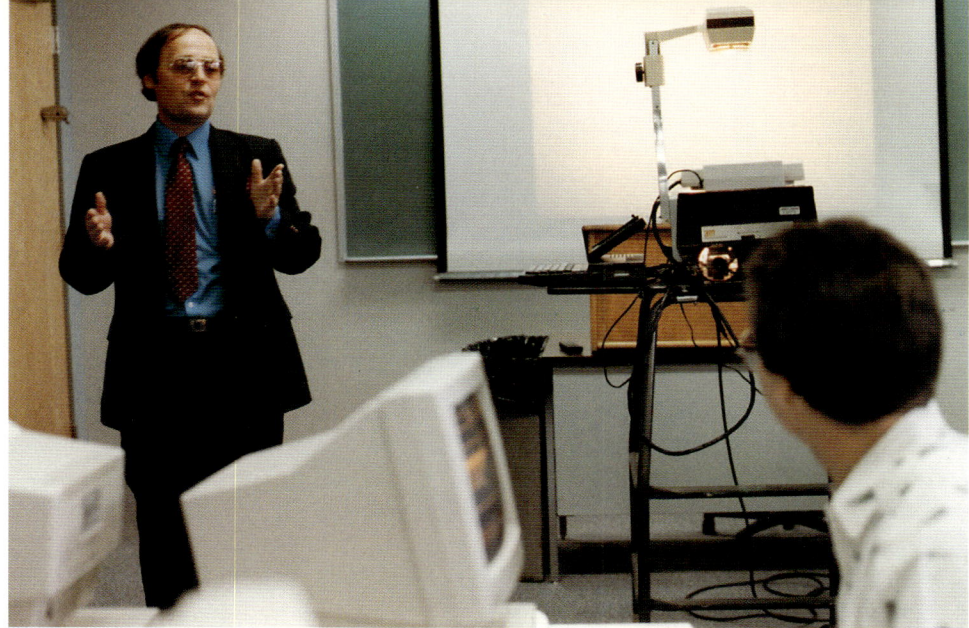

Bryant & Stratton's employees currently serve approximately 8,000 students, providing an extremely low student-to-faculty ratio. Photo by Jim Bush.

of businesses. And as more companies began to turn to computers for communication and interaction, Bryant & Stratton adjusted its emphasis accordingly and prepared students for travel on the information superhighway. The company's Professional Skills Center also offers noncredit contract training in the use of essential computer programs for local businesses. By offering training on networks, insurance, and medical billing, and leadership training for small to medium-sized firms, the school helps to provide the necessary level of education for students and businesspeople alike across the Niagara region.

The company's benefit to the community at large doesn't stop at the classroom walls, however. Campus directors are actively involved in the community, offering free access, free events, and free classes throughout the year to various groups and individuals. Financially, Bryant & Stratton is also a boon to the regional economy, as it uses one-third fewer resources than state-operated colleges, yet offers a graduation rate one-third higher than the average community college. The cost of educating a student in New York is thirty-five percent (35%) higher in state-operated community college systems than the proprietary colleges such as Bryant & Stratton. Bryant & Stratton is also a tax payer, having paid $500,000 in taxes in 1995.

Future plans for Bryant & Stratton include achieving a graduation rate of over 50 percent within four years of matriculation; a placement rate of over 92 percent within six months of graduation; average placement salaries that are the highest of any two-year college; an operating profit of 10 percent of sales revenues, to be reinvested in equipment and research; and the possible addition of several new campuses. By constantly upgrading and updating courses, computers, and other technologies, Bryant & Stratton hopes not only to match the needs of the business world, but also to be viewed by customers and competitors alike as the premier two-year workplace college and the premier center for training third-party organizations.

By encouraging pride in educational outcomes among students, management, faculty, and counselors alike, Bryant & Stratton will continue to be in the vanguard of two-year schools. Bryant & Stratton has generated skilled, adaptable workers for the Niagara region and the world for more than 140 years, and looks forward to continuing its trend-setting pace throughout the 21st century. ◆

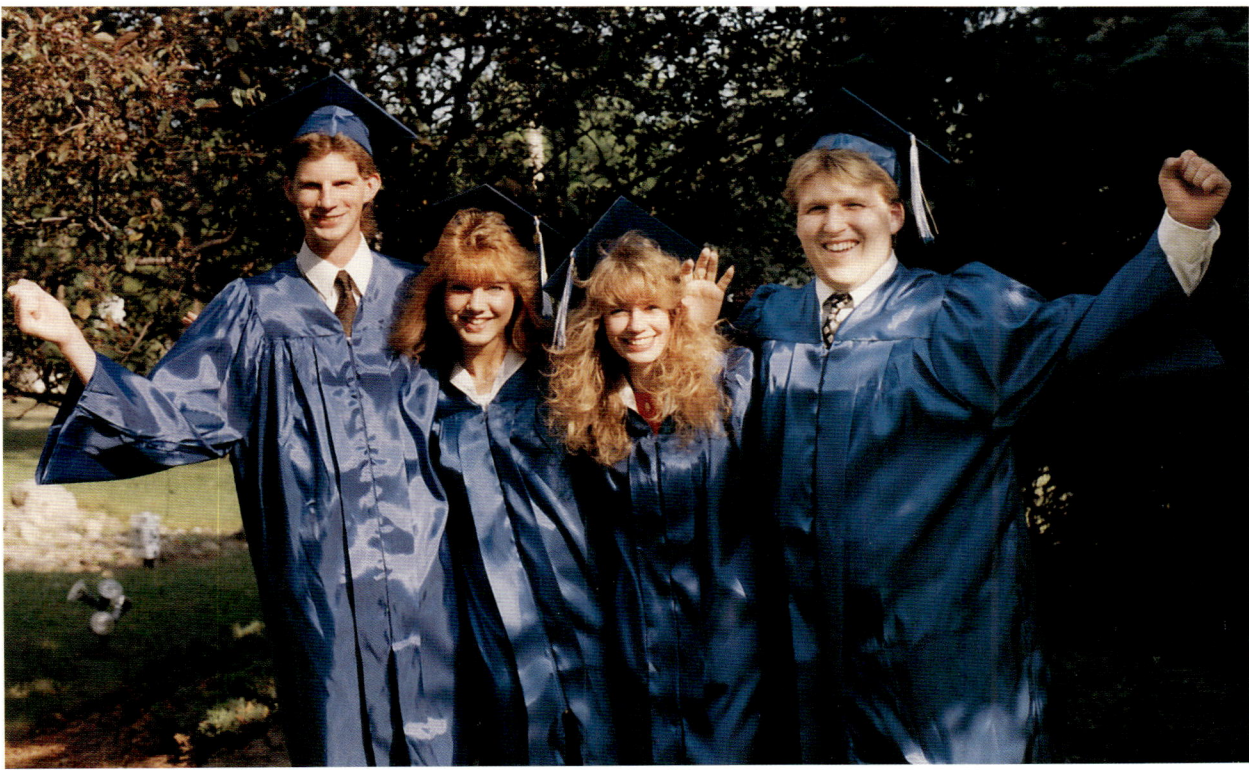

Over the past decade, the school placed more than 90 percent of its students in jobs within six months of graduation. Photo by Jim Bush.

BROCK UNIVERSITY

Brock University is a vibrant, innovative liberal arts university with strong ties to its community and exciting programs that reach out to the world.

Founded in 1964 to provide St. Catharines and the Niagara Region of Ontario with its own university, Brock has grown from 25 students in its first graduating class to more than 11,500 full- and part-time students today. This tremendous growth has brought more than $80 million in new construction to the campus, and the University's operations contribute more than $150 million annually to the local economy.

Even as Brock has grown, it has maintained a unique commitment to extensive contact between faculty and students through small classes and seminar education, with a significant number of undergraduates participating in faculty research projects. Surveys of Brock graduates attest to the close personal attention and instruction each student receives.

Brock is also noted for its innovative learning opportunities, especially in experiential learning programs coordinated with local and regional industry. The Cool Climate Oenology and Viticulture Institute, which began operations in 1996, is a cooperative effort between Brock and the grape-growing and wine-producing industry in Southern Ontario. The first such program of its kind, it has already attracted attention from growers and vintners around the world. Other such programs include the Burgoyne Centre for Entrepreneurship, which has developed Canada's first undergraduate major in entrepreneurship, a co-op accounting program, and a program in sport and exercise management.

The University also is an innovator in the delivery of classes and instructional materials, offering teacher certification upgrade courses via public broadcasting, and is also examining exciting new technologies such as the World Wide Web.

Brock has six faculties: humanities, social sciences, mathematics and science, business, physical education and recreation, and education. Along with undergraduate programs, Brock offers graduate degrees in eight disciplines. The university also provides cross-disciplinary certificates in continuing education.

The campus is located on the scenic Niagara Escarpment in St. Catharines, the Garden City of Ontario. Adjacent to the southern shore of Lake Ontario and only 20 minutes from Niagara Falls and the U.S. border, Brock offers students many opportunities for recreation and entertainment both on and off campus. The university serves as a cultural, academic, and research center for the Niagara Region, attracting visitors from around the region and around the world. Along with regular events, such as concerts, exhibits and performances, Brock has world-class athletic facilities, including the Leo LeBlanc Rowing Centre, Canada's most complete indoor training facility for rowers.

In the future, Brock will continue to work closely with the community it serves, looking for ways to enhance services to its students and the local and regional communities through innovative partnerships with business, government, and graduates. By seeking new opportunities and approaches in cooperation with these constituencies, Brock will continue to meet its educational goals as a university serving St. Catharines, the Niagara Region and beyond. ◆

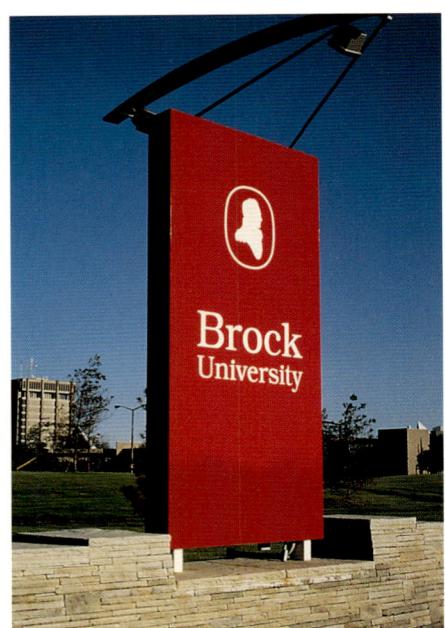

Brock University, a cultural, academic and research center serving the Niagara Region and beyond.

A seminar at Brock University: students get directly involved in the give-and-take that allows real learning.

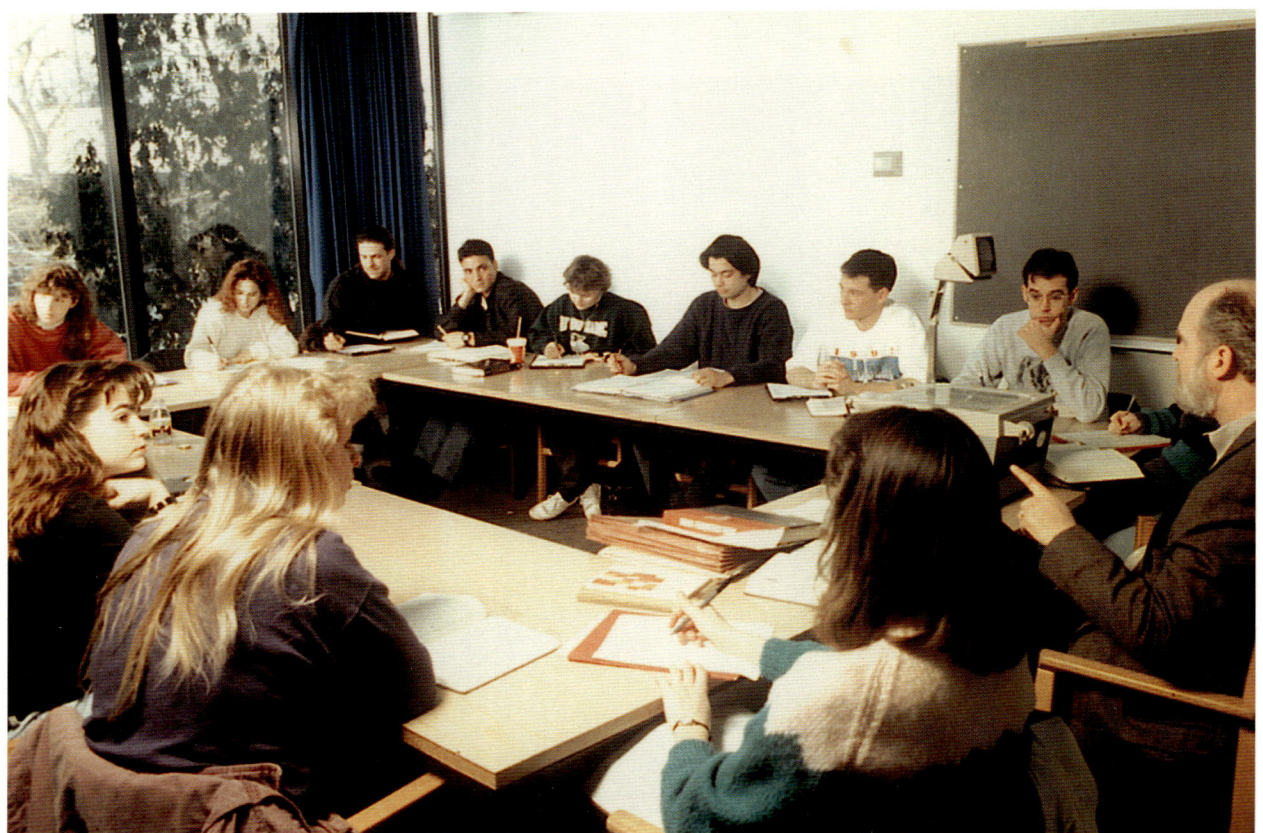

CORNELL
UNIVERSITY
SCHOOL OF
INDUSTRIAL
AND
LABOR
RELATIONS

The Niagara region boasts a wide array of workplaces—factories, stores, offices, schools, health care facilities, and construction sites—and a unique educational resource dedicated to the needs of all workers and employers. Founded in 1945 by the New York State legislature, Cornell University School of Industrial and Labor Relations established its first extension division in Buffalo the following year. Since then, the school has provided practical workplace education, training, research, and technical assistance to large and small business, labor, government, and community organizations in the local area and beyond.

Today, Cornell's Western Region offers an extensive range of services to managers and executives, human resource and labor relations professionals, union officials and workers in all occupations. From public seminars, workshops, conferences, and college-credit certificate courses to customized classes and training sessions tailored to the needs of a particular organization, all programs benefit from the resources of the school's Ithaca-based faculty. With 75 extension faculty and 60 residential faculty on its main campus, the school is the largest single aggregation of industrial and labor relations scholars in the United States, serving more than 45,000 people during a typical year.

As Cornell commemorates its 50th anniversary in the Niagara region, the school continues its commitment to excellence in education on a variety of topics of interest to workers and employers. Innovative Cornell programs contribute to the understanding of workplace cooperation, teaching practical methods of advancing the quality of work-life while increasing organizational efficiency and productivity. Many workplaces have profited from technical assistance and public workshops on mutual gains, on the principles and implementation strategies of interest-based bargaining. Recent initiatives in alternative dispute resolution teach conflicting parties to arrive at mutually acceptable solutions.

A nationally acclaimed program is the Institute for Industry Studies, established in Buffalo in 1986 to conduct specialized research and provide custom-designed education on selected industries or economic sectors. The institute has developed major programs, working with labor and management to set the pace in workforce development, labor-management innovation, and productivity.

Another specialized initiative is the Chemical Hazard Information Program (CHIP). Meeting the growing need for education on occupational hazards and work-related illness, the program helps labor and management in promoting workplace health and safety through training, on-site technical assistance, and expert testimony.

Cornell conferences on economic development have brought together leaders in labor, management, and government to examine the region's economic future, leading to new business initiatives. As the composition of the contemporary workforce changes, Western region programs aid employers, workers, and unions in recognizing the value of an empowered, diverse workforce to build stronger organizations.

Evolving with today's workplace, the school not only functions as "the people's university," helping individuals meet the increasingly complex challenges of the everyday world of work, but also as a cutting-edge resource for all enlightened organizations. As Cornell School of Industrial and Labor Relations marks its first half-century in the Niagara region, it is uniquely positioned to help workers, unions, and employers in the eight counties of Western New York succeed as they compete effectively in the global marketplace of the next 50 years ✦

Cornell's internationally-acclaimed School of Industrial and Labor Relations is a major Western New York workplace education resource, serving employers, workers and unions from offices established in downtown Buffalo in 1946.

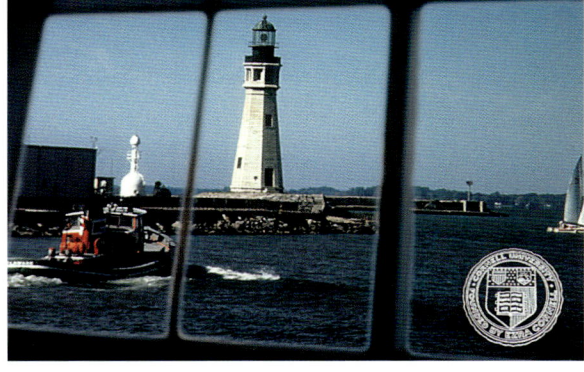

Cornell ILR in Buffalo offers diverse, dynamic programs on topics in human resource management, supervision, career development, labor relations, workplace rights, employee involvement, workplace communication, leadership development and many others.

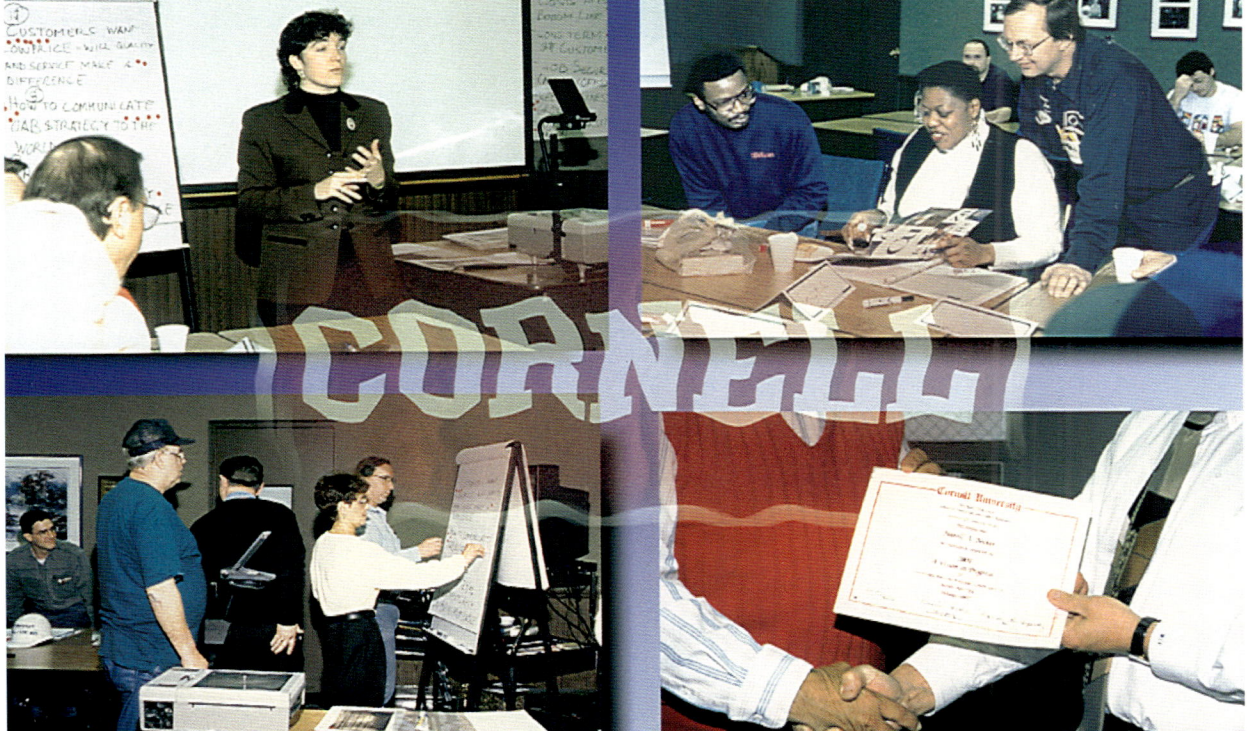

DAEMEN COLLEGE

Originally a women's college established by the Sisters of St. Francis of Penance and Christian Charity, the college is now coeducational and nonsectarian.

Daemen is a small college committed to the personal development of its students.

Founded in 1947, Daemen College has grown into one of the finest private colleges in the Niagara Region, offering a unique combination of liberal arts and professional education at both the undergraduate and graduate levels. As a small college committed to the personal development of its students, Daemen provides a creative balance between career preparation and the development of strong values and lifelong learning skills.

Originally a women's college established by the Sisters of St. Francis of Penance and Christian Charity, the college today is coeducational and nonsectarian. With a student body of 2,000 and more than 150 full-time and part-time faculty, the college offers small classes and individual attention at all levels of study.

The college's four divisions are natural and health sciences, business and commerce, humanities and social sciences, and fine and performing arts. Among the disciplines offered are a nationally renowned program in physical therapy, offering both undergraduate and graduate degrees. A new physician assistant program, a new masters degree in nurse practitioner, along with established undergraduate programs in nursing and medical technology, contributes to the college's exceptional strength in training students for careers in the health sciences. Daemen also offers several dynamic programs in business and commerce, all housed in the division's new state-of-the-art facility.

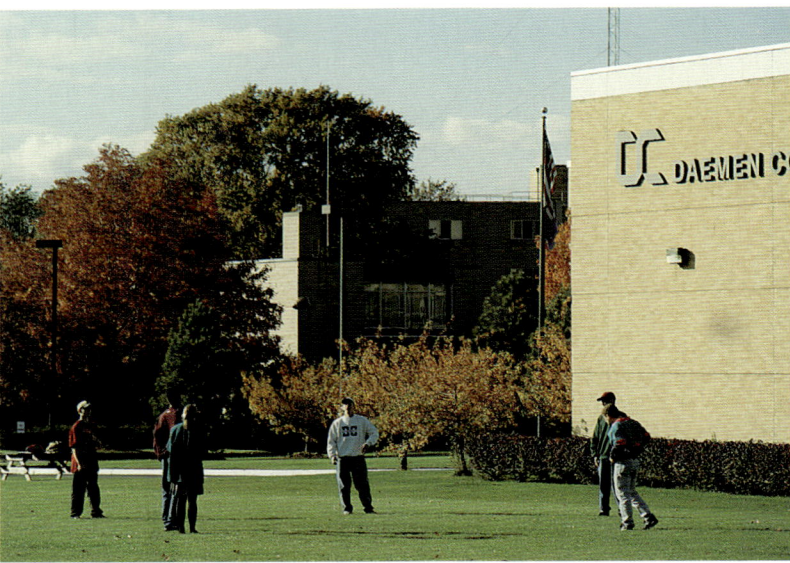

The college's commitment to a modern learning environment is seen in its extensive computer labs and its achievements in new learning techniques, such as a grant received by the physician assistant program for virtual classroom technology, an award to the college's home page on the world wide web, and its continuing construction and renovation of facilities to accommodate new learning technologies.

Daemen also has a strong commitment to serving the community and the Niagara Region. The college has historically attracted many local students and is the choice of many first-generation college students. In addition, the college maintains extensive relations with community service organizations, requiring community service of students in selected courses. With a full-time conference director, the college also attracts many visitors from around the country and the world. A vibrant and growing alumni association further strengthens Daemen's relationships with an extended community that reaches wherever the college's graduates are found.

Daemen's beautiful suburban campus and convenient location only 15 minutes from downtown Buffalo and Canada provide students, faculty, and friends many opportunities to enjoy the best in the region's cultural life. The college hosts many events each year, including an annual film series and productions by Summerfare, Daemen Little Theater's resident acting company.

While the college is committed to strategic growth, especially in extending its mission to include more graduate programs, its first priority is to maintain its excellence in teaching through personal, individual instruction that meets each student's needs. With a stable faculty dedicated to fostering lifelong learning skills in every student, Daemen will continue to offer students from the Niagara Region and around the world a unique learning experience that combines the best of the liberal arts with professional training and prepares every graduate for a lifetime of achievement.

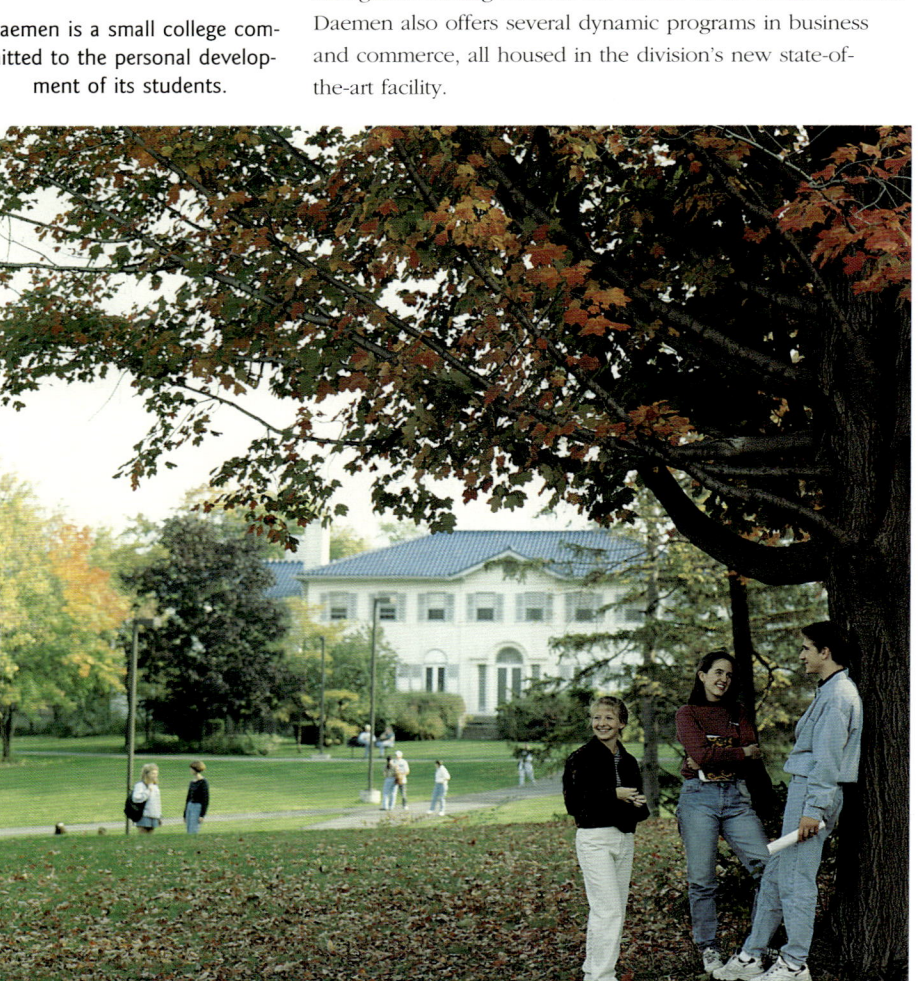

Founded in 1958 by the Sisters of Mercy, Trocaire College traces its mission to the order's foundress, Catherine McAuley, who in 1841 walked the streets of Dublin, Ireland, helping young women find opportunities to support themselves. Throughout its history, the college has continually renewed and revitalized that mission, growing from a two-year liberal arts college for young women entering the order, through its opening to lay women in 1965, and finally to becoming coeducational in 1970.

As the student body grew and diversified, the curriculum also expanded to include health sciences, business, and education. Trocaire's nursing program, affiliated with adjacent Mercy Hospital, was one of the first in the Niagara region, and it was the first to offer a complete evening program, allowing working students to attend. The college also offered the region's first X-ray technology program. Other new and innovative programs include the region's first environmental technology program; a hotel management program, begun with assistance from the Statler Foundation; and an early childhood education program.

Today, Trocaire occupies a unique position in higher education. To maintain its historic mission to the socially, economically, physically, or mentally disadvantaged, the college has chosen to remain a small, urban institution. With a student body of 1,600 and a student/faculty ratio of only 12 to 1, Trocaire offers a warm and caring environment, providing its students, most of whom are first-generation college students, with the personal attention and support they need to succeed.

Trocaire's resources to assist students include a three-phase college success program that helps build the learning skills needed for higher education. In addition, the college's Palisano Learning Center serves the entire student body, receiving more than 8,000 student visits each semester and providing individual assistance, group study sessions, peer tutoring, computer assistance, study guides, and videos to strengthen learning skills. Trocaire also accommodates its many working students, parents, and displaced workers preparing for new careers through flexible scheduling and by offering day, evening, and weekend classes.

Another unique program is the Warde Center, a facility exclusively for women on public assistance. Located off-campus in a low-income neighborhood, the Center combines the college's social outreach and educational missions,

encouraging and assisting women to begin preparation for a college education.

As a two-year college, Trocaire remains flexible, always seeking new opportunities to offer programs that meet the needs of students and the community. Along with Associates of Science, Applied Science, and Arts degrees, Trocaire offers one-year certificates in selected disciplines, providing students with a strong combination of professional and critical thinking skills as they enter the work force, go on to four-year schools, and in many cases progress to graduate studies.

TROCAIRE COLLEGE

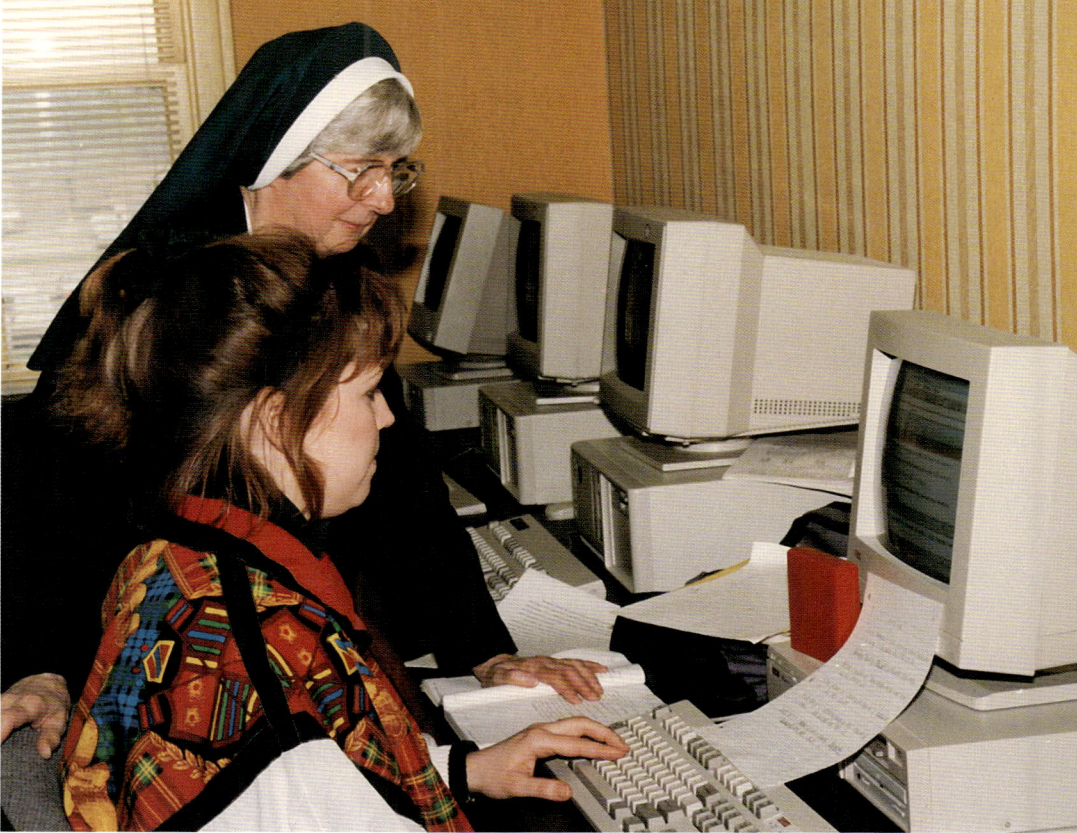

The college has also developed the Lifelong Learning Center, allowing students in health sciences to develop multiple skills, enhancing their opportunities for employment and career advancement. Trocaire graduates are widely recruited by area employers, with 98 percent of the graduates living and working in the community after graduating.

With a recent major renovation of its campus, including a new state-of-the-art library, Trocaire is well-prepared to continue to fulfill its social and educational mission in the Niagara region as a unique place where knowledge and caring come together. ◆

Trocaire was founded by the Sisters of Mercy and the Sisters still play an important role in the college.

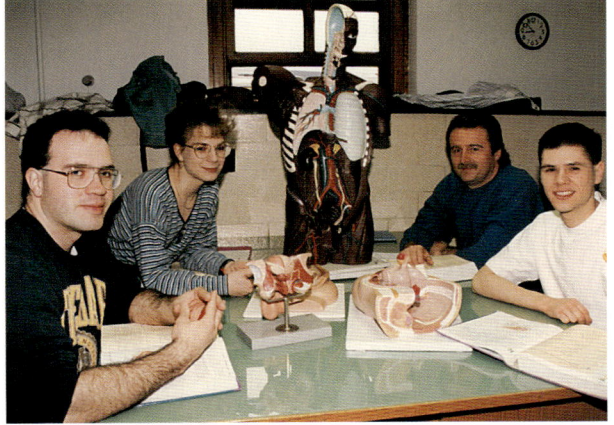

Trocaire Nursing Students get to the "inside" of the subject.

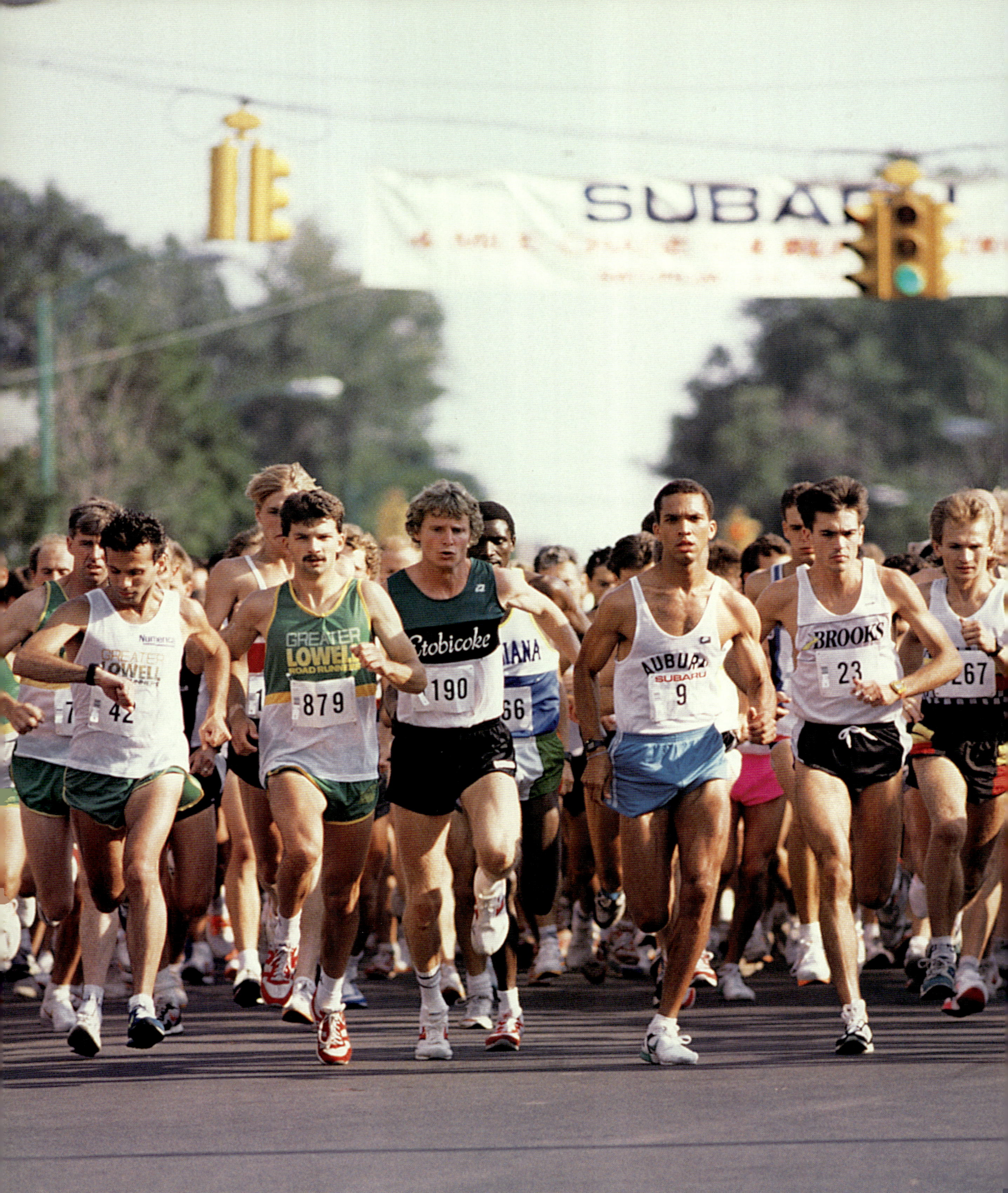

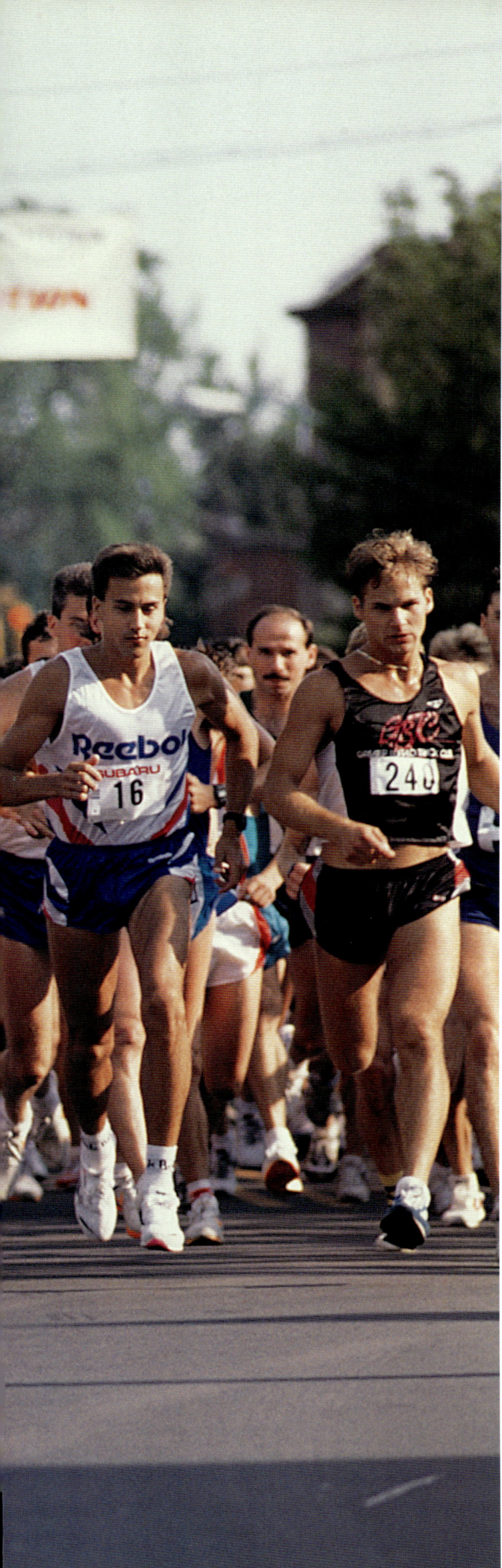

HEALTH CARE

Photo by James P. McCoy.

MILLARD FILLMORE HEALTH SYSTEM

From infants to the elderly, from the heart of Buffalo to the entire Niagara region, Millard Fillmore Health System has been meeting the health care needs of people for more than 125 years.

Growing to meet the changing health care needs of Western New York has made Millard Fillmore Health System, known locally as "the Millard", widely recognized and respected throughout the region, as well as achieving national and international stature for many of its programs. From innovative community-based partnerships, such as the Herman Badillo School Health Center that provides basic health services and education to students and family members in both Spanish and English at this bilingual school, to world-renowned programs in neurosurgery, hand surgery, and endocrinology, the Millard has been a leader in providing essential health care to all parts of the community.

Today, the Millard is one of the primary providers of health care in the region. In addition to its two hospitals, a state-of-the-art laboratory, and three rehabilitation centers, the Millard offers services that reflect its commitment to outpatient treatment, home health care, and proactive wellness care. The Millard Fillmore Surgery Center is the first freestanding site of its kind in Western New York and provides ambulatory surgery services and preadmission testing; the VNA HealthCare Group's network of services provides home health care to the eight counties of Western New York, including nursing services, medication and home health care equipment; and six offices comprise the most extensive primary care network in the area. This comprehensive array of services allows the Millard to touch lives throughout the area.

The Millard is organizing the delivery of health services beyond the traditional medical model. Millard's approach focuses on managing care of the mind, body, and spirit across the continuum of care, and reaches beyond patients to their family and friends. This multidisciplinary approach incorporates a wide array of services to provide seamless coordination among all providers and addresses birth-to-death coverage of needs. For example, parents who lose a baby are offered specialized counseling in bereavement. Another program, Resolve Through Bereavement Sharing, offers training for professionals such as nurses, social workers, clergy, and funeral directors who assist families after the loss of a loved one.

Other programs include annual flu prevention campaigns offering inoculations to thousands in local grocery and discount stores. Individualized outpatient counseling to cardiac patients includes supermarket tours and cooking classes to educate patients and their families about maintaining a heart-healthy lifestyle. A free educational program for high schools and middle schools is designed to help young people avoid head and spinal cord injuries.

Critical to management of care for our community are strategic partnerships with other health service providers in the Niagara region. These long-term, reciprocal relationships allow both the Millard and individual providers to extend services both geographically and into related disciplines while avoiding unnecessary expenditures and duplication of services.

Fundamental to this approach is the ability to organize services around the health needs of the community. The Millard is focusing on identified health concerns: individuals with congestive heart failure or in need of cardiac surgery; individuals who may need joint replacement; and individuals who are dealing with chronic illnesses such as pneumonia and diabetes, or who are at risk for stroke. Targeting these and other community health needs has facilitated the development of centers of expertise within the Millard designed to provide true managed care for people in need. Combining care plans addressing "best practices" with case management techniques reaching

The Millard's Herman Badillo School Health Center's bilingual staff provides primary care and social work services for students.

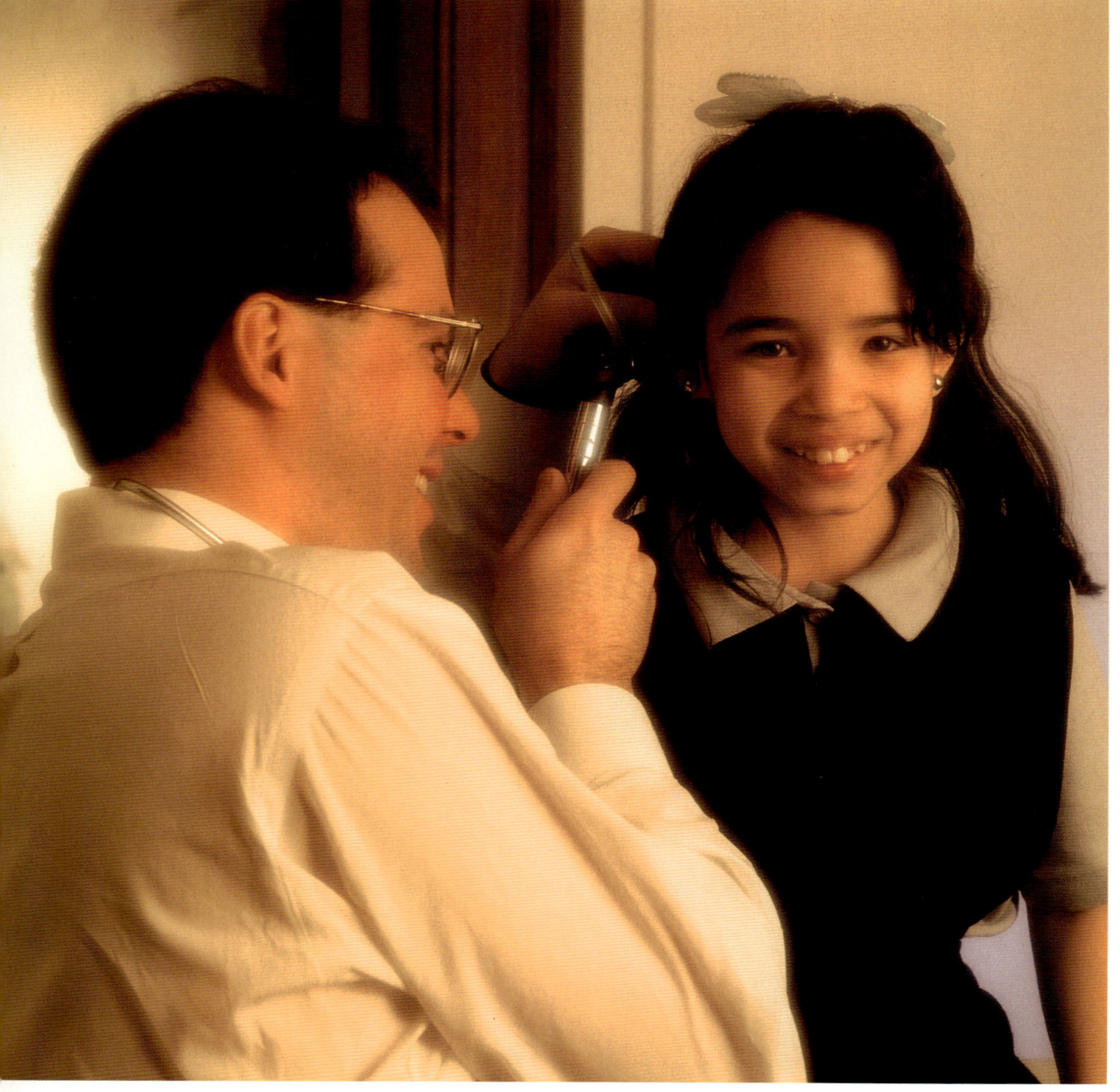

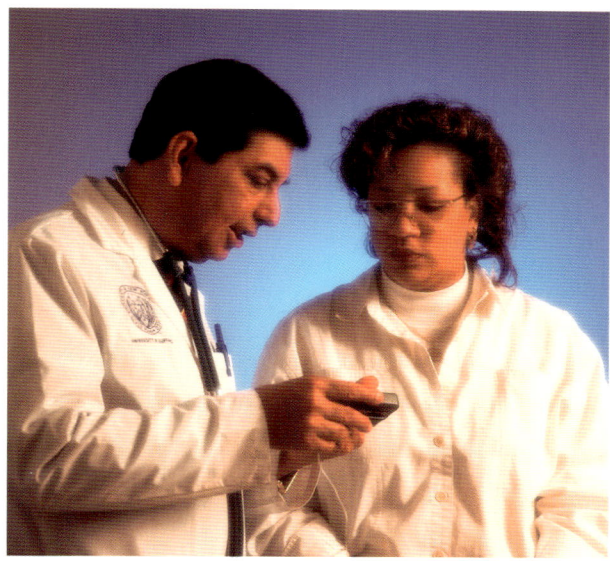

across the entire spectrum of each patient's needs, this unique approach to health care delivery empowers each patient and recognizes the individual's role in achieving the best outcome and highest value in health care services.

Along with this innovative approach to integrated health services delivery, the Millard remains exceptionally strong in its traditional role as a provider of acute care at two hospitals, the Millard Fillmore Hospital at Gates Circle in Buffalo and the Millard Fillmore Suburban Hospital in Amherst. Through its affiliation with the University of Buffalo School of Medicine and Biomedical Sciences, the Millard maintains extensive teaching and research efforts that benefit not only its patients and the community but also the world of medical science, both through the physicians who are trained there and through the advances in treatments and techniques resulting from its research programs. Recognized for the quality of their nursing staff, the Millard hospitals are also home to the Millard Fillmore School of Nursing, one of the oldest and most respected programs in the region. This unique combination of the finest acute care, state-of-the-art

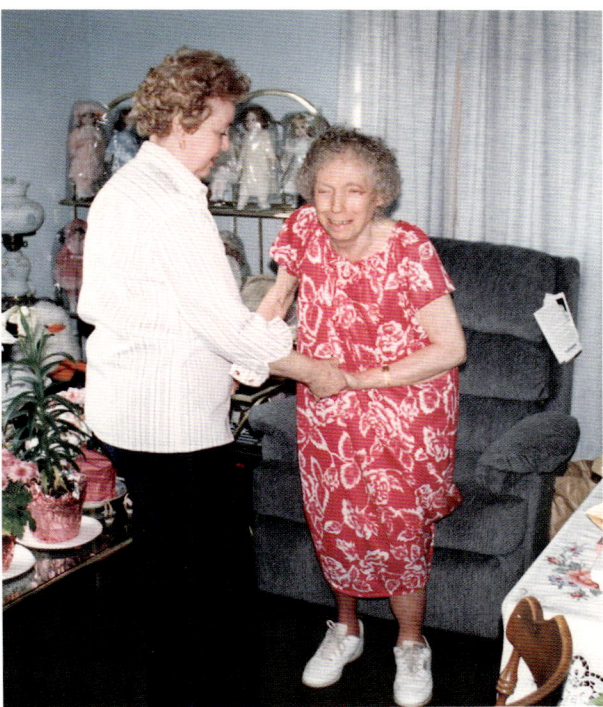

facilities, world-renowned research, commitment to the community, and an innovative approach to integrated health service delivery is embodied in programs such as the Diabetes-Endocrinology Center of Western New York. Established in 1995, the center is the regional leader in the care of diabetes and research in endocrine disorders and the largest program of its kind in upstate New York. Combining patient care with a dedicated research staff conducting clinical and pharmaceutical research, the center is a dynamic and growing part of the Millard's vision for the future of health care.

Headed by Dr. Paresh Dandona, chief of endocrinology and diabetes at the University of Buffalo School of Medicine and Biological Sciences, the center incorporates a team approach to the prevention and treatment of diabetes and complications from diabetes. The goal is to improve the outcome and quality of life for members of the community who suffer from this common and life-threatening disease.

This patient-centered, outcome-oriented approach begins with educating patients about the role they can play in the treatment and management of their disease. While diabetes is the leading cause of blindness, kidney failure, and amputations in the United States, and a leading cause of strokes and heart attacks, these conditions—and the expense of acute care for them—can often be avoided by better prevention and maintenance in which the patient assumes responsibility for and partnership in his or her treatment, by making patients aware of the serious consequences of untreated diabetes and by helping them understand the role of lifestyle, exercise, diet, and medication in managing their disease. This educational, cooperative approach incorporates a Diabetic Patients' Charter to help patients understand their rights and responsibilities, as well as a Diabetic Task Force that reaches out to health care workers and emergency rooms in the region to assist in case management for diabetics.

The center is also leading in innovative new treatment techniques such as the insulin pump; the center was one of the first treatment centers to use the pump to treat blind patients. Another advance is a pancreatic transplant program that provides pancreas transplants for patients who are also receiving kidney transplants, thereby eliminating the need for those patients to use insulin after surgery.

The center also unites professionals in many specialties, including neurology, cardiology, ophthalmology, vascular surgery, obstetrics, and gynecology, all dedicated to the mission of providing a superior level of care for diabetics and others with endocrinological disorders. This multidisciplinary approach attracts many professionals, both regionally and from around the world, who want to contribute to the care of and a cure for diabetes.

Another center of excellence at the Millard is the Hand Center. Led by Dr. Clayton Peimer, this renowned facility for the diagnosis, treatment, and rehabilitation of injuries, disease, and congenital disorders of the hand and upper extremity offers surgical and nonsurgical treatment, acute hand therapy, and work therapy. A multidisciplinary approach includes surgeons, nurses, and physical and occupational therapists who work together to help patients achieve the best possible lifestyle after treatment.

The Millard's Diabetes-Endocrinology Center was one of the first diabetes treatment centers to use the insulin pump in treating blind patients.

The Millard's home care affiliate, the VNA HealthCare Group,Inc. provides home health services to the eight counties of Western New York; including nursing services, medication and home health care equipment.

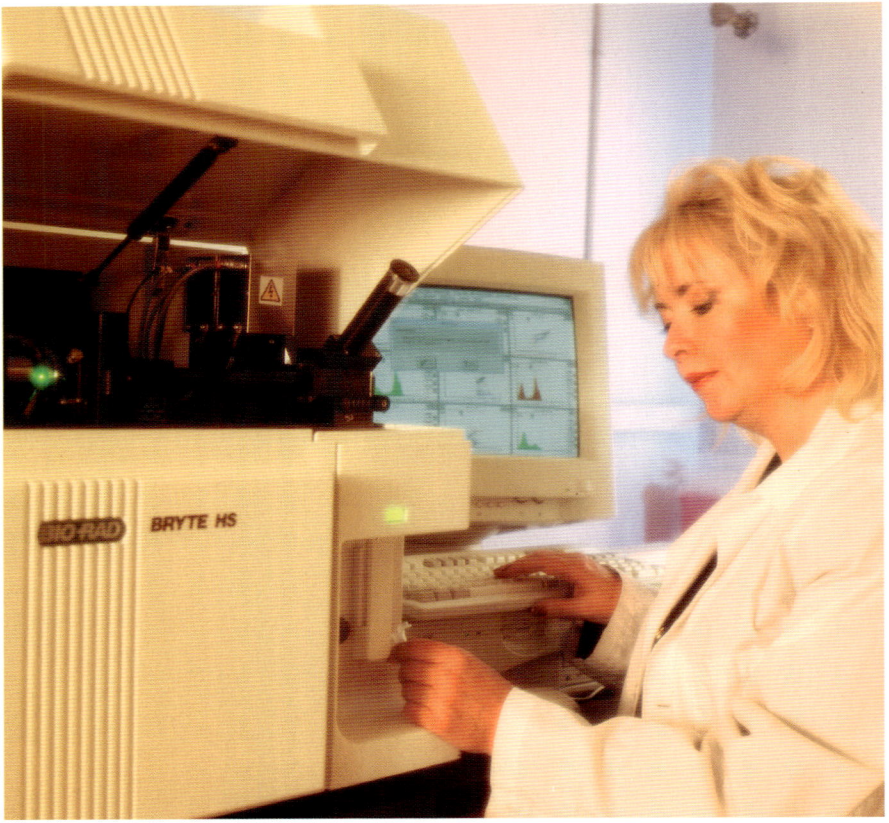

Corporation in the development of the carpal tunnel endoscope, which reduces the pain and post-surgical rehabilitation process for virtually all patients compared to conventional surgical techniques.

In addition to treatment and rehabilitation, the center works actively to educate the community about the values of injury prevention. Innovative and practical, the center has also pioneered cost-effective treatments that can improve outcomes. For example, by adapting an inpatient surgical procedure to an outpatient technique, the center has saved approximately $2,100 per surgery while achieving improved outcomes. Working through the Millard System, the center is reaching out in these and other ways to help improve outcomes for patients and health care providers throughout the region.

Another center of excellence is the Dent Neurologic Institute. Headed by Dr. L. Nelson Hopkins, chairman of neurosurgery at the University at Buffalo School of Medicine and Biomedical Sciences, the institute is a world leader in endovascular treatment of diseases, especially strokes. A minimal invasive surgical procedure, endovascular surgery allows surgeons to work from inside the patient's blood vessels to repair damage caused by strokes, aneurysms, tumors, and a host of other problems.

The institute is also a leader in the diagnosis and treatment of diseases of the spine and spinal cord, and also has a strong program in neuro-oncology to treat brain tumors. The institute was one of the first centers in the United States to treat strokes by injecting medication directly into the clot in the brain. It is one of the leading centers for the treatment of carotid artery disease, a leading cause of stroke, by both surgical and endovascular methods.

Along with treating patients from the region and around the world, the institute is a major center for neurological research. Its advances in research and treatment have attracted grants from around the world, including a $3.65 million grant from Toshiba to fund continuing research in stroke prevention and treatment.

As part of Millard's commitment to research, the Pharmacokinetics Department is using flow cytometry; state-of-the-art instrumentation for the evaluation of drug activity against bacterial and human tumor cells.

Among the center's achievements are the first microsurgical finger, hand, and arm reattachments and the first toe-to-hand transfers in the Niagara region. One of the nation's accredited hand surgery training programs, the center is associated with the University at Buffalo's School of Medicine and Biomedical Sciences and offers a hand surgery fellowship program that trains future hand surgeons. As the only comprehensive upper limb care program in the region, the center performs approximately 2,000 surgical procedures each year and sees more than 13,000 patients, treating a wide variety of disorders and ailments. In addition to treating injuries, the center works closely with hospitals throughout the region, offering reconstructive treatments for patients with upper extremities damaged by tumors and for children with congenital hand and arm defects. Along with micro- and macrosurgery, the center is a regional leader in endoscopic surgery, especially in the treatment of carpal tunnel syndrome. It was one of nine sites in the United States selected to assist 3M

The Millard's Hand Center performed the first microsurgical finger, hand and arm reattachments, and the first toe-to-hand transfers in the Niagara region.

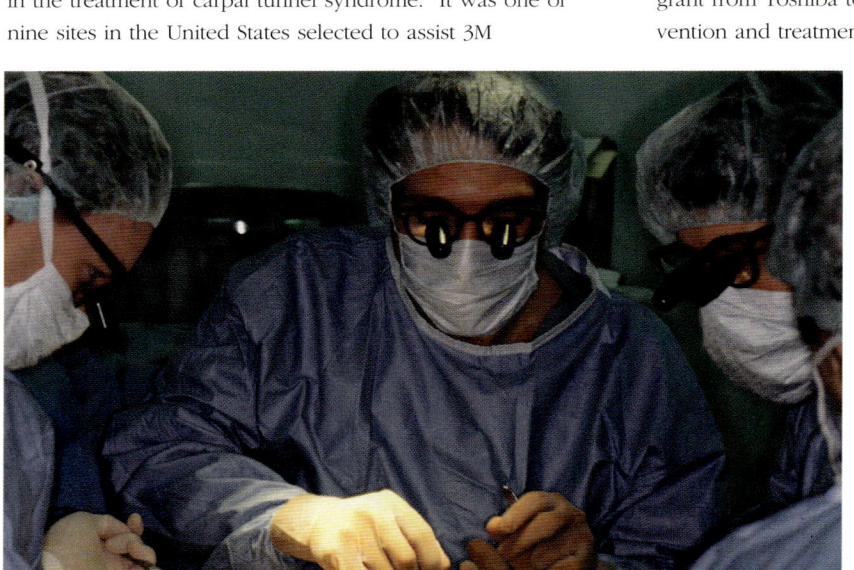

Among the institute's medical advances is its success in actually reversing the effects of strokes in both older and younger stroke victims. Through achievements such as these, and by helping define best practices and outcomes for the worldwide medical community, the institute makes a crucial contribution to the Millard's comprehensive, integrated health services delivery. These are some of the more than 30 areas of special emphasis being developed at the Millard. Others include Neuro-Rehabilitation, the Spine Center, the Eye Center, the Sleep Disorder Center, and many more, all aimed at addressing health issues important to the Niagara region.

Committed. Innovative. Dynamic. Caring. From providing some of the finest acute care in the region to the development of community health service programs, Millard Fillmore Health System has a clear vision for the future as a comprehensive, integrated community of individuals dedicated to improving the wellness of people in the region. That vision is enriched by the values of integrity, mutual respect, innovation, and social responsibility—values that assure Millard Fillmore Health System will continue to meet individual and community needs now and in the years to come.

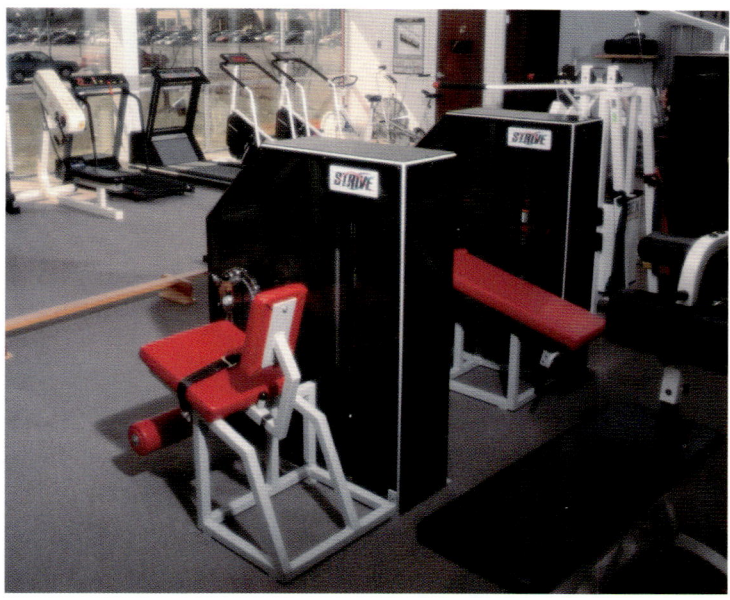

The Millard's rehabilitation programs combine state-of-the- art equipment and caring, one-on-one therapy services to facilitate recovery after injury.

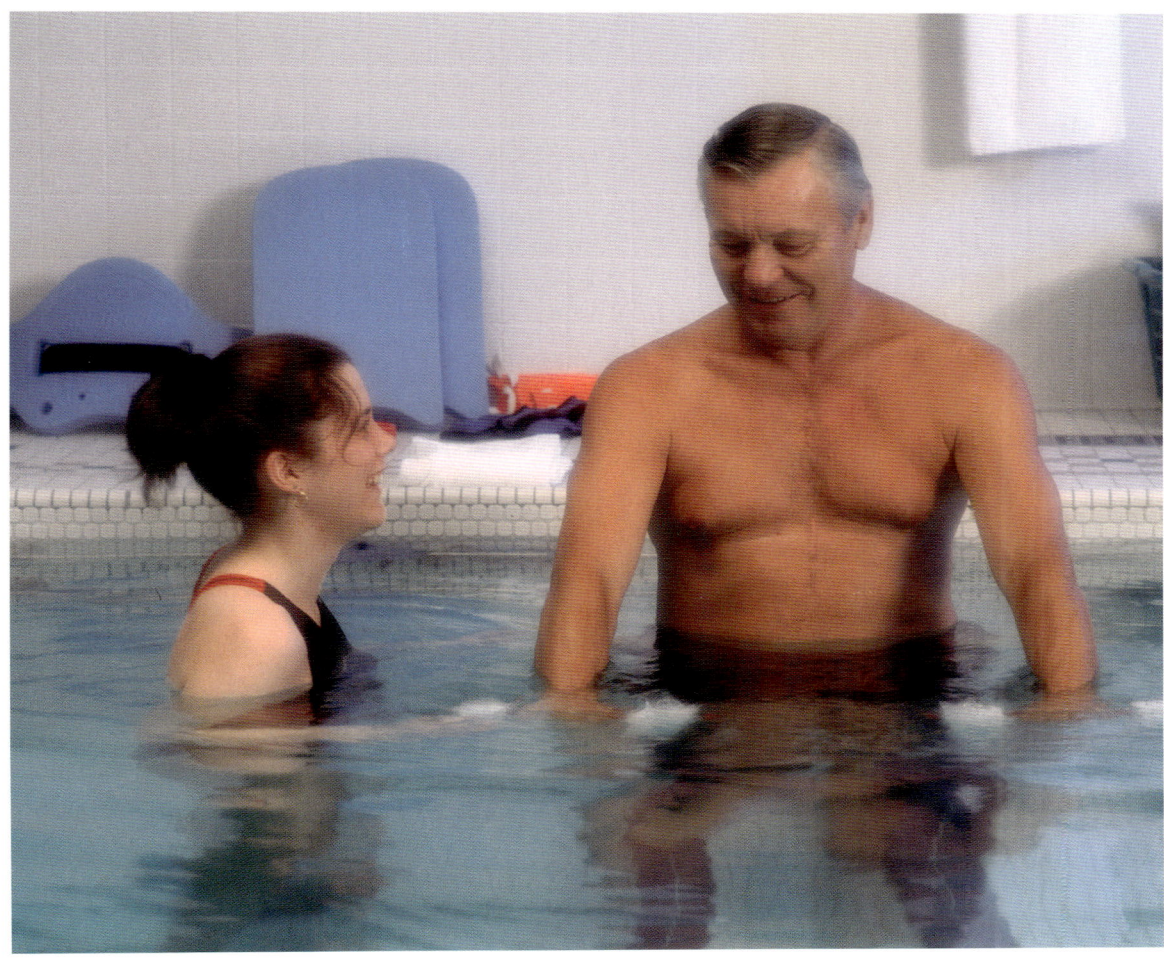

WESTERN NEW YORK'S CATHOLIC HEALTH PROVIDERS

Western New York's Catholic health providers care for more than 50,000 inpatients and more than one million outpatients each year. Its 7,000 employees and 1,200 physicians are dedicated to excellence in health care in the Catholic tradition and to improving the health status of all those they serve. The providers include Catholic Charities of Buffalo, the Mercy Health System of Western New York (Kenmore Mercy Hospital, Mercy Hospital of Buffalo, and St. Jerome Hospital), Mount St. Mary's Hospital, Our Lady of Victory Hospital, St. Joseph Hospital, and Sisters Healthcare.

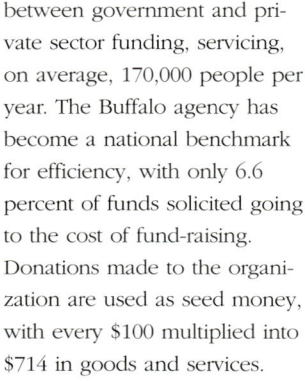

Catholic Charities of Buffalo

Founded in 1923, Catholic Charities is the instrument chosen by the bishops and the people of the Diocese of Buffalo to carry out, in large part, the human service mission of the Catholic Church in Western New York. Catholic Charities is supported by a staff of more than 275 professionals and thousands of volunteers throughout the eight-county region.

As the largest single provider of human services in Western New York, Catholic Charities has worked to fill the void

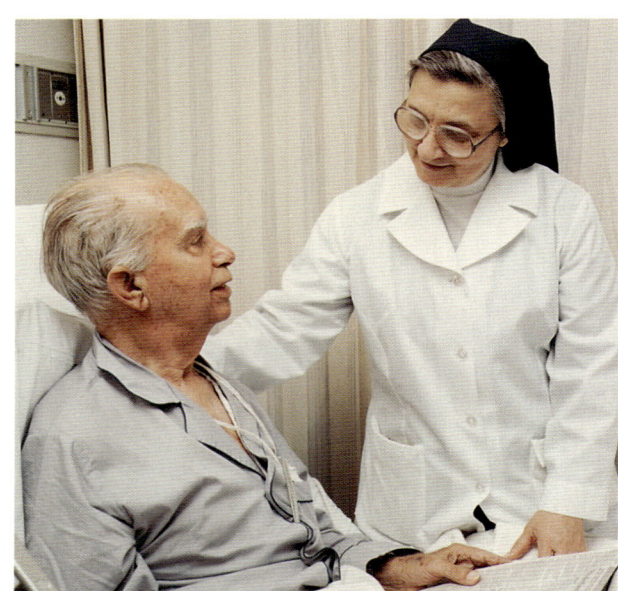

between government and private sector funding, servicing, on average, 170,000 people per year. The Buffalo agency has become a national benchmark for efficiency, with only 6.6 percent of funds solicited going to the cost of fund-raising. Donations made to the organization are used as seed money, with every $100 multiplied into $714 in goods and services.

Catholic Charities' human service delivery system is comprised of eight major departments, including clinical services, services to the aging and institutional services to the aging, and four volunteer organizations. The department of clinical services provides a wide range of programs that serve the counseling, guidance, and treatment needs of the community, including outpatient psychiatric treatment, substance abuse prevention and counseling, developmental disabilities family support, and marriage counseling.

Its departments of services and institutional services to the aging serve the special needs of the elderly and their families through housing and supportive services, home health care, senior day care, foster family care, two adult homes for ambulatory seniors, and five skilled nursing homes.

Every year, people from all over Western New York are faced with the ongoing challenges of hunger, illness, loss of

employment, family violence, and financial and emotional crisis. They come from urban, suburban, and rural communities— from every age, race, religious affiliation, and income level. But they share a common bond: the need for support and assistance to bring about positive change in their lives. For nearly 75 years, Catholic Charities has been there to respond.

The Mercy Health System of Western New York

The Mercy Health System of Western New York is proud of its long-standing dedication to serving the health care needs of families and businesses throughout the Niagara Frontier. Its mission, to promote the Mercy ministry of healing, is firmly rooted in a tradition established by the Sisters of Mercy in Buffalo some 140 years ago: a mission to serve the poor, the sick, and the uneducated with compassion, hospitality, and a commitment to excellence.

Over the years, the Mercy Health System has grown into an integrated health care organization offering a broad continuum of services, including:

Acute Care - With a special emphasis on healing and education, the Mercy Health System operates three acute care hospitals: Kenmore Mercy Hospital, Mercy Hospital of Buffalo, and St. Jerome Hospital. This network of hospitals is dedicated to providing quality medical care at all stages of life. Supported by nearly 1,000 physicians representing a number of medical disciplines, and operating with the latest in state-of-the-art equipment, the Mercy Health System offers a full array of acute care services.

Diagnostic and Treatment - Constantly striving to provide state-of-the-art diagnostic testing and conveniently accessible immediate treatment, the Mercy Health System has expanded its network to include five freestanding diagnostic and treatment Centers: Mercy Ambulatory Care Center—Orchard Park; Mercy Diagnostic and Treatment Center—West Seneca; Mercy Diagnostic Center—East Aurora; Mercy Diagnostic Center—Lancaster, and the Sheridan Healthcare Center—Tonawanda. Services offered include CAT scanning, echocardiography, EKG, laboratory collection, mammography, MRI, preadmission testing, ultrasonography, and x- ray. For medical emergencies, immediate treatment is available at the Mercy Ambulatory Care Center—Orchard Park.

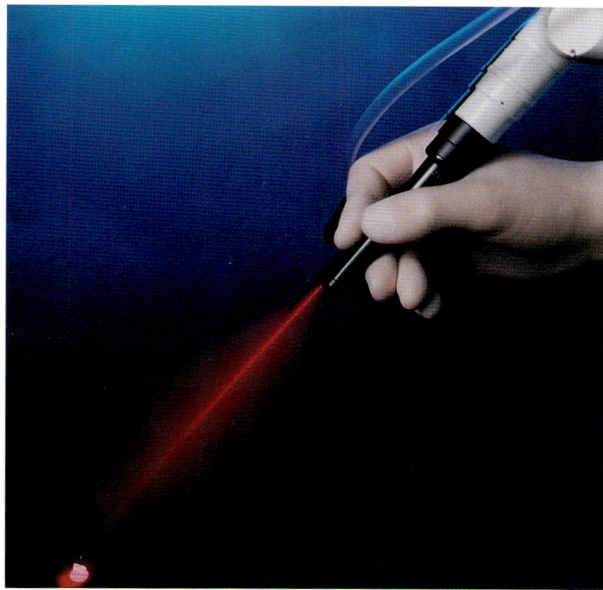

Family Health Care - From routine checkups to the treatment of an illness or chronic medical condition, the Mercy Health System provides a network of family care centers designed to serve the medical needs of children, adults, and seniors. Services available include prenatal care, pediatrics, family medicine, OB/GYN, rheumatology, endocrinology, geriatrics, and podiatry. These centers include Akron FamilyCare, Attica FamilyCare, Batavia FamilyCare, Corfu FamilyCare, Ken-Ton FamilyCare, LeRoy FamilyCare, Mercy/Health Center, Mercy Adult Medical Center, Mercy OB/GYN Center, Mercy Pediatric Center, Riverside/Black Rock FamilyCare, and Tonawanda Seneca FamilyCare.

Health Education and Referral Services - The Mercy Health System offers a wide range of community services. Health Connection, a free telephone referral service, helps callers find physicians, answers health care questions, and puts callers in touch with appropriate community services. Healthy Living offers a variety of health education and wellness programs to help maintain good health or better manage an existing medical condition. Mercy Community Link is an information, assessment, and referral service designed to help individuals remain independent by coordinating needed health care services. Senior Partners is a senior membership program that offers a variety of special benefits. Wellness on Wheels is a mobile health program that offers health education, primary care, and occupational health services in a custom-designed mobile health vehicle.

Home Care - Mercy Health System offers a full range of home care services to assist individuals who need care at home. These services include skilled nursing care, rehabilitation services, private duty nurses, home care aides, and meals-on-wheels provided by Mercy Home Care, Mercy Long Term Home Health Care, and McAuley-Seton Home Care (a joint venture with Sisters Hospital). Complementing these services, Mercy Medical Equipment and Oxygen provides home medical equipment, and Lifeline provides personal emergency response services.

Rehabilitation Services - Mercy Health System offers an array of rehabilitative services that helps individuals reach their maximum level of independence. These include: cardiac rehabilitation, alcohol treatment and rehabilitation, pulmonary rehabilitation, physical therapy and the AthletiCare sports medicine program, and inpatient medical rehabilitation.

Residential Health Care - Medical and nursing services for patients who no longer require hospital care but need daily skilled care are available at three residential health

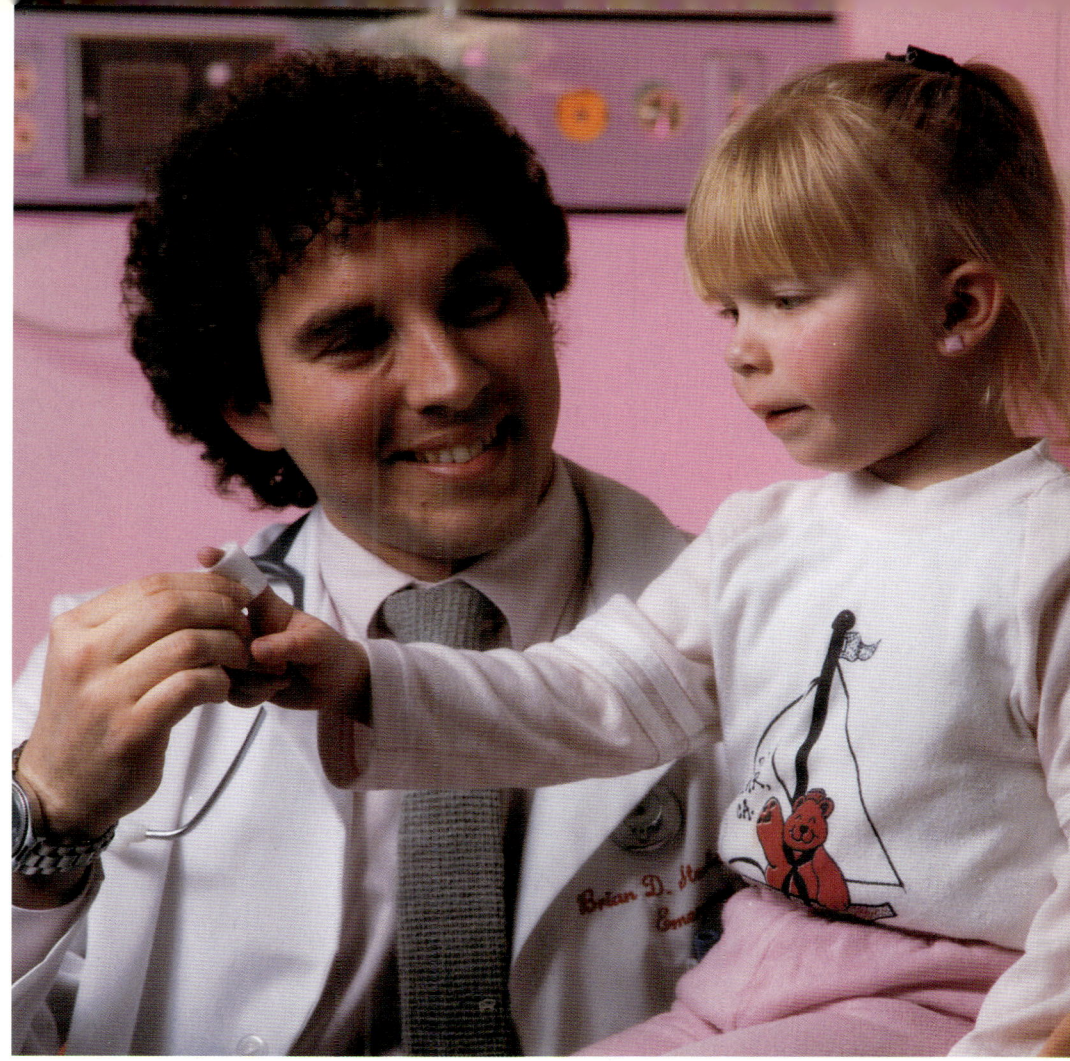

care facilities: McAuley Residence, Mercy Nursing Facility, and Father Baker Manor (a joint venture with Our Lady of Victory and St. Joseph Hospitals). Each facility provides a full array of rehabilitation services, recreational activities, social gatherings, and leisure programs.

Senior Living - Independent living is a unique approach to housing that is attractive to many seniors. The Mercy Health System offers both independent and assisted living options, including Julianna Apartments, Trocaire Place, and Cazenovia Meadows. Residents benefit from the comfort and safety that comes from community living, but maintain their privacy and independence.

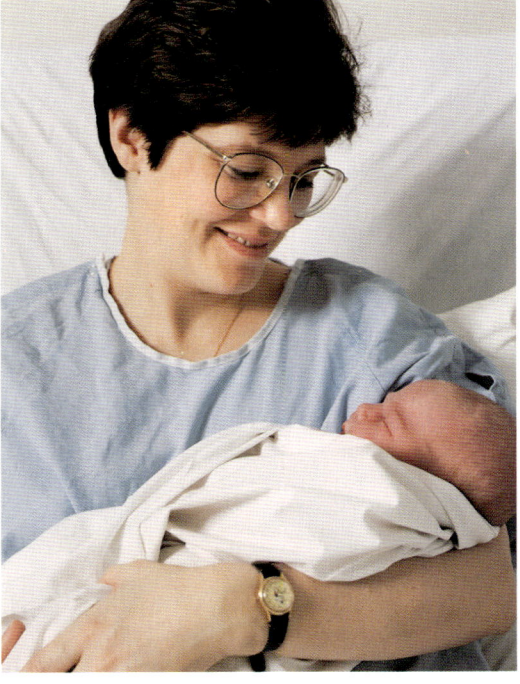

Mount St. Mary's Hospital

Mount St. Mary's Hospital, located at 5300 Military Road in Lewiston, is a 179-bed community hospital founded by the Sisters of St. Francis of Williamsville, New York. It sits on a 28-acre park-like campus located near growing communities with excellent access to major transportation routes. Established in 1907 at the request of the Catholic bishop of Buffalo, the hospital's mission is to provide Niagara County residents with "quality care in a personal manner with total regard for individual human dignity."

Newer additions to Mount St. Mary's include a two-story Medical Arts Building linked to the hospital by a covered walkway. Mount St. Mary's Child Care Center was opened in 1988. A $12 million renovation and building project, commenced in the summer of 1996, includes a new ICU/CCU,

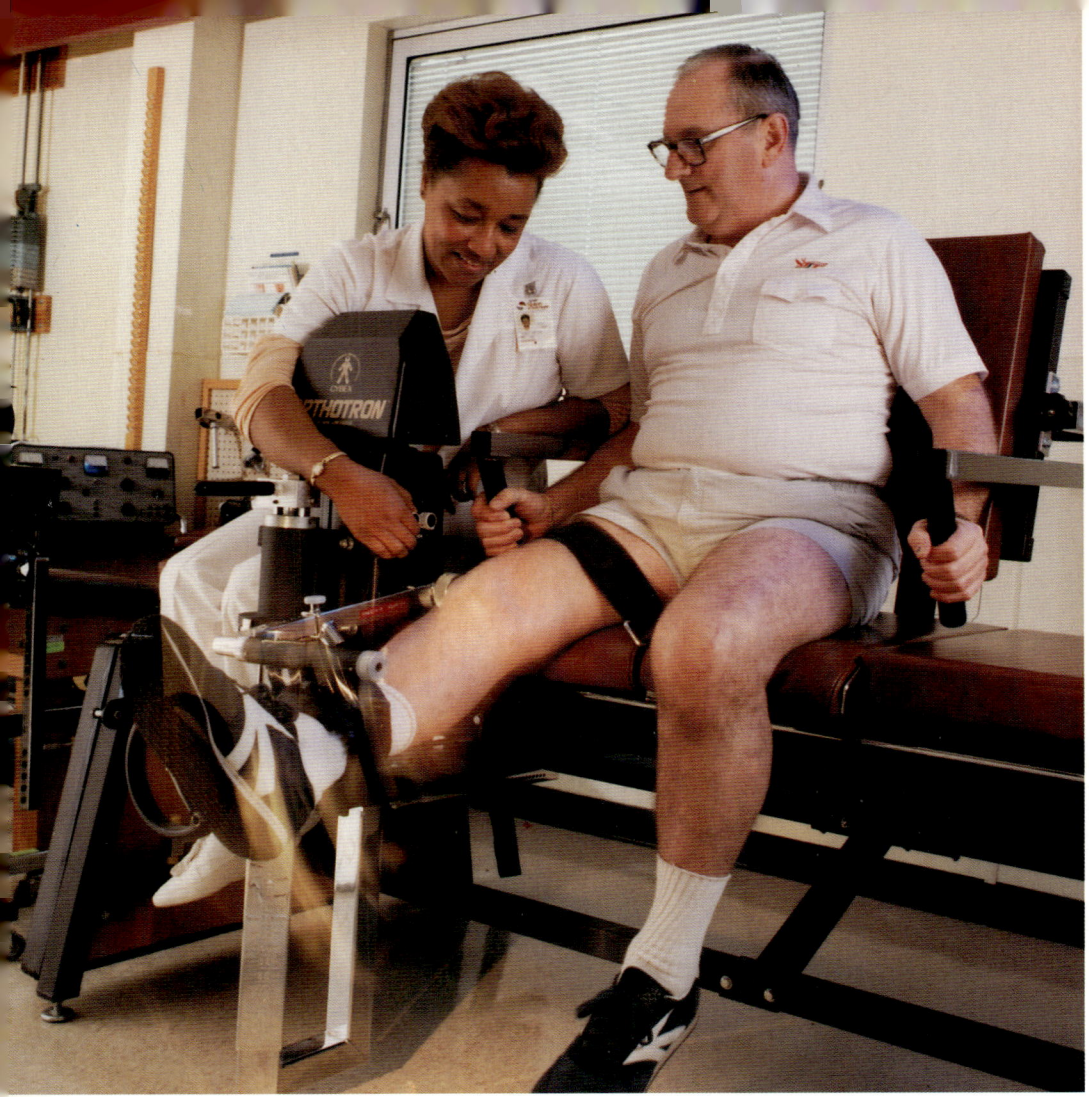

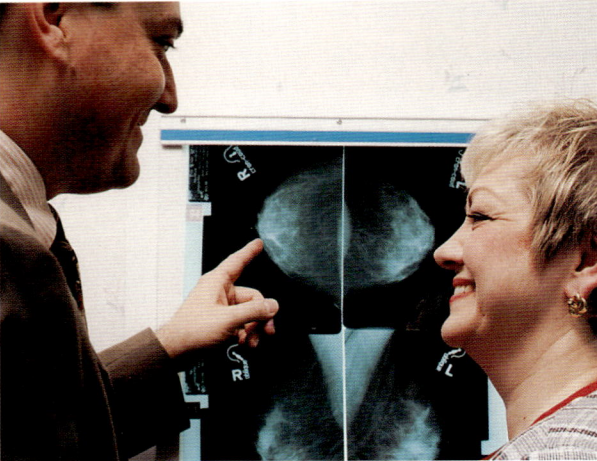

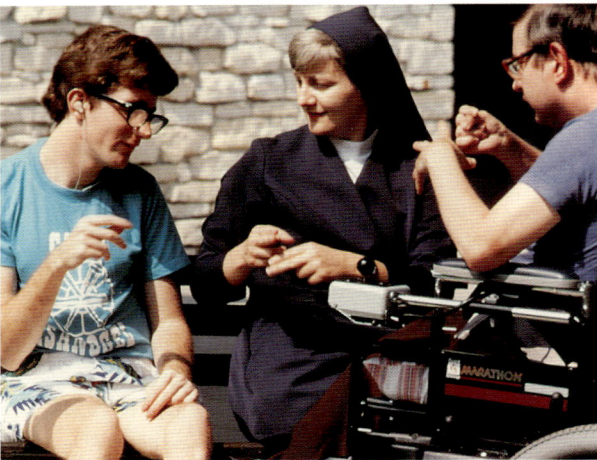

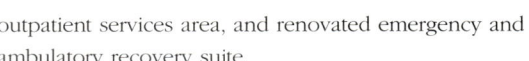

outpatient services area, and renovated emergency and ambulatory recovery suite.

A complete range of health care services is made possible by state-of-the-art medical equipment and a staff of more than 125 physicians, along with a health care team of nearly 630 full-time equivalent hospital employees and 284 hospital-based volunteers. Mount St. Mary's Hospital provides the Niagara community with acute care hospital services, emergency care, outpatient services/surgery, women's health services/programs, senior programs, community health/wellness programs, physical therapy services, cardiac diagnostic services, and diagnostic imaging and laboratory services. Specialized services include: Heartworks for cardiopulmonary rehabilitation; Sleepworks, a sleep disorders clinic; Palliative Care Unit, a hospice unit with Niagara Hospice; Renal Dialysis Unit, in conjunction with the Niagara Renal Center; Clearview for substance abuse services, and Family Healthcare Center neighborhood clinics.

Our Lady of Victory Hospital

Our Lady of Victory Hospital, founded by Father Nelson Baker in 1919, is located in Lackawanna and serves the surrounding area of Blasdell, South Buffalo, West Seneca, Hamburg, and Orchard Park, as well as other Southtowns communities.

The hospital offers the following services: inpatient acute medical-surgical and brain injury rehabilitation, emergency care, primary care, ambulatory surgery, long-term care, and ancillary services providing an appropriate array of accessible diagnostic and treatment modalities for the community. The hospital also provides health services to the special needs population through an extension clinic located at the Infant Home, a population of severely mentally and physically handicapped children and young adults.

In 1991, Our Lady of Victory Hospital established the OLV Primary Care and Surgery Center in Orchard Park to provide Southtowns-area residents with needed additional primary care as well as the opportunity to utilize a freestanding ambulatory surgery center. The hospital also operates an occupational medicine program at the OLV Industrial Medical Center in the Hills Plaza in Blasdell. Here area employers have access to diagnostic testing and treatment services including pre- employment physicals, injury treatment, case management, substance testing, and other work-related health services.

In 1996, the hospital joined with two developers to open the OLV Brierwood Medical Centre, an ambulatory care site in Hamburg, with a family practitioner as its anchor tenant. The facility offers diagnostic imaging and specimen collection services convenient for area residents. It also provides time sharing for selected physician specialists and other specialists as tenants of the facility.

The hospital, along with six other hospitals and their respective radiology groups, entered into a cooperative venture in 1989 to establish a freestanding magnetic resonance imaging facility (MRI) that continues to serve the Western New York community.

Our Lady of Victory Hospital, along with Buffalo Mercy Hospital and St. Joseph Hospital, is a cosponsor of the Father Baker Manor Skilled Nursing Facility in Orchard Park which provides 160 residential health facility beds for the elderly population.

Our Lady of Victory Hospital provides an extensive community education program through its Health Education Department and has taken the lead in planning for the future by cultivating students through educational affiliations for clinical training.

St. Joseph Hospital

St. Joseph Hospital, which opened in 1960, is a 208-bed acute care hospital serving residents and businesses from local communities. Sponsored by the Franciscan Sisters of St. Joseph, the hospital is centrally located in Cheektowaga, near the intersection of the I-90 Thruway and the Kensington Expressway (Rte. 33) and just minutes from the Buffalo International Airport and the Walden Galleria Mall, Western New York's largest retail shopping mall.

In 1996, St. Joseph Hospital completed a $14.1 million renovation and expansion project, featuring seven new state-of- the-art surgical facilities and expanded outpatient and community services. The project also created new patient waiting and visiting areas, a new chapel, and a 150-seat capacity community room.

Each year, St. Joseph Hospital's 306 doctors, 210 volunteers and staff of nearly 900 serve more than 100,000 people on-site and in six off-site primary care centers. Its Emergency Department treats some 21,000 patients annually. Another 9,600 patients come to St. Joseph Hospital for surgeries yearly; more than two-thirds of this total come for same-day (ambulatory) surgeries.

St. Joseph Hospital annually provides wellness and health promotion programming—on-site and at various locations throughout the community—for more than 6,000 people. It also provides clinical training opportunities for more than 120 students and professional interns from area colleges. The hospital is fully accredited by the Joint Commission on the Accreditation of Healthcare Organizations and licensed by the New York State Health Department.

Sisters Healthcare

Buffalo's first hospital is part of Sisters Healthcare, an integrated network of health facilities and programs situated across Western New York. Sisters Hospital dates to 1848, when it was established by the Daughters of Charity of St. Vincent de Paul. Sisters ran different facilities in several locations to serve specific populations. In 1948, the hospital's health care services were merged into one facility, situated at its present Main and Kensington location.

Each year, Sisters cares for thousands of patients in its acute care units, outpatient service areas, affiliated health centers, and chemical dependency offices.

Complete family medical care is offered at the hospital's health centers and physician offices located around the metropolitan area, including Sisters Amherst Health Center and Sisters Amherst Internal Medicine, serving the Northtowns; St. Vincent Health Center, Buffalo; Alden Medical Center, serving eastern Erie County; the Sisters Family Health Center, at Sisters Hospital; Main-Depew Medical Offices, North Buffalo; and Delaware-Brighton Family Medicine, Tonawanda, and West Seneca Family Medicine, West Seneca.

Chemical dependency services are offered through the Amherst, West Seneca, and Buffalo offices of STAR— Substance, Treatment, and Recovery.

The hospital is approved for residency programs in medicine, obstetrics/gynecology, rehabilitation, and osteopathic rotating internships. It also offers fellowships through its Head and Neck Center. In addition, Sisters maintains its

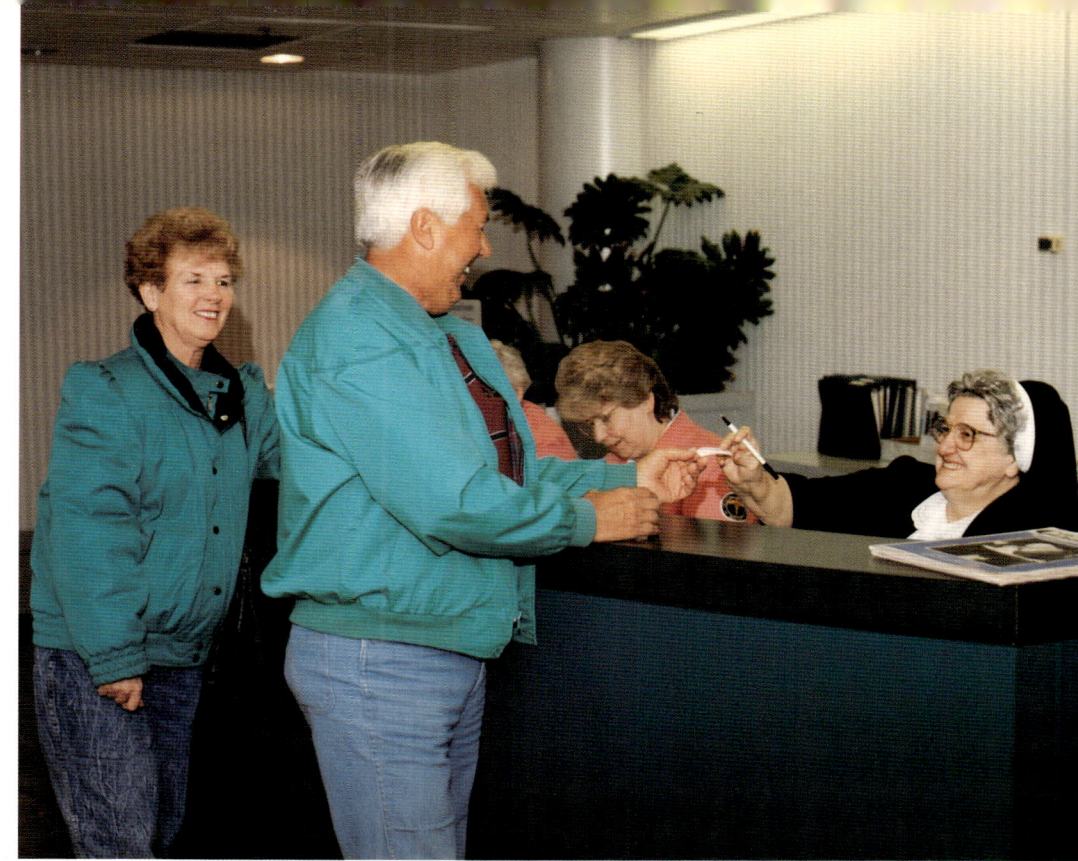

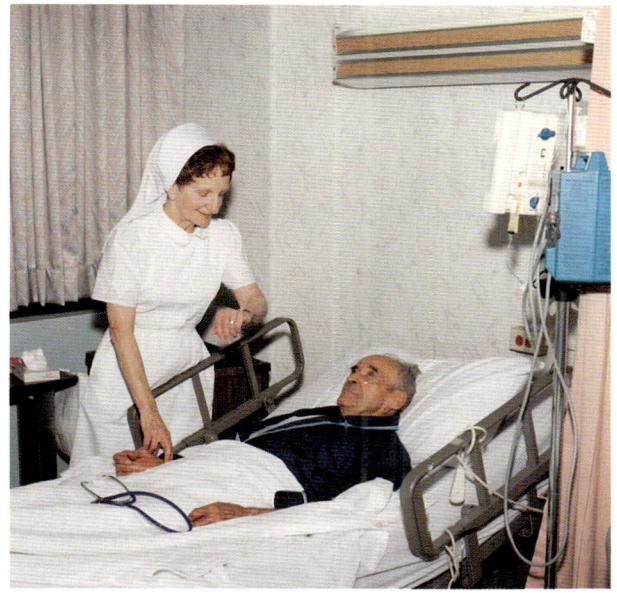

own School of Nursing, graduating 60 students a year with an R.N. and associate's degree.

Sisters is highly regarded for its women's health care programs through its women's services division, Expressly for Women resource and referral program and Specialty Center for Women. A new labor and delivery wing was completed in 1997 offering 10 new labor, delivery and recovery rooms. It's Breast Care Center is staffed by some of the nation's best surgeons, offering an exemplary array of screening, education and treatment.

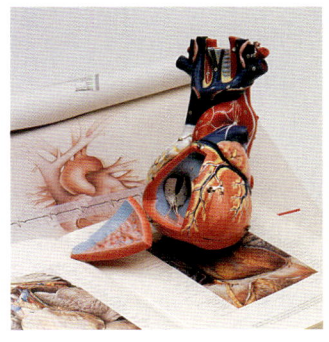

As part of its comprehensive cancer program, Sisters received certification by the American College of Surgeons Commission on Cancer in 1997 as a Certified Cancer Program, one of only two in Buffalo at that time. The hospital's John M. Lore', Jr., M.D., Head and Neck Center, is internationally known in the treatment of head and neck cancer. ✦

ROSWELL PARK CANCER INSTITUTE

Roswell Park Cancer Institute is the world's first cancer research and treatment facility.

From its founding in 1898, Roswell Park Cancer Institute—the world's first cancer research and treatment facility—has been a pioneer in the fight against cancer.

Roswell Park initiated the first cancer chemotherapy program in the world in 1904, and reported the first observations implicating immunological reactions with malignancy that same year. Roswell Park physicians were the first to treat childhood leukemia with high doses of the drug methotrexate, improving the survival rate for childhood leukemia, once a death sentence, to approximately 60 percent. Roswell Park anesthesiologists were the first to describe mouth-to-mouth resuscitation, still acknowledged as the most effective form of artificial respiration. Roswell Park researchers pioneered the first studies using radiolabeled antibodies to localize tumors and were the first to determine the molecular structure of the enzyme ribonuclease, leading to the production of synthetic enzymes nationwide. Scientists at Roswell Park developed photodynamic therapy, a laser/chemical treatment used worldwide to treat skin, breast, lung, bladder, esophageal, and head and neck cancers. And it was at Roswell Park that a human prostate-specific antigen (PSA) was characterized and the PSA blood test to detect prostate cancer was developed.

These are just a few of the many accomplishments that have kept Roswell Park at the forefront of cancer research and treatment worldwide. The institute's influence on cancer research and treatment was recognized when it served as the model for the National Cancer Institute's coveted designation of Comprehensive Cancer Center. Today, Roswell Park is one of fewer than 30 cancer centers in the United States to offer the combination of cancer research, patient care, education, and outreach required for this recognition.

Roswell Park's research continues to enjoy a worldwide reputation. The institute has ongoing research contracts from sources around the world, conducting research ranging from crystallographic studies of the molecular structure of biological substances to preclinical studies of new anticancer agents.

That survival rates for cancer patients are at an all-time high is due, in significant measure, to Roswell Park's leadership in turning research discoveries into effective cancer diagnostic and treatment tools. The PSA blood test for the early detection of prostate cancer, credited by former Senator Robert Dole as saving his life, is one of many such successes.

Along with the millions worldwide who have benefited from advances in cancer detection and treatment pioneered at Roswell Park, more than 19,000 patients are treated annually at the institute. Roswell Park treats patients from almost every

Along with the millions worldwide who have benefited from advances in cancer detection and treatment pioneered at Roswell Park, more than 19,000 patients are treated annually at the institute.

state and more than 20 foreign countries in a typical year, all attracted by the institute's international reputation for excellence in cancer care and treatment. Roswell surgeons report the lowest recurrence rate in the United States for rectal cancer and one of the highest survival rates for malignant melanoma. The institute's Grace Cancer Drug Center is one of only two U.S. centers that shepherds new drugs from conception to manufacture to federally approved clinical trials, offering unique "bench to bedside" opportunities for patients to benefit from the most promising up-to-date treatments.

Along with diagnostic and treatment advances, Roswell Park is a leader in improving the quality of life of cancer patients. The institute pioneered innovative reconstructive surgical procedures for patients with head and neck cancers who have undergone disfiguring surgery, and today houses the Regional Center for Maxillofacial Prosthetics, one of only a dozen U.S. centers using custom-designed prostheses to aid cancer and trauma patient rehabilitation. The institute was also one of the first to offer a Long-Term Follow-Up Clinic

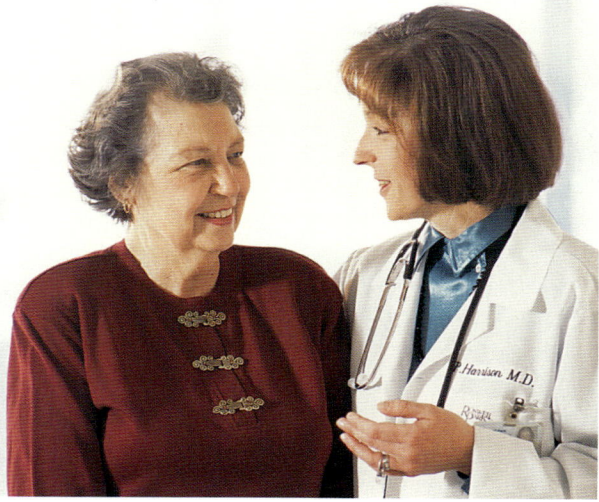

providing specialized medical care and counseling to childhood cancer survivors.

Through its many educational programs, Roswell Park continues to advance the future of cancer treatment and research. The institute has trained thousands of scientists and physicians; two of every three oncologists practicing in the Niagara region are Roswell Park-trained. Roswell Park clinicians and scientists have faculty appointments at the University at Buffalo School of Medicine and Biomedical Sciences. The Visiting Scholars Program, the Postdoctoral Basic Science Program, and many other training opportunities attract scientists and physicians from around the world to work and study at Roswell Park.

Through its outreach program, Roswell Park brings many of the benefits of its world-leading research and patient care to the Niagara region and the international community. Locally, it sponsors services such as free telephone hotlines; free cancer screening clinics, including free mammograms for underinsured women; smoking cessation programs; a speaker's bureau; and support groups for cancer patients and their families. Another important service with national reach is the registries maintained for individuals with a genetic predisposition to certain cancers, including the internationally recognized Gilda Radner Familial Ovarian Cancer Registry.

Roswell Park also has a major economic impact on the region. The centerpiece of downtown Buffalo's medical corridor, the institute's major modernization program has prepared Roswell for another century of greatness, enhancing its facilities so that it can continue to play a worldwide leadership role in cancer research and treatment. This $241 million capital improvement project has had a combined economic impact of $511 million, creating over 1,300 permanent and temporary jobs. In addition, Roswell Park is one of the region's largest employers, with more than 2,100 employees. The institute's ability to attract research grants from national

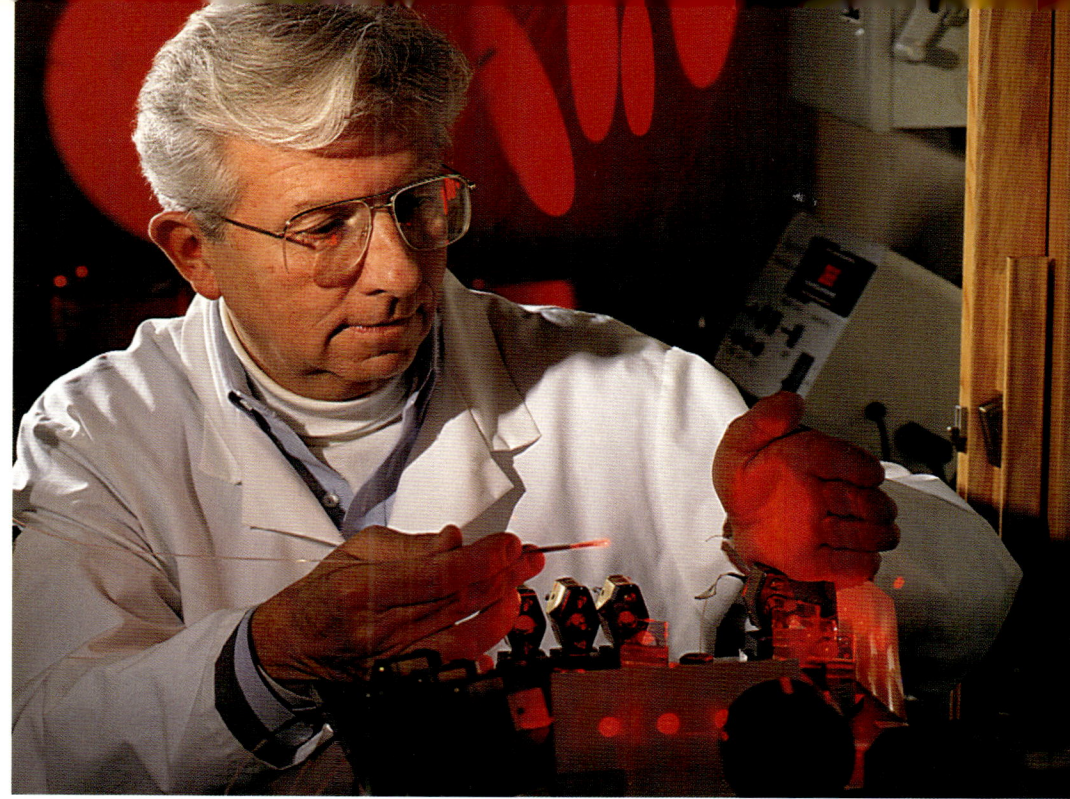

and international sources also has a profound economic effect, with two to three new jobs created for every $100,000 received in grants.

With new facilities such as the Bone Marrow Transplant Unit, new services such as the multidisciplinary Pain Management Program, and new research goals such as genetically engineering the food we eat to help prevent cancer, Roswell is poised for another century of leadership. To meet the challenges of the future, Roswell Park is establishing new "centers of excellence" in experimental therapeutics, molecular genetics, structural biology and molecular medicine, and immunology. And as patient care delivery systems evolve, Roswell Park will remain at the forefront with innovative partnerships, both regionally and nationally, to assure that patients from the Niagara region and around the world continue to enjoy the benefits of the institute's many contributions to the fight against cancer. ❖

Roswell Park's research continues to enjoy a worldwide reputation.

As patient care delivery systems evolve, Roswell Park will remain at the forefront with innovative partnerships, both regionally and nationally.

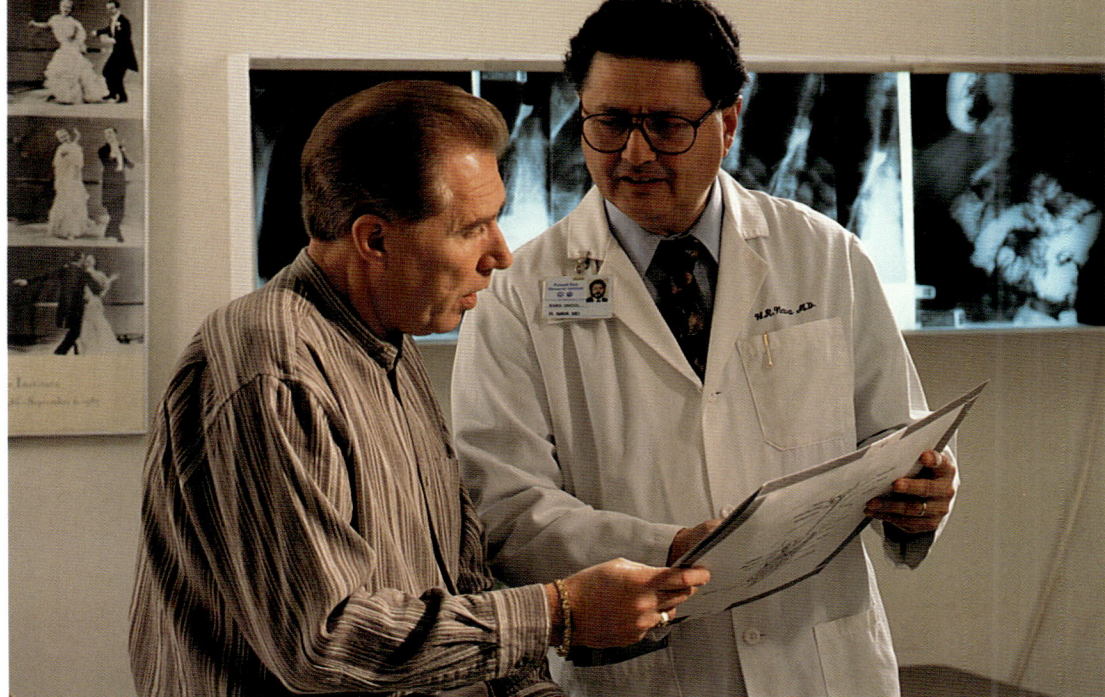

BLUE CROSS AND BLUE SHIELD OF WESTERN NEW YORK

The largest health insurer in this area was formed as the result of the 1992 merger of Blue Shield of Western New York into Blue Cross of Western New York, Inc. The two plans trace their origins to the 1930s, when both not-for-profit organizations were developed to provide area residents with prepaid protection against the costs of hospital and medical care.

In 1936, with the participation of 13 area hospitals, the Hospital Service Corporation of Western New York was established to guarantee prepaid hospital care for employer groups in return for modest monthly payments. Three years later, similar prepayment of doctor bills was made available through the newly formed Western New York Medical Plan, Inc.

The hospital plan took its Blue Cross name from an identification first used by a similar hospital association in Minnesota in 1933 and later adopted around the country. The Blue Shield name and symbol originated with the Buffalo medical plan in 1939, and this identification was also adopted by medical plans nationwide.

Blue Cross and Blue Shield has been an innovator in developing new programs to better serve the people of Western New York. In 1945, they became one of the first in the country to reimburse its member hospitals on the basis of the costs they incurred. That same year, it also recognized the need to avoid any unnecessary costs by forming one of the nation's first medical advisory committees to review claims.

Today, Blue Cross and Blue Shield has established advisory committees representing employers, labor unions, the physician/hospital community, and consumers. All are charged with helping to set policy, make decisions, and effect changes in benefits and procedures that meet the evolving needs of those involved with delivering and receiving health care.

Through the 1950s and 1960s, the two plans worked cooperatively to offer a new Extended Benefits Rider, a forerunner of today's major medical riders; low-cost health care coverage for college students; and over age 65 hospital and medical contracts which covered most of the deductible and co-payment amounts left by Medicare.

In 1985, Community Blue was introduced as an alternative to traditional health insurance. It was an immediate success. As a health maintenance organization (HMO), Community Blue, emphasizes wellness programs and prevention of serious illness. This proactive approach to health care has been expanded to include such current offerings as "Alive & Lively," an award-winning wellness program, and "Breathe Easy," which provides patient education and support on the controllable disease of asthma. In February, 1997, Community Blue earned Full Accreditation from the National Committee

The new Blue Cross and Blue Shield has its headquarters in the former Sears and Roebuck building on Main Street in Buffalo.

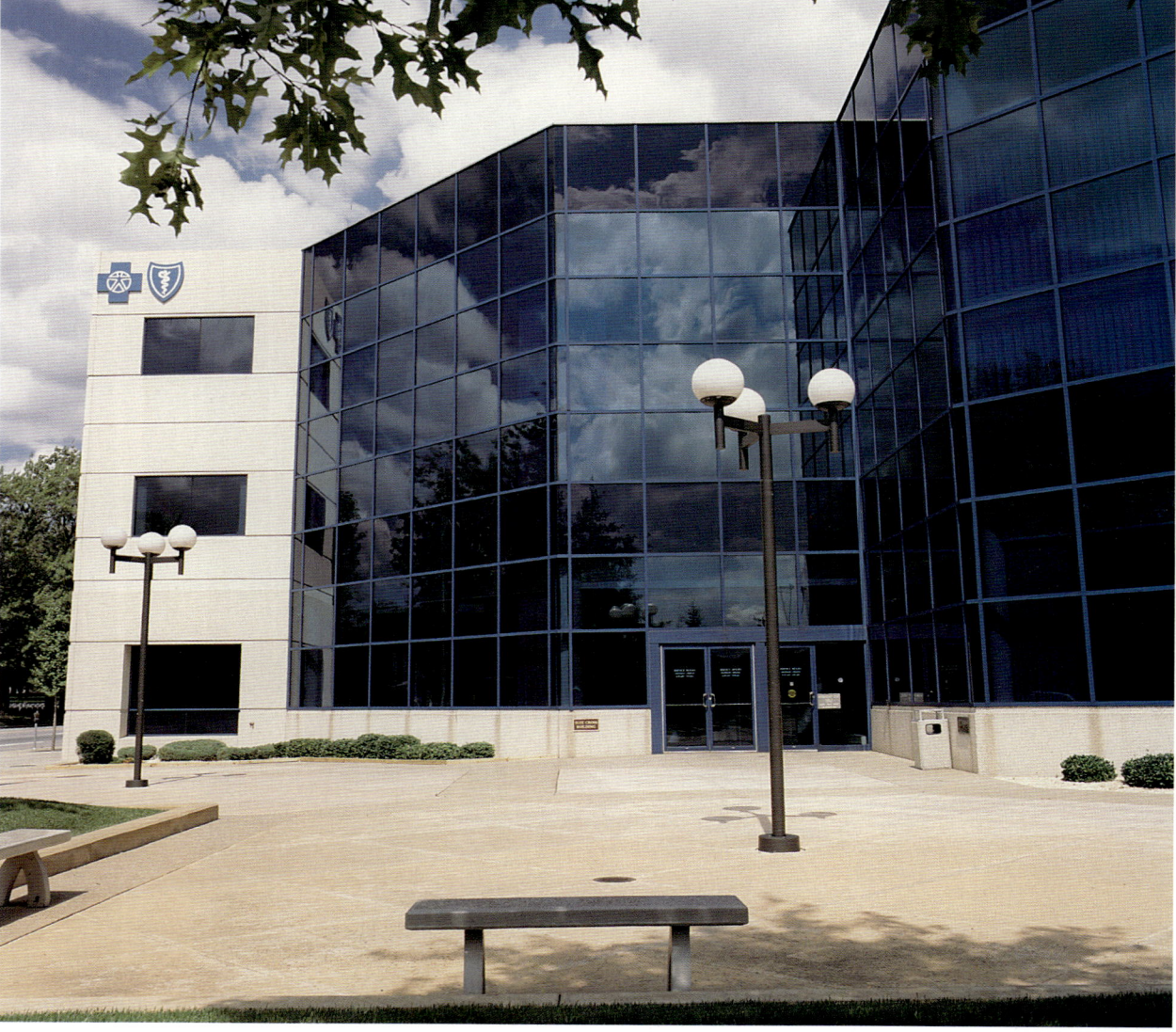

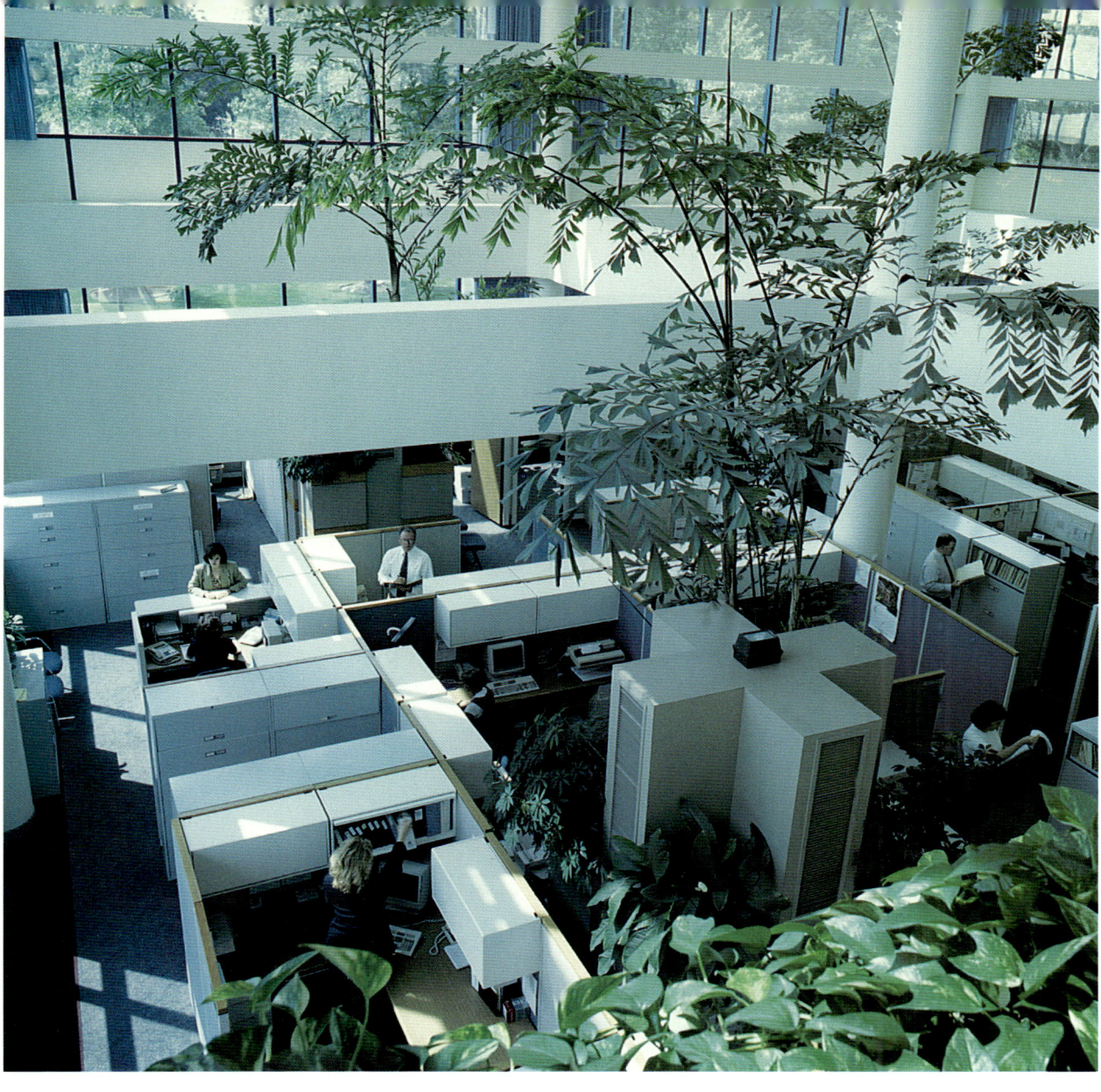

Blue Cross and Blue Shield has been an innovator in developing new programs to better serve the people of Western New York.

for Quality Assurance (NCQA)*. Full Accreditation is granted to plans that have excellent programs for continuous quality improvement and meet NCQA's rigorous standards.

Today's Blue Cross and Blue Shield is a true leader in the managed-care field. with products designed specifically for special populations like children, the elderly, and the poor.

The new Blue Cross and Blue Shield has its headquarters in the former Sears and Roebuck building on Main Street in Buffalo. Divisional offices include one in Albany, Blue Shield of Northeastern New York, and one in Binghamton, the Upstate Medicare Division which processes Medicare Part B claims. Combined the three divisions serve some 700,000 New Yorkers through traditional and managed care coverage, and more than 1.6 million through Medicare Part B claims administration.

In recent years, technological change has altered the internal structure of Blue Cross and Blue Shield. A computerized, electronic-based system has eliminated the old paper "blizzard" of claims-processing, resulting in more efficient, cost-effective delivery of benefits to Blue Cross and Blue Shield customers.

Through all the changes in the health care industry, Blue Cross and Blue Shield has upheld its publicly stated promise to make quality health care coverage available to the greatest number of people at the lowest possible cost.

The company has also maintained a strong tradition of giving back to the community. In 1992, the Blue Cross and Blue Shield Volunteer Squad was introduced. The employee-run project provides opportunities to raise money

for charitable organizations as well as giving hands-on service to the needy. Health care organizations top the list of those that have received Volunteer Squad support. Children's Hospital of Buffalo, the Erie County Home and Infirmary, West Seneca Developmental Center, Roswell Park Cancer Institute, Hospice Buffalo, Our Lady of Victory Infant Home, Ronald McDonald House, and many others have all benefited from Volunteer Squad activities.

Much has changed in the health care business since the days when catastrophic illness meant financial ruin for a family. Offering the pioneering kind of medical costs coverage that would forestall such a tragedy is just one of the reasons Blue Cross and Blue Shield can claim innovative leadership in its field. Two more reasons are the community service exemplified by its staff volunteerism, and the company's continuing commitment to meeting—and anticipating—the unique needs of its subscribers.

In a dynamic and highly challenging business, Blue Cross and Blue Shield has pledged to continue to earn the trust and confidence of the Western New York community for many years to come. It is committed to developing new products and programs designed to fulfill the original purpose for which both plans were organized: To provide people with ready access to quality health care services, wherever they need them. ✣

* This status is effective from 2/97 - 9/98.

WESTWOOD-SQUIBB

Skin care is the business of Buffalo's Westwood-Squibb. This venerable firm, founded as Foster-Milburn in 1876, is today a research-based dermatological company in the Bristol-Myers Squibb pharmaceutical group. Its workforce includes a field sales group that is one of the largest marketing dermatological products. One of the world's largest R&D groups dedicated to dermatological research provides discovery and product development support.

Through the years, Westwood-Squibb has been a leader in the industry. The company first actively reached out to dermatologists more than 50 years ago to develop new products. As a result Westwood-Squibb pioneered moisturizing bath oil, sunscreen products and was the first to market a prescription moisturizing lotion.

Its principle prescription products are LAC-HYDRIN, ULTRAVATE, WESTCORT and DONOVEX. Principle over-the-counter products include MOISTUREL cream, lotion, and cleanser for sensitive skin and PRESUN sunscreen and sunblock.

As a Bristol-Myers Squibb company, Westwood-Squibb carries out its parent's pledge to good corporate citizenship through community involvement. The company and its people have received numerous awards in the past decade as supporters of health and human services, education and the arts.

Today, Westwood-Squibb is working with other Bristol-Myers Squibb operating groups to create a global skin care business. ❖

Westwood-Squibb's research and development is conducted in a 64,000 sq. ft. state-of-the-art complex at the company's headquarters in Buffalo, New York. Here, approximately 100 scientists, technicians and administrative support staff— one of the largest supporting dermatology—discover and develop compounds to treat skin disorders that range from xerosis (dry skin) to psoriasis. The complex underwent a $7 million expansion and upgrade in 1996.

Westwood-Squibb's principle over-the-counter products include MOISTUREL lotion, cream and cleanser for sensitive skin and the PRESUN family of sunscreens and sunblock. Principle prescription products (not pictured), include DOVONEX, LAC-HYDRIN, ULTRAVATE and WESTCORT. Photo by K.C. Kratt Photography.

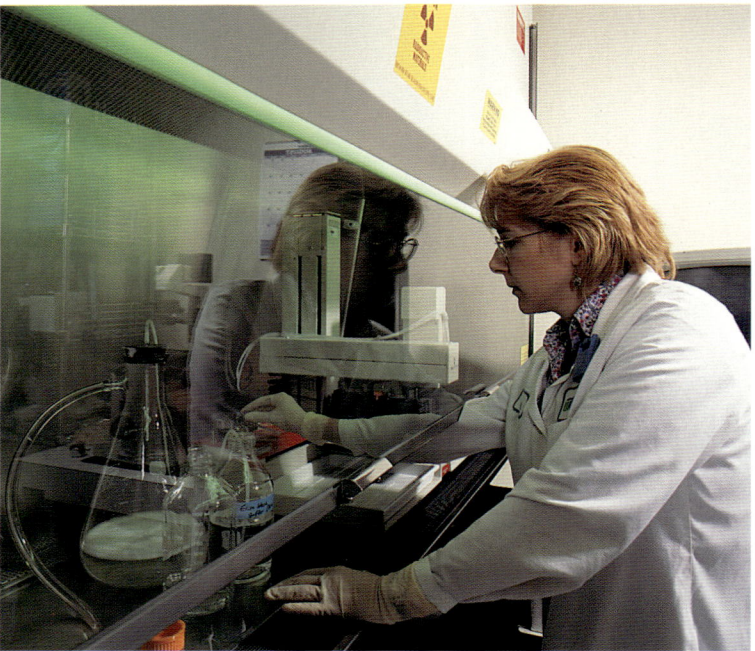

Westwood-Squibb, headquartered in Buffalo, New York, occupies a 21-acre site on the city's upper West Side. Westwood-Squibb is a research-based dermatological company in the Bristol-Myers Squibb Pharmaceutical Group. Working with sister divisions, Westwood-Squibb is playing a key role in globalizing Bristol-Myers Squibb's various skin care business. Photo by James Cavanaugh.

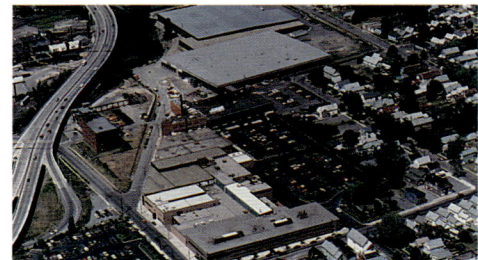

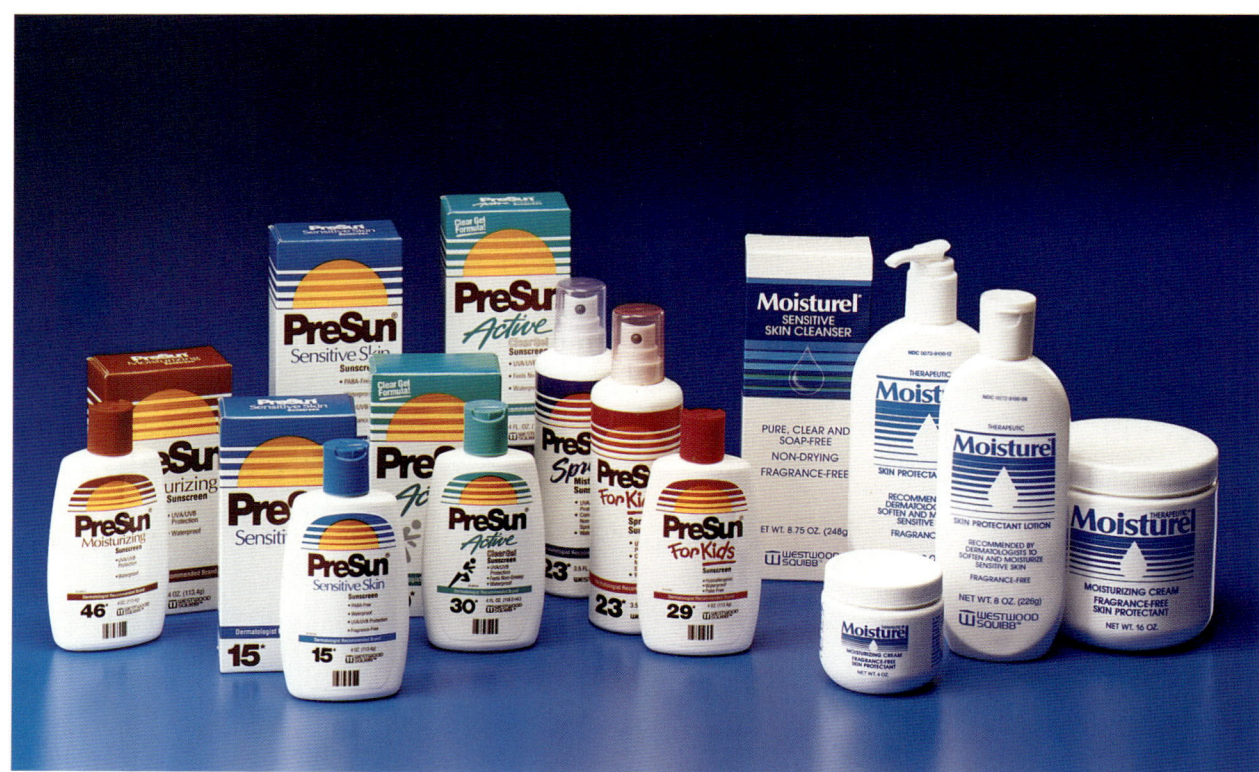

The Buffalo General Hospital, the largest hospital in upstate New York, was founded in 1855. Since admitting its first patient in 1858, it has served Western New York for nearly a century and a half. In that time, the hospital has grown from four small wards to a 772-bed acute care medical center and the flagship of the Buffalo General Health System, an integrated health care delivery system with multiple acute care and long-term facilities, affiliates, and services throughout Western New York.

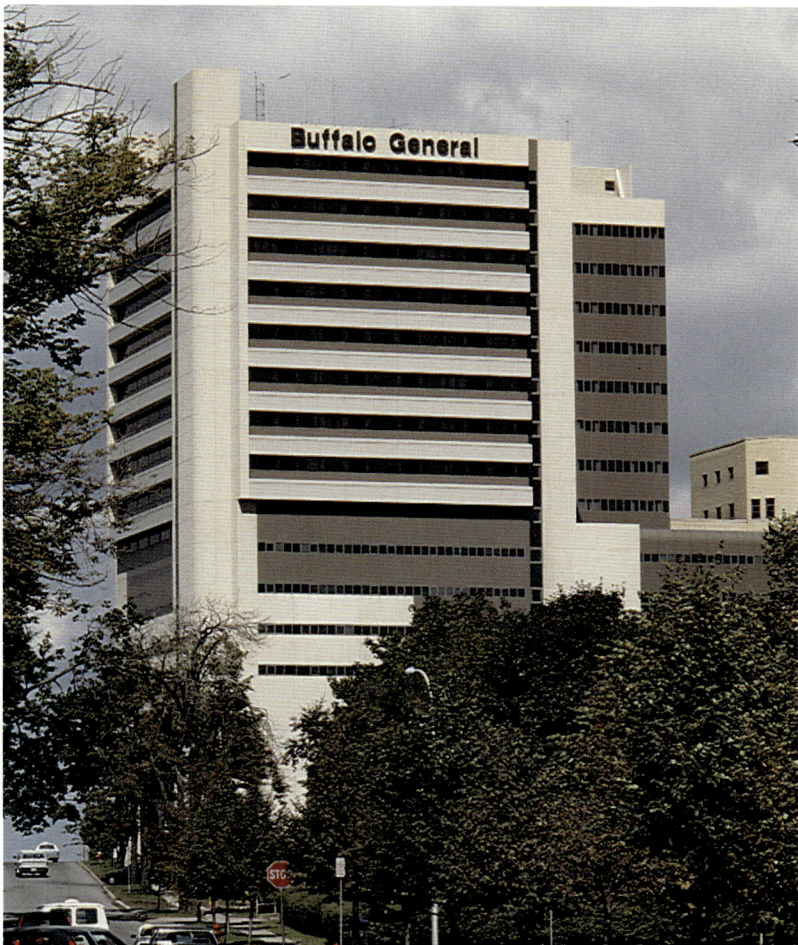

Over the years, Buffalo General has consistently led the area in health services, introducing many procedures now routine. It was the first area hospital to use hypodermic injections, thermometers, electrocardiograms, insulin, 100 percent oxygen, the Drinker respirator, X-ray machines, blood dialyzers in treating kidney disease, and the "patch-graft" technique coronary bypass surgery, minimally invasive coronary artery bypass surgery, and the revolutionary partial left ventriculectomy. The health system continues this leadership role today in its three primary missions: patient care, education, and research.

Providing in excess of 20 percent of all adult medical and surgical services in Erie County, the health system offers a wide range of treatments in 21 clinical inpatient departments and more than 60 outpatient programs. Specialized programs include cardiac and orthopaedic surgery; lithotripsy/urology; oncology; psychiatry, gynecology/obstetrics; dialysis; gastroenterology; cardiac rehabilitation; rehabilitation medicine; kidney, pancreas, heart, and lung transplantation; neurology and neurosurgery.

Always known for the quality of its care, in 1995 Buffalo General was recognized by the Joint Commission on Accreditation of Healthcare Organizations. The national organization gave BGH its highest honor—accreditation with commendation.

A recognized cardiac care center, the health system treats patients from across the United States. Other adult services exclusive to Buffalo General in Western New York include heart and lung transplants; left anterior small thoracotomy (LAST), a minimally invasive single-bypass surgery technique; and lithotripsy, an alternative to the surgical treatment of kidney stones. The hospital is also recognized as a leading center for orthopaedic surgery, including back surgery and reconstructive hip and knee surgery.

Another part of the founding mission that continues today is the hospital's role as a teaching affiliate of the University of Buffalo School of Medicine and Biomedical Sciences. Approximately 800 physicians rotate through the hospital annually in residency or fellowship training. In addition, more than 400 students from academic institutions throughout the region participate in programs such as nursing, nutritional services, pharmacy, medical technology, and radiology.

In research members of the Buffalo General medical staff have made significant contributions in renal medicine, obstetrics and gynecology, neurosurgery, gastroenterology, orthopaedic surgery, rehabilitation medicine, cardiac surgery, cardiac angiography, forensic dentistry, microsurgery, and both heart and kidney transplant surgery. The hospital's Neurology Department also led a four-year nationwide clinical trial that developed the first drug ever to slow the progress of relapsing multiple sclerosis—the most significant breakthrough in the history of multiple sclerosis research and treatment.

The hospital also makes an important economic contribution to the region. As the fourth-largest non-governmental employer, it provides over $450 million in annual value to the local economy and also spends a significant portion of its more than $250 million annual operating budget with local businesses. And, with minority employment at approximately 30 percent of its total work force, it is one of Western New York's largest employers of minorities.

For the future, as the leading institution in the Buffalo General Health System, Buffalo General Hospital will continue to deliver integrated health services to the community and the region, providing a continuum of care for all patients. ❖

Serving Western New York for nearly a century and a half, Buffalo General is the largest hospital in upstate New York

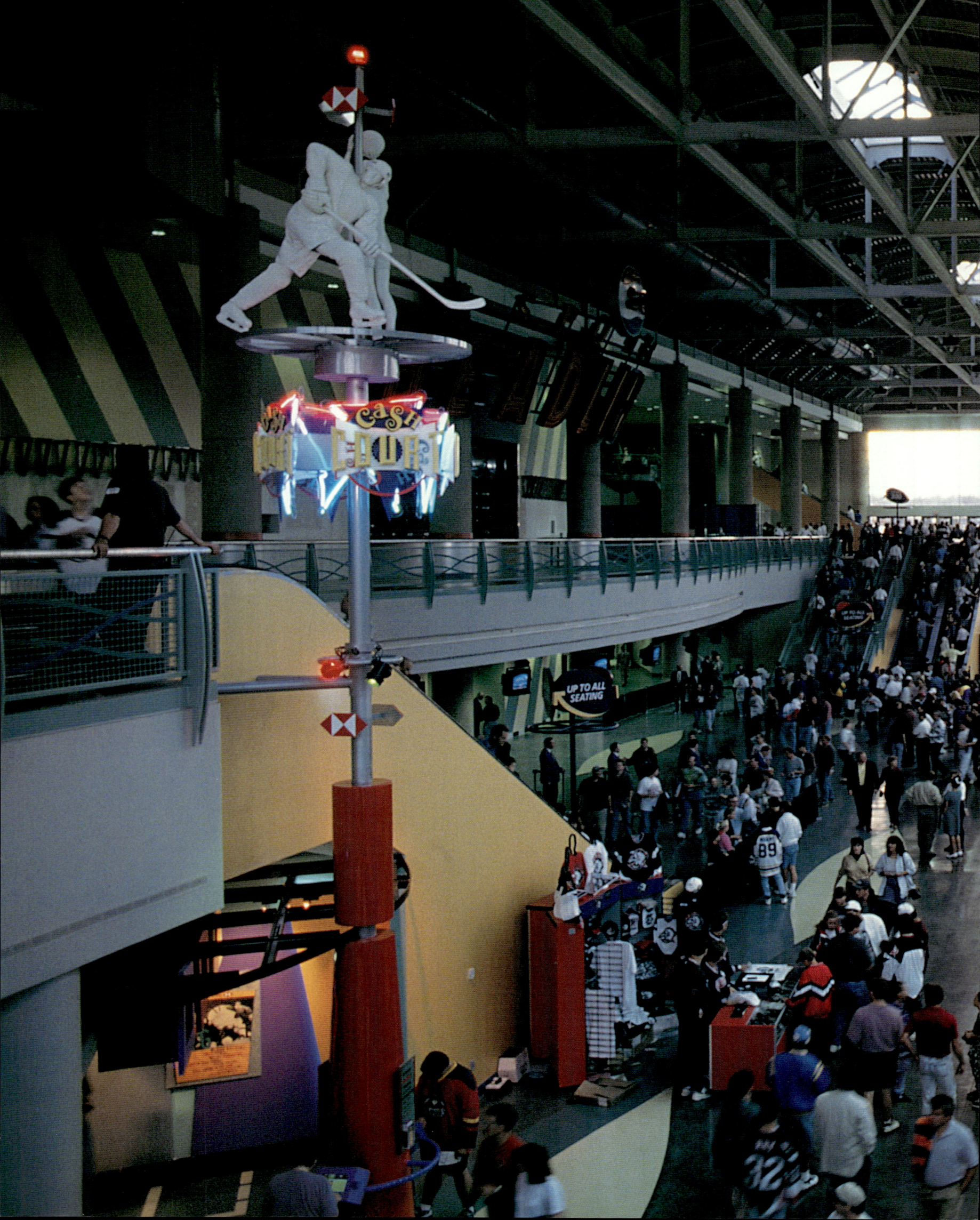

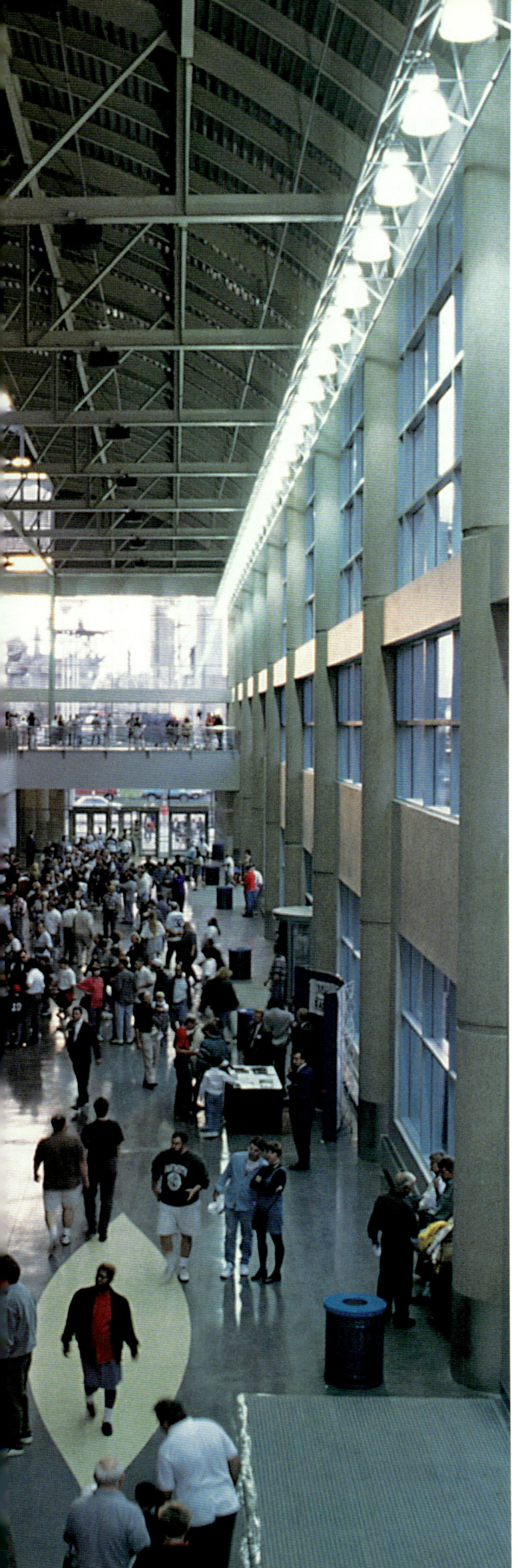

MARKET PLACE

Photo by James P. McCoy.

THE BUFFALO/ NIAGARA MARRIOTT

The Buffalo/Niagara Marriott opened its doors in April, 1981, under the management of one of the Marriott corporation's first franchisees, Boykin Management Company. Founded in 1958 by William J. Boykin, Boykin Management is now in its third generation of family-owned enterprise. Today, the company is owned by Robert and Jack Boykin, who together with the company's executive committee continue to operate with one main objective— to maintain the company's steady and stable growth built on an unswerving dedication to hospitality. Under their leadership, the company owns or operates 22 first-class hotels throughout the United States.

The Buffalo/Niagara Marriott is one of 250 full-service Marriotts worldwide. Committed to providing deluxe hotel accommodations, superior catering, and exceptional service, Marriott is widely recognized as the industry leader in the quality lodging tier and is the hotel company preferred by most business travelers and meeting planners.

Boykin Management chose to build the Buffalo/Niagara Marriott in Amherst, one of Buffalo's most populous, prosperous, and throughout the 1980s, fastest-growing suburbs. With growth projections for the community focused on the rapid growth of the University at Buffalo's north campus, Boykin chose a strategic location for the hotel within walking distance of the university. In addition, Amherst's accessibility to expressways and major highways was ranked first in Western New York by the Buffalo-area business publication

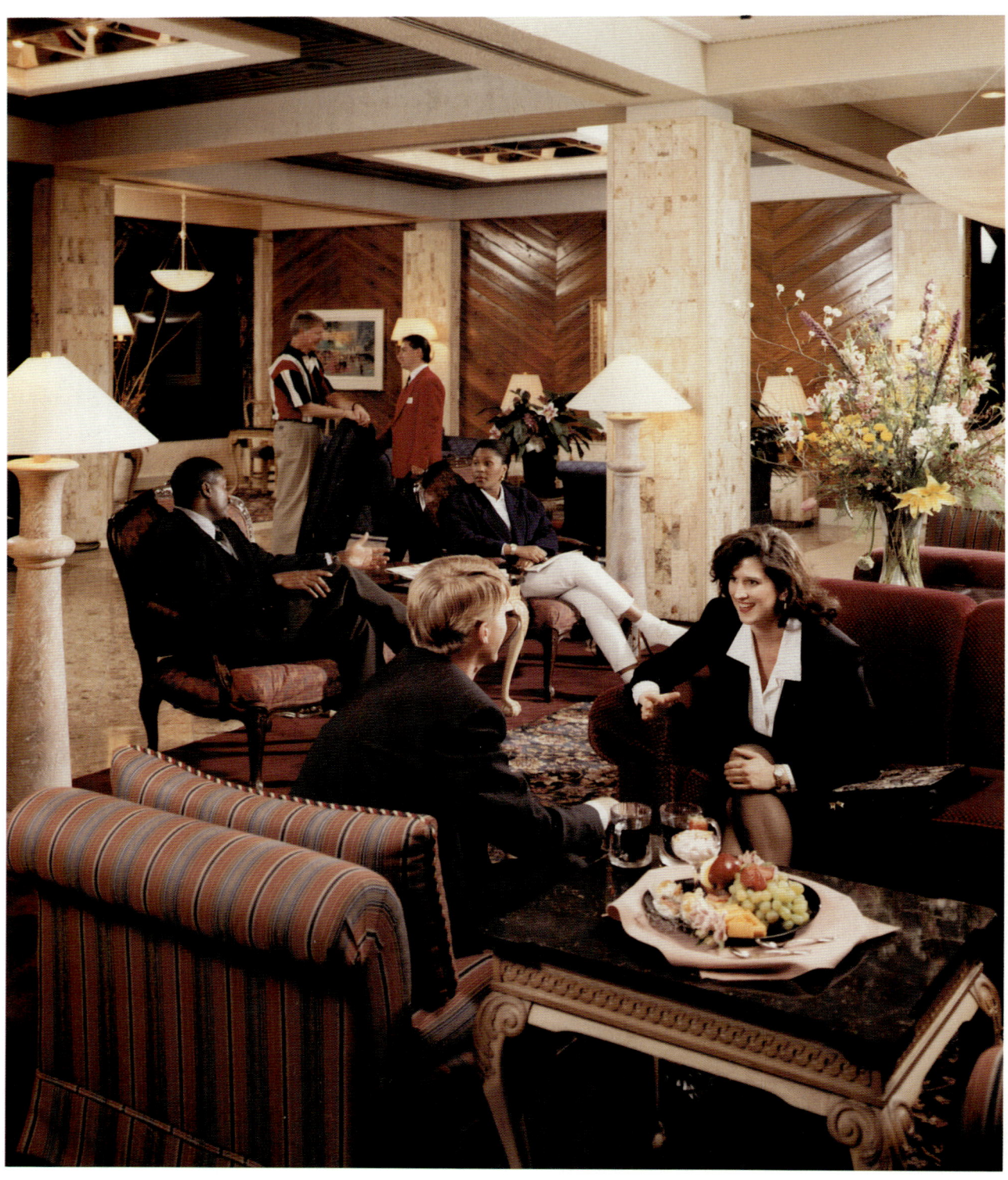

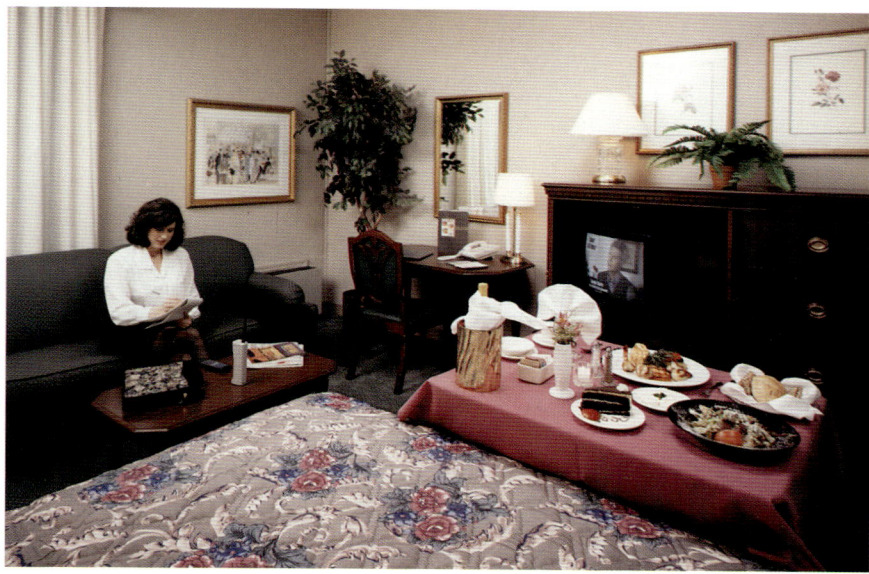

nament were used for a complete renovation of a special "Parent's Room" at the hospital and also funded the purchase of much-needed medical equipment.

The Buffalo/Niagara Marriott remains dedicated to growing along with the Niagara region. A recently completed $3 million renovation saw all guestrooms renovated and all public areas, including ballrooms and salons, completely refurbished, with the highlight of the renovations a beautiful new marble floor in the lobby. Planned renovations of the restaurant and lounge will assure the hotel continues to occupy a premier niche in the region's hospitality industry.

Business First. Amherst has also received top rankings in areas such as public safety and leisure opportunities. Today, the town is the fourth-largest municipality in upstate New York, and the Marriott has played a key role in providing hospitality and accommodations throughout the town's emergence to prominence in the Niagara region.

The Buffalo/Niagara Marriott's key role in the Amherst economy includes employing more than 300 local residents while providing local businesses with upscale lodging and meeting facilities. The Marriott offers 356 deluxe hotel accommodations, including six suites and a beautiful Concierge Level with special accommodations, services, and privileges. Dining and entertainment facilities include the Panache Restaurant, providing fine dining to the community, as well as full lunch and breakfast menus; the Buffalo/ Niagara Marriott Night Club, a popular nightspot for the entire region; and the Blizzards Bar, the perfect spot to relax with a poolside cocktail or snack.

Amenities include both indoor and outdoor swimming pools, a sauna, whirlpool, exercise, and games rooms. Golf, tennis, and racquetball facilities are located nearby. Free parking and courtesy airport transportation are available, along with express check-in and check-out, room service, a gift shop, and valet services.

Conveniently located only 10 minutes from the Greater Buffalo International Airport, only 15 minutes from downtown Buffalo and 30 minutes from Niagara Falls, the Buffalo/ Niagara Marriott offers fast and easy access to virtually every destination in the Niagara region. Convenient access to attractions such as local shopping malls, entertainment complexes, and sporting events makes the Marriott as attractive for tourists as it is for the business traveler. Special plans such as the Honeymoon Package, Two for Breakfast™ Weekend, and Super Saver Weekend attract both out-of-town visitors and local residents seeking an enjoyable and affordable experience.

The Buffalo/Niagara Marriott also plays an important role in the community through numerous donations to nonprofit organizations, schools, and hospitals throughout the region. In addition to direct contributions, the hotel provides organizational expertise and facilities for several events. Every summer, the Buffalo/Niagara Marriott sponsors a charity golf tournament with Children's Hospital of Buffalo, with the proceeds benefiting the hospital. Proceeds from one year's tour-

And the Marriott's dedication to providing superior facilities is matched by its commitment to unparalleled service. By creating an environment that is friendly and supportive for associates, the Buffalo/Niagara Marriott has assembled an outstanding staff. Every associate is provided with the training and support to grow to his or her full potential professionally while maintaining a balance between work and personal needs. Seventeen of the Buffalo/Niagara Marriott's associates have been with the hotel since it opened, attesting to its success in attracting and retaining exceptional associates who provide superior service every day. Marriott recently awarded the hotel a plaque for the most outstanding service in the region, which is proudly displayed in the lobby.

With its modern and attractive facilities, professional and dedicated staff, and its long-term investment in and commitment to the community it serves, the Buffalo/Niagara Marriott will continue to be an important component in the Boykin Management Company's national network of hotels. And it will continue to play a leading role as one of the Niagara region's premier hotels well into the 21st century. ◈

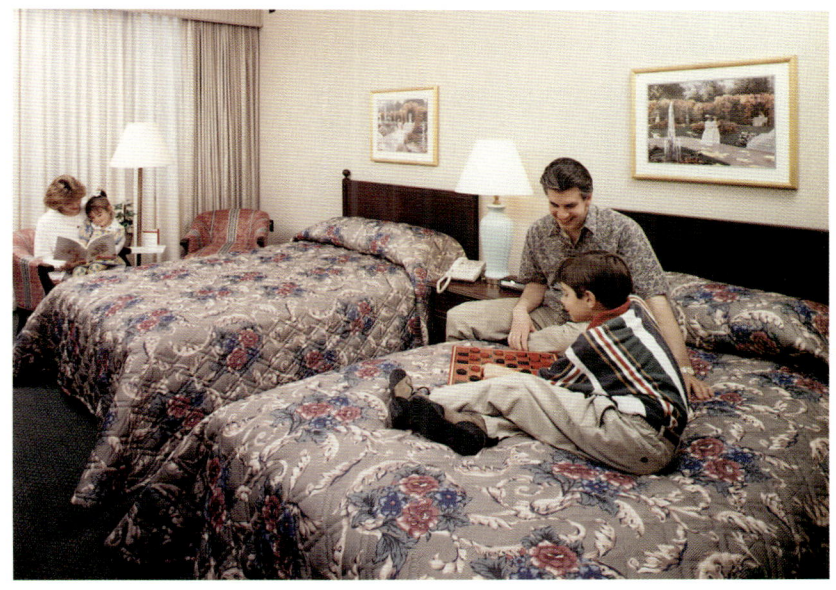

DELAWARE NORTH COMPANIES

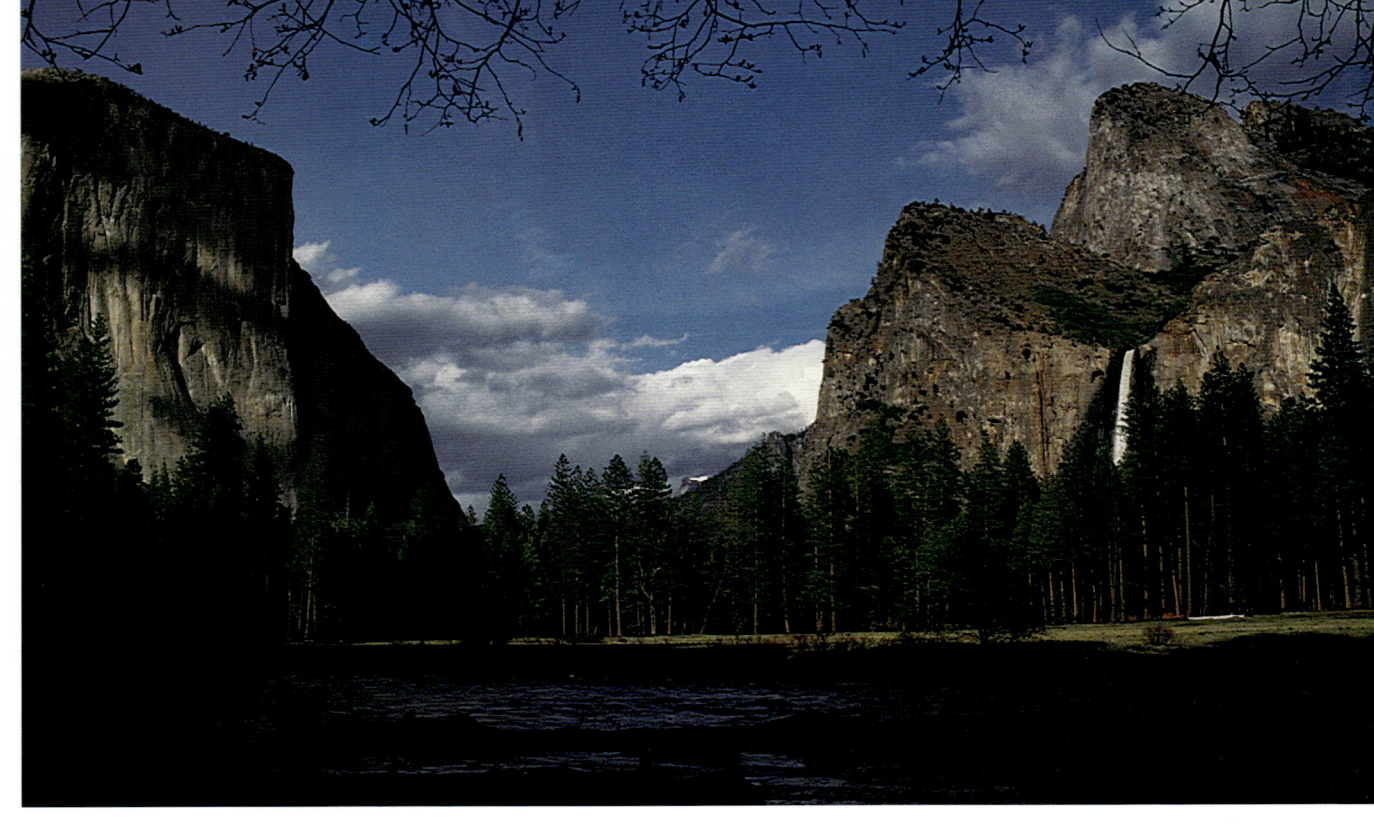

Delaware North Parks Services' manages visitor services at Yosemite National Park, the crown jewel in the nation's park system. The company operates concessions, dining, accomodations, gift shops, and tours for more than four million visitors annually.

CA One Services sets industry standards for food, beverage and retail operations in more than 30 of the nation's airports. The company offers innovative new concepts in airport dining such as Wolfgang Puck Express at the Los Angeles International Airport.

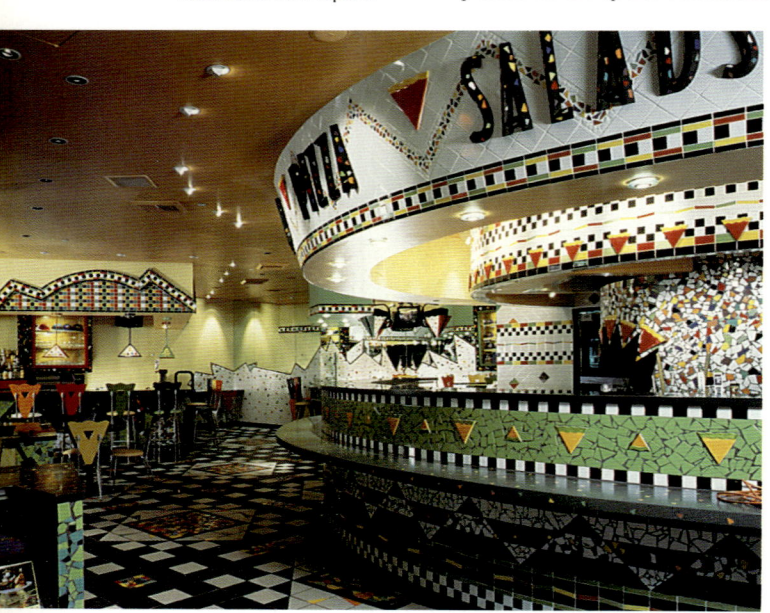

From a modest beginning providing food service for baseball fans, the firm today known as Delaware North Companies Inc. has grown into a billion-dollar-plus international family of businesses that are recognized as leaders in the food and recreation management industry.

Through its subsidiaries, Delaware North provides an array of services at professional sports arenas and stadiums, airports, zoos, racetracks, national and state parks, and other major tourist attractions. The company also owns the new FleetCenter sports and entertainment complex in Boston, and its chairman and chief executive officer, Jeremy M. Jacobs, owns the National Hockey League Boston Bruins team.

Delaware North is nothing if not diverse. The firm's story began more than 80 years ago when brothers Marvin, Charles and Louis Jacobs, peddlers of candy bars and peanuts in Buffalo burlesque houses, expanded their business to theaters in other cities. In pre-air-conditioning days, theaters closed for the summer. Making money year-round meant the Jacobs brothers had to bring their concession business to where the summer crowds were: baseball parks.

It was via this route that the Jacobs' enterprise essentially pioneered the sports concession industry. Known then as Sportservice, the company's first baseball park concession was operated in the old Jersey City park. They broke into major league food service at Detroit's Tiger Stadium in 1926.

Take Me Out to the Ballgame

From those early days of offering hot dogs, beer and peanuts to hungry spectators, Sportservice has grown into one of the largest and most experienced food service management companies in the country. From Chicago-style pizza to Buffalo chicken wings, tenderloin fajitas and vegetarian calzones, today's fan has a gourmet range of appetite-appeasing choices at professional sporting facilities nationwide, thanks to Sportservice.

Using local suppliers and authentic ingredients, the firm's trademark touch in all its facilities is serving a city or region's "signature" foods. With a client base that includes major and minor league baseball, football, basketball, and hockey facilities, racecourses and convention centers, Sportservice maintains affiliations with many professional teams, including the Buffalo Bills and the Buffalo Sabres.

Sportservice served nearly three million meals at the 1996 Centennial Olympic Games in Atlanta. That same year, the firm was selected as long-term master concessionaire for the U.S. Open tennis tournament in Flushing Meadows, New York. Sportservice also operates food service at three of the nation's newest arenas—the Marine Midland Arena in Buffalo, the Tampa Ice Palace in Florida, and the Nashville Arena in Tennessee—all of which opened in 1996.

Delaware North doesn't stop at providing food service for major sporting facilites. It owns and operates the FleetCenter in Boston, the $160-million state-of-the-art sports and entertainment facility and new home of the Boston Bruins and the Boston Celtics. The 755,000-square-foot complex seats 19,600 and was opened in 1995 to rave reviews.

Family Fun and Learning

In 1992, when the National Park Service selected Delaware North to manage visitor services at Yosemite National Park, the decision was based on the company's wide range of hospitality management capabilities. With more than eight decades of expertise in key areas of food service and retail merchandising, and solid experience in still other areas such as accommodations and recreation management, Delaware North brings a full complement of strengths to park concessions management.

With Yosemite as its foundation, Delaware North Parks Services extended its reach to encompass Niagara Reservation State Park in New York, and NASA's Kennedy Space Center in Cape Canaveral, Florida, where comprehensive visitor services include development of state-of-the-art interactive exhibits designed to immerse guests in America's space legacy. The company also secured Roaring River State Park in the Missouri Ozarks and recently added Asilomar State Beach and Conference Center to its roster of attractions.

Satisfied Travelers

CA One Services, Inc. is Delaware North's airport food service and retail operations subsidiary. The division is challenging industry standards with its exciting new food and retail concepts. Private label food products are coming on-line and proving very successful, while proprietary themed concepts are adding extra attractions to airport facilities. Denver International Airport is one example of the new themed concepts, with restaurants like Lefty's Mile High Grill offering regional flavor in a local tavern setting. At Los Angeles International Airport, the company scaled new heights in the airport food business by partnering with famed chef Wolfgang Puck to bring his trademark pizza and salads to airport corridors. Also at Los Angeles is Encounter, CA One's first "eatertainment" restaurant that offers dining for the jet set in a sophisticated sci-fi atmosphere complete with moon rock walls and flowing lava lamps. The company currently manages food and retail outlets at its hometown airport, Greater Buffalo International, and will debut new food and retail operations when the new airport opens in late 1997.

Waging and Gaming

Delaware North's pari-mutuel subsidiary is Sportsystems Corporation. Due to Sportsystems' emphasis on providing exciting, state-of-the-art entertainment, millions of people annually visit and place wagers at the company's greyhound and horse racecourses.

In its most recent innovation, Sportsystems propelled the West Virginia pari-mutuel industry into a new entertainment dimension with the introduction of 700 blackjack, keno, and poker video terminals that turned the Wheeling Downs Racetrack into a full-service gaming facility.

International Connections

In recent years, Delaware North has shown its versatility by entering food service, accommodation and facilities management markets a hemisphere away. Today, through Delaware North (Australia), the company manages a synergistic network of companies: AFS Catering, CA One Services Australia, AVS Catering and Ozray Parking.

AFS manages more than 100 food service outlets throughout Australia, ranging from snack bars to full-scale cafeterias in commercial buildings, industrial plants and commonwealth facilities—including the prestigious Parliament House in Canberra. The company operates hotels which comprise 2,350 rooms nationally, and also provides total facility management for a number of other centers.

CA One Services Australia operations include food and beverage services, as well as gift facilities at Australia's key airports and major railway stations.

AVS caters some of Australia's most prestigious venues. Included are Melbourne Park (formerly the National Tennis

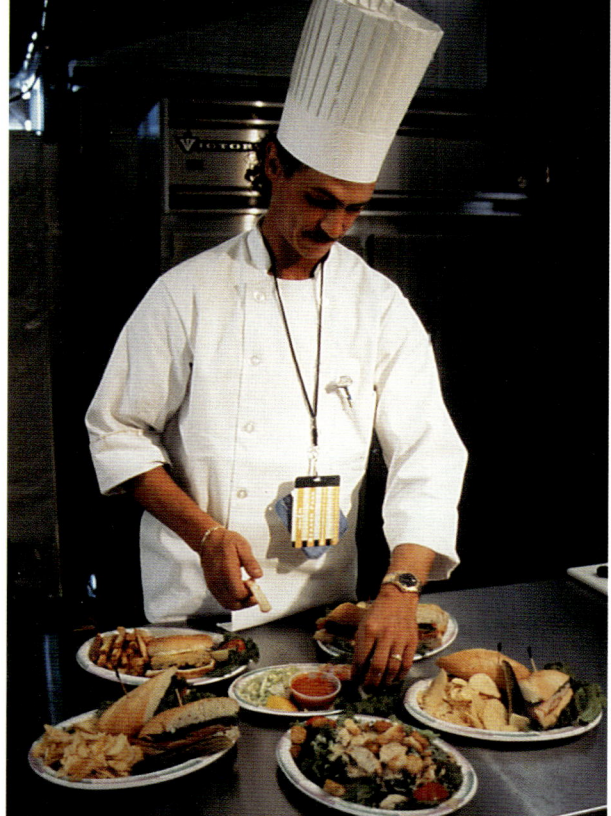

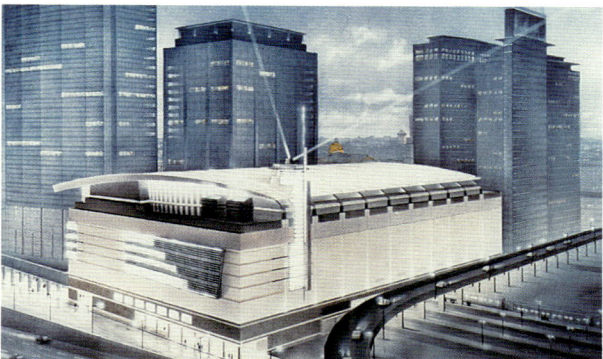

Sportservice Corporation has been serving fan-pleasing fare at ballparks, arenas and stadiums for more than 80 years. From peanuts and popcorn to upscale dining at sporting and entertainment facilities nationwide, Sportservice pleases palates wherever it goes.

Delaware North Companies' NBG Corporation owns and manages Boston's new $160 million FleetCenter, which is home to the National Hockey League's Boston Bruins and the National Basketball Association's Boston Celtics.

Centre), which hosts the Australian Open; Sydney Convention and Exhibition Centre; ANZ and Stockland Stadium; and the Sydney International Aquatic and Athletic Centre at Homebush Bay, site of the Sydney Olympics in 2000.

Shopping Made Easy

Delaware North's newest venture is American Park 'n Swap, a modern version of the ancient open-air marketplace. The concept transforms idle parking lots at public facilities such as convention centers, exhibition halls, racetracks and stadiums into lucrative new income streams.

Conducted on "dark" days (days when no other events occur) at these facilities, the open-air bazaars (more popularly known as "flea markets" in the Northeast) create low-cost events where families can shop at leisure for bargains priced 25 to 50 percent below standard retail prices. Current locations of the enterprise include Apache Junction and Phoenix, Arizona; Little Rock, Arkansas; Myrtle Beach, South Carolina; and Memphis, Tennessee; Pittsburgh, Pennsylvania; and Richmond, Virginia.

Delaware North thrives because it actively pursues opportunities in a changing marketplace. With the assistance of approximately 20,000 full- and part-time employees (1,500 are employed in Western New York), the firm operates across the U.S., in Canada, and as far away as Australia. The annual Forbes 400 list ranks Delaware North in the top tier of privately owned firms. ◆

HYATT REGENCY BUFFALO

When the Hyatt Regency opened its doors in downtown Buffalo's Fountain Plaza in 1984, it signified the first Hyatt hotel for New York State outside of New York City proper. It also pointed to an urban Renaissance in progress, as Hyatts have been associated with the regeneration of American cities.

In Buffalo, the construction of the Hyatt hotel rescued a 60- year-old landmark office building that had been slated for demolition. The unique architectural triumph combined the 15- story, French Renaissance former Genesee Office Building with a new, matching 11-story tower and a contemporary atrium.

The spectacular lobby atrium, once considered a daring design element when it was all the talk at the opening of Atlanta's Peachtree Plaza hotel, is now seen as the signature feature of a Hyatt's property. Ensuring a unique regional character, the developers incorporated part of the neoclassic facade of the Genesee Building into the entrance of the Hyatt's Genesee Sports Bar and Grill. It's a nod to Western New York history that underlies the Hyatt way of doing business.

"We believe in working to benefit the community," says Patrick Sorge, a Niagara Falls native who recently returned to his hometown to work as Hyatt Regency Buffalo's Director of Sales. Thomas R. Pagels is general manager. The Buffalo management team is overseeing a general overhaul of the 12-year- old facility, including modernizing guestrooms and updating business amenities, in addition to a state-of-the-art phone system, which will include voicemail for all guestrooms.

The downtown facility, located in the midst of Buffalo's theatre and financial districts, boasts 400 guest rooms, 12 suites and 18,000 square feet of meeting space featuring a 10,000-square-foot ballroom. It is connected via an enclosed walkway to the Buffalo Convention Center. Close proximity to the new Marine Midland Arena, Studio Arena Theatre, and Shea's Buffalo Center for the Performing Arts make it the hotel of choice for visiting stars of the entertainment world.

The heart of a hotel is not its accoutrements, but its staff, and Hyatt has standardized training to produce the satisfied employees that make for satisfied guests. Staff members are encouraged to take pride in their facility and to participate in the surrounding community via Hyatt F.O.R.C.E., or Family of Responsible Caring Employees. The latter is a Hyatt program designed to give back to the community through volunteer work at area hospitals, projects such as Habitat for Humanity, etc. In Buffalo the Hyatt Regency is host to such charitable endeavors as the American Heart Association's annual dinner and the Share Our Strength/Taste of the Nation benefit for local agencies feeding the hungry.

The construction of the Hyatt Regency in Buffalo rescued a 60- year-old landmark office building that had been slated for demolition.

One of the Northeast's most successful food market chains got its start in Rochester, New York, back in 1915. That was when the grandparents of Chairman of the Board Robert Wegman ran a small store from the front of their Fernwood Avenue home. At the time, their son Walter worked in the store while his brother John peddled fresh produce from a pushcart.

In 1916, John founded the Rochester Fruit and Vegetable Company. Within six years, the brothers had expanded their business to include general groceries and bakery operations. By 1930, the predecessor to the modern-day Wegmans—a full-scale showplace store with canned goods, produce, bakery, meat, and a 300-seat cafeteria—was opened.

In those early days, this enterprising family was committed to bringing quality products to customers, while maintaining a high level of customer service. Not much has changed in Wegmans philosophy, put succinctly in today's store motto, "Every day you get our best."

When he became president in 1950, Robert Wegman was determined to keep up the family standards. He oversaw the addition of new employee benefits, real estate development, and investment in such operations as a company-owned egg farm, a meat-processing center, and a central bakery. In 1971, the Wegmans Consumer Affairs Department was created. Ongoing development has included state-of-the-art technology, such as electronic cash registers and scanners, and the one-stop shopping concept.

In 1976, Robert's son Danny was named president. His granddaughter Colleen is today involved in the family business, giving Wegmans a unique multigenerational family ownership. Wegmans opened its first Buffalo store in 1977 and now has nine locations in the area. Today, the company runs more than 50 food markets throughout New York State and Pennsylvania. Adhering to old-fashioned ideals while keeping abreast with modern developments in the food service industry has earned Wegmans such recent plaudits as a *Fortune* magazine "top supermarket chain in the nation for customer service" designation and a selection as "one of the nation's top produce retailers" by *Supermarket News*, among many other regional and national business honors.

In recognition of its commitment to employees, Wegmans has been recognized as one of the best companies for working mothers, according to *Working Mother* magazine, and has been featured in Levering and Moskowitz's *The 100 Best Companies to Work For in America.*

WEGMANS

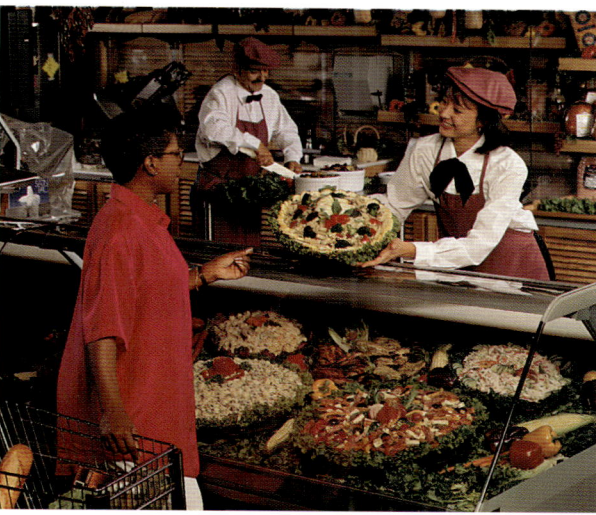

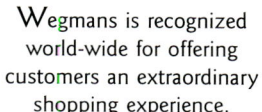

Wegmans is recognized world-wide for offering customers an extraordinary shopping experience.

The company operates more than 50 food markets throughout New York State and Pennsylvania.

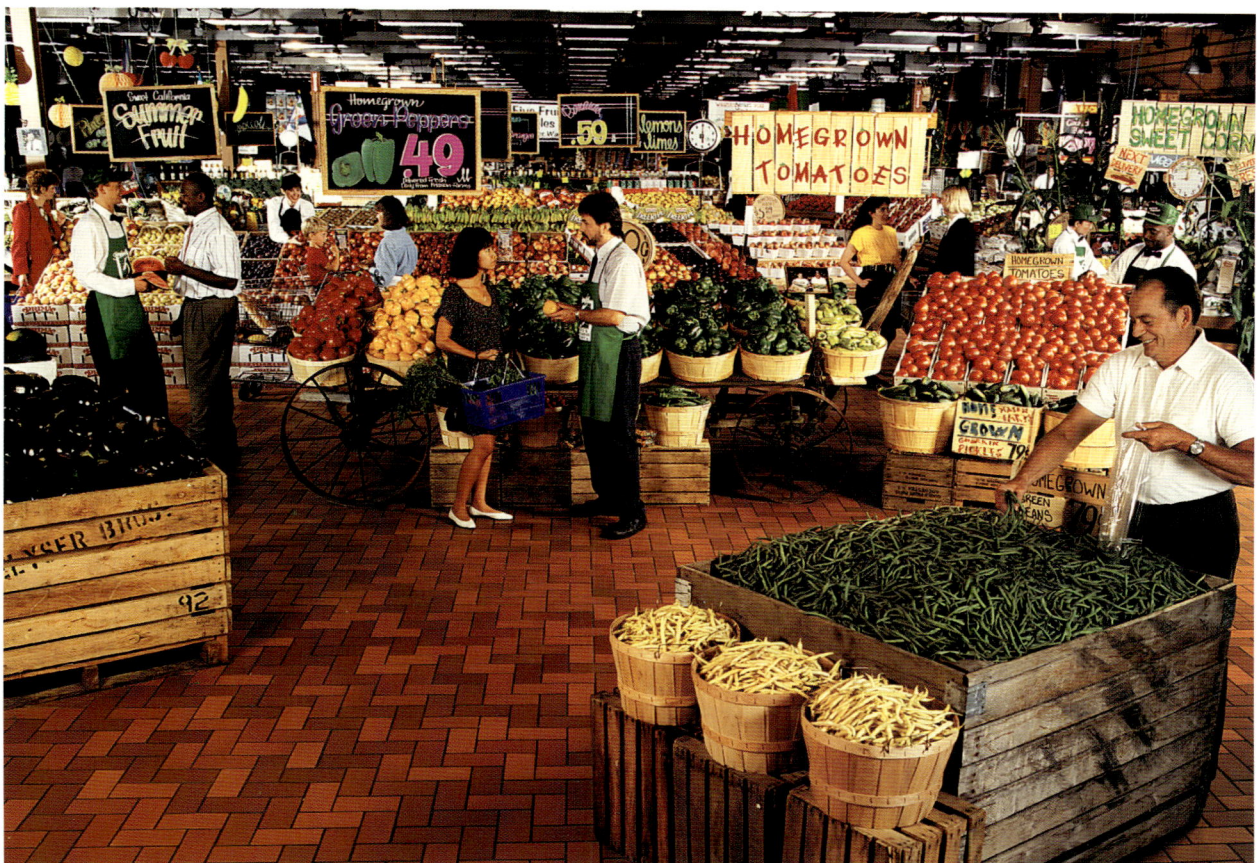

HART HOTELS, INC.

Hart Hotels, an independent hotel management company having franchised affiliations with Holiday Inn Worldwide, Promus Hotels, and Dalts Restaurants, has over 25 years of experience in developing and managing full service, limited feature, and resort hotels in different markets and locations.

Hart Hotels is Western New York's largest hospitality company with 1,200 hotel rooms and 850 employees. Mr. William Hart is chairman of Hart Hotels, and Mr. David Hart is president.

Hart Hotels' local properties include the Holiday Inn-International Airport on Genesee Street; Holiday Inn-Gateway on Rossler and Dingens Streets; Holiday Inn-Downtown on Delaware Avenue; and the Holiday Inn-Amherst on Niagara Falls Boulevard.

As part of the Holiday Inn worldwide modernization program, all of the Buffalo Holiday Inn properties completed a $5 million entire facility renovation in 1996. The lobbies have been dramatically redesigned and amenities added such as expanded pre- conference rooms, meeting rooms, and banquet facilities.

Corporate business travelers will find easier access for communication needs with data ports in all rooms. Other amenities for the executive are new fitness rooms and Jacuzzis. In the King feature rooms, amenities have been added such as hairdryers, coffee makers, and recliners. Security has been improved with the installation of card-activated locks on all doors.

Hart Hotels, Inc. also owns and operates the Hampton Inn Amherst located on Flint Road between Millersport and Maple Road. The Hampton features a Jacuzzi, fitness room, an indoor pool, complimentary continental breakfast daily, and free local telephone calls.

Next to the Hampton Inn is Max Hart's diner, one of Hart Hotels' unique casual restaurants. Max Hart's is a 1950's-style diner with a 1990's sophistication. The restaurant at the Holiday Inn-Airport was recently converted to a Dalts Classic American Grill, which is a franchise of Dalts Restaurants

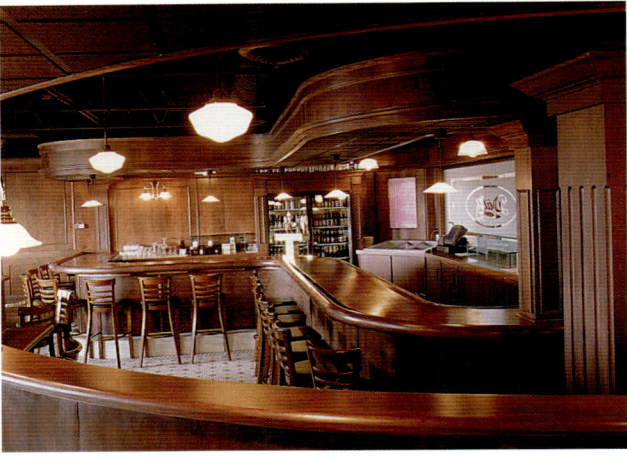

Dalts Classic American Grill at Holiday Inn, Buffalo International Airport.

headquartered in Columbus, Ohio. The restaurant features mahogany booths and is reminiscent of the old neighborhood grill and soda shop. The menu features homemade meatloaf, old-fashioned chocolate malts, and over 30 kinds of imported and domestic beer.

Hart Hotels, Inc. also owns and manages the Holiday Inn-Ithica, New York, and the Yarrow Resort and Conference Center in Park City, Utah. The Yarrow Resort and Conference Center offers 181 guest rooms and suites and an array of amenities, including a year-round swimming pool, hot tub, and fitness center. The Yarrow is located near the Park City Ski area, Utah's largest ski resort. Park City, with Salt Lake City, will host the "2002 Winter Olympics." The Holiday Inn-Ithica is a 178-room hotel located in the heart of the Finger Lakes region. The hotel is near both Ithica College and Cornell University.

Hart Management, a division of Hart Hotels, offers a full range of management services for owners of existing hotels and new owners. Hart Management has successfully operated and managed hotels throughout the United States in downtown, airport, and suburban locations.

Hart Hotels, Inc. has built a corporate web site on the Internet, which provides all of their most current corporate information.

William Hart, David Hart, and Hart Hotels are committed to the Western New York community through various kinds of volunteer work. William is a member of the Greater Buffalo Partnership Board of Directors and of the Buffalo Convention and Visitors Bureau. He is former chairman of the Convention and Visitors Bureau. He is a trustee and treasurer for the Mercy Hospital Foundation, member of the D'Youville College Board of Trustees, and Past President of the International Association of Holiday Inns Worldwide.

David Hart is an Advisory Board member of the Hotel Management programs at both Canisius College and Erie Community College. David currently serves on the Board of the Buffalo Convention and Visitors Bureau. He is Vice-Chairman of the International Association of Holiday Inns Worldwide, Eastern region committee. David was recently recognized for his volunteer work by the Make-A-Wish Foundation of Western New York as "Wish-Maker of the Year." ◊

Lobby at Holiday Inn Buffalo International Airport.

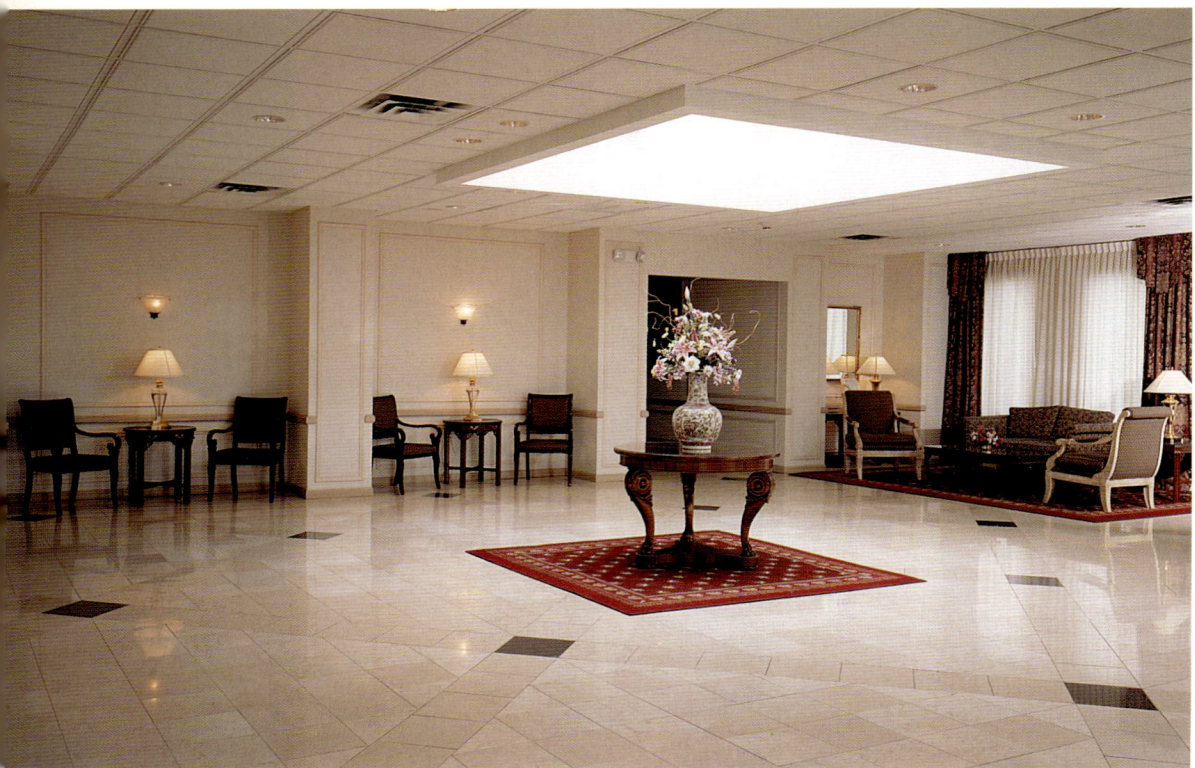

Located near the Greater Buffalo International Airport, the Wellesley Inn of Buffalo provides convenient and enjoyable accommodations to business and government travelers, as well as tourists visiting Niagara region attractions ranging from the grandeur of Niagara Falls to the world-class shopping opportunities afforded by the area's many shopping centers and outlet malls.

Built in 1984, the Wellesley Inn was completely renovated in 1997. It now offers 82 deluxe rooms with amenities including complimentary continental breakfast, remote control TV with HBO, ESPN, CNN, TBS, TNT, USA and Lifetime, and in-room movies, complimentary passes to Bally's Health Spa, in-room telecommunications data ports, facsimile service, same-day valet service, and available microwaves and refrigerators. Additional features include all interior corridors with electronic locks and state-of-the-art fire protection. In-room coffeemakers and AM/FM clock radios round out the many offerings enjoyed by visitors.

For business travelers, the Wellesley Inn offers the right combination of a convenient location and affordable accommodations. Shuttle service to the nearby airport permits access to flights in less than 5 minutes. Only 10 minutes from downtown Buffalo, the Wellesley Inn also offers fast and convenient access to the commercial and government centers of Western New York and the entire Niagara region.

Tourists also enjoy an economical, budget-friendly stay with close proximity to a wide variety of attractions. Only 20 miles from Niagara Falls, 2 miles from both the Eastern Hills and Walden-Galleria shopping malls, 5 miles from North AmeriCare Park and the Albright-Knox Art Gallery, 10 miles from Rich Stadium, McKinley and Boulevard malls, 15 miles from Darien Lake Amusement Park—the list of things to do and places to see makes the Wellesley Inn an excellent base of operations for sightseers and shoppers alike. Again, the airport shuttle service and easy airport access make traveling to and from the area convenient and simple. Travelers by car or bus find similar convenience in the Wellesley Inn's central location and ease of access.

Attesting to the hotel's popularity, each year more than 20,000 visitors make it their home away from home, bringing in over $800,000 in annual revenues and supporting more than 25 full and part-time employees.

One of 30 Wellesley Inns located throughout the northeastern United States and in Florida, the Buffalo Wellesley Inn is owned and operated by Prime Hospitality Corporation of Fairfield, New Jersey. Owner of both the Wellesley Inn and AmeriSuites brands of limited service hotels, the parent company owns or operates more than 120 hotels throughout the United States and the U.S. Virgin Islands. The fifth-largest hotel management company in the world, Prime Hospitality, also manages many well-known hotel brands, including Crowne Plaza, Days Inn, Holiday Inn, Howard Johnson, Marriott, Radisson, Ramada, Sheraton, and Shoney.

As Prime Hospitality grows toward its future goals, the Buffalo Wellesley Inn will continue to play an integral part in its parent company's plans and in the economic life of the Niagara region. Proud to be part of the area's thriving business and tourist trade, the Buffalo Wellesley Inn truly exemplifies the company's motto, "Value never looked so good." ❧

WELLESLEY INN

Completely renovated in 1997, the Wellesley Inn offers 82 deluxe rooms with a wide variety of amenities.

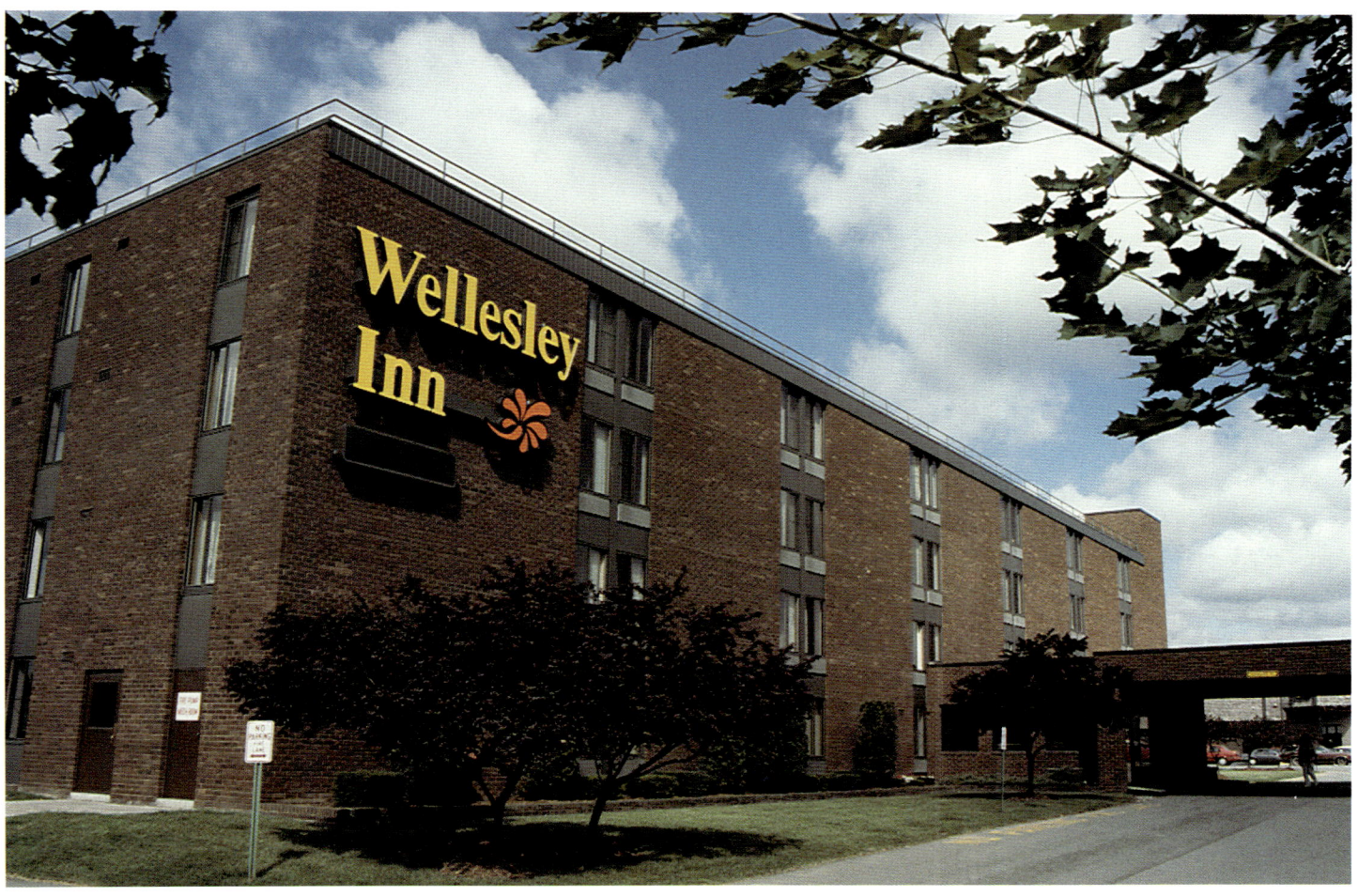

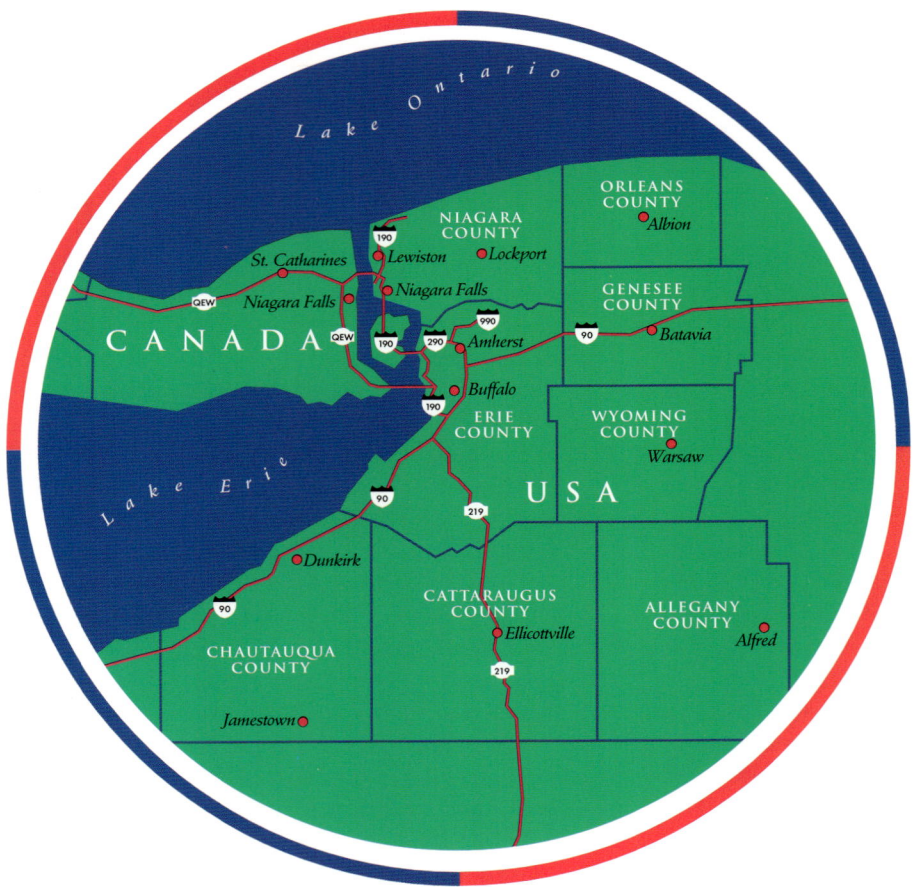

BIBLIOGRAPHY

BOOKS

Bisco, Jim. *A Greater Look at Greater Buffalo*. Northridge, Cal: Windsor Publications, Inc., 1986.

Brown, Richard C. and Bob Watson. *Buffalo: Lake City in Niagara Land*. Northridge, Cal: Windsor Publications, 1981.

Campbell, Marjorie Freeman. *Niagara, Hinge of the Golden Arc*. Toronto: The Ryerson Press, 1958.

Chazenof, William. *Joseph Ellicott and The Holland Land Company: The Opening of Western New York*. Syracuse, N.Y.: Syracuse University Press, 1970.

Cigliano, Jan, and Sarah Bradford Landau, eds., *The Grand American Avenue*. San Francisco: Pomegranate Artbooks, 1994.

Dunnigan, Brian Leigh, and Patricia Kay Scott. *Old Fort Niagara in Four Centuries*, Youngstown, N.Y.: Old Fort Niagara Association, Inc., 1991.

Eberle, Scott, and Joseph Grande. *Second Looks: A Pictoral History of Buffalo and Erie County*. Norfolk, Va.: The Donning Company, 1987.

Fox, Austin, and Lawrence D. McIntyre. *Designated Landmarks of the Niagara Frontier*. Buffalo: Meyer Enterprises, 1986.

Goldman, Mark. *City on the Lake: The Challenge of Change in Buffalo, NY*. Buffalo: Prometheus Books, 1990.

_____. *High Hopes: The Rise and Decline of Buffalo, NY*. Albany: State University of New York Press, 1983.

Graves, Donald E. *Red Coats & Grey Jackets: The Battle of Chippawa*. Toronto & Oxford: Dundern Press, 1994.

Jackson, John N.,and Fred A. Addis. *The Welland Canals, A Comprehensive Guide*. St. Catharines, Ont: The Welland Canals Foundation, 1982.

Kershner, Bruce. *Secret Places: Scenic Treasures of Western New York and Southern Ontario*. Dubuque, Iowa: Kendall Hunt Publishing Co., 1994.

Klinkenborg, Verlyn. *The Last Fine Time*. New York: Alfred A. Knopf, 1991.

Moriyama & Teshima Planners Limited. *Ontario's Niagara Parks, Planning the Second Century*. Toronto: The Niagara Parks Commission, 1988.

Office of the Vice President for Public Service and Urban Affairs, University at Buffalo. *"The Total of All These Acts"*. Buffalo: The University at Buffalo Office of Publications, 1994.

Rounds, Joseph B. *The Time Was Right.* Buffalo: The Grosvenor Society, 1985.

Sellstedt, Lars Gustaf. *Art in Buffalo.* Buffalo: The Matthews- Northrup Works, 1910.

Shea's Buffalo Performing Arts Center, Annual Publication No. 20 Theatre Historical Society, 1993.

Sheridan, Jan, and Kenneth Sheridan. *Buffalo Treasures, A Downtown Walking Guide.* Buffalo: Western New York Wares, Inc., 1995.

Steinberg, Edward. *Introducing the Buffalo Branch of the Federal Reserve Bank of New York.* The Federal Reserve Bank of New York, 1996.

Thomas, William J. *Hey! Is That Guy Dead Or Is He the Skip...* Toronto: Stoddart Publishing Co. Ltd., 1994.

Van Diver, Bradford B. *Roadside Geology of New York.* Missoula, Mont.: Mountain Press Publishing Co., 1935.

Vogel, Michael N. *Echoes in the Mist, An Illustrated History of the Niagara Falls Area.* Northridge Cal: Windsor Publications, 1991.

Wooster, Margaret. *Somewhere to Go on Sunday.* Buffalo: Prometheus Books, 1991.

ARTICLES

Business First of Buffalo:

Debo, David." Auto industry fuels growth of trade." January 22, 1996.

_____. "Labor relations school celebrates 50 years." October 7, 1996.

_____. "Region's trade gates open wide." May 13, 1996.

Franczyk, Annemarie. "Growth in home health care boosts job opportunities." June 17, 1996.

_____. "Health center may hold key to urban rebirth." July 29, 1996.

Thomas, Scott, and Lois Baker. "Biomedical research facility elevates UB to a higher plane." February 19, 1996.

"Working with a customs broker." Executive Business Guide. August 26, 1996.

The Buffalo News:

Brady, Karen. "UB announces plans for stroke center." December 10, 1996.

Buyer, Bob. "Regulations seen hampering area forest industry." February 23, 1994.

Collison, Kevin. "Buffalo wins All-American City designation." June 16, 1996.

Continelli, Louise. "Spreading the word." July 26, 1996.

Davis, Henry L. "Cancer center needs solid foundation." September 1, 1996.

_____. "Institute boasts long record of success in research, patient care." September 1, 1996.

_____. "Plan could cut costs, draw new patients." June 29, 1996.

_____. "Research efforts make cancer center special and important." September 2, 1996.

Madore, James T. "Area plant shows off management-union success." March 29, 1996.

_____. "Canada wants to expand trade with U.S.," BN 10-23-96

McNeil, Harold. "Masiello presents award to Nobel prize winner." November 17, 1995.

Miller, Melinda. "Check it Out (Rodman Hall)." April 25, 1096.

Robinson, David. "Wilson Greatbatch to build new plant in Clarence." April 10, 1996.

Stouffer, Rick. "Cornell school moving to Main-Seneca Building." July 4, 1996.

Vogel, Mike. "A wonder under siege." May 26, 1996.

_____. "Canada draws rising share of tourism." May 27, 1996.

_____. "City ready to launch Inner Harbor project." June 1, 1996.

_____. " Plan envisions parks, homes on waterfront." October 20, 1996.

Other Publications:

Fried, Martin B. "Mark Twain in Buffalo." *Niagara Frontier,* The Buffalo Historical Society, Winter 1959.

"Inventive alumnus honored at MIT program." *UB Today,* The University at Buffalo, Summer 1996.

ENTERPRISES INDEX

INDEX

This book was set in Garamond Light and Light Italic, Goudy Sans Medium and Medium Italic, and Trajan at Community Communications, Montgomery, Alabama, and printed on 80 lb. Warren Flo Text.